CRIMINAL LAW AND PRACTICE

AUSTRALIA
Law Book Co.
Sydney

CANADA AND USA
Carswell
Toronto

HONG KONG
Sweet & Maxwell Asia

NEW ZEALAND
Brookers
Wellington

SINGAPORE and MALAYSIA
Sweet & Maxwell Asia
Singapore and Kuala Lumpur

CRIMINAL LAW AND PRACTICE

First Edition

By

STEPHEN FORSTER, LL.B (Hons)
Lecturer in Law, Lancaster University

LONDON
SWEET & MAXWELL
2008

Published in 2008 by
Sweet & Maxwell Limited of 100 Avenue Road,
http://www.sweetandmaxwell.co.uk
Typeset by YHT Ltd, London
Printed in the UK by CPI William Clowes
Beccles NR34 7TL

No natural forests were destroyed to make this product;
only farmed timber was used and re-planted.

A CIP catalogue record for this book
is available from the British Library

ISBN 978-1-84703-449-6

PREFACE

Reading or working with the depths and complexity of criminal law and practice can be a harsh and unforgiving environment to both the student and practitioner. Some of the more traditional textbooks can be more in depth than is actually needed and in some respects can be a hindrance rather than a benefit. Knowing the fundamentals of criminal law is only part of what makes a promising criminal advocate, a sound working knowledge of the criminal procedure rules is essential to give the confidence to be able to apply the criminal law. Without knowing the practice rules and procedure is like knowing the mechanics of a car but never having learned to drive. Also important to the criminal practitioner is a sound knowledge of the important rules and exceptions to the reception of criminal evidence.

The purpose of the textbook is to provide the reader with all the important and essential principles relating to criminal law, procedure and evidence in one readily accessible source without the loss of the appropriate depth and analysis needed to develop a sufficient awareness in order to bring success. With it now being a common feature of successive Governments to create and introduce more and more confusing and technically drafted criminal legislation, the book is designed to assist the reader in navigating and traversing this legislative quagmire by providing quick reference headings, diagrams, explanations, examples and guidance. The latest in a long line of Criminal Justice Acts to enter the Statute book is the Criminal Justice and Immigration Act 2008 which received the Royal Assent on May 8, 2008 but is yet to be brought into force and is likely to follow a similar pattern experienced with the Criminal Justice Act 2003 of being phased in by Statutory Instrument in a piece-meal manner.

The textbook book should be of real benefit for those studying criminal law, criminal procedure and evidence on the LPC, Bar exams and the ILEX provision. Further it should appeal to those on law and related undergraduate courses, such as criminology and criminal justice. Likewise, it would also benefit those who are newly qualified to the criminal justice profession, including solicitors, barristers, police and other agencies.

To bring together this 1st edition of Criminal Law and Practice has been an immense undertaking and whilst at times almost unbearable, it was my ambition that saw me through those difficult times. It is for that reason I must say a particular thank you to Isabel Owen for her unconditional love, patience and support during those many long nights and weekends when I simply disappeared to fulfill this ambition. My gratitude and sincere thanks must also go to Michelle Walton and Rachel Duckworth for the many hours they dedicated to proof reading the manuscripts. Finally a particular thank you must go to the editorial and marketing staff at Sweet and Maxwell for all their support in the production of the textbook.

The law is as far as it is possible stated as it was on the 25 April 2008. Where possible any recent developments have been added during the proof stage.

Steve Forster LLB
April 2008

CONTENTS

PART III: CRIMINAL EVIDENCE

TABLE OF CASES

*[Paragraph numbers in **bold** indicate where the case has been reproduced]*

R. v Smith. See R. v Edwards (Stewart Dean)
R. v Smith & Tovey. See R. v Tovey (David)
R. v Smith [2006] 2 Cr. App. R. 4 .... 25.11
R. v Smith (Josephine) [2002] EWCA Crim 2671, CA (Crim Div) 3.10
R. v Smith (Lance Percival); R. v Rennie (Stephen Andrew) [2003] EWCA Crim 283; [2003] 1 W.L.R. 2229, CA (Crim Div) 18.44
R. v Smith (Morgan James) [2001] 1 A.C. 146; [2000] 3 W.L.R. 654, HL; affirming [1999] Q.B. 1079; [1999] 2 W.L.R. 610, CA (Crim 3.09, 3.13, 3.14, 3.15
R. v Smith (Patrick); R. v Mercieca (Joseph) [2005] UKHL 12; [2005] 1 W.L.R. 704, HL 18.43
R. v Smith (Shane Stepon) [2003] EWCA Crim 927, CA (Crim Div) 24.29
R. v Smith (Wallace Duncan) (No.3) [2002] EWCA Crim 2907; [2003] Crim. L.R. 398, CA (Crim Div) 20.21
R. v Smolinski (Mark Paul); sub nom. R. v Smolenski (Mark Paul) [2004] EWCA Crim 1270; [2004] 2 Cr. App. R. 40, CA (Crim Div) 28.21
R. v Smurthwaite (Keith); R. v Gill (Susan) [1994] 1 All E.R. 898; (1994) 98 Cr. App. R. 437, CA (Crim Div) 28.12
R. v Smythe (Clive Ormond) (1981) 72 Cr. App. R. 8, CA (Crim Div) 5.40
R. v Soames-Waring (Jonathan Drew) [1999] Crim. L.R. 89, CA (Crim Div) 18.47
R. v Soneji (Kamlesh Kumar); sub nom. R. v Soneiji (Kamalesh Kumar); R. v Bullen (David Frederick) [2005] UKHL 49; [2006] 1 A.C. 340; [2005] 3 W.L.R. 303, HL 13.02, 18.08, 18.19
R. v South East Surrey Youth Court & Ghanbari. See R. (on the application of Crown Prosecution Service) v South East Surrey Youth Court
R. v South Ribble Stipendiary Magistrate Ex p. Cochrane [1996] 2 Cr. App. R. 544; (1996) 160 J.P. 517, DC 23.26
R. v South Worcestershire Magistrates Court Ex p. Roberts, unreported, 2000, DC 16.20
R. v Spear (John); sub nom. Boyd v Army Prosecuting Authority; R. v Williams (David Omar); R. v Saunby (David); R. v Ashby (Mark William); R. v Schofield (John); R. v Hastie (Philip); R. v Boyd (David Morton); R. v Marsh (Peter James); R. v Webb (James Albert); R. v Leese (Henry); R. v Dodds (Andrew Alistair); R. v Clarkson (Lee Martin); R. v English (Paul Anthony) [2002] UKHL 31; [2003] 1 A.C. 734, HL 20.10
R. v Spencer (Alan Widdison); R. v Smails (George Glenville); R. v Ball (Kenneth); R. v Mason (Michael Dennis); R. v White (Paul) [1987] A.C. 128; [1986] 3 W.L.R. 348, HL 18.48, 27.03
R. v Spinks (Mark Lee) [1982] 1 All E.R. 587; (1982) 74 Cr. App. R. 263, CA (Crim Div) 28.08
R. v Spooner. See R. v S
R. v Spratt (Robert Michael) [1990] 1 W.L.R. 1073; [1991] 2 All E.R. 210, CA (Crim Div) 4.10
R. v Stacey (Helen Brenda) [2001] EWCA Crim 2031; (2002) 64 B.M.L.R. 115, CA (Crim Div) 2.22
R. v Stagg, unreported, 1994 .... 28.14
R. v Steer (Dennis) [1988] A.C. 111; [1987] 3 W.L.R. 205, HL 7.14
R. v Stephens (Jerry); R. v Mujuru (Sandra) [2007] EWCA Crim 1249; [2007] 2 Cr. App. R. 26, CA (Crim Div) 8.17
R. v Stipendiary Magistrate for Leicestershire Ex p. Kaur; sub nom. Kaur v DPP (2000) 164 J.P. 127; [2000] C.O.D. 109, QBD 17.12

TABLE OF STATUTES

*[Paragraph numbers in **bold** refer to where legislation is reproduced]*

TABLE OF STATUTORY INSTRUMENTS

*[Paragraph numbers in **bold** refer to where legislation is reproduced]*

CRIMINAL PRACTICE DIRECTION

Part I

CRIMINAL LAW

CHAPTER ONE

INTRODUCTION TO THE CRIMINAL PROCESS

1. THE CRIMINAL PROCESS: PURPOSE, FUNCTION AND THE PUBLIC INTEREST

1.01 The criminal process is the application of the criminal law within the criminal procedure rules in the criminal justice system. The purpose of the substantive criminal law is to ensure that an alleged offender's *culpability* for their prohibited act or omission is properly dealt with and that an appropriate sentence is imposed based on that person's individual circumstances. Criminal law itself operates for and on behalf of the *Public Interest*. Likewise, the purpose of criminal procedure is to ensure throughout an offender's involvement in the criminal process, the fundamental principle of fairness is maintained. Accordingly, *fairness* must be maintained, to the offender, the victim and the community.

Fairness is ensured by having the following:

(1) An independent Criminal Court Structure.

(2) An accountable Police Service.

(3) An independent Prosecution Service (CPS).

(4) A fundamental right to legal representation (Criminal Legal Funding).

(5) Presumptions (i.e. presumption of innocence).

(6) Basic Human Rights, the Human Rights Act 1998, a right to a fair trial.

(7) Strict procedural rules must be followed.

(8) Rules on the admissibility of evidence and the use of s.78 of the Police and Criminal Evidence Act 1984.

(9) An independant jury system.

(10) Victim support and victim impact statements.

In *Hall v Simons* [2000] 3 W.L.R. 543 Lord Hope explained succinctly the purpose of the criminal justice system as follows:

> "Even though the criminal process is formally adversarial, it is of a fundamentally different character to the civil process. Its purpose and function are different. It is to enforce the criminal law. The criminal law and the criminal justice system exists in the interests of society as a whole. It is a directly social function. It is concerned to see that the guilty are convicted and punished and those not proved to be guilty are acquitted. Anyone not proved to be guilty is to be presumed to be not guilty. It is of *fundamental importance* that the process by which the defendant is proved guilty shall be *fair* and it is the public duty of all those concerned in the criminal justice system to see that this is the case. This is the public interest in the system."

Likewise, in *Attorney-General's Reference (No.3 of 1999)* [2001] 1 A.C. 91 Lord Steyn commented:

> "The purpose of the criminal law is to permit everyone to go about their daily lives without fear of harm to person or property. And it is in the interests of everyone that serious crime should be effectively investigated and prosecuted. There must be fairness to all sides. In a criminal case this requires the court to consider a triangulation of interests. It involves taking into account the position of the accused, the victim and his or her family, and the public."

Whilst in *R. v Togher* [2001] 1 Cr.App.R. 457 Lord Woolf noted that:

> "The requirement of fairness in the criminal process has always been a common law tenet of the greatest importance" ... it is not an "abstract concept" nor is it concerned with "technicalities." "If a defendant has not had a fair trial and as a result of that injustice has occurred, it would be extremely unsatisfactory if the powers of this court were not wide enough to rectify that injustice."

It is also worth citing Lord Hope's observation in *Ruddy v Procurator Fiscal* [2006] UKPC 2 that:

> "criminal prosecutions are conducted in the public interest. The factors that have guided judges as to how the principles should be applied in criminal cases are appropriate to that context ... these factors are heavily influenced by considerations of public policy. The considerations operate at large, embracing the need to protect the accused against injustice on the one hand and the need to uphold public confidence in the rule of law on the other. Public policy demands that the accused must be afforded a remedy against injustice. But it also requires the court to balance the rights of the accused against the public interest."

2. The Adversarial System of Justice

1.02 The criminal process in England and Wales is administered and conducted within an adversarial system of justice, as opposed to an inquisitorial system. An adversarial system is based on relevant and admissible evidence, which is then presented by examination in chief and later tested for honesty and accuracy/credibility by way of cross-examination. Rules of evidence, duties and an independent prosecutor, together with an impartial tribunal of fact (jury/magistrates), an appeal system and the independent Criminal

Cases Review Commission, all act so as to ensure that a fair balance is struck between the competing interests.

On the other hand an inquisitorial system (the system preferred by other European Union countries and used by the Coroner's court in England and Wales) is about gathering all the factual evidence which is then assessed not on credibility but on whether the truth can be discovered from that evidence. In *Randall v The Queen* [2003] 1 W.L.R. 56 a Privy Council decision concerning an appeal from the Cayman Islands on the grounds that that the defendant did not receive a fair trial owing to the conduct of prosecuting counsel, Lord Bingham made the following (obiter) observations:

> "A contested criminal trial on indictment is adversarial in character. The prosecution seeks to satisfy the jury of the guilt of the accused beyond reasonable doubt. The defence seeks to resist and rebut such proof. The objects of the parties are fundamentally opposed. There may well be disputes concerning the relevance and admissibility of evidence. There will almost always be a conflict of evidence. Some witnesses may be impugned as unreliable, others perhaps as dishonest. Witnesses on both sides may be accused on exaggerating or even fabricating their evidence".

In *R. v Munnery* [1992] 94 Cr.App.R. 164 Mustill L.J. stated the the strict nature of the adversarial criminal process requires the respective cases for the prosecution and defence to be presented separately in their entirety, first by the prosecution, then by the defence. Although the judge does have discretion to regulate the conduct of the proceedings, only if it is in the interests of justice should there be departure from the normal running order of the proceedings. Any substantial departure is liable to cause confusion. Nevertheless, his Lordship both recognised and accepted that tactics form a legitimate part of the adversarial process, such as where the defence are aware of a gap in the prosecution's case, decide to say nothing about it until the conclusion of the trial, leaving it impossible for the prosecution to be able to rectify the mistake.

3. A Fair Process: "The Triangulation of Interests"

1.03 In order to promote confidence in the rule of law, the criminal process must be seen to be achieving its fundamental aim of convicting the guilty and exculpating the truly innocent. As stated by the Court of Appeal in *R. v Gleeson* [2003] EWCA Crim 3357:

> "a criminal trial is not a game in which a guilty defendant should be provided with a sporting chance. It is a search for the truth in accordance with the twin principles that the prosecution must prove its case and that a defendant is not obliged to inculpate himself, the object being to convict the guilty and acquit the innocent. Requiring a defendant to indicate in advance what he disputes about the prosecution case offends neither of those principles"

The policy of the courts is therefore to strike a fair balance between the public interest in the administration of justice on the one hand and fairness in the criminal process to accused person on the other. In *R. v A (No.2)* [2001] 2 W.L.R. 1546, a case involving the interpretation of s.41 of the Youth Justice and Criminal Evidence Act 1999, the House of Lords spoke of the need to strike a fair balance between the protected rights of the defendant as against the public interest, taking into account the "familiar triangulation of interests of the accused, the victim and society." Sadly, history shows that the lack of fairness can and does lead to serious miscarriages of justice (i.e. the quashing of Sally Clarke's two convictions for the murders of her sons which were obtained on what is now accepted to be seriously flawed expert medical evidence).

The substantive criminal law is a mass of statutory provisions and common law principles of varying complexity. Since Labour came to office in 1997, the Home Office alone has created, amended or modified over 450 criminal offences. Likewise, there has been over 20 major pieces of criminal legislation introduced by the Home Office, and subsequently passed into law, all of which have had a significant impact on the criminal justice system. Take the Criminal Justice Act 2003, which consists of 13 Parts with a total of 339 sections, and 38 schedules, which themselves are split into parts, Schedule 37 having 12 parts. The shear volume of complex legislation and the creation of new criminal offences, (The Sexual Offences Act 2003 created, modified and re-acted 61 criminal offences) makes it difficult for those who practice criminal law to apply and follow such law. Indeed in relation to the Sexual Offences Act 2003 the Court of Appeal in *R. v C* [2006] EWCA Crim 3533 took the view that 2003 will not be identified, were a history of criminal legislation to be written, as a year of "exemplary skill in the annals of Parliamentary drafting" (see Chapter 4 para.4.36). The same can be said for those who study the criminal process. This insatiable appetite of Parliament for introducing complex and over technical legislation with little or no concern for the Rule of Law continues with the Criminal Justice and Immigration Act 2008 which consists of 151 sections and 28 schedules each split into parts. The Act makes numerous amendments, substitutions and insertions to the already over technical and complex Criminal Justice Act 2003 (see the illuminating speech given by Professor Spencer, Q.C. at the 12th Annual Lecture in 2008 entitled "The Drafting of Criminal Legislation: Need it be so Impenetrable?" which can be found at http://www.jsboard.co.uk).

Another problem often encountered is the phased implementation of the provisions themselves over many months, even years, in some instances delaying the implementation date further or only partially implementing a provision. The CJA 2003, for instance, currently has 18 Statutory Instrument Commencement Orders, and still not all of the provisions have effect. This problem is particularly evident in *R. v Rochester* [2008] EWCA Crim 678 (see Part 3 Criminal Evidence, Chapter 23, para.23.17 for a discussion of the case). The case involved the use of the special measures provisions which allow for the hearing of complainant evidence pre-recorded by video.

Although the provision had been brought into force in July 2002 by Commencement Order the problem surrounded the legislative intent behind s.18(2) of the Youth Justice and Criminal Evidence Act 1999, which stated that a special measure shall not be taken to be available until the court has received notification from the Secretary of State. The court concluded that Parliament could not, unless clear language existed, have intended the substantive criminal law to be brought into force by a act of notification by the executive.

The Court noted that the trial involved a serious offence of marital rape with the inevitable distress caused to the complainant by the appeal and the possibility of a re-trial due to a lack of drafting clarity relating to phased implementation not just on a temporal basis but on a geographic basis. If Parliament wished to consider the merits of a change in principle or procedure in certain parts of the country before the changes apply to the whole of England and Wales, then it needed to make that clear in the Act. Further, in must be borne in mind that by doing so there will exist a lack of uniformity in the application of that part of the criminal law.

Nevertheless, the following should always be considered essential to ensuring fair proceedings.

4. The Burden of Proof in a Criminal Trial

1.04 The Prosecution (or the Crown) have the burden of proof. In *Woolmington v DPP* [1935] A.C. 462, 481 Lord Sankey stated that this formed the golden thread of the criminal law and must be observed at all times. This golden thread is also inextricably linked to the common law presumption of innocence which is now stated in art.6(2) of the European Convention on Human Rights as follows:

> "Everyone charged with a criminal offence shall be presumed innocent until proved guilty according to law."

However, in certain circumstances this burden can be reversed and placed on the defendant, and which occurs for a number of offences (for instance, The Offensive Weapons Act 1996 as amended, and the offence of being in possession of an offensive weapon in a public place, requires the defendant to prove that they had good reason or lawful authority for possession of the weapon). However, whilst art.6 preserves the presumption of innocence, ss.75 to 96 of the Criminal Justice Act 2003 which came into effect on April 18, 2005 abolished the double jeopardy rule and allows the Crown to apply to the Court of Appeal for an order quashing a person's acquittal for one of 29 qualifying offences listed in Sch.5 and ordering a retrial for that offence but only if there in now new and compelling evidence (see *R. v Dunlop* [2007] 1 Cr.App.R. 8 and *R. v Miell* [2008] 1 W.L.R. 627).

5. Standard of Proof in a Criminal Trial

1.05 In order to discharge the burden of proof and secure a conviction, the prosecution must, with the presentation of evidence, establish beyond all reasonable doubt so that the jury/magistrates are satisfied so as to be sure that the offender committed the alleged offence. If there is an element of doubt, then the prosecution must fail and the defendant acquitted on the basis that the offence is unproven against them. In *Evans v DPP* [2001] EWHC 369 the High Court quashed the applicant's conviction of assault on the grounds that the magistrates had applied the wrong test. By saying they had weighed up the two different versions (accounts) of events and choosing the complainant over the defendant, they gave the impression that they had applied a test similar to the civil standard of balance of probabilities. Justice had therefore not been seen to have been done. Similarly it was held in *Cooper v DPP* [2002] EWHC 1878, that there was insufficient evidence for the magistrates to find that the defendant was reckless when he had allegedly assaulted a police officer.

6. Unfair Evidence and Section 78 of the Police and Criminal Evidence Act 1984

1.06 The basic proposition in the law of criminal evidence is that if the evidence is relevant to the issue of establishing the ingredients of the offence, then it is prima facie admissible for that purpose, even if the evidence was improperly obtained. Nevertheless, the courts have a discretionary power of exclusion found in s.78 of the Police and Criminal Evidence Act 1984, which provides that the court may exclude any evidence which, having regard to all the circumstances would, if admitted, have an *adverse effect on the fairness of the proceedings* (for instance, the police interview a suspect and refuse them access to a solicitor, or the police find evidence during an unlawful search).

7. Trial Procedure and Article 6

1.07 The defendant must receive a fair trial, the duty of the trial judge is to ensure fairness and that both the prosecution and the defence can present their case properly and be able to test and probe the honesty and accuracy of the other side's case. The rules and procedure within the criminal process exist to ensure fairness to all interested parties and in particular, the defendant. As Lord Bingham said in *Randall v The Queen* [2003] 1 W.L.R. 56:

> "In a criminal trial as in other activities the observance of certain basic rules have been shown to be the most effective safeguard against unfairness, error and abuse."

The passing of the Human Rights Act 1998, which came into force on the

October 2, 2000, gives effect to the European Convention on Human Rights under English Law. Article 6, which enshrines the absolute right to a fair trial, must be protected by the English criminal justice system. Any breach may lead to an unfair conviction. The criminal process can and does maintain its own procedure and principles and has the discretion to alter them. However, at all times the criminal justice process must ensure that this does not in any way infringe the right to a fair trial; if it does then the courts can under s.3 of the Human Rights Act 1998, give a meaning to any conflicting law that ensures compatibility with a Convention right. Nevertheless, if this is unachievable without having to fundamentally change the law, then a declaration of incompatibility can be made and Parliament must seek to make the adjustments.

When dealing with legislation that is potentially in conflict with a Convention right, particularly Art.6, then it is suggested that the three questions outlined by Lord Hope in *Brown v Stott* [2001] 2 W.L.R. 817 ought to be adopted. The first question to be considered is whether the Convention right in question is "absolute"; if not it is open to "modification" or "restriction". If yes, does a "legitimate aim" exist in the public interest? If the answer to this question is yes then is there reasonable proportionality "between the means employed and the aim sought to be realised"? This according to Lord Hope:

> "directs attention to the question whether a fair balance has been struck between the general interest of the community in the realisation of that aim and the protection of the fundamental rights of the individual."

8. Criminal Procedure Rules 2005 (CrPR 2005)

1.08 These came into effect on April 4, 2005 and are specifically designed to bring the procedural rules within a simplified single code, with a greater emphasis on case management, following on the success of the civil procedure rules. The complete rules and updates can be found on the Ministry of Justice website at http://www.justice.gov.uk. Any breach of the rules can amount to an abuse of process and any evidence may be excluded from the trial.

9. Criminal Offences and Legal Certainty

1.09 There exist many hundreds of different criminal offences, some dating back many years. Nevertheless, all criminal offences have a definition. The bulk of criminal offences are defined in *statute law*, law created by our English Parliament, (for instance the definition of theft is found in s.1 of the Theft Act 1968). Nevertheless there still exist a number of offences that are defined in the common law, law created by the appeal courts in England and Wales (for instance the offences of murder and manslaughter are defined in previous Appeal Court cases which have become an established precedent). In *R. v Jones* [2007] 1 A.C. 136 Lord Bingham observed:

> "that there exists no power in the courts to create new criminal offences, as decided by a unanimous House in *Knuller v DPP* [1973] AC 435. While old common law offences survive until abolished or superseded by statute, new ones are not created. Statute is now the sole source of new criminal offences."

Neither does the court, as confirmed by the House of Lords in *R. v Rimmington & Goldstein* [2006] 1 A.C. 459, have a power to abolish existing common law offences. It is for Parliament, following consultation, to decide whether, as in this case, the common law offence of public nuisance still has a purpose in protecting the public. Importantly, Lord Bingham stated that if the alleged facts fall within the ingredients of a statutory offence as well as a common law offence, then as a matter of good practice and respect for the primacy of statute law, the statutory offence ought to be prosecuted unless there is good reason for charging the common law offence instead. What would not generally be a good reason is the prosecution resorting to the common law offence in order to avoid a statutory defence, time limit or procedural step, i.e. mode of trial, or a statutory maximum penalty as opposed to an unlimited common law one. Lord Bingham recognised 11 possible alternative statutory offences, ranging from environmental, public order, terrorism and communication offences to that of common law public nuisance, and that whilst the offence still existed, it would be relatively rare for a prosecution to proceed on the basis of a public nuisance (see s.79 of the CJIA 2008 which abolishes the common law offence of blasphemy).

It is important therefore for the prosecution to charge for the appropriate offence as against the facts and evidence surrounding the allegation. This point is clearly illustrated in *R. v Zafar* [2008] 2 W.L.R. 1013 when the Court of Appeal quashed the conviction of the appellants for an offence under s.57 of the Terrorism Act 2000. The disputed element of the offence was whether the possession of extremist literature electronically stored is for a purpose connected with the commission, preparation or instigation of an act of terrorism. On the facts, the Court held that the prosecution failed to prove a casual connection between the stored information and the suggestion that they were planning to form part of the resistance in Afghanistan. The stored literature could be used for various purposes, such as enjoyment or education.

The Court of Appeal ruled that for s.57 to have the necessary legal certainty, then as a matter of statutory construction within the definition of the offence there must be a requirement for the proof of a direct connection between the article possessed and the alleged act of terrorism to which it is connected. The Court was prepared to re-write the section in order to achieve this by removing the expression "for a purposed connected" and replacing it with "that he intends it to be used for the purpose". This inserts a specific intent (mens rea) in order to give legal culpable certainty. In the instant case, there was no evidence to establish that the appellants had intended the literature to be used by themselves in order to be involved in acts of terrorism abroad. However, the question will remain whether the Court of Appeal has usurped the legislative role of Parliament and breached the separation of powers.

On another construction point, the Court with some hesitation construed the word "instigate" as synonymous with incite, so that so that possessing articles for the intended purpose of inciting (instigating) terrorist acts falls within the definition of the offence, although this may not had formed part of the intention of Parliament. In such circumstances, a better course would be for the prosecution to charge for an offence under s.58 of collecting or making a record of information of a kind likely to be useful to a person in committing or preparing an act of terrorism, or an offence of inciting terrorism overseas under s.59.

One of the important foundational pillars of constitutional law is the rule of law. Within the concept of the rule of law is the requirement that the law must be accessible to all, which means that the law must have certainty and predictability in the sense that all citizens can look at the law, i.e. the criminal offence and be able to indentify the essential ingredients to it, so that they are then in a position to adjust their conduct so as to avoid the commission of the offence. In this context, Lord Bingham, having reviewed the previous authorities, observed that:

> "Vague laws which purport to create criminal liability are undesirable, and in extreme cases, where it occurs, their very vagueness may make it impossible to identify the conduct which is prohibited by a criminal sanction. If the court is forced to guess at the ingredients of a purported crime any conviction for it would be unsafe. That said, however, the requirement is for sufficient rather than absolute certainty."

Article 7 of the European Convention on Human Rights is headed "no punishment without law" and encapsulates two important principles: (i) no punishment can be imposed unless the offence has sufficient clarity so as to allow the alleged offender to be aware of the prohibited conduct, before they embark upon it; (ii) no person should suffer a punishment for an offence that did not exist at the time of the alleged act. This second principle confirms the presumption against the retrospective application of the criminal law. Nevertheless, interference with these two principles is permissible provided it is justified as being "in accordance with the law" if reliance is placed on (art.8) or "prescribed by law" if involving art.10. A State when creating a criminal offence is not required to maintain absolute certainty. Such a requirement would cause the law to become rigid, with an inability to adapt to social change. If the law is sufficiently ascertainable, then there will be no breach of art.7.

Caution must always be adopted, if a criminal offence when created applies retrospectively. The court will need to strike a balance between the differing interests. This point is clearly highlighted in *R. v R* [1991] 4 All E.R. 481 when the House of Lords, affirming the decision of the Court of Appeal, ruled unanimously that Hale's proposition of law that a woman once married cannot retract the implied consent to sex with her husband amounted now to a fiction and that social, economic, and cultural developments rendered it "anachronistic and offensive". The principle could no longer within a system of binding precedent be justifiably sustained in accordance with a statutorily defined offence of rape. This point was challenged in *SW and CW v UK* [1996] 21 E.H.R.R. 363 before the ECHR as breaching art.7 on the grounds, that at the time of the intercourse or attempted intercourse without the consent of his partner, the defendant would not have known this to be an offence and was therefore unable to adjust his conduct. The ECHR rejected this contention in its entirety and endorsed the importance of the English Common Law being able to adapt to changing circumstances and that art.7:

> "cannot be read as out-lawing the gradual clarification of the rules of criminal liability through judicial interpretation from case to case, provided the resultant development is consistent with the essence of the offence and could be reasonably be foreseen."

The very object of the Convention is to maintain respect for human dignity and freedom, the husband's immunity is clearly perverse and at odds with this fundamental objective. It cannot be said that the prosecution of the defendant amounted to an abuse of process or was in breach of art.7, the protection of the wife against inhuman or degrading treatment proportionately outweighed the marriage immunity. Although this development of judicial law making which is now consolidated in to the definition of rape in s.1 of the Sexual Offences Act 2003 was correct, the decision in *R. v C* [2004] EWCA Crim 292 was less so. In this case, the Court of Appeal, approving the unreported decision in *R. v Graham L* (unreported, May 7, 2003), ruled that a man can still be properly convicted for raping his wife which had occurred before the judgment in *R. v R*. In this instance, the Court of Appeal upheld the appellant's conviction for the rape of his wife which had occurred some 25 years earlier in the 1970s. To allow the retrospective prosecution of historic offences would be to render the safeguard contained in art.7, the purpose of which is to prevent arbitrary proceedings and punishment, without meaning.

In *R. v K and R* [2008] 2 W.L.R. 1026 the Court of Appeal rejected the contention of the appellant that the offence of collecting information of a kind likely to be useful to another for terrorist acts, lacked the necessary legality of certainty. The expression "of a kind likely to be useful" is sufficiently certain in that it requires proof that the information is to be used to assist an act of terrorism. Such information, once identified, then demands from the defendant an explanation by raising the defence of reasonable excuse.

It is good practice for any criminal law student or practitioner to look at the legal source of the alleged criminal offence and establish what the prosecution must prove in order to sustain a conviction. Look at the precise wording of the offence; do the words bring about an interpretive dispute as to the meaning and context used; what was Parliament's intention when adopting that word? Does this raise a possible question of law for judicial resolution, consider the prosecution's disclosed evidence, on a question of fact, would a jury convict or can a doubt be established? All offences, unless strictly liable (offences which only require the proof of the prohibited conduct) contain two essential elements of proof together with causation namely:

(i) mens rea, this is Latin and describes the mental element of the offence. The two main words generally used to describe the mens rea are, intention and recklessness. (See Chapter Two)

(ii) actus reus, this again is Latin and describes the prohibited *conduct or omission* in the offence. (See Chapter Two).

It is these two elements found in the definition of a criminal offence, which the prosecution must prove evidentially to exist in order to secure a conviction. If neither or one of them is missing, then the defendant must be acquitted. A paradox of the criminal law is that the role and duty of the prosecution is to prove the ingredients of the offence beyond doubt. This does not necessarily mean that the defendant is guilty or indeed innocent, it simply means that the prosecution, by adducing sufficient evidence to the tribunal of fact, has established the ingredients to the offence and therefore proved its case to the required standard and nothing more is needed.

10. Jurisdiction of Criminal Law

1.10 In terms of the prosecution of criminal offences, this is confined to the jurisdictional boundaries of England and Wales, Scotland and in certain respects, Northern Ireland having in essence its own parallel jurisdiction. Accordingly all criminal acts committed within the territorial boundaries of England and Wales will be prosecuted in either the magistrates' court or the Crown Court. If a British national commits an offence in another jurisdiction, even though such an act would amount to offence in England and Wales, it will be for the relevant prosecuting authority of that State to proceed with a criminal prosecution, subject to extradition proceedings or European Arrest Warrant; the CPS or Ministry of Justice cannot interfere.

This presumption of jurisdiction was clearly affirmed by the House of Lords in *R. v Treacy* [1971] A.C. 536. Nevertheless, Parliament has felt the need to intervene for certain criminal activity which is committed by a UK national in a foreign state to be prosecuted legitimately in England and Wales. A clear example of this is s.72 of the Sexual Offences Act 2003 as amended by s.72 of the Criminal Justice and Immigration Act 2008, when in force. See also the Sexual Offences (Conspiracy and Incitement) Act 1996.

Other exceptions include murder (see *R. v Hamza* [2006] EWCA Crim 2918). Likewise Pt 1 of the Criminal Justice Act 1993 sets out the statutory jurisdiction of fraud and dishonesty offences as amended by the Fraud Act 2006 and any related inchoate offence. Part 1 divides offences into group A and group B. Group A offences are the substantive offences of fraud and allow the prosecution of offenders provided any of the relevant event relating to the definition of the offence occurred in England and Wales, it is immaterial whether other events arose abroad or the offence was initiated here and committed aboard or instead was initiated abroad. Group B offences relate to committing the inchoate offences of a group A offence, i.e. conspiracy to commit a fraud outside England and Wales.

Of notable concern is the ceding of the exclusive sovereignty of Parliament to create and regulate its criminal law and justice system, to the legislature (European Commission) of the EU. This dramatic shift can be seen in the judgment of the European Court of Justice in *Commission of the European Communities v Council of the European Union* [2005] ECR 1-7879 Case C-176/03 in which it was held that the EU can in order to achieve its aim of the protection of the environment impose harmonised criminal sanctions for the offences derived from European law. (See Part 3 of the Consumer Protection from Unfair Trading Regulations 2008 (SI 2008/1277) which came into effect on May 26, 2008. The Regulations implement Council Directive 2005/29 and harmonises the criminal offences relating to unfair business-to-consumer commercial practices.)

11. Definition of Theft: An Example

1.11 Section 1 of the Theft Act 1968 provides that a person is guilty of theft if they dishonestly appropriate property belonging to another with the intention of permanently depriving the other of it. The mens rea consists of two elements: dishonesty and the intention of permanently depriving the other of it. The actus reus consists of the three elements of appropriates, property and belonging to another. The word "appropriates" is defined in s.3 to mean any assumption of the rights of the owner. However, despite this the House of Lords has, on three occasions, had to interpret the legal meaning of the word in respect of whether the prosecution is also required to prove that the owner did not consent to the taking or whether consent is irrelevant (see Theft, Chapter Five, below).

12. The Defence

1.12 It is vital for any defence practitioner to argue that the defendant does not have the mens rea or actus reus, or alternatively the defence may argue their case on one of a number of established general defences as follows: (i) automatism; (ii) insanity; (iii) necessity; (iv) duress; (v) mistake; (vi) intoxication; (vii) self defence. In addition, there also exists the specific partial defences of diminished responsibility and provocation, which can only be raised to an offence of murder, and not any other offence. If established the defendant's culpability, which on the facts amounts to murder, is owing to those extenuating circumstances reduced to what is called voluntary manslaughter.

13. What is Required to be Successful in Examinations/Practice

1.13

The key to success is based on the following two elements:

(i) Knowledge (In-depth awareness of the offences and defences).

(ii) Application of that knowledge (It is one thing having the knowledge but it is of little use to you if you cannot apply that knowledge). This means that you must be able to apply your knowledge to a legal question by stating what the law is and then applying it to a set of facts and providing sound advice to a client.

14. General Approach to Case Study and Problem Type Questions

1.14

Case Studies and problem questions are a popular method of assessment in law courses. Case studies are a method used by the Institute of Legal Executives, in which the student receives in advance a case study file containing documents such as witness statements, police interviews, summary of alleged offence and file notes for the defence. In the exam, the student is then given the questions which relate to the case study. Other law courses use unseen examinations, which contain problem and essay type questions. Problem questions follow the format of a short set of facts which introduce the parties involved. The student is then asked to advise some or all of the parties, of their criminal liability.

When revising for the case study or for problem questions the following is a useful guide to achieve a good result:

Step One: Identify the potential offence(s) of each party based on their involvement

In a criminal law question you first look to identify the alleged offence or offences (of any of the parties in question) (knowledge). What must the prosecution prove to achieve a conviction? i.e. strengths/weaknesses in the evidence, mens rea and actus reus (knowledge). Apply this knowledge to the disputed facts and where necessary refer to any relevant statutory provisions and case authorities.

Step Two: Identify any Possible Defences

It is now important to consider the position of the parties that require your advice. In particular do any of the established defences exist, what must the defence show to establish a defence, i.e. self-defence in order to achieve an acquittal (Knowledge).

Step Three: Causation in Law and Fact

The prosecution must also prove that the prohibited act of the defendant, both in fact and in law (i.e. legal principle), have caused the consequence/result which occurred. The issue that generally arises is was there an intervening event that broke the chain of causation; if so, then the prosecution will have failed to prove the causational link between the defendant's act and the consequence/result which occurred. There are several authorities on this point to consider.

Step Four: Application of knowledge to the facts presented.

In either a case study or examination or indeed in practice you will be presented with a given set of facts relating to the parties in question. You must apply your knowledge to these facts. In other words you need to advise your client (if a problem question) on whether the prosecution can prove the offences or whether they can prove part but not all of the elements, advise the client whether on the facts there exists a good defence, i.e. self defence, then advise on the prospects.

15. Critical Analysis: Essay Questions

1.15 If the question is of the essay type, then usually there is a short statement/assertion, followed by the task, i.e. critically examine, critically assess. In this instance, it is important that you have the proven ability to provide a well-reasoned and convincing analysis of the law. This involves identifying the viewpoint of the statement and then applying to it the strengths/weaknesses, any shortcomings or injustices surrounding that area of law. This must, where the opportunity arises, be supported by case authorities (including conflicting precedent), statutory provisions and judicial interpretation. It is important that each paragraph makes a significant legal point, which is referred directly to the question under review.

Chapter Two

THE ESSENTIAL ELEMENTS OF CRIMINAL LIABILITY

1. Introduction: Basic Requirements of Criminal Liability

2.01 The basic requirement of the criminal law is that in order for the accused to be guilty of a criminal offence, the prosecution must prove that the accused committed the two fundamental elements of an actus reus with the necessary mens rea that exist within the definition of a criminal offence, together with the third element of causation. This requirement is derived from the somewhat imprecise Latin maxim "*actus non facit reum, nisi mens sit rea*". In *R. v Tolson* [1889] 23 Q.B.D. 168, a case involving the offence of bigamy Stephen J. commented:

> "The principle involved appears to me, when fully considered, to amount to no more than this. The full definition of every crime contains expressly or by implication a proposition as to a state of mind. Therefore, if the mental element of any conduct alleged to be a crime is proved to have been absent in any given case, the crime so defined is not committed; or, again, if a crime if fully defined, nothing amounts to that crime which does not satisfy that definition. Crimes are in the present day much more accurately defined by statute or otherwise than they formally were."

When looking at the definition of a criminal offence, it is important to identify which words or expressions define the mens rea and actus reus of the offence. It is these two elements that the prosecution must prove if a conviction is to be obtained. Conversely, the defence may challenge evidentially the existence of the two elements. It is essential therefore to note that it is always necessary, in the first instance, to assess the definition of the offence and what is required to prove the offence. *R. v Rimmington & Goldstein* [2006] 1 A.C. 459 provides a clear example of the need to prove the elements of the alleged offence. The House of Lords quashed the conviction of public nuisance against, first the appellant Rimmington who whilst having sent over 500 racially offensive letters and parcels to several individuals, the accumulative effect of these individual acts did not, no matter how persistent, or objectionable constitute the actus reus of the offence.

An essential element of the offence is that the prosecution must prove that the alleged act of nuisance affected the community or a section of the public, not individuals. The House of Lords felt that the Court of Appeal had incorrectly regarded itself bound by the decision in *R. v Johnson* [1997] 1 W.L.R. 367, by being entitled to consider the cumulative effect of the appellant's act. This approach was mistaken and now overruled. Likewise, the House of Lords quashed the conviction of the second defendant who as a joke aimed at a friend, had sent salt in an envelope through the post. However, the salt seeped out at a sorting office causing major disruption based on a suspicion that the salt was a more sinister substance. In respect of the offence of public nuisance, the House of Lords ruled that the mens rea of the offence required the prosecution to prove that the defendant knew, or ought to have known (because the means of knowledge were available to him) what would be the consequences of what he did, or omitted to do. The House of Lords ruled that the prosecution had on the facts failed to prove the required knowledge element. The appellant, neither intended nor could have known, that the salt would escape, even if he had, he could not have known of the ensuing disruption caused by the leakage.

2. Actus Reus: The Prohibited Conduct of the Offence

2.02 The actus reus of a criminal offence defines the "prohibited act" and if performed will attract criminal liability. In many instances, the actus reus is straightforward. For instance, punching your victim in the face (provided there exists no defence) amounts to an assault, the act of punching causing an injury is the actus reus of the offence and such an act will attract criminal liability. Nevertheless, it will be necessary to look at the concept of the actus reus in more detail in order to provide a greater awareness of its application. The actus reus of all criminal offences will generally fall into one of three possible situations; this is dependant on the nature of the offence itself and the act or conduct that is to be prohibited. The three possible situations are as follows:

(i) where the defendant carries out an unlawful, deliberate, positive and voluntary act; or

(ii) where the defendant fails to act by an omission or a duty owed to another; or

(iii) where there is a given state of affairs.

3. Mens Rea: The Mental Element of the Offence; Culpable Blameworthiness and Morality

2.03 The mens rea of a criminal offence establishes the "mental element" of the offence and means that the defendant had the necessary mental state or degree of fault at the relevant time the actus reus was carried out. To refer to the mens rea as a "guilty mind" is perhaps a somewhat imprecise meaning, since one may have a motive that is morally wrong, i.e. a guilty mind, but this does not necessarily attract criminal liability. For instance, morally it may be considered wrong to have sex with a prostitute in private, morally it may be considered wrong for a man or woman to have an elicit affair, but these moral issues (guilty minds) do not warrant the intrusion of the criminal law. In many instances of the criminal law, it is difficult to distinguish between immorality and law. In *R. v Howe* [1987] A.C. 417, a case concerning the defence of duress, Lord Hailsham himself acknowledged this when he stated:

> "This brings me back to principle. I begin by affirming that, while there can never be a direct correspondence between law and morality, an attempt to divorce the two entirely is and always proved to be, doomed to failure, and, in the present case, the overriding objects of the criminal law must be to protect innocent lives and to set a standard of conduct which ordinary men and women are expected to observe if they are to avoid criminal responsibility."

Nevertheless, in *R. v Hinks* [2000] 1 Cr.App.R. 1, a difficult case concerning whether valid gifts can amount to theft, Lord Hobhouse stated:

> "an essential function of the criminal law is to define the boundary between what conduct is criminal and what is merely immoral. Both are the subject of the disapprobation of ordinary right-thinking citizens and the distinction is liable to be arbitrary or at least strongly influenced by considerations subjective to the individual members of the tribunal. To treat otherwise lawful conduct as criminal merely because it is open to such disapprobation would be contrary to principle and open to objection that it fails to achieve the objective and transparent certainty required of the criminal law by the principles basic to human rights."

It is important to be aware that what amounts to the mental element of a crime, is defined in terms of culpability and seriousness. For instance under s.20 of the Offences Against the Person Act 1861, it is an offence for a person, either to intentionally or recklessly (maliciously) inflict grievous bodily harm on another person or intentionally recklessly (maliciously) wound that person. On conviction, the maximum sentence is one of five years' imprisonment by the Crown Court. However, under s.29 of the Crime and Disorder Act 1998, this offence becomes more serious, if it is proved to be *racially-aggravated* as defined in s.29 and carries this time a maximum sentence of seven years' imprisonment in the Crown Court. Another example is ss.8 and 10 of the Sexual Offences Act 2003, both similar offences of intentionally causing or inciting a child to engage in sexual activity. Section 8 specifically provides for a child under 13 and carries life imprisonment, whereas s.10 deals with a defendant over 18 and a child under 16 and carries a maximum penalty of 14 years' imprisonment. The purpose of the two provisions clearly reflects the intention of Parliament to make a defendant more culpable if the incitement is directed towards a child below the age of puberty (i.e. under 13). This amounts to a more serious offence than that of inciting a child under 16 which of itself is treated seriously (see *R. v Jones* [2007] EWCA Crim 1118).

Nevertheless, ensuring that the appropriate offence to be charged proportionately represents the degree of culpability of the defendant is not always that straightforward. This is well illustrated in *R. v G* [2008] UKHL 37, when Lord Hope in his dissenting judgment felt that it was wrong and clearly disproportionate for a 15-year-old defendant to suffer a conviction for rape of a child under 13 contrary to s.5 of the Sexual Offences Act 2003 in circumstances where the complainant had consented. The appropriate charge which corresponded with the defendant's culpability was a less serious sex offence committed by someone under 18 contained in s.13. The majority of their Lordships, on the other hand were unmoved by the potential stigmatisation of the defendant having a rape conviction for consensual sex. Lord Hoffman found it an "astonishing proposition" that the law should distinguish for the purposes of a s.5 offence between the culpability of a defendant under 18 as opposed to one over 18 and that it would be prejudicial to a young defendant to be guilty unless there was evidence of coercion. Both age and consent are irrelevant elements to the proof of the s.5 offence the primary aim of the offence is the protection of young children from exploitation by a male of any age.

Another point discussed in the appeal was the application of the principle of representative labelling. This means that the label or descriptive name given to the crime such as "rape", should match and correspond with the nature and gravity of the acts carried out by the defendant. The main justification for this rule is that it prevents the defendant from being inappropriately labelled to a particular crime that is wholly unrepresentative of his actions. Is it therefore appropriate to label a 15-year-old boy who as mutual consensual sex with a girl under 13 as a "child rapist"? Baroness Hale observed that whilst the word rape does imply a lack of consent, in this instance, Parliament has chosen to describe penetrative sex with a child under 13 regardless of whether they consented as being justifiably serious enough to amount to rape. This is required in order to protect children under 13 and to ensure that the male whatever their age is fully aware of the need to take responsibility in choosing whom they have sex with in private.

4. Different Words/Expressions that Define the Mens Rea in Terms of Culpability

2.04 The words that define the mens rea to be found in the majority of criminal offences consist of several different mental attitudes, each of which necessarily sets out the degree of culpability to be attached to that offence. The following are the commonly encountered expressions/words that describe the necessary mens rea:

(i) *Intention:* for instance s.18 of the Offences Against the Person Act 1981 states that it is an offence to cause GBH with intent;

or

(ii) *Recklessness:* (maliciously) for instance; s.1 of the Criminal Damage Act 1971 provides that a person commits an offence if they without lawful excuse destroy or damage any property belonging to another *intending* to destroy or damage such property or *being reckless* as to whether a such property would be destroyed or damaged;

or

(iii) *Negligence:* for instance; manslaughter by gross negligence (see below the case of *R. v Adomako* in Chapter Three) or "recklessly or negligently" doing an act which is likely to endanger the safety of an aircraft contrary to art.55 of the Air Navigation Order 2005 (SI 2005/1970);

or

(iv) *Knowledge:* for instance; s.170(2) of the Customs and Excise Management Act 1979 provides for the offence of *knowingly* being concerned in the *fraudulent* evasion of the restriction on the importation of prohibited goods. Another example is s.9 of the Terrorism Act 2000 which creates the offence of providing instruction or training in handling noxious substances, method or technique, or design or adaptation for the purposes of acts of terrorism. The mens rea of the offences is established if the person providing that instruction or training knows that the person receiving it intends to use those skills for the purposes of acts of terrorism;

or

(v) *Willful:* for instance; s.127(1) of the Mental Health Act 1983 makes it an offence to *willfully neglect* a patient. Under s.1(A) of the Children and Young Persons Act 1933 it is an offence for any person 16 years or over who has responsibility for any child or young person under that age, to willfully assault, ill treat, neglect, abandon or expose them, or cause them or procure them to be assaulted, ill treated, neglected, abandoned, or exposed, in a manner likely to cause them unnecessary suffering or injury to health. The word neglect in this offence amounts to a negative act and is qualified by the word willfully, Section 1(2)(a) provides that a parent (or other person legally liable to maintain a child) shall be deemed to have neglected him in a manner likely to cause injury to his health if he has failed to provide adequate . . . medical aid . . . or if, having been unable otherwise to provide such . . . medical aid . . . he has failed to take steps to procure it to be provided under the enactments applicable in that behalf";

or

(vi) *Reasonable Suspicion or likelihood:* ss.57 and 58 of the Terrorism Act 2000 both create criminal liability from either an objective reasonable suspicion, or an likelihood that either articles or information are either intended for the purposes, or are useful to another in the act of terrorism.

5. The Offence of Criminal Damage: An Example

2.05 The offence of criminal damage is found in the Criminal Damage Act 1971, which creates the followings offences:

(i) Simple Criminal Damage: without lawful excuse, destroying or damaging property belonging to another, intentionally or recklessly (s.1(1) Criminal Damage Act 1971).

(ii) Aggravated Criminal Damage: destroying or damaging property belonging to oneself or another intentionally or recklessly, intending to endanger the life of another or being reckless as to whether the life of another is endangered: s.1(2) Criminal Damage Act 1971.

Looking at the offence of aggravated criminal damage, the mens rea is defined by using the words intentionally or recklessly, intentionally being the most culpable of states of mind while recklessly is a lesser state of mind that covers those where it cannot be proved that it was the aim to commit the actus reus, but instead where there was awareness of the risk of endangerment to another from the damage/destruction. Likewise, the mens rea in aggravated criminal damage makes the defendant more culpable than a defendant who has a mens rea for simple criminal damage, since there is no endangerment to the life of another, for simple criminal damage.

6. The Application of the Actus Reus

2.06 Whilst the actus reus of an offence can be explained in simple terms as amounting to the prohibited conduct, it is also important to be aware of and be able to identify the principles that explain the circumstances in which this prohibited conduct can arise. The principles are as follows.

7. The Defendant's Act must be Shown to be a Voluntary, Positive and Deliberate Act

2.07 In order to attract criminal liability, a defendant's conduct or act must be voluntary in the sense that they have complete physical control of their actions, not unconscious involuntary action that is uninitiated and uncontrolled by the defendant. For example, where a motorist whilst driving is suddenly attacked by a swarm of bees or suddenly suffers a muscle spasm or a convulsion without any control by the mind, and crashes killing a pedestrian, this potentially amounts to an involuntary act (this in effect amounts to the defence of automatism). In *Bratty v Att-Gen-for NI* [1961] A.C. 386, Lord Denning in the House of Lords stated:

> "No act is punishable if it is done involuntarily: and an involuntary act in this context.... means an act which is done by the muscles without any control by the mind such as a spasm, a reflex action or a convulsion; or an act done by a person who is not conscious of what he is doing such an act done whilst suffering from concussion or whilst sleepwalking."

It must also be shown that the defendant's act was both a positive and deliberate act. A positive act requires the defendant to have completed the prohibited act, and until such time there is no actus reus for the complete offence. To commit the actus reus of murder requires the positive physical act, which results in death; for instance strangulation with a ligature. A deliberate act requires proof that the defendant wanted to bring about the actual prohibited act. For instance; by placing a ligature around a person's neck after an argument and pulling tightly would be for no other reason, but to bring about death in those circumstances. Secondly, the requirement for the prosecution to show that the act was deliberate, is to distinguish from and allow for a defence of an accident. If a jury should accept that the defendant's act was an accident, then they will not have committed the actus reus of the offence. For example; a person is chopping vegetables in the kitchen, when their friend who is walking towards them with a glass of wine, suddenly slips and falls directly on to the knife held in the defendant's hand who tried to save their friend from the fall, causing fatal injuries. On the facts this would amount to a tragic accident, but not the actus reus for murder or manslaughter.

8. The Defendant's Act must be "Unlawful"

2.08 For many offences there is a specific requirement for the prosecution to prove that the defendant's act was committed "unlawfully", both fatal and non-fatal offences have this requirement. The use of the word "unlawful" is significant and it is important to be fully aware of this requirement. In the context of fatal and non-fatal offences, the defendant is able to claim that they acted in self-defence, which amounts to a legal justification defence. If the jury accepts that the defendant acted in self-defence, then although the defendant had the mens rea and committed the act, this was legally justified and therefore lawful. The defendant will be acquitted since they acted lawfully in the circumstances. Another example is the offence of rape (see Chapter Four), if acquaintance rape the defendant does not deny the actual act of intercourse, but states that the act was not deliberate, it was done with consent.

9. The Defendant's Failure or Omission to Act as Opposed to a Positive Act

2.09 In certain limited circumstances the actus reus of an offence can consist not of a positive act but of an omission or failure to act. The term "omission" basically means a failure to do what is expected in the circumstances when there is some kind of duty to do so, or on the basis of some relationship or role. Accordingly a failure to act where action is required by the criminal law, may give raise to the actus reus. The important issue to be aware of and be able to identify with clarity, is the answer to the question; when in law is someone under a duty to act? This can be a difficult question to determine and it is important to be aware that the answer generally lies in public policy, meaning that it is in the public interest that should a person fail to do some act or closes their eyes to the necessary performance of such an act, criminal responsibility is justified. This is to ensure that, in certain circumstances, those involved will comply with the duty to act and avoid the consequences that would arise if they didn't act.

Lord Mustill in *Airedale National Health Trust v Bland* [1993] A.C. 789 explained succinctly the difficulties in distinguishing criminal liability as between an act and an omission in the following terms:

> "Acts and omissions. The English criminal law, and also it would appear from the cases cited, the law of Transatlantic State Jurisdictions, draws a sharp distinction between acts and omissions. If an act resulting in death is done without lawful excuse and with intent to kill it is murder. But an omission to act with the same result and with the same intent is in general no offence at all. So also with lesser crimes. To this general principle there are limited statutory exceptions, irrelevant here. There is also one important general exception of common law, namely that a person may be criminally liable for the consequences of an omission *if he stands in such relation to the victim that he is under a duty to act*. Where the result is death the offence will usually be manslaughter, but if the necessary intent is proved it will be murder. Precisely in what circumstance such a duty should be held to exist is at present quite unclear. No doubt it would be too stern a morality to place human beings on the same footing as regards criminal responsibility for allowing an undesirable state of affairs to continue as for bringing that state of affairs to being, but even if there is sense in the distinction the current state of law is unsatisfactory, both morally and intellectually, as shown by the troubling case of *R. v. Stone* (1977) QB 354. We cannot however try to put it in order here. For the time being all are agreed that the distinction between acts and missions exists and we must give effect to it."

To add further confusion, the duty to act is found both in the common law and also under statute law. We shall look at each in order to gain a greater awareness of the principles that exist, which establish criminal liability for a failure to act.

10. A Duty to Act that Arises Under Statute Law

2.10 There are many instances where Parliament has decided that on grounds of public policy it is necessary to create a criminal offence to punish not a positive act but a failure or legal requirement to do a certain act. Many of these, for example, exist in road traffic law and are clearly uncontroversial in terms of public safely. Section 170 of the Road Traffic Act 1988, for instance, provides that a driver is under a duty to report an accident involving personal injury to the police, failure to do so (i.e. the omission) amounts to an offence, or failing to stop after an accident and furnish one's details also amounts to an offence. It is also an offence not to have a valid insurance certificate or MOT certificate. It is an offence to fail to produce these documents upon request. Another important uncontroversial example is the failure to provide a specimen of breath in circumstances where there is a suspicion that the driver has been drinking.

The Anti Social Behavour Act 2005 (ASBA 2005) contains a number of statutory failure offences relating to closure orders issued by a local authority in regard to noisy premises. If the person to whom the notice was served fails without reasonable excuse to comply they commit a summary offence punishable with three months' imprisonment and a fine of up to £20,000. Under s.1 of the ASBA 2005, the police have a power to issue a closure notice or in respect of of premises where there are reasonable grounds for believing that they are connected with unlawful drug use. Any person who fails to comply with this notice commits a summary offence. The use of closure notices will, when s.118 and Sch.20 to the Criminal Justice and Immigration Act 2008 come into force, be available for premises associated with persistent disorder or nuisance. Similarly, under ss.58 to 60 it is an offence to fail to comply with a direction of the police concerning trespass on land for the purposes of a rave, or aggravated trespass. Another important provision is the power contained in s.30 of the ASBA 2005, which gives the police a power to issue one of three specified directions for the dispersal of a group of two or more persons in a public place. But only if there are reasonable grounds for believing that members of the public have been intimidated, harassed, alarmed or distressed as a result of the group's presence. A person who knowingly contravenes a lawful direction commits a summary offence. In *R. (Singh) v Chief Constable of West Midlands Police* [2006] 1 W.L.R. 3374, the Court of Appeal ruled that the parliamentary intention behind the dispersal power in s.30 was also to apply to protests and that this was properly prescribed by law and was necessary to prevent disorder and crime. Section 30 is a justifiable and proportionate response in pursuing the legitimate aim of preventing crime and the protection of public safety. For this reason the provision is compatible with art.10 and a right to freedom of expression and does not require being read down by the Court under s.3 of the HRA 1998.

Nevertheless, in *Bucknell v DPP* [2006] EWHC 1888, the High Court ruled that unless there are exceptional circumstances, there must be before a constable can form the necessary reasonable belief, objectively some evidence that the behaviour of the group causes or is likely to cause harassment, intimidation, alarm or distress. To rule otherwise would lead to an unwarranted intrusion into the right of free movement in public, or to pursue legitimate activities in a proper manner. Personal experience and feelings are not sufficient, there must be actual behaviour.

Another interesting example is s.12 of the Criminal Justice and Police Act 2001 which provides that if a constable reasonably believes that a person is, or has been, consuming intoxicating liquor in a designated public place (defined in s.14) or intends to do so, then the constable can require the person,

(i) not to consume in that place anything which is, or the constable reasonably believes to be, intoxicating liquor;

(ii) to surrender anything in his possession which, is or which the constable reasonably believes to be intoxicating liquor or a container for such liquor (other than a sealed container).

A person who fails without reasonable excuse to comply with the requirement commits a summary offence. Continuing with this theme, s.27 of the Violent Crime Reduction Act 2006 provides a uniformed police officer with a power to give written directions requiring a person aged 16 or over to leave the locality of a public place (defined in s.27(8)) and prohibit them from returning for a period of up to 58 hours. Before giving the direction the officer must be satisfied in all the circumstances that the person's presence is likely to cause or contribute to the occurrence of alcohol related crime or disorder and the direction is necessary to reduce that risk. Any failure to comply with such directions amounts to a summary offence punishable by fine only at level 4.

Other notable examples include s.19 of the Terrorism Act 2000 which makes it an offence for a person to fail to disclose as soon as is reasonably practicable to the police their belief or suspicion and any information relating to money offences for the purpose of terrorism in ss.15 to 18. There exist other examples relating to environmental offences contained within the Environmental Protection Act 1990 and Clean Neighbourhoods and Environmental Act 2005. Section 20 of CNEA 2005 gives a principal litter authority a power to issue a "litter cleaning notice" in relation to any open air land. A person to whom the notice is served who fails without reasonable excuse to comply with the notice requirements commits a summary offence. Another offence within the CNEA 2005 exists in relation to non-compliance with a "dog control order" under s.55.

When in force s.119 of the Criminal Justice and Immigration Act 2008 creates a new offence of causing without reasonable excuse a nuisance or disturbance on NHS premises and refusal to leave when asked to do by a constable or NHS staff member constitutes a summary offence.

11. A Duty to Act that Arises Under the Common Law

2.11 The general rule of the common law is that there is no duty to act, a point firmly recognised in *R. v Miller* [1982] Q.B. 532, when May L.J. stated:

> "unless a statute specifically so provides, or the case is one in which in the criminal context the common law imposes a duty to act in a particular way towards another ... then, a *mere* omission to act, with nothing more cannot make the person who so fails to so something guilty of a criminal offence."

In *Stephen's Digest of the Criminal Law* (1887) there is found the following well-known example of the general rule:

> "A sees B drowning and is able to save him by holding out his hand. A abstains from doing so in order that B may be drowned, and B is drowned. A has committed no offence"

It is important that the student starts with and considers the general rule of the common law and then further considers the exceptions created by the common law to the general rule, which are based on grounds of public policy. The exceptions are generally uncontroversial and arise in limited circumstances. What is required for a failure or omission to act to attract criminal liability under the common law, is generally the establishment of a duty of care owed to the complainant and it is this that the student should focus on. The principles of law are found in a number of case authorities, which for ease of learning, are better referred to as the "Duty Owed Cases". However, other examples do exist, as with the common law offence of public nuisance. The House of Lords in *R. v Rimmington* [2006] 1 A.C. 459, having reviewed the development of the offence, confirmed it as an offence with sufficient legal certainty. The principles to the offence are (i) the defendant did an act not warranted by law, or (ii) *omitted to discharge a legal duty*, (iii) the purpose of the act or omission was to endanger the life, health, property or comfort of the public, or (iv) obstruct the public in the exercise of rights common to everyone.

12. Exceptions: The "Duty Owed Cases" and the Offence of Gross Negligence Manslaughter

2.12 The one clear example of an exception under the common law to the general rule that there is no duty to act, is the offence of gross negligence manslaughter and it is this offence that attracts criminal liability to those who are generally seen as decent and honest people, but have failed in an important duty they owed to another generally, more vulnerable person. For instance, a teacher who takes a group of students on a trip are both contractually and by assumption, owes those students a duty of care to ensure at all times they are not exposed to any obvious risk of injury. The principles of law in establishing the common law offence of manslaughter by gross negligence, are found in the speech of Lord Mackay in *R. v Adomako* [1995] 1 A.C. 171 and that the jury should be directed to consider the following questions:

(i) Was there in the circumstances a duty of care owed by the defendant to the deceased (assuming that the judge has ruled that on the facts such a duty was capable of arising)?

(ii) Was there a breach of that duty?

(iii) Did that breach cause the death of the deceased?

(iv) Was the breach so gross so as to be characterised as amounting to a criminal act?

13. "Assumption of Responsibility": Case Examples

2.13 Criminal liability will only arise as an exception to the general rule where it is established that the defendant owed the complainant a duty of care (question 1 above). Such a duty generally arises by assumption of a responsibility to the complainant. For instance a parent assumes responsibility for their child(ren), if they have a party for their child(ren) and invite other children, then they further assume a responsibility and a duty of care for that period of time to the other children also. In *R. v Gibbins and Proctor* [1918] 13 Cr.App.R. 134, a father and his girlfriend where convicted of murder by omission in that they had together deliberately withheld food from their child intending its death. Whilst this is an example of an offence of murder being committed by omission, it must be recognised as being one decided on its own particular facts, since the greatest difficulty of proving murder in these circumstances is a deliberate intent to kill by starvation.

R. v Miller [1983] 2 A.C. 161, is a case which is often cited as an example of criminal liability for the greater consequences that can arise out of the initial positive minor act of the defendant, but the defendant then fails to prevent the greater danger from occurring. In this case, the defendant, a tramp, went into a building, lay down on a mattress, lit a cigarette but fell asleep. He then woke up to find the mattress was smouldering, and ignoring this clear risk decided to go into another room, the fire being left caused considerable damage to the building. The defendant was convicted of the more serious offence of arson. He appealed on the grounds that his criminal liability was that of simple criminal damage to the mattress and not the greater damage, since he was under no obligation to prevent such damage. This argument was rejected by the House of Lords which upheld his conviction on the basis that when he became aware of what he had done in setting the mattress on fire at that point he was under a duty to take such steps as were within his power to prevent or minimise the damage to the house.

R. v Pittwood [1902] 19 R.T.R. 37 is a case that is often used to identify criminal liability for a failure to perform a contractual obligation, which results in death. The defendant was a rail-crossing gatekeeper; he failed to close the gate resulting in the death of a car driver, which was struck by a passing train. The offence is clearly one of manslaughter by gross negligence, as stated by the Court of Appeal, in dismissing the defendant's appeal:

> "that there was gross and criminal negligence, as the man was paid to keep the gate shut and protect the public.... A man might incur criminal liability from a duty arising out of contract."

The following case authorities are well established examples of where a duty arises through caring for another and should be noted by the student for that reason, since they clearly identify the factual circumstances where the courts have imposed a duty of care. In *R. v Instan* [1893] 1 Q.B. 450, the defendant lived with and was looked after by his 73-year-old aunt, who unfortunately became ill herself and in the last 12 days of her life developed gangrene in her leg. The defendant sadly never helped her or provided her with food. The defendant's failure to call medical help accelerated her death. The defendant was charged with and convicted of manslaughter, on the basis that they had lived together for both their benefit and for this reason the defendant had assumed a duty to care for his aunt and had failed to act on that assumption of responsibility.

2.14 A somewhat more controversial case is *R. v Stone and Dobinson* [1977] Q.B. 354 in which the defendants had voluntarily taken in to their household Stone's younger sister, who was suffering from anorexia nervosa. After time, the sister became unwilling and unable to leave her room, in consequence she developed a fatal illness. Both defendants ignored the seriousness of the situation which was developing and failed to summon medical attention, which resulted in the sister's death. Both defendants were convicted of manslaughter and appealed against their conviction on the grounds that the general rule applied. The Court of Appeal upheld their conviction stating that both of them had voluntarily assumed a duty of care to the sister, to ensure she was properly cared for. Failing to care for the sister amounted to an obvious risk of injury to health which both defendants should have foreseen or to which they had shown an indifference.

In *R. v Khan and Another* [1998] Crim. L.R. 830, a case with distressing facts, the Court of Appeal had to quash the conviction of the defendant for manslaughter of the victim, to whom he had sold and supplied drugs and who overdosed. The appellant, realising that the deceased had overdosed, left the flat without summoning medical help which was clearly needed. He returned the next day to find the young girl dead and he and an accomplice then dumped her body on some waste ground and set fire to the body, to destroy any evidence. The judge, in his summing up of the law, adopted the principle from *R. v Miller* that that the defendants had created a chain of events which give rise to a risk of harm to the deceased and failed to prevent that risk. The judge did not consider or leave for the jury's determination whether there was a duty of care owed to the victim and therefore an offence of gross negligence manslaughter.

The Court of Appeal highlighted that in cases of this nature, the offence to be charged is that of "manslaughter by gross negligence" not an "offence of manslaughter by omission". Such an expression, although commonly found in legal writings, is merely a descriptive title to help explain and identify an area of law. It is not an actual offence known under the common law and it was therefore wrong to charge it as such.

The Police Service already assumes a responsibility to the general public within the resources they have. In *R. v Dytham* [1979] Q.B. 722, a police constable witnessed a man being assaulted outside a nightclub, he remained in his police car and failed to intervene. The Court of Appeal upheld his conviction for the common law offence of misconduct in a public office; to carry out his duty to protect citizens from violent assault, by omitting to take steps to preserve the peace and to prevent the actual assault. The ingredients to this particular offence were extensively reviewed by the Court of Appeal in *Attorney-General's Reference (No.3 of 2003)* [2004] EWCA Crim 868 which involved the acquittal of police officers for the death of a detained person in police custody. It was stated that to establish the offence, it must be proved that the public officer without reasonable excuse or justification, willfully neglects their duty or willfully misconducts themselves, to such a degree as to amount to an abuse of the public's trust in that person. This does not require reference to "bad faith" on the part of the defendant.

14. Actus Reus as a State of Affairs

2.15 This simply means that where the defendant is found to be in a given prohibited circumstance, then that amounts to the actus reus. Within the criminal law there exist only a few offences that have a state of affairs that amount to the actus reus. One offence that is commonly encountered by the police, as a state of affairs actus reus, is the offence of being drunk and disorderly in a public place contrary to s.91 of the Criminal Justice Act 1967. The state of affairs is simply being drunk coupled with disorder. In many instances the defendant, come the morning, will be unable to remember being in such a state of affairs, but this is irrelevant for the commission of the offence. This point can be seen in *Winzar v CC OF Kent The Times, March 28, 1983*, where the defendant was drunk and being a nuisance in a casualty department. The police came, took him outside, put him in the police car and then arrested him for being drunk on an highway. The defendant's conviction was upheld on appeal on the basis that the actus reus of this offence did not require any act, just a state of affairs.

15. The Actus Reus and the Mens Rea must Coincide in Time

2.16 In order to attract criminal liability it is an established principle of criminal law that the accused not only committed the actus reus with the necessary mens rea, but that both elements are shown to exist at the same time. In many respects this principle amounts to no more than an academic moot point. It is rarely encountered as a legal argument in criminal practice.

Nevertheless, it is an important point to be aware of and be able to apply. The principle of coincidence is explained and identified in the old authority of *R. v Pembiton* [1874] L.R. 2, where the defendant was charged under the old Malicious Damage Act (now the Criminal Damage Act 1971) of intentionally damaging a window. During a fight, the defendant decided to throw a stone intending it to hit someone in the crowd. However, it missed and smashed a window instead. The defendant's conviction for criminal damage was quashed on appeal when applying the principle of coincidence. It was accepted that whilst the defendant had, at the time of throwing the stone, the actus reus of criminal damage, he did not have the necessary mens rea for the damage, only that for an assault.

Since this decision, and to avoid a too rigid application of the principle of coincidence which could create factual absurdities, the common law has developed the principle with a certain degree of flexibility, recognising that a person's act may be one of a series of different acts that taken together amount to one overall act. Alternatively, a person's act, when started, will continue over a period of time before it is completed. This means that the actus reus, once embarked upon and in progress is one continuous act or consists of a series of acts, which together with the mens rea completes the commission of the offence.

16. A Series of Acts

2.17 This principle applies where the defendant embarks upon a series of acts and then argues that each act is a separate completed act. Therefore, at the particular time of that particular act, neither the mens rea nor actus reus coincided. To deal with this argument, the common law developed the series of acts principle which provides that although a defendant may commit several different acts, if those acts, albeit a series of acts, form part of the overall conduct of the defendant, then in those circumstances they will be treated as one complete act. The operation of the principle is well illustrated in *Thabo Meli v R.* [1954] 1 W.L.R. 228, where the four defendants violently assaulted the victim, and in so doing they believed that they had killed him. In order to make it look like an accident, they decided to throw the victim off a cliff. However, the victim was, in fact, still alive and instead died of exposure. All four were convicted of murder and appealed on the grounds that the actus reus and mens rea did not coincide in time and did not therefore commit murder. They contended on two points of law that:

(i) by violently assaulting the victim, they had the mens rea of intent to kill or do serious bodily harm at that time, but this did not coincide with the actus reus since the victim was still alive;

(ii) equally when they pushed the victim over the cliff, they at that time had the actus reus of causing death, but this did not coincide with the mens rea of intent since they already thought they had killed the victim due to the assault.

The Privy Council upheld their convictions by applying the series of acts theory, which meant that what the four defendants did was, from the outset, one whole act and that to separate the actus reus and mens rea from what is clearly one overall act in an attempt to seek an acquittal, would be manifestly absurd. Accordingly, the Privy Council held that it was impossible to divide up what was really one series of acts. The crime was not to be reduced from murder to a lesser crime merely because the appellants were under some misapprehension for a time during the completion of their criminal plot. The appellants were guilty of murder. Similarly in *R. v Church* [1966] 1 Q.B. 59, the appellant met a woman whom he invited to his van for the purpose of sexual intercourse. He was unable to perform, and the woman made derogatory remarks and slapped him. A fight ensued in which the appellant inflicted serious injuries to the woman. The appellant, believing the woman to be dead, threw her into the River Ouse. In fact the woman was not dead at the time but was probably unconscious, she died instead of drowning.

The appellant was indicted for murder; the jury acquitted but instead convicted of manslaughter after the judge had directed them that if they were satisfied that he held an honest belief that the woman was dead when he threw her in the river, he could not be guilty of murder, but of manslaughter. The defendant appealed against his conviction on the basis that his mens rea and actus reus did not coincide at the time of the offence. The Court of Appeal, in dismissing the appeal, approved the principle derived from *Thabo Meli v R.* Edmund Davis J. commented that the jury should have been directed that a conviction for murder would arise, despite the honest belief of the defendant:

> "if they regarded the appellant's behaviour from the moment he first struck her to the moment when he threw her into the river *as a series of acts* designed to cause death or grievous bodily harm."

By way of contrast, the Court of Appeal in *Attorney-General's Reference (No.4 of 1980)* [1981] 1 W.L.R. 705, ruled on a point of law that the defendant's act which caused the victim's death could not be established. In brief the defendant had: (i) caused a girl to fall over a banister, and (ii) believing her to be dead dragged her upstairs by a rope tied around her neck to dispose of her body. The girl died, but it was impossible to say factually whether she was killed by act (i) or act (ii). If the first act caused death, there was evidence for a jury that the defendant had caused death by an unlawful and dangerous act and so was guilty of manslaughter. If the second act caused death, there was evidence on which a jury might have found that he was guilty of manslaughter by gross negligence. The trial judge ruled that on the facts it was impossible to prove which act caused death and therefore directed an acquittal. On a reference by the Attorney-General to seek the opinion of the Court of Appeal on whether the trial judge's ruling on the law was correct the Court of Appeal held that the jury should have been told to convict if they were sure that both the fall was caused by the defendant's unlawful and dangerous act, and that he was guilty of gross criminal negligence when he dragged the girl's body upstairs. They would then have been sure that he was guilty of manslaughter either on occasion (i) or on occasion (ii) and that was enough.

17. The Continuous Act Theory and the Offence of Assault

2.18 Another proposition established by the courts through the common law to link both the mens rea and actus reus is the continuing act theory. This establishes that the actus reus of the offence is not one isolated act but an act that continues over time and the offence is considered to be in progress until the act itself is completed. Accordingly, a defendant may initially embark upon the actus reus without the necessary mens rea to complete the offence. However if the actus reus is an act deemed to be ongoing or continuous and during that relevant period the defendant forms the necessary mens rea the offence will then have been completed and will not fail for lack of coincidence of mens rea and actus reus.

A vivid illustration is *Fagan v Commissioner of Metropolitan Police* [1968] 1 Q.B. 439 in which the appellant was convicted in the magistrates' court for assaulting a constable in the execution of his duty. He appealed by way of case stated to the High Court (QBD) against conviction on the ground that he lacked the mens rea for assault although he had embarked upon the actus reus. The appellant was requested by a police officer to pull over to the kerb in regards to a motoring matter. The appellant had parked some way off the kerb and so the police officer gave precise instructions to move closer to the kerb where the officer was stood. On doing so the appellant drove the vehicle so that the offside wheel stopped on the police officer's left foot. The officer shouted to the appellant to move the vehicle as it was on his foot. The appellant replied with strong language and turned off the ignition. As a result of the appellant's act or omission the officer suffered an injury.

At trial the appellant contended that his act was not done deliberately, it amounted to an accident. It was also contended that when the appellant drove the vehicle onto the officer's foot he was not aware of this fact and that the moment the vehicle mounted the officer's foot, the actus reus of assault came to an end. The appellant only formed the mens rea of assault (either intentionally or recklessly causing someone to apprehend that unlawful and immediate violence will be used against them) after the actus reus was completed. Accordingly no offence in law had been committed. The High Court dismissed the appellant's appeal on the basis that allowing the car to remain on the officer's foot was a continuing act of assault and that once the appellant was aware of this, the mens rea of intent coincided and therefore constituted the offence of common assault.

18. The Continuing Act of "Appropriation" in the Offence of Theft and Robbery

2.19 The basic offence of theft is found in s.1 of the Theft Act 1968 and provides that a person commits theft if they dishonestly appropriate property belonging to another with the intention of permanently depriving the other of it. The offence of robbery is an aggravated form of basic theft and is found in s. 8 of the Theft Act 1968 which states that "a person is guilty of robbery if he steals, and immediately before or at the time of doing so, and in order to do so, he uses force on any person or puts or seeks to put any person in fear of being then and there subjected to force". Accordingly, to be convicted of robbery the prosecution must prove that the defendant "steals"; this means basic theft and that in order to commit that theft, the defendant used force. Robbery is an indictable only offence, whilst theft is an either way offence. Naturally, robbery is a more serious offence and therefore the defendant culpability is greater, usually resulting in a sentence of imprisonment if convicted.

In *R. v Lockley* [1995] Crim. L.R. 656, the appellant, together with two others, entered an off-licence and took cans of beer; the owner confronted them, whom they assaulted in order to escape. Both were convicted of robbery. The appellant appealed against his conviction on the ground that he had not committed robbery, since the act of theft of the cans of beer was completed before force was used. Accordingly, the appeal turned on whether the act of appropriation in theft was still continuing when violence was used against the owner and therefore the force used was in order to steal. The Court of Appeal dismissed the appeal and held that the case of *R. v Gomez* [1993] A.C. 442, in which the House of Lords had to consider the legal meaning of the word "appropriation" and whether property could be appropriated, even if the owner consented, had not overruled the principle in *R. v Hale* [1978] 68 Cr.App.R. 415, in which it was held that appropriation is a continuing act. The matter of an appropriation as a continuing act is a question of fact for the jury to determine in each particular case, should the matter arise.

A somewhat more difficult question of a continuing act appropriation arose in *R. v Atakpu* [1994] Q.B. 69. The defendants were charged with conspiracy to steal vehicles they had hired in Germany by use of false documents and brought back to England. The legal question that arose was whether the cars had been appropriated in Germany, or England. if the appropriation took place in Germany then the prosecution may fail since the offence was not committed in England. On this point the Court of Appeal held that a thief can only steal goods once, if this was not the law then on every occasion the thief used the goods, they will be guilty of theft again. Accordingly, the cars were stolen in Germany and although the continuous act of appropriation was a question for the jury, in this instance the cars had been stolen many days before and therefore the theft was completed in Germany not England.

19. The Mens Rea of Criminal Intention

2.20 All criminal offences, unless strictly liable type offences, will have in the definition, words or expressions that identify the mens rea and the actus reus of the offence. There are various words that describe the mens rea, the word that describes the most culpable of state of mind in the criminal law is that of intention. It is a word in common usage in the English language, that requires no elaboration or technical explanation when used generally or in most criminal trials. Conversely, the word reckless is used within the criminal law to describe unjustifiable risk taking, a less culpable state of mind to that of intention. Common examples of offences with intention as part of the mens rea are:

(i) Murder under the common law, the mens rea being an intention to kill or cause serious bodily harm.

(ii) Section 18 of the Offences Against the Person Act 1861, which provides "whosoever shall unlawfully and maliciously by any means whatsoever would or cause any grievous bodily harm to any person *with intent*".

(iii) Section 1 of the Theft Act 1968 states that a person is guilty of theft if they dishonestly appropriate property belonging to another with the *intention of permanently depriving the other of it*.

(iv) Section 1 of the Criminal Damage Act 1971 provides that a person who without lawful excuse destroys or damages any property belonging to another *intending* to destroy or damage any such property or being reckless as to whether any such property would be destroyed or damaged shall be guilty of an offence.

20. The Difference Between Direct and Indirect Intent

2.21 The word intention, when in common usage, causes no difficulties in knowing what the speaker meant when using the word, i.e. "It was my intention to go to town today to pay a bill, but my car broke down". Notwithstanding this common usage, the criminal law had real difficulties in giving a legal meaning to the word intention that appropriately identified the degree of culpability of the offence. These difficulties have arisen in regard to the difference in culpability between the offence of murder to that of manslaughter and deciding on the evidence where a defendant's mens rea lies, in order to secure a conviction for murder or, lacking the intent to kill, an offence of manslaughter.

In this regard, the courts have spilt the word intention into two types, namely, direct intent and indirect intent. It is the development of the legal test for indirect intent that has caused the greatest difficulties for the courts and indeed, the criminal law student, with confusing and perplexing judgments in the House of Lords. It is important to remember that, in terms of culpability, there can be a significant difference between murder and manslaughter and the criminal law must ensure that a defendant's mens rea reflects properly the seriousness of the offence, whilst taking into account the complainant and the public interest in bringing the appropriate charge in the first instance.

Direct Intention in law relates to the defendant's aim or purpose and generally causes no difficulties for the jury. Conversely, indirect intention (known also as oblique intention) relates not to the defendant's specific aim or purpose, but instead to the defendant's foresight of the consequences that might result from his act. For example the defendant is said to have this type of intention where he sees the consequences as virtually certain to happen from what he does. Although he does not physically desire it, he goes ahead with his actions anyway. It is important therefore to be aware of the reasons why this type of intention exists. The word indirect is used to suggest that although the defendant does an act, evidentially cannot be proven that it was their specific (direct) aim or purpose. They must still have known (indirectly) by doing what they did it, that it was a virtual certainty that death or serious injury would occur and therefore intended to kill.

2.22 There are two reasons why the common law recognises indirect intention as a second type of criminal intention:

(i) the difference in the degree of culpability between the two homicide offences of murder and manslaughter, and

(ii) on grounds of public policy.

If there is an unlawful death, then the defendant will either be charged with murder, manslaughter or both. The Crown Prosecution Service have the responsibility of deciding what the appropriate offence is, based on their view of the evidence, the defendant's culpability for their act and the public interest. Both the offence of murder and manslaughter can be committed with various degrees of seriousness, i.e. from the serial killer to the premature killing of a terminally ill relative or in respect of manslaughter, a vicious assault causing death, to a one punch tragic death. If the death was caused by an unlawful act, then the defendant is criminally liable for the act which caused death. The important question that unlocks the meaning of indirect intent, lies in the proof of the mens rea for murder.

To secure a conviction for murder the prosecution must prove that the defendant, at the time of causing the death: (i) intended to kill, or (ii) intended to do serious bodily harm to the victim. The difficulty in determining the relevant mens rea for murder as distinct from manslaughter is well illustrated in *R. v Harris and Others* [2005] EWCA Crim 1980, in cases of shaken baby syndrome, especially where during a period of anguish, a mother or child minder violently shakes an infant causing death. The evidence of shaking may not necessarily furnish the requisite intent to do GBH for murder, but may instead and undoubtedly will furnish the mens rea for unlawful and dangerous act manslaughter (see also *R. v Stacy* [2001] EWCA Crim 2031).

If this direct intention cannot be proved, then provided the act which caused death was an unlawful act, the defendant will be guilty not of murder but of manslaughter. A significant difference for the defendant in terms of culpability and their likely sentence if found guilty of manslaughter in the alternative to murder. Most cases of murder and manslaughter are evidentially and factually distinguishable. However, a limited number of cases blur the culpability distinction between the two offences. Take an extreme example: A wishes to kill B. A is aware that B every morning catches the 7:30 train to work. A decides on the extreme method of placing a small but crude incendiary device in the carriage occupied by B. A detonates the device at the precise moment, killing B instantly. However, in the mayhem the bomb kills two other innocent commuters and injures dozens more. A's direct intention, i.e. his purpose, was to kill B, this result was achieved and A will be charged with B's murder.

The question now arises what offence should A be charged with in relation to the two other deaths, since those are a consequence of A actions. A's only direct intent was to kill B, he never desired or intended to kill other commuters. Clearly he is liable for their manslaughter but would such a charge be in the public interest, since to the layperson these must also amount to murder. However, evidentially the prosecution has real difficulties in proving a direct intent to kill and is unlikely to succeed. This is where the prosecution will rely on indirect intention to secure a conviction for murder, as opposed to a conviction for manslaughter.

21. Difficulties in Determining the Correct Legal Test to Establish Indirect Intent

2.23 The confusion on the issue of foresight of consequences as sufficient proof for murder had developed initially through several divided House of Lords judgments in which their Lordships could not agree on what expression should be used to determine the degree of foresight needed. It is quite extraordinary that with regard to what is considered to be the most serious offence in the criminal hierarchy, the House of Lords, despite visiting this point of issue in terms of degree and culpability, failed to agree on a simple test to assist the jury. It wasn't until the decision in *R. v Nedrick* [1986] 1 W.L.R. 1025, that the law was finally given the clarity needed, but this still needed a further House of Lords decision in *R. v Woollin* [1999] 1 A.C. 82, to perfect the *Nedrick* direction. A quite unacceptable state of affairs and a compelling indictment of an area of common law that needs to be reformed, in terms of the recommendations set out by the Law Commission in its recent report "Murder, Manslaughter and Infanticide". A second problem that also confronted the courts in the development of the concept of "foresight of consequences" (i.e. death) is whether or not it forms part of the substantive law and therefore amounts to a third specific mental element to murder, or simply forms part of the law of evidence from which a jury may find a direct intent proved, i.e. an intent to kill or cause GBH.

22. Historical Development of the Meaning of Intention in Murder

2.24 The offence of murder is defined by the common law in case authorities and legal writings and has been developed over several centuries. Historically, murder was committed with "malice aforethought". In *R. v Vickers* [1957] 2 Q.B. 664, Lord Goddard took this to be a term of art and simply meant that the mens rea for murder consisted of two elements, namely;

(i) an intention to kill (expressed malice)

or

(ii) an intention to cause serious bodily harm causing death (implied malice).

Prior to its abolition by s.1 of the Homicide Act 1957, a person could be found guilty of murder under the application of the principle of "constructive malice". A somewhat distorted principle, which meant that in circumstances where a person intended to commit any offence and whilst committing that offence caused a death, would amount to murder. Although the Appeal Court in *Vickers* set out the mens rea requirement for murder, the Court neither discussed nor mentioned the concept of "foresight of consequences" and the degree required to convict for murder in terms of expressed malice; i.e. an intent to kill. The Court approved the concept of implied malice and the grievous harm rule as a second element, to prove mens rea for murder.

DPP v Smith [1961] 3 W.L.R. 546, was the first case in which the common law encountered the creation of the foresight of consequences test. The defendant, Smith, in an attempt to escape arrest, killed the police officer who tried to stop him by sitting on the bonnet of his car. Smith accelerated and threw the officer off into the path of oncoming traffic, which caused his fatal injuries. At his trial, Smith claimed that he had no intention to kill or cause GBH, he simply became frightened and instinctively reacted as he did. Smith appealed against his conviction for murder on the basis that he lacked the necessary intent for murder and a material misdirection of the trial judge, who told the jury that intention to kill/cause GBH could be found by:

> "inference from the surrounding circumstances including the presumption of law that a man intends the natural and probable consequences of his acts"

and that if a reasonable person would have appreciated the risk of serious injury to the officer, then this inference could be drawn by the jury. The House of Lords affirmed Smith's conviction and approved the legal direction of the judge, therefore confirming the application of foresight of consequences, as part of proving the mens rea for murder, but in doing so created an objective test of the reasonable man to infer the necessary intent to kill, not a subjective test of what was in the mind of the defendant. The decision received strong criticism on this point and led to Parliament enacting s.8 of the Criminal Justice Act 1967, to remove this part of the decision in Smith, of the objective criteria and impose a subjective test; both as to foresight of consequences and direct intention.

2.25 Matters remained settled until the House of Lords decision in *R. v Hyam* [1975] 2 All E.R. 41, which highlighted the difficulties in creating a legal test for indirect intent on a charge of murder. The defendant Hyam was having an intimate relationship with a Mr Jones until an operation prevented her from having sexual intercourse. Hyam became jealous of a Mrs B with whom Jones was having a relationship and was believed to have proposed to marry. Hyam went to Mrs B's house at night where B and her three children were sleeping. Hyam set fire to the house with petrol. B and one child escaped, but sadly the other two children died in the fire. Hyam was Indicted and convicted of murder, the trial judge gave the basic direction of an intent to kill or cause GBH, and that this was proved if they were sure that when Hyam set fire to the house she knew that it was *highly probable* this would cause serious harm and that it mattered not if her motive was to frighten Mrs B. Hyam appealed against conviction on the ground that knowledge of a consequence from an act as being highly probable, did not prove an intent to bring about the result of death. The defence contended that the required proof of murder is an intention to kill or endanger life, not GBH alone.

The House of Lords was divided on the correct legal test required to establish a foresight of consequences. By a majority (Lord Hailsham, Viscount Dilhorne, and Lord Cross) dismissed the appeal and upheld the defendant's conviction (Lord Diplock and Lord Kilbrandon dissented but concurred with each other). Confusion arose in the speeches of the majority, who gave different versions as to what they believed to be the correct test of establishing the necessary degree of foresight to convict of murder. Lord Hailsham felt that where the defendant realised there was a "serious risk" of death that would be sufficient, whilst in contrast Viscount Dilhorne adopted a "highly probable" test and for Lord Cross it was just a test of probability. If this wasn't enough, two of their Lordships disagreed as to whether foresight formed not part of the substantive law of mens rea for murder, but was simply evidence that entitled the jury to infer the necessary intent to kill or cause GBH. This confusing judgment caused real difficulties in the lower courts as to how to explain the correct test to juries to be applied in murder cases where the prosecution presents their case to prove murder by indirect intent.

The next opportunity for the House of Lords to clarify the law, but where they failed to do so, was *R. v Moloney* [1985] A.C. 905. The defendant (Moloney), a soldier, tragically killed his father during a drunken argument over a challenge who could draw a gun quicker. Moloney, in his defence, claimed that he had no intention to either kill his father or cause him serious harm, since when he pulled the trigger he was not aware that the gun was pointing directly at his father. When the appeal reached the House of Lords, the court quashed the defendant's conviction on the grounds that there was an imbalance in the trial judge's summing up of the defence case, and sought to use the opportunity to clarify the divided opinion in *Hyam*. Lord Bridge, who gave the leading judgment on the point of intention, firstly stated that in a trial of a specific intent offence such as murder, the trial judge "should avoid any elaboration or paraphrase of what is meant" by direct intent, and simply "leave it to the jury's good sense to decide whether the accused acted with necessary intent" unless something further was necessary to avoid misunderstanding. In such circumstances, "clarity and simplicity" were of paramount importance.

2.26 On the issue of the correct degree of foresight test, Lord Bridge posed two questions for the jury's determination, which became known as "The Maloney Guidelines" The first question required the jury to consider whether death or serious injury was a "natural consequence" of the defendant's act. If yes on the second question, did the defendant foresee death as a "natural consequence" of his act. His Lordship also confirmed that in his opinion, the foresight of consequence test forms not part of the substantive law of mens rea, but of the law of evidence that entitles the jury to determine that mens rea of intent. Nevertheless, the *Moloney* guidelines as they stood failed to create a simple and appropriate test to be applied.

To express the test as being a "natural consequence" of the defendant's act and nothing more did little to assist a jury in its difficult task of having to decide between murder to that of manslaughter. Although Lord Bridge had earlier said in his judgment that this meant something little short of overwhelming, he failed to mention this in the guidelines. In *R. v Hancock and Shankland* [1986] 1 A.C. 455, the trial judge directed the jury exactly in accordance with the two *Moloney* questions, which resulted in a conviction for murder being secured against a low degree of foresight and therefore a clear injustice to the defendants. Both *Handcock* and *Shankland* were striking miners who were vehemently opposed to any miner going to work. Together, they decided to push a concrete block over the parapet of a bridge which smashed through the windscreen of an on-coming taxi, killing the driver, whose passenger was a non-striking miner.

They were both indicted and convicted of murder. The defence at trial was that they had no intention to kill, or cause GBH, their intention was to push the block on to the middle lane, not the nearside lane in which the taxi was travelling, so as to block the path of the taxi or to frighten the occupants. The trial judge adhered to the *Moloney* guidelines, directing the jury to consider "was death or serious injury a natural consequence of what was done?" As a result, they both appealed against their conviction on the grounds that the direction was inadequate and misleading, in that the judge failed to explain to the jury the degree of foresight of a natural consequence needed to convict of murder.

2.27 The House of Lords dismissed the appeal by the prosecution from the decision of the Court of Appeal to quash the defendants' murder convictions and substituting a manslaughter conviction. Lord Scarman disapproved of the *Moloney* guidelines in that "as they stand are unsafe and misleading" since there is no clear reference in the guidelines to the degree of foresight needed in terms of probability, necessary to convict not of manslaughter but murder. On that basis the judge's failure to explain this mislead the jury to focus, not on the defendants' mind set, but on whether the death of the non -striking miner was a natural consequence caused by the defendant's act of pushing the stone over the bridge.

Although, the outcome of the appeal in *Hancock* was right in terms of culpability, the House of Lords still failed to seize on the opportunity to clarify the correct test of foresight. This did not happen until the Court of Appeal decision in *R. v Nedrick* [1986] 2 All E.R. 1, in which the facts were almost identical to those which occurred ealier in *Hyam*. The appellant (Nedrick) poured petrol through the letter box of a Mrs C, who he had a grudge against and ignited the petrol; as a consequence a child in the house died. He was indicted with and convicted of murder of the child and appealed against his conviction on the grounds that the judge had misdirected the jury on the issue of foresight in that the judge, by telling the jury that for an intent to kill "there is an alternative state of mind" which the jury must consider, namely that if he knew it would be highly probable that his act would result in serious injury to someone in the house, even though he did not desire that result there is a sufficient state of mind to convict of murder, had effectively placed foresight of consequences as forming part of the mens rea to prove murder, when he should have directed the jury that it was evidence from which they could infer the necessary intent. The Court of Appeal quashed the conviction for murder and substituted a verdict of manslaughter.

Lord Lane finally devised a clear and simple test to assist the jury in its task of having to determine the issue of indirect intent in a murder trial brought by the prosecution and who present their case on that factual point. Lord Lane set out the test in the following way:

> "Where the charge is murder and in the rare cases where the simple direction is not enough, the jury should be directed that they are not entitled to *infer* the necessary intention, unless they feel sure that death or serious bodily harm was a *virtual certainty* (barring some unforeseen intervention) as a result of the defendant's actions and that the defendant appreciated that such was the case" *and that* the decision is one for the jury to reach upon the consideration of all the evidence".

Lord Lane's direction on the legal test to be applied in cases where the prosecution rely on foresight of consequences as proof of murder, finally brought clarity to this troublesome area of law, but was again revisited in the sad case of *R. v Woolin* [1999] A.C. 82, where the appellant, owing to the constant crying of his three-month-old son lost his temper and threw him against the wall with tragic consequences, causing the death of the boy. At his trial for murder, the Crown presented its case not on direct intent to kill, but that the defendant had the intention to cause serious harm. The trial judge directed the jury to consider the virtual certainty test established in *Nedrick*, but towards the end of his summing up, the judge deviated and told the jury that if they are satisfied that the appellant must have realised when he threw the child there was a *substantial risk* that he would cause serious injury, then the jury could find the necessary direct intent to convict of murder.

2.28 The appellant was convicted of murder and appealed against conviction on the grounds that the judge had misdirected the jury when he used the words "there was a substantial risk". This, according to the defence, unacceptably widened the mental element for murder by allowing the jury to convict on a state of mind of recklessness and that this would have confused or mislead the jury as to the degree of foresight required. The House of Lords, in quashing the appellant's conviction for murder and substituting one of manslaughter, held that the *Nedrick* direction had been applied for a number of years without problems and was therefore the correct test to be applied, subject to one modification in that the word "infers" should be substituted by the word "find" and this is what the jury should be told. Although since the decision in *Nedrick* and *Woolin*, the relevant legal test of indirect intention is simple and clear; problems were encountered in the tragic case of *R. v Matthews & Alleyne* [2003] 2 Cr.App.R. 461, in which the two defendants, who initially robbed the deceased for his credit cards, but were unable to obtain money, later by misfortune and coincidence came across the deceased again. This time they kidnapped him, took him to Tyringham Bridge and threw him off despite his plea that he could not swim.

On the basis that the defendants at trial claimed the death was unintended and accidental, the judge gave a *Nedrick* direction as to virtual certainty. The defendants where subsequently convicted of murder and appealed on the grounds that the judge misdirected the jury in giving a direction that suggested that the virtual certainty test of indirect intent amounted to a specific mens rea to prove murder and not, as he should have said, a question of evidence that entitled them to find the defendant had the necessary mens rea of intent to kill or cause GBH. The Court of Appeal dismissed the appeal and upheld the defendants' conviction, the Court was unconvinced that the jury would have misunderstood the legal test of intention as explained to them by the judge, and that if the jury accepted that the defendants appreciated, barring some unforeseen event, that the death was a virtual certainty, they were entitled to convict, since they must have rejected the defendants' claim that this was a prank that went terribly wrong. The Court also confirmed that at present, the legal test explaining the meaning of indirect intent is not a substantive rule of law in terms of mens rea for murder, but a question of evidence for the jury to find the necessary mens rea.

23. Law Reform of the Meaning of Criminal "Intent"

2.29 The Law Commission in its report entitled "Murder, Manslaughter and Infanticide" November 2006 Law Com.No.304, provides an in-depth analysis on the law of homicide, its shortcomings, perplexities and anomalies. On the issue as to the legal meaning of criminal intention, the Commission recommended that the word be codified as follows:

(i) A person should be taken to intend a result if he or she acts in order to bring it about.

(ii) In cases where the judge believes that justice may not be done unless an expanded understanding of intention is given, the jury should be directed as follows: an intention to bring about a result may be found if it is shown that the defendant thought that the result was a virtually certain consequence of his or her action.

This definition of intention recommended by the Law Commission embraces both direct intention in (i), by bringing about a result and indirect intent in (ii), where the defendant knew that result was a virtually certain consequence of what they did. In essence this amounts to and follows Lord Lane's direction in *Nedrick*.

24. In Summary

2.30 The meaning of indirect intention can be conceptually difficult to apply, especially for the criminal law student. Most exam questions on intent are of the essay type and usually ask the student to provide a critical analysis of the development to the meaning of intent. This requires the student to have a thorough awareness of, and a confident ability to discuss, the authorities and the confusion that has surrounded those decisions in terms of the lack of clarity and a settled definitive principle leading up to the decision in *Nedrick*. The Court of Appeal managed in this case to bring some clarity to this conceptually difficult area of law, The Court stated that when indirect intention is in issue at trial, the jury should be directed that they may find the defendant guilty of murder if, having heard the evidence, they are sure that the defendant foresaw as a consequence of their conduct that death of the victim was a *virtual certainty*. If so, then the jury may find the defendant had intended that death or to cause serious injury leading to death, even though they may not have desired that outcome. Given the confusion, should the law continue to recognise indirect intent, or for murder should the mens rea simply be a specific intent to kill and nothing else?

25. The Mens Rea of Criminal Recklessness

2.31 As already stated, the most culpable of mental elements within the definition of a criminal offence is that of intent, namely a person's aim or purpose. We have shown that although a person may not have a direct intention to achieve a particular result, should it be established that such a person's foresight of that particular result/circumstance/consequence is virtually certain to happen, then the jury are entitled from that evidence to find the defendant had the necessary direct intent. The mental element of adjective recklessness, on the other hand, is something less and covers unjustifiable risk-taking, which is prohibited by the criminal law. Some risks are lawfully undertaken, such as medical operations, with the consent of the patient. Until recently there had been established by the common law two legal tests that defined the term recklessness when used to identify the mens rea of a criminal offence. The two legal tests are:

(i) subjective recklessness;

and

(ii) objective recklessness (now abolished by the House of Lords in *R. v G* [2004] 1 A.C. 1034).

26. The Meaning of Subjective Recklessness: "Foresight of Consequences of a Particular Kind of Harm"

2.32 The criminal law is based on notions of fairness and culpability, those who are criminally culpable are justifiably to be convicted and appropriately punished for their unlawful acts. When looking at the mental element of the defendant there is a need under these notions for the jury to enquire and look into the defendant's mind at the material time they are alleged to have committed the unlawful act. This requires a subjective assessment of the defendant's state of mind by the jury. Like the word intention, reckless as an ordinary English word requires no elaborate interpretation when used generally. However, it is important to be aware that the legal meaning of reckless differs from its common usage. The legal meaning of reckless is found in the common law and the interpretation of the word "maliciously" used to describe the mental element in the range of offences of violence and assault, enshrined in the outdated Offences Against the Person Act 1861 (OAPA 1861).

The word malicious was often used to describe the mens rea for a number of offences, but in modern language it is both an unhelpful and obscure way of defining the necessary mental element. However, despite repeated calls, in particular from the Law Commission, for Parliament to repeal the OAPA 1861 and replace it with a coherent and concise structure of offences where the mental element corresponds with the gravity of harm suffered, the OAPA 1861 still operates today as the main substantive piece of criminal legislation covering the main non fatal offences against the person. In *R. v Cunningham* [1957] 2 Q.B. 396, the Court of Appeal held that the correct legal meaning of the word maliciously was that expostulated by Professor Kenny in that what must be proved is either:

(i) an actual intention to do the particular kind of harm that was done; or

(ii) recklessness as to whether such harm should occur or not in the sense that the defendant foresaw that a particular kind of harm might be done and carries on regardless of the risk.

In *Cunningham* the Court quashed the appellant's conviction under s.23 of the OAPA 1861 of maliciously causing a poison or other destructive or noxious thing to be administered by any person so as to endanger that person's life, due to a misdirection by the judge of the legal meaning of maliciously when he said it meant "wickedly doing something which he has no business to do and perfectly well knows it". In this instance Cunningham had decided to remove a gas meter from a wall in a flat in order to steal its contents causing a gas pipe to fracture in which gas escaped and seeped through a party wall and partially asphyxiated the woman occupant, who was asleep in her bedroom.

Leading on from *Cunningham*, the House of Lords in *R. v Savage and Parmenter* [1992] 1 A.C. 699, had to address the meaning of maliciously in s.20 of the OAPA 1861 which creates the offence of malicious wounding or inflicting GBH. In this context the House of Lords approved the use of subjective *Cunningham* recklessness as the mens rea for a s.20 offence, with the added qualification that it is enough to prove that the defendant foresaw that some physical harm to some person, albeit of a minor character, might result from their conduct.

27. The Meaning of Objective Recklessness: "The Obvious Risk Test"

2.33 In contrast to subjective recklessness, objective recklessness focused not on what the defendant actually foresaw as a consequence of their conduct in terms of risk but whether there was an obvious risk that would have been apparent to a reasonable and prudent man (the reasonable man being either the magistrates or the jury in the Crown Court). If the answer is yes, then the accused must be convicted even though they themselves may not have foreseen the consequences of their conduct as obvious. The creation of a objective recklessness as forming part of the criminal law arose in *R. v Caldwell* [1981] A.C. 341, in which the House of Lords had to address what the legal meaning was of the mens rea of recklessness in the two offences of simple criminal damage and aggravated criminal damage found in s.1 of the Criminal Damage Act 1971. Lord Diplock was concerned that if a subjective recklessness test applied to recklessness in criminal damage, then a defendant who was so intoxicated as to not being aware of what they where doing, could be acquitted of the offence despite still being culpable and therefore give rise to an injustice on public policy grounds.

To avoid this possibility Lord Diplock felt that an objective meaning to recklessness was required for criminal damage and that the prosecution must prove objective recklessness based on the "reasonable man". This required the prosecution to prove that the defendant gave no thought to an unreasonable and obvious risk of damage that would have been apparent to a reasonable man. In *Caldwell* the defendant became drunk and set fire to an hotel based on a grievance with the owner. There were guests in the hotel; the fire was discovered and extinguished with no casualties. Caldwell was indicted on two counts of arson, he pleaded guilty to the offence of simple criminal damage but not guilty to the aggravated offence, since he claimed that due to his intoxication he had given no thought to the element of endangerment to the life of another. Soon afterwards, the House of Lords in *R. v Lawrence* [1982] A.C. 510, applied the objective test of recklessness to the now repealed offence of death by reckless driving.

It is important to note that two problems developed over the application of an objective test as opposed to a subjective test. The first concern related to culpability; in that a defendant should only be liable for the consequences which they themselves subjectively foresaw as a risk. An objective test, on the other hand, convicts a defendant not on what they foresaw as a risk, but on an obvious risk to a sober and reasonable person. The second, more fundamental problem with the objective test was that it was unfair to young and vulnerable defendants. This was highlighted in *Elliot v C* [1983] 1 W.L.R. 939, when the defendant, who was 14 and of limited intelligence, had entered a shed, found white spirit, poured it on to a piece of carpet and set fire to it. The High Court upheld the defendant's conviction for arson and ruled that in whether the risk created was obvious, is to be determined by an adult reasonable person, not a reasonable person sharing the same age and sex of the defendant. The decision in *Elliot* was later, albeit with a degree of regret, followed in *(R) Stephen Malcolm* [1984] 79 Cr.App.R. 334 and *R. v Coles* [1995] 1 Cr.App.R. 157.

28. *R v G* [2004] the House of Lords Departed from *R v Caldwell* [1981]

2.34 The House of Lords in *R. v G* [2004] 1 A.C. 1034, after many years of criticism of the objective recklessness test especially if the defendant is a young or vulnerable person, accepted that this created a real injustice and therefore departed from the decision in *Caldwell* and replaced the objective recklessness test for criminal damage with a subjective test. In this case the two defendants who, aged 11 and 12, decided to camp out one evening, and unable to sleep entered the rear of a Co-op shop. They then opened the bundle of morning papers and used a lighter to set fire to some of the papers. They then left the lighted paper this engulfed a plastic wheelie bin which then spread to the actual building causing extensive damage. They were both charged with arson and convicted on an application of the *Caldwell* objective test, even though they subjectively were not aware of this risk created, although such a risk was obvious to a reasonable and prudent man.

The defendants appealed against their conviction on the grounds the *Caldwell* test was wrong and flawed. This was rejected by the Court of Appeal, which felt regrettably bound by the decision in *Caldwell*. The House of Lords, in the judgment of Lord Bingham, agreed with the contentions of the defence; having analysed the historical background to the offence of criminal damage, his Lordship concluded that the intention of Parliament in the use of the word recklessly in the Criminal Damage Act 1971 was that of subjective recklessness, as confirmed in the Law Commission report which preceded the Act itself. Although the decision in *Caldwell* had stood for over 20 years it was not free of criticism and amounted to a "misinterpretation" of the word recklessly which was "offensive to principle and is apt to cause injustice. That being so, the need to correct the misinterpretation is compelling". The House of Lords quashed the defendants' convictions and ruled that the meaning of recklessly in the offence of criminal damage now required the prosecution to prove either of the following:

(i) that the defendant themselves created a circumstance in which they where aware of a risk that exists or will exist, or

(ii) is aware that their act or omission will result in damage, and in the circumstances known to the defendant it was unreasonable to take that risk.

29. The Distinction between Criminal Recklessness and Plain Stupidity

2.35 A person is only criminally liable if they do a prohibited act which causes injury to another and that their state of mind was criminally culpable when so acting. In *R. v G* [2004] 1 A.C. 1034, Lord Bingham recognised this as a "salutary principle" of criminal law in the proof of serious crime. His Lordship identified intention and recklessness as culpable states of minds and made the following observation:

> "it is clearly blameworthy to take an obvious and significant risk of causing injury to another. But it is not clearly blameworthy to do something involving a risk of injury to another of (for reasons over than self-induced intoxication) one genuinely does not perceive the risk. Such a person may fairly be accused of stupidity or lack of imagination but neither of those failing should expose him to conviction of serious crime or risk of punishment."

In *R. v Brady* [2006] EWCA Crim 2413, the appellant, who was drunk in a nightclub, climbed on the railings from a balcony that overlooked the main dance floor. He then jumped off, landing onto the complainant's head. The blow tragically broke her neck, rendering her a lifelong quadriplegic. The appellant was convicted of recklessly inflicting GBH, contrary to s.20 of the OAPA 1861, and appealed on the grounds that the trial judge had misdirected the jury as to the meaning of recklessness. Firstly, the defence contended that since the decision in *R. v G*, the judge was now required, as a matter of law, to qualify the word risk with the expression "obvious and significant" when explaining to the jury the meaning of foresight of consequences. The Court of Appeal disagreed and rejected this contention.

On a second point, the appellant contended at trial that he genuinely believed that he was secure by sitting on the rail and that therefore he did not perceive any risk of injury to any other person and that by falling off was an unintentional accident not a deliberate act. The Court of Appeal quashed the appellant's conviction as unsafe on the basis that the judge gave a limited direction, explaining to the jury that the only issue for them to decide was whether the appellant had acted recklessly. The jury should have been directed to look at recklessness based on the possible different versions of events in which the appellant fell. In other words if the jury accepted that the appellant had jumped, then was this a criminally reckless act in a subjective context as explained in *Cunningham* or was it a stupid or very tragic un-blameworthy act?

30. The Concept of Transferred Malice

2.36 If a defendant deliberately intends to injure any person or foresees the risk of such an injury to another, then the mens rea is proven. However, factually difficulties may arise where a defendant intentionally or recklessly wants to injure a particular person but instead injures another, then the defence could claim to lack the necessary mens rea in respect of the injured person on the basis that this was neither intended nor foreseen. To overcome this perceived difficulty, the criminal law has developed a concept called "transferred malice" in which the prosecution can rely on the defendant's mens rea directed to a particular result or consequence, being transferred to another result or consequence which occurred during the factual events. A vivid illustration is *R. v Mitchell* [1983] Q.B. 741, where the defendant, Mitchell, went into post office and deliberately jumped the queue, another person in the queue remonstrated with Mitchell who assaulted him and who from the force of the assault fell against an old lady, who in turn broke her leg in her fall and died of a pulmonary embolism. Mitchell was convicted of manslaughter and appealed on the grounds that his mens rea was directed not that the old lady but the other person and therefore he could not be liable for the death. The Court of Appeal rejected this contention, applying the transferred malice principle, where Mitchell's mens rea was directed to the person he assaulted and then transferred to the old lady.

Another example of the application of the principle is *Latimer* [1886] 17 Q.B.D. 359, in which two men where arguing in a pub; one struck the other with a belt, and a glancing blow caught both the man he was aiming it, as well as an innocent bystander causing injury to them both. Latimer's conviction for assault on the innocent bystander was upheld under the transferred malice principle. In *Attorney-General's Reference (No.3 of 1994)* [1997] 3 W.L.R. 4251, the House of Lords reviewed the rationality of the principle of transferred malice, and agreed that the principle had a sound basis in law, but found it difficult to base a modern law of murder on such a concept. Lord Mustill observed that the concept is long out of date and that:

> "to speak of a particular malice which is transferred simply disguises the problem by idiomatic language. The defendant's malice is directed at one objective, and when after the event the court treats it as directed at another object it is not recognizing a 'transfer' but creating a new malice which never existed before."

The defendant in this case was acquitted of the murder of his baby daughter on the direction of the judge. The Attorney-General sought the opinion of the court on a point of law under s.72 of the Criminal Justice Act 1972. The defendant had violently stabbed his girlfriend, who was pregnant, in the abdomen causing the premature birth of the foetus, which later died as a result. Part of the actus reus of murder is that the death most be of a person in being. This caused difficulties for prosecution, who contended that the transferred malice principle could be used to transfer the defendant's mens rea that was directed at the mother, to the foetus, and then to the baby born as a living being. This was rejected in its entirety by the House of Lords, Lord Mustill considered it was going too far to deploy the transferred malice principle since this requires "a double transfer of intent" The defendant only intended to injure his girlfriend, he did not intend to injure either the foetus or the baby subsequently born. To convict would mean transferring the intent directed to the murder not once but twice, namely from the mother to the foetus and then from the foetus to the baby born. This would, according to his Lordship be stretching the old law too far and creating new law. In response, the prosecution tried to then argue that the foetus was part of the mother just like or arm or leg and therefore the defendant's mens rea would only be transferred once from the mother to the born baby. This too was rejected by the House of Lords who held that medically, a foetus is a separate entity to the mother and does not form part of the mother as the prosecution claimed.

31. The Meaning of Legal Causation and the Novus Actus Interveniens Principle

2.37 The prosecution must not only prove the mens rea and actus reus of the offence, they must also prove that the defendant's act/omission caused the consequence/result. In other words, they must prove an unbroken chain of causation, which started with the defendant's initial act and ended with the result or consequences which arose due to the act. It is possible for a defendant to argue that although they started the chain of events, an unforeseen intervening act was the actual cause of the result or consequence that occurred, thereby breaking the chain of causation. This is known as a *novus actus interveniens*, and medical negligence is often argued to be an intervening act. The issue of causation is rarely brought into issue at trial, but if it is, the criminal law requires the prosecution to prove there is: (i) causation in fact; (ii) causation in law.

32. Defining Causation in Fact and the Act of "Escape"

2.38 In all criminal trials, the prosecution is required to establish beyond doubt that on the facts it was the defendant's act which caused the outcome. In some cases the defendant may not deny it was them who caused, say the injuries in an assault case, but may claim they were justified in doing so in self defence. One point the courts have had to give a ruling on in terms of causation in fact and in law, is whether or not a defendant who attacks the complainant, who then tries to escape but is seriously injured in their own pursuit of escape, caused those injuries on the facts or was the escapee the cause of their own injuries. The Court of Appeal ruled in *R. v Roberts* [1971] 56 Cr.App.R. 95, that the act of escape completes the actus reus of the crime and that it was an objective question for the jury to decide whether or not, on the facts, the defendant had caused the injuries suffered in the act of escape. The defendant, *Roberts* gave a lift to the complainant in his car and then during the journey placed his hand on the complainant's leg to sexually assault her. The complainant, in fear of further assault opened the door of the car and jumped out suffering injuries as result. The Court upheld the defendant's conviction for those injuries since factually he had caused them from the initial sexual assault.

33. Defining Causation in Law

2.39 Factually the prosecution must prove causation, but if the defendant raises as an issue that they did not cause the result or consequence which is alleged to have occurred, then the trial judge will have to decide on whether or not to give a legal direction on when in law a defendant has caused the outcome. The legal principle of causation is found in *R. v Pagett* [1983] 76 Cr.App.R. 279, where a gunman, while firing at police, used a woman as a shield and she died as a result of gunfire returned by the police. The Court held that the legal test for causation in law is that the judge should direct the jury that the defendant's act/omission need not be the sole cause, or even the main cause, of the victim's death (or other result or consequence) *it being enough that his act contributed significantly to that result.* An interesting case where both causation on law and fact were brought into issue was *R. v White* [1910] 2 K.B. 124, in which the defendant decided to murder his mother, so he put cyanide in her drink intending to kill her. However, she instead died naturally of a heart attack before drinking it. The Court held that in causation he was not guilty of his mother's death, but was guilty instead of attempted murder.

In *R. v JT and others* [2007] EWCA Crim 3133, the Court of Appeal quashed the manslaughter convictions of the appellants on the grounds that factually from the pathological evidence adduced at trial, it was impossible for the jury to exclude the sole cause of death by arrhythmia as being from the insults and spittle directed towards the deceased and not the later throwing of the stones. This case aptly demonstrates the distinction that needs to be drawn between scientific/medical proof which cannot exclude other possibilities and that of legal proof, and in this case an unlawful and dangerous act.

34. The "Thin (Egg) Skull" Rule and Causation

2.40 The thin skull rule together with the maxim "he who assumes the risk must suffer the consequences" is a principle of the common law and simply means that the accused takes his victim as he finds them. The application of the principle is well illustrated in *R. v Blaue* [1975] 1 W.L.R. 1411, where B stabbed a girl not knowing she was a Jehovah's witness. In order for her to survive from the wound, she was told that a blood transfusion was necessary. To this request the victim refused and subsequently died. Medical evidence showed that had the victim agreed to a transfusion then she would have survived. Despite this B was charged with murder, which was later at trial reduced to manslaughter on the grounds of diminished responsibility. B appealed on the basis that the victim had caused her own death. Dismissing his appeal, Lawson L.J. pronounced firmly, "that those who use violence on other people must take their victim as they find them". Applying the rule to Mr Blaue clearly made him liable for all the consequences that naturally flowed from his initial prohibited conduct, despite his lack of knowledge about the peculiarities of his victim.

35. Novus Actus Interveniens and Medical Intervention

2.41 The defendant assaults the complainant but later at hospital, they die as a result of medical negligence. The question arises did the defendant cause the victim's death, or was the medical negligence an intervening act such as to physically break the chain of causation and exonerate the defendant from criminal liability? The legal principle on whether medical negligence amounts to an intervening act is found in *R. v Cheshire* [1991] 1 W.L.R. 844, where the defendant had shot the victim who subsequently died from "cardio respiratory arrest" due to his injuries. At trial the defendant raised medical evidence that the victim had in fact died of a rare, but unknown complication due to the treatment received. The defendant was convicted of murder and appealed on the grounds that the judge had misdirected the jury on the issue of causation. The Court of Appeal dismissed the appeal and held that the jury should be directed that the act of the defendant need not be the sole cause of death, it need only be a significant contribution to the death.

Medical negligence is evidence that a jury can consider in their determination only where the negligence is so independent and so potent a cause of death, to make the defendant's act insignificant so as to exclude their act and therefore liability for those injuries (see also the tragic facts in *R. v Brown* [2001] EWCA Crim 1043, in which the Court of Appeal dismissed the appellant's appeal against his murder conviction, since, although the deceased's treatment at hospital was negligent to an appalling degree, the defendant's violent assault upon him was still a significant cause of his death).

In *R. v Rafferty* [2007] EWCA Crim 1846, the deceased had suffered an appalling undignified death by drowning in the sea, but beforehand had suffered a severe beating by the defendant and two other co-defendants. However, the Court of Appeal quashed the defendant's conviction for manslaughter on the grounds that he had been involved in causing injury by beating the deceased on the beach. But while the defendant had left the scene to use the deceased's bank card in an attempt to withdraw money, the other two co-defendant's dragged the deceased into the sea and left him to drown. Accordingly, although the defendant had been part of and caused the earlier injuries, the act of the two co-defendants in dragging the deceased to his death amounted to a intervening act which broke the casual link between the defendant's violent act and the actual death of the victim, so that no reasonable jury could conclude other than the acts of the co-defendant's as being an intervening act. It is a clear principle of law that if person A violently injures another, and walks away, but then person B, unconnected to A, violently assaults an already lame victim causing death, although A started the chain of events, they cannot be held liable for the death, since this was caused by the unconnected intervening act of B. Of course, if A and B where proven to be acting as a joint enterprise then both would be liable for either murder or manslaughter.

36. Absolute (Strict) Liability Offences

2.42 An offence that is defined as a strict liability offence means an offence which consists only of an actus reus element. No mens rea exists in a strict liability offence, and the prosecution is therefore not required to prove a mental element, only that the defendant committed the actus reus. The word absolute or strict means that once the defendant has committed the actus reus of the offence, regardless of what was in their mind at the material time, they are liable at that point. A common example is the road traffic offence of speeding; once it is proven that the driver contravened the speed limit the offence is complete, regardless of whether or not the driver knew they were in fact speeding. The basic reasons behind the creation of a strict liability offence is to ease the burden of proof which normally rests with the prosecution to save court time, to provide a more realistic prospect of a conviction and eliminate any possible legal issue as to what the defendant was thinking or not thinking at the material time.

The majority of such offences are well established and clearly justified as a regulatory and preventative measure in areas such as health and safety, trading legislation (see for example s.1 of theTrade Descriptions Act 1968 and *Newman v Hackney London Borough Council* [1982] R.T.R. 296) and consumer law, where more often than not the criminal breach can be considered a technical one and the punishment is more likely to be punishable be a fine. Such offences in many instances do not cause any social disgrace or obloquy against the offender. It is important to be able to identify a strict liability offence as opposed to an offence that requires the prosecution to prove both mens rea and actus reus. For most offences this is obvious but less so for others. The distinctions are sometimes difficult to establish since when Parliament creates a strict liability offence, it doesn't expressly state this in the offence creating provision. Parliament generally leaves the offence provision silent as to the need to prove mens rea and therefore by this omission would have intended the offence to be one of strict liability. Another common element to a strict liability offence is the insertion of a statutory defence usually expressed as taking all reasonable precautions and exercising all due diligence to avoid the commission of the strict liability offence (i.e. see s.33(7) of the CNEA 2005 concerning the depositing of controlled waste without a licence, other examples are found in the Trade Descriptions Act 1968) in order to ensure that the offence does not offend fairness.

37. The Offence of Dropping Litter: An Example

2.43 Section 18 of the Clean Neighbourhoods and Environment Act 2005 (CNEA 2005), creates the offence of dropping litter. Section 18(1) provides that "A person is guilty of an offence if he throws down, drops or otherwise deposits any litter in any place to which this section applies and leaves it". Place means an area open to the air to which the public have access and this includes land and water. Reading the definition of the offence, the section is silent on mens rea, no words exist to describe a mental element, only to describe the actus reus. For this offence the actus reus can be committed in three ways as follows: (i) throws down; (ii) drops or; (iii) otherwise deposits. So what of the situation where a person walking in a public park accidentally drops a crisp packet and leaves it, the person has completed the actus reus and is guilty at this point.

The offender cannot at court claim he was not aware that the crisp packet had fallen out of his pocket. This is irrelevant; the offence is clearly strictly liable and is justified in that rubbish is blighting communities generally and therefore the law imposes a high preventative duty on any person to ensure that they do not drop litter. In other words the crisp packet offender should have ensured that the crisp packet would not fall, even accidentally, out of his pocket. A statutory defence exists for the offence and is contained in subsection (4A) which provides that no offence is committed if the person is authorised by law to drop litter or has the consent of the owner of the place in question. Another more serious offence can be charged under s.33 of depositing controlled waste or knowingly causing or permitting controlled waste to be deposited in or on any land without a waste management licence. This can include depositing waste from a vehicle, i.e. throwing waste out of the window. This amounts to an either way offence punishable by a maximum two years' imprisonment on indictment. Nevertheless, the Secretary of State does have a power to exclude any deposits deemed to be small enough or temporary in nature or innocuous.

38. The Common Law Presumption of Mens Rea Guidelines and the Principle of Legality

2.44 In *B (a minor) v DPP* [2000] 2 W.L.R. 452, the House of Lords held that within the common law there existed a presumption of mens rea which applied to all criminal offences, unless that presumption was excluded by Parliament either (i) expressly or; (ii) through necessary implication. It is important to be aware that the common law treats all offences as having a mens rea element, but this is only a presumption and can therefore be excluded. In this instance the courts recognise that Parliament may want to establish a strict liability offence, but if Parliament intends to do this, it needs to exclude the presumption in one of two ways either expressly saying so in the legislation or alternatively impliedly through the wording and the nature of offence.

In deciding whether or not an offence which is silent as to the need of mens rea Lord Steyn stated that whilst parliamentary sovereignty is a fundamental principle of our constitution, Parliament must still legislate within the principle of legality exemplified by Lord Hoffmann in *R. v Home Secretary Ex p. Simms* [2000] 3 W.L.R. 328, which meant that, "parliament must squarely confront what is it doing and accept the political cost".

His Lordship then added that:

> "in the absence of express language or necessary implication to the contrary, the courts therefore presume that even the most general words were intended to be subject to the basic rights of the individual."

Section 3 of the Human Rights Act 1998 incorporates the principle of legality as a rule of statutory construction involving a potential violation of a Convention right. Article 6(2) is the relevant provision on the issue of offences of strict liability. This protects the presumption of innocence and requires the prosecution to establish all elements by applying general principles of law. To confirm the principle unequivocally Lord Steyn in *R. v K* [2002] 1 A.C. 462, stated that:

> "it is well established that there is a constitutional principle of general application that whenever a section is silent as to mens rea there is a presumption that, in order to give effect to the will of Parliament, we must read in words appropriate to require mens rea ... The applicability of this presumption is not dependant on finding an ambiguity in the test. It operates to supplement the test. It can only be

displaced by specific language, i.e. an express provision or a necessary implication"

39. Guidelines on Deciding whether the Presumption has been Displaced/Excluded by "Necessary Implication"

2.45 If the offence is silent on the issue of mens rea and it is argued that the necessity to prove mens rea is excluded by necessary implication, the question that then arises is what is meant by necessary implication and what factors give rise to the displacement of the common law presumption. In *Gammon v Att-Gen* [1985] A.C. 1, Lord Scarman, considering the decision in *Sweet v Parsley* [1970] A.C. 132, set out five proposals to decide on whether the offence requires proof of mens rea. These are as follows:

(i) There is a presumption of mens rea required (where the definition of the offence omits any reference to an appropriate *mens* rea then it is the court's duty to imply such an element unless contrary is shown).

(ii) The presumption is strong where the offence is *"truly criminal"* in nature and character.

(iii) The presumption applies to all statutory offences unless displaced either *expressly* or *by necessary implication.*

(iv) Presumption is displaced if the offence is concerned with an issue of *social concern and public safety* (this requires the court to look at the mischief the offence is trying to prevent. If the offence is one which as a specific social concern and public safety purpose then mens rea can be displaced.

(v) Even at point (iv) the presumption of mens rea, applies unless the offence requires *strong vigilance* from the defendant. (This requires the court to still apply presumption of mens rea to offences with a specific social concern and public safety, unless that offence requires strong vigilance from the defendant to ensure that they do not commit the offence).

In *B v DPP* [2000] 2 A.C. 428, Lord Nicholls stated that necessary implication set out in guideline (iii) above:

> "connotes an implication, which is compellingly clear. Such an implication may be found in the language used, the nature of the offence, the mischief sought to be prevented and any other circumstances which may assist in determining what intention is properly to be attributed to Parliament when creating the offence."

One such relevant factor is the statutory context of the offence. Lord Nicholls referred to the seriousness of the offence and the severity of any punishment as indictors, requiring proof of mens rea. Accordingly, the more serious the offence is in terms of culpability, the more that offence is of a truly criminal nature and therefore a mens rea element, although not expressly set out in the offence, is essential and the court's duty is to insert such a mens rea into the offence to avoid unfairness to the defendant. Likewise, if the offence carries a substantial sentence of imprisonment, then there is a clear requirement for the need of a mens rea for the offence.

40. Strict Liability and the Presumption of Innocence

2.46 Article 6 of the Convention on European Human Rights provides for the absolute right to a fair trial; within this right is art.6.2, which states that any person charged with a criminal offence "shall be presumed innocent until proved guilty according to law". On a simple view, the creation of a strict liability offence conflicts with the presumption of innocence principle and is therefore a breach of the defendant's right to receive a fair trial. The basis for this argument relies on the point that if the prosecution are not required to the prove a mental element of knowledge or awareness, then the defendant does not have the benefit of an innocent mind defence and therefore cannot from the outset be presumed innocent.

In *Barnfather* v *London Borough of Islington* [2003] 1 W.L.R. 2318, the appellant was convicted under s.444 of the Education Act 1996 which provides that if a child of compulsory school age fails regularly to attend school, then the parent is guilty of offence. On appeal to the High Court the appellant contended that s.444(1), being a strict liability offence; breached art.6.2 and was therefore unfair and unlawful. The High Court, on this important point, rejected it in its entirety. Referring to European Court of Human Rights decision in *Salabiaku v France* (1988) 13 E.H.R.R. 379, the Court held that art.6.2 did not apply to the substantive criminal law, it related to criminal procedure, in terms of how the offence is proved, not the actual elements to the offence itself. The House of Lords in *R. v G* [2008] UKHL 37 have now put the matter beyond doubt that the creation of strict liability as with the offence of raping a child under 13 contained in s.5 of the Sexual Offences Act 2003 is not incompatible with art.6.2 and that member states are free to decide what the necessary proof elements of an offence will be. Accordingly, the drafting of the criminal law was a matter for the domestic State, and that the creation of a strict liability offence did not offend art.6.2 in that context.

In *R. v Muhamad* [2002] EWCA Crim 1856, the defendant was convicted of an offence under s.362 of the Insolvency Act 1986 which provides that if a bankrupt who within a two-year period before the order of bankruptcy, "materially contributed to, or increased the extent of his insolvency by gambling or by rash and hazardous speculations is guilty of an offence". The Court of Appeal ruled that although the offence had a maximum two-year sentence of imprisonment this still amounted to one of strict liability on the basis that it "will encourage greater vigilance to prevent gambling which will or may contribute to insolvency".

Another similar summary strict liability offence is contained in s.54 of the

Anti-social Behavour Act 2005, which makes it an offence to sell aerosol paint contain to a person under the age of 16. To ensure there is no breach of art.6, subsection (4) provides a statutory defence of taking reasonable steps to determine the purchaser's age and that the person reasonably believed the purchaser was not under 16. If the offence was committed by an employee, then the trader is vicariously liable for that offence, but does have a defence, if they can prove that they took all reasonable steps to avoid the commission of the offence.

CASES WHERE THE PRESUMPTION WAS HELD TO APPLY		
	CASE NAME	**OFFENCE**
1	*Sweet v Parsley* [1970] A.C. 132	Section 5 of the Dangerous Substance Act 1965 which provided that a person who, being the occupier of premises, permits those premises to used for the purpose of taking drugs shall be guilty of an offence. The Court of Appeal held that the presumption of mens rea applied and that the prosecution must prove that the defendant "knew" (mental element) the premises were being used for such use. The presumption was not rebutted on the grounds that the offence was serious and "truly criminal" in nature with a substantial sentence of imprisonment.
2	*B (a minor) v DPP* [2000] 2 W.L.R. 452	Section 1 of the Gross Indecency with Children Act 1960 provided that a person who commits gross indecency with a child under the age of 14 if they incite that child to commit such an act and shall be guilty of an offence. The House of Lords held that for this offence the presumption applied and that the prosecution were required to prove that the defendant knew or genuinely believed the child to be under 16. The presumption was not rebutted on the grounds that the offence was "truly criminal" in nature a serious offence with a 10-year sentence of imprisonment.
3	*R. v K* [2002] 1 A.C. 462	The House of Lords followed the decision in *B v (a minor) v DPP* and held that for the offence of indecent assault with a person under 16 found in the now replaced s.14 of the Sexual Offences Act 1956.

CASES WHERE THE PRESUMPTION OF MENS REA HAS BEEN DISPLACED		
	CASE NAME	**OFFENCE AND GUIDELINES**
1	*Harrow BC v Shah* [1993] 3 All E.R. 302	Sections 11 and 12 of the National Lottery Act 1993 provides that a person is guilty of an offence if they sell a lottery ticket to a person under the age of 16. The Court held that the prosecution need only prove that the actus reus of the offence. It is irrelevant whether or not the defendant believed that the person was under 16. Presumption of mens rea rebutted on grounds that the offence is of a specific social concern and public safety preventing underage gambling and possible addiction with strong vigilance from lottery outlets to ensure they do not sell a ticket to a person under 16. This equally applies to selling alcohol (binge drinking and violence). Off licences must show strong vigilance to ensure they do not commit the offence.
2	*Barnfather v London Borough of Islington* [2003] 1 W.L.R. 2318	Section 144 of the Education Act 1996 provides that if a child of compulsory school age fails to attend regularly at school their parents are guilty of an offence. The Court held that the prosecution need only prove the actus reus and what the parents believed or didn't believe is irrelevant Presumption of mens rea is rebutted on the gounds that the offence is of a specific social concern and public safety preventing truancy and lack of social development.
3	*R. v Bezzina* [1994] 1 W.L.R. 1057	Section 3 of the Dangerous Dogs Act 1991 creates the offence of having a dog dangerously out of control in a public place. If the dog injures another person, then the offence is charged as an aggravated offence. The Court of Appeal held that the presumption of mens rea had been rebutted, since the offence required strong vigilance from dog owners not to be careless or complacent.

4	*R. v Doring* [2002] EWCA Crim 1695	Section 11 of the Companies Directors Disqualification Act 1986 creates the offence of acting as a company director whilst being an undischarged bankrupt. The Court of Appeal held that this amounted to a strict liability offence and that the prosecution was not required to prove any element of dishonesty.
5	*Grundy v Halton Magistrates' Court* [2003] EWHC 272	Involved the offence of felling trees without a felling licence from the Forestry Commission contrary to ss.9 and 17 of the Forestry Act 1967. The High Court held that the offence, being regulatory and not truly criminal, amounted to a strict liability offence.
6	*R. v Matudi* [2003] EWCA Crim 697	Involved Regulations 21 and 37 of the Products of Animal Origin (Import and Export) Regulations 1996, which creates the offence of importing any animal product without first giving notice to the relevant authority. The High Court ruled that the offence amounted to one of strict liability, despite the possibility of a two-year sentence of imprisonment. The Court reasoned that the offence involved concerned a matter of considerable importance, social concern and health with potential serious economic consequences.
7	*R. v Harrison* [1996] 1 Cr.App.R. 138, and *R. v Waller* [1991] Crim L.R. 381	Involved s.1 (possessing a firearm without a certificate) and s.19 (having a firearm with ammunition in a public place) of the Firearms Act 1968. The Court in both cases held that the offences to be of strict liability and that the prosecution need not prove any element of knowledge.
8	*R. v Deyemi* [2007] EWCA Crim 2060	Involved s.5 of the Firearms Act 1968, possessing a prohibited weapon (a electrical stun gun). The Court of Appeal considered itself bound by the decision in *Bradish* [1990] 90 Cr.App.R. 271 and ruled that the offence was one of strict liability. Therefore, no defence of innocent possession can be claimed (defendant believed it to be a torch).

Chapter Three

UNLAWFUL HOMICIDE: MURDER AND MANSLAUGHTER (FATAL OFFENCES)

1. Unlawful Homicide Offences

3.01 When a death occurs, the important issue to be aware of and be able to identify is whether that death was lawful or unlawful. If the death was unlawful, then the question will arise as to whether that death was murder or manslaughter. Other unlawful homicide offences also exist, which are committed in specific circumstances. These are as follows:

(i) Infanticide contrary to s.1 of the Infanticide Act 1938.

(ii) Assisting a suicide contrary to the Suicide Act 1961.

(iii) Causing death by dangerous driving contrary to s.1 of the Road Traffic Act 1991.

(iv) Death by careless or inconsiderate driving contrary to s.20 of the Road Safety Act 2006.

Both murder and manslaughter are common law offences and are defined in the decisions of the Appeal Courts and as we have already seen, the issue of the legal meaning of indirect intent has caused difficulties for the law of murder. This point is encapsulated in the observations of Lord Mustill in *Attorney General's Reference (No.3 of 1994)* [1996] 2 W.L.R. 412 as follows:

> "Murder is widely thought to be the gravest of crimes. One could expect a developed system to embody a law of murder clear enough to yield an unequivocal result on a given set of facts, a result which conforms with apparent justice and has a sound intellectual base. This is not so in England, where the law of homicide is permeated by anomaly, fiction, misnomer and obsolete reasoning."

The current definition of murder is clearly unsatisfactory and does not have a sound, fair or coherent structure. This is highlighted in the application of the mens rea for murder (see below at para.3.03). It is important to note that, as a general rule explained in *R. v Treacy* [1971] A.C. 536, criminal proceedings cannot be commenced where the commission of a criminal offence occurred outside the jurisdiction of the justice system in England and Wales. However, an exception to this rule exists for murder, in that, provided the alleged defendant is a British national, they can be indicted for a murder committed outside England and Wales (see the obiter comments in *R. v Hamza* [2006] EWCA Crim 2918, for confirmation of this exception).

2. Actus Reus of Murder

3.02 It is important at this point to be aware that the actus reus is the same for both murder and involuntary manslaughter. In this regard, for both offences, the prosecution must establish the following;

(i) the defendant did an act

This is an obvious question. On this point the defendant will usually run an "absolute denial" defence, in that it was not them who committed the act, such as in a case of "mistaken identity".

(ii) the act was deliberate, not accidental or involuntary

This is not confined to the initial deliberate act, it includes all the consequences of that act, but it will not be deliberate if that death occurred as a result of an accident, or that the defendant was at the time acting involuntarily. This means that the defendant had no control over their conduct due, to for example, insanity or automatism.

Prior to 1996 for a death to be murder it had to occur within a year and a day from the alleged act. Owing to advances in medial preservation of life, the Law Reform (Year and a Day Rule) Act 1996 abolished this requirement. Nevertheless, the Act contains two safeguards for the defendant. If the death occurs more than three years after the act causing death, or the defendant has been convicted of a different offence before the death (i.e. s.18 wounding with intent) then before a prosecution for murder can be commenced the consent of the Attorney-General must be sought.

(iii) the act was unlawful

The act causing death will not be unlawful if the defendant used reasonable force and was therefore justifiably acting in self defence.

(iv) the death was of a person in being

The victim must have been alive at the time of the defendant's act. In general this is a straightforward point. However, a sensitive point which we explored in the previous chapter arose in *Attorney-General's Reference (No.3 of 1994)* [1996] 2 W.L.R. 412, where the House of Lords held that a child in utero is not a person in being, until subsequently born; neither is a foetus part of the mother in order to allow the principle of transferred malice to apply. Their Lordships ruled that based on developments in fertility treatment:

> "an embryo is in reality a separate organism from the mother from the moment of conception" and "this individuality is retained by it throughout its development unit it achieves an independent existence on being born".

Accordingly the House held that a foetus does not form an integral part of the mother, even though it is dependant upon the mother for survival until birth. (For the facts of the case see the discussion of the concept of transferred malice in Chapter Two at para.2.36.)

(v) the act was a substantial cause of the death

(see earlier cases on *novus actus intervenes*, i.e. *R. v Pagett, R. v Cheshire* concerning medical negligence, *R. v Blaue* (egg shell skull rule) in Chapter Two at para.2.41).

3. Mens Rea for Murder

3.03 The mens rea for murder was defined as unlawful killing with "*malice aforethought*". In *R. v Vickers* [1957] 2 Q.B. 664, as affirmed in *R. v Moloney* [1985] A.C. 905 and *R. v Woolin* [1999] A.C. 82, the House of Lords has stated that malice aforethought means; (i) an intention to kill; (ii) an intention to cause grievous bodily harm (really serious harm). We have already in Chapter Two looked in detail at the perplexing issue of indirect intent. Another anomaly relating to the mens rea for murder is the ability for the prosecution to rely on an intent to cause grievous bodily harm as a sufficient mens rea to secure a conviction for murder.

In *R. v Smith* [1961] A.C. 290, the House of Lords ruled that the word "grievous" in this context simply means "really serious". The anomaly regarding this part of mens rea can been seen in the judgment of Lord Steyn in *R. v Powell* [1999] 1 A.C. 1, a case involving liability in terms of the necessary mens rea required for a secondary offender, as part of a joint enterprise where the primary offender in the course of committing the agreed offence, commits a further more serious offence. His Lordship stated:

> "In English law a defendant may be convicted of murder who is in no ordinary sense a murderer. It is sufficient if it is established that the defendant has an intent to cause really serious bodily injury. This rule returned murder into a constructive crime. The fault element does not correspond to the conduct leading to the charge."

This means that the criminal law allows a person to be convicted of murder with a mandatory life sentence, when at the time of death they did not intend to kill, but did intend to cause serious injury, a less culpable state of intent. Accordingly, although the defendant foresaw serious injury they did not foresee death or intend it. On this basis, and what Lord Mustill believed to be a principle which "no longer rests on any intellectual foundation", this part of the mens rea for murder does not reflect the defendant's culpability, neither does it reflect the popular conception of murder.

It is important to be aware that should this part of the mens rea be removed, it would not lead to a defendant being inappropriately punished, since below murder is the immediate offence of involuntary manslaughter, which carries a discretionary life sentence. Nevertheless, the mens rea of intent to cause GBH in murder was authoritatively confirmed in *R. v Cunningham* [1982] A.C. 566, as forming part of the law of murder. The justification for the rule is the unpredictability of the outcome of a vicious assault and that on public policy grounds, a defendant should not be able to complain if convicted of murder on evidence that shows the death occurred as a direct result of their attack.

4. Meaning of "Grievous Bodily Harm"

3.04 The expression GBH, which is found in both s.18 and s.20 assault offences in the Offences Against the Person Act 1981, is an unhelpful expression for juries to comprehend the degree of harm needed to convict. In *DPP v Smith* [1961] A.C. 290 the House of Lords in the judgment of Viscount Kilmuir L.C. stated that the expression GBH should be given its ordinary and natural meaning of "really serious harm (injury)", and that what amounts to serious is a question of fact for the jury to determine in the assessment of the evidence. In *R. v Ashman* [1858] 1 F. & F. 88 it was held that the prosecution do not have to prove that the harm was life-threatening, dangerous, or permanent, neither is there any requirement in law that the victim should require treatment, or that the harm should extend beyond soft tissue damage. This decision gives the expression GBH a wide application and can create difficulties in this regard since what might be serious to one person may not necessarily be serious to another.

To some extent this was resolved in *R. v Bollom* [2004] 2 Cr.App.R. 6, where the defendant had caused numerous bruising injuries on the body of his 17-month-old step-daughter. His conviction for s.18 causing GBH with intent was quashed on the grounds that the judge had failed to direct the jury that where considering the seriousness of the "cumulative" injuries suffered, they would have to be satisfied that these occurred during a single, or continuous attack. In the present case, there was no evidence of this and further, the injuries themselves required no medical intervention. Accordingly, in determining the seriousness of the injuries suffered, the jury will need to assess such injuries in the context of the person who suffered the injuries and whether or not such injuries are serious individual to them. By example, what may be minor injuries to a 17 stone 6′ 2″ man would conversely, if caused to a young child or a lesser bodied person, be deemed serious to them.

5. Voluntary Manslaughter: A ''Concession to Human Frailty''

3.05 Voluntary manslaughter arises when a defendant has both the actus reus and mens rea to convict of murder. However, this is reduced to voluntary manslaughter on the grounds of either diminished responsibility or provocation. Both diminished responsibility and provocation are known as partial specific defences to a charge of murder. Partial in the sense that if successfully pleaded, it will not lead to an acquittal for murder, but reduce this to that of voluntary manslaughter. They are specific in the sense that they can only be relied upon to a charge of murder. They cannot be relied for any other criminal offence. The word voluntary is used to show that the defendant carried out the actus reus of the offence with the necessary mens rea, but owing to a human frailty their culpability for murder is reduced to a conviction of manslaughter, which carries a discretionary life sentence. It is important to be aware that both defences exist to provide an excuse as to why the defendant committed murder.

The reason, namely provocation and diminished responsibility, are indicative of a human weakness or imperfection. In such circumstances it would be unjust for the criminal law to impose the ultimate sanction of mandatory life imprisonment on a defendant who would not have otherwise committed murder. But for this human frailty and therefore in terms of culpability, they are not totally to blame for their actions. This is the justification of the existence of the defences, but that is not to say they are without criticism, in certain instances the defences are controversial. In provocation for example; the defendant is contending that the victim must take some responsibility for their own death. Had they not through conduct or words caused the defendant to lose control, then the defendant would not have acted in the way they did by killing them. This suggests that the criminal law is perverse in the sense that the victim is to a certain extent considered to be the cause of their own misfortune.

An example would be where an husband returns home only to be told by his wife that she's been having an affair with his boss and that she is leaving him. An argument ensues and there is an exchange of derogative and demeaning remarks about the other's performance and ability. The husband suddenly snaps and grabs a knife, fatally wounding his wife. The issue for the jury will be to determine whether the husband was provoked by what his wife said or did, causing him to lose his self-control and in so doing killing her, or as the prosecution may claim he did not lose his self control, but acted in a jealous rage leading to the deliberate killing of his partner and therefore he was nothing other than a cold blooded murderer. This factual circumstance also reveals another criticism of provocation in that it is biased towards men in domestic violence deaths, since a man is more likely to snap and kill. Whereas, the woman is likely to kill when the man is no threat, leading to the problem that the loss of control lacked the necessary suddenness required for the defence.

In regard to diminished responsibility, the defendant is contending that they would not have committed murder had it not been for the development of an abnormality of the mind, which substantively impaired their mental responsibility and it is this human weakness which reduces their culpability from murder to manslaughter. The criticism here is that other factors may have contributed to the mind defect, such as abuse of intoxicants and that this defect can be temporary. Accordingly, at trial the defendant would appear to be normal, but at the time of death, their mind was substantively impaired and therefore they had an inability to account for their unlawful conduct. The final controversy surrounding these two defences is the actual length of sentence the defendant receives, which is proportionately far less than what would have been given in the tariff for murder. This has led to the sentencing advisory council issuing sentence guidelines to improve justice in sentencing and the Law Commission to make recommendations for the abolition of the two defences.

6. Partial Defence of Provocation: Section 3 of the Homicide Act 1957 and the Difficulties in Applying the "Reasonable Man" Test

3.06 The partial defence of provocation was originally defined in the common law and existed to show clemency to a defendant who killed, but only did so in extenuating circumstances, so as to avoid the death penalty. The defence is now contained statutorily in s.3 of the Homicide Act 1957 and provides that where, on a charge of murder, there is evidence on which the jury can find that the person charged was provoked (whether by things done, or things said or both) to lose their self control, the question whether the provocation was enough to make a reasonable man do as he did shall be left to the jury.

Section 3 did not, however, repeal the common principles, it simply amended them and recognised the existing objective test as established in the common law. One important modification made by s.3 to the common law was the removal of the discretionary power of the trial judge on whether to leave the partial defence for the jury's determination. Section 3 provides that if there is sufficient causative evidence of provocation, then as a matter of law, the issue of provocation must be left for the jury's determination.

Although the meaning of provocation in s.3 appears simple, the House of Lords has in several appeal decisions been called upon to address the question; who in law is a reasonable man? This has until recently led to divided opinion in the House of Lords, bringing inconsistency, uncertainty and unfairness to a controversial area of law that focuses on a human frailty as a justification to reduce criminal culpability from murder to manslaughter. It is important therefore to be aware of, and be able to critically analyse the development of provocation and the principles that establish the partial defence.

7. Evidential Basis Needed for Provocation to be Left to the Jury

3.07 If a defendant is charged with murder and provided that the factual evidence indicates that the victim may have provoked them to lose their self-control, the defence will present their case based on provocation. Nevertheless, this does not necessarily mean that the jury will be directed to consider provocation. It is for the trial judge to assess the evidence and decide if this raises an evidential issue of provocation, which ought to be left for the jury's determination. In *R. v Acott* [1997] 2 Cr.App.R. 94, the House of Lords ruled that if there exists sufficient evidence to show a causative link between the alleged provocative conduct and the loss of control, then the judge must leave the issue of proportionality to the jury, even if the defence place no reliance on this defence. Only if the evidence of provocation is minimal or fanciful so as to be insufficient, should a judge refuse to leave provocation as an issue for the jury.

8. Provocation Direction to the Jury

3.08 If there is an evidential basis for a partial defence of provocation, then the trial judge in his summing up will give the jury the legal direction on the application of provocation. This direction will consists of two questions and it is for the jury, having heard the evidence, to consider the questions and decide if a plea of provocation is made out and therefore return a verdict of not guilty of murder, but guilty of manslaughter by reason of provocation. It is these two questions that are essential to the application of provocation and therefore it is important to be aware of them, to be able to critically analyse the case authorities that exist behind them. The two questions are as follows:

(i) Was the defendant provoked into losing self-control? (Factual Ingredient)

This amounts to a subjective factual test, in which the jury must determine whether the gravity of provocative words or conduct of the victim caused in the defendant a "sudden and temporary loss of self control" as stated in *R. v Duffy* [1949] 1 All E.R. 932, under the common law prior to the passing of s.3. The jury are told when considering this question of fact that they must look at all the circumstances including not only the age and sex of the defendant, but also take into account, (if raised) any evidence of any mental or other abnormal characteristic of the defendant, upon which the gravity of the provocation would have had an impact. It is important to be aware that this does not include weak emotions, such as violent outbursts, pugnaciousness, jealousy, or intoxication, all of which amount to inexcusable behavour over which the law expects all persons to have a sufficient degree of control. If the answer to this question by the jury is no, then the defence will fail, if on the other hand the jury answer is yes, then the next question must be considered.

(ii) Would a reasonable man have reacted as the defendant did? (Evaluative Ingredient)

This amounts to an objective test and exists as a safeguard against defendants who are violent or pugnacious in claiming that they were provoked. The jury are told to look at the circumstances and decide whether the reasonable man would have lost his self-control and reacted as the defendant did. In *Att-Gen of Jersey v Holley* [2005] 2 A.C. 351, Lord Nicholls stated that this evaluative ingredient consists of two elements namely; (i) assessment of the *gravity* of the provocation; (ii) external standard of self control; "whether the provocation was enough to make a reasonable man do as he did"? The concept of the reasonable man is used to provide a point of standard in which the defendant's self-control can be measured in deciding whether or not their plea of provocation is justified.

9. Behaviour Which does not Cause Loss of Self-Control in the Defendant

3.09 Both in *R. v Camplin* [1978] A.C. 705, and the judgment of Lord Hoffmann in *R. v Smith* [1999] 2 W.L.R. 610, the House of Lords stated clearly that the law of provocation is based on public policy and that for this reason all persons must be able to exercise a sufficient degree of control over commonly encountered human emotions. The defence provides an excuse not to those who have a tendency to be pugnacious, excitable, or jealous, go into violent rages, or become intoxicated, but to those who have as a direct result of what the deceased said or did lost self control at that moment, leading to the act of causing death. In *R. v Pearce* [2001] EWCA Crim 2834, the Court of Appeal dismissed the appellant's appeal, who had killed his brother during a drunken argument by stabbing him three times. The appellant had argued on appeal that the trial judge should have directed the jury that his alcoholism was a relevant characteristic to be shared by the reasonable man. The Court of Appeal affirmed the murder conviction stating that the consumption of alcohol or drugs, especially if knowingly taken in large quantities that invariably leads to reprehensible behaviour, does not amount to a sufficient excuse to cause one to lose one's self-control.

10. Meaning of "Sudden and Temporary" Loss of Self Control in the Context of the "Final Straw" Cases

3.10 The common law definition of provocation as modified by s.3 is set out in *R. v Duffy* [1949] 1 All E.R. 932. Although s.3 simply states that the defendant lost self-control this is qualified by the existing principle stated in *Duffy* that such loss of control must be "sudden and temporary". This principle is an essential ingredient to the application of the defence and exists to limit the defence to those who at the moment of causing death were not in control of their mind set. This amounts to a question of fact for the jury to decide on the available evidence and to distinguish between a provoked response and a deliberate act.

In many cases this issue will be obvious, but in the particular context of domestic violence difficulties have arisen. Where there is a delayed reaction to the provocative conduct, the jury will need to consider the time for reflection. The longer time passes between the provocative conduct and the act of causing death, the more likely the defendant festered over being humiliated, the stronger the evidence becomes that the attack is motivated by revenge and not by loss of control. This amounts to a pure question of fact for determination by the jury, not a question of law. Each case will ultimately depend on its own particular facts.

In *R. v Ahluwalia* [1992] 4 All E.R. 889, the appellant, having allegedly suffered from years of abuse and violence from her partner, decided to throw petrol into his bedroom where he was asleep and then set it alight, resulting in his death. The appellant appealed against her conviction for murder on the ground that the judge should have directed the jury to consider the cumulative abuse and violence, which led to the killing by a "slow burn" effect as opposed to it being sudden and temporary. The Court of Appeal rejected this contention on the basis that the *Duffy* direction is a clear principle of law to which the court is bound to follow.

To rule otherwise would mean a change to the law, which on public policy grounds is a matter for Parliament, not the courts. Nevertheless the Court accepted that the jury when considering provocation it could take into account background evidence from the intervening period between the provocative conduct and the defendant's reaction to it. The court quashed the appellant's conviction for murder and substituted one of manslaughter on the basis that medical evidence of a serious depressive illness, which was not advanced at trial, could now be received by the court under s.23 of the Criminal Appeal Act 1968 as coming within the ambit of diminished responsibility.

In *R. v Thornton (No.2)* [1996] 1 W.L.R. 1174, the defendant killed her violent husband who had physically and mentally abused her over a number of years. At the time of the attack he was drunk and threatened to kill her. He fell asleep, where upon the defendant calmly went to the kitchen, took a carving knife, sharpened it and then stabbed him, killing him. The appellant's first appeal, *R. v Thornton* [1992] 1 All E.R. 306, was rejected on the *Duffy* principle. However on a second appeal, the Court of Appeal accepted the existence of "battered women's syndrome" as a medical condition which the jury could take into account as part of the historical background and which was therefore relevant, dependant on its severity, to the issue of sudden and temporary, where loss of self control could be triggered even by a minor incident as a "last straw".

In *R. v Smith* [2002] EWCA Crim 2671, a case referred to the Court of

Appeal by the Criminal Cases Review Commission, the appellant had, with a shotgun taken from her father's house, killed her husband whilst he was asleep. The Court of Appeal, although with some hesitation, quashed her conviction for murder and substituted one of manslaughter on the basis that the judge had, in directing the jury on provocation, restricted the jury's attention to the evidence of a long row that occurred immediately before the killing. This potentially misled the jury to conclude that the appellant's medical history of depression and "learned helplessness" arising from abuse and control of her by the deceased, was not relevant to the defence of provocation.

11. What in Law is Meant by the Reasonable Man

3.11 Section 3 of the Homicide Act 1957 does not provide a statutory meaning of the phrase "reasonable man". Accordingly, the appeal courts through the common law have had to interpret and provide a legal meaning for this expression. Unfortunately, this has caused the greatest difficulties, with divided opinions in the judgments of both the Court of Appeal and the House of Lords, causing inconsistency and unfairness in a controversial area of law. It is important therefore to be aware of and be able to critically assess the divided opinions and to judge whether, as the current law stands, it is satisfactory or unsatisfactory in terms of justice and fairness.

The leading interpretive authority on the reasonable man concept is *R. v Camplin* [1978] A.C. 705, in which the House of Lords departed from its previous decision in *Bedder v DPP* [1954] 1 W.L.R. 1119, where it was held that the defendant's impotence was not a material factor for the reasonable man in determining whether he had been provoked into killing the deceased prostitute. In *Camplin* the defendant, a 15-year-old was, charged with the murder of a man. His defence of provocation was based on the fact that the man had forcibly buggered him and then afterwards laughed at him, causing him to lose his self control and kill. Lord Diplock explained the expression reasonable man:

> "ordinary person of either sex, not exceptionally excitable or pugnacious, but possessed of such powers of self control as everyone is entitled to expect that his fellow citizens will exercise in society as it is today."

Once the jury have determined the subjective question and concluded that the defendant lost their self-control, in terms of the second question and the concept of the reasonable man, they should be directed that this is a:

> "person having the *power of self-control to be expected of an ordinary person of the sex and age* of the accused, but in other respects *sharing such of the accused's characteristics* as they think would affect the gravity of the provocation to him."

Lord Diplock did not elaborate further on what he meant by the jury being entitled to share with the reasonable man such of the accused's characteristics as they think would be relevant to the gravity of the provocation. Subsequent House of Lords rulings have had to determine precisely what characteristics, if any, of the accused the law would be allowed to be embodied in the reasonable man. It is this legal issue that has divided the House of Lords in three conflicting judgments, causing misinterpretation and misunderstanding. It is important to be aware that there are difficulties surrounding whether the reasonable man should be completely detached from the accused, or whether there should be some reflection of the accused in terms of shared characteristics with the reasonable man. The answer becomes one of justice, on the one hand, if the reasonable man (as determined by the jury) shares no characteristics with the defendant, then the reasonable man in such circumstances is unlikely ever to lose self control, thus creating an injustice to the defendant. Whilst on the other, if the reasonable man is deemed to share the same characteristics as the defendant, then the assessment of objectivity is lost with the reasonable man and the defendant simply becoming the same person.

3.12 Following *Camplin*, the Court of Appeal in a series of authorities ruled that the jury were entitled to consider, when applying the reasonable man test, certain permanent characteristics of the defendant that distinguished them from the ordinary person, and such characteristics formed part of the provocation. The Court of Appeal in *R. v Newell* [1980] 71 Cr.App.R. 331, followed and approved an obiter observation in *McGregor* [1962] N.Z.L.R. 1069 a New Zealand authority in which it was held that characteristics of a permanent nature, relating to the defendant's mental and physical qualities, form part of the reasonable man, provided there is some connection between those characteristics and the alleged provocation. In *R. v Doughty* [1986] 83 Cr.App.R. 319, it was ruled that there was evidence to establish a causative link between the deceased child's persistent crying and the response of the father (defendant) in killing the child and therefore the judge was wrong in his refusal to leave provocation to the jury.

Likewise, in *R. v Baillie* [1995] 2 Cr.App.R. 31, provocation should have been left to the jury when the defendant (who very drunk), having learned that his son had been threatened by a local drug dealer, proceeded to arm himself with a shot gun and cut throat razor, visited the home of the drug dealer, and killed him. In *R. v Dryden* [1995] 4 All E.R. 987, the defendant had killed a local authority planning officer who had visited his home over a planning dispute. The Court of Appeal ruled that obsessiveness and eccentricity were characteristics of the defendant that the jury should have considered as part of the reasonable man test. In *R. v Thornton (No.2)* [1995] 1 W.L.R. 1174, the Court of Appeal had ruled that battered women's syndrome was a relevant characteristic of the reasonable man. Whilst in *R. v Ahluwalia* [1992] 4 All E.R. 889, the Court stated that the mental and personality disorders of the defendant amounted to relevant characteristics. Likewise in *R. v Humphreys* [1995] All E.R. 1008, abnormal immaturity and attention seeking by the defendant slashing her wrists, also amounted to relevant characteristics shared by the ordinary person.

The first post-*Camplin*, House of Lords authority on the meaning of the reasonable man was *R. v Morhall* [1996] A.C. 90, in which the defendant, an habitual glue sniffer, had killed his friend who had persistently told him to stop. The issue on appeal was whether the glue sniffing characteristics of the defendant should be shared by the reasonable man in the sense that the reasonable man will be a glue sniffer having ordinary powers of self-control. The House of Lords, by a majority, allowed the appeal, quashing the defendant's conviction for murder and substituting one of manslaughter, stating that the judge was entitled to tell the jury that they must take into account "the entire factual situation", including the self induced addition of the defendant in the objective ordinary person test. According to the House of Lords, if these glue sniffing characteristics were not taken into account, then this would render the objective ordinary person test pointless, given that the provocative words were directed to the characteristic in question.

3.13 Shortly afterwards, the Privy Council was again faced with the same legal point in *Luc Thiet Thuan v The Queen* [1997] A.C. 131. An appeal from Hong Kong, in which the judge refused to allow the jury to consider the appellant's brain damage that he claimed, caused him to respond badly to even minor provocation. By a majority of four to one the Privy Council rejected the appeal and ruled that the characteristics of the accused can be taken into account in the subjective question, but only age and sex can be characteristics shared by the ordinary person in the objective test. To rule otherwise would be a misinterpretation of s.3. Lord Steyn, on the other hand, delivered a powerful dissenting judgment based on logic and fairness, referring to several previous Court of Appeal decisions including *R. v Ahuwalia* [1992] 4 All E.R. 889, *R. v Humphreys* [1995] 4 All E.R. 1008, and *R. v Thornton (No.2)* [1996] 1 W.L.R. 1174 as being correctly decided. His Lordship considered the development of legal principle in these cases as simply being an extension of the ratio of *R. v Camplin*, and that these cases were underpinned by ensuring justice, as opposed to legal logic, for the defendant who possesses a particular characteristic that is relevant to the gravity of the provocation.

The law on the meaning of the reasonable man, despite the majority decision in *Luc Thiet Thuan*, still remained unsettled, given the lack of unanimity in their Lordships' opinion and that a Privy Council decision is not binding on English courts but only persuasive. For this reason, the subsequent decisions of the Court of Appeal in *R. v Campbell* [1997] 1 Cr.App.R. 199 and *R. v Parker* [1997] (unreported), ruled that they were bound, not by the Privy Council decision, but the previous Court of Appeal authorities on the meaning of the reasonable man in provocation. This led to the issue being revisited by the House of Lords in *R. v Smith* [2000] 3 W.L.R. 654, in which the defendant, who had a severe depressive illness, killed his friend whom he believed had stolen some of his tools and that despite repeated denials by the friend the defendant killed him, convinced that he had stolen them. The defendant at trial relied on his depressive illness as being susceptible to the provocative words of the deceased, causing him to lose his self control and kill. The trial judge ruled, based on the majority decision in *Luc Thiet Thuan*, that severe depressive illness was not a matter for the jury to take into account when considering the reasonable man test in provocation. The defendant was convicted of murder and appealed on the grounds that there was a misdirection by the judge on the meaning of the reasonable man.

The Court of Appeal allowed the defendant's appeal and quashed his conviction, the matter then went to the House of Lords who by a bare majority of three to two agreed with the Court of Appeal. The majority in the judgment of Lord Hoffman ruled that s.3 required the judge to ensure justice, direct the jury that they may take into account certain characteristics of the defendant, whether temporary or permanent, when considering the objective standards of an ordinary person in terms of exercising a sufficient degree of self control that society would expect in those circumstances. Lord Hobhouse, giving a dissenting judgment, felt that to interpret the meaning of the ordinary (reasonable) person so as to share certain characteristics of the defendant, amounts to a "strained construction" of s.3 in order to avoid a potential injustice was misplaced since those with certain mental defects can rely on diminished responsibility instead.

3.14 The lack of resolution, with previous conflicting decisions and the fact that the majority opinion in *Smith* refused to follow the majority ruling in *Lu Theit Thuan* created more uncertainty, which led yet again to the statutory construction of s.3 coming before the Lordships in *Att-Gen for Jersey v Holley* [2005] 3 W.L.R. 29 a Privy Council appeal decision from the Court of Appeal in Jersey. To endeavour to bring some finality and certainty in to this unrelenting area of law, the Appeal Committee consisted of nine Law Lords. Unfortunately, their Lordships still remained divided by a six to three majority. In this instance the majority concluded that *R. v Smith* had been wrongly decided and that the majority decision in *Luc Thiet Thuan* had stated the law correctly.

The majority concluded and ruled that the jury, having assessed the gravity of the provocation to the defendant, must then consider the standard of self control by which his conduct is to be evaluated, for the purpose of the defence of provocation is the external standard of a person having and exercising ordinary powers of self control, and nothing more in terms of the characteristics of the defendant other then sex and age. This is what Parliament intended when it amended the law on provocation in s.3 of the Homicide Act and the common law cannot be developed in any way to depart from what Parliament meant. Despite the lack of unanimity on the correct interpretation of s.3 all their Lordships agreed that the present law on murder and indeed provocation is flawed, principally as a result of its development and difficulties in its application. To this extent it was highlighted by their Lordships that statutory reform by Parliament was now imperative, of the law of murder generally, if potential injustice in individual cases is to be avoided under the present law.

On another point, despite the majority decision returning the law to that postulated in *Lu Theit Thuan*, (itself a Privy Council decision) and now in direct conflict with the House of Lords decision in *Smith*, this now brought into issue the established principles of precedent on which decision a Court of Appeal is bound to follow, given that decisions of the Privy Council are only persuasive, whereas decisions of the House of Lords are strictly binding on the lower courts. In this sense a Court of Appeal would have to ignore the ruling in *Holley* and follow that in *Smith*, which would bring more turmoil to the law.

This issue of precedent came before the Court of Appeal in *R. v James and Karimi* [2006] 1 Cr.App.R. 29 requiring the constitution of five Lord Justice's of Appeal to decide this point. Lord Phillips L.C.J., giving the leading speech of the Court, ruled that although the Court of Appeal was bound by decisions of its own and that of the House of Lords, in this instance the Court of Appeal was bound to follow the majority decision in *Holley*, on the basis that the nine Law Lords had purposely been constituted to "clarify definitively" this difficult area of law and, secondly, their Lordships through the decision in *Holley* had changed the common law rule of precedent, by confirming that if necessary a decision of the Privy Council can depart from a decision of the English House of Lords to create an established principle of law binding on lower courts.

12. Burden of Proof and Summary of Provocation

3.15 It is important to be aware that on a plea of provocation the defendant simply has to raise an evidential issue before a jury. It is for the prosecution to negate the elements of the defence. To do this the Crown must satisfy the jury beyond reasonable doubt that the defendant was not provoked, but in fact was the aggressor and the attacker. Accordingly as stated in *R. v Smith* [2005] 3 W.L.R. 654 the burden of proof lies with the prosecution to disprove provocation, not the defence to prove it, only raise it evidentially. On the subjective question of provocation, the jury are entitled to take into account all mental and physical characteristics of the defendant in the loss of self control.

On the second objective question the law is now set out in *Holley* in that the only characteristics relevant to the reasonable man are sex and age. It is important to be aware that all previous authorities on what characteristics could be shared by the reasonable man which conflict with this decision are now wrongly decided and no longer good law. For the practitioner, these cases are now of little importance, but to the criminal law student they have relevance in terms of being able to critically assess a controversial area of law. Most essay questions on provocation will require the student to review critically the previous law leading up to the decision in *Holley* and indeed consider whether *Holley*, albeit now the law, was correct in rejecting the majority opinion in *Smith*.

13. Sentencing Guidelines in Cases of Provocation

3.16 If a jury accept that a defendant was provoked into losing their self control and therefore return a verdict of not guilty of murder, but guilty of manslaughter by reason of provocation, or the Crown, having reviewed the evidence; accepts a guilty plea to manslaughter on the grounds of provocation then s.3 provides that the sentence available to the court is "discretionary life". This means that the trial judge, having taken account of both the aggravated and mitigating factors, can impose a sentence ranging from discharge up to life imprisonment. In the context of domestic violence provocation cases particularly, this can cause real difficulties for the sentencing judge, since they need so far as possible to reflect in the sentence that a balance has been struck between the acceptance that the offender acted under provocation as against their actual criminal culpability.

In *Attorney-General's Reference* (*Nos 74, 95 & 118 of 2002*) [2002] EWCA 2982, the Court of Appeal was referred several cases in which the Attorney—General believed that the sentences imposed were unduly lenient and invited the court to issue guidelines on appropriate sentences in cases of provocation. The Court declined to give guidance but stated that in these type of cases the sentencing judge must make four assumptions in favour of the defendant as follows:

(i) That the defendant lost control, and did not act in a jealous rage or with loss of temper;

(ii) That this was caused by things said or done by the victim;

(iii) That the loss of control was reasonable in all the circumstances;

(iv) And that this amounts to a sufficient excuse to reduce the defendant's culpability from murder to manslaughter.

The assumptions arise to ensure that when determining sentence the judge does not depart from the actual verdict of the jury. In each of the three domestic violence provocation cases under review the Court of Appeal refused to interfere with the sentences that ranged from three and a half years to seven years. In 2005 the Sentencing Guidelines Council, in order to clarify the sensitive issue of sentencing, issued definitive guidance which must now be considered by judges in the sentencing process. The guidelines provide that the starting point is a custodial sentence. In determining the length of that sentence in terms of seriousness, the critical factor for the sentencing judge is that they are required to assess the degree of provocation in terms of its nature and duration. In this regard, the guidelines identify three sentencing ranges, low, substantial and high.

If the degree of provocation is low then the sentencing range is 10 years to life, with a starting point of 12 years. For substantial degree of provocation, the sentencing range is four years to nine years with a starting point of six years. For cases with an high degree of provocation then the sentencing range is zero to four years with a starting point of three years. For each sentencing range the guidelines identify certain additional aggravating and mitigating factors which can either increase or decrease the actual sentence from the starting point term. Furthermore, manslaughter is categorised as a "serious offence" under the Criminal Justice Act 2003 when dealing with dangerous offenders and the imposition of a sentence under the prescribed procedure for the protection of the public.

14. Partial Defence of Diminished Responsibility: Section 2 of the Homicide Act 1957

3.17 Section 2 of the Homicide Act 1957 provides that a person who at the time of killing another, was suffering from (1) *abnormality of the mind* of such a nature caused by one of three occurrences, so as to have (2) *substantially impaired* their mental responsibility with respect to the act or omission of the killing or being a party to the killing, shall not be convicted of murder but instead voluntary manslaughter. The application of this partial defence to murder requires the jury to consider two questions as follows:

(i) Is there an *abnormality of the mind* from one of the specified causes (set out in s.2), these being whether it arose from a,

   (a) condition of arrested or retarded development or
   (b) inherent cause, or
   (c) it may have been induced by a disease or injury.

(ii) If the answer to the first question is yes then the second question that must be considered is; was it such as *substantially to impair* the defendant's mental responsibility?

It is important to be aware that whereas provocation is concerned with provocative conduct, under this partial defence, this issue becomes one of an "abnormality of the mind". If a defendant places reliance on this defence then they are bringing into issue their mental responsibility, evidentially this will require the existence of expert medical evidence usually in the form of two or three psychiatric reports. It is the relevance of this evidence that the jury will either accept or reject when forming a decision on whether the defence exists or not.

15. What is Meant by an Abnormality of the Mind

3.18 Section 2 is silent on what is meant by an "abnormality of the mind". This led to the expression being considered and explained in *R. v Byrne* [1960] 2 Q.B. 396. Byrne was a sexual psychopath who strangled a young woman and then mutilated her body. Medical evidence showed that he suffered from violent perverted sexual desires which he could not control and this caused him to kill. The Court of Appeal held that an inability to control impulses could amount to an abnormality of the mind. The Court in the judgment of Parker L.C.J. then ruled that the phrase abnormality of the mind:

> "means a state of mind so different from that of ordinary human beings that a reasonable man would term it abnormal" *and* "was wide enough to cover the minds activities in all its aspects, not only the perception of physical acts and matters, and the ability to form a rational judgement as to whether an act is right or wrong but also the ability to exercise will power to control physical acts in accordance with rational judgment".

This means that where a defendant is shown to

(i) have an inability to perceive the consequences of their physical act, or

(ii) an inability to rationalise on the difference between right and wrong, or has an

(iii) inability to exercise a sufficient degree of will power over the above two,

then provided this inability arises from one of or more of the three specified causes, the defendant will be deemed to have been suffering from a abnormality of the mind. Nevertheless, it is important to be aware that whether an accused person was at the time of the act which results in the victim's death suffering from any abnormality of mind, is a question for the jury. Although medical evidence is important on this question, the jury are not bound to accept medical evidence, if there is other material before them, from which, in their judgment, a different conclusion may be drawn.

16. Specified Causes of the Abnormality

3.19 Under s.2 the abnormality of the mind can only arise from one or more of three possible occurrences, this can either be from a defect in that person's development, or is exists inherently, or brought about at some point by a disease or injury. Again s.2 is silent on what is meant by each cause and it is generally left to medical expert evidence to show that whatever abnormality is claimed, falls within one of the three causes. In *R. v Sanderson* [1993] 98 Cr.App.R. 325, the appellant had inflicted appalling injuries upon his girlfriend which caused her death. He appealed against his conviction for murder on the basis that the trial judge had misdirected the jury on diminished responsibility. In quashing the appellant's conviction the Court of Appeal was "inclined" to the view" that the statutory expression "induced by disease or injury" embraces both organic or physical injury and "disease of the body including the brain". Functional mental illness such as paranoia, if medically classified as a disease, would clearly come within "any inherent cause" and therefore within the ambit of s.2.

17. Inherent Causes: Alcohol and Drugs

3.20 Inherent means a condition that is intrinsically part of the defendant such as paranoia. However, in *R. v Fenton* [1975] 61 Cr.App.R. 261, and confirmed in *R. v Gittens* [1984] 79 Cr.App.R. 272, the Court of Appeal ruled that both alcohol and drugs do not, as a matter of law, come within the concept of any inherent cause and therefore on the question whether the defendant suffering from abnormality of the mind arising from an inherent cause, the jury must be told to disregard the effect of alcohol and drugs. This general rule was approved by the House of Lords in *R. v Dietschmann* [2003] 2 W.L.R. 613.

18. Exception: Alcohol Amounting to a Disease

3.21 If the defendant can show themselves to be diagnosed as suffering from alcohol dependence syndrome, then based on the principle in *R. v Tandy* [1988] 87 Cr.App.R. 45, this can amount to a disease that induced the abnormality of the mind. Although the Court of Appeal ruled that alcohol dependency is a disease for the purposes of diminished responsibility, the defendant must show either that their alcoholism was to such a degree so as to damage the brain and its rational and emotional responses, or that they are unable to control their craving for alcohol to such an extent that drinking it becomes an involuntary act. This must go beyond an inability to resist an impulse to drink. In *Tandy* the appellant, having almost consumed a bottle of vodka, killed her 11-year-old daughter by strangulation. The Court of Appeal refused to quash her conviction for murder on the basis that evidentially she had failed to establish that the first drink she had consumed was involuntary. Accordingly, her drinking binge on the day of the killing was consumed voluntary at her own will.

In *R. v Wood* [2008] EWCA Crim 1305 the Court of Appeal in quashing the appellant's conviction for a brutal murder and substituting one of manslaughter on the grounds of diminished responsibility, criticised the literal and prescriptive way in which the *Tandy* principle had been applied generally. To place a person who has ADS but lacking any brain damage from it into a legal straight jacket requiring them to establish that their craving was to such an extent or degree, so as to render them in a state of unconscious knowledge before their act of drinking becomes involuntary as opposed to being voluntary, is clearly at odds with human behaviour. Even a chronic alcoholic which an uncontrollable craving for alcohol will abstain from drinking at certain points, either to eat, wash or sleep for instance, but does this mean to say that in doing so, they made a free choice and as a result their alcoholism is no longer involuntary for the purposes of establishing an abnormality of the mind? In light of the decision in *Dietschmann* the Court felt that a re-assessment of the *Tandy* exception is now needed on public policy grounds.

19. What is Meant by "Substantial Impairment"

3.22 In *R. v Byrne* [1960] 2 Q.B. 396 it was stated that substantial impairment is a question of degree and essentially one for the jury. Medical evidence is, of course, relevant, but the question involves a decision not merely as to whether there was some impairment of the mental responsibility of the accused, but whether such impairment can properly be called "substantial, a matter upon which juries may quite legitimately differ from doctors". The issue of self-control and inability to resist impulses is incapable of scientific proof and are scientifically insoluble. Accordingly, the jury can only approach this in a somewhat broad common sense way based on the facts and medical evidence.

20. Substantial Impairment and the Effect of Self-Induced Intoxication: *R. v Dietschmann* [2003]

3.23 In *R. v Dietschmann* [2003] 2 W.L.R. 613 the House of Lords had to address the difficult issue of to what extent, if any, self induced intoxication through drink or drugs is a factor relevant to the substantial impairment question. In other words, is the defendant required to satisfy the jury that regardless of his self induced intoxicated state at the time of killing, his abnormality of the mind would still have arisen, even in a state of sobriety, and substantially impaired his mental responsibility leading to the actus reus of murder? The appellant, as a result of an unhealthy relationship with an aunt who had died, was suffering from a grief reaction and an abnormality of the mind.

The appellant treasured a watch given to him as a present from the aunt. Whilst at a party in which the appellant had consumed a large quantity of alcohol, the victim had accidentally bumped into the appellant causing the watch to break. In response, the appellant launched a sustained a vicious attack causing death. The appellant was convicted of murder and appealed, contending that the judge was wrong to direct the jury that the defence of diminished responsibility would only arise if they were satisfied that the defendant had proved that he would still have killed as a result of his abnormality, even if he had not been drunk at the time.

The House of Lords accepted this contention and quashed the appellant's conviction for murder and substituted one of manslaughter. The statutory interpretation of "substantially impaired" and the effect of voluntary intoxication had arisen in several previous conflicting Court of Appeal decisions. In *R. v Turnbull* [1977] 65 Cr.App.R. 242, the Court of Appeal did not disapprove of the trial judge's direction that amounted to the defendant having to prove that he would still had killed, if sober. This conflicted with an earlier Court of Appeal decision in *R. v Fenton* [1975] 61 Cr.App.R. 261, which had held that the jury should be told to look at the combined effect of the intoxication and the abnormality and decide whether even with the drink the abnormality substantially impaired the defendant's responsibility.

In *R. v Gittens* [1984] Q.B. 698, the Court of Appeal approved the *Fenton* interpretation and stated that *Turnbull* should not be followed in the future. However, further inconsistency arose when Professor Smith, commenting in the Criminal Law Review on the *Gittens* case, presented two questions which the jury should consider. These amounted to the jury being told, as in *Turnbull,* that the defendant had to satisfy the jury that had he not taken drink, he would still have killed, and that he was suffering an abnormality at the time.

This then led to the Court of Appeal in *R. v Atkinson* [1985] Crim. L.R. 314, and *R. v Egan* [1992] 4 All E.R. 471, approving Professor's Smith's summary as the correct two questions on which to direct a jury on this point. This conflict of authority on the interpretation of "substantively impaired" was resolved by the House of Lords in *Dietschmann* in which their Lordships disapproved of the decisions in *Turnbull, Atkinson* and *Egan* as erroneous and that the correct legal interpretation is found in *Gittens.* The House of Lords ruled that looking literally at the expression "substantially impairs" means that the abnormality need not be the sole cause of the defendant's impaired mental responsibility, provided it was the substantive cause, then the defendant was acting under diminished responsibility even if he was intoxicated at the time of the killing.

Importantly, Lord Hutton gave the following guidance as to how a trial judge should direct the jury on this issue:

> "Assuming that the defence have established that the defendant was suffering from mental abnormality as described in s.2HA 1957, the important question is: did that abnormality substantially impair his mental responsibility for his acts in doing the killing?
>
> You know that before he carried out the killing the defendant had had a lot to drink. Drink cannot be taken into account as something which contributed to his mental abnormality and to any impairment of mental responsibility arising from that abnormality. But you may take the view that both the defendant's mental abnormality and drink played a part in impairing his mental responsibility for the killing and that he might not have killed if he had not taken drink.
>
> If you take that view, then the question for you to decide is this: has the defendant satisfied you that, despite the drink, his mental abnormality substantially impaired his mental responsibility for his fatal acts or has he failed to satisfy you of that. If he has satisfied you of that, you will find him not guilty of murder but you may find him guilty of manslaughter. If he has not satisfied you of that, the defence of diminished responsibility is not available to him."

21. Burden and Standard of Proof

3.24 Unlike provocation on a plea of diminished responsibility, s.3 provides that it is for the defendant to prove on a balance of probabilities, (i.e. more likely than not or more probable than not) they were suffering from an abnormality of the mind and this substantially impaired their mental responsibility. The prosecution simply have to challenge the medical evidence adduced by the defence at trial.

22. Common Law Offence of Involuntary Manslaughter

3.25 Criminal liability for involuntary manslaughter can occur in three different situations as follows:

(i) unlawful and dangerous act manslaughter (also known as constructive manslaughter);

(ii) gross negligence manslaughter;

(iii) Reckless manslaughter.

All three offences are defined in the common law. The word involuntary means that the defendant, although liable for the death of another, did not in the circumstances intend or even realise the risk of death resulting from their initial prohibited act. It is important to be aware that the actus reus for involuntary manslaughter is the same as that for murder, the distinction between the two common law offences is in the mens rea. For murder there is a specific intent to kill or cause serious bodily harm, whilst for manslaughter it is an unintentional killing, this in effect can range from that which is almost murderous to that which is almost accidental. Another distinction between the two offences is the available sentence, for murder it is a mandatory life sentence, whilst for manslaughter it anything from a discharge to a discretionary life sentence.

23. The Offence of Unlawful and Dangerous Act Manslaughter

3.26 The offence of unlawful and dangerous act manslaughter is sometimes referred to as constructive manslaughter. This means that the defendant's culpability for the offence of manslaughter is constructed out of less serious circumstances. For instance, a defendant punches a rival in the face, his mens rea and therefore culpability is that of an assault. However if as a result of that punch the rival falls backwards, banging his head on a kerb stone causing death, the law will now construct from this less serious offence culpability for the more serious offence of manslaughter.

The criticism of this particular offence is that the defendant's culpability does not correspond with the more serious consequence and therefore it is unfair to hold a defendant liable for something they neither intended, nor realised the risk of death. Nevertheless, an important principle of the criminal law is that a defendant who assumes the risk must suffer the greater consequences that arise. In *DPP v Newbury* [1976] 62 Cr.App.R. 291, two boys had pushed into the path of an oncoming train a piece of paving stone, which had been left on the parapet of a railway bridge, killing a train guard. The boys' convictions for manslaughter were upheld by the House of Lords, even though they did not foresee that their act might cause harm to another.

24. The Essential Ingredients of the Offence

3.27 The essential ingredients to manslaughter by an unlawful and dangerous act are found in *R. v Larkin* [1942] 29 Cr.App.R. 291, which was later approved in, *R. v Church* [1965] 49 Cr.App.R. 206 and *DPP v Newbury* [1976] 62 Cr.App.R. 291. The principles are as follows:

(i) that the accused is guilty of manslaughter if it is proved that he intentionally did an act which was unlawful and dangerous and that the act inadvertently caused death, and

(ii) that it is unnecessary to prove that the accused knew that the act was unlawful or dangerous.

25. The Meaning of an Intentional Unlawful Act

3.28 This element requires the prosecution to prove a basic intent, namely the defendant either intended or recklessly did an act. This act must be unlawful, in the sense that the act itself amounts to a criminal offence no matter how minor (see *R. v Lamb* [1967] 2 Q.B. 981). It is important to be aware that the word unlawful is not surplus to the offence. It exists to allow a defendant to claim, if evidence exists, that they acted in self defence, which would turn an unlawful act into a lawful and justifiable act and an acquittal. For example, whilst in a night club a fight breaks out between two young men, punches are exchanged, one of them then punches the other with a sufficient degree of force causing the other to lose his balance and tragically strike his head on the way down on a chair, resulting in death. The unlawful act is clearly an offence of assault, this act of assault was intentionally or recklessly committed by the other male. However, in the circumstances he could claim that whilst he had assaulted the other, he was acting with lawful justification in self defence (see *R. v Scarlett* [1994] 98 Cr.App.R. 290).

26. Supplying of Drugs to Another: An Unlawful Act

3.29 Problematic issues have arisen in a series of cases where the defendant has either (i) supplied drugs to another, or (ii) supplied drugs and assisted in the administration of the drug of which the user dies as a consequence. In each situation, the issue was what constituted the unlawful act to sustain a conviction for manslaughter. In *R. v Dias* (2002) 2 Cr.App.R. 5, *R. v Rogers* [2003] 1 W.L.R. 1374, *R. v Finlay* [2003] EWCA Crim 3868 and *R. v Kennedy (No.2)* [2005] 1 W.L.R. 2159, it is a clear point that if the defendant had injected the drug into the deceased, this would amount to an unlawful act under s.23 of the Offences Against the Person Act 1861 which creates the offence of intentionally or recklessly (i) administering to, or (ii) causing to be administered to, or (iii) taken by any other person, "any poison or other destructive or noxious thing thereby endangering life". In this instance the unlawful act is dangerous, but could such an act in law have caused the user's death? Although, this legal point of issue, has now been settled unanimously by the House of Lords in *R. v Kennedy* [2008] 1 A.C. 269. It is worth considering the previous authorities which highlight very well the difficulties, the courts sometimes face, in ensuring justice, between the conflicting interests of the public interest, the complainant and the defendant. On this difficulty the House of Lords stated:

> "much of the difficulty and doubt which have dogged the present question have flowed from a failure, at the outset, to identify the unlawful act on which the manslaughter count is founded. It matters little whether the act is identified by a separate count or counts under s.23 or by particularisation of the manslaughter count itself. But it would focus attention on the correct question, and promote accurate analysis of the real issues, if those who formulate, defend and rule on serious charges of this kind were obliged to consider how exactly, in law, the accusation is put."

Given that the s.23 offence can be committed in one of three ways, it is, as the House of Lords are suggesting, essential for the prosecution to frame the count in the indictment properly, spelling out on what offence they are purporting to rely, rather than a vague reference to s.23. Problems have arisen when trying to establishing an unlawful act where the defendant simply supplied the drugs to the user who then administered the drug themselves, resulting in their death. In *R. v Dalby* [1982] 1 W.L.R. 425 the Court of Appeal stated that a supply of a prohibited drug alone would not in itself directly caused harm to the deceased and therefore would not constitute manslaughter. Conversely in *R. v Kennedy* [1999] Crim. L.R. 65 although the defendant's conviction was upheld. Waller L.J., giving the judgment of the Court, stated that self injection of drugs amounted to an unlawful act and that those who assisted or encouraged that act would be equally liable as a secondary party.

However, this statement was misplaced and flawed since there is no offence of self injection of drugs under the Misuse of Drugs Act 1971, the only offence is simple possession, or supply of drugs with intent. In *R. v Dias* [2002] 2 Cr.App.R. 5, the trial judge felt bound by *Kennedy* and gave a direction to the jury to that effect. Dias who had prepared the syringe and then passed it to the deceased had his conviction quashed, due to this misdirection of the judge and the failure to leave the issue of causation to the jury. The Court of Appeal distinguished the decision in *Kennedy* and followed *R. v Cato* [1976] 62 Cr.App.R.41, as correctly stating the law that there is no offence of self injection of a prohibited drug. Similarly, in *R. v Richards* [2002] EWCA Crim 3175, the trial judge had directed the jury in accordance with *Kennedy*; the Court of Appeal quashed the appellant's conviction in following the decision in *Dias*.

The confusion that arose in *Kennedy* was resolved by the Court of Appeal taking a different legal route in *Rogers* in that if the accused, whilst not directly being involved in the injection process, was still nevertheless elementary to the preparation in readiness for injection, then the law of joint enterprise will apply. This means that the deceased and the accused are acting with a common intention to administer a drug and are both principals to the offence under s.23. In *Rogers*, the Court of Appeal stated that if active participation is established and death was as a result of the administration of the drug in those circumstances, then as a matter of law no issue of causation arises. As a result of the disapproval of the original decision, the Criminal Cases Review Commission referred back to the Court of Appeal the case of *Kennedy* [2005] 1 W.L.R. 2159. The Court of Appeal affirmed the conviction by following the approach in *Rogers*, but also accepted that the prosecution could rely on the unlawful act of supplying a prohibited drug with intent, but would then need to establish causation, while in other circumstances there may arise a case of gross negligence manslaughter.

On appeal to the House of Lords in *R. v Kennedy* [2008] 1 A.C. 269, this was unanimously rejected and the appellant's conviction quashed. Their Lordships firstly emphasised that the "the criminal law generally assumes the existence of free will" with several recognisable exceptions where this is not possible, such as with the young, vulnerable persons, duress and necessity, deception and mistake. The House of Lords then ruled explicitly that if, on the evidence, the deceased was a, "fully informed and responsible adult" who freely and voluntarily administered the injection of drugs themselves, then in such circumstances it is never appropriate to find someone guilty of manslaughter. The question of causation does not arise. The House of Lords, in referring to the decision in the pollution case of *Environment Agency v Empress Car* [1999] 2 A.C. 22, clearly expressed that although a question of causation arises in many aspects of law it is "not a single, unvarying concept to be mechanically applied without regard to the context in which the question arises". On the point of using the propositions of law relating to principal and secondary offender liability to establish an unlawful act for the purposes of on manslaughter the House observed that:

> "if the conduct of the deceased was not criminal he was not a principal offender, and it of course follows that the appellant cannot be liable as a secondary party. It also follows that there is no meaningful legal sense in which the appellant can be said to have been a principal jointly with the deceased, or to have been acting in concert."

The Court of Appeal was therefore wrong not to consider the issue of informed voluntary choice and personal autonomy.

27. The Meaning of Dangerous: An Objective Test

3.30 The meaning of dangerous for the purposes of the offence was clearly defined in *R. v Church* [1965] 49 Cr.App.R. 206, (for facts see above at para.2.17) Edmund Davies J. said of dangerous:

> "The conclusion of this Court is that an unlawful act causing the death of another cannot, simply because it is an unlawful act, render a manslaughter verdict inevitable. For such a verdict inexorably to follow the unlawful act must be such as all sober and reasonable people would inevitably recognise must subject the other person to at least risk of some harm resulting there from, albeit not serious harm."

This means that for a conviction of manslaughter to arise, an unlawful act alone causing death will not be enough, the act must be one that is dangerous, this being an act that the sober and reasonable person objectively looking at the act considered it to subject the victim to some risk of injury, which need not be seen as a risk of serious injury. Ultimately this is a question of fact for the jury to determine. The issue between an unlawful act that is not considered dangerous, to one that is, was highlighted in the tragic case of *R. v Carey* [2006] EWCA Crim 604. The victim was with her friends at a local beauty spot when she encountered the defendants, who made fun of them and then chased them, caught them and attacked them, two boys turned up and told the defendants to stop and they then ran off. The victim then ran away only to and collapse and die within 109 metres of ventricular fibrillation. It was revealed at the post mortem that, unknown to the victim and her family, she had a severely diseased heart.

The defendants were convicted of unlawful and dangerous act manslaughter and appealed on the grounds that the prosecution had failed evidentially to establish that the defendants had caused the victim's death. The Court of Appeal agreed and quashed the defendants' conviction for manslaughter on the basis that although the defendants had assaulted the victim and therefore were guilty of affray, their act, whilst clearly unlawful, was not dangerous for the purposes of manslaughter (as set out in *R. v Church*) in the circumstances of this case (the risk of death was unforeseeable from the assault) and that the physical harm from the assault was slight and had not caused the death.

In *R. v Dawson* [1985] 81 Cr.App.R. 150, the defendant took part in an attempted violent armed robbery on a petrol station and subjected the 60-year-old attendant to fear of violence. Shortly after making their escape, the attendant collapsed and died of an heart attack linked to shock from the robbery. The defendant was charged and convicted of manslaughter. The Court of Appeal quashed the defendant's conviction stating that although the deceased had heart disease this was unknown to the defendant and therefore the "sober and reasonable person" when objectively assessing the dangerousness of the act, would just like the defendant, not be aware of the medical susceptibility of the deceased.

Similarly, in *R. v DJ and Others* [2007] EWCA Crim 3133, the deceased had been playing cricket with his son on a fenced tennis court when it is alleged that the appellants first traded insults and spittle followed by throwing stones over the fence. The deceased collapsed and died of an arrhythmia due to a previous heart by-pass operation. The pathological evidence at its strongest could only conclude that the condition was likely to have been brought about by the combination of the events that took place.

In consequence it would not be possible for the jury to be able to exclude that the insults and spittle were the sole cause of death and if so, such acts do not amount to dangerous acts for the purposes of manslaughter. Accordingly the appellants' convictions for manslaughter had to be quashed.

Conversely in *R. v Watson* [1989] 1 W.L.R. 684, the defendant burgled the home of an elderly man (87 years old) who lived alone and had a serious heart condition. during the course of the burglary the defendant subjected the man to verbal abuse and ultimately left without stealing anything. Ninety minutes later the elderly man had died of an heart attack. Although the defendant's appeal against his conviction for manslaughter was allowed on a separate point, the Court of Appeal rejected the defence's contention that the knowledge available to the sober and reasonable person was confined to the knowledge of the defendant at the time of entry, at which point the defendant would not have been aware of the elderly occupant. The Court ruled that the knowledge attainable to the sober and reasonable person in the test of dangerousness was that knowledge gained by the defendant during the commission of the burglary offence, which would have meant that the defendant became aware of the frailty of the occupant. From these two authorities, if a conviction for manslaughter is to be sustained in circumstances where the death occurred, not as part of the direct commission of an unlawful act, but instead as a consequence of it happening, the knowledge or lack of knowledge gained in the course of the unlawful will be essential.

28. Summary of Manslaughter by an Unlawful and Dangerous Act

3.31 In order for the prosecution to secure a conviction for unlawful and dangerous act manslaughter the following four elements must be established:

(i) Was the act done intentionally?

(ii) Was it unlawful?

(iii) Was it also dangerous because it was likely to cause harm to somebody?

(iv) Was that unlawful and dangerous act the cause of the death?

One of the main criticisms of the current definition of dangerous act manslaughter is its potentially wide application from almost murderous acts at one end of the culpability scale to minor acts with the unforeseeable consequence of death at the other end (accidental death).

29. Manslaughter by Gross Negligence (Duty Owed Cases)

3.32 The principles that established the offence of gross negligence manslaughter were originally stated in *Andrews v DPP* [1937] A.C. 576, and later approved by the House of Lords in *R. v Adomako* [1994] 1 A.C. 171, in which the defendant anaesthetist during an operation had failed to notice that the tube which enabled the patient to breathe during the operation had become disconnected, resulting in his death. The House of Lords ruled that the offence of gross negligence manslaughter consists of the following elements:

(i) There must be an existence of a duty of care owed by the defendant to the victim which was breached.

(ii) In deciding whether a duty of care is owed is a question of fact by the jury based on whether the defendant had or assumed a responsibility for the deceased. This duty will be breached if on the evidence the defendant failed to fulfil that responsibility, by falling below a standard one would expect of a person in those circumstances.

(iii) The negligent breach of duty exposed the victim to a risk of death.

(iv) The jury must consider that the breach of duty is one of being "grossly negligent" and therefore so reprehensible as to amount to gross criminal negligence. By gross negligence it is meant that there is a serious departure from the accepted standards of care that is placed upon the defendant, having regard to the risk of death and seriousness of the breach of duty.

We have already reviewed this offence in the context of criminal omissions to act in Chapter Two.

30. Gross Negligence Manslaughter and Legal Certainty

3.33 In *R. v Misa and Another* [2004] EWCA Crim 2375, the defendants, who were house doctors, were convicted of gross negligent manslaughter when they failed to appreciate that the deceased who was in hospital for a routine operation, had fallen seriously ill which eventually led to his death due to toxic shock syndrome. They both appealed against their convictions on the grounds that the ingredients to the offence lacked legal certainty and therefore breached art.7 of the European Convention of Human Rights. Article 7 prohibits criminal offences to be applied retrospectively, but it also provides that no punishment can arise if the act or omission does not constitute an offence at the time the alleged offence was committed.

This means that all criminal offences must be sufficiently precise in terms of prohibited conduct, which would then allow a person to be aware (with legal advice if necessary) at what point their actions will incur criminal liability and therefore properly regulate their conduct, so as to avoid such liability. If the definition of the offence is too vague, it will lack this necessary precision to its application and be unfair to the potential defendant. In *Misa* the Court of Appeal rejected that argument, stating that the ingredients to the offence are clearly established in *Adomako*. The jury are clearly told to consider the available evidence and decide as a question of fact whether the defendants' conduct was negligent to such a degree that it was criminal.

The Court accepted that uncertainty and vagueness may arise in the decision-making process of the jury, but there is no uncertainty about the offence itself. Accordingly, a doctor knows that they owe a duty of care to a patient. If they fail in that duty, they also know should the matter come before a jury and is determined to amount to a serious breach, constituting a gross failure, this will bring criminal liability for manslaughter. The Court of Appeal also rejected the defence's contention that the offence lacked a form of mens rea, by holding that although negligence is concerned with failures which fall below the standards of a reasonable man, it clearly incorporates a fault element that must be gross and therefore determines the defendant's degree of culpability.

31. Criminal Enterprise and Public Policy

3.34 In *R. v Wacker* [2003] 2 W.L.R. 374 a Dutch national was convicted of 58 offences of gross negligent manslaughter of illegal immigrants, concealed in his truck with no air supply. He appealed on the basis that given that they were part of a joint criminal enterprise of which he himself was a party, they had by committing a criminal offence accepted a degree of risk, and consequently in law he owed them no duty of care. This was rejected by the Court of Appeal, holding that the criminal law would not decline to hold a person to be criminally responsible for the death of another simply because the two were engaged in some joint unlawful activity at the time or because there might have been an element of acceptance of a degree of risk by the victim in order to further the joint enterprise. Secondly, the duty to take care owed could not, as a matter of public policy, be permitted to be affected by the countervailing demands of the criminal enterprise.

32. Reckless Manslaughter

3.35 At para.2.26 the Law Commission in its paper "Legislating the Criminal Code: Involuntary Manslaughter" consider that as well as unlawful and dangerous act manslaughter and gross negligence manslaughter there exists a third offence of subjective reckless manslaughter. To secure a conviction for this offence the prosecution must prove that the defendant was aware that their conduct involved a risk of causing death or serious injury and they unreasonably took that risk. The Law Commission accept that no case authority exists that confirms and sets out this offence, and that in practice defendants in these circumstances are charged with unlawful act manslaughter. An example might be found in the circumstances surrounding death arising out of a road traffic collision, the consequences of which are of such gravity as to justify a prosecution for manslaughter.

33. Corporate Manslaughter

3.36 Where a death or deaths occur due to the failings of a corporate entity there will potentially be breaches of health and safety legislation. If the failings are serious in the sense that the corporate entity fell far below a standard that a reasonable person (company) would expect in such circumstances, then the offence of corporate manslaughter could be considered. Originally, the offence was defined in the common law and one significant shortcoming in the application of the offence was the need to identity within the company from Chief Executive down, a person who evidentially was grossly negligent.

The problem arises that under company law, a business that is incorporated with limited liability status becomes its own separate legal entity from those who in reality administer the business. In other words, the company itself is treated as a legal being and it is the company which is responsible for acts of the company and that those who commit those acts can hide behind the corporate veil. Putting this difficulty to one side, trying to isolate one identifiable individual responsible (the identification principle) is virtually impossible, if the death was as a result of a systemic failure of the overall management structure (see *Attorney-General's Reference No.2 of 1999*) [2000] 3 W.L.R. 195.

In response to the recommendations of the Law Commission (Legislating the Criminal Code: Involuntary Manslaughter" Law Com.237) to reform this area of law, Parliament passed the Corporate Manslaughter and Corporate Homicide Act 2007, which received the Royal Assent on the July 26 2007 and came into force on April 6, 2008 (see the Commencement Order (SI 2008/401)). Section 20 abolishes the common law principles of corporate manslaughter and is replaced by a new statutory offence contained in s.1. This creates a new offence of corporate manslaughter (if in England, Wales and Northern Ireland) and corporate homicide (if in Scotland) which applies only to those organisations listed in s.1(2) and Sch.1 and that organisation; owing to its managerial activities, (which must be a substantial element of the breach and by the senior management team, s.1 (3)) causes a person's death and this amounts to a gross breach of a duty of care owed (note that the new offences have not yet been brought into force).

The extent of the duty of care is set out in s.2 (1) of the Act and includes those held in custody see s.2(2). Sections 3 to 7 limited the imposition of a duty of care for certain public authorities and agencies. Section 7 provides that the jury must consider evidence that shows the defendant organisation failed to comply with health and safety law that is relevant to the breach and its seriousness. Subsection (3) provides that the jury may consider the extent of any evidence concerned with attitudes, policies or practices that encouraged the failure or tolerance of it. The jury may also take into any health and safety guidance relevant to the breach.

Before a prosecution can be commenced, s.17 provides that the consent of the DPP must be first obtained. The offence is classified as an "indictable only offence" and on conviction in the Crown Court punishable by a fine only. In addition the Court has the power under s.9 to make a "remedial order" the terms of which will require the organisation to take certain specified steps. Section 10 allows for the court to make a "publicity order" which will require the organisation to publicise details of the conviction as specified in the order. A failure by a defendant organisation to comply with either of these two orders amounts to an indictable only offence punishable by a fine.

34. THE OFFENCE OF INFANTICIDE

3.37 This sensitive offence is found in s.1 of the Infanticide Act 1938, it is used as either as offence in its own right (being an alternative to murder) or as a partial defence to a charge of murder. It can only be committed by a woman in circumstances where by a wilful act or omission causes the death of her child under the age of 12 months, and it is established at the time of that act or omission:

> "the balance of her mind was disturbed by reason of her not having fully recovered from the effect of giving birth to the child or by reason of the effect of lactation consequent upon birth, notwithstanding that the circumstances were such that but for this Act the offence would have amounted to murder."

There is no requirement on the defence to adduce evidence that there is a causal link between the female defendant's disturbed mind and the act/omission of killing the child. The burden of proof is upon the prosecution to disprove any disturbed mind and that if it is alleging murder a clear intent to kill. In *R. v Gore* [2007] EWCA Crim 2789, a case with tragic facts, the Court of Appeal rejected the defence's contention that the prosecution had to prove the mens rea for murder to secure a conviction for infanticide as being too restrictive, the mens rea for the offence is clearly set out in the provision of "wilfully". The Court observed that the offence is purposely wide in order to avoid a situation where a mother in severe distress would have to accept that they have murdered the child before they can benefit from the offence of infanticide; that was not the intention of the offence.

However, other difficulties exists with the application of the offence and according to the Court of Appeal in *R. v Kai-Whitewind* [2005] 2 Cr.App.R. 31, requiring a thorough review given that current definition of the offence is unsatisfactory and outdated. An unsatisfactory limitation to the offence is that the disturbed mind must be as a consequence of not having fully recovered from the birth. This does potentially not take into account other factors such as environmental stress and personality disorders. A further problem which arose in *Kai-Whitewind* is that if the mother denies the killing and does not consent to a psychological assessment, then it becomes impossible to accept a plea or conviction for infanticide. This leaves the defendant mother vulnerable to a conviction for murder if the jury reject her defence. The Law Commission in its report on Homicide No.304 have recommended the current offence remains unchanged, but that should the defendant be convicted of the new offence of first or second degree murder, then the judge trial ought to have the power to order a medical examination to determine whether the is evidence indicating infanticide allowing then the opportunity to appeal.

The offence is an indictable only offence with a maximum possible sentence of life imprisonment. However, in the sentencing authority of *R. v Sainsbury* [1989] 11 Cr.App.R. (S) 533, the mitigating factors are generally so strong, so as to justify the imposition of a non custodial sentence. A separate or alternative offence of child destruction exists is s.1 of the Infant Life (Preservation) Act 1929. Whilst for abortion there are ss.58 and 59 of the OAPA 1981, or the offence of concealment of a birth in s.60.

35. Law Reform of Unlawful Homicide

3.38 The Law Commission in its report "Murder, Manslaughter and Infanticide" (2006) (Law Com. No.303) recommends that in order to give the law of homicide a more coherent and comprehensive structure, Parliament should draft a new Homicide Act to replace the existing Act of 1957. Within the new Act there should be a hierarchy of offences that properly reflect the gravity of injury caused, proportionate to the defendants' culpability. The Commission recommends the following structure,

(1) First Degree Murder (mandatory life sentence)

This will consist of the following mental elements:

(a) Killing intentionally (same as current law);
(b) Killing where there was an intention to do serious injury, coupled with an awareness of a serious risk of causing death (different to the current law on indirect intent).

(2) Second Degree Murder (discretionary life sentence)

This will amount to a new homicide offence and will consist of the following mental elements,

(a) killing where the offender intended to do serious injury; under current law this forms part of the mens rea for murder, but would now come within the new second degree murder offence;
(b) killing where the offender intended to cause some injury or a fear or risk of injury and was aware of a serious risk of death. Under current law this amounts to manslaughter but new structure would be second degree murder (i.e. pouring petrol through letterbox causing death but only intended to frighten);
(c) killing in which there is a partial defence (provocation, diminished responsibility) to what would otherwise be first degree murder.

Under current law the two partial defences would reduce murder to manslaughter, whereas under the new structure both defences would be modified in their application, and would reduce culpability from first degree murder to that of second degree murder.

(3) Manslaughter (discretionary life sentence)

This would replace the current common law involuntary manslaughter offences with the following:

(a) killing through gross negligence as to a risk of causing death
(b) killing through a criminal act:

(i) intended to cause injury; or
(ii) where there was an awareness that the act involved a serious risk of causing injury.

Further, the Law Commission recommends the reform of both the essential elements to the partial defences of provocation and diminished responsibility. In respect of provocation this is based on a subjective and objective assessment. The subjective element is based on a response to gross provocation causing a justifiable sense of being seriously wronged, or fear of serious violence to them or another or a combination of both. The objective test will not encapsulate a reasonable man, but will be determined by a person of ordinary temperament in terms of tolerance and self restraint, who is the same age of the defendant, might have reacted in the same, or similar way in the circumstances of the defendant. All the circumstances of the defendant, other than those relating to capacity of self control, should be taken into account. Provocation will not be available, if self induced, or if there is a desire for revenge.

In regard to diminished responsibility, the Law Commission recommended that the partial defence should be based on impaired capacity to understand the nature of their conduct, or form a rational judgment or control themselves. Further, that this capacity was substantially impaired by an abnormality of mental functioning, due to a recognised medical condition, developmental immaturity, if under 18 and each or both provide an explanation for the killing.

Finally, the Law Commission recommended that the defence of duress should become a full defence leading to an acquittal for both first and second degree murder and attempted murder, but that the defendant carries the legal burden of proof, based on a balance of probabilities, to establish all the elements to the defence.

Chapter Four

NON-FATAL OFFENCES AGAINST THE PERSON AND THE DEFENCE OF CONSENT

1. Introduction

4.01 The present law relating to offences of assault and violent assault is still enshrined in the nineteenth century Offences Against The Person Act 1861. For the last 25 years there have been repeated calls for Parliament to repeal this badly drafted, archaic and incomprehensible Act which creates confusion and injustice. The Law Commission, both in 1980 and 1991, have criticised the Act for poor draftsmanship, and called upon Parliament to repeal and replace the 1861 Act with a comprehensive series of offences. Parliament has yet to implement this recommendation, and in the meantime the courts and the common law will have to grapple with the lack of clarity that emanates from the provisions of the 1861 Act. Subsequently, the Act has become the victim of much judicial interpretation and as such has caused contradiction, inconsistency and uncertainty in a branch of law that occupies much of the magistrates' and Crown Court's time.

2. Hierarchy of Offences and the Mens Rea of "Maliciously"

4.02 Although in a somewhat illogical structure, the main offences, which are taken in order of the gravity of injury suffered, are as follows;

(i) Section 18: Wounding or causing grievous bodily harm with intent.

(ii) Section 20: Recklessly wounding or inflicting grievous bodily harm.

(iii) Section 23: Administering poison or other noxious thing.

(vi) Section 47: Assault occasioning actual bodily harm.

Other assault offences exist such as common assault and battery, defined within the common law. There is also the offence of assaulting a police officer in the execution of his duty under s.89 of the Police Act 1996, and under s.38 of the OAPA 1861 assault with intent to resist arrest. Sections 32 to 34 cover specific offences of endangering railway passengers. Section 35 deals with an offence of causing injury by furious driving of a carriage. Little known but recently interpreted in a modern context is s.31, which creates an offence of (i) setting or placing, or (ii) causing to set or place, any spring gun (i.e. a shot gun set to go off with a device connected to a door), man trap (i.e. large animal trap), or other engine calculated to either (i) destroy life with intent, or (ii) inflict GBH with intent on, (iii) a trespasser or other person. In *R. v Cockburn* [2008] EWCA Crim 316, the Court of Appeal was asked to address the meaning of "other engine" in the context of the preceding devices. The Court rejected the defence's contention that other engine was restricted to a device which produced its own force or energy. Accordingly, the home made device consisting of metal spikes rigged up by the appellant that derived its force from gravity alone and was activated by the opening of the door did not constitute an engine. The Court of Appeal considered the decision in *R. v Munks* [1964] 1 Q.B. 304, where it was held that a device rigged up by the appellant involving wires did not form an engine given that it was an electrical as opposed to a mechanical contrivance. Whilst accepting the decision in *Munks*, the Court of Appeal ruled that the statutory language was not intended to be construed too narrowly, it can include a tool or implement. The contraption created by the appellant was a contrivance and it was mechanical. If this question arises again then close attention will need to be given to the object in question and the method, if any, of activation. In an obiter comment the Court was inclined to agree that a disguised deep hole with spikes placed at the bottom would constitute a man trap but that a shallow hole may not, given the unlikely infliction of GBH.

Other serious offences against the person include rape and sexual assault in the Sexual Offences Act 2003. It is important to be aware that within the definition of ss.18 and 20, the word "maliciously" is used to describe the relevant mens rea of the offence. This identifies a clear defect in the Act since the word itself lacks legal substance or logical application. Accordingly, as we discussed in Chapter Two, the Court of Appeal in *R. v Cunningham* [1957] 3 W.L.R. 76 formulated a subjective recklessness test to establish the mens rea for a s.20 offence. This means that the word "maliciously", although used in s.20, is interpreted to mean intention or recklessness and is therefore ignored when directing the jury as to the mens rea of the offence.

3. Section 18: Wounding or causing Grievous Bodily Harm (GBH) with Intent to do so

4.03 The offence in s.18 is the most serious offence and carries a sentence of life imprisonment. It is important to be aware that the offence can be committed in two ways, with the prosecution claiming either that the defendant (i) wounded the complainant with intent to do them GBH, or (ii) the defendant caused the complainant GBH with intent to do so. The individual facts of each case will determine whether the defendant is charged with wounding or causing. If the injuries are as a result of a stabbing, then the likely charge will be wounding, whereas if the injuries are sustained in a vicious attack with punching and kicking, then the likely charge will be causing GBH. The mens rea for this offence is that of intention only; this means that s.18, like murder, is known as a specific intent crime. This is important when we come to look at the effect of intoxication on the ability to form the necessary mens rea of intent, and whether or not a conviction can be sustained in such circumstances. The word "maliciously" does appear in s.18 but is superfluous to its application. On this point Lord Diplock in *R. v Mowatt* [1967] 1 Q.B. 421, made the following observation:

> "In Section 18 the word 'Maliciously' adds nothing. The intent expressly required by that section is more specific than the element of foresight of consequences as is implicit in the word 'maliciously' and in directing the jury about an offence under this section the word 'maliciously' is best ignored."

4. The Meaning of the Words "Cause" and "Wound"

4.04 In *R. v Mandair* [1995] 1 A.C. 208, the House of Lords upheld the appellant's conviction, even though the judge had, at the appellant's trial for s.18, directed the jury that they could find him guilty of the alternative offence of "causing bodily harm" contrary to s.20. An offence not known to law, since the word "cause" does not appear in s.20. On this point Lord Mackay stated:

> "In my view 'cause' in s18 is certainly sufficiently wide to embrace any method by which GBH could be inflicted under s20 and since causing GBH in s18 is an alternative to wounding I regard it as clear that the word 'cause' in s18 is wide enough to include any action that could amount to inflicting GBH under s20 where the word 'inflict' appears as an alternative to 'wound' For this reason following the reasoning in *R .v. Wilson* an alternative verdict under s20 was open on the terms of the indictment ... In my opinion ... the word 'cause' is wider or at least not narrower than the word 'inflict.'"

In *JJC (a minor) v Eisenhower* [1983] 3 All E.R. 230, the High Court, on appeal by way of case stated in respect of a s.20 offence, reviewed the previous old authorities on the meaning of "wound" and concluded that there must be a break in the continuity of the whole skin, and this can include not just the outer skin but also the internal cavity of the body. In this case, the Court ruled that internal injuries of rupturing of blood vessels do not amount to a "wound", since it was impossible for the court to determine on the evidence that there had been any break in the continuity of the skin. Although this case involves s.20, the legal meaning of "wound" is the same as that of s.18; the difference in the offences is the criminal culpability. It is important not to become overtly technical, clearly the defendant in *Eisenhower* was guilty of inflicting. Further the Crown Prosecution Service readily use guidelines on charging standards, to ensure that the appropriate offence is charged that sufficiently reflects the defendant's culpability.

5. The Meaning of the Expression "Grievous Bodily Harm"

4.05 We have already assessed the interpretation of GBH in the context of the mens rea for murder. In *R. v Smith* [1961] A.C. 290, the House of Lords had said that it should be given its natural and ordinary meaning of "really serious harm". In *R. v Brown and Stratton* [1998] Crim. L.R. 485, the Court of Appeal adopted the same approach in the following terms:

> "It cannot be too often emphasized that grievous bodily harm should be given its ordinary natural meaning of *really serious harm* and it is undesirable to attempt any further definition of it."

In *R. v Ashman* [1858] 1 F. & F. 88, it was held by the Court that the prosecution do not have to prove that the harm was life-threatening, dangerous, or permanent, neither is there any requirement in law that the victim should require treatment or that the harm should extend beyond soft tissue damage. In *R. v Bollom* [2003] EWCA 2846, it was established that the concept of seriousness is determined as against the impact of the injuries on the victim, in terms of age, condition and sex. It is clear that when the jury are determining whether or not the gravity of the physical harm suffered amounts to serious bodily harm, it is a question of fact based on the available evidence adduced at trial.

6. What must the Prosecution Show to Sustain a Conviction?

4.06 In summary, for the prosecution to secure a conviction for this offence the following elements must be proved:

(i) The accused did an deliberate act (actus reus).

(ii) The act was unlawful in the context that the defendant was not lawfully acting in self defence, if raised (actus reus).

(iii) The act caused a wound or other serious physical injury (actus reus).

(iv) When the accused did the act, are the jury satisfied they intended to cause a wound or other really serious physical injury (mens rea)?

The Sentencing Guidelines issued by the Sentencing Guidelines Council in February 2008 provide that the starting point for a very serious injury is five years within a range of four to six years' custody. In respect of life threatening injuries dependant on pre-meditation there is a sentencing range of seven to 16 years' custody.

7. Section 20: Intentional/Reckless Wounding or Infliction of GBH

4.07 Section 20 is the next offence in the hierarchy, and can be committed in one of two ways as follows:

(i) unlawful and reckless (malicious) wounding;

(ii) unlawfully and recklessly (maliciously) inflicting GBH.

Like s.18, the word "maliciously" is used to describe the mens rea of the offence. However, as we have seen in Chapter Two this was interpreted in *R. v Cunningham* [1957] 3 W.L.R. 76, to mean intention or recklessness, that the accused "has foreseen that a particular kind of harm might be done and yet has gone on to take it". This interpretation was approved and affirmed by the House of Lords in *R. v Savage and DPP v Parmenter* [1991] 3 W.L.R. 914, which makes it clear that "maliciously" in s.20 means:

> "...an actual intention to do the particular kind of harm which was in fact done or recklessness as to whether such harm should occur (i.e. the accused has foreseen that the particular kind of harm *might* be done and yet had gone on to take the risk of it. It is enough that the accused foresaw that some physical harm to some person, albeit of a minor character, *might* result from his action"

The House of Lords approved the principle derived from the Court of Appeal decision in *R. v Mowatt* [1967] 1 Q.B. 421, when Diplock L.J. stated that the expression "particular kind of harm" meant that the prosecution do not have to prove that the defendant foresaw their act might cause harm of the gravity required for GBH. The prosecution need only prove that the defendant foresaw that some physical injury to some person, even if this is only of a minor character, might result from their act.

Put simply, the prosecution only need prove that the defendant foresaw the risk that some bodily harm (however slight), might result from what they were going to do and yet, ignoring that risk, the defendant went on to commit the offending act. Accordingly, if a defendant punches the victim in the face resulting in a broken jaw and cheekbone, the prosecution does not have to prove the defendant actually foresaw these particular injuries, simply that they foresaw some injury, even if minor, such as bruising from the punch, this is enough to establish the mens rea for s.20.

8. The Meaning of the Word "Inflicts" in the Context of Harm and Sexual Diseases

4.08 On the meaning of "inflicts", the legal issue arises as to whether the prosecution must prove some direct application of force to the victim's body by the accused whether the accused inflict an injury on another by an act that does not involve direct physical injury. The starting point is *R. v Martin* [1888] 8 Q.B.D. 54, in which the defendant's conviction for unlawfully and intentionally inflicting GBH on two theatre goers was upheld. The defendant had extinguished the gas lights on the stairway in a theatre which caused a great panic. He had also placed a bar on the door to prevent escape, causing injury to several people. Lord Coleridge, giving the leading speech, ruled that the defendant had inflicted the injuries within the context of s.20, even though there was no direct application of force by the accused upon the victims.

In *R. v Ireland and Burstow* [1998] 1 Cr.App.R. 177, the House of Lords gave the word inflicts, a wide meaning. The House rejected the appellant's argument that the word inflicts requires the prosecution to prove that there was some form of direct or indirect application of force to the victim. Their Lordships, accepted that the word inflicts is not totally synonymous with the word cause in s.18. The two words are as confirmed in *R. v Mandair* interchangeable, and contextually the word inflicts embraces acts that lead to the victim suffering harm, there is no necessary ingredient of force. This is the natural meaning of the word in a practical sense and it is therefore clear that a person can inflict psychiatric harm upon a victim without any application of force being felt by the victim.

Counsel in *Ireland* had sought to rely on the old decision of *R. v Clarence* [1888] 22 Q.B.D. 23, in which it was held by a majority of nine to four that the defendant who, knowing he was suffering from a venereal disease, had consensual sexual intercourse with his wife who was unaware of his condition, had not inflicted harm upon his wife for the purposes of s.20 since the infection did not result from direct or indirect application of physical violence. For Lord Slynn, whilst *Clarence* provided some weight to the appellant's arguments it was a "troublesome case" and no longer assisted in the development of the law. In a significant development of the criminal law on contemporary grounds, the Court of Appeal in *R. v Dica* [2004] EWCA 1103, held that the decision in *Clarence* amounted to an unsatisfactory principle and no longer represents the law. The Court of Appeal followed the decision of the House of Lords in *Ireland & Burstow* and ruled unanimously that although the appellant had not directly applied physical force to the victims, his act of sexual intercourse had indirectly inflicted on the victims an injury, which was clearly detrimental or adverse to their health.

9. The Causation Element in the Offence of Inflicting GBH must be Applied Objectively

4.09 In *R. v Marjoram* [2000] Crim. L.R. 372, the Court of Appeal ruled, in dismissing the appeal, that for a s.20 offence the prosecution have to prove that the defendant's conduct caused or significantly contributed to the injury suffered by the victim. This is an objective test of whether the injury was a *natural result* of what the accused said and did, and that a reasonable person could have foreseen the injury as a natural consequence of what the defendant did. In the case where the victim was trying to "escape", it was stated following *R. v Roberts* [1971] 56 Cr.App.R. 95 that if a reasonable person would have foreseen the victim's conduct in attempting to escape as a possible outcome of what the defendant said or did, then the defendant caused those injuries. The prosecution does not have to prove that the defendant himself actually foresaw what occurred as a possibility in order to establish causation. The maximum sentence for a s.20 offence is five years' imprisonment.

It is important to remember that causation is just one element that the prosecution must establish, if brought into issue. The prosecution must always prove in addition to causation the following:

(i) The defendant did a voluntary and deliberate act.

(ii) The act was unlawful.

(iii) The complainant suffered the relevant gravity of injury, i.e. grievous bodily harm.

(iv) That the defendant either intentionally or recklessly foresaw some bodily harm, even of a minor character.

The sentencing guidelines for this offence provide that the starting point for a typical offence with grave injury and a weapon used is 18 months' custody, within a range of 12 months to three years. For those offences of particularly grave injury, there is a starting point of three years' custody within a range of two to four years. For assaults with no weapon there is a a range from Community Order to 18 months' custody. If the offence is racially aggravated then this must be an added factor to take into account.

10. Section 47: Assault Occasioning Actual Bodily Harm

4.10 Section 47 provides that a person is guilty of this offence if they assault another occasioning actual bodily harm (ABH). The drafting weaknesses in the OAPA 1861 were well illustrated when the Court of Appeal in *R. v Spratt* [1990] 1 W.L.R. 1073 and *R. v Savage* [1991] 2 W.L.R. 418; unwittingly on the same day delivered judgments that reached opposite conclusions in the interpretation of s.47 on what must be proved in terms of mens rea. In *R. v Spratt* the Court held, approving the decision in *R. v Venna* [1976] Q.B. 421, that *Cunningham* subjective recklessness furnished the correct test for both s.20 and s.47 alike. Conversely, a conflicting view was reached in *R. v Savage* where the Court ruled that the mens rea for s.47 was not *Cunningham* recklessness, but was the same as that for common assault. In addition, unknown to the Court in *Savage*, it had upheld the decision of an earlier Court of Appeal in *R. v Roberts* [1971] 56 Cr.App.R 95. Soon afterwards, the Court of Appeal in *R. v Parmenter* [1991] 2 W.L.R. 408, was faced with this outright conflict of authority. It was held, quashing the defendant's conviction under s.20 and refusing to substitute a s.47 offence, that the approach in *Spratt* was to be prefered. In the joint appeals of *R. v*

Savage; DPP v Parmenter [1991] 3 W.L.R. 914, the House of Lords was called upon to clarify the confusion that had arisen as a result of the earlier Court of Appeal decisions.

In *Savage*, the defendant decided to throw the contents of her beer glass over a Miss Beal; whilst doing this the glass, unaware to Savage, somehow broke, causing Miss Beal to suffer a cut. The jury convicted her under s.20 of intentionally or recklessly inflicting GBH. This was set aside by the Court of Appeal and a s.47 conviction substituted. Mrs Savage appealed to the House of Lords on the grounds that she had no mens rea for the injury under s.47 as she was not aware of the glass breaking. The House of Lords upheld her conviction. Lord Ackner, who gave the leading speech, confirmed that in regard to a s.47 offence the prosecution have to prove two elements:

(i) *mens Rea* for common assault, namely that the accused intended to cause the victim to apprehend immediate and unlawful violence or was reckless as to such apprehension being caused, and

(ii) the assault occasioned ABH. This solely raised an objective question of causation. Accordingly, if the ABH suffered was a natural consequence of the assault then the offence is complete.

From this decision it is quite clear that the word "assault" in s.47 means the commission of a common assault. Accordingly, the mens rea for a s.47 offence is the same as that for common assault. This simply requires the prosecution to prove that the defendant had an intention to cause the victim to apprehend immediate unlawful personal violence or recklessness as to whether such apprehension is caused. Consequently, the prosecution is not required to prove any mens rea for occasioning ABH. This simply raises an objective question of causation, and that if the ABH suffered was a natural consequence of the assault then the offence is confirmed.

The sentencing guidelines provide that for a typical s.47 offence with relatively serious injuries, a starting point of 36 weeks or 12 months within a sentence range of Community Order to two years' custody. For an assault just short of GBH or with use of weapon there is a starting point of 30 months' custody in a sentencing range of two to four years.

11. Meaning of "Actual Bodily Harm" (ABH)

4.11 Like Grievous Bodily Harm, the phrase Actual Bodily Harm (ABH) lacks clarity and as an expression, does not necessarily convey in clear terms the gravity of harm needed to sustain a conviction under s.47. The Act itself does not give a statutory meaning to ABH and it has been left to the courts to provide guidance on its application. In *R. v Donovan* [1934] 2 K.B. 498, the Court of Appeal stated that ABH should be given:

> "its ordinary meaning and includes any hurt or injury calculated to interfere with the health or comfort of the victim, which need not be permanent, but must be more than merely transient and trifling."

In *R. v Chan-Fook* [1994] 2 All E.R. 552, the House of Lords observed that:

> "these are three words of the English language which require no elaboration and in the ordinary course should not receive any. The word 'harm' is a synonym for 'injury' and that the word 'actual' indicates that the injury (need not be permanent,) and should not be so trivial so as to be wholly insignificant. It is not limited to 'harm to the skin, flesh and bones of the victim' it applies to all body parts 'including the victim's organs, nervous system and his brain.'

12. Bodily Harm includes Loss of Consciousness

4.12 In *R. (T)* v *DPP* [2003] EWHC 266, the defendant was involved in an altercation with the complainant during which the appellant had kicked the complainant, who momentarily lost consciousness, but suffered no other physical injury. The appellant was convicted in the magistrates' court for a s.47 assault and appealed to the High Court by way of case stated contending that a momentary loss of consciousness did not amount to ABH. Relying on the obiter statement in *Donovan*, the appellant argued that such loss of consciousness was no more than "merely transient". The High Court rejected this argument in its entirety and ruled that a loss of consciousness clearly amounts to harm which was bodily since, "it involved an injurious impairment to the victim's sensory functions" and that this was "actual".

The High Court relied on the ruling given by Lynskey J. in *R v Miller* [1954] 2 Q.B. 282, that ABH is not limited to physical injury, but includes injury to a person's state of mind which, in the instant case, was hysteria and shock suffered by the victim having been thrown down the stairs by her partner three times. Further, in an obiter observation, Kay J. noted that the statement in *Donovan* should not be treated as if they amounted to words of a statute. The Court of Appeal in that case, was excluding from the definition of ABH harm which was no more than "transient *and* trifling"; not, as the appellant argued, transient *or* trifling. It follows therefore that physical pain consequent on an assault is not a necessary ingredient of the offence.

13. Bodily Harm includes Cutting a Person's Hair without Consent

4.13 An interesting legal point on the application of ABH arose in *DPP v Smith* [2006] 2 Cr.App.R. 1, where the defendant had pinned his girlfriend down on the bed, used a pair of scissors and cut off her pony tail; she was later seen in a distressed state. The magistrates ruled that there was no case to answer and accepted the defence's argument that cutting hair does not amount to ABH. The DPP appealed against this ruling by way of case stated to the High Court. In allowing the appeal and remitting the case back to the magistrates, the Court held that hair is an attributable part of the human body, even if above the surface of the scalp it is dead tissue, it remains part of the body and is attached to it and therefore falls within the meaning of "bodily" in of ABH.

14. Both GBH and ABH include "Psychiatric Injury"

4.14 The legal issue arose in several "stalking" cases whether the actus reus of GBH and ABH are wide enough to encompass not just physical injury, but also psychiatric injury. In *R. v Chan-Fook* [1994] 1 W.L.R. 689, the defendant had imprisoned a suspected thief and questioned him aggressively. On appeal against his conviction for a s.47 offence, the Court of Appeal had to address, as a matter of statutory construction, whether the legal meaning of ABH amounted to and included psychiatric injury. Approving the ruling in *R. v Miller* [1954] 2 Q.B. 282 (see para.4.13 above), the Court of Appeal concluded that the word "bodily" does not limit the "harm" suffered to the skin, flesh and bones of the complainant but included all parts of the body such as bodily organs, the brain and the nervous system. Hobhouse L.J. concluded that ABH is capable of including psychiatric injury to the victim, but his Lordship qualified this by stating that it does not include mere emotion, nor does it include a state of mind that does not have some identifiable clinical condition. Accordingly, unless there is some psychiatric evidence, the matter should not be left to the jury.

In *R. v Ireland and R. v Burstow* [1998] 1 Cr.App.R. 177, the House of Lords confirmed this extended meaning of "bodily harm". Lord Steyn approached the question of interpretation of "bodily harm" on the basis that Acts of Parliament are "always speaking" and that the court is rightly entitled to give the words a meaning that embraces current contemporary conditions. His Lordship concluded by stating that the decision in *Chan-Fook* [1994] 1 W.L.R. 689:

> "was based on principled and cogent reasoning and it marked a sound and essential clarification of the law. I would hold that 'bodily harm' in sections 18, 20 and 47 must be interpreted so as to include recognizable psychiatric illness."

In *Ireland*, it was held that silent telephone calls made to the victim constituted assault, since they were capable of causing terror and apprehension of violence; this included palpitations, breathing difficulties, stress and a nervous skin condition, anxiety and sleeplessness. In *Burstow* it was held that bodily harm in s.20 included psychiatric injury, and therefore an offence under s.20 could be committed in the absence of physical violence applied directly or indirectly to the body of the victim; the victim suffered from severe depression, with marked features of anxiety that amounted to grievous harm of a psychiatric nature. It is important to be aware that whilst the legal meaning of "bodily harm" extends beyond physical injury to include psychiatric injury, a prosecution will only arise if evidentially there is a "recognisable psychiatric illness". This would require the complainant to be assessed by at least two psychiatrists, a process that some would find discouraging from a labelling point of view.

15. Grievous Bodily Harm includes Transmission of a Sexual Disease

4.15 In *R. v Dica* [2004] EWCA Crim 1103, the Court of Appeal upheld the appellant's conviction under s.20 by recklessly infecting his girlfriend with HIV. In referring to the development of the law in relation to the meaning of bodily injury in respect of psychiatric damage, the Court concluded that this clearly includes a sexual disease and it was open to the jury to convict, if satisfied that the injury to health arising from the disease was serious in the context of the gravity of harm required for a conviction under s.20.

16. Common Assault and Battery under s.39 of the Criminal Justice Act 1988

4.16 The most minor offences in the hierarchy of non-fatal offences are common assault and battery. Although both offences are defined in the common law, s.39 of the Criminal Justice Act 1988, in a procedural context, classifies them as amounting to summary only offences. Both the mens rea and actus reus for Common Assault are indistinguishable; meaning that a defendant with the necessary mens rea will also be committing the prohibited act. In *R. v Savage* [1991] 3 W.L.R. 914, the House of Lords, approving the decision in *R. v Venna* [1976] Q.B. 421, held that an offence of common assault is made out if it is proved that the defendant intentionally or recklessly caused the victim to apprehend that immediate unlawful violence would be used against them. There is no requirement of any physical violence to be proved; simply that the victim apprehended that violence might be used against them. An example of an offence of common assault is where the defendant either uses words such as "if you don't shut up you will get it", or by conduct where the defendant aggressively waves their clenched fist at the victim. If from these potential common assaults, the victim suffers an injury, then the offence potentially becomes assault occasioning ABH.

Conversely, the common law offence of battery requires the prosecution to prove the actual infliction of unlawful force on another person, either intentionally or recklessly, as confirmed by Goff L.J. in *Collins v Wilcock* [1984] 3 All E.R. 374. An example would be deliberately slapping the victim's face, if this act was done without the victim being aware of it, such as from behind, then this is the offence of battery alone. If, on the other hand, this act is done from the front, then immediately before the actual act of slapping, the defendant has already committed the offence of common assault, provided the victim feared the slap. Once slapped, the victim suffered an injury and the defendant committed a battery. In this instance the common assault includes a battery.

In *DPP v Little* [1992] 1 All E.R. 299, the High Court, in a case stated appeal, ruled that the two offences are entirely separate and that from a charging point, if the facts reveal both a common assault with a battery and the injury is insufficient for a s.47 offence, then the defendant should be charged with "assault by beating". In *Haystead v Chief Constable of Derbyshire* [2000] Crim. L.R. 750, the High Court, following the line of authorities on the meaning of inflicts in s.20, held that for an offence of battery there in no requirement for the prosecution to prove a direct application of force when the defendant, having punched a mother holding a child, dropped the child as a consequence. The Court held that the magistrates were wrong to accept a submission of no case to answer on this basis; the force applied to the mother was the same force that caused the child to fall causing injury. The sentencing guidelines provide a range from a fine to custody bearing in mind that the maximum is six months' custody.

17. Offences within the Protection of Harassment Act 1997

4.17 The Protection from Harassment Act 1997, as amended by s.125 of the Serious Organised Crime and Police Act 2005, was passed in direct response to the mischief of individuals who harass another by stalking them and the recommendations in the consultation paper from the Home Office entitled "Stalking-The Solutions" and more recently "Animal Welfare-Human Rights—protecting people from animal rights extremists" (2004). However, the breadth of the application of the offences within the Act has been applied extensively across a range of social harassment incidents and the Act clearly applies to harassment in the workplace and indeed, to the constant demands and threats of a creditor upon a debtor.

Within the Act there exist two criminal offences. Sections 1 and 2 provide that a person is guilty of a summary only offence if they pursue a course of conduct which amounts to harassment of another and that they know or ought to have known that this amounts to harassment. A new s.1(A) amends this and extends harassment not just of another, but to harassment of two or more persons on separate occasions. The purpose behind the extension is to prohibit threats and intimidation to prevent an individual(s) from doing a lawful activity, i.e. entering a sensitive place of work (animal testing laboratory). Section 4 on the other hand, creates a more serious offence where the course of conduct, on at least two occasions, puts the victim in fear that violence will be used against them, and the defendant knows or ought to have known this would happen. Section 7 provides interpretive guidance for "harassing" a person which includes alarming that person or causing them distress; "course of conduct" means conduct on at least two occasions and "conduct" includes speech. Since August 1, 2001 and in accordance with s.44 of the Criminal Justice and Police Act 2001, course of conduct includes conduct by another if it is aided, abetted, counselled or procured by the defendant.

18. Harassment and "Duplicity"

4.18 In *DPP v Dziurzynski* [2002] EWHC 1380, the High Court ruled as a matter of statutory construction that the singular words of "person" and "him" in the Act include the plural so that more than one person can be harassed. However, to avoid "duplicity" and unfairness to the defendant in knowing precisely what is alleged, the victims must form part of "a close knit definable group" and that in the instant case, the charge simply referring to employees of B & K was too imprecise and vague. Accordingly, the District Judge in the magistrates' court was right to rule that there was no case to answer.

19. What Amounts to "Harassment"?

4.19 In *Sai Lau v DPP* [2000] Crim. L.R. 580, the High Court observed that the fewer the incidences of harassment and the more such incidences are separated in time, the less likely such incidences could reasonably constitute harassment under the Act. In *King v DPP* [2000] (unreported), the High Court ruled that the magistrates were wrong to conclude that an unwanted gift of a plant and an non offensive rambling letter amounted to harassment; they amounted to background evidence that suggested the appellant wanted to form a relationship with the complainant. However, in remitting the case back to the magistrates they must consider whether the evidence that the appellant had filmed the complainant and rummaged through her bin bags, amounted to harassment by applying the relevant test in ss.1 and 7.

Importantly, in *R. (Simon Howard) v DPP* [2001] EWCA 17, Woolf L.C.J., giving the leading speech in the High Court, stated that under s.4 whether a course of conduct caused fear of violence amounted to a question of fact based on the individual facts of each case. The issue is not whether specified conduct falls within or outside the ambit of the offence, it is whether the complainant feared violence and the defendant knew or ought to have known this. Accordingly, in the instant case, a direct threat to the complainant's dogs did not constitute conduct for the purposes of s.4, since such threats were not directed at the complainant. However, these threats against a background of previous threats made to the complainant, could give raise to a fear of personal violence.

20. Harassment of a Person in their Home

4.20 Section 42 of the Criminal Justice and Police Act 2001, as amended by s.126 of the Serious Organised Crime and Police Act 2005, creates an offence committed by a person who is outside or in the vicinity of any premises used as a dwelling, with the purpose of persuading the resident or another individual to stop doing something, or do something they are not obliged. The mens rea of the offence is that the prosecution must prove that the accused intends their presence to amount to harassment, alarm or distress or that they know or ought to have known that their presence is likely to cause such harassment. The purpose behind the offence is to prevent protesters such as animal rights activists from targeting the homes of those in the industry. The difficulty will always be the sensitive issue of striking the right balance between peaceful protest and activities that cross the threshold into criminal harassment.

21. Racially Aggravated Offences Against the Person

4.21 Section 29 of the Crime and Disorder Act 1998, which came into force on September 30, 1998, allows the prosecution to use the existing ss.20 and 47, and common assault offences, as explained above and charge the defendant with a racially aggravated form of the offence, if this can be proved, i.e. "racially aggravated inflicting GBH contrary to s.20". Likewise, in s.32 of the Crime and Disorder Act 1998, there are created racially-aggravated forms of the two offences found in the Protection of Harassment Act 1997. In order to be convicted of the offence of aggravation, the prosecution must first prove all the elements to the basic offence under s.20 and s.47 and common assault. The prosecution must then proceed to adduce sufficient evidence to satisfy the racial aggravation test set out in s.28.

Accordingly, it must be shown that there was "racial hostility" based on the victim's membership or presumed membership of a racial group, at the time of committing the offence or immediately before or after doing so, or the basic offence was motivated, wholly or partly by such hostility. Racial group is defined in s.28(4) as being a group of persons defined by reference to race, colour, nationality or ethnic or national origins. The offence is still committed where the defendant perceived the victim to be of a certain racial group, but that perception is wrong. Section 18 is not included, since if there is evidence of racial hostility, this is taken directly as an aggravating feature for the purposes of sentencing. If the racially aggravated offence is under s.20 and s.47 then the sentence available to the Crown Court is increased to seven years, whilst for common assault it is two years.

In *Attorney-General's Reference (No.4 of 2004)* [2005] EWCA 889, the trial judge had ruled that there was no case to answer against the defendant for racially aggravated assault by beating, when she took her child to the doctor's, and immediately before the assault called the complainant "an immigrant doctor". The judge had ruled that the word immigrant did not come within the meaning of s.28 as forming part of a specific racial group. The Attorney-General, under s.36 of the Criminal Justice 1972, sought the opinion of the Court of Appeal on whether the judge was right to rule as he did as a matter of law. The Court of Appeal applied and adopted a "contextual approach" to the construction of the statutory meaning of "racial group" and found that the judge erred in the ruling he gave:

> "whether Mrs D's use of the term "immigrant doctor" towards Dr N was only an allegation of non-Britishness or was part of a demonstration by her of hostility to him within the terms of s.28(1)(a) because she perceived his non-Britishness to derive from his race and/or colour and/or his nationality and/or his ethnic or national origins involved a question of fact for the determination by the jury on the facts of the case."

4.22 Accordingly, the judge should have left the matter for the jury to determine as a question of fact as to whether the defendant had committed the aggravated offence. The Court of Appeal applied the broad non technical approach to the meaning of "racial group" adopted in *DPP v M (a minor)* [2004] EWHC 1453 (Admin), in which the High Court, in an appeal by case stated from the magistrates' court, ruled that the expression "bloody foreigners" used by the defendant just before committing criminal damage may depending on the context in which they are used (whether relating to an inclusive or non-inclusive group) as demonstrating hostility based on that person's membership of a racial group i.e. a non inclusive group of "foreigner." The House of Lords in *R. v Rogers* [2007] 2 A.C. 62 had to address the same expression of "bloody foreigners" in relation to the racially aggravated form of s.4 Public Order Act 1986, in which the appellant had directed the words at three young Spanish women. In confirming his conviction, Baroness Hale observed that the non technical approach to the racial aspect of the offence was both right as a matter of language and on public policy grounds, given that the mischief of the offences is aimed at racism and xenophobia and to ensure equal respect and dignity to those who are deemed to be the "other". Her Ladyship then stated:

> "this is more deeply hurtful, damaging and disrespectful to the victims than the simple version of these offences. It is also more damaging to the community as a whole, by denying acceptance to members of certain groups not for their own sake but for the sake of something they can do nothing about. This is just a true if the group is defined exclusively as it is if it is defined inclusively."

Likewise, in *R. v White* [2001] 1 W.L.R. 1352, the Court of Appeal adopted the same approach to the adjective "African" in the offending comment "African bitch" as capable of being part of a racial group dependant on the context in which it is used. Applying the decision in *DPP v M*, the High Court in *DPP v Balham Youth Court* [2004] EWHC 2990, took the same approach concerning the comment "you . . . foreigner, bloody bastard" said by the defendant before assaulting the complainant. It is immaterial, as explained in *DPP v McFarlane* [2002] EWHC 485, that the pejorative words are directed to a small or large group on colour, race, or origin, since such words can be equally offensive regardless of the number of other persons sharing those characteristics. In a different context the Divisional Court in *DPP v Stoke–on–Trent Magistrates* [2003] EWHC 1593, ruled that away supporters' chants of "you're just a town full of pakis" at Oldham football club amounted to "a statement of a racial nature" and therefore constituted an offence under s.3 of the Football (Offences) Act 1991 (see also *Johnson v*

DPP [2008] EWHC 509 and *DPP v Howard* [2008] EWHC 608 in relation to the racially aggravated offence of causing harassment, alarm or distress under s.5 of the Public Order Act 1986).

Other related offences of stirring up racial and religious hatred in the Public Order Act 1986 as amended by the Racial and Religious Hatred Act 2006 which came into effect on October 1, 2007, include a public performance of a play that is intended to stir up racial religious hatred. When in force s.74 and Sch.16 of the Criminal Justice and Immigration Act 2008 will include hatred directed towards a person's sexual orientation. These offences will not be discussed in depth here, save to say that they are sensitive as whether they strike a fair balance between allowing freedom of expression as to against inflammatory words, performance or material.

22. Maliciously Administering Poison so as to Endanger Life or Inflict GBH

4.23 Section 23 of the OAPA 1861 creates three separate offences as follows:

- (i) administering any poison or other destructive or noxious thing to any other person;
- (ii) causing any poison or other destructive or noxious thing to be administered to any other person;
- (iii) causing any poison or other destructive or noxious thing to be taken by any other person.

For each offence the prosecution must prove the mens rea of intention or recklessness; that the act was unlawful and would endanger the life of any other person or would inflict GBH on such a person. In *R. v Gillard* [1988] 87 Cr.App.R. 189, the Court of Appeal, in dismissing the appeal, applied the same approach to the word "administer" as taken in *R. v Maginnis* [1987] 85 Cr.App.R. 127 to the word "supply" and therefore required as a matter of law a legal meaning to define its application. The Court ruled that "administer" does not require the prosecution to prove any element of direct physical contact by the defendant with the complainant; it is sufficient to cover the spraying of a noxious thing whereby the vapour then comes into contact with the complainant either endangering life or inflicting GBH (see the problems encountered with the offence of unlawful and dangerous act manslaughter in Chapter three at para.3.26)

23. The Defence of Consent and the Issue of Public Policy

4.24 The issue that arises is whether the defendant can, at trial for an assault offence, claim that the victim consented to their injuries and that therefore they have committed no offence. This also sometimes brings into existence a defence of mistaken belief, i.e. where the defendant argues that they honestly and genuinely believed that the victim was consenting at the time, albeit that belief was a mistaken belief.

24. General Rule and the Ground of Public Policy

4.25 The general rule is unequivocal in that consent will only amount to a defence in exceptionally limited circumstances and only where the victim suffers an injury that taken at its worst, would be merely trivial or transient. Where any injury suffered amounts to actual bodily harm or more, consent cannot amount to a defence on grounds of public policy. This means that it can never be in the interest of the public to allow consenting adults to violently assault each other. To allow such behaviour would be unjustifiable for reasons of health, safety and what is acceptable and expected in terms of values and standards. The general rule is set out clearly in the judgment of Swift J. in *R. v Donovan* [1932] 2 K.B. 498, in which the defendant's conviction of indecent assault was upheld when the defendant had, in private, beaten a girl of 17 for the purposes of sexual gratification with her consent. His Lordship stated:

> "it is an unlawful act to beat another person with such a degree of violence that the infliction of bodily harm is a probable consequence and when such an act is proved, *consent is immaterial.*"

Likewise, in *Attorney–General's Reference (No.6 of 1980)* [1980] Q.B.D. 715, the Court of Appeal ruled that a consensual fist fight, whether in public or private, which results in actual bodily harm or worse, amounts to an offence regardless of consent. It cannot, according to Lane L.J., be in the public interest to cause bodily injury to each other for no reason. Based on the limited application of the general rule of consent, only minor, almost unascertainable injuries such as standing on another passenger's foot on a busy train or bumping into someone in a busy shopping mall or queue, would allow for a defence of implied consent to be raised. As a matter of law, unless a recognisible exception exists a person cannot consent to the infliction of bodily harm.

25. Acts of Sexual Gratification in Private

4.26 The limited application of a defence of consent raised sensitive and difficult legal issues, especially in regard to extending the intervention of the criminal law into people's private lives, as can be seen in the controversial House of Lords decision in *R. v Brown and Others* [1994] 1 A.C. 212 and other subsequent authorities. This involved a group of sado-masochists, all of whom willingly and enthusiastically participated in the commission of acts of violence against each other for sexual pleasure. They each pleaded not guilty to s.47 and s.20 offences, and aiding and abetting such offences. One of the defendants was charged with keeping a disorderly house, a common law offence. The trial judge ruled that the prosecution did not have to prove lack of consent. In consequence of this ruling, the defendants changed their plea to guilty and appealed on the ground that the ruling was wrong. The House of Lords, by a majority of three to two, held that the defendants, who had engaged in consensual homosexual sado-masochistic behaviour, could not claim consent as a defence to the assaults they had inflicted upon each other.

Lord Templeman, giving judgment for the majority, stated that the previous authorities dealing with the intentional infliction of bodily harm did not establish that consent is a defence to a charge under the OAPA 1861; they establish that consent is a defence to injury suffered during some lawful activity, and that as a matter of policy and public interest, a defence of consent cannot be extended to sado masochism. His Lordship then observed that:

> "I am not prepared to invent a defence of consent for sado-masochistic encounters which breed and glorify cruelty and result in offences under s.47 and 20 of the Act of 1861."

Lord Mustill, in a dissenting judgment, felt that the criminal law should not interfere with the private lives of adults, a right respected in art.8; a right to a private life. Likewise, Lord Slynn, who also dissented, agreed, the matter was one of important public policy, since social and moral factors were involved and that for this reason, it was a matter for Parliament not the courts, to decide whether such conduct should be brought within the ambit of the criminal law. This divided ruling led to Brown, Laskey and Jaggard appealing to the European Court of Human Rights (ECHR), arguing that their right to a private life had been breached. In *Laskey and Others v UK* [1997] 24 E.H.R.R. 39, the ECHR ruled that there had been no violation under art.8 of a right to a private life, since such a right is a qualified right and can be interfered with, provided such an interference was justified and proportionate to the legitimate aim of securing in a democratic society the protection of health and morals. Sado-masochistic acts involved a significant degree of injury and wounding and that the UK was entitled to act within a margin of appreciation to regulate such behaviour, for the protection of health and morals. Ultimately, the case had major ramifications on the issue of the involvement of the criminal law in the private sexual lives of people generally, and whether it was more to do, not with the sexual proclivities of the defendants, but the extreme nature of what they were doing.

4.27 Nevertheless, in *R. v Wilson* [1996] 2 Cr.App.R. 241, the Court of Appeal quashed the defendant's conviction under s.47 when he had branded his initials on his wife's buttocks with her consent. The Court refused to follow *Brown* and *Donovan* by distinguishing them on the facts. The Court observed that Mrs Wilson not only consented to the appellant's act, she had in fact instigated it. Further the Court recognised that there was no deliberate intent to injure, quite the opposite, the appellant simply wanted to assist his wife in her desire for personal adornment, which is no different in character to body piercing/tattooing, a recognised exception to the general rule in consent. Importantly, Russell L.J. noted that:

> "Brown is not authority for the proposition that consent is no defence to a charge under s.47 of the 1861 Act, in all the circumstances where actual bodily harm is deliberately inflicted."

Brown was concerned specifically with sado-masochistic acts and their Lordships in *Brown* recognised there are a number of exceptions to the general rule. The decision in *Wilson* clearly identifies that consensual activity between husband and wife in the privacy of the matrimonial home, is not a proper matter for a criminal investigation or prosecution.

Conversely, in *R. v Emmett* [1999] EWCA Crim 1710, in which more sinister facts arose in respect of sexual activities between husband and wife, the Court of Appeal followed the ruling in *Brown*, coming to the conclusion that the evidence in *Emmett* was:

> "in striking contrast to that in Wilson, made it plain that the actual or potential damage to which the appellant's partner was exposed, plainly went far beyond that which was established by the evidence in Wilson."

It was therefore held that the defendant, who engaged in sexual asphyxiation with his partner with her consent, was still guilty of a s.47 assault offence and could not rely on consent since to decide otherwise would be an affront to public policy, given the danger and degree of injury sustained. In the *R. v Coutts* [2006] UKHL 39, the House of Lords considered *Emmett* and confirmed that the appellant's act of placing tights around the victim's neck during consensual sexual asphyxiation resulting in death was a dangerous act and that the consent of the victim does not prevent this act from being unlawful. In *R. v Dica* [2004] EWCA Crim 1103, Judge L.J. observed that the authorities restricting sexual gratification:

> "can too readily be misunderstood. It does not follow from them, and they do not suggest, that consensual acts of sexual intercourse are unlawful merely because there may be a known risk to the health of one or other participant."

In these circumstances and regardless of the sexual overtones, there was deliberate and intentional infliction of bodily harm which is unlawful:

> "to date, as a matter of public policy, it has not been thought appropriate for such violent conduct to be excused merely because there is a private consensual sexual element to it."

26. Exceptions to the General Rule

4.28 In *R. v Brown* the House of Lords recognised and confirmed that there exist a number of exceptions to the general proposition, where on the facts, consent can be used as a legal justification for the injuries inflicted. The following are the recognisable exceptions.

27. Justifiable Sports, i.e. Football

4.29 All justifiable contact sports which are properly regulated and controlled and where, as part of the essence of the game, it is inevitable that players come into contact with each other and injury results, there will be a defence of consent to the offending player in such circumstances. The injured player and all the other participating players have impliedly consented to those foreseeable injuries that might arise during the game. However, the defence of consent will not pray in aid of a player who either intentionally or recklessly goes beyond the accepted rules of conduct of the game and causes grave injury. *R. v Barnes* [2004] EWCA Crim 3246 involved a violent attack during a football match. Although the defendant at trial contended that the tackle was fair and that the injuries caused were accidental, he was convicted of a s.20 offence. He appealed against his conviction on the grounds that the judge had summed up inadequately to the jury.

Giving the leading judgment, Woolf L.J. provided guidance for the prosecution of this type of incident. His Lordship stated that as a starting point, it is undesirable for there to be criminal intervention in organised sports, and that criminal proceedings should only arise in the situations "where the conduct is sufficiently grave to be properly categorized as criminal". If criminal intervention is justified, then dependant on the gravity of the injuries suffered, all offence options are available. For contact type sports, public policy limits the defence to such injuries that fall within the implicit consent given by the player. Whether the conduct of the offending player amounts to criminal liability is a question of fact dependent on all the circumstances of the case. His Lordship then noted that the question whether the conduct reaches the threshold level for criminal liability is an objective one, which disregards the individual views of the players but does take into account:

> "the type of sport, the level at which it is played, the nature of the act, the degree of force used, the extent of the risk of injury, the state of mind of the defendant."

For those "grey area" cases, the jury will need to assess:

> "other questions whether the contact was so obviously late and/or violent that it could not be regarded as an instinctive reaction, error or misjudgment in the heat of the game."

If the conduct in question does not reach the criminal liability threshold level, then any injury suffered from that conduct is deemed lawful and justifiable, as part of the implicit consent given and therefore there exists no unlawful act.

28. Lawful Consent to a Medical Procedure, including Tattooing

4.30 Both in *R. v Brown*, and *R. v Barnes,* the House of Lords and the Court of Appeal confirmed respectively that a patient can lawfully consent to a medical procedure, despite the fact that they will invariably suffer an injury. This includes tattooing/body piercing.

29. Rough "Horseplay"

4.31 In *R. v Brown*, Lord Mustill confirmed that the criminal law should not, as a matter of public policy, interfere with the generality of community life and that rough "horseplay", such as exists in the school playground, or in the barracks room, obviously involves a mutual risk of deliberate physical contact in which one of the participants may come off worse, but in such circumstances there in no unlawful act to attract criminal intervention provided of course that matters do not go to far. Nevertheless, his Lordship noted that the general social acceptance of criminal intervention in regulating people's individual private lives may change with the passage of time and so:

> "the assumptions of the criminal justice system about what types of conduct are properly excluded from its scope, and what it meant by 'going to far' will remain constant".

In *R. v P* [2005] ECWA Crim 1960, the Court of Appeal affirmed the appellant's conviction of manslaughter when he had claimed that throwing the victim off a bridge, from which he died of drowning, was part and parcel of larking around and horseplay. The Court acknowledged the lawfulness of horseplay, but this was a matter for the jury and that the judge had directed them correctly as to this in his summing up (see also *R. v Jones* [1986] 83 Cr.App.R. 375 and *R. v Aitken* [1993] 95 Cr.App.R. 304).

30. Consent Obtained by Fraud or Mistake and the Offences of Rape and Assault

4.32 In *R. v Clarence* [1889] QBD 23, it was held by a majority that consent obtained by fraud does not, as a matter of law, lead automatically to the negation of the consent, to make the act of rape or assault unlawful. Consent would be destroyed by fraud in circumstances where the consent was not properly and freely obtained, on the basis that had the victim known of the true nature and quality of the act and/or the identity of the person doing it, they would not have consented. In simple terms the true consent of the victim is lacking. In *R. v Linekar* [1995] Q.B. 250, the Court of Appeal quashed the defendant's conviction of rape of a prostitute when he made off without paying her the agreed fee of £25; it was argued that she would not have consented to the sexual intercourse had she known that he wouldn't pay. The Court held that the false representation that he would pay, had not in the circumstances vitiated her consent, since this did not distort her true consent as to the nature of the act of sex or the identity of the person involved. In *R. v Richardson* [1998] 2 Cr.App.R. 200, the defendant (a suspended dental practitioner), had her conviction for assault on patients who were not aware of the suspension quashed by the Court of Appeal on the grounds that, although their consent to treatment had been procured by her failure to inform then that she had been suspended, did not extend to criminal liability for assault under s.47, since in law, they were not mistaken as to the identity of the defendant.

However, in *R. v Tabassum* [2000] 2 Cr.App.R. 328, the defendant's conviction for indecent assault was upheld when he had asked several women to take part in a breast cancer survey to enable him to prepare a data base for sale to doctors. The women consented to him examining their breasts; the defendant had no medical qualifications or relevant training. The victims stated that they would not have consented had they known the true facts. The Court of Appeal held that the complainants were only consenting to touching for medical purposes, not to the act of indecency and that the women only gave their consent to the nature of the act (i.e. breast examination) not the quality of that act, namely for indecent purposes. The Court refused to follow the decision in *Richardson* and distinguished it on the facts, as a case that raised the sole issue of identity not the nature and quality of the act. The differing approaches adopted by the Court of Appeal in *Richardson* and *Tabassum* are somewhat irreconcilable, since in *Richardson*, had the complainants known the truth, then they would not have consented to the dental procedure, and therefore the nature and quality of that act, meaning they suffered an unlawful assault.

However, it would seem the Court of Appeal was concerned to extend the ambit of the criminal law to acts that whilst reprehensible in the context of the facts, in *Richardson* amounted only to civil liability. On the application of the law on the issue of consent in terms of nature and quality, there is little to distinguish the two cases, other than looking at the motives of each defendant; those belonging to *Tabassum* are far more sinister and reprehensible than those of *Richardson*. The Court of Appeal adopted an approach of not changing the current principles of law, by contextual application to differing culpable motives.

4.33 Taking account of these principles, in regard to the common law offence of kidnapping, the Court of Appeal in *R. v Hendy-Freegard* [2007] 2 Cr.App.R. 27 followed the ruling in *R. v Wellard* [1978] 67 Cr.App.R. 364 that the definition of kidnapping as set out by the House of Lords in *R. v D*

[1984] A.C. 778, which requires the proof of four elements as follows; (i) the taking or carrying away of one person by another; (ii) by force or fraud (iii) without the consent of the person so taken or carried away; and (iv) without lawful excuse. For elements (i) and (ii) the prosecution must prove that there was a "deprivation of the complainant's liberty".

The Court disproved the ruling given in *R. v Cort* [2003] EWCA Crim 2149; the appellant was convicted for kidnapping and attempted kidnapping. He had stopped at several bus stops in his car and said falsely to the complainants stood waiting that the bus had broken down, he then offered them a lift. Two women agreed and the appellant took them to their correct destination, one woman asked him to let her out which he did. In such circumstances, although the complainant's consent had been obtained by fraud the Court failed to go further and consider the need that the taking and carrying away included a deprivation of liberty, given that the appellant had not prevented either complainant from leaving his vehicle, there had been no deprivation of liberty. The Court noted that: "precedent been properly applied, the appellant (Cort) should not have been guilty of kidnapping".

Phillips L.C.J. in *Hendy-Freegard* also rejected the Court's justification for reaching its decision in *Cort* in that that the appellant's conduct was not trivial and society ought to be able to control such conduct that could lead to other serious consequences. On this point His Lordship noted that:

> "it is open to the court to develop the common law to accommodate change and car ownership affords an opportunity for the types of objectionable behaviour envisaged by the court. We are not however, persuaded that these considerations justified the radical change that appears to haven been made in Cort to the offence of kidnapping."

In *Hendy-Freegard*, the appellant had managed to persuade the complainants that he was a secret agent, and over a period time convinced them to travel around the country whereby he would financially exploit them. The appellant had not, on the occasions in dispute, accompanied the complainants. The Court of Appeal quashed the appellant's conviction for kidnapping owing to a misdirection by the judge, who had failed direct the jury to properly as to the correct principles and the need for proof of deprivation of liberty. It is not enough to establish the offence on lack of consent by fraud or misrepresentation; voluntary movement by the complainant does not amount to a deprivation of liberty.

31. Deliberate Infliction of a Serious Disease and Risk Taking

4.34 In *R. v Clarence* [1889] 22 Q.B. 23, the Court stated that the complainant, who was the wife of the defendant, had consented freely to the act of sexual intercourse and that consent was not negated by a fraud of the husband who deliberately concealed the the fact that he had a sexual disease. There was no fraud as to the nature of the act or the identity of the defendant and therefore no assault under s.20. In *R. v Dica* [2004] EWCA Crim 1103 the Court of Appeal ruled that *Clarence* was no longer authoritative on the meaning of "inflicts". In the context of the issue of consent the facts of this case and *Clarence* were indistinguishable. The defendant (Dica) was an AIDS sufferer who had consensual sexual intercourse with two women, who subsequently themselves became HIV positive. The Court of Appeal rejected the appeal, which relied upon the principle in *Clarence*, since *Clarence* was based on the now disapproved fiction of "deemed consent" that a wife could not refuse to have sex with her husband and was therefore no longer authoritative.

The Court of Appeal ruled that where a person, who knows themselves to be suffering from a serious sexual disease and conceals this condition, either intentionally or recklessly infects another person, then as a matter of public policy they will be liable to conviction of unlawfully inflicting GBH under s.20, where the complainant did not know of their condition or consent to the risk of contracting the disease. However, the Court stated clearly that the infected person would have a defence; if they made the complainant aware of their condition, and with this knowledge, they were still prepared to accept the risk involved and consented to sexual intercourse. On the basis that the judge had withdrawn the issue of consent from the jury, the appellant's conviction was quashed and a re-trial ordered.

The decision is *Dica* was further approved in *R. v Barnes* [2004] EWCA Crim 3246, and applied in *R. v Konzani* [2005] EWCA Crim 706, where the Court of Appeal refused to interfere with the appellant's conviction for infecting the complainants with HIV on the grounds that the trial judge had failed to direct the jury; that notwithstanding, his non disclosure, they had impliedly consented to the risk of infection and that the appellant had genuinely and honestly believed they were consenting, even if that belief was unreasonable. Judge L.J. stated explicitly that from the authority of *Dica* and the observations in *Barnes*, consent will only provide a defence if there is the informed consent of the complainant. In other words, the complainant, having knowledge of the risk, assesses it and still gives consent to the dangerous consequences of that risk if taken. Implied consent is insufficient. In trials of this nature, the issue for the jury's determination is that of whether the complainant gave an informed consent. Consent can never be properly informed in ignorance of the truth of a person's sexual health, and that the honest belief of the defendant in a complainant giving their informed consent would rarely arise.

It is Important to note that Judge L.J., who gave the leading speech, observed that there are potential risks to health, if participating in acts of sexual gratification or simple sexual intercourse, but "modern society has not thought to criminalise those who have willingly accepted the risks". To extend criminal liability to all consensual sexual risk taking would undermine the public's perception of the boundaries in their own personal and private lives and that it would be an oddity to criminalise sexual risk taking to health, but not other every day risk taking decision as to a person's health. To criminally interfere with personal autonomy to this level and extent is a matter for Parliament, not the courts. From the new principles of law in *Dica*, the issue that may arise as a consequence is whether other less dangerous sexually transmitted diseases such as chlamydia will attract criminal liability. Based on an obiter statement by Judge L.J., the answer is yes. On this point His Lordship said:

> "We shall confine ourselves to reflecting that unless you are prepared to take whatever risk of sexually transmitted infection there may be, it is unlikely that you would consent to a risk of a major consequent illness if you were ignorant of it. That said, in every case where these issues arise, the question whether the defendant was or was not reckless, and whether victim did or did not consent to the risk of a sexually transmitted disease is one of fact, and case specific."

It is important to note that the public policy considerations in *Dica* are right in terms of an offence of intentional or reckless infliction of GBH. However in regard to the application of consent in the context of rape in the Sexual Offences Act 2003, evidence of the defendant having HIV is irrelevant to the issue of consent (see *R. v B* [2006] EWCA Crim 2945 at para.4.36 below).

32. Reasonable Chastisement

4.35 Until recently, a parent who hit a child could rely on the defence of reasonable chastisement, as identified and explained in *R. v H* [2001] 2 F.L.R. 431, where the Court of Appeal recognised that in law a defence of reasonable chastisement had existed since *R. v Hopley* [1860] 2 F. & F. 202, to an allegation of assault. If relied upon, the Court stated that the jury must be given directions as to the reasonableness of the punishment and whether it was proportionate to the degree of misbehaviour. The issue of reasonableness would be a question of fact for the jury. However the defence of reasonable chastisement is now as a matter of public policy, unjustifiable in certain circumstances. To this extent, the defence is restricted by s.58 of the Children Act 2004, which provides that reasonable chastisement as a defence cannot be relied upon as justification to a s.47, s.20 and s.18 offence. The defence is unaffected in regard to offences of common assault and battery; in these circumstances reasonable chastisement can be relied upon as lawful justification. Section 58 is yet to be brought into force.

33. Sexual Offences against the Person

4.36 Parliament has long been concerned with the need to strike a fair balance between the seriousness of rape, a decline in rape conviction rates and ensuring a fair trial for the defendant. Against this background and the recommendations made by the CPS and the Inspectorate of Constabulary in a joint inspection into the investigation and prosecution of cases involving allegations of rape, and the Law Commission's report into consent in sexual offences, the Sexual Offences Act 2003 (SOA 2003), came into effect on May 1, 2004. The purpose of the Act is to codify the existing law concerning sexual offences. However, in *R. v C* [2005] EWCA Crim 3533, the Court of Appeal, in determining a terminating ruling of the judge under s.58 of the CJA 2003, held that s.140 of the SOA 2003 had simultaneously repealed the offences found in the Sexual Offences Act 1956. But the Secretary of State had failed under s.141 to create relevant transitional provisions.

Accordingly, given that the prosecution were unable to prove whether the offences of gross indecency occurred before or after May 1, 2004, then no offence could have been committed because of its repeal. The Court further stated that owing to the omission of the Secretary of State to ensure the operation of the 1956 Act, it was not open to the Court to adopt a purposive approach or any other method of interpretation to cure an absurdity caused by the inactivity of the Secretary of State. The legislation was unequivocal and clear in that regard. In the result, Parliament itself has had to cure the defect with the implementation of s.55 of the Violent Crime Reduction Act 2006, which brings into effect the difficulty observed by the court in *R. v C.*

This now ensures continuity of sexual offences in that it allows for the prosecution to place pre-2003 Act commencement offences as separate counts in the indictment to post May 1, 2004 offences, and that the only thing preventing a conviction is that the jury are not convinced beyond doubt in relation to each offence of the time when it was committed. Put simply, if the jury is not sure it was committed after May 1, 2004, but sure it was before then they will convict the defendant of the pre-commencement offence and acquit of the post-2003 Act offence, and visa versa.

Professor Spenser Q.C. in the 12th Annual Lecture to the Judicial Studies Board entitled "The Drafting of Criminal Legislation: Need it be so Impenetrable" (to be found at http://www.jsboard.co.uk) raises concerns about the authoritarian tone and the overburdening technical drafting of some of the offences. He gives the example of the offence of voyeurism contained in ss.67 and 68 as using 334 words to create three separate offences, but which then fails in certain respects to deal with the very act the offence was designed to criminalise. This is aptly illustrated in *R. v Hamiltion* [2008] 1 W.L.R. 107, as to whether the acts of the defendant by surreptitiously filming up women's skirts, would amount to the offence of voyeurism given the actus reus of one of the offences is recording another person doing a private act, but does not use the words "private parts".

34. Statutory Rape

4.37 Section 1 of the Sexual Offences Act 2003 provides for a new offence of rape that is wider than the old offence. A person commits rape if he intentionally penetrates the vagina, anus or mouth of another person with his penis and that at the time, the complainant did not consent to this act, and the defendant did not reasonably believe that the complainant was consenting.

In considering the defendant's belief, the jury must have regard to all the circumstances and any steps the defendant took in order to ascertain whether the complainant was consenting. Section 5 creates the same offence but with a person under 13.

35. Meaning of Consent and Statutory Presumptions of Fact

4.38 Section 74 provides a general meaning of consent and consists of a person who has a capacity to make an agreement, reached by freedom of choice. A significant development in the conduct of a rape trial are the wide reaching implications of s.75. This section provides that once it is proved that the defendant committed the actus reus and one or more of six evidential circumstances are shown to exist and the defendant knew of the circumstances, then unless there is sufficient evidence to the contrary, it will be evidentially presumed that in such circumstances, the complainant did not consent or that the defendant held a reasonable belief. The six presumptions are:

(i) At the time or immediately before the act, violence was used against the complainant or the complainant feared that violence would be used against them.

(ii) As above but the violent or fear of violence was directed towards another person.

(iii) The complainant but not the defendant was at the time unlawfully detained.

(iv) The complainant was asleep or otherwise unconscious at the time of the act.

(v) A physical disability of the complainant prevented them from communicating whether they consented or not.

(vi) Administering or causing to be administered without complainant's consent a substance rendering the complainant to be stupefied or overpowered.

If, on the evidence any of the above exist, then it will, at that point in the trial, be presumed that the complainant did not consent and factually the defendant is deemed not to have a reasonable belief that the complainant was consenting at the time. In order to avoid a conviction, there is placed upon the defence an evidential burden to produce sufficient evidence in rebuttal of the presumptions about consent. If no evidence is forthcoming, then the defendant is at real risk of being found guilty of rape.

If the allegation is one of acquaintance rape, then the conduct of such trials and the difficult and sensitive task of the jury are profoundly delicate. The defendant will not deny that sexual activity took place, it will be his defence that such activity was with the free consent of the complainant.

Conversely, the prosecution will present its case on lack of consent and reasonable belief in consent. The issue of consent is purely fact based and in cases where the crucial evidence is essentially the testimony of the complainant and the defendant, then the jury's task is to decide who is telling the truth and who is telling a lie. If the complainant cannot be believed, then the only alternative is to acquit. The difficulties in the prosecution of such cases are clearly illustrated in *R. v Thompson* [2001] EWCA Crim 486, a case based on its own exceptional facts.

Consent is an essential ingredient for establishing the actus reus for a number of offences within the Act. However, in relation to certain specified offences where the complainant is under 13, then the issue of consent is irrelevant. For instance, the offence of sexual assault a child under 13, in s.7, requires the proof of intentional sexual touching to sustain a conviction, consent and reasonable belief do not form part of the offence.

36. Un-rebuttal (Conclusive) Presumptions

4.39 Going a step further from the ambit of s.75 is s.76, a far reaching provision, which provides that once it is proved the defendant committed the actus reus, and one or both of two specified circumstances exist, then as a matter of law it is to be presumed conclusively that the complainant neither consented, nor could the defendant have held a reasonable belief of consent. The two specified circumstances are:

(i) an intentional deception by the defendant against the complainant as to the nature and purpose of the act;

(ii) impersonating a person known to the complainant with the intention of inducing the complainant to consent.

In *R. v Jheeta* [2007] EWCA Crim 1699, the Court of Appeal ruled that the application of the s.76(2)(a) presumption is limited to the actual sexual act. Accordingly, the conclusive presumption will only apply to situations where the deception of the defendant is as to the nature and purpose of that actual act. In the present case, the appellant had, in somewhat bizarre circumstances, deceived the complainant into having sexual intercourse with him, an act she was fully aware of. The Court concluded that:

> "no conclusive presumptions arise merely because the complainant was deceived is some way or other by disingenuous blandishments of or common or garden lies by the defendant."

Nevertheless, the appellant's convictions for rape were still safe given his guilty plea on the basis that he accepted she had not, on the occasions in question, consented to the act.

37. Consent and Self-Induced Intoxication

4.40 Although s.74 provides a meaning of consent, the factual circumstances where and when someone is not consenting can range from a truly passionate encounter to outright physical objection. If self-induced intoxication plays a significant part in the reduction of a person's inhibitions, followed by regret, rejection and emotional distress, then the issue of consent can and does become a difficult task for a jury to resolve. The practical reality of human behaviour in these circumstances came to be addressed by the Court of Appeal in *R. v Bree* [2007] 3 W.L.R. 600. The appellant had, along with the complainant, consumed large quantities of alcohol, both returned at the end of the evening to the defendant's brother's flat where it was not disputed that sexual intercourse took place. The disputed issue was that of consent.

The prosecution had originally claimed lack of capacity to choose due to intoxicated unconsciousness. Instead, they based their case on the complainant having capacity not to consent, but owing to the degree of intoxication, the complainant suffered lack of recollection, and therefore an inability to resist; she was aware of what was happening and did not consent to it. The defence however, maintained that whilst intoxicated, the complainant voluntarily consented to sexual intercourse. In quashing the appellant's conviction on the grounds of an inadequate summing up to the jury by the judge, the Court of Appeal ruled that, as a matter of construction, s.74 in the context of intoxicated consent is clear; if the complainant temporarily losses her capacity to freely consent whether through drink or other means, this will not be consenting and amount to rape, subject to proof of the defendant's state of mind. Conversely, if the complainant voluntarily consumes large quantities of alcohol but is still capable of reaching an unequivocal free decision as to intercourse, this is consenting and is not rape.

The issue at trial in such cases will always be for the jury to determine whether or not the complainant had the capacity to consent. Each case will depend on its own particular facts and circumstances. Nevertheless, following the Court of Appeal decision in *Bree*, the defence will be able to raise evidence that a complainant, whilst drunk, still had the capacity to give the necessary consent and did so in that drunken state. A drunken mind can still be a mind capable of consent. In *R. v Wright* [2007] (unreported), in which similar facts arose, the Court of Appeal considered the *Bree* ruling and dismissed the appeal on the basis that the issue of consent is for the jury to determine in a case of this nature, between whether the complainant was partially unconscious by intoxication and therefore incapable of making a choice or alternatively, although drunk, she was still capable of making that choice freely. Essentially, where two versions of events are in stark conflict, it comes down to which one of them the jury will accept is telling the truth.

38. Consent and Non Disclosure

4.41 In *R. v B* [2007] 1 W.L.R. 1567, the Court of Appeal ruled that as a matter of law, the non disclosure by the appellant of his HIV status was not relevant to the issue of consent to sexual intercourse under s.74 in an allegation of rape. Accordingly, the trial judge was wrong to admit evidence of the appellant's HIV condition and to direct the jury that this is relevant to the issue of whether the complainant consented. Allowing the admission of such evidence was highly prejudicial to the appellant's case and should have been excluded under s.78 of the Police and Criminal Evidence Act 1984. The Court of Appeal referred to the wording of s.74 of the Sexual Offences Act 2003 and acknowledged there is no statutory reference to "implied deceptions" being relevant to the issue of consent in terms of the complainant's capacity to choose whether or not to have intercourse. The Court gave its ruling as follows:

> "Where one party to sexual activity has a sexually transmissible disease which is not disclosed to the other party any consent that may have been given to that activity by the other party is not thereby vitiated. The act remains a consensual act."

Further, in *R. v Dica* [2004] Cr.App.R. 28, Judge L.J. stated, on the assumed facts of the case, that the victims had consented to sexual intercourse and therefore the defendant was not guilty of rape, but had not consented to the infliction of injury. The Court of Appeal did however, recognise the perplexities in the application of consent to different offences and observed that such consequences:

> "requires debate, not in a court of law but as a matter of public and social policy, bearing in mind all the factors that are concerned including questions of personal autonomy in delicate personal relationships."

The Court further acknowledged the findings of the Law Commission that non disclosure of a sexually transmitted disease is of such importance that it should form part of the capacity to consent. Whether or not to criminalise the sexual activities of those with a sexual disease as amounting to either rape or new offences of sexual deception is a matter for public debate.

39. Offence of Assault by Penetration

4.42 Section 2 creates a new offence of assault by penetration. To secure a conviction for this equally serious an offence as rape, with a maximum sentence of life imprisonment, the prosecution must prove the:

(i) mens rea of intention to penetrate the vagina or anus of another with a part of the (defendant's) body or anything else;

(ii) that the act of penetration was sexual in nature;

(iii) that the complainant did not consent to such an act; and

(iv) the defendant at the time did not have a reasonable belief that the complainant was consenting.

For the act to be sexual it must be shown in accordance with s.78 that a reasonable person (objective test) would consider the penetration regardless of its circumstances, (i.e. misunderstanding or perception) or purpose to be because of it nature a sexual act. Or alternatively, because of it nature and or circumstances or purpose, it is sexual. In comparison to the offence of rape, this offence is narrower in application by not including penetration of the mouth. Conversely, it is wider than the offence of rape in that the penetration can result from any part of the defendant's body (i.e. fingers) or anything else, which would embrace the utility of all conceivable natural and man made objects. Also, the s.2 offence can be committed by both a man, or woman whereas for rape this is limited to a man by the use of the words "with his penis". On the issue of consent both presumptions in ss.75 and 76 apply. Section 6 creates the same offence but with a person under 13.

40. The Offence of Sexual Assault

4.43 Section 3 creates a new offence of sexual assault that replaces specifically the old offence of indecent assault. The ingredients to this offence are similar to those in the s.2 offence. The only difference is that instead of having to prove penetration, the prosecution has to prove intentional touching and that the touching itself is sexual in accordance with its meaning in s.78 (see para.4.24). This is less serious than rape and assault by penetration since both are indictable only offences, whereas sexual assault amounts to an either way offence with six months' imprisonment on summary conviction or on conviction in the Crown Court, 10 years' imprisonment. Section 7 creates the same offence but with a child under 13. In *R. v Heard* [2007] 3 W.L.R. 475, the Court of Appeal observed that the s.3 offence is clear; the prosecution must prove that the defendant deliberately intended to touch the complainant and that touching was sexual within the meaning of s.78. Reckless touching in not sufficient and does not from part of the statutory offence. Accordingly, to recklessly fall, stumble or barge around which results in the unintentional touching of another, although objectively sexual, cannot amount to an offence in those circumstances, due to the lack of mens rea.

In *R. v Court* [1988] 2 W.L.R. 1071, the House of Lords, in considering the previous offence of indecent assault, ruled that evidence of the sexual motives of the accused is admissible to assist in establishing whether or not the purpose of the assault was indecent. With the new offence, based on this decision, the prosecution ought to be able to adduce evidence of a sexual motive to prove that the defendant had a deliberate intent to touch the complainant sexually. In *Court* this was a "buttock fettish". Likewise in *R. v H* [2005] 1 W.L.R. 2005, the Court of Appeal in dismissing the appeal against conviction, ruled that touching in the context of the new offence of sexual assault included, as the appellant did, grabbing the complainant's tracksuit bottoms, having asked her if she fancied sex. The Court of Appeal made it clear that it could not have been Parliament's intention, when it used the expression "through anything" in s.79(8), to limit the commission of the offence to actual touching of the body, and not the clothes the complainant was wearing at the time.

41. Defence of Mistaken Belief and Lack of Consent

4.44 Each offence in relation to a complainant of 13 or over requires the prosecution to prove that the defendant, at the time of the alleged offence, did not have a reasonably held belief as to consent of the complainant. However, using the word "reasonably", narrows the application of the defence of mistaken belief and repeals the wider common law principles found is *Morgan v DPP* [1976] A.C. 182 and *DPP v B (a minor)* [2000] 2 A.C. 428, which had held that the prosecution must disprove any genuinely held belief as to consent/age, even if the belief was unreasonably held. If the complainant is under 13 for the purposes of either rape (s.5), assault by penetration (s.6), sexual assault (s.7) sexual activity (s.9) and causing or inciting sexual activity (s.10) the prosecution is relieved of the burden of disproving or proving that the defendant did or did not have a reasonable belief as to age. For all the offences contained in ss.5 to 13, in relation to a complainant under 16, whether or not the complainant consented is irrelevant as to proof of the offence.

42. Criticism of Current Law and Law Reform

4.45 The weakness of the law of non-fatal assault offences is that it lacks any coherent structure; there is no logical hierarchy of offences, the expressions used in the definition of the offences are archaic and antiquated, which has led to much of the present confusion surrounding the application of each offence. The word "maliciously" serves no useful purpose and has had to be replaced with the modern mens rea of "recklessness". The application of the words "inflicts" and "bodily" have required judicial interpretation. The expression "GBH" is used to describe the actus reus for both s.18 and s.20, leading to inconsistency in setting out the relevant degree of injury required for each offence. In practice, the prosecution, when deciding on the appropriate charge in terms of culpability, apply the criteria in charging standards for assault offences.

Another clear illogical inconsistency is that although s.47 is deemed less culpable than s.20, the punishment of five years' imprisonment is the same for each offence. To avoid potential injustice the culpability distinction is made at sentencing. Finally, inconsistency also arises between a s.47 offence and that of common assault; although, an offence of ABH is culpably more serious than common assault, the mens rea for each is the same, as a consequence of the House of Lords ruling in *R. v Savage*. It is clear that the OAPA 1861 is flawed and overdue for replacement; to this extent the Law Commission in 1992 formulated a comprehensive Criminal Law Bill setting out proposals for three new non-fatal offences. Section 18 would be replaced with offence of intentionally causing serious injury, whilst s.20 would be replaced by an offence of intentionally or recklessly causing serious injury and s.47 would be replaced by an offence of intentionally or recklessly causing injury. If these proposals were ever to be adopted, then there is no doubt they would bring clarity and simplicity to these often encountered offences.

CHAPTER FIVE

PROPERTY OFFENCES PART 1: BASIC THEFT, ROBBERY AND BURGLARY

1. THEFT OFFENCES

5.01 The law of theft and its many related offences are found in the Theft Act 1968, the Theft Act 1978 now partially repealed and the recently enacted Fraud Act 2006, which simplifies the offences of deception. The Theft Act 1968 was passed in order to remove the technical difficulties found in the old Larceny Act 1916 and to modernise and simplify the application of the offences. Given that theft involves property, which belongs to another, its application is linked inextricably to civil law concepts of possession, ownership, consent and the vitiating elements of mistake and misrepresentation. Ultimately what distinguishes a civil dispute over a contractual obligation from that which attracts criminal liability, is the existence of dishonesty. The public needs protection from the thieves and deceivers who may try to hide beyond the civil law.

A useful illustration is where a local builder attends at the home of an elderly gentleman and convinces him that his roof is dangerous and needs immediate replacement. The elderly gentleman agrees for the builder to do the work, who charges him £25,000 and takes him to the bank to obtain the money. In fact the original roof is safe and the builder only replaced a few tiles. Looking at these facts, there is a contract between the elderly gentleman and the builder, there is clearly a civil dispute based on breaches of the implied term in that the work must be carried out with reasonable skill and care. Further, there is a strong case for a voidable contract tainted by fraudulent misrepresentation. If as in this case, that fraudulent misrepresentation is criminally dishonest, then the criminal law must, on public policy grounds, intervene in what is a contractual arrangement.

For this reason the law of theft is based on civil concepts, it is important to be aware that such concepts deliberately form part of the definition of the offence. For example, the offence of burglary requires the prosecution to prove that the defendant was a "trespasser". In many instances like the one above, civil liability is clearly and rightly distinguishable from criminal liability. However considerable difficulties have been perceived in separating the legal and factual distinction between the two liabilities where there exist fine distinctions, especially when assessed against moral deplorability. A vivid illustration of this inextricable dilemma is found in the divided judgment of the House of Lords in *R. v Hinks* [2001] 2 A.C. 241, and whether accepting valid gifts can amount to theft in given circumstances.

2. The Offence of Basic Theft

5.02 The offence of basic theft is found in s.1 of the Theft Act 1968 (Basic s.1 Theft Offence) which provides that:

> "A person is guilty of theft if s/he dishonestly appropriates property belonging to another with the intention of permanently depriving the other of it."

It is important to be aware that the mens rea and actus reus for theft consist of five elements. It is these five elements that the prosecution must prove to exist if a conviction for theft is to arise. It is important to be aware that if one or more of any of the five elements of the offence is missing, then the defendant must be acquitted.

The actus reus for basic theft consists of:

(i) Appropriates

(ii) Property

(iii) which Belongs to another.

The mens rea for basic theft consists of:

(i) Dishonestly

(ii) Intention to permanently deprive.

To assist in the proof of both the mens rea and actus reus, ss.2 to 6 of the Theft Act 1968 provide a statutory meaning for each individual element. Despite this statutory aid, all five elements have come before the appeal courts for judicial interpretation of what each word or expression means in the context of theft. It is important therefore to first look at the actual definition of basic theft, the relevant interpretation section for the element in issue and then any case authorities that provide further, interpretive guidance on the application of the offence. It is necessary therefore to assess the legal meaning of each individual element of the offence.

3. The Meaning of "Appropriates"

5.03 The House of Lords, just like with the meaning of "indirect intention" and the concept of the "reasonable man" in provocation, have had to address on three separate occasions the legal meaning of "appropriates" and its general application in the context of theft. The starting point is to consider s.3(1), the interpretive section for the word "appropriates" This section provides that any *assumption* by a person of the rights of an owner amounts to an *appropriation* and this includes, where that person comes by the property (innocently or not) without stealing it, any later assumption of a right to it by keeping it as owner.

The critical question that the House of Lords had to address and resolve on three occasions with divided opinion, is whether or not a person can for the purposes of theft, still appropriate property that belongs to another, even in circumstances where the actual owner consents to the appropriation. Section 3 is silent on the issue of "consent" and simply provides that there is an "appropriation" if the defendant is proved to have assumed the rights of the owner. The difficultly with this meaning is whether in law there can still be such an assumption even if the owner consents and allows the defendant to exercise their own rights of ownership of the property either by transfer of that ownership through contract, or alternatively by a simple gift.

The first House of Lords decision to address this point is *R. v Lawrence* [1972] A.C. 626, where the appellant, a taxi driver, took an £6 extra from an Italian passenger who because he could not speak English, invited the appellant to take the relevant money from his wallet. In fact the journey should have only cost 52p. The appellant was convicted of theft and subsequently appealed against his conviction on the grounds that he could not as a matter of interpretation have committed theft since by the victim giving consent for him to take £6, he could not in such circumstances have assumed the rights of the owner. The House of Lords unanimously rejected this contention and held that in law there is still an appropriation for the purposes of theft, even if the owner had permitted or consented to the property being taken. For Viscount Dilhorne the Theft Act 1968 was passed to simplify the application of theft and that his Lordship saw:

> "no ground for concluding that the omission of the words 'without the consent of the owner' was inadvertent and not deliberate, and to read the subsection as if they were included is, in my opinion, wholly unwarranted. Parliament by the omission of these words has relieved the prosecution of the burden of establishing that the taking was without the owner's consent. That is no longer an ingredient of the offence."

The House of Lords ruled that the issue of consent was not a relevant factor in the proof of "appropriates", but a matter relevant to the element of dishonesty. The ratio in *Lawrence* is clear in that the prosecution is not required to prove in respect of appropriation that the taking was without the consent of the owner. The second case is which the issue of appropriation came before the House of Lords was *R. v Morris and Anderton* [1984] A.C. 320, in which the appellant took goods from the shelves in a supermarket and switched the price labels for labels which displayed a lower price, with the intention of paying this at the check-out. Both were convicted of theft on the basis that switching the labels amounted to appropriation. They each appealed on the ground that they had not appropriated the goods by applying the invitation to treat principle in contract law, in that the shop had impliedly invited them (i.e. consented) to take the goods and make an offer at the till which could be accepted or rejected. Although the House of Lords confirmed the appellant's convictions, it was the legal approach taken in reaching that decision which caused subsequent confusion. The judgment of Lord Roskill encapsulated this approach in the following terms:

> "If one postulates an honest customer taking goods from a shelf to put in his or her trolley to take to the checkpoint there to pay the proper price, I am unable to see that any of these actions involves any assumption by the shopper of the rights of the supermarket. In he context of section 3(1), the concept of appropriation in my view involves not an act expressly or impliedly authorized by the owner but an act *by way of adverse interference with or usurpation of those rights.*"

5.04 This observation was seen to be in direct conflict with the decision in *Lawrence*. By using the words *adverse interference*, it was considered that the prosecution must prove lack of consent in the appropriation, if there was consent then there could be no adverse inference with the owner's rights. Owing to this difference of opinion, the law was unsettled which needed to be resolved. *Dobson v GAF and L Assurance* [1990] 1 Q.B. 274, a civil case, concerned the refusal of an insurance company to pay a claim against the loss suffered by the claimant of a valuable ring under a contract with a deceiving rogue, as not amounting to theft as required under the policy. Ruling in favour of the claimant, Parker L.J. observed the conflict between *Lawrence* and *Morris* and preferred the ratio in *Lawrence* and stated obiter that *Morris* could not be regarded as:

> "having overruled a very plain decision in Lawrence, that appropriation can occur even if the owner consents".

Although not binding on a criminal appeal court, this ruling was applied by the House of Lords in *R. v Gomez* [1993] A.C. 442, in which the conflict was settled. The appellant was the assistant manager of an electrical goods shop. A customer wishing to purchase electrical goods valued at £16,000 approached him and offered to pay with two worthless cheques, which the appellant (Gomez) knew to be stolen. The appellant then deceived the manager into authorising the sale. The appellant pleaded guilty to theft after an unfavourable ruling by the trial judge and appealed on the ground that an appropriation involved an unauthorised transfer, so the consent of the shop manager to the transfer of the electrical goods even though obtained by fraud, was not an appropriation for the purpose of theft.

By a majority of four to one, the House of Lords, in confirming the appellant's conviction for theft, held that the decision in *Lawrence* correctly represented the law and that their Lordships in Morris had not intended to say anything in their judgment to be in direct conflict with *Lawrence*. What Lord Roskill had said in the context of adverse inference, was both unnecessary to the decision in the case and an incorrect interpretation of the law.

Lord Keith, giving the leading speech of the majority, felt it would serve no useful purpose to seek guidance from the Eighth Report of the Criminal Law Revision Committee on Theft and Related Offences (1966) (Cmnd. 2977), since the decision in *Lawrence* was clear on the construction of "appropriates" which had according to his Lordship:

> "stood for 12 years when doubt was thrown upon it by obiter dicta in Morris. Lawrence must be regarded as authoritative and correct, and there is no question of it now being right to depart from it."

On the other hand, Lord Lowry, in a dissenting judgment, felt it was right to consult the Committee Report, and stated that the word "appropriates" should be given its ordinary and natural meaning found in the dictionary, which provides for taking without authority.

It is important to note that the interpretative difficulties encountered by the House of Lords as to the legal meaning of "appropriates", arose as a result of the prosecution deciding to indict the defendants in *Lawrence* and *Gomez* with theft, as opposed to obtaining property by deception in s.15 of the Theft Act 1968. To have interpreted in favour of the defendants would have allowed what was clearly a criminal act to go unpunished and not in the public interest. The result of these two authorities was to blare the distinction between the two offences, especially in situations were consent was obtained by a fraud or misrepresentation, since the offender can at the same time either be a thief or a deceiver.

4. Valid Gifts: An Issue of Dishonesty not Appropriation

5.05 The third case in which the House of Lords had to again consider appropriation, involved the question of whether a person can appropriate property belonging to another, where that other person makes an indefeasible (valid) gift of that property, to the person who is now accused of stealing. In this situation there is no suggestion that the complainant's consent was obtained by a fraud, deception or misrepresentation. The legal difficulty arises between the element of appropriation with that of dishonesty, in the sense that where a person receives money or other property as a gift, can they ever be held to be acting dishonestly in such a situation regardless of how morally reprehensible they are in accepting the gift.

A clear illustration of this sensitive issue between establishing criminal fault as opposed to undesirable moral fault can be seen in *R. v Mazo* [1997] 2 Cr.App.R. 518. The appellant had worked as a maid of an 89-year-old lady and had received cheques and valuables from the complainant. The appellant had contended at her trial for theft that these amounted to simple gifts, the prosecution however claimed she had stolen them. She was convicted and appealed on the basis that the trial judge had failed to properly put her defence to the jury, in that she had received valid gifts of which she was entitled to accept and that no offence of theft arose. The Court of Appeal agreed and quashed her conviction on the grounds that if a person makes a gift with full knowledge of the circumstances in the making of the gift, the defendant could never have acted dishonestly.

However, in *R. v Kendrick and Hopkins* [1997] 2 Cr.App.R. 524, a different Court of Appeal refused to follow *Mazo* and distinguished it on the facts. The two appellants ran a small residential home for the elderly, the complainant was a 99-year-old blind lady, the appellants after the death of the complainant's daughter, had taken power of attorney. They liquidated her assets of £127,000 and paid the proceeds into an account, which they alone controlled. They subsequently withdrew large sums of money, which they contended was with the complainant's consent and for her benefit. Both were convicted of conspiracy to steal and sentenced to 30 months' imprisonment and ordered to pay compensation of £27,500 to the complainant. The Court dismissed the appeals on the basis that the judge's direction to the jury on the issue of valid gifts was sufficiently adequate and that the issue for the jury was one of whether there was a dishonest appropriation of the money and that the lack of mental capacity of the victim related, not to the question of appropriation, but to the question of dishonesty. Given the implausible explanation of the appellants in this case the Court of Appeal was right to reject their appeal, since to have done so would have been an affront to justice. However, as can be seen in *Mazo*, although the public interest demands that any alleged act of dishonesty should be prosecuted, there is an evitable danger of what is an undesirable immoral act, still attracting criminal liability. Morally sinister acts even in the face of public distaste are not criminal acts, but there lies the difficulty for the criminal law in ensuring that a distinction in the interests of justice is maintained between each.

5.06 On this issue in respect of valid gifts, the House of Lords in *R. v Hinks* [2001] 2 A.C. 241, felt the interests of justice demanded that the jury should be entrusted with maintaining this distinction as a question of fact with appropriate legal directions. The appellant in *Hinks* was a single mother who became a friend of the complainant, a man of low intelligence. At trial *Hinks* claimed to be a carer of the complainant and during a period of some five months, the complainant withdrew £60,000 from his Building Society account, which was then placed into the account of the appellant. The complainant had also made on a daily basis withdrawals of up the maximum of £300. By the end of the year the complainant had lost virtually all his savings. The appellant was charged with six counts of theft relating the withdrawal of money and one count in relation to the transfer of a TV.

At trial the prosecution claimed that the appellant had coerced and influenced the complainant to withdraw the money. A substantive volume of evidence was adduced including the testimony of Building Society employees who claimed that the appellant did all the talking. A Consultant Psychiatrist assessed the victim to have a below average IQ and described him as not being aware of the value of his assets or calculation, although he accepted the complainant was capable of making gifts and understood the concept of ownership, but could not make this decision alone. The defence in turn argued that there was no case to answer, that the money was a gift and that title had validly transferred to the appellant in which there was no appropriation to convict of theft. This was rejected by the trial judge who refused to direct the jury on this point. The appellant was convicted and received 18 months' imprisonment. She appealed up to the House of Lords against her conviction. The House of Lords by a majority of three to two confirmed the conviction and dismissed the appeal. Lord Steyn giving the leading speech for the majority, ruled that a distinction needed to be maintained between appropriation and dishonesty:

> "and that the defendants belief or lack of belief that the owner consented to the appropriation, is relevant to the jury's determination of whether the defendant acted dishonesty".

Both Lord Hutton and Lord Hobhouse in dissenting judgments, stated that this distinction could lead to an injustice in the sense that a jury may convict on the basis that the defendant, whilst accepting money, did so in circumstances that was clearly deplorable and morally reprehensible and not on whether such conduct was criminally dishonest. Accordingly, their Lordships in the minority felt that if there is a valid gift then there can never be any act of dishonesty in accepting it and no offence of theft. It is only when there is evidence of whether or not the donee is mentally capable of making the gift, does the issue of dishonesty arise and a criminal trial. Despite this strong minority view, the clear and unequivocal principle of law is that the transfer of ownership in property with the original owner's consent to another person amounts to, in law, appropriation for the purposes of theft, and that the issue of whether the defendant acted dishonestly is a question for the jury to determine.

5. Appropriation and Purchases in Good Faith: Section 3(2) of the Theft Act 1968

5.07 Section 3(2) provides that a person who purchases property for valuable consideration in good faith, but subsequently discovers that the property was in fact stolen is not guilty of theft. The later assumption of the rights of the owner by the purchaser does not amount to appropriation for theft by reason of the defect in the transfer of ownership of the property. In *R. v Adams* [1993] Crim. L.R. 72, the appellant's conviction for theft was quashed under s.3(2). The appellant, a motor cycle enthusiast, had purchased, unknowing to him, stolen parts, he was told and honestly believed that they were from a "write off". A few days later he found out their true identity. The factual issue arising under this section for the jury is whether or not the defendant "acted in good faith". This will depend on the particular circumstances of the case, such as the environment in which the purchase was made and the actual price paid against the available information to the defendant to make a decision as the legitimacy of the purchase.

6. The General Meaning of "Property" in the Act

5.08 The word "property" for the purposes of theft is defined in s.4, which gives a wide general statutory meaning to what amounts to property. Subsection (1) provides that property includes money and all other property, real or personal, including things (chose) in action and other intangible property. It is important to be aware of what is meant for the purposes of theft by the expression "thing (chose) in action". In *R. v Marshall* [1998] 2 Cr.App.R. 282, Mantel L.J. explained that a:

> "chose in action is a known legal expression used to describe all personal rights of property which can only be claimed or enforced by action and not by taking physical possession; see *Torkington v Magee* [1902] 2KB 427."

The expression a thing (chose) in action is a legal description of a particular transaction and nothing more. A simple example would be a written cheque for a specified amount of money. The actual cheque is nothing more than a piece of paper giving the account holder the authority to a bank to pay a fixed amount of money to another person. This person has the right to the amount of money stated in the cheque, but in order to obtain its monetary value he must take action by presenting the cheque to his bank for processing. Another important point to be aware of is that in *Low v Blease* [1975] Crim. L.R. 513, the Court held that electricity does not for the purposes of theft, constitute "other intangible property". A separate offence exists in s.13 of abstracting electricity. Likewise, in *Oxford v Moss* [1978] 68 Cr.App.R. 183, the Court held that confidential information does not constitute property for the purpose of theft and that therefore a student was not guilty of theft when he photocopied the answers to the exam questions from the original examination paper.

7. Body Parts as Amounting to Property in Certain Circumstances

5.09 The question arose in *R. v Kelly and Lindsay* [1999] 2 W.L.R. 384, whether body parts formed part of "all other property" within s.4. The appellants took between 35 to 40 body parts from the Royal College of Surgeons including three heads, part of a brain, six arms 10 legs and three torsos, Kelly, a sculptor, made casts of the parts which were later exhibited at an art gallery. Both where convicted of theft and appealed against their convictions on the basis that the trial judge was wrong to rule in law that an exception existed to the common law rule, that there is no property in a corpse as set out in *R. v Sharp* [1857] D. & B. 160. The Court of Appeal upheld their convictions and stated in the judgment of Rose L.J. that "parts of a corpse are capable of being property within s4 if they have acquired different attributes by virtue of the application of skill, such as dissection or preservation techniques, for exhibition or teaching purposes". The Court placed significant reliance on the Austrialian authority of *R. v Doodward and*

Spence [1908] 6 C.L.R. 406, in reaching its decision as creating an exception to the common law rule. It would be a matter for Parliament to abolish the old common law rule. Nevertheless, in an interesting obiter statement the Court noted:

> "Furthermore the common law does not stand still. It may be that if, on some future occasion, the question arises, the courts will hold that human body parts are capable of being property for the purposes of s4, even without the acquisition of different attributes, if they have a use or significance beyond their mere existence. This may be so if for example, they are intended for use in an organ transplant operation, for the extraction of DNA, or for the matter, as an exhibit in a trial."

As an observation, the possession of human remains is controlled and governed by the Anatomy Act 1984. Section 4 allows the use of bodies for anatomical examination for the purpose of research or teaching. There is nevertheless a statutory period of limitation of three years after the death of the deceased in s.4(8). There exist specific offences under the Act itself.

8. The Meaning of Property in Specific Situations

5.10 The remainder of s.4 provides for the meaning of property in specific and less commonly encountered situations, but where clarity is needed to ensure the correct application of the law of theft. Subsection (2) provides that a person cannot steal land or things forming part of it or removed from the land by them, except if that person is:

(i) a trustee;

(ii) a personal representative;

(iii) authorised by power of attorney;

(iv) a liquidator; or

(v) an agent and acts in breach of confidence (i.e. Estate Agent).

Subsection (3) of s.4 provides that a person who picks:

(i) mushrooms (includes any fungus) growing wild on any land, or

(ii) flowers, fruit or foliage from a plant(includes any shrub or tree) growing wild on any land.

does not steal them, unless they deliberately picked such property for reward or for sale or other commercial purpose.

Subsection (4) provides that wild creatures tamed or untamed amount to property for the purposes of theft. However, if a person takes a wild creature which is not tamed or normally kept in captivity or the carcass of such a creature, does not steal them, provided the wide creature is not reduced into possession by or on behalf of another and that possession has not been lost or abandoned.

9. The Meaning of Belonging to Another: Section 5(1)

5.11 In order to sustain a conviction for theft, the prosecution must, as part of the actus reus, prove that the property alleged to have been stolen "belonged to another". In many instances the owner is clearly identifiable and will not be disputed, the prosecution will simply state in the particulars of the offence in the indictment, the name of the owner, to whom the property belonged. If there is a factual dispute over who the property belongs to, then s.5 gives a wide statutory definition of what in the context of theft is meant by belonging to another. Property belongs to any person who has: (i) possession or control of it, or (ii) a proprietary right or interest in it.

10. A Person's Own Property can Belong to Another

5.12 Given the wide application of the definition of property belonging to another, it is quite possible for a person to actually be guilty of theft of his own property in circumstances as confirmed in *R. v Turner (No.2)* [1971] 2 All E.R. 441, in which the defendant took his car to a garage for repair, a few hours later he removed it, without paying the bill and without the garage proprietor's knowledge. The Court of Appeal upheld his conviction for theft and stated that the sole question for the jury was whether the garage proprietor had "possession or control" of the car and that there is no need or justification to qualify these words with civil legal issues of "lien" or "hire purchase" arrangements. The question for the jury is simply whether the person from whom the property is appropriated had at that time possession or control over the property. If yes, then that property belonged to another. The Court of Appeal upheld his conviction for theft acknowledging that the judge was correct to direct the jury that the essential question was did he act dishonestly. There was no ground to qualify the words "possession or control". It is sufficient if it is found that the person from whom the property is appropriated, was at the time in fact in possession or control.

11. Retrieving Lost Golf Balls: Property Belonging to Another

5.13 It is quite common for many who play golf to accept that once they have lost a golf ball it is abandoned and that should someone later retrieve the golf ball to keep it as their own is not guilty of theft, since the golf ball does not belong to another. However, In *Hibbert v McKiernan* [1948] 2 K.B. 162, the Court ruled that where golf balls are lost or abandoned within the area of a golf course, then the balls belong to the golf club on the basis that they have possession and control of any lost golf balls for their own purposes, even if those balls may never be found.

In *Rostron and Collinson* [2002] EWCA Crim 1397, the Court of Appeal approved and applied the principle in *Hibbert v McKiernan* and rejected the appellant's appeal against conviction for stealing golf balls from golf courses and also going equipped to steal. Both appellants were found by the police in diving suits and in possession of a sack containing retrieved golf balls from a lake used as a water hazard. The Court of Appeal although accepting the general proposition of law with regard to lost golf balls, noted that each case will depend on its own facts and on whether there is evidence to establish that the balls do in fact belong to the club itself. Such evidence could arise from the terms of the membership of the club that makes it clear that any balls lost would become the ownership of the club.

12. Property Held in a Trust: Section 5(2)

5.14 Section 5(2) makes it clear that although the property is clearly owned by the person who placed it in the trust, it also includes any person who has a right to enforce the terms of the trust, i.e. a beneficiary of the trust, and that any intention by the trustees to defeat the terms of the trust, will for the purposes of theft amount to an intention to deprive the beneficiary of the property.

13. Property Received Under a Contractual Obligation or Credit Agreement: Section 5(3)

5.15 Section 5(3) specifically provides that for the purposes of theft, if a person receives property from or on account of another person, and under that agreement is under an obligation to that person to "retain and deal with that property or its proceeds in a particular way", then that property still belongs to the other if they act contrary to that obligation. In *R. v Hall* [1973] 1 Q.B. 126, the Court of Appeal, in quashing the appellant's conviction for theft, held that on the facts there was insufficient evidence to establish an obligation to retain and deal for the purposes of s.5(3). The appellant a travel agent having received deposits from clients for air trips to be arranged by him had subsequently paid the money into the firm's account, but did not then arrange the trips and later could not repay the money. The Court stated the money did not belong to the clients and so the appellant had not committed theft. This would amount to a civil breach of contract dispute.

In *R. v Breaks and Huggan* [1998] Crim. L.R. 349, the defendants received insurance premiums from clients, which should have then been paid to the insurance broker but the defendants failed to do this and were therefore charged with theft. The Court of Appeal quashed the appellant's convictions for theft due to misdirection of judge. The Court stated that it was well settled that the expression "obligation to the other to retain and deal" means a legal obligation, which can only arise under the civil law. The contractual obligation in this case did not amount to more than a debt, and therefore could not be stolen. For s.5(3) to apply, it most be proved that there was a legal obligation to kept the property or its proceeds separate from the defendant's other property. It is as a matter of law for the judge to decide whether there is a legal obligation and for the jury to decide on the facts, whether the defendant has failed to fulfill that obligation.

One example of a situation that would engage s.5(3) is where, for instance, an investor decides to place a fixed amount of money into the possession of an investment broker and directs that broker to deal with the money in a particular way, i.e. by stating that they must only invest the money in certain shares. Should the broker ignore that obligation and deal with the money in another unauthorised way, then at that point, the money belongs to the original investor, and should the broker lose the money, they are potentially liable for theft and will not be able to claim that the money belonged to them as under the agreement.

5.16 This is exactly what occurred in *R. v Paul Adrian Smith* [1997] (unreported), where the Court of Appeal affirmed the appellant's conviction of 10 counts of theft in the misuse of funds obtained from elderly clients. The appellant acted as a mortgage broker trading as Intercity Associates. He acted also as an appointed representative under an agency agreement with Guardian Royal Exchange (GRE) to promote and assist elderly clients in an "equity release scheme" which allowed them to raise money, (locked funds) on the security of their homes. To relieve a capital shortage he had, instead of paying the cheques obtained from the elderly clients of which he was under an obligation to invest in a bond from Guardian Royal Exchange, he paid them into his own account. House prices fell where it was then alleged that he stole £136,000 from GRE. The appellant denied acting dishonestly and that, s.5(3) had no application to the facts of this case in that the money did not belong to GRE and that like the travel agent in *Hall* he was entitled to pay the cheques into his bank account and use the money as he chose.

The Court of Appeal rejected this contention since the money from the elderly clients was property, which the appellant received on account of GRE and observed:

> "this appellant unlike the appellant in Hall was bound by a agency agreement, the terms of which are not in dispute, so there were no relevant facts for the jury to find which made the application of s5(3) conditional, and as Edmund Davies LJ said in Hall 'what cannot of itself be decisive of the matter is the fact that the A paid the money into the firm's general trading account.'"

However, in *R. v Dyke and Munro* [2001] Cr.App.R. 30, the appellants were indicted with theft of monies belonging to a person or persons unknown. It was alleged that the appellants had stolen substantial sums of money collected in tins from the public for a children's charity. The Court of Appeal quashed their convictions on the grounds that the indictment was defective, since s.5(3) provided that the person who collected the money was under an obligation to give that money, in accordance with the donor's intention to the charity. This created a trust. In this situation therefore the appellants had not stolen from the donor member of the public as alleged in the indictment, but from the beneficiaries of the charity.

14. Mistake and the Need to Make Restoration: Section 5(4)

5.17 Section 5(4) specifically provides for the situation where a person obtains property due to the mistake of another and is then under an obligation to make restoration of that property, or its proceeds, or its value. To the extent of this obligation the property still belongs to the person entitled to its restoration. If there is an intention not to make restoration, then such an intention will be regarded as an intention to deprive the other of their property. A simple example for the application of s.5(4) is where a person orders a round of drinks in a pub which comes to £7.50, and pays with a £10 note. The bar assistant then mistakenly gives change for a £20, the person who orders the drinks realises the mistake, but says nothing. The person is clearly under an obligation to make restoration of the over change. The over change is property that still belongs to the pub owner, by failing to return the money, could amount to theft provided all other elements are proven.

In *Attorney-General's Reference (No.1 of 1983)* [1985] 1 Q.B. 182, the defendant, a police officer had her bank account credited with £614.11 salary, £74 of which was an overpayment to which she was not entitled in consequence of a mistake by her employer. At trial the judge, having agreed with a defence submission that the overpayment belonged to the bank, not the employer, ordered an acquittal. The Attorney–General sought under s.36 of the Criminal Justice Act 1972, the opinion of the Court of Appeal, on whether the trial judge's ruling was correct in law. The Court of Appeal gave the opinion that the overpayment amounted to a chose in action and therefore amounted to property in s.4(1). This property therefore under s.5(4) belonged to the Metropolitan Police and the defendant was under an obligation to restore the value of the overpayment. Accordingly, the defendant would be guilty of theft if she intended not to make restoration, had appropriated the property, and had acted dishonestly. In *Gilks* [1972] 1 W.L.R. 1341, the court of Appeal held that "obligation" in s.5 must be a *legal* obligation not a *moral* obligation. In this case the appellant, a punter, had been overpaid his winnings. He knew of this, but did not return the money to the bookie. It was held that for the purposes of s.5 he was under no legal obligation to restore the money, as it had been made from a wagering contract which cannot be enforced in contract law since they are based on honour and good faith, i.e. moral not legal obligations.

15. Setting Out the Mens Rea

5.18 The mens rea for the offence of theft consists of two elements each of which the prosecution must prove beyond doubt. The two elements are as follows:

(i) dishonesty, and

(ii) intention to permanently deprive.

We will look at each element in turn.

16. The Meaning of Dishonesty and Section 2

5.19 Section 2 of the Theft Act 1968 provides for several situations where in law, if a person holds a particular belief then they will not have acted dishonestly. The three beliefs are set out as follows:

(i) If the person appropriates property in the belief that they have, in law, the right to deprive the owner of the property either on behalf of themselves, or a third person.

(ii) If the person appropriates property in the belief that they would have had the owner's consent, if the owner knew of the appropriation and the circumstances of it.

An example of this belief is where a person who regularly takes an early morning paper from outside the shop and then later pays. The paper shop owner knows of this taking and the circumstances in which it happens should then the person be charged with theft, they can rely of this belief as evidence to show they have not acted dishonestly.

(iii) If the person appropriates property in the belief that the person to who the property belongs cannot be discovered by taking reasonable steps.

An example of this belief would be where a person comes across a £10 note on the floor and nothing in the way of identifying the owner through reasonable steps. However, if the person sees the money fall out of the owner's pocket, then a reasonable step would be to catch up with the owner and return it, or where a wallet is found, then a reasonable step would be to hand it in to the police. The above three beliefs are based on specific circumstances and that if a defendant relies on one of these belief, whether or not this is an honest person or a dishonest person, is a matter of fact for the jury to decide on the evidence presented. An important point to be aware of is that under s.2(2), it is made clear, that even if a person is willing to pay for property they have appropriated, which belongs to another they may still be acting dishonestly. An example would be where a person takes a CD belonging to a friend and then when found out says they are willing to pay for it but then break down in tears, which leads to the owner refusing to accept that payment.

17. *R. v Ghosh* [1983] Known as the "Ghosh Test of Dishonesty"

5.20 If none of the three beliefs above are in issue, but the defendant still claims that the have not acted dishonesty, then in these circumstances a "*Ghosh* direction" may be given to the jury, which explains when in law a person is dishonest for the purposes of theft.

In *R. v Ghosh* [1982] 1 Q.B. 1053, the Court of Appeal stated that if dishonesty is disputed, the jury should be directed to consider the following two questions in regard to what the defendant did:

(i) whether according to the ordinary standards of reasonable and honest people was what the defendant did dishonest? (This amounts to an objective test.)

If this question is answered yes then the jury must ask the second question,

(ii) did the defendant himself realise that what he was doing was dishonest according to those standards?

If the answer is yes to this question then they are dishonest for the purposes of the offence of offence.

It is important to be aware that the *Ghosh* test does have potential shortcomings and in its application can be misleading, especially when looking at the first objective question. This is potentially vague, since it places emphasis on what each particular jury considers to be the ordinary standards of honest people. Every person has their own standards of honesty in particular circumstances some will be less honest than others. The potential injustice risks to the application of the *Ghosh* test, is clearly seen in the dissenting judgments of their Lordships' opinion in *R. v Hinks*, where there was a risk that the jury may have deemed what could be morally reprehensible behaviour as amounting to dishonestly in theft. In *Atkinson v R.* [2003] EWCA Crim 3031, the Court of Appeal having referred to *R. v Roberts* [1987] 84 Cr.App.R. 117, and *R. v Price* [1990] 90 Cr.App.R. 409, accepted that where dishonestly is alleged, a *Ghosh* direction is not only unnecessary, but also misleading. The *Ghosh* direction should only be given in cases where the defendant might have believed that what they were alleged to have done was in accordance with the ordinary person's idea of honesty, namely subjectively the defendant is contending that they in their own mind believed what they did was not dishonest assessed against the standard of the reasonable and honest person.

18. The Meaning of Intention to Permanently Deprive

5.21 The second element of the mens rea for theft is that it must be proved that the defendant had an intention to permanently deprive the other of the property. Section 6 of the Theft Act 1968 provides a interpretative meaning to the expression. The first part of s.6 provides that where a person who has appropriated property belonging to another does so without meaning the other permanently to lose the property, can still be regarded as intending to permanently deprive, if it is shown that their intention was to treat the property as their own to dispose of it regardless of the other's rights to it.

In *R. v Lloyd* [1985] 81 Cr.App.R. 182, Lord Lane observed that the first part of s.6 is aimed at the situation where a defendant takes property from the owner and then offers them back to the owner for payment. However, in *R. v Fernandes* [1996] 1 Cr.App.R. 175, the Court of Appeal rejected the defence's contention that this gave a limited application to s.6(1) to the taking of property for re-sale to the owner or attempted re-sale. The Court ruled that s.6(1) was expressed in general terms and was not limited to the illustrations given by Lord Lane in *Lloyd* neither did Lord Lane suggested such limitations and that it might apply to a person as in the instant case takes possession or control of an other property (i.e. money) and dishonestly deals with that property for their own purposes and knowing that in doing so, there is a risk of loss of some or all of that property.

It is important to be aware that whether or not a defendant had the necessary intent of permanent deprivation is a question of fact for the jury. The longer the period of depriving the owner of their right to use their property, the stronger the evidence of an intent will be. Of course, the shorter the period, the less likely the defendant formed such an intention. The second part to s.6(1) provides a specific illustration when a person is deemed to have an intention to permanently deprive the owner of the property in the context of borrowing or lending. In this situation a borrowing or lending of property can amount to an intention to permanently deprive, "if but only if, the borrowing or lending is for a period and in circumstances making it equivalent to an outright taking or disposal". This is clearly a question of fact for the jury to determine, but an intention can only be established, if there is sufficient evidence to prove that the period of borrowing was such, as to make it an outright taking or disposal of the property. A simple example would be where a neighbour borrows a lawn mower, moves to another area and takes the lawn mover with them and treats it as theirs and uses it at their disposal with the result that the lawn mover is no longer in the condition it was in when borrowed.

In *R. v Lloyd* [1985] 81 Cr.App.R. 182, the Court of Appeal quashed the appellant's conviction for theft, where he had secretly taken films from the cinema where he worked as a projectionist. These were then passed to a friend who copied them and later returned back to the cinema. The Court of Appeal observed that mere borrowing cannot alone be sufficient to establish the relevant intention, unless the property is returned "in such a changed state that it can truly be said that all its goodness or virtue as gone". On the facts the Court concluded that the film themselves where returned in the same condition as borrowed, and that the period in which the appellant had borrowed the films was insufficient to constitute an outright taking of them.

In *R. v Raphael and Johnson* [2008] EWCA Crim 1014, the Court of Appeal, considering the decision in *Hall* [1848] 1 Den. 381, ruled that the taking of property and then later offering to sell it back to the original owner, even if that offer was "wholly genuine" can amount to an intention to permanently deprive for the purposes of theft.

19. Theft in Sale of Unexpired Travel Ticket

5.22 In *R. v Marshall and Others* [1998] 2 Cr.App.R. 282, the appellants audaciously obtained underground tickets or travel cards from members of the public, passing through the barriers and then re-sold the still remaining valid tickets to other potential customers entering the underground at a discount. The Court of Appeal affirmed the appellants' conviction and rejected the defence's contention that s.6(1) should be narrowly interpreted and confined to the examples given by Lord Lane in *Lloyd*. The Court applied the reasoning in *Fernandez* and ruled that the ticket was property which belonged to London Underground (LU), as stated on the back and that LU had the exclusive right to sell tickets. By doing what the appellants did, they assumed the rights of the owner (LU) and therefore appropriated the ticket in which the appellant's by acquiring and re-selling the ticket had an intention to treat the ticket as their own to dispose of, regardless of LU right to issue the ticket. The fact that at some point LU would have the ticket returned to them, did not negate the intent of the appellants, since the appellant's clearly intended to deprive LU of the profit that would have been made on the sale of a properly purchased ticket by the traveling public.

Another example would be where a person takes a concert ticket from the owner's desk, goes to watch the concert and then returns the ticket to the owner, and then claims that they never intended to deprive the owner of the ticket. To allow this contention would create an absurdity, and as Lord Lane stated in *Lloyd*, the ticket albeit returned is now worthless and that whilst the defendant may never have intended to deprive the owner of the paper ticket itself, they clearly intended to deprive the owner of the chose in action, i.e. the value of it, and that amounts to theft in such circumstances.

20. Section 8 and the Offence of Robbery

5.23 The offence of robbery is contained in s.8 of the Theft Act 1968 and it is important to be aware that robbery is simply an aggravated form of theft, in that what distinguishes robbery from a theft is the use of force or the threat of force. It is this that clearly makes the offence far more serious than a basic theft offence in s.1. Further, robbery can range from something little more than a theft, i.e. a street robbery by snatching a bag right through to an armed robbery in which firearms are used. Section 8 defines robbery as follows:

> "a person is guilty of robbery if he steals, and immediately before or at the time of doing so, and in order to do so, he uses force on any person or puts or seeks to put any person in fear of being then and there subjected to force."

The maximum sentence for robbery is life imprisonment.

21. "Steals" Requires Proof of "Basic s.1 Theft"

5.24 In order for the prosecution to secure a conviction for robbery two elements must be proved:

(i) that the accused committed the offence of basic theft (steals) (prosecution must prove all five elements of the offence of basic theft);

and

(ii) that the aggravated element of force or fear of force was used in order to commit that theft.

It is important to be aware that the prosecution must first prove all the elements of the offence of basic theft. If the prosecution is unable to prove basic theft then there can be no offence of robbery, even if the threat of force or actual force is used against the complainant. On the other hand, if the prosecution are able to prove basic theft, then at this point the defendant is guilty of that offence, to secure a conviction for the more serious offence of robbery, the prosecution must prove the aggravated element of force or fear of force. In *R. v Robinson* [1977] Crim. L.R. 173, the Court of Appeal ruled that for the purposes of honest belief in s.2(1) of the Theft Act 1968, the defendant is only required to show that they held an honest belief that they were entitled to take the property that they believed was owed to them, not an honest belief in the legality of the method used in order to take the property. The Court quashed the appellant's conviction for robbery, since he had held an honest belief that the complainant owed him a debt, even though he knew by using a knife in order to secure its return was a criminal act in itself. For this reason he was not guilty of basic theft as the element of dishonesty was missing. Therefore, with no theft there can be no robbery.

22. Uses Force or Puts or Seeks to Put Any Person in Fear of Force: Actus Reus

5.25 The Theft Act 1968 does not provide a definition of what is meant by force and it is therefore to be given its ordinary and natural meaning. Whether or not what the defendant did amounts to force for the purposes of robbery, is a question of fact to be decided by the jury, using their knowledge, experience and common sense.

In *R. v Dawson* [1976] 64 Cr.App.R. 170, the Court of Appeal made it clear that whether or not force was used is a sole question of fact for the jury, and requires no legal meaning being applied to it. Accordingly, whether a defendant uses some sort of tactic of distraction, or a simple pushing or nudging motion are not legal issues, but form part of the evidence for the jury to decide on whether such incidents amount to force. Likewise in *R. v Clouden* [1987] Crim. L.R. 56, the Court of Appeal took the view that where force is used only to gain possession of property from the victim, still amounts to force used on a person. The defendant did not directly use force against the victim, but instead wrenched the shopping basket from her hands. This amounted to the use of indirect force. Accordingly, the Court of Appeal refused to interfere with the defendant's conviction.

As well as deciding whether the defendant's act amounts to force or the fear of force the act must be directed at "any person". It is clear that this not only includes the actual robbery victim, but any other person, such as a armed robber who enters a bank with a firearm orders customers to the ground and then tells the cashier to hand out the money threatening to kill a customer if they don't, or puts the firearm to the head of a child in a pram and then demands money. Another example would be where an armed gang kidnap the wife and family of a bank manager, tie them up, use violence against them and tell the bank manager if he doesn't open the safe they will be killed.

It is important to be aware that the offence of robbery is not limited to the use of direct or indirect force, it is still sufficient for the offence if the defendant instead puts or seeks to put any person in fear of being then and there subjected to force. The expression "then and there" requires the prosecution to establish evidentially that the act of putting or seeking to any person in fear of force was designed to give the frightened victim the impression that such force would be used almost immediately, based on the realism of the threat and the circumstances in which it is delivered. Again this amounts to a pure question of fact for the jury to decide based on the admissible evidence. It is irrelevant whether force was used or not or that the defendant never in fact intended to use such force. The factual issue is whether the victim was in fear of being subjected there and then to the use of force.

23. Immediately Before or at the Time of Doing So and in Order to Do So: Actus Reus

5.26 It is important to be aware that s.8 makes it clear that the prosecution must prove that the use of force, or putting or seeking to put any person in fear of force, was either immediately before or at time of the stealing and that force or fear of force, used in order to steal from the victim. If the force occurs after the actual offence of theft (stealing) then this will not amount to robbery, or that any force was not used in order to steal. For example A assaults B due to a long standing grudge money falls out of B's pocket of which A decides to take. This may not amount to robbery, since the assault is separate to the offence of theft. It was not used in order to steal.

Accordingly in such circumstances A is not liable for robbery but is liable for two separate offences of assault and theft. Nevertheless, it is important to consider the "continuous act of theft" as applied in *R. v Lockley* [1995] Crim. L.R. 656, in which the defendant took cans of beer from an off license and when approached by the shop owner on leaving the premises he used violence against him. The defendant was found guilty of robbery and appealed on the basis that the force he had used occurred after committing the theft and he could not be guilty of robbery. The court of appeal held, dismissing his appeal that the element of appropriation in the offence of basic theft is a continuing act, that the theft is not complete until the property has been taken from the complainant and that the defendant is physically making off with it. Therefore, any force used upon the complainant during the actus reus of theft, or before the defendant makes good his escape, is sufficient for the offence of robbery. In these circumstances, the question for the jury would be was the defendant still engaged in the act of stealing when he used force against the complainant. If yes then he is guilty of robbery.

24. Mens Rea of Robbery

5.27 Whilst s.8 does not specifically set out a mens rea for the offence, it is implicit within the definition of the offence that the prosecution must prove the use of force or fear of it. To prove this important element would also require proof that the defendant intended to use such force or was reckless by using it, but also that the defendant intended the use of such force for the purposes of stealing from the complainant.

25. Other Possible Offences

5.28 It is important not to look at or approach criminal acts in isolation. If one particular offence cannot be proven there are usually other offences available either as separate offences or as alternatives to the more serious offence. With robbery other offences include assault, criminal damage, blackmail, attempted robbery, threats to kill and firearms charges.

26. The Offence of Burglary: Sections 9 and 10

5.29 The offence of burglary is contained in s.9 of the Theft Act 1968, and replaced the old larceny offence of "breaking and entering". The offence of burglary can be committed, dependant on the state of mind of the accused in two ways. The prosecution will, based on the evidence, either charge the accused with a s.9(1)(a) burglary or alternatively with s.9(1)(b) burglary. Burglary is a somewhat confusing offence, in that the different ways in committing the offence are distinguished based on intent at the point of entry. Further, the offence applies the civil concept of trespass to the commission of the actus reus. It is also important to be aware that the law, especially in regard to drafting the indictment and for the purposes of sentencing, distinguishes between a "dwelling house" burglary with a "commercial premises" burglary. There is a further more serious offence of aggravated burglary contained in s.10.

27. The Section 9(1)(a) Offence

5.30 A person is guilty of a s.9(1)(a) offence if it is proven that they enter a building or part of a building as a trespasser and with intent to commit one or more of several offences:

(i) stealing anything there,

or

(ii) inflicting GBH on any person there,

or

(iii) doing unlawful damage to the building or to anything in it.

The offence of rape originally formed part of the offence of burglary, but was removed by the Sexual Offences Act 2003 (see Sch.7, which came into effect on May 1, 2004 and replaced with a specific wider sexual offence contained in s.63). This creates a new offence: trespass with intent to commit a sexual offence, and provides that a person is guilty of an either way offence if as a trespasser on any premises, they intend to commit a relevant sexual offence and knows that, or is reckless as to whether they are a trespasser. A relevant sexual offence is any of the offences listed in Pt 1 of the Act. This includes rape sexual penetration and sexual assault. Premises means a structure or part of a structure, which in turn means, a tent, vehicle or vessel or other temporary or movable structure. If convicted on indictment, then the maximum sentence is 10 years while a summary conviction will attract a maximum of six months.

28. The Section 9(1)(b) Offence

5.31 Under s.9(1)(b) a person commits this form of burglary if it is proven that having entered a building or part of a building as a trespasser they:

(i) steal or attempts to steal anything from it,

or

(ii) inflict or attempts to inflict GBH on any person in it.

29. The Different Elements between the Two Offences

5.32 It is important to be able to distinguish between the two offences, since in practice the prosecution must decide for which particular offence to charge and draft the indictment on and present their case to that effect. The differences are as follows:

(i) In s.9(1)(a) the actus reus of the offence arises on "enters" combined at that point of entry with a specific intent to commit one of several offences. Whereas for s.9(1)(b) the actus reus occurs when the person "having entered", with no specific mens rea requirement.

(ii) Further under s.9(1)(a) the prosecution can rely on an intent to commit one or more of three possible offences. Whereas under s.9(1)(b), only two offences are capable of being committed, but expressly include attempting to commit such offences.

If the prosecution have strong evidence that when the accused enters a building, they either before and at that point, as a deliberate intent, when in the building to commit one of the three specified offences, then the accused will be charged with s.9(10(a) burglary. If by contrast there are evidential difficulties concerning what the accused's purpose or aim was at the point of entry, then if having entered that building (i.e. on the premises) and either attempts or commits one or both of the two specified offences, then the accused will be for that reason charged with a s.9(1)(b) burglary. The two offences are drafted in wide terms, to ensure that the law encapsulates all possible factual situations that may arise. Parliament also choose not to limit the offence of burglary to stealing, but to widen its meaning to include other offences that can be charge separately as a substantive offence.

30. Actus Reus Common to Both Offences of Burglary

5.33 Common to both s.9 offences is that the prosecution, based on whether the accused "enters" or "having entered", must also prove that this entering was in a building or part of a building as a trespasser. What amounts to a trespasser in the context of burglary was considered by the Court of Appeal in *R. v Collins* [1972] 3 W.L.R. 243, a case with somewhat incomprehensible facts. The complainant was initially asleep, only to be awoken by a naked figure at her bedroom window. Believing this to be a man she was regularly having sex with, she let him in and consented to sexual intercourse with him. However, she later discovered the mistake she had made in that the man was not whom she believed him to be and would not have invited him in to her bedroom for sex, had she known his true identity. The appellant was convicted of burglary with intent to rape, and appealed on the grounds that he was not a "trespasser" and therefore could not have committed burglary as alleged. The Court of Appeal agreed and quashed the appellant's conviction. Edmund Davies L.J., who gave the leading speech, observed that whilst s.9 was passed to remove the technical difficulties of the old breaking and entering offence, Parliament had omitted to provide a meaning as to "trespasser". Given the serious nature of the offence:

> "burglary should be held to require a mens rea in the fullest sense of the phrase: D should only be liable for burglary only if he knowingly trespasses or is reckless as to whether he trespasses or not."

It is clear from *Collins* that the prosecution for the element "trespasser" must prove a mens rea of either:

(i) the defendant knows he is entering as a trespasser, or

(ii) is (subjectively since the House of Lords authority *R. v G* [2004] 1 A.C. 1034) reckless as to whether or not his is unlawfully entering.

31. Entering in Excess of Permission given can Amount to being a Trespasser

5.34 A situation may arise where a person may at first have entered a building with lawful authority or permission from the owner or occupier, but then subsequently decided to exceed that authority or permission and commit one of the specified s.9 offences. In *R. v Jones* [1976] 1 W.L.R. 672, the appellant's father gave his permission for him to enter his bungalow at any time as he pleased. However, the appellant and his friend entered his father's bungalow as permitted and decided to take two TV sets. The father reported the burglary to the police. The appellant appealed against his conviction for burglary on the grounds that the judge had misdirected the jury, by telling them if they had a dishonest intent when entering the building they would be trespassers. The Court of Appeal rejected the appellants' contention that they could not for the purposes of s.9 be trespassers, when they had the owner's permission to enter. James L.J., giving the leading speech, applied the ruling in *R. v Collins* and stated if a person:

> "enters premises of another knowing that he is entering in excess of the permission that has been given to him or being reckless as to whether he is entering in excess of the permission given to him to enter then. Provided the facts are known to the accused which enable him to realize that he is acting in excess of permission given or that he is acting recklessly as to whether he exceeds that permission, then that is sufficient for the jury to decide that he is in fact a trespasser."

32. The Meaning of Entry

5.35 The word "enters" or "entered" is not defined in s.9 and is therefore given its ordinary and natural meaning. It is a question of fact and degree for the jury to decide whether or not a defendant sufficiently enters or entered a building, for the purposes of burglary. Nevertheless in *R. v Brown* [1985] Crim. L.R. 212, the Court of Appeal ruled that where the defendant had put part of his body through a shop window and stole goods this amounted to an effective entry for burglary. Likewise in *R. v Ryan* [1996] Crim. L.R. 320, the Court of Appeal applied the decision in *Brown* and ruled that the appellant's conviction for burglary was safe, since although he had become physically lodged in a window unit, with half his body in the building and his lower half outside the building, this still amounted to entering for the purposes of burglary, even if it is impossible to steal anything, since under s.9(1)(b) attempts to steal are sufficient. It is clear from these two authorities that whether or not a defendant has entered, or enters, is a question of fact for the jury, but that factually an insertion of any part of the body would be sufficient to establish this element to the offence.

33. The Meaning of Building or Part of a Building.

5.36 The Act itself does not define the word "building". Therefore the word is simply given its ordinary and natural meaning. Nevertheless the Court in the old authority of *Stevens v Gourley* (1859) C.B.N.S. 99, gave a general meaning to what amounts to a building as:

> "a structure of considerable size and intended to be permanent or at least to endure for a considerable time".

It would seem therefore, for the s.9 offence, that a building has at least to be a structure that as some degree of permanence. In *R. v Walkington* (1979) 1 W.L.R. 1169, the Court of Appeal dismissed the appellant's appeal against conviction for a s.9(1)(a) burglary. The appellant had entered a Debenham's store in London, he then entered a three-sided moveable rectangular counter not fixed to the floor, where he opened the till intending to steal its contents, but the till was empty. The appellant had sought to argue that he could not be guilty of burglary since the sale counter could not form part of a building. The Court of Appeal rejected this contention and ruled that the store gives customers an implied consent to enter their store to pursue goods for purchase they do not give consent to any prohibited area. The appellant was therefore a trespasser, and that the sales counter as a structure had sufficient physical demarcation for the jury to determine whether or not it amounted to part of a building, of which the public need not have agreed access.

34. The Mens Rea of Burglary

5.37 The mens rea for a s.9(1)(a) burglary offence consists of the following: an intention on the part of a trespasser to do the following:

(i) steal anything in a building or part of it, or

(ii) inflict Grievous Bodily Harm on any person in it, or

(iii) do unlawful damage to the building or anything in it.

The prosecution must prove a specific intent of the defendant, in that at the point of entering the building, or part of a building the defendant had an intent to carry out one of the three specific offences listed in the section. In *R.* v *Walkington* [1979] 1 W.L.R. 1169, The Court of Appeal made it clear that a defendant cannot claim he only had a conditional intention, in that he only an intention to steal if in fact there was something to steal. The Court ruled that a reading of s.9(1) simply requires the prosecution to prove and for the jury to be satisfied, so as to be sure that the defendant:

> "that at the moment of entering he intended to steal anything in the building or that part of it, the fact that there was nothing in the building worth his while to steal seems to us immaterial. He nevertheless has the intent to steal ... to hold otherwise would be to make a nonsense of this part of the Act and cannot have been the intention of the legislature at the time when the Theft Act 1968 was passed."

The second specific offence is that of "inflicts" grievous bodily harm, which would suggest that this is restricted to a s.20 offence. However, since it was held in *R. v Mandair* [1995] 1 A.C. 208, by the House of Lords that the word cause includes inflicts it is submitted that if a defendant has an intention to inflict upon somebody in the building GBH, then this includes either a s.18 or a s.20 offence under the Offences Against the Person Act 1861. However, it is important to note that reckless infliction of GBH is not sufficient and the defendant will have to be charged with the substantive assault. Likewise, if the injury amounts to a s.47 or common assault, then the defendant cannot be charged with burglary. In these circumstances, they will have to be charged with the separate assault offences. Also, it is important to note that if a defendant enters a building with the intention of causing GBH or does, then the prosecution is likely to proceed by charging the defendant with the actual s.18 offence, as opposed to burglary. While this offence is available, it is rarely used in this situation.

The third specific offence of criminal damage is contained in s.1 of the Criminal Damage Act 1971. The word unlawful is used in the sense that it is not an offence for a person to damage property belonging to himself under the basic criminal damage offence. If the offence is aggravated criminal damage, then it is still unlawful to damage property, whether it belongs to the defendant or not, if the damage endangers the life of another. It is also important to be aware that there exists a specific defence of lawful excuse to an offence of criminal damage in s.5 of the Criminal Damage Act 1971. For a s.9(1)(b) burglary offence, the prosecution are not required to prove any specific intent, but they are required to prove the mens rea for the specific offences listed in the section for the offence, namely steals or attempts to steal. This would require proof of the basic s.1 theft and the mens rea for that offence attempted stealing is an offence under the Criminal Attempts

Act 1981. The third offence of inflicts or attempts to inflict GBH clearly includes a s.18 offence and also the s.20 offence, which, in contrast to an offence under s.9(1)(a), will include reckless infliction of GBH.

35. Section 10 and the Offence of Aggravated Burglary

5.38 Section 10 provides that a person who commits the primary offence of burglary contained in s.9 and in the course of committing that offence has with them one or more of the specified items listed, to assist them, shall be guilty of aggravated burglary.

The statutory specified items are as follows:

(i) Any firearm or imitation firearm, weapon of offence

"Firearm" includes an airgun or air pistol, and "imitation firearm" means anything which has the appearance of being a firearm, whether capable of being discharged or not.

(ii) Weapon of offence

"Weapon of offence" means any article made or adapted for use for causing injury to or incapacitating a person, or intended by the person having it with them for such use.

(iii) Any explosive

"Explosive" means any article manufactured for the purpose of producing a practical effect by explosion, or intended by the person, having it with them for that purpose.

36. The Mens Rea for Aggravated Burglary

5.39 Section 10 and the issue of what must be proved by the prosecution in regard to mens rea for the offence, was considered in *R. v Stones* [1989] W.L.R. 156. The appellant was caught with a kitchen knife within the vicinity of a house burglary. When questioned, he claimed it was for self-defence, not to assist in the burglary. He was convicted of aggravated burglary and appealed. Dismissing his appeal, the Court of Appeal ruled that in order to commit the s.10 offence, it must be shown that the defendant *knew* he was carrying a knife and that his *intention* was to use it, even if he did not do so. From this decision it is clear that not only must the prosecution need to show mens rea for the basic burglary offence, they must also establish intention for the more serious aggravated form of burglary also.

Further, in *R. v Kelly* [1993] 97 Cr.App.R. 245 the appellant had entered a dwelling house using a screwdriver to gain entry. He was disturbed by the occupants whilst stealing a video recorder of which he left the house in one hand and the screwdriver in the other. On appeal against his conviction for aggravated burglary, the appellant contended that the expression "has with him" should be interpreted to require the prosecution to prove that the defendant had with him the weapon of offence with intent to cause injury, before the need arose for him to use the weapon. This was rejected by the Court of Appeal in its entirety who considered itself bound by the earlier decision in *R. v O'Leary* [1986] 82 Cr.App.R. 341, in which it was held:

> "that under this particular charge, the time at which the defendant must be proved to have had with him a weapon of offence to make him guilty of aggravated burglary was the time at which he actually stole."

Conversely in *R. v Klass* [1998] 1 Cr.App.R. 453, the Court of Appeal quashed the appellant's conviction for aggravated burglary and substituted one of s.9 burglary, when the appellant and another man used a piece of pole to break into a caravan. At the time of doing, the occupier came out, from whom they then demanded money, but he did not have any. They hit him with the pole and repeatedly hit him as he ran away. The Court of Appeal first noted that a s.10 offence can be committed in a joint enterprise by a co-accused who does not have the weapon or indeed uses it, or by a person who aids and abets the offence. Nevertheless, the Court adopted a purposive approach to s.10 by stating that:

> "the gravamen of this offence is entry into the building with a weapon. The purpose of the section is to deter people from taking weapons into buildings whilst committing burglary. The fact that a getaway driver has a weapon with him in the car would not, in our judgment, be sufficient to turn an offence of burglary into one of aggravated burglary."

It is clear from these three authorities, if a defendant has a weapon of offence, either before entering the building with an intent to use it to gain entry, or as in *O'Leary* picks up a knife from the kitchen, the prosecution have only to prove that the defendant had the weapon of offence at the time at which they embark on the stealing, with an intention to use it, even if they don't. Nevertheless, the defendant must enter with the weapon.

37. Recent Possession Evidence as Proof of Substantive Offence

5.40 If the defendant is found in possession of goods or other items from the theft, robbery or burglary soon after the offence was committed, then in accordance with authorities such as *R. v Seymour* 38 Cr.App.R. 68, and *R. v Smythe* 72 Cr.App.R. 8, the judge can in law give to the jury a recent possession direction, in that the jury are entitled to draw an inference from the fact that the defendant, by being in actual possession of the stolen property, was soon after the alleged offence, the actual offender of the theft, robbery or burglary.

Chapter Six

PROPERTY OFFENCES PART 2: HANDLING STOLEN GOODS, BLACKMAIL AND FRAUD

1. The Offence of Handling Stolen Goods

6.01 The offence of handling stolen goods is defined in s.22 of the Theft Act 1968. It is an important offence in the sense that it is treated more seriously than that of basic theft in terms of punishment, with a possible sentence of imprisonment on conviction on indictment not exceeding 14 years. The reason for this is based on public policy, with the clear assumption that if you severely punish and deter the person who is prepared to dispose of the fruits of the thief, then the thief cannot operate without a network of those who handle the goods, thereby making it difficult for them to operate and in theory at least, reduce the commission of theft offences. An interesting side note is s.23 which creates a summary offence committed by anybody who by way of public advertisement seeks the return of goods stolen in return for money or immunity from prosecution.

2. The Meaning of Goods

6.02 Section 24(1) provides that on a jurisdictional point the goods (defined in s.34(2)(b) as including money and every other description of property except land) can be the subject of a theft in England and Wales or elsewhere. Accordingly, it matters not in which country the goods were stolen, for the purposes of the offence, if the handler resides in England and Wales the offence is still committed.

The first important point to be aware of is that the goods which are alleged to be handled by the defendant must in terms of the actus reus of the offence, be proved to be stolen in the first instance. If the prosecution cannot prove that the goods are in fact stolen, then the defendant will need to be charged with the offence of attempted handling stolen goods (see *R. v Shivpuri* [1987] A.C. 1). In addition, s.24(4) gives an extended meaning to the word "stolen", its effect is that for the purpose of the offence of handling, goods are to be regarded; stolen, not only if they have been the subject of theft as defined in s.1, but also if they have been obtained by blackmail or by fraud as provided by Sch.1 to the Fraud Act 2006.

To avoid any narrow application of the meaning of goods, s.24(2) provides that for the purposes of the offence, any other goods proved to represent or have at any time represented either directly or indirectly the original stolen goods *in the hands of the thief* or parts of them will constitute goods stolen. This covers the situation where the thief disposes of, or realises the goods into other goods, and further covers the situation where the handler disposes of or realises the goods being handled into other goods. For example: a thief A steals a flat screen TV and swops it for an X Box, and then sells this to B the handler who then swops it for a football match ticket. In *R. v Forsyth* [1997] 2 Cr. App.R. 299, the Court of Appeal ruled that in the hands of the thief was wide enough to mean in the possession or under the control of the thief and not literally in their hands. Important in this situation is the application of s.24(3) which expressly provides that goods cease to be stolen if (i) they are restored to the victim or to the other lawful possession or custody (i.e. the police), or (ii) where the person claiming entitlement losses their right to restitution of the goods from the theft.

3. The Actus Reus of the Offence

6.03 Provided there is evidence that establishes the goods to have been stolen then assuming that the defendant has the necessary mens rea they will be guilty of handling if (otherwise than in the course of the stealing) (which means that the offence cannot be committed during the act of appropriation of stealing), they:

(i) receive stolen goods,

(ii) arrange to receive stolen goods,

or

(iii) undertake or assist in one or more of four specified prohibited acts: (1) retention, (2) removal, (3) disposal or (4) realisation of the stolen goods by or for the benefit of another,

or

(iv) arrange to act as in (iii).

The prohibited conduct in the context of the offence is deliberately wide and needs to be in order to cover all possible outcomes of what might happen when goods are stolen, or passed into the hands of the handler. In particular, (iii) is wide and covers the situation where the handler agrees with or helps another by retaining (storing) or removing (transporting) or disposing (destroying, dumping, giving away or transforming stolen goods i.e. melting down) or realising (cashing a stolen cheque).

4. The Meaning of "by or for the Benefit of Another"

6.04 The prosecution must prove that the defendant's involvement in the specified prohibited acts was "by or for the benefit of another person" In using the word "by" this means that another is physically participating in the prohibited acts and the defendant simply assists. On the other hand, in using the words "for the benefit of another", this means that the defendant themselves are undertaking to participate in any of the prohibited acts.

This statutory expression came to be considered by the House of Lords in *R. v Bloxham* [1983] A.C. 109, in regard to the situation where an innocent purchaser of a motor car subsequently realises that it is stolen and so decides to sell it on cheap. The question which arose was whether in such circumstances the seller, now knowing or believing the car to be stolen, is guilty of handing the stolen car, if when they sell the car on they do so by undertaking, or assisting in its disposal or realisation by or for the benefit of the new purchaser.

On this point the House of Lords, allowing the appeal against conviction, ruled that a person who sells stolen goods does not assist the buyer to dispose of it since the buyer does not dispose of it, nor does the seller undertake the realisation or disposal for the benefit of another as they sell it for their own benefit. The buyer benefits from the purchase, but not from any realisation in the goods. In the context of the offence, the purchaser on any sensible analysis does not constitute "another person" since their act of purchase cannot be described as a disposal or realisation of the goods by him. Lord Bridge stated that the critical words in the provision of "undertakes ... their ... disposal or realisation ... for the benefit of another" cannot be construed in isolation, but must be construed in their context.

It would require the court to give a strained meaning to the statutory language to hold that A, who sells his own goods to another B amounts to an act of disposal or realisation of the goods for the benefit of B. If there are any ambiguities in the construction of this expression, then in the opinion of Lord Bridge, a narrow construction is to be preferred when dealing with an ambiguous provision in a criminal statute. It is plain from this decision that a seller does not sell goods "for the benefit of" his purchaser, unless they are acting as an agent for another. The House of Lords was further fortified in its decision by reference to s.3(2) which protects an innocent purchaser from being liable for theft if acting in good faith.

In *R. v Gingell* [1999] 163 J.P. 648, the Court of Appeal ruled that on a plain meaning of the expression "of another", this cannot logically include a co-defendant. If a defendant is charged with others with handling a stolen car and the prosecution case is presented on the basis that the defendant is handling the goods for the benefit of their co-accused, any conviction will be unsafe. The word "another" in the context of the offences means somebody other than a co-defendant.

5. The Mental Element to the Offence

6.05 The prosecution are required to prove that the defendant either (i) knows, or (ii) believes that the goods are stolen goods at the time when they do the prohibited act which constitutes handling. In regard to either undertaking or assisting, the knowledge or belief can arise during the act of retention, disposal, removal or realisation, and if the defendant continues with that knowledge or belief, then they have the mens rea. Whereas, for receiving, it must be proved that the knowledge or belief existed at that time, otherwise no criminal liability arises. The third mental element is like that for all theft related offences, that of dishonestly which if in issue, the *Ghosh* test will apply.

6. The Meaning of "Knows or Believes"

6.06 There have been several authorities expressing how best to sum up to a jury instances when a defendant knows or believes (see *Atwal v Massey* [1971] 56 Cr.App.R. 6 and *R. v Hall* [1985] 81 Cr.App.R. 260). However, the Court of Appeal in *R. v Forsyth* [1997] 2 Cr.App.R. 299, having considered the authorities, felt that the suggested direction in *Hall* was cumbersome in distinguishing between mere suspicion and knowledge or belief. The better approach is to adopt what was said in *R. v Moys* [1984] 79 Cr.App.R. 72, by Lord Lane:

> "the question is a subjective one and it must be proved that the defendant was aware of the theft or that he believed the goods to be stolen. Suspicion that they are stolen, even coupled with the fact that he shut his eyes to the circumstances, is not enough, although these matters may be taken into account by the jury when deciding whether or not the necessary knowledge or belief existed."

Beldam L.J. in *Forsyth* observed that "the ordinary meaning of belief is the mental element of a fact as true or existing". In other words, the jury must be satisfied that there is actual knowledge or belief, not just suspicion. Each case will be different and the judge will need to tailor their summing up on what is meant by knows or believes to the particular facts presented in the evidence to the case. It is better to avoid any elaborations on the distinction between what is and what is knowledge, belief or suspicion (see also *R. v Adinga* [2003] EWCA Crim 3201).

7. Previous Convictions

6.07 Section 27 of the Theft Act 1968 provides that where a person is being proceeded against for an offence of handling stolen goods and not any other offence, then evidence of previously handling stolen goods in the last 12 months from the offence charged is admissible to prove they knew or believed the goods to be stolen. Additionally, provided seven days' notice is given to prove the conviction, evidence that they have within the last five years been convicted of theft or handling stolen goods is admissible at trial for the same reason. The purpose of this provision is to allow a jury to draw an inference that if the defendant claims lack of knowledge or belief then the fact that he has recently handled stolen goods suggests that the defendant must have known or believed on the occasion now alleged.

The section came to be considered by the House of Lords in *R. v Hacker* [1994] 1 W.L.R. 1659, where the Court rejected a restrictive interpretation of the provision and held that read together with s.73(2) of PACE 1984, s.27 allows the admission of not only the certificate of the previous conviction(s) but also the evidence relating to the type of goods involved in those convictions which are the same or similar to the goods forming part of the current charge. In this case it was a Ford RS Turbo (*R. v Fowler* [1988] 86 Cr.App.R. 219).

8. Recent Possession and "Otherwise in the Course of Stealing"

6.08 Similar to the offence of burglary, the prosecution may seek to rely on doctrine of recent possession to prove the offence of handling stolen goods, whereby the jury are told that if the defendant is charged with receiving goods that have recently been stolen, then in the absence of any reasonable explanation they may find them guilty of handing the goods (see *R. v Abramovitch* [1916] 11 Cr.App.R. 45). Further, in *R. v Cash* [1985] 1 Q.B. 801, the Court of Appeal, approving the application of recent possession evidence, ruled that when relied upon by the prosecution there is no requirement to prove that the defendant was not the thief or the burglar or fraudster (i.e. otherwise in the course of stealing). To place such an additional burden upon the prosecution would be to defeat the very object of recent possession evidence.

If there is no issue raised at trial as to whether the defendant had done the original stealing, then the judge does not need to give a direction, the jury can properly assume that the defendant came into possession of the goods otherwise than in the course of stealing. To do so would be wrong and indeed confusing to the jury. If it is raised as an issue, then a direction will need to be given. For instance, if the defendant is discovered with the goods within a very short time of the stealing, then the jury will need to decide if the defendant is the actual person who did the stealing or infer from the recent possession that they where handling. If the only count on the indictment is handling stolen goods and the jury are satisfied the defendant was not handling, then they must acquit.

In these circumstances the prosecution will need to decide whether to charge with theft, burglary or fraud, with alternative counts of handling. If there is a time lapse between the stealing and the handling offence, then a judge is likely to leave only the handling offence to the jury. In *R. v Bosson* [1999] Crim. L.R. 596, the Court of Appeal commented on not confusing matters by overloading the indictment. If the prosecution seek to present their case on theft by a second appropriation, i.e. the goods having been stolen once or stolen again by the defendant, in these circumstances, it is better to leave the possibility of an alternative count of handling to theft until all the evidence has been concluded and then make a decision as to whether to leave the count or discharge the jury from giving a verdict. If the prosecution feel that the defendant is either the initial thief or the second thief, then two counts of theft on the indictment is permissible, but duplicity most be avoided and the defendant must know precisely what is being alleged.

9. The Offence of Blackmail

6.09 The offence of blackmail constitutes a serious indictable only offence carrying a sentence of imprisonment not exceeding 14 years as contained in s.21. This provides that the offence is committed if the prosecution can prove the actus reus of the making of any unwarranted demand with menaces coupled with the mens rea of doing so with a view to gain for themselves or another or with intent to cause a loss to another. Further, there is a presumption that a demand with menaces will be unwarranted unless the defendant(blackmailer) can show evidentially they did so in the subjective belief:

(i) that they had reasonable grounds for making a demand; and

(ii) that the menaces were a proper means of them having to reinforce a demand that was reasonable. Once this is raised then it is for the prosecution to prove beyond doubt no such belief could exist.

To ensure the wide application of the offence s.21(2) provides expressly that the nature of the act or indeed an omission is irrelevant, as is the particular action taken by the blackmailer as forming part of the menaces. For instance, A has been having a elicit affair with a prominent celebrity, is then rejected and decides to demand a series of payments which, if not forthcoming, will lead them to take action by informing the media. This would clearly amount to an improper threat. However, to simply publish the scandal on its own would not. Gain or loss for the purposes of the offence is defined in s.34 as meaning in money or other property, either temporary or permanent. Gain can include keeping what the blackmailer already as and loss includes not obtaining what the blackmailer expected to get.

The terms of the offence are deliberately left silent, menaces is exactly that, a serious or significant threat. In terms of belief it was suggested in *R. v Harvey* [1980] 72 Cr.App.R. 139, by the Court of Appeal that a threat made knowing it to be criminally unlawful would not amount to an proper means of enforcing the demand. Always consider the possibility of attempted blackmail. Another similar offence is the frequent demand for payment made by a creditor of a debtor which are calculated to subject the debtor or members of their family or household to alarm, distress or humiliation. This is a summary offence found in s.40 of the Administration of Justice Act 1970.

10. A New Framework for Fraud Offences

6.10 The Fraud Act 2006 received the Royal Assent on November 8, 2006 and the whole Act came into effect on January 15, 2007. The Act itself is as a result of the recommendations made by the Law Commission in its report on *Fraud* Law Com. No.276, to provide a modern and comprehensive framework of new offences relating to fraud. The proposals of the Commission were considered by way of consultation with interested parties through the Home Office Consultation Paper *Fraud Law Reform* (May 2004). Schedule 1 to the Act abolishes the previous offences contained in s.15 of the Theft Act 1968, obtaining property by deception, s.15A obtaining a money transfer by deception, s.16 obtaining pecuniary advantage by deception, s.20(2) procuring the execution of a valuable security by deception. In the Theft Act 1978, the offence of obtaining services by deception and the evasion of liability by deception offences in s.2 are also abolished. It is important to remember that any allegation of deception prior to January 15, 2007 will need to be charged as one of the old offences, so it is still important to have an awareness of these offences. However, as time passes this will become less significant and for this reason these old offences will not be discussed.

11. Section 1 Fraud

6.11 Section 1 of the Fraud Act 2006 (FA 2006) provides that the offence of fraud can be committed in one of three situations, as set out in ss.2 to 4. For the purposes of classification the offence of fraud constitutes an either way offence, and on summary conviction a sentence of 12 months' imprisonment and/or a fine of £5,000, whilst a conviction on indictment can attract a sentence of imprisonment not exceeding 10 years and or a fine.

12. Fraud by False Representation

6.12 Section 2 sets out the first situation in which the offence of fraud can be committed. This provides that if a person makes a dishonest false representation with the intention of making a gain for themselves or another or to cause loss or the exposure to a risk of such loss to another is guilty of fraud. In regard to what amounts to a representation, the prosecution must prove that this relates to any fact or law and includes the state of mind of its maker or indeed any other person. This is clearly very wide and can either be made expressly or by implication, in any form or any system or device designed to receive, convey or respond to communications. This would seem to clarify the previous uncertainty about whether a person could deceive a machine.

For the representation to be false, the prosecution will need to establish that it was either untrue or misleading and the author of it knows that it is, or that it might be. The mens rea of this category of the offence consists of three elements (i) dishonesty, (ii) intention, and (iii) knowledge. The actus reus is that of (i) representation, (ii) make a gain, or (iii) cause a loss.

13. Fraud by Failing to Disclose Information

6.13 Section 3 sets out the second situation in which the offence of fraud can be committed and provides that a dishonest failure to disclose information to another, where the defendant is under a legal duty to do so and their intention in that failure is to make a gain or cause a loss or an exposure to such a loss, they are guilty of the offence. The mens rea is that of dishonesty and intention, whilst the actus reus amounts to an omission in the failure to provide information that they have a legal duty to disclose and from which a gain is made, or a loss is suffered. The Act does not define what constitutes a legal duty. This will fall to be determined at trial against the particular facts of the case, with particular reference to the Law Commission Report. Examples of when a legal duty arises includes a duty created by statute, or under either oral or written contracts including contracts of utmost good faith (insurance contracts), or from the implied or expressed terms of a contract generally, or a custom arising out of a trade or market, or where there is a fiduciary relationship between the parties (i.e. agent and principal). The explanatory notes to the Act give two classic examples: the withholding of information by a solicitor from his client in order to gain money or other property, or the withholding of detrimental medical information from an insurance company.

14. Fraud by Abuse of Position

6.14 Section 4 sets out the third and final situation and provides that if the defendant dishonestly abuses a position of trust in which it is expected of them to safeguard rather than act against the financial interests of another they are guilty of fraud, if by abusing that position, they intended to make a gain, or cause a loss or the exposure to such a loss of another. Section 4(2) provides specifically that the abuse can occur either through a positive act or by an omission to act. The mens rea is that of dishonesty and intention, while the actus reus is the act or omission or abuse. The explanatory notes to the Act make reference to the examples in the Law Commission Report as to when somebody would be in a position of trust. These include the relationship between trustee and beneficiary, director and company, professional person and client, agent and principal, employer and employee, or even between partners, in the context of the family or through voluntary work, "or in any context where the parties are not at arm's length". The report makes the point of resorting to the civil law concept of fiduciary duty in order to give assistance in deciding whether a person is in a position of trust. Whilst this is a matter of fact, it may become necessary for the judge to make a ruling in a particular case whether such a relationship subsists or not.

Two clear examples given in the explanatory notes are obvious and rightly culpable, where an employee at an IT company clones software with the intention of selling it for gain and to cause loss. The other example is where a carer for the elderly or vulnerable obtains a power of attorney or otherwise gains access to such a person's account or other property and makes transfers.

15. The Meaning of "Gain" and "Loss" and "Dishonesty"

6.15 Section 5 gives a statutory meaning to the words gain and loss in the context of the three situations in which the offence of fraud can be committed. First, the gain or the loss is limited to money or other property. However, this can be either permanent or transitory. Property like its predecessor is widely defined and includes real and personal property, things in action (i.e. cheques) and other intangible property (such as gas, electricity, or company shares). A gain for the purposes of the offence covers the situation where the defendant is able to keep the money or property they already have, as well as the benefit of gaining that money or property. Conversely, a loss amounts to not receiving what should have been received as well as losing the benefit of the money or property that a person already has. This would seem to raise no issue of ownership, if the person has it and it is lost through a fraud that is a loss whether they owned it or not.

The Act deliberately does not define what is meant by dishonesty and the explanatory notes to the Act state clearly that if dishonesty is in issue then the *Ghosh* test is to be used.

16. Obtaining Services Dishonestly

6.16 Section 11 creates a new offence to replace the old offence of obtaining a service by deception in s.1 of the Theft Act 1978. A person is guilty of the new offence if by doing a dishonest act either for themselves or another, they obtain a service. The expression "service" is not specifically defined but to be guilty, the service must be made available on the basis that payment has been, is being, or will be made for in respect of the service being provided, and the defendant knows that such payment is required or might be required, but intends by obtaining the service to avoid making payment for them at all or not in full. The explanatory notes give the example of this offence being committed by somebody who climbs a wall and watches a sports game without paying or where a person inserts a decoder in the television device to access cable or sky free of charge. The offence is classified as an either way offence with a 12-month sentence of imprisonment and or a £5,000 fine on summary conviction, while on conviction on indictment a sentence of imprisonment not exceeding five years and or a fine.

17. Preventative Offences

6.17 Section 6, like "going equipped", is a preventative offence, and captures criminal conduct that falls short of more than merely preparatory conduct needed for a conviction of criminal attempts. The offence is committed if it is proved that the defendant has in their possession or under their control any article for use in the course of or in connection with any fraud. This offence is purposively wide and covers the very early stages right up to the threshold for attempted fraud. The offence amounts to an either way offence with 12 months' imprisonment and or a fine of £5,000 on summary conviction, whilst a conviction on indictment will attract a sentence not exceeding five years and or a fine. In *R. v Ellames* [1974] Cr.App.R. 7, the Court of Appeal, in regard to the offence of going equipped, ruled that the prosecution are not obliged to prove an intention to use the article in a specific burglary, theft or cheat, it being sufficient to prove a general intention to commit any burglary, theft or cheat, and that intention can cover the article being used by some other person.

Section 7 makes it an offence for a person to make, adapt, supply or offer to supply any article provided it is proved they have the mens rea of knowing it is designed or adapted for the use in the course of or in connection with a fraud offence or they intend it to be used to commit, or assist in the commission of a fraud offence. This offence has an actus reus that covers (i) makes, (ii) adapts, (ii) and supplies. In terms of supply the prosecutor will need to have in mind the decision in *Fisher v Bell* [1961] 1 Q.B. 394, and frame the charge to supply and not offers to supply if there is an issue over whether the person is not in fact offering but inviting others to make offers to him. The mens rea requires the proof of knowledge or intention. The meaning of knowing is likely to be the same as with that in handling stolen goods and other statutes, which means that the prosecution will need to prove a belief. A mere suspicion is not sufficient.

18. The Offence of Making off Without Payment

6.18 Although the Fraud Act replaces the bulk of the offences contained in the Theft Act 1978, s.3 remains in place. This provides that a person who knowing that payment on the spot for any goods supplied or service done is required or expected from him, dishonestly makes off without having paid as required or expected and with intent to avoid payment of the amount due shall be guilty of an offence. This is classified as an either way offence with a sentence of imprisonment not exceeding two years on conviction on indictment or six months and/or a fine of £5,000.

To secure a conviction for this offence the prosecution must prove the following:

(i) that the defendant in fact made off without making payment on the spot; (actus reus) together with,

(ii) the following mental elements of (mens rea);

(a) knowledge that payment on the spot was required or expected of them; and
(b) dishonestly; and
(c) intent to avoid payment (of the amount due).

The purpose of this offence is very clear, it exists to capture those who go into a restaurant, order a meal and leave intentionally to avoid payment. It is not designed to criminalise those who have had a meal and refuse to pay because of incompetent service or poor quality of food. It is designed to capture those who fill their fuel tank and drive off without paying, or use a taxi, but at the end of the journey jump out without paying.

19. Dishonestly Makes Off: Civil Debt or Criminal Liability?

6.19 Undoubtedly with this offence, in certain circumstances, there can arise a fine factual distinction between what amounts to a civil debt owed in terms of a breach of contract and thus attracting only civil liability with that a dishonest avoidance of payment attracting criminal liability. It is for this reason that the prosecution is required to prove strictly three different mental elements to secure a conviction, namely knowledge, dishonestly and intent. If any are missing then the offence is unproven and must fail. In *R. v Brooks* [1982] 76 Cr.App.R. 266, it was held that the expression "dishonestly makes off" is straightforward for a jury to consider and no elaboration is needed as to what may or may not be "making off" from the judge.

Nevertheless the fine distinction between civil and criminal liability is well illustrated in *R. v Allen* [1985] A.C. 1029, in which the appellant had left a hotel he had stayed at without paying his bill. At trial the judge refused to leave to the jury the contention raised by the defence that he could not at that time pay the money owed, but that with money which was due to him shortly, he intended to return and settle in full. The House of Lords quashed his conviction on the grounds that the judge was wrong to refuse to allow the defendant's explanation to be put before the jury and held that the prosecution must prove that the defendant intended to permanently to avoid payment altogether and not merely an attempt to delay or defer payment.

Similarly in *R. v Vincent* [2001] 2 Cr.App.R. 150, the appellant had stayed at two hotels in Windsor and had left both hotels without paying the full bill, but had made a part payment at the second hotel. The appellant claimed that he had reached an agreement with each hotel to postpone payment and settle the bill later. The issue on appeal was whether when the defendant left the hotel, payment was at that time "required or expected from him" and therefore whether that requirement or expectation was defeated by the financial arrangement made between the defendant and the hotel proprietor before he left, even if that agreement had been dishonestly obtained by the defendant, since he had no intention to pay.

The Court of Appeal held, quashing the conviction, that an agreement made before payment is required or expected of the defendant is capable of defeating the expectation of payment and therefore no offence can be committed. The words "made off" suggests some surreptitious departure, (leaving without anybody knowing) and that s.3 does not require or permit an analysis of whether the agreement actually made was obtained by deception:

> "If the expectation is defeated by an agreement, it cannot be said to exist. The fact that the agreement was obtained dishonestly does not reinstate the expectation."

Nevertheless, it is clear on the plain wording of the new offence of obtaining a service dishonestly that the conduct of the two appellants above may be caught. However, to ensure the distinction between civil and criminal liability, the prosecution must prove for the new offence the three mental elements of knowledge, intention and the all-important requirement of dishonesty. It is not necessarily being dishonest, if a person defers payment, for instance.

20. Other Offences

6.20 Section 13 creates the offence of abstracting of electricity. This offence is committed if it proved that the defendant did without due authority the actus reus of causes to be wasted or diverted, any electricity, together with the mens rea of being dishonest. This amounts to an indictable offence which carries an sentence of imprisonment not exceeding five years. It is not proposed to discuss them but other similar offences that may be encountered are found in the Forgery and Counterfeiting Act 1981 and the Social Security Administration Act 1992, as amended by the Social Security Fraud Act 1994.

Chapter Seven

PROPERTY OFFENCES PART 3: CRIMINAL DAMAGE

1. Introduction

7.01 The offences relating to either damaging or destroying property are contained in the Criminal Damage Act 1971 (CDA 1971). The purpose of this Act was to replace the old offences of "malicious damage", contained in the Malicious Damage Act 1891 and to provide a modern comprehensive range of offences that are simple to apply in practice. Within the CDA 1971 there are several different offences of criminal damage which identify the differing degrees of culpability, based on the different methods in which the offence can be committed as follows:

Simple Criminal Damage

7.02 This offence is committed when a person without lawful excuse, destroys or damages property belonging to another, intentionally or recklessly; s.1(1) Criminal Damage Act 1971. Although this offence is classified as an either way offence, with a maximum sentence of 10 years on conviction on indictment, it is also a relevant offence for the purposes of s.43 of the Anti-social Behavour Act 2003, as amended by s.28 of the Clean Neighnourhoods and Environment Act 2005. If the offence is low level graffiti or fly-posting then an enforcement officer employed by the Local Authority or a CSO can, provided they have reason to believe that a person had committed simple criminal damage, offer them the opportunity so as to avoid a conviction to accept a penalty notice of £75 to be paid within 14 days.

Under s.48 a local authority can serve a "graffiti removal notice" on any person who is responsible for a relevant surface area as defined in subsection 9 that as been defaced by graffiti which is detrimental to the amenity of the area. The notice requires the named person to remove, clear or otherwise remedy the defacement within a period of not less than 28 days of the notice being served.

Racially Aggravated Criminal Damage

7.03 Section 30 of the Crime and Disorder Act 1998, creates the offence of racially-aggravated criminal damage. To prove this offence the prosecution must first prove the elements of s.1(1) criminal damage, and secondly that the offence was racially aggravated within the meaning contained in s.28 of the Crime and Disorder Act 1998. If convicted for this more serious offence on indictment, the maximum sentence is 14 years' imprisonment.

Aggravated Criminal Damage

7.04 This offence is committed when a person destroys or damages property belonging to themselves or another intentionally or recklessly, intending to endanger the life of another or being reckless as to whether the life of another is endangered; s.1(2) CDA 1971.

Section 1(3) Arson

7.05 If the aggravated offence in s.1(2) is committed by fire then the defendant must be charged with arson.

Other Offences Under the Act

7.06 Two other offences exist under the Act as follows:

Threats to Destroy or Damage Property

7.07 Section 2 creates the offence of making threats of criminal damage without lawful excuse. The threat can be committed in two ways, but it must be proved that the person making the threat intended another to fear that the threat would be carried out. The threat must relate either to (i) destroying or damaging any property belonging to the person threatened or third person; or (ii) destroying or damaging their own property in a way which they know is likely to endanger the life of that person or a third person.

Possessing Anything with Intent to Destroy or Damage Property

7.08 Section 3 creates the offence of a person who has anything in their custody or under their control, intending without lawful excuse to use it or cause, or permit another to use it to either (i) destroy or damage any property belonging to another; or (ii) to destroy or damage their own or the user's property in a way which they know is likely to endanger the life of another.

Other Related Offences

7.09 Section 75 of the Criminal Justice and Immigration Act 2008 and Sch.17 creates a new indictable only offence of damaging the environment. This offence is committed if without lawful excuse a person who receives, holds, and deals with nuclear material, either intends to cause or enable another to cause damage to the environment with that material, or does so recklessly. A second covers a act directed at a nuclear facility either intending to cause damage to the environment by the emission of ionising radiation or the release of radioactive material or doing so recklessly.

2. Actus Reus for Basic Criminal Damage: Section 1(1)

7.10 The actus reus of this offence amounts to the prosecution having to prove "destroying or damaging property belonging to another". This can be committed in one of two ways; that the defendant by their act either destroys or damages. Giving the word destroys its ordinary meaning would require that the property is beyond use or no longer exists in its original format and cannot be repaired. A simple example would be where a person throws a stone directly at a window, shattering the glass. Alternatively, to simply damage property raises the question of whether this must be permanent or temporary in nature. This point was considered in *Samuel v Stubbs* [1972] 4 S.A.S.R. 200, where in was held that criminal damage had been done to a policeman's helmet when it had been jumped upon, causing a temporary functional derangement. Walters J. stated that no "precise and absolute rule as to what constitutes damage" can be laid down.

What amounts to damage is based on "the circumstances, of each case, the nature of the article, and the mode in which it is affected or treated". Similarly, in *Hardman v CC of Avon & Somerset* [1986] Crim. L.R. 330, an appeal heard in the Crown Court against conviction from the magistrates' court, it was held, applying what was said in *Samuel v Stubbs*, that writing on a pavement using water soluble chalks constituted damage, when the local authority was involved in expense in cleaning the pavement. It is clear from these two authorities that what amounts to damage is a question of fact and degree, based on the circumstances, for the jury or magistrates to determine.

A defendant can only be liable for criminal damage to "property", s.10 defines property as property of a tangible nature whether real or personal including money and includes wild creatures which have been tamed or are ordinarily kept in captivity. This also extends to wild creatures or their carcasses, "but only if they *have been reduced into possession which has not been lost or abandoned or are in the course of being reduced into possession*." It is important to note that this definition differs to that of property in the offence of theft, since theft can include intangible property, so for instance shares in a company cannot be damaged or gas cannot be damaged, since such items are clearly of intangible quality. Neither does the definition include, unlike theft, mushrooms growing wild or flowers or fruit.

7.11 Nevertheless, an intriguing point arose in *Cox v Riley* [1986] 83 Cr.App.R.54, in which the defendant had deliberately erased a computer program from a printed circuit card so as to render in inoperable. He was convicted in the magistrates' court and appealed by way of case stated to the High Court, on a point of law that the computer program was not tangible property within the meaning of s.10 and therefore his conviction was wrong. The High Court held, in dismissing the appeal and applying the authority of *Henderson and Battley* [1984] (unreported), that the erasing of a computer program did amount to damage to property of a tangible nature. By such an act the defendant had temporarily rendered the computer useless which amounted to damage, since to rectify such damage necessitated time, labour and expense by the complainant in restoring the relevant program, which all amounted to tangible actions.

In *Cresswell v DPP* [2006] EWHC 3379, the Divisional Court, by way of case stated from the Crown Court, was asked to give an opinion on whether the badger as a wild creature amounts to property for the purposes of criminal damage. The appellant had damaged badger traps set by the Environment Agency for the purpose of culling in order to prevent the spread of TB amongst the cattle population. The appellant relied on the s.5 lawful excuse defence so as to protect property, namely the badger, which was rejected by the Crown Court as badgers do not amount to property. The appellant appealed against the ruling. In dismissing the appeal, the Divisional Court considered that the badgers in question were wild and untamed and were "not in the course of being reduced into possession" by the enticement of food and even against the objective of ultimately being killed.

The Court further derived support from the concept that the property must belong to another and that in this instance the badger would belong to DEFRA, and if shot by the farmer on whose land the traps are set, not only would he be guilty of an offence under the Protection of Badgers Act 1992 but also of criminal damage, which could not be the purpose of the provision. The Court concluded that in terms of wild creatures it was necessary to "identify with some degree of precision which animal(s) are in the course of being reduced into possession". In this case that degree of precision could not be achieved since it was not possible to identify which particular badger would be so reduced until the stage at which the badger was entering the trap. Therefore by damaging the traps pre capture, the potential unidentified badger was neither property nor belongs to another. If this interpretation is legally correct then the appellant would only have a defence of lawful excuse for damaging the traps in order to release an already captured animal.

3. The Distinction between "Simple Criminal Damage" and the "Aggravated Offence"

7.12 It is important to observe that for the s.1(1) basic criminal damage offence, the prosecution are required to prove that the destroyed or damaged property in fact belongs to another, whereas this element of the actus reus in not required for the more serious aggravated offence. This distinction is deliberate in that Parliament did not wish to criminalise an act of damaging one's own property; if a person like Basil Faulty in "Faulty Towers" wishes to flog to death his car with a tree branch, causing damage, then that is a matter for them. However, if such an act of damaging or destroying one's own property endangers to the life of another, then in such circumstances that will amount to the more serious aggravated offence, for instance; setting fire to your furniture is likely to endanger the life of another. For the purposes of the basic offence "belonging to another" is defined in s.10 and is similar to, but not the same as, belonging to another in theft. Section 10 provides that belonging to another means somebody who has:

(i) custody or control of it;

(ii) any proprietary right or interest not equitable;

(iii) a charge on it.

Difficult factual issues may arise over ownership, especially in situations of property held under joint ownership such as where a couple decide to separate and one resorts to cutting the stereo and other shared property in half. If the other had custody or control of it, regardless of ownership, this would amount to criminal damage or if jointly purchased then the other would have a proprietary right in it and again this would amount to criminal damage.

4. The Mens Rea for Basic Criminal Damage: Section 1(1)

7.13 The prosecution, having proved that the defendant committed the actus reus, must also prove the required mental element of the two offences which consists of either intentionally or recklessly and without lawful excuse. Both the meaning of intention and recklessness in the context of criminal damage were reviewed extensively in Chapter Two and it is not intended to repeat it here other than to state that the test for recklessness is now subjective recklessness as set out in *R. v G* [2003] 1 A.C. 1034, in which the House of Lords departed from its own previous decision of objective recklessness in *MPC v Caldwell* [1981] A.C. 341. The House of Lords ruled that recklessness in criminal damage requires the prosecution to prove:

(i) with respect to a circumstance of damage that the accused themselves were aware of a risk that exists or will exist;

(ii) with respect or a result of damage, when they are aware of a risk that it will occur;

(iii) and it is in the circumstances known to them, unreasonable to take the risk.

It is important to be aware that in terms of culpability a mental element of intent is clearly more blameworthy than that of a reckless subjective mind in terms of the seriousness of the offence. Further, it ought to be noted also that self-induced intoxication cannot be relied upon by a defendant so as to negate the element of mens rea, since criminal damage for the purposes of the application of self-induced intoxication amounts to a basic intent offence (see *DPP v Majewski* [1976] 2 All E.R. 142).

5. The Mens Rea for the Aggravated Offence of Endangerment: Section 1(2)

7.14 Section 1(2) of the CDA 1971 creates the more serious offence of either intending by the damage or destruction to endanger life of another, or being reckless as to such endangerment. It is important to note that the prosecution must first prove the basic offence of criminal damage and the mens rea of that offence, in order to secure a conviction for the aggravated offence. The prosecution must further prove that the defendant intended by that destruction or damage to endanger the life of another or was subjectively reckless as to whether such endangerment would arise from their act of damage or destruction. The issue that arises for this more serious aggravated offence is what is meant by "endangers". In *R. v Steer* [1987] 3 W.L.R. 111, the appellant had a grudge against a business partner, went to his house, knocked on the door and then shot several times at the window with a rifle. At his trial for aggravated criminal damage, he argued that there was no case to answer, since the danger to life had not come from the damage, but from the actual shots.

This was rejected by the trial judge and he was subsequently convicted. He appealed on the same legal point in the House of Lords, which allowed his appeal against conviction and ruled that the prosecution, in relation to the offence of aggravated criminal damage, must prove that the danger to life resulted directly from the actual destruction or damage to property. It is not sufficient for the prosecution to prove that the danger to life arose from the act of the defendant. In this case, the actual damage to the window did not endanger the life of another, and therefore amounted only to the basic offence of criminal damage, not the aggravated form. It would seem that the prosecution charged for the wrong offence and should have considered other offences under the Firearms Act 1968 of which he was guilty. This principle of law was later applied in *R. v Asquith and Others* [1995] 1 Cr.App.R. 492, when the defendants pushed a coping stone from the parapet of a railway bridge, which hit a train and showered the passengers with glass fibre from the roof but did not enter the compartment.

6. The Specific Defence of "Lawful Excuse" in Section 5 to a Section 1(1), 2 and 3 Offence

7.15 Section 5 of the CDA 1971 provides for two situations where a defendant who on the facts criminally destroyed or damaged property can have a "lawful excuse" to that act of damage or destruction. In other words, the act of damage or destruction becomes a lawful act since the excuse for the act of damage or destruction is one that the law will allow. It is important to be aware that when applying the two situations for lawful excuse, s.5(3) states that "it is immaterial whether a belief is justified or not if it is honestly held". It is important to be aware that s.5(1) provides specifically that the defence of lawful excuse is only available to the offences of basic criminal damage in s.1(1), threats to damage s.2 and possessing anything with intent to damage in s.3. It is not available for the more serious offences of aggravated criminal damage in s.1(2) and arson in s.1(3).

7. Section 5(2)(a): Honest Belief that the Owner would have Consented to the Damage

7.16 Section 5(2)(a) provides that a person will have a lawful excuse, but only if they believed that the person(s) whom they believed to be entitled to consent to the destruction of, or damage to the property would have consented to that act. What is meant by an honest belief when formed mistakenly as a result of self-induced intoxication was considered in *Jaggard v Dickinson* [1981] Q.B. 52. On the facts the appellant, after an heavy night of drinking, went to a house which she mistakenly believed belonged to a friend who would have consented to her damaging two windows and a curtain in order to gain entrance. In fact the house, albeit identical to the friend's house, belonged to the complainant. The magistrates held that she could not rely on the defence of lawful excuse since her mistaken belief was formed not with sobriety but as a direct result of her intoxication and convicted her. The appellant's appeal by way of case stated was allowed by the High Court. Mustill J., giving the judgment of the Court, distinguished the House of Lords' decision in *DPP v Majewski* [1976] 2 All E.R. 142, which clearly applied on public policy grounds to the proof of mens rea in criminal damage, but in the context of the s.5 lawful excuse defence:

> "Parliament has specifically required the court to consider the defendant's actual state of belief, not a belief which ought to have existed."

The court is therefore:

> "required by s.5(3) to focus on the existence of the belief, not its intellectual soundness; and a belief can be just as much honestly held if it is induced by intoxication as if it stems from stupidity, forgetfulness or inattention."

The Court held that the magistrates ruled in error and allowed the appeal against conviction.

8. Section 5(2)(b): Honest Belief that Property was in Immediate Need of Protection

7.17 The second situation in which a defendant can rely on a lawful excuse defence for criminal damage is contained in s.5(2)(b) which provides the protection of a lawful excuse defence for a defendant where it is established that they:

(i) damaged or destroyed the property in question; in order

(ii) to protect property belonging to them or another, or a right or interest in property which they believed to be vested in themselves or another (See *Chamberlain v Lindon* below); and

(iii) at the time of committing criminal damage, they honestly believed (this belief need not be justified, provided it is honestly held by the defendant) that

(1) the property was in immediate need of protection; and
(2) that the means of protection adopted were *reasonable* having regard to all the circumstances.

On the application of this part of the defence, the issue arose concerning the correct test that the court should apply to the honest belief in the need to protect the property, in the sense as to whether it required a subjective test, i.e. what the defendant themselves honestly believed, or, on the other hand, did it require an objective assessment in that would a reasonable person have held such an honest belief. This legal point was raised and considered in *R. v Hunt* [1978] 66 Cr.App.R. 105, *R. v Ashford & Smith* (1988) (unreported), and *R. v Hill & Hall* [1988] 89 Cr.App.R. 74.

In *R. v Hill and Hall*, the defendants were charged with possessing an article intending to damage property, namely the perimeter fence of a US Naval facility. They claimed that they had to do this act of damage in order to protect their own property and that of others from nuclear destruction. Both were convicted and appealed. The appeal was dismissed, the Court of Appeal held that the trial judge had rightly refused to put the lawful excuse defence before the jury, since the link between the proposed damage to the fence and the alleged protection was so tenuous and nebulous that the acts could not objectively have amounted to protection in law: it was simply too remote. Lane L.J., who gave the judgment of the Court, concluded that when considering the lawful excuse defence the trial judge should apply a two stage test as follows:

(i) What was in the defendant's mind at the material time(subjective test)?

(ii) Whether as a matter of law on the facts believed by the defendant, the act of damage/destruction done was an objectively reasonable measure taken because of an immediate need to protect another's property (objective test taken by the judge looking at the evidence as a whole, the weaker the link between the damage to the immediate need of protection, the less likely it is in law that the defence exists).

More recently, this part of lawful excuse was reviewed by the Court of Appeal in *R. v Kelleher* [2003] EWCA Crim 3525, in which the appellant held strong political beliefs that the capitalist and individualistic polices of the USA and UK were leading directly to world destruction. For this reason he was very concerned for the future of his son. He held Margaret Thatcher personally responsible for creating the prevailing policies of materialist values, individualism, and selfishness. He visited the Guildhall Gallery, armed with a cricket bat, and proceeded to destroy a statue of Lady Thatcher which cost of £150,000 to replace. He was charged with simple criminal damage. He claimed he had a defence of lawful excuse based on the need to damage the statue, in order to protect property belonging to him or others against globalisation. The trial judge ruled that this did not amount to a lawful excuse, and directed the jury to convict if they were satisfied so that they were sure that the defendant had committed criminal damage. He was sentenced to three months' imprisonment.

The appellant appealed against conviction. The Court of Appeal dismissed his appeal and held that they were bound by the decisions in *Hunt, Ashford* and *Hill* and that the question whether or not a particular act of destruction or damage or threat of destruction or damage was committed in order to protect property belonging to oneself or another, must be considered by way of an *objective test*. In other words, taking into account the defendant's subjective state of mind at the time he damaged property, looking objectively at what he did, was it done in order to protect property that was in immediate need of protection? If the damage was not caused in order to protect property with such immediacy then there existed no lawful excuse and no defence. Clearly, on the facts, neither the appellant's nor any other's property was at immediate threat from the political policies of Margaret Thatcher, or would be so in the foreseeable future.

9. What is Meant by Reasonable in all the Circumstances?

7.18 For a defence of lawful excuse to be pleaded successfully at trial, not only must the defendant show that they honestly believed that damage or destruction was necessary in order for the immediate protection of their or another's property, but they must also show that the method of protection adopted was reasonable, i.e. the damage caused was proportionate to the property that needed immediate protection, having regard to the circumstances of what happened. For instance, it may not be considered reasonable to cause £100,000 worth of damage to protect property that is only worth £500, nevertheless this could, taking into account the circumstances, be reasonable. This is clearly a question of fact for the jury or magistrates to determine.

In *Chamberlain v Lindon* [1998] 1 W.L.R. 1252, the defendant had destroyed a wall built on land belonging to his neighbour, believing it was necessary in terms of immediacy to protect his own right of vehicular access across that land rather than commence a civil action to enforce his right, which would take time. In a rare instance, Chamberlain brought his own private prosecution by summoning the defendant to answer the allegation of criminal damage before the magistrates' court. The magistrates' court dismissed the prosecution on the basis that s.5(2)(b) was satisfied. The prosecutor (Chamberlain) appealed by way of case stated seeking the opinion of the High Court on whether the justices were entitled on the facts to find that the defendant had a lawful excuse.

The High Court applied the two stage test in *Hill and Hall* and concluded that, subjectively, he honestly believed that his right of way (a right or interest in his property) was in immediate need of protection. Secondly, objectively considering the defendant's act it did in law, amount to a reasonable and proportionate response to protect his right; that whilst his act of damaging the wall may have allowed him to avoid the need to take legal action, this did not convert the purpose in his act of damage from protecting his right into avoiding specifically such litigation. On a further point, the Court stated that taking in all the circumstances, the defendant should not be penalised for his attempt through correspondence to persuade the prosecutor to remove the wall and that the longer the wall remained the more urgent was the need to protect his right and that, based on the attitude of the prosecutor, the defendant believed it would have resulted in protracted litigation in the courts.

10. Committing Criminal Damage with Intent to Commit a Sexual Offence

7.19 An interesting development of the criminal law on clear grounds of protection and public policy is the new offence under s.62 of the Sexual Offences Act 2003, which creates the either way offence of committing any offence with the intention of committing a relevant sexual offence. Accordingly, a person who writes a message on a toilet wall, for instance inviting boys under 13 to make contact for sexual activity, will potentially be committing criminal damage with intent to commit a sexual offence.

11. Removing a Wheel Clamp as a Lawful Excuse

7.20 Another issue raised in the courts is whether, as a matter of law it is reasonable so as to amount to a defence of lawful excuse to damage a wheel clamp in order to release a vehicle. In *Lloyd v DPP* [1992] 1 All E.R. 982, and *Steer v Scott* [1984] (unreported), the High Court ruled that if a motorist parks their car without permission on another person's property knowing that by doing so they run the risk of being clamped, then they have no right to damage or destroy the clamp. To suggest that such action amounted to a lawful excuse was "wholly untenable". If a person damages a clamp, then they will be guilty of criminal damage. In *Steer v Scott* (unreported) the Court rejected the argument that the forceful removal of a clamp was justified, even in circumstances where the clamping of the unlawfully parked car was itself a trespass. Likewise, in *R. v Mitchell* [2004] R.T.R. 14, the Court rejected the argument that the civil defence of recaption of property, in which a person is entitled to use reasonable force to recover property of which they had been wrongfully deprived, was available to allegation of criminal damage. The Court followed the decision in *Lloyd* and expressed concern about the courts extending the right of self help in this area of law and that it should happen only on an incremental case by case basis. The Court concluded that a motorist confronted by a clamp should pay the release fee and then commence a civil claim to recover it.

CHAPTER EIGHT

PARTICIPATORY LIABILITY AND INCHOATE OFFENCES

1. INTRODUCTION

8.01 Criminal offences are committed in various ways, either by a sole offender or several offenders. When there is more than one offender, the issue of secondary party liability arises. Secondary participation simply consists of assisting or encouraging the commission of an offence by the principal offender. Invariably such offenders are described as being "accomplices", "accessories" or "secondary parties". Dependant upon the facts of the case, the secondary participant will either be charged as an aider and abetter, i.e. providing assistance generally to the "principal offender" prior to or at the time of the actual commission of the offence, or alternatively be "jointly charged" as part of a *joint enterprise* with another or others.

It is important to be aware of the differences between these two situations. An aider and abetter may not be involved in the actual commission of the offence. For instance; A wishes to commit a burglary of some commercial premises, B is an ex employee and at the request of A, draws a diagram of the external and internal structure of the building. A is clearly the principal offender who commits the actual offence on his own. Although B does not become involved in the actual commission of the offence, he provided assistance and is therefore equally and criminally liable as a secondary party to the offence of burglary and will be charged with aiding and abetting that offence.

Conversely, in a joint enterprise situation all the offenders involved are treated as being both principal and secondary offenders in relation to each other, regardless of the degree of involvement. For instance; A and B agree to commit a domestic burglary together, between them it is arranged that B will enter the premises, whilst A will wait in the van outside ready to drive away quickly. Both A and B are actively involved in the commission of the offence and are therefore the principal offenders to the offence, regardless of their active roles; just because A is the getaway driver and did not enter the premises will not reduce his criminal liability. As a joint enterprise they are equally and criminally liable for the offence of burglary. This causes no difficulties and it is clearly right as a matter of public policy that all participating offenders are charged and tried with the same offence.

Difficulties however, can arise in a joint enterprise situation, when one of the participants goes beyond committing the agreed offence and commits a further, more serious offence. In this situation there is now a principal offender for the greater offence, the question arises; can the other offender(s) still be jointly liable for that greater offence? For instance; A and B decide to commit a domestic burglary and they agree to carry knives but only to be used to frighten any occupant. A states that he will steal from the upstairs rooms, whilst B steals from the down stairs rooms. During the commission of the burglary, B hears a commotion from upstairs, with A making his way down stairs with the knife in his hand and blood on it and him. Both panic and leave the premises. The following day, the elderly resident is reported to have died from his injuries sustained in the knife attack. Both A and B are clearly and unequivocally jointly liable for the offence of burglary as a joint enterprise; they each acted as a principal. However, A goes beyond the scope of the enterprise and commits a more serious offence of either, murder, or manslaughter, he and he alone is a principal offender for this offence. B is now potentially a secondary offender for that greater offence and may be jointly liable for that more serious offence, even though he never formed any intent to kill for murder. He could still be charged tried and convicted of that murder or manslaughter. In this instance, it is important to be aware that the mens rea for a secondary offender is different and lesser to that of the principal offender. Similar problems also arise in spontaneous violent group attacks.

In relation to incohate offences, the Law Commission, at the request of the Government, has now published its extensive consultation review into the current principles relating to the offences of conspiracy and criminal attempts. The report, "Conspiracy and Attempts", Paper No.183, covers 234 pages which outline the shortcomings in the current law, noting in particular that the principles of both offences are at the moment too generous to the defendant, requiring reform.

2. Section 8 Accessories and Abettors Act 1861 and Section 2 of the Suicide Act 1961

8.02 The principles of law relating to a party, who is deemed to act as an aider and abetter to the principal offender, are still to be found in the common law. Section 8 of the Accessories and Abettors Act 1861, as amended by the Criminal Law Act 1977, provides that:

> "whosoever shall aid, abet, counsel or procure the commission of any *indictable offence* ... shall be liable to be tried, indicted and punished as the principal offender".

This does not set out the law, its purpose is procedural in that anybody who aids, abets, counsels, or procures the commission of an indictable offence (this means either an either-way offence or an indictable only offence), is to be tried, indicted and sentenced as if they were the principal offender. In other words, the principal offender and the secondary offender will sit in the dock together, indicted with the same offence, they will stand trial together for it and if both are convicted, will be sentenced together for it. It is important to note that a separate provision exists under s.44 of the Magistrates' Court Act 1980 to create the same liability for secondary participation in summary only offences.

In *Attorney-General Reference (No.1 of 1975)* [1975] 3 W.L.R. 12, the defendant had secretly laced the drink of a friend, who then drove their car over the prescribed legal drink limit and was guilty of that offence. The defendant was charged with aiding and abetting that offence within s.8. The trial judge accepted that there was no case to answer and directed the acquittal of the defendant on the basis that there was no evidence to establish a common intention between the two offenders, (i.e. that there was no established meeting of minds). The Attorney–General sought the opinion of the Court of Appeal under s.36 of the Criminal Justice Act 1972, on whether as a matter of law, on the facts, the trial judge was correct to acquit the defendant. Lord Widgery, giving the opinion of the Court of Appeal, stated that the four words should be given their ordinary meaning and accepted that there was a difference in the meaning between each of them. The Court approached the issue in the case as one of procurement and said that:

> "to procure means to produce by endeavour. You procure a thing by setting out to see that it happens and taking the appropriate steps to produce that happening."

Accordingly, there was a case to answer, since the defendant knew that the friend was going to drive and that by adding more alcohol this caused the friend to commit the offence of drink driving, even though he was unaware of this risk. Giving "aids" its ordinary meaning covers any form of assisting the principal offender to commit the offence; "abetting" means any incitement or encouragement to do so, whilst "counselling" means advising or soliciting the principal offender to take a particular course of conduct.

Section 2 of the Suicide Act 1961 creates a specific offence committed by a person who aids, abets, counsels or procures the suicide, or attempted suicide of another. This amounts to an indictable only offence with a maximum sentence of 14 years. Before a prosecution can commence, the consent of the DPP must first be obtained. In the tragic case of *Pretty v UK* [2002] 35 E.H.R.R. 1, the European Court of Human Rights upheld the ruling of the House of Lords, that the refusal of the DPP to give an undertaking to the husband that he would not be prosecuted for this offence, if he assisted his terminally ill wife to commit suicide, was correct. Tragic though the facts were, this did not breach any human rights, since whilst art.3 protects a right to a life, there is no corresponding right to die, to allow the creation of such a right would be contrary to public policy.

3. Actus Reus and Mens Rea of "Aids, Abets, Counsels, or Procures"

8.03 In terms of the actus reus, the prosecution must establish the following two elements:

(i) The accessory did a *deliberate act or omission* which aids, abets, counsels, or procures and that this; and

(ii) assisted the later commission by the perpetrator of the actual offence.

In regard to the mens rea it is the same for aiding, abetting, counselling and procuring. The prosecution must prove that:

(i) the defendant did the act deliberately, *realising* that it was capable of assisting the offence;

(ii) the defendant at the time of doing the act, *contemplated* the commission of the offence by perpetrator, i.e. they foresaw it as a "real and substantial risk" or "real possibility"; and

(iii) the defendant when doing the act, *intended or knew* that it would assist perpetrator in what he was doing. (see the judgment of Devlin J. in *National Coal Board v Gamble* [1959] 1 Q.B. 11).

The prosecution are not required to prove that the accessory at the time of the act of aiding, abetting, counselling, procuring, intended the offence to be committed; simply that they realised, contemplated and intended to assist in its commission. A good illustration is found in the speech of Devlin J. in *National Coal Board v Gamble* [1959] 1 Q.B. 11, as follows:

> "If one man deliberately sells to another a gun to be used for murdering a third, he may be indifferent whether the third man lives or dies and interested only in the cash profit to be made out of the sale, but he can still be an aider and abetter."

It makes no difference if the accessory prays in vain that the principal will not succeed. In terms of knowledge, it must be proved that the accessory at least knew the essential matters of the principal offence (see the judgment of Lord Goddard L.J. in *Johnston v Youden* [1950] 1 K.B. 544), it need not be proved that they actually knew the offence has been committed. The question is one of fact for the jury, who are entitled to draw inferences from all the admissible surrounding evidence.

4. The Position of the "Passive Spectator"

8.04 Many will remember a school ground fight, which attracts a baiting crowd, with some giving specific support and encouragement to one or another of the fighters, whilst others would just generally encourage with no allegiance and some would remain impassive and silent. At what point in law and fact does a person convert from a passive spectator to that of a person who aids and abets, thereby potentially attracting criminal liability? This point is illustrated vividly by the disturbing case of *R. v Clarkson* [1971] 1 W.L.R. 1402, in which three soldiers who had been drinking became aware that a woman was being raped by other soldiers. They entered the room where the offence was taking place and simply watched, there was no evidence of any participation or encouragement of the principal offender.

The Court of Appeal allowed the appeal and quashed the appellant's conviction of aiding and abetting a rape, on the basis that the judge had failed to emphasise in his direction to the jury, that the prosecution must prove that where there is a non accidental presence at the commission of an offence by the principal offender, the defendant had intended by their presence to give encouragement. Especially if the defendant is in a drunken state; mere intention is not sufficient. The Court of Appeal applied the ruling of what must be proved in non-accidental presence cases stated by Hawkins J. in *R. v Coney* [1882] 8 Q.B.D. 534, as follows:

> "to constitute an aider and abettor some active steps must be taken by word or action, with intent to instigate the principal(s). Encouragement does not of necessity amount to aiding and abetting, it may be intentional or unintentional, a man may unwittingly encourage another in fact by his presence, by misinterpreted words, or gestures, or by his silence, or non-interference, or he may encourage intentionally by expressions, or gestures, or actions intended to signify approval. In the latter case he aids and abets, in the former he does not. It is no criminal offence to stand by, a mere passive spectator of a crime, even if a murder. No—interference to prevent a crime is not itself a crime. But the fact that a person was voluntarily and purposely present witnessing the commission of a crime, and offered no opposition to it it, although he might reasonably be expected to prevent and had the power so to do, or at least to express his dissent, might, under some circumstances afford cogent evidence upon which a jury would be justified in finding that he wilfully encouraged and so aided and abetted. But it would be purely a question for the jury he did so or not."

In *R. v Alford Transport Ltd* [1997] 2 Cr.App.R. 326, two lorry drivers employed by a transport company pleaded guilty to offences of making false entries on a tachograph contrary to s.99 of the Transport Act 1968. The defendants, the company itself, were convicted after trial of aiding and abetting those offences. The Court of Appeal allowed the appeal against conviction on the basis that the judge had materially misdirected the jury by not explaining the required mens rea of knowledge, simply that negligence would be sufficient.

The Court of Appeal held that there was no evidence to infer properly that the defendant company encouraged the commission of the offences by its drivers. The Court did, nonetheless, observe that the prosecution was required to prove knowledge of the principal offence, together with the ability to control the action of the offender and the deliberate decision to refrain from doing this. Nevertheless, the Court noted that, if the management had turned a blind eye in order to keep the drivers happy or encourage the creation of false entries rather than accurate ones, and that knowing this they continued to supply the lorries, would amount to them being an aider and abettor.

An important case to note at first instance was heard at Leeds Crown Court (see *The Times*, February 15, 2008, "Girl faces jail for happy slap"). This reports a jury convicting a 15-year-old school girl who, although not physically taking part, had by filming a vicious unprovoked assault in which the victim died on her mobile phone, aided and abetted the offence of manslaughter.

5. Proof of "Causation" and an "Intervening Event"

8.05 The prosecution must not only prove the mens rea and actus reus of an offence. They must also establish, if the issue is disputed, that the defendant's act caused the result or consequence, both in fact and law. There is no difference between the causational burden of securing a conviction either against a principal offender, or an "accessory". This point is well illustrated in *R. v Bryce* [2004] 2 Cr.App.R. 35, the appellant (B) was convicted of murder not as the principal but as an accessory. B had transported X (the murderer, principal offender), along with the gun with which X used to kill the victim to a caravan site so that X could wait for an opportunity to carry out the killing. The Court of Appeal dismissed the appeal against conviction by ruling that the delay of some 13 hours between the assistance relied on and the actual killing did not break the chain of causation. This did not amount to an intervening event. The prosecution were not required to prove that B's act of assistance occurred at the time when X had formed the necessary intent to kill. All that was necessary for secondary liability is *foresight of the real possibility* that an offence will be committed by the person to whom the accessory's act of assistance is directed.

In *R. v Anderson and Morris* [1966] 2 W.L.R. 1195, Lord Parker L.J. in an obiter statement said that there may well be situations where, as a matter of causation some overwhelming supervening event was of such a character as would break the chain of causation. For instance; where two co-defendants embark jointly in the commission of a burglary and one of them had, in a moment of crisis, formed the intention to kill. In other words, the death was caused solely by the sudden action of that person, which breaks any causative link between the initial joint acts of the defendant, to the act of murder by the other party.

6. Causation and the Issue of "Withdrawal"

8.06 One of the issues that may arise in the proof of causation is whether by withdrawing the aider and abetter have themselves intervened and broken the chain of causation of encouragement and thus redeemed themselves from criminal liability. If a secondary party is to avoid liability for assistance rendered to the perpetrator in respect of steps taken by the perpetrator towards the commission of the offence, then only an act taken by them which amounts to countermanding of their earlier assistance and a withdrawal from the common purpose will suffice. Repentance alone, unsupported by action taken to demonstrate withdrawal, will be insufficient. Accordingly, if the secondary party has the necessary mens rea at the time of the act of rendering their advice or assistance, the fact that their mind is "innocent" at the time when the offence is committed is no defence.

In *R. v Becerra* [1976] 62 Cr.App.R. 212, the Court of Appeal dismissed the appellant's conviction for murder, which occurred when he and two other men, whilst in a common venture of committing a burglary, were disturbed by the occupant. The appellant shouted "let's go" and jumped out of the window, one of the other men then stabbed the occupant to death. Roskill L.J., giving the leading judgment, analysed the principles of law relating to withdrawal from an enterprise as dating back to *Sanders and Archer* [1577] 2 Plowd 473. The principles of law are plain, it is a question of fact for the jury to be satisfied that the defendant had withdrawn (abandoned) the illegal enterprise. There is required, save in exceptional circumstances, to be something more than a "mere mental change of intention or physical change of place". Where it is practicable and reasonable there must exist, "timely communication" of an intention to abandon, either verbally, or otherwise, that will serve "unequivocal notice" upon the other party to the common unlawful cause that, if he proceeds upon it, he does so without the further aid and assistance of the withdrawing party.

There is no requirement that reasonable steps must be taken to prevent the offence from being committed. Whether a defendant has done enough to have withdrawn, within the application of the law, is a question of fact for the jury based on all the circumstances of the case. In the instant case to simply say, "let's go", did not amount to a sufficient "countermand" or "repentance" the actions of another. In *R. v Grundy* [1977] Crim. L.R. 543, the Court of Appeal, in quashing the appellant's conviction for burglary, applied the principle in *Becerra* and ruled that the judge erred in refusing to direct the jury concerning the appellant's only defence of withdrawal, and that such evidence was a matter for the jury to consider, who can then, either accept or reject it.

In *R. v Rook* [1997] 1 W.L.R. 1005, the appellant had arranged with the husband to have his wife killed for £15,000. The appellant recruited two others (also discussed was the method for the killing, i.e. knife and piece of wood) and arranged with the husband the place and time for the murder. The appellant absented himself from the scene of the murder, the husband drove his wife to the scene where the other two men brutally murdered her.

The appellant was convicted as part of a joint enterprise to commit murder. On appeal against conviction, he contended that by changing his mind and deliberately absenting himself from the scene of the murder, he had withdrawn from the criminal enterprise. The Court of Appeal, in dismissing the appeal, applied the principle of law clearly set out in *Becerra* and ruled that the appellant had not expressly informed the others that he did not wish to continue with the crime. The fact that he absented himself on the day of murder did not amount to "unequivocal communication" of his withdrawal sufficient to break the chain of causation. Further, in *R. v O'Flaherty* [2004] 2 Cr.App.R. 20, the Court of Appeal stated that as a matter of law:

> "a person who unequivocally withdraws from the joint enterprise before the moment of the actual commission of the crime by the principal, shall not be liable for that crime,"

and that for there to be a withdrawal:

> "mere repentance does not suffice. To disengage from an incident a person must do enough to demonstrate that he or she is withdrawing from the joint enterprise. This is ultimately a question of fact and degree for the jury."

Nevertheless, it is important to be aware that any acts of the secondary party committed before their withdrawal can, on their own, amount to other offences, such as public order offences.

7. Liability of a Secondary Party without Conviction of Perpetrator

8.07 A somewhat paradoxical outcome in the criminal law is that the "accessory" principle allows the prosecution to secure a conviction of a secondary offender, even though the principal offender is acquitted of committing the actual offence. This point is clearly highlighted in *R. v Cogan and Leak* [1975] 3 W.L.R. 316, where the Court of Appeal dismissed the appeal against conviction for rape. The appellant (Leak) had invited his friend (Cogan) to have sexual intercourse with his wife. The wife did not show any resistance but had not consented to the intercourse. Both where convicted of rape, on appeal Cogan's conviction was quashed on the basis of the principle in *R. v Morgan* [1975] 2 W.L.R. 913, in which the House of Lords had held that a mistaken belief as to consent is still a defence, even if that belief is held unreasonably, provided that the defendant honestly and genuinely believed that the complainant was consenting, this will amount to a mistaken belief.

Nevertheless, the Court of Appeal upheld Leak's conviction, that although Cogan was innocent of rape, the actus reus of rape had still been procured by Leak, the wife had never consented to that act. Leak had the necessary mens rea of intention to procure that offence. Lawton L.J., on the contention of the appellant that such an outcome creates an anomaly stated, "in the circumstances of this case it would be more than anomalous: it would be an affront to justice and to common sense of ordinary folk", if the secondary offender was not liable for this reason.

Conversely, in *Thornton v Mitchell* [1940] 1 All E.R. 339, the High Court quashed the appellant's conviction of aiding and abetting the principal in careless driving. The appellant was a bus conductor who gave signals for the driver who could not see to reverse; unfortunately two people were injured, one fatally. On the basis that the driver had to rely on the appellant's signals, the magistrates found him not guilty of careless driving, but the appellant guilty of aiding and abetting it. Hewart L.C.J. approved and applied the statement of law derived from *Morris v Tolman* [1931] 1 K.B. 166, that:

> "in order to convict, it would be necessary to show that the secondary party was aiding and abetting the principal, but a person cannot aid another in doing something *which that other has not done*."

In other words, a person can never be guilty of aiding and abetting a principal who does not commit the actus reus of the offence. If the prosecution can prove the principal had committed the actus reus, then provided they can prove that the secondary offender had the relevant mens rea of an accessory, it matters not whether the principal is acquitted or indeed prosecuted.

In *DPP v K and B* [1997]1 Cr.App.R. 36, a case with disturbing facts, the High Court allowed an appeal by the prosecution from the Youth Court and ruled that the two defendants aged 14 and 11, were liable for procuring the offence of the rape of another girl, whom they had falsely imprisoned, even though the principal offender, an unknown young boy, was never traced.

8. Assisting Offenders and the Notification Requirements under the Road Traffic Act 1988

8.08 There exists within the criminal law the right against self incrimination; no person is under a legal duty to disclose knowledge of an offence, or of the person who perpetrated it. Nevertheless, there are clear exceptions to this rule: namely perjury, perverting the course of justice and assisting an offender. Section 4(1) of the Criminal Law Act 1967 provides that where a person has committed a relevant offence, any other person who knowing or believing them to be guilty of the offence, or some other relevant offence, does without lawful authority or reasonable excuse any act with intent to impede their apprehension or prosecution is guilty of an offence. Relevant offence for the purposes of this section means murder, or an offence with a minimum sentence of five years or more.

Accordingly, there is no specific offence of assisting an offender for a relatively minor offence, but the offence of perverting the course of justice, or an offence under s.172 of the Road Traffic Act 1988, can arise, as is clearly illustrated in *O'Halloran and Francis v UK* [2007] (Application No.15809/02). The registered vehicles of each appellant were caught speeding by a speed camera. Both appellants contended that s.172 of the Road Traffic Act 1988 breached their right against self-incrimination enshrined in art.6, a right to a fair trial. Section 172 creates the offence of failing to comply with a requirement from the police to give such information as to the identity of the driver, or which may lead to their identification, who has committed a specified offence (speeding is one such offence).

In *Mohindra v DPP* [2004] EWHC 490, the High Court reluctantly quashed the appellant's convictions for failing to give the notification requirement on the grounds that the prosecution lacked the necessary evidence to prove that the requirement to give notification of the identity of the driver was made by, or on behalf of a Chief Officer of Police; an essential element of the offence under s.172. To resolve this difficulty the s.9 statement used to prove service should always be attached to the notice of intended prosecution and the notice requirement which does not have to be signed personally (see *Arnold v DPP* [1999] R.T.R. 99). If a defendant wishes to contend the legality of the notice, then they should bring this to the attention of the court, before the close of the prosecution case, so that the court can then, at its discretion allow the prosecution to re-open its case and prove that element of the offence. Section 12 of the Road Traffic Offenders Act 1988 allows for the standard reply statement purported to be signed by the accused to be admissible as evidence that the accused was the driver. In *Francis v DPP* [2004] EWHC 591, the High Court held that an omission to sign properly or complete the form amounts to a failure to comply with the requirements issued by the Chief Police Officer and therefore the offence is committed.

A statutory defence exists in that, if a person can show that either they did not know or they are unable to ascertain who the driver was with reasonable diligence, they are not guilty. By a majority of 16 to two, the European Court of Human Rights in *O'Halloran* ruled that s.172 does not violate art.6. The Court referred to the Privy Council ruling in *Brown v Stott* [2001] 2 W.L.R. 817 and stated that the owning or driving of vehicles, like shotguns, can, if used irresponsibly cause grave injury. For this reason car owners and drivers are taken to accept the regulatory regime in place to ensure public safety on the roads. The information sought from the duty to disclose is limited to a simple fact; there is no intense interrogation and the penalty is "moderate and non-custodial" (see also *Charlebois v DPP* [2003] EWHC 54, and *DPP v Wilson* [2002] R.T.R. 37).

Thus the s.172 inference with the right to silence and privilege against self incrimination is justified and proportionate to the legitimate aim of preventing serious injury and death on the roads and ensuring public safety. In a powerful dissenting judgment, Judge Pavlovschi stated that the requirements of fairness and the presumption of innocence should be observed, regardless of the culpability of the offender and that to compel a suspect to confess, or incriminate, runs contrary to the notion of fairness. Section 172 amounted to an unjustifiable blanket statutory deprivation of a large portion of the population of their fundamental rights under criminal law and procedure.

9. Criminal Liability of those being Part of a Joint Enterprise

8.09 A joint enterprise arises where two or more persons act under a "common venture" to commit an offence and are both at the scene. Both are equally liable for the offence, being part of their common intention, since they both have the mens rea and actus reus of the offence. Equally, if the primary party commits the offence whilst the secondary party is elsewhere both are equally liable for the offence committed. However, problems arise where the primary offender, or if a number of persons, act together, the primary offender or one out of a group does an act which then results in a greater offence being committed by them, are the others still criminally liable for that greater offence? The issue with joint enterprise is determining the mens rea of the secondary party in contrast to that of the principal. What is clear, is that it need not be established that the secondary offender shares the same mens rea as the primary offender.

The liability of a secondary party does not require the proof by the prosecution of the actual offence committed by the primary party but whether the secondary party subjectively foresaw/realised that the primary offender might commit that greater offence. The question is whether the primary offender acted outside the scope of the joint enterprise. Accordingly, the mens rea of a secondary party can be of a lesser form to that of a primary offender but they can still be guilty of the greater offence. Looking at the "accessory principle", it is suggested that this creates a form of "constructive criminal liability", whereby a defendant is liable for a greater offence, with only a mens rea for a lesser offence.

Likewise, the principle creates an "anomaly" in the criminal law, in that a defendant who is a secondary offender is liable equally with a principal offender, even though the secondary offender's culpability is less than that of the principal offender. Both these contentions where rejected by the House of Lords in *R. v Powell and English* [1997] 3 W.L.R. 959, Lord Steyn stated that the principle is supported by practical and policy considerations and if the prosecution were required to prove that the secondary offender possessed the mens rea for the greater offence, then, "the utility of the accessory principle would be gravely undermined".

10. General Liability of a Joint Enterprise and Evidential Difficulties that can Arise

8.10 The principles of law are clear and unequivocal and were fully explored in *R. v Hyde* [1991] 1 Q.B. 134, and by the House of Lords in *R. v Powell and English*. Where two or more persons, either expressly or tacitly form a common venture/purpose/intention to commit an offence, then it is irrelevant, as far as criminal liability is concerned, what the precise amount of participation of each person was. All, if the prosecution can prove the common purpose, are equally liable for the commission of the offence. There exists no controversy surrounding this principle and it is clearly justified on public policy grounds. Nevertheless, the prosecution must prove beyond doubt that the defendant was in fact part of the enterprise and either expressly or tacitly agreed to its purpose.

R v O'Flaherty and Others [2004] 2 Cr.App.R. 315 was a case involving the use of gang street violence that occurred in two separate incidents, which resulted in the stabbing to death of one of the participants. The Court of Appeal ruled that the prosecution must prove:

(i) that the injuries which were sustained occurred when the joint enterprise was still continuing and that the defendants were still participating in that enterprise;

(ii) the act(s) which caused the death where within the scope of the enterprise and not acts that were fundamentally different from those expressly or tacitly agreed.

In cases where there was no pre-planned violence, but violence erupted spontaneously resulting in a joint group attack on a specific victim, the existence and scope of the enterprise can, by the jury, be ascertained from the knowledge and actions of the participating parties. This may require the jury to draw relevant inferences from the evidence, whether there was a separate incident, or one continuing incident, is evidence to assist the jury in deciding whether the participant no longer formed part of the enterprise, or had physically withdrawn from it. This is a question for fact in each individual case for the sole determination of the jury.

In spontaneous group violent attack situations, the prosecution's case can be significantly weakened by lack of evidence, especially when the incident occurs over a matter of minutes, combined with poor observations. Such evidential difficulties are well illustrated in the sensitive case of *R. v Miah and Others* [2004] EWCA Crim 63, the appellant's conviction for s.18 causing grievous bodily harm with intent on a young white man, an assault that was cowardly and unprovoked and involved the use of a broken bottle being stabbed into the victim's throat, was deemed unsafe. The Court of Appeal held that, if guilt of a joint enterprise was to be established, it had to be shown evidentially that each defendant was present with the relevant mens rea. In the instant case, the prosecution was unable to prove evidentially by identification that any of the appellants were actually present and took part in the attack. None of the prosecution's eyewitnesses were able to pick out any of the appellants as those being responsible.

11. Liability for the Commission of Offences that did not form Part of the Enterprise: Mens Rea of Foresight is Sufficient for Secondary Party Liability

8.11 This refers back to the "Introduction" at para.8.01, and the burglary offence example where one of the participants steps outside the scope of the enterprise and commits a greater offence, such as murder, to the one that was expressly or tacitly agreed, i.e. burglary. In regard to that defendant (who is now a principal offender) the prosecution must prove the necessary mens rea and actus reus for the offence of murder. The other participants are equally liable for the burglary offence; the question arises whether these other participants although they did not physically commit the actus reus of murder, can as secondary participants to it, still be equally liable for it. The principle of law is settled and found in *Chan Wing-Siu v The Queen* [1985] A.C. 168, which was later applied by the House of Lords in *R. v Powell and English* [1997] 3 W.L.R. 959. Lord Steyn confirmed the principle as follows:

> "the established principle is that a secondary offender to a criminal enterprise may be liable for a greater criminal offence, committed by the principal, of a type which the former foresaw but did not necessarily intend. Criminal culpability lies in participating in the criminal enterprise with that foresight, which is a necessary and sufficient ground for liability of the secondary offender."

Accordingly, in respect of a secondary participant, the House of Lords ruled unanimously that the prosecution do not need to prove the mens rea or actus reus for murder; in respect of a secondary offender. It is sufficient to prove a lesser form of mens rea of foresight in that they (subjectively) realised or contemplated that during the course of the joint enterprise, the principal offender might kill with intent to do so or with intent to cause grievous bodily harm unless the risk was so remote that the jury take the view that the secondary party genuinely dismissed it as altogether negligible. The degree of foresight required to impose liability is that of a realisation or contemplation that another might commit a different offence.

The actus reus of the secondary party is the act of participation within the scope of the enterprise and therefore, to avoid the actus reus, the secondary party must show that they joined after the commission of the greater offence or had withdrawn altogether from the enterprise before its commission. The facts in each appeal are brutal: Powell along with two other men went to the house of a drug dealer to purchase drugs. The drug dealer was shot dead when he came to the door. Evidentially the prosecution were unable to prove which one of the three carried out the fatal shooting and therefore presented their case on the basis that each of them knew one of them was carrying a gun and realised that he might use it to kill.

The House of Lords dismissed Powell's appeal against conviction on the ground that it was unsafe. Conversely, owing to a mis-direction by the trial judge, the House of Lords allowed the appeal against conviction of English who along with his co-defendant, as part of a common venture, decided to attack a police officer with wooden posts. During the attack the co-defendant produced a knife and killed the officer. English had contended that he had no foresight of his co-accused producing such a weapon and using it to kill. The judge had not qualified his direction to the jury to provide that English would not be guilty of murder if this was an unforeseen event which took it outside the scope of the enterprise itself.

The application of the principle that a secondary party cannot be liable for any unseen act by another to the enterprise which results in another offence being committed, is well illustrated in the Northern Ireland case of *R. v Gamble* [1989] N.I. 268. Two of a gang of four, who were members of the terrorist organisation the Ulster Volunteer Force which had agreed, as part of a joint enterprise, to inflict punishment on the victim, either by a severe beating or kneecapping were held to be not guilty of murder when the other two members of the gang instead produced a knife and brutally cut the victim's throat, leading to rapid death. This act of brutality was, for the two defendants, an event they had not foreseen and could not have contemplated or realised the others would commit.

Nevertheless, the House of Lords ruled that if the secondary offender realises the principal offender has a weapon and foresees that he might use it, then they are equally liable. If although realising that the principal offender is carrying a particular weapon but instead produces a different weapon to commit the other offence, i.e. murder, then the secondary party will only be equally liable if the jury accept the weapon used was equally dangerous to the one contemplated by the secondary party. If the weapon used is fundamentally different and less dangerous, then the secondary party will not be liable for the greater offence.

12. Group Attack with Spontaneous Violence

8.12 Where a number of persons become involved in a group attack on another, or others, each individual is committing their own individual offences, such as assault and public order offences, i.e. violent disorder. They are at the same time acting as both principals and secondary parties to each other. The prosecution are not required to distinguish between who is acting as principal and who is acting as secondary participant. They are all in such circumstances, albeit spontaneously and becoming involved at different times, maybe withdrawing and then rejoining, acting as part of a common purpose to inflict/cause injury to another. All are equally liable for the injuries sustained during their continued involvement in the violent enterprise. In regard to each participant, the prosecution simply have to prove the mens rea for a secondary participant, in that each individual realised subjectively that the other participants might use violence, even if the other is not known to them. If however, one of the many in the group attack produces a weapon and uses it to seriously injure or cause death, then the others will endeavour to disassociate themselves from such an act by contending that such an act was unforeseen to them and therefore was an act which they did not contemplate.

The relevant principles of law are found in *R. v Uddin* [1998] 3 W.L.R. 1000, the facts of which are not uncommon but tragic. The victim, as a matter of chance, became involved in a road rage altercation with another vehicle. By an unfortunate coincidence the victim was confronted by the driver from the earlier incident, who had by this time called a number of associates to the area with the intention of attacking the victim. All were aware of this and their involvement; some had armed themselves with wooden posts and iron bars. However, one of the attackers produced a knife and fatally stabbed the victim. The appellant was convicted of murder and appealed against his conviction on the grounds that the judge had misdirected the jury as to the required foresight. The Court of Appeal allowed the appeal and ordered a re-trial on the basis that the judge had not directed the jury to focus on the point of whether the knife used was fundamentally different to that contemplated by the appellant in the actual attack, with the use of posts and bars as weapons. Beldam L.J., giving the judgment of the Court, stated that there were five principles applicable to cases of this type (see summary at para.8.12 below).

A similar event occurred in the earlier authority of *R. v Hyde* [1991] 1 Q.B. 134, where the three appellants had violently attacked another man with fists and kicks; no weapons were used and the victim later died from his injuries. On the evidence it was not possible to establish who had struck the fatal blow. The Court of Appeal held, approving Sir Robins Coke's obiter statement in *Chan Wing Siu v The Queen* [1985] A.C. 168, that if a secondary offender realises that the other party may do certain prohibited acts (for instance commit murder), beyond that which was tacitly agreed, i.e. assault, and nevertheless continues to participate in the criminal enterprise, this will provide a sufficient mental element to convict the secondary offender.

13. Summary of the Applicable Principles of Law for Secondary Offender Liability

8.13 The following is a summary of the principles of law to be derived from the authorities as applicable to secondary participation, either in a pre-planned enterprise or a spontaneous attack:

(i) Where two or more offenders either expressly or tacitly agree with each other to commit an offence as part of that common purpose, all are equally liable as principals for that offence, unless the act of one of the participants is of a type that is entirely different from that which the other participants foresaw as part of the enterprise (the "fundamentally different" rule, see below at para.8.14).

(ii) If one of the participants acts outside the agreed enterprise and commits a different and generally more serious offence, then in respect of that participant, the prosecution must prove the necessary mens rea and actus reus for that offence. In respect of the other participants, if the prosecution can establish that they subjectively foresaw (realised) that the other during the course of the agreed enterprise might commit another offence, i.e. might kill during the course of a burglary, then they are equally liable for that other offence committed by the principal offender. Only if the risk was so remote that the jury take the view that the secondary party genuinely dismissed it as altogether negligible, will they be acquitted for that offence.

(iii) If, during the course of the enterprise the principal offender suddenly produces a weapon and uses it, then the principal is again liable for that other offence if proved by the prosecution. In respect of the remaining participants, if they where not aware of the weapon and therefore did not foresee or contemplate its use, then they are not liable for the greater/other offence, but will each be individually liable for other possible offences.

(iv) If, however, the secondary offender is aware that the principal offender has the weapon and it is proven that they subjectively foresaw, i.e. realised/contemplated that they might use it during the course of the enterprise, then they are equally liable, along with the principal, for the particular offence, unless the jury accept that the secondary party genuinely dismissed it as altogether negligible.

(v) If the secondary offender knows that the principal offender has a particular weapon, but then produces a different weapon to the one the secondary party believed they had, then in such circumstances the secondary party will only be liable if the jury are satisfied that the weapon used and unknown to the secondary party is equally dangerous to the one believed to be in their possession. If, however, the weapon used is fundamentally different to the one believed to be in the principal's possession, then the secondary party will not be liable for the other offence committed by the principal offender, since such an act is committed outside and not in the contemplation of the enterprise.

(vi) If, during the course of a concerted group attack a weapon is suddenly produced by one of the participants, provided the other participants know that they have the weapon and might use it during the course of the attack and regardless of this continue to participate in the attack they will be equally liable for the greater offence caused by the use of the weapon.

14. Withdrawal from Spontaneous Violence

8.14 If violence flares up and many participants become involved, each playing a part in the violence, or a number of persons agree to cause, or inflict serious injury on another, or others, then at the moment a person embarks in that common enterprise, they will attract criminal liability for the assault. If, however, a particular individual participant realises that others who are involved, are going beyond what was agreed, or that matters are simply getting out of hand or control, and no longer wish to be part of the enterprise, then they must, in order to avoid liability for any greater offence that might be committed, make an effective withdrawal from the enterprise.

The principles of withdrawal from a spontaneous attack are different to those from a pre-planned enterprise and are found in *R. v Mitchell and King* [1998] 163 J.P. 75. It was held that whilst communication of withdrawal is a necessary condition for disassociation from a pre-planned violence, it is not necessary when the violence is spontaneous. Accordingly, a defendant who effectively disengages or withdraws before the fatal injury is inflicted, is not guilty of the offence because he was not party to and did not participate in any unlawful violence which caused the fatal injury or injuries. The Court stated that sufficient action on the part of the secondary offender which could amount to effective withdrawal in a spontaneous attack, would be ceasing to fight, throwing down one's weapons, or walking away. There is no requirement that reasonable steps must be taken to prevent the crime. This decision was followed by the Court of Appeal in *R. v O'Flaherty* [2004] 2 Cr.App.R. 315 (see above at para.8.09).

15. Alternative Verdict of Manslaughter: Degree of Foresight needed by the Secondary Party: The "Fundamentally Different" Principle

8.15 Since the decision in *Powell and English*, the one question that remained unresolved is whether and in what circumstances a secondary party can still be convicted of the alternative offence of manslaughter, the principal having been convicted of murder. Alternatively, if the principal offender is convicted of manslaughter can the secondary party be convicted of murder? For instance; A, B and C agree to give D a slap, A and B catch up with D, C being elsewhere. A and B launch in to a violent attack, killing D. The principal offenders A and B are convicted of murder. The question is; can C under the principles in *Powell and English*, if not liable for the murder, since he did not foresee the deliberate intent to kill, still nonetheless be guilty of manslaughter given he may have foreseen the unlawful act of assault, which was dangerous and caused the death? In *R. v Robert Day and Day* [2001] Crim. L.R. 984, the Court of Appeal held that the judge has a discretion, based on the evidence in the case, to direct the jury that it is possible to convict some parties of murder and others of manslaughter, if the secondary party contemplated the act of violence by the other which caused the death.

The issue was explored further by the Court of Appeal in *Attorney-General's Reference (No.3 of 2004)* (2005) EWCA Crim 1882, on a point of law reference arising out of the acquittal of Van Hoogstraten (VH). The Court stated that to resolve the critical issue of a secondary party's liability for manslaughter when the principal offender committed murder is to apply the "fundamentally different" test. Did the secondary party foresee the possibility that the primary party would do what he had done, or was that act said to be of a fundamentally different character to what the secondary party had contemplated? In such circumstances the secondary party is neither guilty of murder, nor manslaughter. The reference involved the defendant VH, a wealthy property owner, who had a dispute over money with the victim. The prosecution had alleged that VH had recruited K and C to kill the victim. K and C went to the victim's house, when he answered the door they shot him dead, both where later convicted of murder. VH was acquitted of murder but found guilty of the victim's manslaughter.

His appeal against conviction was quashed by the Court of Appeal on the grounds that the judge had failed to direct the jury properly that they could only convict him as a secondary party if they were sure that he had contemplated the use of a lethal weapon in the attack; i.e. the defendant is only responsible for the consequences of the actus reus he specifically, or tacitly agreed to with the others, VH had claimed that he only agreed to frighten the victim not injure him. The Court of Appeal ordered a re-trial, a fresh indictment was preferred, but the trial judge acceded to a defence submission of no case to answer, since on the assumed facts that VH did not intend physically to injure or kill the victim nor had he foreseen that possibility, then this revealed no basis upon which a jury could conclude that VH contemplated that the act done by K and C would cause death.

The application of the "fundamentally different" principle was considered recently by the Court of Appeal in *R. v Rahman* [2007] EWCA Crim 342, a tragic case in which the deceased, a young man, was stabbed in the back during an attack on him by a group of other men. The appeal against conviction on the grounds that the judge had misdirected the jury on the fundamentally different principle was dismissed. The Court of Appeal, "albeit with trepidation", formulated a series of questions for the jury to determine in cases where the victim dies during a group attack and the prosecution are unable to establish the identity of individual killer and therefore present their case as a joint enterprise to commit murder.

Before any of the participants can be convicted of murder, the jury must first be sure that one of the participating attackers had the mens rea and committed the actus reus of murder. If so the questions for the jury are as follows:

"1. Are you sure that D intended that one of the attackers would kill V intending to kill him or that D realised that one of the attackers might kill V with intent to kill him? If yes, guilty of murder. If no, go to 2.

2. Are you sure that either:

(a) D realised that one of the attackers might kill V with intent to cause him really serious bodily harm; or
(b) D intended that really serious bodily harm would be caused to V; or
(c) D realised that one of the attackers might cause serious bodily harm to V intending to cause him such harm?

If no, not guilty of murder. If yes, go to question 3.

3. What was P's act which caused the death of V? (e.g. stabbing, shooting, kicking, beating) Go to question 4.

4. Did D realise that one of the attackers might do this act? If yes, guilty of murder, if no, go to question 5.

5. What act or acts are you sure D realised that one of the attackers might do to cause V really serious Harm? Go to question 6.

6. Are you sure that this act or those acts (which D realised one of the attackers might do) is/are not of a fundamentally different nature to P's act which caused the death of V? If yes guilty of murder. If no, not guilty of murder."

The Court of Appeal commented that the fundamentally different principle is an "objective test" in that "it is used to compare the acts which D realised one of the attackers might do and P's (the unidentified killer) which caused the death" (see also *R. v Rafferty* [2007] EWCA Crim 1846). It is important to be aware that another problem which can arise when a jury convict one participant of murder and the other of manslaughter, or convict one and acquit the other, is that the verdict could be deemed to be unsafe on the grounds of inconsistency, as explained in *R. v McGill* [2005] EWCA Crim 1252 and *R. v Green* [2005] EWCA Crim 2513.

16. Cut Throat Defences and Incrimination

8.16 As can often be the case, especially in spontaneous group violence situations, each defendant may, as part of their defence, claim that they were a mere bystander or that if involved in the violence, they were not part of the incident that lead to the injuries. By making such contentions, this will invariably conflict with the contentions raised by the other co-accused in their defence. In *R. v Jones and Jenkins* [2003] EWCA Crim 1966, the Court of Appeal observed that in situations such as this and even if the cut throat defences are mirror images of each other, i.e. each blames the other, then the judge should direct the jury to consider each defendant's contentions separately, bearing in mind to warn the jury that a co-defendant will have a purpose of their own to serve. Finally, the jury should assess the honesty and accuracy of the co-defendants, as they would with any other witness. Further, the Court ruled that the decision in *R. v Burrows* [1999] Crim. L.R. 48, that a warning was not necessary where two defendants blamed each other in evidence, was limited to its facts and did not provide any principle of law (see also the decision of the House of Lords in *R. v Hayter* [2005] 1 W.L.R. 605).

17. Children: Their Non-Accidental Death or Serious Injury

8.17 For the prosecution, evidential difficulties would often arise where a child was killed or suffered serious injury whilst in the company of both parents who blamed each other, and therefore it could be proved which of the two was directly responsible and which one was not and therefore must have been an accomplice. In *R. v Abbott* [1955] 3 W.L.R. 369 it was stated:

> "If two people are jointly indicted for the commission of a crime and the evidence does not point to one rather than the other, and there is no evidence that they were acting in concert, the jury ought to return a verdict of not guilty in the case of both because the prosecution has not proved its case. If, in those circumstances, it is left to the defendants to get out of the difficulty if they can, that would put the onus on the defendants to prove themselves not guilty."

This led the Law Commission to review and propose a change in the law (See "Children: Their Non- Accidental Death or Serious Injury (Criminal Trials) Law Com. No.279). Parliament adopted these reforms which are to be found in ss.5 and 6 of the Domestic Violence, Crime and Victims Act 2004 which came into effect on March 21, 2005. Section 5 creates a new homicide offence of causing or allowing the death of a child or vulnerable adult. This provides that a person is guilty of an offence in two situations. First, if the child (a person under 16) or a vulnerable adult (a person 16 or over whose ability to protect themselves from violence, abuse or neglect, is significantly impaired through physical or mental disability or illness or old age or otherwise) dies as a result of the unlawful act (i.e. any criminal act, such as an assault, act also includes a positive act or an omission) of a person who at the time of the act is a member of the same household as the deceased (household in this context will mean a domestic one, the defendant does not have to live there), and had frequent contact with him.

Secondly, at the time of the unlawful act there was a significant risk of serious physical harm being caused to the deceased by such a person and that person either caused the death or was or ought to have been aware of the risk of serious harm, or failed to take such steps to protect the deceased from the risk as could be reasonably been expected of them (this amounts to an objective test) and that the person foresaw or ought to have foreseen, in the circumstances, the unlawful act (this amounts to the mens rea, which would seem to have a subjective element, i.e. foreseen and an objective element, i.e. ought to have foreseen). In *R. v Stephens* [2007] EWCA Crim 1249, the Court of Appeal ruled that the expression "significant risk" in the context of the offence should be given its ordinary and natural meaning and that just like the word "insults" in *Brutus v Cozens* [1973] A.C. 854, it is in general usage. Accordingly, the judge was wrong to direct the jury that it meant something "more than minimal"; he should have said that it is a question of fact for them to decide.

A person who is under 16 at time of the unlawful act and is not the mother or father of the victim, cannot be charged with the offence. Sub-section (7) classifies the offence as an indictable only offence with a maximum penalty of 14 years' imprisonment. Section 6, to ensure that proceedings are not too readily dismissed, makes several evidential and procedural changes specific to the s.5 offence, namely the drawing of inferences from a refusal to give evidence or answer questions. This also applies to murder or manslaughter, even though for those offences there may be no case to answer, a submission of no case to answer, which is usually heard at the close of the prosecution case, can only be heard at the close of all the evidence.

18. Inchoate (Incomplete) Offences

8.18 The criminal law exists in the public interest and is deliberately wide in its application. It is just as important to punish those who embark upon acts that, if successful, would lead to the commission of a criminal offence, as it is to punish those who have committed an offence. This is the very essence and justification for the availability of inchoate or incomplete offences. Accordingly, the criminal law readily attaches criminal liability to those in the preliminary stages of committing a complete offence, no matter how significant or insignificant is their involvement. The relevant offences are (i) incitement; (ii) soliciting; (iii) conspiracy; (iv) attempts.

19. The Common Law Offence of Incitement

8.19 The common law definition of incitement was explained by Clarke L.J. in *R. v Goldman* [2001] EWCA Crim 1684, in which his Lordship stated obiter:

> "The ordinary meaning of 'incitement' as adopted in the authorities is that it encompasses encouragement, persuasion or inducement. The following definition was graphically given by Holmes JA in *Mkosiyana* (1966) 'An inciter ... is one who reaches and seeks to influence the mind of another to the commission of a crime. The machinations of criminal ingenuity being legion, the approach to the other's mind may take many forms, such as a suggestion, proposal, request, exhortation, gesture, argument. Persuasion, inducement, goading or the arousal of cupidity.'

The Court of Appeal upheld the defendant's conviction for attempting to incite another to distribute indecent photographs of children under the age of 16, contrary to s.1 of the Criminal Attempts Act 1981. The defendant responded to an advertisement for material from a company in Amsterdam, he paid by cheque, but did not receive the material. The Court held that the defendant attempted to incite another, namely the company, to do an act of sending to him indecent photographs, which would have involved the commission of an offence namely the distribution of indecent photographs and that he had the relevant intent or belief.

In *R. v Tompkins* [2007] Crim. L.R. 234 the Court of Appeal dismissed the appeal, stating that a person could be guilty of incitement to commit an offence where the person that they sought to incite was in another jurisdiction (country). In this case, the offence was incitement to distribute indecent photographs of children, in which the person to be incited was situated abroad. The appellant argued that he had committed no offence in this country and therefore could not be prosecuted in this country; he relied on the criminal law presumption of jurisdiction. However, the Court of Appeal ruled in this instance that, in the circumstances in which the offence had been committed, the presumption was rebutted on public policy grounds.

20. The Statutory Offence of Incitement: Part 2 of the Serious Crime Act 2007

8.20 The Law Commission, in its report "Inchoate Liability For Assisting and Encouraging Crime; Law Com. No.300 (2006), reviews extensively the existing law relating to secondary offender liability and inchoate liability. The Commission considered that the common law on incitement is defective, complex, unsatisfactory and arbitrary. A person who assists another to commit a crime incurs no liability if the person they assisted does not or is prevented from, actually committing the crime. Parliament agreed that the common law needed to be simplified and therefore has adopted the recommendations from the Commission with the creation of three new statutory offences contained in Pt 2 of the Serious Crime Act 2007 which received the Royal Assent on October 30, 2007, but has yet to be brought into force.

Section 59 expressly abolishes the common law offence of incitement. Section 44 creates the new offence of intentionally encouraging or assisting an offence and is committed if a person does an intentional act capable of encouraging or assisting the commission of an offence. This amounts to a specific intent crime and it is made clear in subsection (2) that foresight of consequences is not enough to prove the required mens rea. Section 45 creates the new offence of encouraging or assisting an offence, believing it will be committed. The actus reus is the same as for the s.44 offence, the mens rea however, is that the person "believes" the offence will be committed and their act will encourage or assist its commission.

Section 46 creates the all embracing offence of encouraging or assisting offences believing one or more will be committed. Again, the actus reus is the same as for the other offences, but relates to "one or more of a number of offences". The mens rea is that of "belief". The prosecution are not required to prove belief as to a particular offence, just a belief that one or a number of offences would be committed. Procedurally, the indictment must specify the believed category of offence, but not every single offence needs to be specified.

8.21 Section 47 further sets out what the prosecution must prove in terms of the mens rea of the defendant (for all three new offences) who does an act of encouragement or assistance of another, to commit an offence that requires "proof of fault"; for instance, if a defendant provides a knife to another to be used to commit a serious assault on a love rival, then the prosecution must prove that the defendant either:

(i) believed that the act (namely the assault would be done with the necessary fault, i.e. if s.18 an intent to cause/wound with GBH) required for that offence, or

(ii) was reckless as to whether such an act would be done, or

(iii) if they were to commit the offence they would have the necessary fault elements, i.e. the defendant, a woman, encourages or assists a man to rape another person.

The same except (iii) applies to offences that require the prosecution to prove particular circumstances or consequences of the offence, i.e. involuntary manslaughter.

It is important to be aware that the act done by the person who is being encouraged or assisted, includes:

(i) a failure to act, i.e. gross negligence manslaughter;

(ii) the continuation of an act;

(iii) an attempt to do an act.

Further, s.49(1) expressly states that a person still commits any of the three new offences, regardless of whether the offence encouraged or assisted is committed or not. Equally, subsection (2) provides that for an offence in ss.44 and 45 the defendant can commit separate offences, for each encouraged or assisted offence (i.e. A provides B with a breaking in tools which B uses to commit three burglaries in the same night, A will be guilty of three offences of encouraging or assisting a burglary) Likewise, a person can, in the one act of encouraging or assisting, commit some, or all of the three offences. However, certain "listed offences" in Sch.3 are precluded in the commission of an offence under ss.45 and 46, whilst the offences listed in Sch.4 require the consent of the Attorney-General before a prosecution can be commenced. Section 50 provides for a specific statutory defence of reasonableness for any of the three offences.

It is important to be aware that s.51 maintains both the previous common law rules and statutory provisions that provide protection to a class of persons, and that where such a person is the actual victim, they cannot be liable for aiding and abetting that offence. This section is designed to maintain the rule in *R. v Tyrrell* [1894] 1 Q.B. 710, in which it was held that the defendant cannot aid, abet solicit or incite another to have unlawful sexual intercourse with a person under 13, when in fact the defendant was the actual victim of the offence committed by the other defendant. The law protects those who, as in this case, are under a specified age, as being incapable of consenting (even though on the facts they did consent) so as to provide the necessary protection from exploitation. It would be absurd if a victim, who is not the perpetrator, to lose that protection and the actual person who is inciting to use the protection, to escape criminal liability (see also the particular ruling in *R. v Claydon* [2006] 1 Cr.App.R. 20.

8.22 Section 52 allows for all three offences to be widely applied, in that the defendant can be outside England and Wales at the time of their act of encouragement or assistance; provided they know or believe the anticipated offences might take place wholly or partly in England and Wales. Section 54 determines the rules regarding the institution of proceedings and provides, in particular, that general powers of seizure, retention and forfeiture of property apply to all three offences, and that a non-UK owned internet service provider can still commit the offences. In terms of mode of trial, s.55 provides that an offence under ss.44 and 45 is triable in the same way as the anticipated offence, i.e. if the defendant encourages B to commit theft, then A, if charged with a s.44 offence, will be dealt with as being charged with an either way offence, whereas for a s.46 offence this must proceed as an indictable only offence.

Section 57 provides expressly for the rules on alternative verdicts in s.6(3) of the Criminal Justice Act 1967, in that if the prosecution present their case that under s.44 the defendant intended to encourage or assist B to commit GBH with intent, but the jury are not satisfied that the defendant intended GBH, but had a mens rea for ABH instead, then they convict them under s.44 for encouraging ABH as an alternative to the count alleging the more serious offence of GBH. Subsection (10) allows for the defendant to plead guilty to the less serious anticipated offence. Section 58 states expressly that in terms of punishment, the defendant can be sentenced to the same level of punishment for the anticipated offence.

Finally, ss.65, 66 and 67 provide that the defendant's act of encouragement or assistance includes a "course of conduct" and also any steps taken by them so as to reduce the risk of criminal proceedings being brought, in respect of the anticipated offence or failing to take reasonable steps to discharge a duty owed, i.e. a police officer watches a street robbery but fails to intervene. Further, an act of threatening another or putting pressure on them to commit an offence amounts to encouraging or assisting the commission of that offence. Section 66 ensures that liability for the three offences will still arise against a person who makes arrangements for another person, B, to encourage or assist a third person C; this indirect encouragement or assist is aimed at gang leaders who instruct one of their lieutenants to encourage another to kill the victim.

21. Other Statutory Encouragement Offences

8.23 Section 1 of the Terrorism Act 2000 creates the offence of intentionally or recklessly publishing or causing to be published a statement that is likely to be understood by those members of the public to whom it is published as encouraging or inducing them, either directly or indirectly, to commit, prepare or instigate an act of terrorism. The encouragement can include the glorification of past or future acts of terrorism. Proof of the encouragement can be inferred from the contents of the statement, circumstances and manner in which it was published. A defence exists in s.1(6), but only to recklessly publishing a statement. The statutory defence places the burden on the defendant to show that the statement neither expressed their views, nor had their endorsement and that this is clear in all the circumstances surrounding the publication. This amounts to an either way offence with a maximum sentence of seven years' imprisonment on conviction on indictment.

Section 2 creates a similar offence that catches specifically intentional or reckless conduct that involves the dissemination of terrorist publications which directly or indirectly provide encouragement or inducement to others to become involved in acts of terrorism. This carries the same custodial penalties as for s.1. Section 3 of the 2000 Act deals specifically with statements made in connection with a service provided electronically. Section 59 of the 2000 Act creates the offence of inciting another person to commit an act of terrorism which amounts to a specified offence, i.e. murder wholly or partly outside the UK. Section 2 of the Terrorism Act 2006 creates an offence committed by a person who engages in conduct intended to give, either direct or indirect encouragement or other inducement to acts of terrorism.

Other statutory offences of incitement, which arise separately to the three new offences, include those contained in the Sexual Offences Act 2003, namely, s.8 causing or inciting a child under 13 to engage in sexual activity, s.10 in regard to a child under 16 and s.26 inciting a child family member to engage in sexual activity.

22. The Offence of Conspiracy

8.24 The offence of conspiracy is a "catch all" type of offence, where the prosecution are unable to prove the alleged substantive offences, or where there is insufficient evidence to prove that certain participants committed any substantive offence, but there is evidence to link them to it, then it would in those circumstances be appropriate to charge with conspiracy. For instance, the police have had under surveillance a gang of men, who they believe have been breaking into houses to obtain the keys to the expensive cars parked on the driveways. When the lock up is raided, the police find various car parts and documentation that suggests the cars had been sent abroad by container. The police arrest a number of the gang, but have no evidence to prove they actually committed the burglaries or theft of cars, but there is evidence to establish their involvement to some degree. In this instance, in order to have a more realistic prospect of securing a conviction, it would be more appropriate to charge them all with conspiracy to steal motor vehicles.

The offence of conspiracy is defined in s.1 of the Criminal Law Act 1977 as follows:

> "if a person *agrees* with any other person(s) that a *course of conduct* shall be pursued which, if the agreement is carried out in accordance with their intentions either,
>
> (i) will necessarily *amount to* or invoke the commission of *any* offence(s) by the parties to the agreement *or*
> (ii) would *do so but* for the existence of facts make it *impossible* to commit the offence
>
> is guilty of conspiracy to commit the offence(s)."

To secure a conviction for a conspiracy, the prosecution must prove that there are two or more persons involved, that these persons agree to pursue a course of conduct (actus reus) with an intent (mens rea) to commit an offence, even if that offence is impossible to commit. Section 5(8) makes it clear that if there are only two conspirators and one of them is acquitted, this acquittal does not preclude the conviction of the remaining conspirator, provided that their conviction is not shown to be inconsistent with the acquittal of the other, so as to make that conviction unsafe for inconsistency. Likewise, the prosecution are not required to indict two or more persons; one person can be indicted for having conspired with others unknown.

However, s.1(2) limits the application of the statutory conspiracy contained in s.1(1), in that where liability for the substantive offence which "may be incurred without knowledge", i.e. no mens rea of the defendant, and then no conspiracy offence can be committed, unless the defendant "and at least one other party to the agreement intend or know that a fact or circumstance shall or will exist at the time when the conduct constituting the offence is to take place". The purpose behind s.1(2) is to exclude from liability offences of strict liability and offences with a mens rea of recklessness, unless the actual conspirator intends or knows that the fact or circumstance of the substantive offences exists at the time of the conduct of the conspiracy. Although the offence of conspiracy is an inchoate offence, designed specifically to attach criminal liability to acts in the future, the prosecution, to avoid falling foul of the rule of duplicity (i.e. overloading the indictment with numerous counts), will charge conspiracy so as to encapsulate the defendant's overall conduct in one count, even though the substantive offence has indeed been committed. By doing this, the defendant's culpability can be reflected in the sentencing process.

8.25 However, routinely taking advantage of this procedural practice led the prosecution into the legal difficulties in *R. v Saik* [2007] 1 A.C. 18, concerning the offence of money laundering contained in s.93C of the Criminal Justice, Act 1988 as amended. This decision is now largely academic, because of the later amendments by the Proceeds of Crime Act 2002. The earlier version of the offence of money laundering required proof of either knowing or having reasonable grounds to suspect that any property represents another person's proceedings of crime. In *R. v Montila* [2004] 1 W.L.R. 3141, the House of Lords had ruled that the prosecution must prove that the property does amount to proceeds from an actual crime. The appellant Saik had pleaded guilty on the basis that he only had a suspicion that money which was being brought to his money exchange business, to be exchanged into another currency, was money from a crime.

Having accepted the basis of the plea on these terms, the prosecution were bound. The House of Lords quashed the appellant's conviction on the grounds that by virtue of s.1(2), suspicion was not enough; the provision required the prosecution to establish that the appellant either intended, or knew that the the money, when he exchanged it, was the proceeds of a crime. Lord Nichols was not prepared to avoid an unattractive outcome by producing a distorted interpretation of s.1(2), "it is not for the courts to extend the net of criminal conspiracy beyond the reach set by Parliament".

The prosecution could have avoided this outcome by either charging the appellant with the substantive offence, or framing the particulars of the conspiracy, so that the appellant, when exchanging the money, was in an agreement which when carried out with that intention, would necessarily amount to or involve the commission of, the money laundering offence. In *R. v Griffiths* [1965] 3 W.L.R. 405, the Court stated that a conspiracy offence should not be added as a separate count to that alleging the substantive offence; a conspiracy allegation should, unless it is not in the interests of justice to do so, be tried separately (for pre-*Saik* convictions see *R. v Ramzan and Others* [2006] EWCA Crim 1974).

8.26 Further, the Court of Appeal stated that the prosecution must prove that those who they allege form part of the conspiracy do so as one agreed conspiracy; it need not be established that the entered the agreement at the same time, each can join at different times. Neither must it be shown that each knows the other, but it is fundamental that it is proved that they was all acting in common, to pursue a course of criminal conduct. This is sometimes referred to as a "wheel conspiracy" where A is situated in the centre, who then invites others, B,C and D to join him to pursue a common course of conduct. Likewise, a "chain conspiracy" occurs where A conspires with B, B then conspires with C and so on, but again, it is vital for the prosecution to prove they each knew of the common purpose of the conspiracy. If this cannot be proved, then there exists no conspiracy between the parties involved (see also *R. v Mintern* [2004] EWCA Crim 7).

As is often the case with conspiracy trials, the prosecution, in terms of proving that the defendants were in agreement to pursue a course of criminal conduct, will adduce evidence of the "overt acts" of the defendant, from which the prosecution will invite the jury to draw or infer from such acts the existence of a continuing agreement between them all. Originally the s.1 offence only included offences that could be triable in England and Wales, s.5 Criminal Justice (Terrorism and Conspiracy) Act 1998 inserts a new s.1A into s.1 of the 1977 Act which provides that if the following four specified conditions are satisfied:

(i) the event is intended to take place outside the UK;

(ii) the offence constitutes an offence under the jurisdiction of the other country;

(iii) the elements of conspiracy are there

(a) two or more persons
(b) agreement
(c) course of conduct
(d) any offence;

(iv) the parties must have done something in the UK in agreement,

then the person(s) will be guilty of conspiracy for an offence to be committed outside jurisdiction of the UK.

23. Common Law Offence of Conspiracy to Defraud (Dishonesty)

8.27 The House of Lords in *Scott v MPC* [1974] 3 W.L.R. 741 confirmed the existence and application of the common law offence of conspiracy to defraud, and that s.32 of the Theft Act 1968 had not repealed it (the offence is now preserved by s.5(2) of the Criminal Law Act 1977). The elements for establishing a conspiracy in the context of a fraud are the same as for statutory conspiracy. If the prosecution are able to establish a conspiracy, then if the complainant is a private individual, it must be proved that the purpose of the conspiracy was to dishonestly (*Ghosh* test to be applied) cause that person economic loss by depriving them of some property or injure some proprietary right to which they are entitled.

In terms of dishonesty, the prosecution are not required to prove that there was a deceit, simply that the conspirators acted dishonestly. If the complainant of the conspiracy is a person who is performing a public duty (i.e. a local councillor), then the prosecution need only prove that the purpose of the conspiracy was to dishonestly cause this person to act, contrary to their public duty. There is no requirement in this situation for the prosecution to prove an economic loss. Section 12 of the Criminal Justice Act 1987 provides that the common law offence of conspiracy to defraud, is an indictable only offence with a maximum sentence of 10 years' imprisonment.

24. Conspiracy to Corrupt Public Morals/Outrage Public Decency

8.28 In *Shaw v DPP* [1962] A.C. 220, the House of Lords, by a majority of three to two, confirmed that there existed in the common law an indictable offence of conspiracy to corrupt public morals. The appellant's conviction for publishing a female contact magazine ("The Ladies Directory") was upheld. What is meant by public morals is a question of fact for the jury by applying the current standards/values of society. This decision was upheld by the majority in *R. v Knuller* [1973] A.C. 435, in which the facts where similar to *Shaw* but involving gay men. However a second count against *Knuller*, charging a conspiracy to outrage public decency of which he was convicted, was quashed on the basis of a mis-direction.

By a majority, the House of Lords ruled that an offence of outraging public decency was known in the common law, but that the courts do not have a residual power to create new common law criminal offences. Although this offence still exists, in the context of the facts of *Shaw* and *Knuller*, a prosecution is unlikely to be commenced given the liberal and indeed human rights approach to the exercise of values in our current society. Both *Shaw* and *Knuller* were accused of public debauchery and the destruction of moral values that existed at the time. Today, such standards have become more liberalised with greater exposure to sexual imagery. Nevertheless, s.63 of the Criminal Justice and Immigration Act 2008, when in force, creates a new offence of possessing extreme pornographic images. This is in response to the disturbing facts that arose in *R. v Coutts* [2006] 1 W.L.R. 2154. In a different context, the offence of outraging public decency is often used to prosecute men who have sex with a prostitute in public, but it did not cover the growing problem of watching sexual activity in public such as "dogging". This type of public nuisance led to Parliament creating the offence of voyeurism contained in s.67 of the Sexual Offences Act 2003. This consists of observing, recording or operating equipment for the benefit of a third person of another doing a private act, who they know would not have consented, for the purpose of sexual gratification.

The application of the common law offence of outraging public decency had to be addressed by the Court of Appeal against the somewhat unsettling facts in *R. v Hamilton* [2008] 1 Cr.App.R. 13. The appellant, a practising barrister, had surreptitiously and strategically placed a digital camcorder in a bag and filmed under female skirts in a supermarket; this included a 14-year-old complainant. The appellant on appeal contended that he could not be guilty of the common law offence of outraging public decency, since on the facts it was impossible for the prosecution to prove the two person public element rule of the actus reus.

This was rejected by the Court of Appeal who adopted a mischief rule approach to the application of the principles in that the public needs protecting from such intrusive conduct. Having reviewed the previous authorities, the Court concluded that the prosecution, in order to secure a conviction for the offence, must prove (i) that the act took place in public which is accessible to the public; (ii) that the act was lewd, obscene or disgusting (means causing the annoyance or loathing or distaste of an onlooker) and that it outrages public decency, this requires evidence that the act offends the recognised standards of propriety in contemporary society; (iii) the public element requirement that the act is capable of being witnessed by at least two persons who are present. For this element the Court of Appeal refused to adopt a restrictive interpretation, holding that the prosecution are not required to prove that the two people present actually saw the act, only that it was capable of being witnessed. This is a difficult offence, given the lack of mens rea and the possible uncertainty of what constitutes public decency and now requires the House of Lords to clarify its application.

25. Conspiracy and Impossibility

8.29 Section 5 of the Criminal Attempts Act 1981 amended the definition of statutory conspiracy by providing that even if it is impossible, or has become impossible, for the conspired offence to be committed, the parties involved are still guilty of the offence of conspiracy of the impossibility. Accordingly, there is no available defence of impossibility to an allegation of statutory conspiracy.

Nevertheless, such a defence is still available for the common law offence of conspiracy to defraud, as set out in *DPP v Nock* [1978] A.C. 979, in which the House of Lords held that there could be no common law conspiracy to defraud where, unknown to the alleged conspirators, the object of the conspiracy was impossible to achieve. In *R. v Gleeson* [2003] EWCA Crim 3357, counsel for the defence sought to gain a tactical advantage, when the prosecution had charged conspiracy to defraud, but on the facts this was impossible to commit, since the police became involved in an undercover investigation and therefore there could be no victim. The judge accepted the defence's submission of no case to answer based on the *Nock* decision, but allowed (which was confirmed by the Court of Appeal) the prosecution to amend the indictment to include a statutory conspiracy count.

26. Conspiracy to Import Prohibited Drugs

8.30 In *R. v Taylor* [2002] Crim. L.R. 205, it was held by the Court of Appeal that the name of the particular drug alleged to be part of conspiracy need not be specified in the indictment. Accordingly, if the indictment alleges a conspiracy to import a class A drug, it does not matter that the person who joined the conspiracy thought it concerned a different drug, provided it was of the same class. Further, if the prosecution can prove that the defendant joined the conspiracy to import drugs and in their own mind cared not whether they were heroin or cannabis, they would be guilty of whatever drugs were in fact imported. This principle was confirmed and received approval by the Court of Appeal in *R. v Ayala* [2003] EWCA Crim 2047.

27. Conspiracy to Commit Criminal Damage

8.31 A similar issue can arise with the Criminal Damage Act 1971, which consists of basic criminal damage and aggravated damage, with a mens rea of intention or recklessness and arson. Accordingly, there exists between the offences differing degrees of culpability and levels of sentencing. In *R. v Roberts and Others* [1998] 1 Cr.App.R. 441, the Court of Appeal quashed the conviction the on a single count of "conspiracy to commit criminal damage" which involved a campaign of various types of damage, including using petrol bombs against exporters of live animals. The Court ruled that the presentation at trial was inappropriate for basic (simple) criminal damage and that the indictment failed to identify the aggravated form of criminal damage. For this reason, it was impossible for the judge to impose an appropriate sentence based on the appellant's culpability.

28. Criminal Attempts: Section 1 of the Criminal Attempts Act 1981

8.32 Where a person attempts to commit an offence but fails to complete that offence, then they will be charged with attempting to commit that offence under s.1 of the Criminal Attempts Act 1981.

This provides that:

(a) if with *intent* to commit an *"indictable offence"* but not conspiracy or being an accessory a person does an act which is more than merely preparatory to the commission of the offence, they are guilty of attempting to commit the offence

(b) a person is still guilty of attempting to commit that offence even if on the facts it is impossible to commit.

The mens rea of a criminal attempt is that of *specific intent*, it is not sufficient to have a reckless mind when attempting to commit an indictable offence. The Act further limits the offence of attempt to those that are classified as indictable offences (i.e. either way and indictable only). Accordingly, as a matter of law, it is not possible to attempt to commit a summary only offence unless such an offence is specifically created as such (i.e. s.5(1)(a) of the Road Traffic Act 1988 creates the offence of attempting to drive a motor vehicle on a road being over the proscribed limit, see also s.3 of the Criminal Attempts Act 1981 which allows for specific statutory exceptions). A good illustration of this limitation is the offence of driving whilst disqualified, which amounts to a summary only offence.

If driver A is disqualified and takes the keys to his car and places the keys in the door to open it, he is committing no offence of attempting to drive whilst disqualified, only until he starts the engine and drives on a public road will he commit an offence. It is also important to be aware of the paradoxical distinction between the mens rea for murder and that of attempted murder, which would be charged under s.1 of the Criminal Attempts Act 1981, although the mens rea for murder is an intent to kill or an intent to cause GBH, for attempted murder, as confirmed in *R. v Morrison* [2003] 2 Cr.App.R. 37, the prosecution must prove a specific intent to kill, it is not sufficient for attempted murder to have an intent to cause GBH. If the prosecution cannot prove an intent to kill, then the defendant cannot be guilty of attempted murder but possibly a lesser alternative assault offence.

8.33 In order to establish the actus reus of a criminal attempt, the prosecution must prove that the defendant did an act which is more than merely preparatory to the commission of the offence, even if that offence is impossible. Section 4(3) makes it clear that whilst the judge may determine whether or not there is sufficient evidence to allow a jury to determine properly whether an attempt was committed, once the matter is before the jury it becomes a question of fact and degree for the jury to decide whether the prosecution has proved its case. Ultimately, the jury must decide on the facts whether the defendant is still in mere preparation mode or has moved in the execution stage and therefore into the ambit of attempts.

In *R. v Campbell* [1991] 93 Cr.App.R. 350, the appellant, having been observed by police officers, was stopped outside a post office and found to have sunglasses, an imitation firearm and was threatening to the officers. The Court of Appeal allowed the appeal and quashed the conviction for attempted robbery, stating the judge was wrong on the evidence to allow the case to be put before a jury. Watkins L.J. observed that as a matter of guidance, an attempt occurs:

> "when the merely preparatory acts come to an end and the defendant embarks upon the crime proper."

His Lordship further noted that a trial judge should avoid giving any illustrations of what can and cannot amount to an attempt, it is a matter for the jury to decide whether the act alleged was more than a act of preparation to commit the offence.

Similarly, in *R. v Geddes* [1996] Crim. L.R. 894, the Court of Appeal quashed the appellant's conviction for attempted false imprisonment of a child. He had been seen in the toilets of a school, but left the premises when challenged by a police officer. A rucksack belonging to the appellant was later found to contain some distressing items, namely a large knife, rope and masking tape. Although the Court was uneasy about quashing the appellant's conviction and whilst his intention was to falsely imprison or kidnap a child, he had not, on the evidence, gone beyond the mere preparation stage. Conversely, in *R. v Tosti* [1997] Crim. L.R. 746, the Court of Appeal dismissed the appeal against conviction for attempted burglary, since the evidence of having and concealing cutting equipment near the farm premises and then inspecting the lock of the barn they intended to burgle, was sufficient to allow a jury to properly determine the line between mere preparation and actually trying to commit the offence. In terms of punishment of conviction of an attempted offence, s.4 provides expressly that if a person is convicted of attempted murder, then the court may impose a discretionary life sentence, whilst for attempts of other offences, the sentence available is the same as that for the offence that was attempted.

8.34 Section 1(2) states that even if the complete offence is impossible to commit, a defendant can still be guilty of attempting to commit it. The House of Lords, as a matter of statutory construction, considered whether attempting the impossible covers situations where the defendant does an act which is "objectively innocent". In *Anderton v Ryan* [1985] A.C. 560, the House of Lords, by a majority, ruled that Parliament had not intended to criminalise a person who although they do a legal act, had mistakenly believed that such an act was unlawful. In *R. v Shivpuri* [1987] A.C. 1, the appellant attempted to smuggle through London Airport what he thought was heroin, which he later admitted into in an interview.

However, after forensic analysis it was found that the substance he attempted to smuggle was in fact vegetable matter, not drugs. The appellant was indicted and convicted of attempting to commit a s.170 of the Customs and Excise Management Act 1970 offence of being knowingly concerned in dealing with a controlled drug, the importation of which was prohibited. The House of Lords agreed unanimously that the decision in *Ryan* had wrongly interpreted the law and therefore their Lordships used the 1966 practice statement to depart formally from the decision. Lord Bridge readily accepted that he had erred in *Ryan* and that the concept of "objective innocence is incapable of sensible application in relation to the law of criminal attempts".

It was regretted that the House had not taken note of para.2.97 of the Law Commission report, which led to the creation of the Criminal Attempts Act 1981. This makes it clear that provided a defendant has the necessary intent and does an act of more than mere preparation to the commission of the complete offence, it is irrelevant whether that act later turns out to be an innocent act; the liability of attempt lies with the mens rea of intent together with preparation. In *R. v Jones* [2007] EWCA Crim 1118, the appellant was convicted of a number of offences, one particular offence was that of attempting to commit an offence under s.8 of the Sexual Offences Act 2003 by causing or inciting a child under 13 to engage in penetrative sexual activity. The background to the offence was that various written messages were left at railway stations inviting eight to 13 year-old-girls for sex. A journalist made contact with the appellant and through a series of text messages was asked for a naked photograph and to meet after school for oral sex. This was passed on to the police who set up an undercover sting operation using a police officer as a girl called Amy aged 12, further explicit text messages were exchanged.

On appeal against conviction, the appellant sought to distinguish the ruling in *Shivpuri* on the basis that in *Shivpuri*, the defendant had a "real" intent to smuggle drugs whereas the appellant (Jones) only had a "fictional" intent since the actual person he sought to incite was not a child under 13, but an adult police officer. The Court of Appeal rejected this contention in its entirety and concluded that provided all the elements to the offence existed, the fact that the police had substituted the child with an adult did not provide an escape from liability just as Shivpuri could not escape liability for drug smuggling. Even though it was impossible for the appellant to commit the complete s.8 offence, he had done an act which was more that mere preparation (i.e. arranging to meet the unknown child), together with the relevant intent this amounted to offence known to law and was a criminal attempt.

29. Other Incomplete Offences

8.35 If there is no attempt of a theft offence, then the defendant may still be potentially liable for another offence of going equipped to steal under s.25 of the Theft Act 1968, in which it must be proved that he was not at his place of abode and has with him any article that can be used in the course of or in connection with a burglary, theft or cheat. Under s.16 of the Offences Against the Person Act 1861, there exists the offence of threats to kill, which is committed if a person, without lawful excuse, makes a threat to kill another, with the intention of causing that person to fear such a threat would be carried out against them, or a third person. Such a person is liable to a maximum of 10 years' imprisonment.

Section 4 of the OAPA 1861 establishes the offence of solicitation of murder which is committed when a person solicits, encourages, persuades or endeavours to do so or propose to any person, to murder any other person regardless of whether that person is British or living in Britain. Such a person is guilty of an offence and liable to a maximum of life imprisonment. In *R. v Hamza* [2007] 1 Cr.App.R. 227, the Court of Appeal rejected the contentions of the defence that the appellant could not be guilty of soliciting others to commit murder directly through his speeches of hatred, since the solicitation was for other foreign nationals to commit murder outside the jurisdiction of England and Wales. The Court of Appeal affirmed the general rule of the common law set out in *Board of Trade v Owen* [1957] A.C. 602, "that an inchoate offence is not committed unless the conduct planned or incited would, if carried out, be indictable in England and Wales".

However, the Court held that s.4 is a statutory exception to this rule and that by giving the words in the section a broad natural meaning, the offence is still committed, even though those who are so solicited are foreign nationals and even though the potential victim is a foreign national, provided the act of solicitation arose in England and Wales, the offence is still committed, even if that person is a resident alien. Sections 61 to 63 of the Sexual Offences Act 2003 create several new specific preparatory offences where there is an intention to commit a sexual offence. Section 61 creates the offence of administering a substance with intent; s.62 creates the offence of committing any offence with intent to commit a sexual offence; and s.63 creates the offence of trespass to premises with intent to commit a sexual offence.

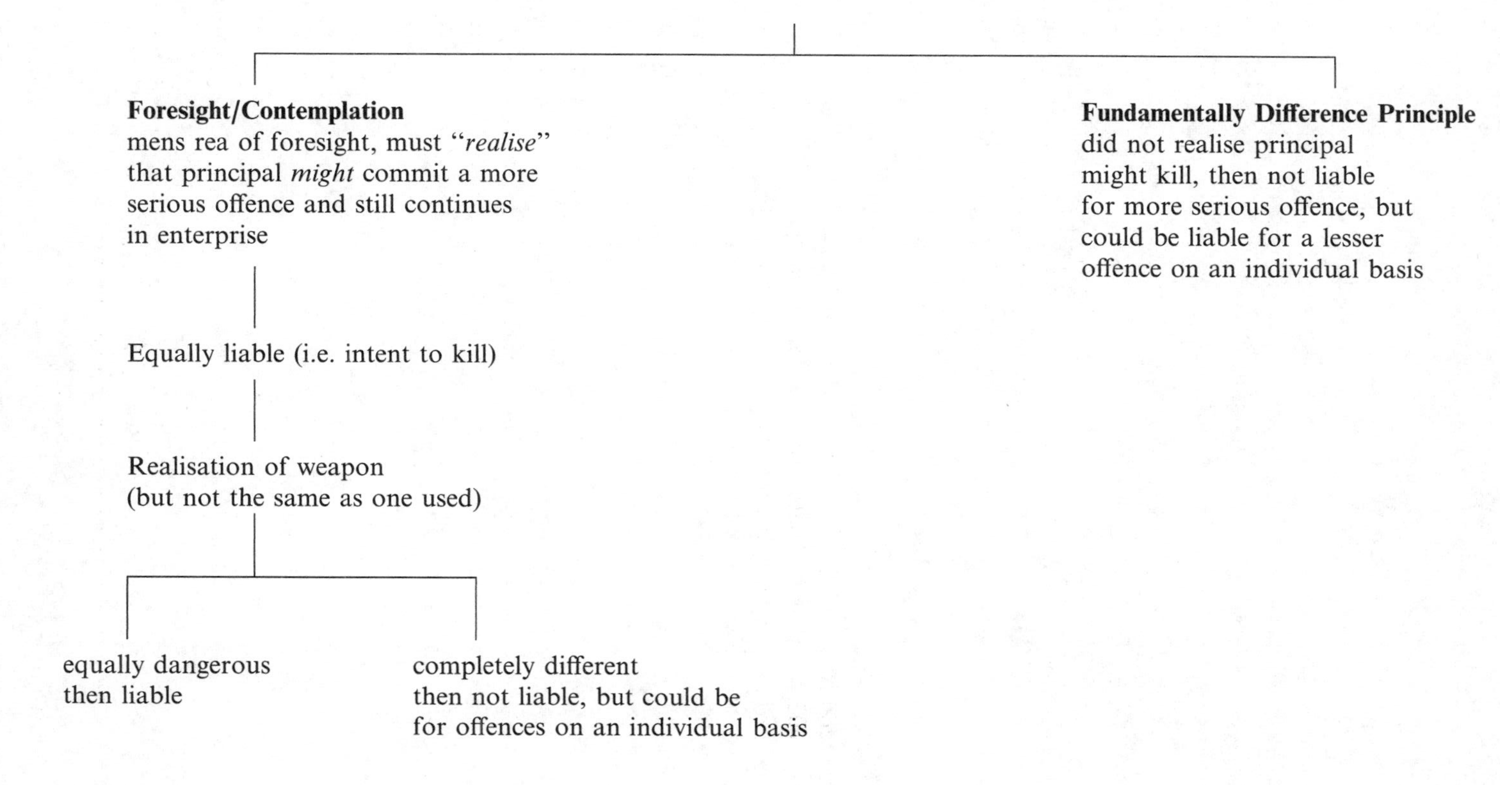
MENS REA FOR SECONDARY OFFENDER
(Authority R. v Powell & English [1997] 3 W.L.R. 959)
Foresight/Contemplation
mens rea of foresight, must "realise" that principal might commit a more serious offence and still continues in enterprise
Equally liable (i.e. intent to kill)
Realisation of weapon (but not the same as one used)
equally dangerous then liable
completely different then not liable, but could be for offences on an individual basis
Fundamentally Difference Principle
did not realise principal might kill, then not liable for more serious offence, but could be liable for a lesser offence on an individual basis

CHAPTER NINE

GENERAL DEFENCES
PART 1: NECESSITY AND DURESS

1. INTRODUCTION

9.01 Within the criminal law, there exist two types of defence:

(i) *Specific Defences*: Provocation and diminished responsibility that are specific to the offence of murder.

(ii) *General Defences:* These are defences that are available to all offences, including murder, and if successful then the defendant will either be excused from criminal liability or owing to the circumstances they found themselves in, they were justified in committing the offence (i.e self defence).

Both the defences of necessity and duress have some similarities with those of provocation and diminished responsibility in that they are a response to a human frailty or weakness, compared with the need to show tolerance, fortitude and self resilience/restraint. Each defence contains a situation where a defendant is faced with an unfortunate choice, neither of which is beneficial, both have an evil outcome. The question for the defendant is one of having to make a choice between the lesser (arguably) of two evils, that they have been compelled to make by another person, or circumstance. It is that choice and the evidence surrounding it that the jury are asked to determine. It is important to be aware that necessity and duress are exculpatory defences and not legal justifications. In other words, what the defendant is saying is that whilst they accept that they committed the criminal offence which is being alleged, they now seek to be excused for their behaviour on the basis that they had no other alternative but to commit that offence in extreme and compelling circumstances.

2. Defence of Necessity and Duress

9.02 The defence of necessity allows a defendant to claim that they had no alternative but to commit the offence since it was necessary in order to avoid some other greater consequential evil. For instance, a homeless person has not eaten for several days and in desperation steals a tin of beans from a food store. This causes a dilemma for the criminal law, since it can never be justified to steal; however, given the extreme circumstances the homeless defendant found himself in, could it be acceptable for the public to legally excuse him from his liability of theft? It was a necessity for him to eat, or face illness or death from starvation. The general rule of the criminal law is that there is no available defence of necessity to a criminal offence. The policy reasons for this are aptly illustrated in the classic and old authority of *R. v Dudley and Stephens* [1884] 14 Q.B.D. 273, in which three sailors and the cabin boy had been shipwrecked and on the 20th day the sailors decided to kill and eat the boy in their desperation to survive. The Court held that the sailors were still guilty of murder, the necessity they faced was not a justification to kill, since they chose the weakest and the youngest. Was it more necessary to kill the boy than one of them: the answer is no. Lord Coleridge observed that whilst law and morality do not always amount to the same thing, it would be of a "fatal consequence" to separate the two concepts in this case and allow an absolute defence of necessity for murder. His Lordship stated:

> "to preserve one's life is generally speaking a duty, but it may be the plainest and the highest duty to sacrifice it . . . In this case the weakest, the youngest, the most unresisting, was chosen. Was it more necessary to kill him than one of the grown men? The answer must be no."

The general rule received further support in *R. v Howe* [1987] A.C. 417, when Lord Hailsham went as far as saying that to allow a general defence of necessity would result in its abuse and "mask anarchy" by the unscrupulous:

> "to see their own moral judgment and self-interest above the protection of their fellows and of the law. The ill, the starving and the homeless must look to the good, the charitable, and the public services, not a defence of necessity."

3. Exception to the General Rule: Medical Necessity

9.03 Although the general rule rests plainly on public policy grounds, both a medical and legal inexorable dilemma arose in the highly sensitive case of *Re A (children) (conjoined twins: surgical separation)* [2000] 4 All E.R. 961. Both J and M were conjoined twins at birth; however sadly, one was stronger than the other, and if there was no attempt to separate them both would die. If successful, one would survive but the other would die as a consequence. The parents of J and M refused to consent to the operation. The hospital applied to the Court for a declaration to make the operation lawful and not murder, the High Court granted the declaration and the parents appealed. A substantial amount of previous case authority was referred to and considered by the Court of Appeal.

The leading judgment was given by Ward L.J. and provides an extensive review of the interlinking principles of medical, family and criminal law in the context of the issue to be resolved. The Court of Appeal analysed the law of homicide and concluded that, in the circumstances, if the doctors operated to separate, this would amount to an unlawful positive act that would cause death with an intent to kill and therefore murder. In dismissing the appeal by the parents, the Court of Appeal ruled that the principle in *Dudley and Stephens* did not envisage a situation of separating twins as a necessity. Brooke L.J. applied the legal writings of Sir James Stephen, who had said in his digest of criminal law (1887), that there existed three requirements for the application of necessity within the criminal law:

(i) The act (i.e. in this case a separation of the twins) is needed in order to avoid inevitable and irreparable evil.

(ii) That no more should be done than is necessary for the purpose to be achieved.

(iii) That the evil inflicted must not be disproportionate to the evil to be avoided.

Brooke L.J., having also reviewed the developing principles surrounding a defence of duress of circumstances, expressed the view that allowing a limited exception of medical necessity would not create a risk that people would try to excuse themselves of otherwise criminal conduct, since such operations of sacrificial separation would be "an exceptionally rare event" and that the medical profession can always present the evidence before a court and seek a lawful order to proceed. The Court fully recognised the sanctity of life and the protection of life by the law of homicide; and that currently euthanasia is unlawful. Further, the law does not recognise an opposing right to die (see *Pretty v UK* [1997] 24 E.H.R.R. 423), but in the circumstances both family law and medical evidence justified the separation as being in the interests of the stronger child over the conflicting interests of the weaker child who could not survive.

In a different situation the House of Lords ruled in *Airedale NHS v Bland* [1993] 1 A.C. 789, that when a doctor who decides to switch off the life support machine of a patient who is medically assessed to be in a permanent vegetative state (PVS), this neither amounts to a positive act nor a culpable omission to act, for the purposes of the criminal law. Such an act will not be unlawful unless it constitutes a breach of duty of care to the patient. In respect of a patient in a PVS, to continue to treat them would be of no benefit to them, despite their inability to consent or voice an opinion, and that although the principle of sanctity of life is of fundamental importance, it is not an absolute principle. As Lord Keith observed, it does not compel a doctor to treat a patient against their consent (i.e. a patient's right to self determination) who will otherwise die if they do not act, to do so would amount to an assault both criminally and in a civil context. Neither does it authorise the forcible feeding of a person refusing to be feed (on hunger strike in prison) or require the sustaining of life of a terminally ill patient, if this were to prolong their pain and suffering. However, for a doctor to deliberately reduce the life of a patient, even a terminally ill patient and for humanitarian reasons, is an unlawful act. Euthanasia is not lawful under the common law.

4. Medical Necessity to Take a Prohibited Drug to Relieve Pain is not Available

9.04 Although the common law in *Re A (conjoined twins)* and *Bland* set out plainly the restrictive application of a defence of medical necessity to exceptionally rare cases, the Court of Appeal had to address the possible legal extension of this defence so as to allow the taking of a prohibited drug to relieve pain and suffering, as amounting to a necessity on medical grounds and therefore lawfully justifying the possession of those drugs. In *R. v Altham* [2006] 2 Cr.App.R. 127, the Court of Appeal applied the decision in *R. v Quayle* [2005] 1 W.L.R. 3642 and stated that the exception of medical necessity or duress of circumstances to the general rule cannot be applied to legitimise conduct contrary to the clear legislative policy and scheme of the Misuse of Drugs Act 1971, which prohibits in s.5 the simple possession of a specified drug or possession with intent to supply. Neither did it breach the defendant's right to a private life (art.8), nor did it breach art.3 by causing the defendant to suffer inhuman or degrading treatment by preventing him taking cannabis in order to relieve the pain from MS or any other illness. The Court of Appeal considered and applied the obiter observations of Lord Bingham in *R. v Hason* [2005] 2 W.L.R. 314 on the principles of law relating to a defence of necessity or duress. In *Quayle* the defendant was a leg amputee and had cultivated cannabis for his own use to relieve the pain.

5. Duress of Circumstances and Duress of Threats

9.05 Duress is a common law defence narrowly defined on grounds of public policy for two reasons:

(i) so as to avoid a situation were any excuse can be used to plead the defence; and

(ii) that it is easy for a defendant to claim they were compelled to act as they did, but difficult evidentially for the prosecution to disprove, since it is based on inferences drawn from assertions in evidence.

It is against this background that the principles of the defence have developed to deal with specific factual cases that have come before the appeal courts. This has inevitably led to a defence that is now shrouded in a mass of various principles, applicable to various cases as they are presented to the court.

The common law has come to recognise two types of duress: (i) duress of threats; and (ii) duress of extraneous circumstances. A defence of duress of threats arises where the defendant was compelled to do an unlawful act by reason of threats of death or serious injury to themselves or another, if they refused (i.e. A threatens B with death, if B does not commit a street robbery) (see *Lynch v DPP for Northern Ireland* [1975] 61 Cr.App.R. 6). Conversely, a duress of extraneous circumstances arises when the compulsion to act unlawfully manifests itself from the circumstances (facts) in which the defendant found themselves (i.e. A's wife is pregnant and about to give birth prematurely, A drives his wife to hospital at speed and carelessly).

It is important to be aware that a defence of duress amounts to an exculpatory defence and if accepted by the jury, is an absolute defence in that the defendant must be acquitted of the criminal offence which they were either by threats or circumstances compelled to commit. Like provocation and diminished responsibility, the rationale for the defence is an acceptance and concession to a human frailty or weakness and therefore excuses the criminal conduct of the defendant. Further, it is also important to be aware that whilst the law readily recognises that duress can be pleaded in two different ways, the principles of law are of general application to both situations.

9.06 Equally, it is also important to be aware that Woolf L.J. in *R. v Conway* [1989] Q.B. 290 observed that a defence of duress of circumstances is but an example of necessity and whether it is called duress or necessity is unimportant. What is important, according to his Lordship, is that, "it is subject to the same limitations as the 'do or else' species of duress". The appellant, Conway, was sat in a car along with his passenger who feared a serious attack from someone who was out to get him. Whilst stationary, two men approached their vehicle; the passenger thinking he was going to be attacked, shouted to Conway to make off. In fact the two approaching males were police officers wishing to make enquiries, who then gave chase in an unmarked car. Conway was charged with and convicted of reckless driving and appealed against the ruling of the judge, who refused to allow a defence of duress to be put to the jury.

The Court of Appeal held, quashing the conviction, that a defence of duress of circumstances will arise where the defendant was compelled by the circumstances to do what he did so as to avoid death or serious injury. Similar observations were made in *R. v Martin* [1989] 1 All E.R. 652, where the Court of Appeal quashed the appellant's conviction for disqualified driving (now a summary only offence), stating that the judge was wrong to refuse to leave a defence of necessity to the jury when the appellant had claimed to have been compelled to drive his son to work due to him oversleeping; with the risk of him losing his job and that his wife who was suicidal had threatened to kill herself if he didn't.

It is clear from these two authorities that a limited defence of necessity does albeit in the form of duress of circumstances exist and based on the observations of Kennedy L.J. in *R. v Pommell* [1995] Cr.App.R. 607, is not limited to road traffic offences, but given its close association with duress of threats, is available to all criminal offences except murder, attempted murder and treason. This point of general application of the defence was approved and confirmed by the Court of Appeal in *R. v Abdul-Hussain* [1999] Crim. L.R. 570, and is therefore available for hijacking contrary to s.1 of the Aviation Security Act 1982. It is important to be aware that the Court of Appeal in several judgments, such as *Abdul-Hussain*, has conceded that the current common law principles are complex and unsatisfactory and has expressly called upon Parliament to legislate and create a clear and simplified statutory defence of duress and its availability.

6. Relevant Principles of Law of Duress

9.07 Rose L.J. in *R. v Abdul-Hussain* [1999] Crim. L.R. 570, by way of obiter dictum, referred to the principles of law developing on a case by case basis and that the current principles relevant to both types of the defence of duress can be found in eleven propositions of law as explained in *R. v Martin* [1989] 1 All E.R. 652. Further, in *R. v Hasan* [2005] 2 A.C. 467, Lord Bingham also found that it important, whilst not forming part of the question of law under review in the appeal, to identify the various common law principles of the defence. In order to make sense of the principles of law, it is perhaps for ease of simplicity to set the defence out in logical steps as follows.

7. Step 1: Duty of Judge to Assess Evidence of Duress

9.08 When a defence of duress either by circumstances (necessity) or by threats is raised by the defence or brought into issue at trial, the trial judge is under a duty to decide whether or not the defence exists on the evidence. The judge must decide whether the defence evidentially can be left for the jury's determination or alternatively, it does not arise on the evidence and therefore refuse to put the defence before the jury. In this assessment of the evidence, the trial judge will need to consider the following questions:

(i) Was the defendant acting reasonably and proportionately in order to avoid a threat of death or serious injury?

This amounts to an objective question and requires the judge to assess whether the evidence (if any) of threats or circumstances, was of such a magnitude so as to amount to the defendant's criminal act being reasonable and proportionate in order to prevent an act of greater evil. Within this assessment the Court of Appeal ruled in *R. v Safi* [2003] Crim. L.R. 721 that the actual threat or circumstance, need not exist factually; it is enough that the defendant reasonably believed there to be a threat or circumstances. In other words, it is not necessary for the threat or circumstances to have existed on the facts.

If the defendant objectively reasonably believed that the threat did exist when in fact it didn't, this is sufficient for the defence to be determined by the jury. *Safi* involved the appellant's hijacking a plane from Afghanistan and forcing it to land at Stansted. To the offence of hijacking, the appellant claimed duress on the basis that they had no alternative but to act has they did, since the Taliban had discovered they were part of an opposing group and they were at risk of torture and death. The Court of Appeal quashed the appellant's conviction on the basis that firstly, the defence applied to hijacking and second the judge had misdirected the jury by telling them no threat existed and therefore the belief of the appellant's was legally irrelevant (see also *R. v Cairns* [2000] Crim. L.R. 473).

9.09 (ii) That there was an imminent peril of death or serious injury to the defendant, or those to whom they have responsibility, or persons for whom the situation makes them responsible. These people need not be known or ascertainable but it must be possible to describe them by reference to the action which is threatened by in which they would become victims, unless the defendant acts as they is compelled to do.

This point of principle is derived from *R. v Shayler* [2001] 1 W.L.R. 2206. The appellant was charged with an offence of disclosing documents or information (during his time working at MI5) to a national newspaper without lawful authority under the Official Secrets Act 1989. At a preparatory hearing, the trial judge refused to leave a defence of duress to the jury since it did not extend to the Official Secrets Act 1989. Before the Court of Appeal, the appellant contended that this was wrong and claimed that the disclosure was necessary to protect the public from death or serious injury, for which he had a responsibility. The Court of Appeal dismissed the contention, on the grounds that the appellant was unable to show or describe the people whose lives were at risk if he did not disclose. The Court gave the example of a person threatening to explode a bomb in a crowded building if the defendant did not act as ordered. Clearly the defendant has a responsibility to those occupying the building.

(iii) The death or serious injury (peril) from threats or circumstances does not have to be shown to be immediate but must be imminent.

This principle determines the required degree of urgency between the threat or believed threat or circumstances being realised and the commission of the criminal offence which the defendant commits under the compulsion of the threat or circumstance. In *R. v Abdul- Hussain* [1999] Crim. L.R. 570, the Court of Appeal followed the ruling in *R. v Hudson & Taylor* [1971] 56 Cr.App.R. 1, that the occurrence of the threat or circumstance does not have to be shown to be immediate, simply that it was imminent. The decision in *R. v Cole* [1994] Crim. L.R. 582, which had concluded that there must be a degree of directness and immediacy was incorrect and not the law. In *Abul-Hussain,* the Court of Appeal quashed the appellant's conviction of hijacking a Sudanese plane and forcing it to land in the UK. The appellant had claimed he and his family where terrified that the Sudanese authorities would deport them back to Iraq, where they would be tortured by the Sadam Hussain regime. The Court of Appeal stated the judge had applied that law too strictly and was therefore wrong to refuse to put the defence before the jury.

Nevertheless, Lord Bingham in *R. v Hason* [2005] 2 A.C. 467, disapproved of the relaxation of the degree of the necessity or circumstance to act in the commission of offence as against the peril of death or serious injury. His Lordship stated that it should be made clear to juries that unless the threat:

> "is not such as he reasonably expects to follow immediately or almost immediately on his failure to comply with the threat, there may be little if any room for doubt that he could have taken evasive action, whether by going to the police or in some other way to avoid committing the crime with which he is charged."

(iv) That the threat or circumstances is extraneous to the defendant.

This principle requires that the threat or circumstance came not from the defendant themselves but from some other external agency. In other words, there must be evidence to show that the circumstance/threat was causative of the defendant committing the alleged offence and was extraneous to the offender, otherwise the defence is not available. This point of principle is derived from the decision in *Rodger and Rose* [1998] 1 Cr.App.R. 143, in which the Court of Appeal dismissed the appeal against conviction for escaping from prison. Both appellants; having had their sentence tariff increased, broke out of Parkhurst prison on the basis that if they remained there they would commit suicide. In referring to the authorities of *Pommell, Martin* and *Conway*, Sir Patrick Russell, who gave the leading judgment, stated those authorities possessed a common feature that the causative threat/circumstance was extraneous to the offender himself. In contrast in this case:

> "it was solely the suicidal tendencies, the thought processes and the emotions of the offenders themselves which operated as duress. That factor introduced an entirely subjective element not present in the authorities."

It would be an unjustifiable development in the law and not in the public interest to allow a defendant to avail themselves of criminal liability in such situations as arose in *Rodger and Rose*.

8. Step 2: Direction Questions to the Jury on the Defence of Duress

9.10 When a judge is required to provide a relevant legal direction on the application of the defence of duress in their summing up to the jury, they have to assist them with what are known as specimen directions, issued by the Judicial Studies Board. The classic statement on the appropriate directions to the jury are found in the authorities of *R. v Graham* [1982] 1 W.L.R. 294, *R. v Martin* [1989] 1 All E.R. 657 and *R. v Bowen* [1996] 2 Cr.App.R. 157. The judge will direct the jury to consider two questions; one subjective and the other objective. The jury will be told that it is essentially a matter for them as a question of fact, to decide whether the defence exists or whether the prosecution have negated it existence. The two questions are as follows:

(i) Was the defendant impelled to act as a result of what he reasonably believed to be the situation by fearing death or serious injury?

This amounts to a subjective question in the sense that the jury look at the evidence as a whole and assess whether the defendant themselves had in their mind a reasonable belief that if they did not so act as compelled by the threat or circumstance they or another person to whom they were responsible would suffer death or serious injury. The threat or circumstance does not have to exist in fact, it is sufficient for the defendant to believe it could exist.

If the jury answer this question as no, then the defence will fail and the issue will be whether the prosecution have proved the relevant elements to the alleged criminal offence committed by the defendant. If however, the jury answer the question in the affirmative, then they must consider the second question:

9.11 (ii) Would a sober person of reasonable firmness, sharing certain characteristics (if identified) of the defendant have responded to that situation as the defendant did (as explained in *R. v Howe* [1987] 1 A.C. 417)?

This amounts to a clear objective test very similar to that used in the partial defence of provocation and it is important to be aware that it exists for the same public policy reason; in that a defendant must be assessed to have the necessary standard of self-restraint that one would expect of an ordinary person in such a situation. This objective criterion, as with provocation, is essential so as to ensure that justice is achieved and determined by the jury. In each case the jury will set a standard objectively to be expected and decide whether, in the factual situation they are trying, a reasonable person would have reacted in the same way as the defendant.

However, it is important to be aware that the shared characteristics for a defence of duress are wider than the limited characteristics of sex and age in provocation. In *R. v Bowen* [1996] 2 Cr.App.R. 157, the Court of Appeal stated expressly that the reasonable/ordinary person, as a matter of law, will not share the characteristics of a defendant who is identified to be more pliable, vulnerable, timid or susceptible to threats. Nevertheless, the Court did recognise that certain characteristics of a defendant may reduce their ability to resist the threat/circumstances and that such characteristics could be shared by the ordinary person. Those identified by the Court are age, possibly sex, pregnancy, serious physical disability, recognised mental illness or psychiatric conditions; i.e. post traumatic stress disorder. Further, the Court emphasised that sexual orientation is irrelevant, along with self-induced abuse through alcohol, drugs or glue sniffing.

In regard to mental illness, impairment or a recognised psychiatric illness as being a possible shared characteristic, the Court in *Bowen* stated that psychiatric evidence may be admissible at trial. Provided only if it would assist the jury in determining that owing to that particular illness (condition) of the defendant and therefore the ordinary person sharing it, they fall into a vulnerable category of persons who would be more susceptible to the threats or circumstances and therefore more likely to be impelled to act, unlike a person without such an illness. In *R. v Rogers* [1999] (unreported), the Court of Appeal ruled that "asperger's syndrome" amounted to a recognised mental or psychiatric illness and therefore, medical evidence was admissible at the appellant's re-trial for possession with intent to supply a prohibited drug, such evidence having not been available at his first trial. In *R. v Walker* [2003] EWCA Crim 1837, the Court of Appeal quashed the conviction for theft, stating that the judge was wrong to rule inadmissible psychiatric evidence relating to his "social anxiety"; the Court did however observe that this was border line inadmissible/admissible.

9. Step 3: Limitations on the Application of the Defence of Duress

9.12 The common law, in accordance with public policy, has placed specific limitations on the application of the defence of duress in certain situations. Dependant on the particular facts of the case, the trial judge, having given the jury the standard two question direction on duress as explained above, must direct the jury to consider the following further two questions amounting to limitations on the application of the defence and if established the defence will fail. The two further questions are as follows:

(i) Was it possible on the facts for the defendant to seek protection of the police?

In *Lynch v DPP for Northern Ireland* [1975] 61 Cr.App.R. 6, Lord Morris stated that if on the evidence the defendant can avoid the duress by taking a "safe avenue of escape", then the defence cannot be relied upon. If therefore, the jury answer yes to this question, the defence of duress will fail. If on the other hand they answer no, then the jury must consider the next question:

(ii) Whether on the facts the defendant had voluntarily placed themselves to be subjected to the threats or circumstances.

At first glance, these two questions seem to cause little difficulty as to how the defence is to be limited against defendants who can either avoid the duress or who voluntarily place themselves in a position to be subjected to duress. These two limitations are clearly justified on public policy grounds. However, difficulties had arisen on the issue of whether the defendant, in terms of voluntarily placing themselves to be subjected to threats to commit a criminal offence, must be shown to have known the type of offences that they would be threatened with; or is it simply enough to prove that they were aware of the risk of threats to commit any offence minor or serious. This particular point of law resulted in several conflicting Court of Appeal decisions (known as the drug debt cases), and ultimately the House of Lords having to settle the principle.

The starting point is *R. v Sharp* [1987] 85 Cr.App.R. 207, in which the defendant's conviction for an armed robbery of a post office was upheld. The defendant had claimed that the gang leader had threatened to "blow his head off" if he did not partake in the offence. The Court of Appeal ruled that:

> "where a person has voluntarily, and with knowledge of its nature, joined a criminal organisation or a gang which he knew might bring pressure on him to commit an offence and was an active member when he was put under such pressure, he cannot avail himself of the defence of duress."

9.13 Conversely in *R. v Sheppard* [1987] 86 Cr.App.R. 47, the Court of Appeal quashed the appellant's conviction for theft (shoplifting) in which a sting type operation was used where one of the gang distracted the owner, whilst the others stole. After the first time, the appellant said he wanted to leave the gang; one of the gang members who had introduced the appellant threatened him and his family with violence if he refused to carry on. The Court of Appeal, considering *Sharp,* accepted that the trial judge should have left the defence of duress to the jury, given there was evidence that the appellant failed to appreciate the risk of duress of threats of violence, since the criminal enterprise in which he had joined was non violent. The Court made it plain that this would not necessarily result in a conviction being quashed since the jury would have to consider the nature and timing of the threats against the offence committed. It was that fact that such questions were never put to the jury that made the conviction unsafe.

In *R. v Baker and Ward* [1999] 2 Cr.App.R. 335, the Court of Appeal stated that on the question of whether the defendant had voluntarily placed himself at risk of being coerced into committing an offence against their will, the jury should be directed that the limitation only applies if it is established that the defendant was aware of a risk that the group he joined voluntarily might try to coerce him into committing offences "of the type for which he is now being tried by the use of violence or threats of violence". In this case, the appellant had been convicted of robbery at a superstore. He claimed that he was impelled to commit the offence owing to threats made against him and his family from a violent drug dealer to whom he owed £10,000 for cannabis. The Court of Appeal quashed his conviction on the basis that the judge had refused to assist the jury, who had sought greater assistance on the application of the limitations.

Soon afterwards, a similar issue arose in *R. v Heath* [2000] Crim. L.R. 109, in which the Court of Appeal ruled that the trial judge was right to refuse to leave a defence of duress to the jury, since the appellant admitted himself that in the drugs world "people collect their debts in one way" and that therefore he was clearly aware of the risk of threats. The Court of Appeal, in distinguishing *Baker and Ward* stated that:

> "it is the awareness of the risk of compulsion which matters. Prior awareness of what criminal activity those exercising compulsion may offer as a possible alternative to violence is irrelevant."

Accordingly, a person who becomes indebted to a drugs supplier has voluntarily exposed themselves to the threat of violence, and could not therefore rely on those threats as duress to excuse them from liability for any subsequent criminal conduct. A similar approach was taken by the Court of Appeal in *R. v Harmer* [2001] EWCA Crim 2930, another drug debt case, in which the Court followed the decision in *Heath* and dismissed the appeal.

9.14 This conflict of authority came to be addressed in *R. v Hasan* [2005] 2 A.C. 467, in which the appellant appealed against his conviction for aggravated burglary, claiming that a man called Sullivan, he had described as a "lunatic yardie", threatened him and his family with violence if he didn't commit the burglary. The trial judge directed the jury that if they were satisfied that the appellant, by associating with Sullivan, had voluntarily put himself in a position where he was aware of being subject to threats, the defence of duress was not available to him. The Court of Appeal, considering the conflict of opinion in *Baker and Ward* and that in *Heath*, preferred the decision in *Baker and Ward* over that of *Heath* and therefore quashed his conviction. The prosecution appealed against this ruling to the House of Lords, in which their Lordships unanimously allowed the appeal and reversed the decision of the Court of Appeal. Lord Bingham first stated that the Court in *Baker and Ward* had mis-stated the law and that there is no requirement in law for the prosecution to prove that the defendant had a foresight of coercion to commit offences of the type of which the defendant is charged; the only requirement is that the prosecution must prove that there was a foresight of risk of coercion.

The question then remained of whether this foresight should be determined by a subjective or an objective test. Lord Bingham made it clear that, on public policy grounds, the law should be seen to be discouraging criminal associations and slow in excusing their criminal conduct. With this in mind his Lordship stated:

> "if a person voluntarily becomes or remains associated with others engaged in criminal activity in a situation where he knows or ought reasonably to know that he may be the subject of compulsion by them or their associates, he cannot rely on the defence of duress to excuse any act which he is thereafter compelled to do by them."

Lord Bingham left open the question on whether this principle would apply to an undercover agent of the State (i.e. police officer) who, for genuine law enforcement purposes integrates into a criminal organisation but is then compelled by the gang to commit criminal offences.

10. Step 4: The Defence of Duress is not Available for the Following Offences

9.15 The common law has determined that, for public policy reasons, the defence cannot be raised when the alleged offence is either murder or attempted murder. The sanctity and preservation of life are sacrosanct, both legally and morally, and are indistinguishable when a person is faced with the threat of death if they do not kill another person. To perform the killing to save one's own life amounts to murder and legally and morally the law cannot excuse such conduct.

This point of principle is explained in clearly the appalling case of *R. v Howe and Others* [1987] 1 A.C. 417, in which two of the appellants were involved in a joint enterprise, in which two of the victims were taken to a remote spot and subjected to violence, sexual depravity and then killed. Howe claimed that he acted under duress from a co-accused called Murray, and believed that if he didn't follow his instructions, he too would be murdered. The House of Lords, exercising its power in the Judicial Precedent Practice Statement (1966) departed from the previous decision in *DPP for Northern Ireland v Lynch* [1975] A.C. 653, that conflicted with the Privy Council decision in *Abbott v The Queen* [1977] A.C. 755, and held that a defence of duress is not available to an offence of murder on public policy grounds, this includes the actual killer and also those who participate in the murderous enterprise.

In *R. v Wilson* [2007] 2 Cr.App.R. 31, the 13-year-old defendant had participated with his father in an appalling murder of a neighbour using various weaponry, but claimed at trial that he feared violent repercussions from his father if he did not and therefore did not form the specific intent to kill. In dismissing his appeal against his conviction for murder, the Court of Appeal plainly ruled that regardless how susceptible a person is to duress, including a 13-year-old boy, the principle that duress is not available applied equally. Likewise, the Court of Appeal in *R. v Gotts* [1991] 1 Q.B. 660 ruled, applying several obiter observations found in the judgment of their Lordships in *Howe*, that given attempted murder involved a greater evil in terms of mens rea, to that of murder; the defence of duress does not extend to an offence of attempted murder and is therefore neither available for this offence.

Neither is the defence available against the exercise of the Crown's prerogative powers, or to a crime committed outside the jurisdiction of England and Wales. This point of law was confirmed in *R. v Jones and Others* [2006] 2 W.L.R. 772 in which the defendants were all charged with conspiracy to commit criminal damage at RAF Fairford. Before trial at a preparatory hearing the judge rejected their claim that they were acting out of necessity or under duress of circumstances on the basis that the war in Iraq was an unlawful act, and one which they were compelled to prevent. The House of Lords affirmed the decision of the Court of Appeal who rejected this also and therefore left them with no defence on the ground that the prerogative powers of the Crown taken in Parliament to commence a war is a lawful act and that the defence is only available to a domestic crime.

11. Duress/Necessity Defence Specific to Road Traffic Offences

9.16 In common parlance, the defence of duress of circumstances or necessity is often raised as a defence to road traffic strict liability offences, which has resulted in the High Court having to deal with a number of case stated appeals against a ruling of the magistrates on its applicability in particular circumstances. In *DPP v Hicks* [2002] EWHC 1638, the High Court allowed an appeal by the prosecution against the ruling of the magistrates, that the defendant could rely on duress to the offence of driving whilst over the prescribed alcohol limit, when he claimed that he was compelled to drive to a chemist for calpol because his child was sick. The Court stated that in these circumstances there was no risk of death or serious injury. Similarly *DPP v Tomkinson* [2001] EWHC Admin 182 and *DPP v Bell* [1992] R.T.R. 334, were both drink driving offence cases in which the magistrates were held to have erred in allowing a defence of duress.

The High Court ruled in these situations that it is important when deciding whether the defendant was impelled to drive over the limit, to look at the circumstances stage by stage and the court must consider the compulsive circumstances at the time of the actual offence. So whilst a driver may initially be driving under duress, this does not automatically mean that he does so throughout the whole of the driving. The moment the driver realises that the duress ceases is the moment he should stop driving.

In *DPP v Mullally* [2006] EWHC 3448, the Divisional Court, allowing an appeal by the DPP by way of case stated, ruled that the magistrates were wrong to conclude that the defendant was acting under duress when she had driven over the limit to her sister's, and was assaulted by her sister's partner. She called the police and then drove off from the scene. The Court stated expressly that the defence of necessity had to be strictly controlled, neither the defendant nor her sister were in immediate danger of death or serious injury. In *R. v Backwell* [1999] Cr.App.R. 35, it was ruled that the defence was available for an offence of careless driving, (see also *DPP v Harris* [1995] R.T.R. 100 concerning duress and the use of emergency vehicles).

12. Burden of Proof

9.17 In *R. v Hasan* [2005] 2 A.C. 467, and also in *R. v Bone* [1968] Q.B. 546, both the House of Lords and Court of Appeal ruled that if there is sufficient evidence to raise at trial an issue of duress, then the burden of proof rests clearly with the prosecution to establish the criminal standard of beyond all reasonable doubt that the defendant was not, when committing the alleged offence, under duress. In other words, the defendant simply has to adduce sufficient evidence (evidential burden) to justify the jury considering the defence of duress, it is for the prosecution to disprove (negate) the existence of the defence (persuasive burden) it is not for the defendant to prove it.

Chapter Ten

GENERAL DEFENCES
PART 2: INSANITY AND AUTOMATISM

1. Introduction

10.01 Mental Disability is often raised in three situations:

(i) The defendant claims at the time of the alleged offence that they were insane and therefore lacked both mens rea and actus reus, but is fit to stand trial for the offence.

(ii) The defendant claims that they were sane at the time of the alleged offence, but is now unfit to enter a plea.

(iii) The defendant was insane at time of the offence and is unable to enter a plea.

The defences of insanity and automatism are, in essence, the same defence but with a different description. The reason behind this anomaly is that pleading a defence of insanity is not ideal with the possible outcome of an indefinite hospital order. In order to avoid the consequences of not guilty by reason of insanity, those defendants who brought into question their state of mind as a method of negating their criminal liability would often use automatism as an alternative. The reason for this was that general automatism amounted to a complete defence and so resulted in the defendant being acquitted. Such outcomes had the potential of being perverse, especially if the defendant's mental condition meant that if untreated they constituted a risk to the public.

This resulted in the two defences becoming one and the same, with the defence of automatism being split into two categories of insane and non insane automatism. Accordingly, when assessing the relevant principles of law in relation to insanity and insane automatism, they are equally applicable to each defence. Ultimately, it will be the defence who decide to plea insanity or alternatively plead automatism, in which case the trial judge will have to make a ruling based on the evidence whether the defendant's alleged state of automatism amounts to insane or non-insane. If the judge rules that it is insane automatism, then the defence is one of insanity.

2. Fitness to Plead: Procedural Steps

10.02 A defendant, regardless of the offence of which they are charged, has an absolute right to a fair trial as enshrined in art.6 of the Convention on Human Rights. Likewise, the prosecution are required to establish beyond doubt the elements of the alleged offence. If at the commencement of their trial a defendant's mental ability is brought into question, then it must first be determined that they are in fact fit to enter a plea and are able to follow the proceedings. If they are not then the trial cannot proceed for reasons of fairness until such time as they become fit. However, this leaves the issue of disposal, since it could never be in the public interest to allow an unconvicted, but potentially dangerous defendant to remain free. This issue of determining actual fitness and disposal in these circumstances is a matter of procedure set out in s.4(A) of the Criminal Procedure (Insanity) Act 1964, as amended by the Criminal Procedure (Insanity and Unfitness to Plead) Act 1991, and further by ss.22 to 26 of the Domestic Violence, Crime and Victims Act 2004 which came into effect on March 31, 2005. It is not intended to assess the procedural requirements in any depth, but to simply give an overview of what happens, should fitness to plead become an issue.

Section 4(A) set out the following procedural steps:

(i) The issue of a defendant's fitness to plead may be raised by the defence, prosecution or the court.

(ii) The question is whether the defendant is *under a disability*. This question is determined by a judge (prior to March 31, 2005 this was a jury) on the evidence of at least two registered psychiatrists and if so determined, this involves looking at the relevant criteria of understanding, the nature of the plea, the nature of the offence, the court procedure, the ability to follow the court process, to give evidence and also give instructions to their legal team. A statutory right of appeal exists to the Court of Appeal against the decision on disability.

(iii) If the judge concludes that the defendant is under a disability, then a jury is empanelled ("the trial on the facts") to consider on the evidence whether they are satisfied that the defendant "did the *act* or made the omission charged against them". If not, then the defendant is to be acquitted, if yes then they will be dealt with in accordance with s.5.

(iv) Under subsection (4) if a defendant is found to be unfit, but later recovers they can be tried for the offence.

Although the procedure is relatively straightforward both the Court of Appeal and the House of Lords have had to define what is meant by "*act*" in the context of what the prosecution must prove, against the availability of a defence that would have been raised on behalf of the defendant had they not been under a disability, to negate the unlawful act and mens rea. In *R. v Antoine* [2000] 2 Cr.App.R. 94, the House of Lords ruled that the decision in *R. v Egan* [1998] 1 Cr.App.R. 121, is no longer to be followed and that the decision in *Attorney-General Reference (No.3 of 1998)* [1999] 3 W.L.R. 1194 stated the law correctly. Their Lordships ruled unanimously that the word "act" meant that the prosecution need only to prove and the jury to be sure that the defendant committed the actus reus of the alleged offence. It does not require proof of the requisite mens rea to the offence. Accordingly, the defendant cannot under s.4(A) raise a defence of diminished responsibility, since this relates to the negation of mens rea to murder not the actus reus.

Likewise, if diminished responsibility were available under s.4, it could lead to the possibility, on a single count for murder, of the jury finding that whilst a defendant had committed the act of killing, they where not guilty of murder owing to them suffering diminished responsibility and therefore acquit the defendant, to be at liberty; an outcome Parliament could not have possibly intended to arise from s.4. The problem with this is that it is not always clear or indeed possible to distinguish precisely between the mens rea and actus reus of the offence and the possible defence to it. Such difficulties could arise when defences of accident, mistake, or self-defence are raised. For instance, the defence of self defence, if established, justifies the defendant's act as lawful, but within the defence the jury are required to consider the defendant's honest belief as a mental state. Lord Hutton in *Antoine* observed that in order to resolve this difficulty fairly, provided that there is "objective evidence" from a witness that brings into issue a defence of mistake, accident or self defence:

> "then the jury should not find that the defendant did the "act" unless it is satisfied that beyond reasonable doubt on all the evidence that the prosecution has negatived that defence."

His Lordship made it clear that the defendant cannot raise any of these defences by way of suggestion alone, in the absence of other evidence to support the defence, the jury under s.4 are not required to consider it.

Likewise in *Grant v DPP* [2001] EWCA Crim 2611, the Court of Appeal, considering *Antoine*, ruled that a defendant cannot raise under s.4 the possibility of a defence of provocation, since this involves an issue of mens rea in that it requires the jury to consider an intent to kill, and whether, in the circumstances, the defendant had suddenly and temporarily lost their self control, a subjective state of mind. Rose L.J. observed that:

> "it would be unrealistic and contradictory, in relation to a person unfit to be tried, that a jury should have to consider what effect the conduct of the deceased had on the mind of that person. Parliament cannot have intended that question to be included within the determination of whether the person 'did the act' charged."

In *R. v H* [2003] 1 W.L.R. 411, the House of Lords was called upon to decide whether the s.4 procedure was incompatible with art.6 of the Convention on Human Rights and therefore breached the defendant's right to a fair trial.

Their Lordships ruled unanimously that in applying the determination of a criminal charge test in *Engels v The Netherlands (No.1)* [1976] 1 E.H.R.R. 647, the s.4 procedure does not engage art.6 since the defendant is not charged with a criminal offence under s.4. The s.4 procedure does not result in a conviction, or the imposition of a criminal sentence. The purpose of s.4 is both to protect the defendant and the public.

If fitness to plead is an issue for a summary only offence at either the magistrates' or Youth Court, then the procedure is that contained in s.37(3) of the Mental Health Act 1983 and s.11 of the Powers of Criminal Courts (Sentencing) Act 2000 which provides that if the magistrates are satisfied that the defendant did the act or omission, after a medical examination the magistrates may make a hospital or guardianship order without convicting them (see *R. (P) v Barking Magistrates' Court* [2002] EWHC 734 and *CPS v P* [2007] EWHC 946).

3. The Defence of Insanity: *M'Naghten Rules* [1843]

10.03 If a defendant decides to bring into issue the state of their mind at the time of the alleged offence, then the trial judge, as a matter of law, must determine whether the defendant is raising the defence of insanity or automatism. The legal definition of insanity is found in the answers given by the court to several questions raised in the old case of *M'Naghten* [1843] 10 Clarke & Finnelly 200. Tindall C.J. pronounced:

(i) In all cases the defendant is *presumed to be sane* and to possess a sufficient degree of reason to be responsible for the offence (presumption of sanity).

(ii) However this presumption can be rebutted provided it is proved clearly by the defendant on balance of probabilities, that at the time of committing the offence they were insane.

(iii) The defendant was suffering from a *defect of reason* arising from a *disease of the mind* which meant that they did not know the *nature and quality* of their act(s), or if they did, they did not know that such act(s) were *wrong*.

If proven, the defendant is to be found not guilty by reason of insanity (for disposal of the defendant on this finding of the jury see para.10.05 below). In *R. v Antoine* [2000] 2 Cr.App.R. 94, Lord Hutton stated expressly that a plea of insanity under either limb of the *M'Naghten Rules* negates the mens rea to the offence. It is important to be aware that the Divisional Court, on an appeal by way of case stated held in *DPP v H* [1997] 1 W.L.R. 1407, stated that procedurally a defence of insanity is available and can be pleaded in the magistrates' court but only if the offence charged has an element of mens rea. In this case the magistrates were wrong to allow a defence of insanity to a defendant (who suffered manic depressive psychosis) for the offence of drink driving contrary to s.5 of the Road Traffic Act 1988, since the offence is one of strict liability requiring no proof of mens rea.

In summary, the requirements of the defence are that the defendant must prove on a balance of probabilities three elements:

(i) defect of reason;

(ii) disease of the mind;

(iii) ignorance of nature and quality of act, or that it was wrong. It is the defect of reason requirement that in essence, distinguishes this defence from that of an abnormality of the mind for diminished responsibility, which focuses on an inability to control impulses.

In *R. v Clarke* [1972] 1 All E.R. 219, the appellant was alleged to have stolen food items from a store; at trial she adduced medical evidence relating to depression to support her defence that she had no intention to deprive. The trial judge had wrongly ruled that her defence was insanity; in consequence she changed her plea to that of guilty. The Court of Appeal quashed her conviction stating that the evidence did not raise insanity. Ackner J. stated that the rules do not apply to those who, whilst retaining their reasoning power, have a lapse of confusion or absent-mindedness and therefore at that time, fail to utilise their powers of reason. The appellant was not suffering from any defect of reason, her defence was simply a lack of mens rea for theft.

4. The Defence of Insane Automatism

10.04 This element to the defence of insanity has caused the greatest difficulty for the courts. The case authorities that have dealt with the meaning of a disease of the mind have arisen were the defendant has tried to argue that they were suffering from automatism, not insanity, in the hope of gaining a complete acquittal. The defence of automatism is usually raised where the defendant claims that through an unforeseeable mental malfunction or state of (un)consciousness, they suddenly lose the ability to voluntarily control their actions. The defendant is therefore claiming that in this situation, they have failed to commit the actus reus, since their act is an involuntary act as opposed to a voluntary one. It is for this reason that the principles relating to automatism are in a quagmire and are confusing because of the difference in factual circumstances that allow the defence to be raised.

On the one hand, the defendant may bring the state of their mind in issue as amounting to automatism, whilst on the other, instead bring into issue not their mind but a conscious, uncontrollable act. It is for this reason that the House of Lords in *Bratty v Attorney-General for NI* [1963] A.C. 386 stated that as a matter of law there exist two categories of automatism as follows; (i) insane automatism (ii) non-insane automatism. In *R. v Quick* [1973] 3 W.L.R. 26, the nature of automatism and whether the raising of such a plea amounts to a defence of insanity or simple (non-insane) automatism was described by Lawton L.J. as a:

> "quagmire of law, seldom entered nowadays save by those in desperate need of some kind of defence."

In *R. v Burgess* [1991] 2 Q.B. 92, the Court of Appeal observed that when the defence of automatism is raised by the defence, the trial judge must consider two questions before leaving defence with the jury:

(i) Is there a proper evidential foundation for the defence of automatism? It will always be for the judge to decide whether the evidence given in a particular case is sufficient to raise an issue of automatism so as to be left to the jury.

(ii) Does this evidence show the case to be one of insane automatism and therefore falls with the *M'Naghten Rules* or does the evidence show a defence of non-insane automatism?

The dividing line between whether the defendant's unconsciousness amounts to a claim of insane or non-insane automatism is determined by whether that mental malfunction or state of unconscious comes within the meaning of a defect of reason arising from a disease of the mind.

5. Meaning of Disease of the Mind: The External Factor Theory

10.05 The Court of Appeal in *R. v Kemp* [1957] 1 Q.B. 399 and *R. v Quick* [1973] 1 Q.B. 910 together with the House of Lords in *Bratty v AG for NI* [1963] A.C. 386 and *R. v Sullivan* [1984] A.C. 156, encapsulated the legal meaning of disease of the mind as consisting of the following elements:

(i) A malfunctioning (impairment) of the mind, not the brain, and mind is given its ordinary meaning of mental faculties of reason, memory and understanding) caused by a disease.

(ii) That the source of the malfunction/impairment derives from some internal body factor, this can either be organic, i.e. epilepsy or functional, i.e. psychoses such as schizophrenia which manifests in violence.

(iii) It does not include the application of external factors to the body, "such as violence, drugs, including anaesthetics, alcohol and hypnotic influences" (see decision in *Quick* [1973] 1 Q.B. 910)

(iv) That the impairment need not be permanent, it can be transitory, or intermittent, provided that it subsisted at the time of the commission of the act. (see the decision in *Sullivan* [1984] A.C. 156)

In *Quick* Lawton L.J. noted:

> "that the law should not give the words 'defect of reason from disease of the mind' a meaning which be regarded with incredulity outside a court."

and gave the example of a person who had just received dental treatment under a local anaesthetic and suffered a bad reaction to it, who could not be expected to be deemed legally insane, yet such a logical outcome has not been achieved with regard to those who have diabetes.

6. The Diabetic Cases: A Problematic Issue of Fairness

10.06 The creation of the external factor theory so as to provide a workable legal meaning of the expression disease of the mind, has led to the development of a legal anomaly which is both illogical and potentially unfair, dependant on what type of diabetes the defendant happens to suffer from. This point is well illustrated in *R. v Quick* [1973] 3 W.L.R. 26, in which the appellant, a nurse at a psychiatric hospital, assaulted a patient. He was charged with a s.47 ABH offence, to which he claimed that at the time of the assault he was in a state of automatism due to the fact that he was suffering from hypoglycaemia; a deficiency in his blood sugar level caused by him injecting too much insulin. The trial judge ruled that the appellant's condition amounted to a disease of the mind and therefore only a defence of insanity was available to him. In consequence of this ruling the appellant changed his plea to guilty and later appealed against the ruling as incorrect in law.

The Court of Appeal had to decide whether or not the appellant's condition amounted to a disease of the mind for the purposes of insanity. Lawton L.J. giving the judgment of the Court, ruled that appellant's:

> "alleged medical condition, if it ever existed, was not caused by his diabetes but by his use of the insulin prescribed by his doctor. Such malfunctioning of his mind as there was, was caused by an external factor and not a bodily disorder in the nature of a disease which disturbed the working of the mind."

The Court quashed the appellant's conviction, stating that a defence of non-insane automatism should have been allowed. In contrast, the decision in *Quick* is irreconcilable with the subsequent decision of the Court of Appeal in *R. v Hennessy* [1989] 1 W.L.R. 287. Unlike *Quick*, the appellant was a hyperglycaemia diabetic and was charged with two offences of taking a conveyance without the owner's consent under s.12 of the Theft 1968 and also disqualified from driving. The appellant claimed at the time of the offences, he was in a state of non-insane automatism having failed to take his proper dosage of insulin which caused stress, anxiety and depression and therefore he wasn't aware of what he was doing.

The Court of Appeal, distinguishing *Quick* but relying on a obiter statement, held that whilst stress, anxiety and depression can be caused by other external factors, they cannot in law, either separately or together, be capable of amounting to external factors for the purposes of automatism. Alone or together, they represent at state of mind that is "prone to recur" and lack the relevant features of novelty or accident. In this respect the Court ruled that the appellant's hyperglycaemic episode amounted to a malfunction of the mind due to an internal factor, namely the diabetes itself, which was an internal defect not corrected by insulin. Although the two authorities clearly review and apply the principles of law relating to what amounts to a disease of the mind, the results of each are not easy to reconcile in terms of justice and fairness. In Quick's situation the law deems such a person to be classified as non-insane and therefore entitled to be acquitted absolutely, whilst those in Hennessy's position are to be classified as legally insane and therefore can be acquitted by reason of insane automatism but are then subject to the special verdict.

7. Epilepsy and Sleeping Disorders both Amount to Disease of the Mind

10.07 In *R. v Sullivan* [1984] A.C. 156, the appellant had violently assaulted the elderly complaint whilst suffering an epileptic seizure. He was charged with s.18 causing GBH with intent and contended that he had a defence of non-insane automatism. This was rejected by the judge, who ruled that his condition amounted to a defence of insanity. He subsequently changed his plea to guilty and appealed against this ruling. The Court of Appeal dismissed his appeal and ruled that epilepsy can be a disease of the mind and therefore only insane automatism or insanity was available to the appellant. Lawton L.J. in this regard stated that epilepsy amounts to a morbid inherent (internal) condition of the brain, resulting in a total lack of understanding and memory and therefore constitutes legal insanity. Significantly, Lawton L.J. noted that this decision may come across as being harsh, but that it must:

> "be remembered that persons who, through disease, cause injury to others and may do so again, are a potential danger to all who may come into contact with them. It is in the public interest that they should be put under medical care for as long as is reasonably necessary for the protection of others, but no longer."

The ruling in Sullivan was approved and applied by the Court of Appeal in the somewhat rare case of *R. v Burgess* [1991] 2 Q.B. 92, in which the appellant had violently assaulted a female friend for whom he had affection, with a video machine. At his trial for a s.18 GBH offence, the appellant did not deny causing the injuries but instead claimed that he lacked the necessary mens rea of specific intent, on the basis that, at the time of the offence, he was in a state of non-insane automatism, namely a state of unconsciousness during an episode of sleepwalking, medical evidence was adduced to support this claim. The judge ruled that on the evidence, the defence was one of insanity on which the jury agreed and found him not guilty by reason of insanity. The Court of Appeal dismissed his appeal against this verdict stating that on the evidence:

> "the judge was right to conclude that this was an abnormality or disorder, albeit transitory, due to an internal factor, whether functional or organic, which had manifested itself in violence. It was a disorder or abnormality which might recur, though the possibility of it recurring in the form of serious violence was unlikely."

In an interesting legal move, a jury at Norwich Crown Court (unreported, 2003) found the defendant, Reginald Pull, who had multiple sclerosis, to be not guilty of causing death by dangerous driving by reason of insanity as opposed to non-insane automatism. The defendant had, owing to his illness, suffered a muscle spasm which caused his foot to jam on the accelerator and the car to go out of control, killing a pedestrian.

8. Combination of both External and Internal Factors

10.08 Similar to the issue faced by the House of Lords in *Dietschmann* so too the Court of Appeal in *R. v Micheal Roach* [2001] EWCA Crim 2698, in regard to what is the legal position if evidentially there exists both a combination of external and internal factors which caused a malfunctioning of the defendant's mind. In this case, the appellant was convicted of s.18 wounding with intent when he stabbed a work colleague who he disliked. The appellant contended at trial that he had no knowledge or memory of the incident itself but was aware of the events leading up to it and after the stabbing. The trial judge considered that the appellant had an anti-social (mixed) personality disorder of the psychogenic type, which amounted to insane automatism.

The appellant, on appeal against his conviction, argued that this disorder played a causative role when combined with the contributory external factors of alcohol and prescribed medication, and therefore he should have been allowed to plead the defence of non-insane automatism before the jury. The Court of Appeal accepted this was a "borderline case" between the two types of automatism, but on careful consideration held that if external factors are operative upon an underlying condition which would not otherwise produce a state of automatism, then a defence of non-insane automatism should be left to the jury.

9. Meaning of the Nature and Quality of the Act and Wrong

10.09 As with the other elements of insanity, whether or not the defendant, as a result of their disease of the mind, did not know the nature and quality of their act or if they did know, they were not in the circumstances aware that it was wrong to do it, will be determined by psychiatric medical evidence which the jury can accept or reject. In *R. v Codere* [1916] 12 Cr.App.R. 21, the appellant was convicted of a murder in which the deceased suffered appalling injuries. On appeal, the appellant argued that he should have been found not guilty by reason of insanity, since the jury should have been directed that the word "quality" meant that the accused did not know that his act was immoral. This was rejected by the Court which ruled that the expression "nature and quality" referred to only the physical character of the act, and that the Law Lords in *M' Naghten* had not intended in the use of those words to distinguish between the physical and moral aspect of the act committed.

In *R. v Windle* [1952] 2 Q.B. 826, the appellant killed his wife (who herself was considered insane) by giving her a fatal dose of pills. The appellant claimed that his wife had persistently nagged him and that due to her own mental health he considered it a morally and kind act to bring her life to a premature end. At a time when the death penalty was the only sanction for murder the appellant's plea of insanity was rejected by the trial judge. Dismissing the appeal the court ruled that the word "wrong" meant:

> "contrary to law and not wrong according to the opinion of one man or of a number of people on the question whether a particular act might or might not be justified."

In this case, *Windle* clearly knew what he was doing was wrong in law and he knew the punishment for murder was death. In *R. v Johnston* [2007] EWCA Crim 1978, the Court of Appeal ruled on this important point that the statement of what is meant by wrong in *Windle* is unequivocal. The meaning of wrong is settled and the strict position applies. Accordingly, although the appellant (a paranoid schizophrenic) did not believe it was morally wrong to attack two people, he knew it was legally wrong and therefore the defence of insanity was not available to him.

It is ultimately a question of fact for the jury to decide whether the defendant at the time of the offence did not know the nature and quality of their act or if they did they did not know it was wrong. These factual questions are well illustrated in the facts that arose in *Attorney-General's Reference (No.3 of 1998)* [1999] 3 W.L.R. 1194. Although the case involved a point of law, relating to fitness to plead, the medical evidence agreed that the defendant was legally insane at the time when he committed the offence of aggravated burglary, in which he had armed himself with a snooker cue, smashed down the front door of the complainant's house and attempted to assault him. The defendant had stated that he believed that he was Jesus Christ, who was confronted by both evil and danger and that he was looking for a house with a light on which he believed would be a safe place and protect him from the presence of evil. The psychiatric evidence confirmed that the defendant did not know the nature and quality of his act or if he did, he did not know it was wrong legally.

10. Burden of Proof for Insanity and Insane Automatism

10.10 The burden of proof to establish a defence of insanity rests upon the defendant. This amounts to a persuasive burden in that it must be shown by the defendant that the elements to the defence of insanity are satisfied on a balance of probabilities. This means that the defendant must adduce expert psychiatric evidence at trial, to establish that more likely than not, or more probably than not at the time of the offence they were insane. The prosecution need only adduce conflicting medical evidence. This reversed burdened of proof is stated clearly in *Woolmington v DPP* [1935] A.C. 462 and in *R v Quick* [1973] 3 W.L.R. 26 for insane automatism.

11. Disposal if Shown to be Unfit to Plead or Legally Insane

10.11 Section 24 of the Domestic Violence, Crime and Victims Act 2004 (DVCVA 2004) amends s.5 of the Criminal Procedure (Insanity and Unfitness to Plead) Act 1991 by inserting a new s.5(A), which creates a new range of disposals available to the court for a defendant found either to be unfit to plead or where they are found not guilty by reason of insanity. These new disposal orders will allow for the defendant to receive treatment and support if the court thinks that this is appropriate in the circumstances of the particular case. The court has three options:

(i) To make a hospital order in accordance with the Mental Health Act 1983. This can be accompanied by a restriction order under s.41. A hospital order cannot be imposed without supporting medical evidence under s.37 of the Mental Health Act 1983 which shows that the defendant is mentally disordered and requires specialist medical treatment.

(ii) To make supervision order; this allows for treatment for both physical and mental disorder, but can not compel a defendant to receive treatment as an in-patient unless they consent. This order is designed to provide a framework of treatment and is therefore non-punitive in nature. Accordingly, there is no punishment, should a defendant breach the order.

(iii) To order an absolute discharge; this means that the defendant is discharged of liability absolutely and would only arise where the offence committed was trivial, or the defendant does not require any treatment.

Section 25 of the DVCV Act 2004 provides for a right of appeal to the Court of Appeal against a supervision or hospital order. The Court of Appeal then has the power to quash the order imposed and either substitute or amend the orders originally imposed. Also under s.12 of the Criminal Appeal Act

1968 a defendant as a right of appeal to the Court of Appeal against a verdict of guilty by reason of insanity.

12. The Defence of Non-Insane Automatism

10.12 Lord Denning in *Bratty v Att-Gen for NI* [1963] A.C. 386 explained succinctly the general meaning of non-insane automatism in the following terms:

> "No act is punishable if it is done involuntary: an involuntary act (automatism) means an act which is done by the muscles without any control by the mind, such as a spasm, a reflex action or convulsion."

Similarly, in *Hill v Baxter* [1958] 1 Q.B. 277, the Divisional Court observed that a temporary loss of consciousness arising accidentally would not amount to insanity. Non-insane automatism is usually raised as a defence to a road traffic offence, in which the defendant will rely on some form of physical involuntary act that does not bring into issue their state of mind. Although there exists no clear authority; an example of non-insane automatism would be where a defendant is charged with careless driving, but at the time of the alleged offence suffered a bout of sneezing, this could be relied upon even without the requirement of medical evidence.

The issue of sleep deprivation as amounting to a state of automatism, was addressed in *Attorney-General's Reference (No.2 of 1992)* [1993] 97 Cr.App.R. 329, in which the defendant, a lorry driver, had been driving for six hours out of 12, suddenly drove down the hard shoulder and hit a broken down vehicle killing two people. At his trial for causing death by dangerous driving, the prosecution alleged that he was in the process of falling asleep or had already done so. The defence presented expert evidence to say that he was in a state of "driving without awareness" and therefore in a state of automatism. The trial judge left the defence of automatism to the jury based on this expert evidence. The defendant was acquitted.

The Attorney-General, using his power under s.72 of the Criminal Justice Act 1972, referred the case to the Court of Appeal for its opinion on whether the judge was right to rule as he did. The Court of Appeal gave the opinion that, as a matter of law, for the defence of automatism to be left to the jury, there had to be a total destruction of voluntary control on the defendant's part, impaired or reduced control was not enough and that therefore driving without awareness did not involve a total destruction, as there remained an ability to steer and a capacity to react. The trial judge was therefore wrong to leave the defence of automatism to the jury.

Similarly in *Attorney-General's Reference (No.4 of 2000)* [2001] 2 Cr.App.R. 417, the defendant was a bus driver who drove at speed out of the bus station and in doing so had to turn sharply to the right. He accelerated by inadvertently placing his foot on the accelerator instead of the brake, as a result he killed two people. At his trial for causing death by dangerous driving the judge accepted there was no case to answer since his action was involuntary due to his mistaken belief as to the nature of the pedal he was pressing and therefore the prosecution could not prove the actus reus of a deliberate act. The Attorney-General sought the opinion of the Court of Appeal as to the correctness of the judge's ruling. The Court of Appeal gave the opinion that the judge's ruling was wrong and that a mistaken belief as to the possible consequences of a conscious action did not render that act involuntary. The purpose of the actus reus of the offence of dangerous driving is captured in situations where the driver, as in this case, made a mistake of that nature.

13. Burden of Proof in Non-Insane Automatism

10.13 In contrast to insanity or insane automatism, the burden of proof for non-insane automatism is upon the prosecution to disprove beyond all reasonable doubt that the defendant's act was a voluntary act and not involuntary due to a state of automatism. The defence simply have an evidential burden, in the sense that they simply have to adduce evidence to support their claim of an involuntary act of automatism. Another important distinction is that if the jury are satisfied that the defendant did an involuntarily act due to a state of automatism, then they must acquit the defendant absolutely, which means they are able to walk freely from court without a stain on their character (see the decision in *Hill v Baxter* [1958] 1 Q.B. 277).

14. Fault Liability no Excuse to both Insane and Non-Insane Automatism

10.14 The common law will not allow a person to avoid criminal liability in circumstances where they themselves are at fault in causing their own state of automatism to arise. In *R. v Quick* [1973] 1 Q.B. 910, the Court of Appeal referred to the decision in *R. v Lipman* [1970] 1 Q.B. 152, (in which the defendant had voluntarily taken LSD and killed under an illusion of being attacked by snakes) that a self induced incapacity will not, in law, amount to excuse:

> "nor will one which could have been reasonably foreseen as a result of either doing, or omitting to do something, as for example, taking alcohol against medical advice after using certain prescribed drugs or failing to have regular meals while taking insulin. From time to time difficult boarderline cases are likely to arise."

In such cases there is no defence of automatism available to the defendant; this point is illustrated clearly in *R. v Marison* [1997] R.T.R. 457, in which the Court of Appeal dismissed the appellant's appeal against conviction for causing death by dangerous driving, which occurred when he lost consciousness during an hypoglycaemic episode (the same as in *Quick*). The

Court of Appeal stated that on the evidence a defence of automatism did not arise, since it was clear that having suffered a previous attack it could be reasonably foreseen that he might suffer an hypoglycaemic attack and therefore he was at fault for his own loss of consciousness.

In causing death by dangerous driving cases or other similar road traffic offences, it is for the defence to:

(i) adduce evidence that there was at the time a total loss of control (this need not be throughout the whole journey). If no such evidence the defence fails, if there is then the second question is considered;

(ii) was the total loss of control unforeseen, namely that the defendant could not have reasonably foreseen either through advance warning or advance blood/sugar test? If yes the defence ought to be left to the jury, if not then the defence does not arise.

These issues can become problematic in practice as highlighted in *R. v JG* [2006] EWCA Crim 3276, a tragic case in which the defendant, an insulin dependant diabetic, caused the death of another motorist during an hypoglycaemic attack. The judge had withdrawn the case at the conclusion of the defence's case. The prosecution appealed against the ruling to the Court of Appeal which held, based on the medical evidence in terms of whether the defendant had properly managed her condition, that there was no proof of fault of the defendant in not checking her blood sugar levels. Accordingly, the defendant was acquitted of causing death by dangerous driving.

In *R. v C (prosecution right of appeal)* [2007] EWCA Crim 1862, the Court of Appeal made it plain that it is for the defendant to adduce evidence that there was a total loss of control at the time of the collision. Only if such evidence exists should the second question of whether the defendant could have reasonably avoided the unforeseen attack through advance testing and management of the diabetes be considered. The Court emphasised that if a judge is asked to rule on the availability of the defence, it is important that they do not make a premature ruling on the point. Whilst not wanting to be prescriptive, the Court took the general view that the appropriate time would be when the defence has had an opportunity to adduce evidence in relation to the issue as to the degree of loss of control, if it is in issue, and its cause, if that too is controversial.

For the prosecution, unless and until the defence adduce evidence of a total loss of control, the case is a straightforward issue of driving dangerously. If the defence call evidence as to loss of control and unawareness, then at that stage the prosecution would adduce rebuttal evidence to the contrary. Accordingly, the judge fell into error by ruling that there was no case to answer by the defendant for causing the death of a pedestrian he had collided with. The Court of Appeal quashed the ruling and ordered a fresh trial to take place.

Chapter Eleven

GENERAL DEFENCES
PART 3: INTOXICATION AND MISTAKE

1. Introduction

11.01 Within the criminal law there exist a number of defences that are generally available to all criminal offences. These defences exist, on the one hand, to excuse the criminal conduct (duress), whilst, on the other, to provide a justification for such conduct (self-defence). Alternatively, the defence can instead adduce at trial evidence of intoxication. This is strictly not a defence; when raised the defence are claiming that due to the intoxicated state of the defendant at the time of the alleged offence, it was not possible for them to have formed the necessary mens rea. The criminal law has come to recognise two types of intoxication, namely voluntary and involuntary intoxication; if successful, intoxication negates the element of mens rea. However, difficulties have arisen for the common law in determining the actual application of intoxication and its effect on mens rea generally. Such difficulties are more profound when intoxication is linked inextricably to other defences. For this reason, the Court of Appeal in *R. v Hatton* [2006] 1 Cr.App.R. 16, was asked to reconsider the previous authorities in relation to the effect of an intoxicated mistaken belief in self defence.

2. Voluntary Intoxication (self-induced) and the Specific/Basic Intent Dichotomy and Grounds of Public Policy

11.02 Where the defendant voluntarily takes drugs or alcohol with the result that they are incapable of knowing what they are doing and therefore incapable of forming the mens rea this amounts to intoxication by self inducement. However, to allow such a claim in all circumstances would amount to an unjustifiable excuse and the lack of culpability. The leading authority on intoxication is *R. v Majewski* [1977] A.C. 443, in which the defendant had consumed considerable quantities of drugs, then went to a pub where he became involved in a fight. Having been convicted under s.47 of the OAPA 1861, he appealed on the grounds that by reason of self induced intoxication, he neither intended to nor acted recklessly in what he did.

The House of Lords affirmed his conviction and held that a defendant can only use evidence of voluntary intoxication to negate mens rea if the offence is one of *specific intent*. If the offence is one of *basic intent* then the defendant cannot put forward evidence of self induced intoxication to support a claim that they did not form the necessary mental element. Lord Diplock stated that a specific intent crime is one where "the prosecution must in general prove that the purpose for the commission of the act extends to the intent expressed or implied in the definition of the crime". Conversely, a basic intent crime amounts to offence that consists of both "intention" and "recklessness" or other states of mind describing the mens rea to the offence and does not go beyond the actus reus of the offence (i.e. common assault). Intoxication is not available for basic intent offences on public policy grounds. In *R. v Majewski*, Lord Elwyn-Jones set out the limited application of intoxication to specific intent crimes and not those of basic intent in the following terms:

> "if a man of his own volition takes a substance which causes him to cast off the restraints of reason and conscience, no wrong is done to him by holding him answerable criminally for any injury he may do while in that condition. His course of conduct in reducing himself by drugs and drink to that condition in my view supplies the evidence of mens rea, of guilt certainly sufficient of basic intent. It is a reckless course of conduct and recklessness is enough to constitute the necessary mens rea in assault cases. The drunkenness is itself an intrinsic, an integral part of the crime, the other part being the evidence of the unlawful use of force against the victim."

The categorisation of offences into specific and basic intent crimes was contextually analysed in some depth by the Court of Appeal in *R. v Heard* [2007] EWCA Crim 125. The appellant had rubbed his penis against an police officer whilst in a drunken state, the trial judge ruled that the offence sexual assault was a basic intent crime and therefore the appellant's drunkenness was irrelevant. The appellant was convicted and appealee against his conviction on the grounds that this ruling was wrong.

The Court of Appeal, in dismissing his appeal, stated that the House of Lords in *Majewski* was not seeking to clinically categorise individual offences into either specific intent or basic intent for the purposes of voluntary intoxication, since some offences have different elements as to proof of the mens rea. The Court of Appeal confirmed that the logical way to separate offences for the purposes of intoxication is, as was said in *Majewski* and also in *DPP v Morgan* [1976] A.C. 182, that for an offence to constitute a specific intent crime, the mens rea must be identified as having a "ulterior intent" in the sense that the required mens rea to prove the offence is one of intent only; if the mens rea contains any other states of mind, whether recklessness or belief, then these offences will amount to basic intent crimes, based on clear grounds of public policy. Although the offence of sexual assault cannot be committed with a reckless mind, this does not mean that it is a crime of specific intent; there exist other elements to the offence such as deliberate touching (i.e. that the defendant's act, whether drunk or not, is done on purpose) which must be objectively sexual, there must be a lack of consent or a unreasonable belief as to consent. Accordingly, the Court of Appeal ruled that the offence of sexual assault, as with all comparable sexual offences, amounts to basic intent crimes and that Parliament, when passing the Sexual Offences Act 2003, had not intended to change the previous law on this point.

Likewise, the House of Lords in *R. v Kingston* [1994] 3 W.L.R. 519, relied on the same public policy grounds by refusing unanimously to extend the limited application of intoxication to situations where the defendant has the requisite mens rea but lack any moral fault on the basis that they would not have committed the offence had it not been for another surreptitiously drugging them, so as to be in a state of involuntary intoxication. In *Kingston*, the House of Lords upheld the appellant conviction's for indecent assault on a young boy and said that he had no defence of involuntary intoxication when he claimed that had he not been drugged by his co-accused, who then hoped to photograph him in a sexual act with the complainant so as to blackmail him, he would not have committed the act itself. It would be an affront to justice to allow a defendant, who had paedophiliac tendencies, to be able to claim that whilst he possessed the mens rea, he was not morally at fault since had it not been for the act of another in drugging him, he would not have otherwise developed a need to satisfy his sexual appetite of young boys.

3. A Drunken Intent is Still an Intent in Law: *Sheehan and Moore* Direction

11.03 Whilst the defence may endeavour to adduce evidence of intoxication at trial, it is for the trial judge to decide whether such evidence should be left to the jury. In *Sheehan and Moore* [1960] 60 Cr.App.R. 308, the Court of Appeal gave guidance to trial judges on the issue of intoxication. The general rule is that if there is evidence that intoxication might be relied upon by the defence, then the judge should leave the issue to the jury. But such a direction is not always needed since a drunken intent can still be an intent to commit the offence; if a direction is given then the jury are told to take this into account. Likewise in *R. v McKnight, TheTimes*, May 5, 2000 the Court of Appeal approved the *Sheehan* Direction and added that following the Privy Council decision in *Sooklal (Narine) v Trinidad and Tobago* [1999] 1 W.L.R. 2011, there must exist a "proper factual basis" before a *Sheenan* Direction is required. In *R. v Alden* [2001] EWCA Crim 804, the Court of Appeal rejected defence counsel's submission that both *McKnight and Sheenan* were in conflict with each other and that *Mc Knight* was therefore wrongly decided. The Court held that:

> "the crucial question in every case where there is evidence that a defendant has taken a substantial quantity of drink, is whether there is an issue as to the

defendant's formation of specific intent by reason of the alcohol which he has taken."

4. Alternative Offences

11.04 Although a claim of intoxication may relieve the defendant of liability for more serious conduct, lesser alternative offences exist to capture that conduct regardless of intoxication. In *R. v Lipman* [1969] 3 W.L.R. 819, the defendant was acquitted of murder but instead convicted of manslaughter when he had killed his partner by stuffing bedclothes down her throat under the illusion, induced by the hallucinatory drugs he had taken, that he was fighting for his life against snakes. Widgery L.J. on the issue of alternative offences, noted that:

> "if the drunken man is so drunk that he does not know what he is doing, he has a defence to any charge, such as murder or wounding with intent, in which specific intent is essential, but he his still liable to be convicted of manslaughter or unlawful wounding for which no specific intent is necessary."

In relation to offences against the person where the common defence relied upon is self defence and the alleged offence is often as a direct or indirect consequence of intoxication, it is a settled principle of law found in *R. v Wilson* [1984] A.C. 242, *R. v Maxwell* [1990] A.C. 242, *R. v Mandair* [1995] 1 A.C. 208 and more recently in *R. v Lahaye* [2005] EWCA Crim 2847, that within the hierarchy of offences there can be, either within the indictment or at the judge's own discretion under s.6(3) of the Criminal Law Act 1967, an alternative direction as to the offence should the jury not be able to convict on the more serious specific intent crime.

5. Intoxication Combined with a Mistaken Belief as to Facts Defence

11.05 It is a well established principle of criminal law that if a person genuinely holds a mistaken belief as to the facts, even if that belief is in certain circumstances unreasonable, provided it is genuinely held by the defendant this will provide a defence. These principles were reviewed extensively by the House of Lords in *B (a minor) v DPP* [2000] 2 A.C. 132. The appellant a 15-year-old boy had asked a 13-year-old girl on a bus to give him a shinner (blow job), the magistrates ruled that his belief of the girl being 14 was irrelevant. The House of Lords held, applying the decision in *R. v Morgan* [1976] A.C. 182, and referring to the old authority of *R. v Tolson* [1889] 23 Q.B.D. 168, that the common law presumption of mens rea applied to all criminal offences unless it was excluded by Parliament either expressly or through necessary implication. Their Lordships stated that this exclusion did not exist for an offence of gross indecency under s.1 of the Indecency of Children Act 1960 and that the prosecution must disprove any genuinely held belief as to age, even if the belief was unreasonably held. The question that arises is what factors give rise to the displacement of the common law presumption? Lord Nicholls stated:

> "necessary implication connotes an implication, which is compellingly clear. Such an implication may be found in the language used, the nature of the offence, the mischief sought to be prevented and any other circumstances which may assist in determining what intention is properly to be attributed to Parliament when creating the offence."

The decision in *B (a minor) v DPP*, was later applied in *R. v K* [2002] 1 A.C. 462, to an offence of indecent assault with a girl under 16 in which the House of Lords held that the prosecution are required to disapprove a defence of honest belief that the complainant was 16 or over, since as a matter of law, a girl under 16 cannot consent to the assault. Likewise the Court of Appeal in *R. v Kumer* [2005] 1 W.L.R. 1353 applied the same principle to the offence of buggery with a person under 16.

One such factor is the statutory context. Lord Nicholls referred to the seriousness of the offence and the severity of any punishment as indictors requiring proof of mens rea. His Lordship identified that the original punishment under s.1 was one two years' imprisonment. This was subsequently increased to 10 years by s.52 of the Crime (Sentences) Act 1997 and that any convicted person will be subject to the notification requirements under the Sex Offenders Act 1997. It is important to note that this offence was repealed and replaced by ss.9 and 13 of the Sexual Offences Act 2003 which creates the offence of sexual activity with a child in which the prosecution must prove that the complainant is under 16 and the defendant does not reasonably believe that they are 16 or over. Nevertheless, if the complainant is under 13 there is no reasonable belief requirement as to age. The same applies with the offence of gross indecency which was repealed and replaced by s.10 by causing or inciting a child to engage in sexual activity.

11.06 In *R. v Aitken* [1992] 1 W.L.R. 1006, and *R. v Richardson* [1999] 1 Cr.App.R. 392, the Court of Appeal held that through self-induced intoxication the defendant, who had formed a mistaken belief that another person who had earlier consented to "horseplay" but then subsequently withdrew their consent and was still assaulted, had a defence and the jury should be directed to take this into account. In contrast the Court of Appeal in *R. v Fotheringham* [1989] 88 Cr.App.R. 206, held that self-induced intoxication was no defence to a defendant who mistakenly believed that he was having sex with his wife but in fact it was with the 14-year-old baby sitter, since rape is a basic intent crime and therefore self-induced intoxication does not arise. In relation to the offence of having sexual intercourse with a girl under 16 contained in s.6(3) of the Sexual Offences Act 1956, there exists a specific young man's defence where they are under 24 and have not previously been charged with a like offence and have a reasonable belief that the complainant is over 16.

In *Kirk and Russell* [2002] EWCA Crim 1580, it was ruled that this defence, although limited to men under 24, is not discriminatory in its application to older men, since the legitimate aim behind the offence is to protect young girls. Conversely, in *Attorney-General's References (Nos 74 & 83 of 2007) (Foster and Fenn)* [2007] EWCA Crim 2550, an unduly lenient sentence referral, the Court of Appeal observed that the alternative offence of having sexual intercourse with a girl under 13 in s.5 amounted to an absolute offence since in law, a girl under 13 can not give consent to such activity and that a defendant's belief, even if reasonably held as to the complainant's age, is irrelevant. Nonetheless the Court observed that the apparent age or belief in it could amount to mitigating factors as to sentence, as if there had been consent.

The legal meaning of self defence was defined by the Privy Council in *R. v Palmer* [1991] A.C. 814, amounting to two questions, namely an honest belief that it was necessary to act in self defence, and secondly whether that act, in terms of force used, was reasonable and proportionate to the degree of threat applied. It is now well established in *R. v Williams* [1984] 78 Cr.App.R. 276, that as part of the question whether the defendant honestly believed that it was necessary to defend themselves or another, the jury are entitled to consider the defendant's mistaken view of the facts, regardless of whether objectively such a view was unreasonable or not.

However, the acceptance in *Williams* of mistaken belief in self-defence caused considerable difficulties when that mistaken belief is formed not with sobriety, but as a direct result of intoxication. This point in issue was first addressed by the Court of Appeal in *R. v O' Grady* [1987] 3 All E.R. 420, where it was held that a defendant could not rely on self-defence if, because of his self-induced intoxication, he had formed a mistaken belief as to the amount of force reasonably necessary to defend himself and had used more force than was necessary. Lane L.J. referred to the decision in Williams and distinguished it on the facts. His Lordship then found clear support for the Court's conclusion in the speeches of Lord Simon and Lord Edmund-Davies in *R. v Majewski* [1976] 2 All E.R. 142, and that to rule otherwise would result in an absurd outcome in a case like *Lipman* of the defendant being acquitted, on the basis that he believed he was defending himself from attack by serpents. His Lordship stated:

> "it is significant that no one seems to have considered that possibility" and that the decision of the court is right for the "reason recoils from the conclusion that in such circumstances a defendant is entitled to leave the court without a stain on his character."

Soon afterwards, the Court of Appeal re-visited the *Grady* decision in *R. v O'Connor* (1990) Crim. L.R. 135, where the defendant was convicted of murder when, through a drunken mistake, he believed that the deceased was about to attack him. Had it not been for the drink, no such mistaken belief could have been formed. The defendant appealed against his conviction on the grounds that the judge had failed to direct the jury in relation to the effect of drink on his mistaken belief. On this point, the Court applied and followed the decision in *O'Grady* and held that it was unnecessary for the judge to provide a direction on drunkenness as it affected the defendant's mistaken belief.

6. An Un-Repentant Court of Appeal in *R. v Hatton* [2005]

11.07 Professor Smith, in his commentary on *O'Connor*, described the decision in *O'Grady* as an illogical dictum and one which causes unnecessary complexities for the jury. Such illogicality is found when the jury are told that they are not entitled to consider the effect of drink on a mistaken belief in self-defence, but are then told that, when assessing the specific intent in murder, they are this time entitled to consider the effect of drink as negating that mens rea. Professor Smith believed that the decision in *O'Grady* was obiter dicta since *O'Grady* was convicted not of murder but of manslaughter so the Court in *O'Connor* was not bound by the *O'Grady* decision. Additionally, Professor Smith was in agreement with the Law Commission (No.177, see later report "Intoxication and Criminal Liability" (1995) (No.229) HC153) in that evidence of intoxication, when raised with a general defence, should be treated the same as intoxication with a specific intent crime. Professor Smith concluded by saying:

> "It is not too late for the Court of Appeal to repent and establish a sound basis for the law—the ruling in the present case seems to be scarcely less obiter than that in *O'Grady*."

In *R. v Hatton* [2006] 1 Cr.App.R. 16, the facts were not dissimilar to those of *O'Grady* in that the appellant was alleged to have unlawfully killed the deceased in his flat with a sledgehammer but had no recollection of this due to the consumption of a large amount of alcohol. The trial judge considered that he was bound by *O'Grady* and therefore, when summing up, made no reference to the appellant's intoxication in the self defence direction. Defence counsel, on appeal against the murder conviction, argued that the observations in *O'Grady* were wrong in principle and were obiter, which was not binding and ought not to be followed. In rejecting this submission, the Court, in the judgment of Lord Phillips L.C.J., stated that the Court in *O'Grady* made no express distinction between the offence of murder and that of manslaughter and that the decision to refuse to allow an intoxicated mistaken belief was not being narrowly applied.

Accordingly, Lord Phillips L.C.J. considered that the observations in *O'Grady* amounted to a general principle and not obiter dicta and therefore the Court in *Hatton* was "obliged to follow *O'Grady*". The Court also felt that the trial judge could not have directed the jury on drunken mistake since there was doubt as to whether a defence of self defence in fact existed at all. Accordingly, in this instance the Court of Appeal refused to follow Professor Smith's suggestion and repent of itself. However, the Court recognised those criticisms and those of the Law Commission, and therefore felt that it was for the House of Lords to change the law, not for the Court of Appeal to repent by ignoring well established principles of precedent. Parliament has now put this point beyond doubt and agreed with the decisions in *Hatton* and *O'Grady* by reinstating the principle in s.75(9) of the Criminal Justice and Immigration Act 2008, which provides that a defendant cannot rely on a voluntarily intoxicated mistaken belief for the purposes of self defence.

Accordingly, the decisions in *O'Grady, O'Conner* and *Hatton* are right, based on common sense and the need to ensure justice within the triangulation of interests of those of the community, victim and defendant. For this reason, the Court had to create a general principle of law since to allow an intoxicated mistake to amount to a defence, would be to make such a defence an excuse for inexcusable conduct. These were the precise fears held by Lord Diplock in *Caldwell* [1980] A.C. 341, on the meaning of recklessness, albeit now misplaced by the House of Lords' decision in *R. v G* [2004] 1 A.C. 1034, on a defendant being able to claim intoxication as a defence to aggravated criminal damage. Nevertheless, the decisions in *O'Grady* and *Hatton* are more difficult to reconcile with the decisions in *Richardson* and *Aitken*, which allow a defendant to raise an intoxicated mistaken belief defence to the withdrawal of consent, since both are a misunderstanding of the facts.

7. Mistake as to the Law: *Ignorantia Juris Haud Excusat*

11.08 Although the common law recognises that a mistaken but honest belief as to the facts amounts to a defence, there is no corresponding rule for a mistake as to the law. The proposition of law in this situation is that enshrined in the maxim *ignorantia juris haud excusat*, which means that ignorance of the law is no defence to an alleged offence. For instance, a person cannot plead ignorance to a law of theft by taking some property without paying for it. The application of this clear principle of law is well illustrated in *R. v Lee* [2001] 1 Cr.App.R. 293 in which the Court of Appeal dismissed the appeal against conviction for an assault with intent to resist arrest. The appellant had argued that he honestly believed that his arrest by the police officer in question was unlawful, and therefore that he was entitled to use reasonable force to resist the arrest. The police officer in the circumstances was using his powers of arrest lawfully under the Police and Criminal Evidence Act 1984. Accordingly, the appellant's belief amounted to an honest but mistaken belief as to the powers of arrest. The Court concluded that the defendant's mistaken belief was not as to the facts but as to the law relating to arrest and that this ignorance could not be a defence. The Court applied the principles in *Blackburn v Bowering* [1994] 1 W.L.R. 1324, where it was held that for a defence of mistake to exist, that mistake must be one relating to the facts and not a mistake as to the law.

A similar approach was taken by the High Court in *Birch v DPP* [1999] All E.R. 1431, in which the defendant's appeal by way of case stated against his conviction for the offence of obstructing the highway under s.137 of the

Highways Act 1980 was dismissed. He and others sat deliberately in the middle of the road at the premises of SARP UK, where they were demonstrating. The offence is not committed if the obstruction is due to a lawful activity; sitting in the road in this instance does not constitute a lawful activity. Accordingly, the defendant sought to argue that whilst his activity was unlawful, he had an honest and reasonable belief that his activity was preventing crime and was therefore lawful. The Court distinguished the previous authority of *Hirst and Agu v Chief Constable of West Yorkshire* [1987] 85 Cr.App.R. 143, where it was held that handing out leaflets at a animal rights demonstration was a reasonable activity providing a lawful excuse. In the instant case, that was not the case and it therefore ruled that to sit in the road was an obstruction, that it was wilful, i.e. deliberate, and that the prosecution had proved that it was without lawful authority or excuse.

CHAPTER TWELVE

GENERAL DEFENCES
PART 4: SELF DEFENCE AND AGE CAPACITY

1. SECTION 3 OF THE CRIMINAL LAW ACT 1967

12.01 The defence of self defence is a common law defence, but is also found in s.3 of the Criminal Law Act 1967 which provides that a person may use such force as is reasonable in the circumstances, in the prevention of crime or in effecting or assisting in the lawful arrest of offenders of crime. What amounts to reasonable force is determined now by s.75 of the Criminal Justice and Immigration Act 2008 which consolidates the common law principles into a statutory format. If a defendant is successful in pleading self defence, it will provide a lawful justification to the commission of an offence and therefore, the defendant is entitled to be acquitted. Self defence is most commonly raised to the range of assault offences found in the Offences Against the Person Act 1861 and also to the fatal offences of murder and manslaughter. It is nevertheless, important to note that s.3 allows for a defence of self defence in the prevention of crime, which means clearly that a person can act in defence of a third person, known or unknown and also act in defence of property, i.e. from a burglar.

The word "crime" therefore clearly means any crime within the criminal law of England and Wales, and causes no difficulties in its application. Nevertheless, an important legal issue arose in *R. v Jones* [2007] 1 A.C. 136, as to whether the intentional crime of aggression, established as part of customary international law, forms part of domestic law. The appeal involved 20 appellant's who appealed against their convictions for criminal damage and aggravated trespass. All argued that their acts where legally justified in preventing a crime of aggression in Iraq by the British Government and or the USA. The House of Lords ruled unanimously that the word crime, used in the context of the 1967 Act, would not have been intended by Parliament to include the international crime of aggression; the courts cannot create new criminal offences, it is a matter for Parliament to incorporate crimes under international customary law into domestic law, This has not occurred and therefore the appellants could not rely on s.3 as a defence to their unlawful acts.

The principles relating to self defence have caused public outcry, particularly in situations where a homeowner has killed an intruder and then subsequently been found guilty of that person's murder or manslaughter, such as in *Martin* and *Clegg*. A tragic case that highlights this controversy well is *R. v Hastings* [2003] EWCA Crim 3730. The appellant had attended at the home of his ex partner and child who, not known to him, were out. The appellant was confronted by the victim (an habitual offender who was in breach of license for a previous offence) who was in the process of burgling the premises. During this confrontation the victim received 12 stab wounds to his back and head of which he later died. At trial the jury rejected the appellant's contention that he had used force that was proportionate to the threat he was under from the victim, whom he mistakenly believed was carrying a machete. The Court of Appeal upheld his conviction for manslaughter, albeit that the appellant had appealed on grounds not relating to the use of self defence. The Court did however reduce his sentence from five years to that of three years' imprisonment.

There have been several unsuccessful attempts through the private member's bill procedure to amend the current law in terms of those who use excessive force in the protection of their home. The last attempt was that of Anne McIntosh with the Criminal Law (Amendment) (Protection of Property) Bill, which was presented to Parliament in 2005; had this bill been successful it would have amended s.3 of the CLA 1967, so as to provide that a person who uses force against a burglar shall not be guilty of any offence unless the degree of force used was grossly disproportionate and that this was or ought to have been apparent to the person using the force. Also, no prosecution could be commenced without the consent of the Attorney-General. A similar failed attempt was that of Roger Gale with the Criminal Justice (Justifiable Conduct) Bill 2004.

However, the Ministry of Justice, rather than adopt these reforms to extend the defence in specific circumstances, in s.75 of the Criminal Justice and Immigration Act 2008 simply consolidates the common law principles on reasonable force. Both s.3 of the Criminal Law Act 1967 and the common law principles remain, s.76 applies when self defence in relied upon, but only in the context of the second question for the jury's determination; namely that of reasonable force. Other than giving reasonable force a statutory meaning already found in the common law, the provision is superfluous, it gives no more protection to home owners than that which already exists.

2. Burden of Proof and the Constituent Components of Self Defence

12.02 It is for the Crown to negate self-defence. The burden is upon the prosecution to convince the jury, so as to be sure, that the defendant did not use reasonable force and therefore was not acting in self defence. In the context of s.18 wounding/causing GBH with intent and s.20 reckless infliction of GBH and s.47 assault occasioning ABH, the prosecution must establish beyond doubt that the act of the defendant was unlawful. This is established clearly in *R. v Abraham* [1973] Cr.App.R. 799, when the defendant's conviction of a s.20 offence was quashed on the grounds that the judge had failed to explain to the jury that the onus of proof was upon the prosecution to disprove self defence, not for the defence to prove it. Edmund Davies L.J. stated:

> The judge needs to give a clear, positive and unmistakeable general direction as to onus and standard of proof; then immediately follow it with a direction that in the circumstances of the particular case there is a special reason for having in mind how the onus and standard of proof applies and go on to deal ... with the issue of self-defence as follows ... members of the jury, the general direction which I have just given to you in relation to onus and standard of proof has a particularly important operation in the circumstances of the present case. Here the accused has raised the issue that he acted in self-defence. A person who acts reasonably in his self-defence commits no unlawful act. By his plea of SD that accused is raising in special form the plea of not guilty. Since it is for the Crown to show that the plea of not guilty is unacceptable, so the crown must convince you beyond reasonable doubt that SD has no basis in the present case. Having done that the judge can then proceed to deal with the facts of the particular case.

See *R. v Stokes* [2003] EWCA Crim 2977, in which the trial judge had, in his directions to the jury, given the impression that the burden of proof as to reasonable force rested with the defendant when in fact, he should have made it clear it was for the prosecution to negate. The appellant's conviction for a s.20 unlawful wounding was ruled unsafe and was quashed.

When raised, self defence consists of two constituent components the determination of reasonableness:

(i) necessity, and

(ii) proportionality under s.75 of the CJIA 2008 (reasonableness) in that force cannot be justified unless it is proportionate, i.e. reasonable in relation to the degree of threat the defendant is placed under.

This requires the trial judge, as identified in *Norman Shaw v The Queen* [2000] 1 W.L.R. 1519, by Lord Bingham, to pose two essential questions (however expressed) for the jury's consideration:

(i) Did the defendant honestly believe or may he honestly have believed, that it was necessary to defend himself? This amounts to a subjective test.

(ii) If so, and taking the circumstances and the danger as the appellant honestly believed them to be, was the amount of force which he used reasonable? This amounts to an objective test.

3. Question 1: Was it Necessary to Act in Self Defence and Mistaken Belief?

12.03 This amounts clearly to a subjective question for the jury's assessment, in that the jury, considering the facts, determine whether the defendant themselves, as a state of mind, honestly believed that they found it necessary to act in self defence. This includes a belief that later turns out to be mistaken, provided it was honestly held, that is sufficient. This point of principle is derived from *R. v Williams* [1983] 3 All E.R. 411and now reinstated in s.75(8) of the CJIA 2008. In *Williams*, a Mr Mason (M) witnessed a street robbery and gave chase; he caught the offender and endeavoured to detain him. The offender broke free, M caught him again and knocked him to the ground and placed the offender's arm up his back. The offender continued to struggle and cried for help. The appellant (Williams) at this point intervened (unaware of what had previously happened), M informed the appellant that he had arrested the offender for robbery and that he (which he was not) was a police officer. The appellant asked to see his warrant card which he could not produce, thereupon the appellant physically intervened from which M sustained a facial injury and the real offender escaped.

The appellant was indicted of a s.47 offence of assault occasioning ABH and raised a defence of self defence of another in that he honestly believed that the youth was being unlawfully assaulted. The judge directed the jury that such a belief must be based on reasonable grounds. He was convicted and appealed on the grounds of a misdirection by the judge. The Court of Appeal allowed the appeal and quashed the conviction by holding that the defendant's belief was to be determined by his mistaken view of the facts, regardless of whether objectively such a view was unreasonable or not. In giving the main judgment Lord Lane, relying on the authority of *Kimber* [1983] 1 W.L.R. 1118, as binding upon the Court said:

> "The reasonableness or unreasonableness of the D's belief is material to the question of whether the belief held by the defendant at all. If the belief was in fact held, its unreasonableness, so far as guilt or innocence is concerned, is neither here or there. It is irrelevant. Where it otherwise, the defendant would be convicted because he was negligent in failing to recognise that the victim was not consenting or that the crime was not being committed and so on. In other words the jury should be directed first of all that the prosecution have the burden or duty of proving the unlawfulness of the D's actions; secondly, if the defendant may have been labouring under a mistake as to the facts, he must be judged according to his mistaken view of the facts; thirdly, that is so whether the mistake was, on an objective view, a reasonable mistake or not.
>
> In a case of SD, where the SD or the prevention of crime is concerned, if the jury come to the conclusion that the D believed, or may have believed, that he was being attacked or that a crime was being committed, and that force was necessary to protect himself or to prevent crime, then the prosecution have not proved their case. If however, the D's alleged belief was mistaken and if the mistake was an unreasonable one, that may be a powerful reason for coming to the conclusion that the belief was not honestly held and should be rejected. Even if the jury come to the conclusion that the mistake was an unreasonable one, if the D may genuinely have been labouring under it, he should be entitled to rely on it."

This proposition of law was soon afterwards approved by the Privy Council in *Beckford v R.* [1987] 3 All E.R. 425. It is important to be aware that a defendant cannot rely on a mistaken belief if formed due to being intoxicated. This restriction is based on clear public policy grounds as stated in *R. v O'Grady* [1987] 3 All E.R. 470 and now reinstated in s.75(9) of the CJIA 2008 which prohibits a defendant from relying on a mistaken belief formed not with sobriety but due to voluntary intoxication (see Chapter Eleven)

4. Question 2: Was the Degree of Force used Proportionate to the Threat Applied

12.04 Section 75 of the Criminal Justice and Immigration Act 2008 (CJIA 2008) (not yet in force) now defines what amounts to reasonable force. This does no more than consolidate the existing common law principles and therefore reference to the well-established authorities will still be required.

This question is essentially an objective assessment of the actual force the defendant adopted and involves the jury deciding whether that the force used was reasonable in all the circumstances, taking into account the subjective belief of the danger the defendant perceived to arise from the threat being applied. Section 75(3) of the CJIA 2008 incorporates this subjective belief, providing that whether the degree of force used by the defendant was reasonable is to be assessed by reference to the circumstances as the defendant believed them to be. This must be applied subject to subsections (4) and (5) which consolidate the principle of law decided in *Palmer v R.* [1971] A.C. 814.

The partial subjective element forms part of which is essentially an objective assessment of deciding whether the force used amounted, in the circumstances, to being reasonable and therefore lawful or instead amounts to excessive (disproportionate) force, and is unlawful under s.75(4) of the CJIA 2008. Lord Morris in *Palmer v R.* [1971] A.C. 814 stated that a jury, when considering whether the amount of force used by the defendant was proportionate to the degree of threat applied, should take into account that:

> "If there as been an attack so that defence is reasonably necessary, it will be recognised that a person defending himself cannot weigh to a nicety the exact measure of his defensive action. If the jury thought that in a moment of unexpected anguish a person attacked had only done what he honestly and instinctively thought necessary that would be the most potent evidence that only reasonable defensive action had been taken."

Accordingly, when considering the objective test of reasonableness, the jury are entitled under s.75(5)(a) to take into account the fact that the defendant would not have had time to consider precisely the right amount of force needed when acting for a *legitimate purpose* to deal with the threat applied to them. In this sense, there is a certain amount of flexibility and it is still reasonable for a defendant to use more force that was in fact necessary, provided that force does not exceed what is proportionate force and therefore the defendant becomes the attacker rather than the defender. Section 75(5)(b) provides, as stated in *Palmer*, that evidence of a person reacting in a way that they honestly and instinctively thought was necessary amounts to strong evidence showing that the force was reasonable. Legitimate purpose is defined in s.75(10) and simply refers to when a defendant is acting in self defence under the common law, or in the prevention of crime under s.3 of the CLA 1967. It is vital for the trial judge to explain and give the two legal direction questions, and failure to do so may lead to any subsequent conviction being unsafe, as occurred in *R. v Pinnock* [2003] EWCA Crim 1903.

5. Excessive and Disproportionate Force

12.05 The demarcation between what is and is not reasonable force is a question of fact for the jury, based on the particular facts and circumstances of the case. For instance, whilst in a pub A realises that B is present. There exists bad blood between them; B proceeds to approach A with a pint glass in his hand, fearing attack A instinctively grabs hold of a pool cue and hits B with it as he is about to smash the glass in A's face, causing serious head injuries to B. A is charged with a s.18 wounding with intent and raises self defence. It is for the jury first to decide whether A honestly believed, even if mistaken, that it was necessary to use force to defend himself. If yes, the jury must then decide whether objectively the force used, i.e. the pool cue, was reasonable/proportionate to the threat of being glassed, taking into account that A had little or no time to weigh up the nicety of the situation. So if A used slightly more force than was needed to displace the threat, this will still amount to reasonable force. However if, having hit B with the pool cue, who falls to the ground, A decides to launch in with several kicks to B's head and body, this is now clearly an unjustifiable and excessive use of force. So whilst A may have initially acted in self defence, the later kicks amount to a clear unlawful assault as forming part of a revenge attack for which A is criminally liable.

In *R. v Scarlett* [1994] 98 Cr.App.R. 290, the landlord of a pub decided to eject a drunken customer and in the course of doing so, the customer fell down some steps and died from the injuries received. The prosecution alleged that the defendant had used excessive force and was therefore was guilty of manslaughter. The Court of Appeal, quashing his conviction, ruled that if excessive force is alleged then the prosecution must prove the requisite mens rea for the assault and that in this case the judge had failed to direct the jury as to this burden. A similar approach was taken by the Court of Appeal in *R. v Owino* [1996] 2 Cr.App.R. 128, in which the High Court affirmed the conventional approach to the application of the defence of self defence in terms of reasonable force, as set out in *Palmer*. This was again addressed by the High Court in *DPP v Armstrong-Braun* [1999] 163 J.P. 271, in which the appellant's contention that the issue of reasonable force should be assessed substantially by a subjective test, was rejected. The High Court observed obiter that the common law of self defence should be codified, since its current un-codified state caused difficulties and complexities for the lower courts in its application when there was an attempt to modify or adjust the principles to the given facts of individual cases.

In *R. v Clegg* [1995] 1 All E.R. 334, the appellant was a British solder serving in Northern Ireland at a check point. When a stolen car drove directly at the soldiers, the appellant opened fire killing the front seat passenger, who had been hit in the back. The appellant was convicted of murder, the jury having rejected his claim of self defence, as amounting to excessive force, on the basis that at the time of his last shot the vehicle was not longer a threat. The House of Lords refused to create a new defence of the use of "excessive force" as a partial defence to murder which would reduce it in extenuating circumstances, as in the appellant's case, to voluntary manslaughter. Lord Lloyd, who gave the leading judgment, stated that:

> "I am not averse to judges developing law, or indeed making new law, when they see their way clearly, even though questions of social policy are involved. A good recent example would be the affirmation by the House of the decision of the Court of Appeal that a man can be guilty of raping his wife *R v R* [1992] 1 AC 599. But in the present case I am in no doubt that your Lordships should abstain from law-making. The reduction of what would otherwise be murder to manslaughter in a particular class of case seems to me essentially a matter for the decision of the Legislature, and not by this House in its judicial capacity."

His Lordship further noted that the development of a new defence forms part of the wider sentencing issue of a whether the mandatory life sentence should still be applied, a matter only Parliament could decide. The House of Lords maintained the same view in *R. v Martin* [2002] 2 W.L.R. 1, in which the appellant, a Norfolk farmer, had shot and killed an intruder as he was fleeing. Their Lordships, on the issue of self defence, refused to interfere with the jury's verdict of murder and that the defendant must have used excessive force when he discharged the fatal shot.

6. No Requirement for the Defendant to Show Retreat

12.06 The common law does not directly require the defendant, when claiming self defence, to show that they had taken positive steps to avoid the potential threat, since a defendant is very much entitled to take necessary and reasonable preventative action. This point is illustrated clearly in *R. v Bird* [1985] 81 Cr.App.R. 110, where a fight broke out at a party during which the appellant, a young woman, struck her former boyfriend in the face with a glass, inflicting a severe injury which caused the loss of a eye. The boyfriend had turned up with his new girlfriend; the appellant resented this and an argument resulted in which the appellant was asked to leave, which she did, but later returned at which time a second argument occurred. On this occasion the appellant claimed that she had been held up against a wall by the victim and that she therefore retaliated. The Court of Appeal held that there is no duty on the defendant to demonstrate that she had done everything in order to retreat from the situation. This is just one element that the jury can consider and that the more the defendant can show they retreated, the more it is that the force used was reasonable in the circumstances. Accordingly, the appellant's conviction for a s.20 wounding was quashed due to a misdirection on this point by the judge.

7. Revenge, Aggression and Retaliation: Directions to Jury

12.07 Given that the burden of proof is upon the prosecution to negate a lawful act of self defence, it will be claimed by the prosecution under its duty to discharge the burden that the defendant either used excessive force or that they and not the complainant are the aggressor and may have wanted to extract their own revenge. This question arises if the defendant does seek revenge but then a fight breaks out between them and the complainant, but the complainant then themselves retaliates; can the defendant in this situation still rely on self defence? This principle is found clearly in *R. v Rashford* [2005] EWCA Crim 3377, in which the Court of Appeal held, approving the proposition of law found in the Scottish case of *Burns v HM Advocate* [1995] S.L.T. 1090 as an accurate statement of the law, it that a person who killed someone in a quarrel that he himself had started by provoking it or entering into it willingly, could still plead self defence if his victim then retaliated. The issue in cases of this nature as to whether a plea of self defence was available, depended on whether the retaliation was such that the defendant was entitled, in all the circumstances, to defend themselves in terms of necessity and reasonable use of force. An essential issue for the jury will be whether the gravity of the violence from the complainant was far greater than that initially shown by the defendant, so as to cause him to honestly believe that he was in immediate danger from which he could not escape.

8. Age Capacity

12.08 Section 50 of the Children and Young Persons Act 1933 provides for the presumption in law that a child under 10 is incapable of committing a criminal offence and therefore cannot be subject to any criminal proceedings, even though factually they may have the mens rea and actus reus of the alleged offence. Section 34 of the Crime and Disorder Act 1998 abolishes the presumption of *doli incapax* which had applied to young persons between the ages of 10 and 14. It was presumed that such young persons were incapable of knowing that their criminal act was wrong. This meant that the prosecution had not only to prove the elements of the offence but also had to rebut the presumption by having to prove beyond doubt that the child defendant knew their act was "seriously wrong" and not merely naughty. To maintain such a rule was both illogical and absurd.

The common law was extensively reviewed in *C v DPP* [1996] 1 A.C. 1, an appeal by way of case stated from the magistrates' court heard by the House of Lords in which their Lordships refused to remove a well-established principle of the criminal law by the use of judicial law making. This therefore led to the passing of s.34. Uncertainty as a matter of construction had still existed as to the extent of s.34. At the same time as abolishing the presumption, the question remained: did it also abolish the general common law defence of *doli incapax*, where a child 10 or over can claim as a defence that they did not know that their act was wrong? *In R. v T* [2008] EWCA Crim 815 the Court of Appeal ruled that the Parliamentary intention behind s.34 when abolishing the presumption also included the defence of *doli incapax* and that therefore the judge was right to rule that no such defence was available to the young defendant. The Court rejected the obiter observations found in *CPS v P* [2007] EWHC 946 which had suggested otherwise.

Part II

CRIMINAL PROCEDURE

Chapter Thirteen

AN INTRODUCTION TO CRIMINAL PROCEDURE

1. Introduction

13.01 Criminal litigation is the process in which a defendant takes once a decision to prosecute them for an alleged offence has been taken by the CPS or other prosecuting agency. There are various steps that are taken from the commencement of an investigation by the police, through the court proceedings, to sentencing and appeal. For the busy practitioner and the student a sound knowledge of the main procedural rules is essential in order to ensure that the client is advised properly and that the case is prepared properly for trial. The objective of this chapter is to introduce the rules of procedure, where to find them, the hierarchy and jurisdiction of the criminal courts, classification of offences and other methods of dealing with criminal acts.

2. Criminal Procedure Rules 2005 and Procedural Irregularity

13.02 Sections 69 to 74 of the Courts Act 2003 created the Criminal Procedure Rule Committee (CPRC). The CPRC has the power to make rules governing practice and procedure in the criminal courts. In exercising this power, the CPRC must endeavour to ensure that the criminal justice system is accessible, fair and efficient, and that the rules are both simple and clearly expressed. The previous rules of procedure were unnecessarily perplexing and overwhelmingly confusing, having been constantly amended with the result that the different rules were to be found in 50 different statutory instruments.

The new Criminal Procedure Rules 2005 (CrPR) codify these rules within one simple code, with a glossary and notes to help the reader. The new rules came into force on April 4, 2005, and can be found on the Ministry of Justice website. The rules apply to proceedings both in the magistrate's court and Crown Court. The emphasis of the rules is on clear case management and require the judge to exercise an extensive managerial role in order to ensure that the case is prepared and presented properly at trial and also to avoid unnecessary delay (see the important observations of Judge L.J. in *R. v Jisi and Others* [2004] EWCA Crim 696, in that whilst justice is the starting point for all parties, resources are limited, including time, which requires judicial management and control, see also *R. v L* [2007] EWCA Crim 764). In *R. v K* [2006] 2 All E.R. 552, it was observed that a judge is not bound to allow oral submissions; they can order written submissions if if good management demands this and limit those submissions. The rules themselves are divided into 78 parts, with practice directions and protocols.

In an important ruling the Court of Appeal in *R. v Ashton and Others* [2006] EWCA Crim 794, had to address the consequences for criminal proceedings, if a procedural mistake has been made. Fulford J., following the principles found in the House of Lords' decision in *R. v Soneji* [2005] 3 W.L.R. 303, and the Court of Appeal decision in *R. v Sekhon* [2003] 1 W.L.R. 1655 (confiscation cases), ruled unequivocally that:

> "In our judgment it is now wholly clear that whenever a court is confronted by a failure to take a required step, properly or at all, before a power is exercised ('a procedural failure'), the court should first ask itself whether the intention of the legislature was that any act done following the procedural failure should be invalid. If the answer to that question is no, then the court should go on to consider the interests of justice generally, and most particularly whether there is a real possibility that either the prosecution or the defence may suffer prejudice on account of the procedural failure. If there is such a risk, the court must decide whether it is just to allow the proceeding to continue. On the other hand, if the court acts without jurisdiction if, for instance, magistrates' court purports to try a defendant on a charge of homicide, then the proceedings will usually be invalid."

In *R. v Thwaites* [2006] EWCA Crim 3235, the High Court ruled that despite the judge not following the correct procedure of holding a mode of trial hearing when either way offences of burglary where added to the indictment in the Crown Court this did not nullify the proceedings since the defendant would have pleaded not guilty and was not in any way prejudiced. It was further ruled that the Court was no longer bound by the decisions in *R. v Hayle* [2002] EWCA Crim 2476, and *R. v Gayle* [2004] EWCA Crim 2937, but was instead bound by the more recent decision by the Court of Appeal in *Ashton*. This decision may now need to be treated with caution since the decision of the House of Lords in *Clarke* [2008] UKHL 8, see below).

However, the radical sea change towards substance as opposed to formality, directory over mandatory, has been tempered significantly by the House of Lords in *R. v Clarke* [2008] UKHL 8, in respect at least of the operation of s.2 of the Administration of Justice (Miscellaneous Provisions) Act 1933, in which the intention of Parliament is made inescapably clear that an bill of indictment, in order to become an valid indictment, must be checked and properly signed by the Court Officer. It will be interesting to see, in other procedural respects, what approach the court will take, particularly when balancing the triangulation of interests. The approach taken to s.2 by the House of Lords was right and based not on whether a procedural step is simply directory rather than mandatory, but on what lies behind Parliament's intent when introducing that procedural requirement (see Chapter 18 para.18.15).

3. Part 1: The Overriding Objective and Enforcement

13.03 To give the rules a fundamental purpose and in order to ensure compliance, in Pt 1 of the Rules there is an "overriding objective" similar to the one found in the Civil Procedure Rules. Without the overriding objective, the rules would lack structural coherence. Every part of the rules must be considered together with the overriding objective. The overriding objective of the new rules is all embracing and provides that:

> "Criminal cases be dealt with justly, this includes the following
>
> (a) acquitting the innocent and convicting the guilty
> (b) dealing with the prosecution and defence fairly
> (c) recognising the rights of a defendant, particularly a right to a fair trial
> (d) respecting the interests of witnesses, victims and jurors and keeping them informed
> (e) dealing with the case efficiently and expeditiously
> (f) ensuring that the appropriate information is available to the court when bail and sentence is considered
> (g) dealing with the case in ways that take into account,
>
> (i) the gravity of the offence alleged
> (ii) the complexity of what is in issue
> the severity of the consequences for the defendant and others affected and
> (iii) the needs of other cases."

Following on from the success of the Civil Procedure Rules the emphasis within criminal litigation is "active case management". Part 3 of the rules deals with the duty of the court and the parties involved. Rule 3.2 sets out the duty of the court in the furtherance of the overriding objective in terms of active case management, and provides an non-exhaustive list of priorities such as:

(i) early identification of the real issues;

(ii) setting an early timetable for progression;

(iii) ensuring evidence is presented in the shortest and clearest way;

(iv) discouraging delay and avoiding unnecessary hearings.

More significantly the court has a discretion to issue any direction to the parties involved, requiring them to complete certain specified tasks by a specified time which are deemed necessary to ensure that the case is prepared in readiness for trial (see in particular rr.3.5 and 3.10). The Criminal Procedure (Amendment No.3) Rules 2007 (SI 2007/3662) which came into effect in April 2008 inserts a new r.3.5 which gives the court the necessary enforcement measures to deal with a party who fails to comply with either a rule or a direction. The three enforcement measures are:

(i) re-set an hearing date;

(ii) make a cost order; and

(iii) impose any other sanction deemed appropriate.

An interesting and worthwhile development is the requirement for both the prosecution and defence, under r.3.4, to designate a person to be responsible for the progression of the case. In many respects, most defence solicitors already do this as part of their quality of service and the funding contract. The court itself will also designate a case progression officer whose role will be to monitor the progress of the case and ensure compliance with any court directions. With active case management being one of the central key elements in the operation of the new rules, it is important to note that a shift in emphasis has occurred, with control and conduct of case progression now being in the hands of the trial judge and not the parties.

4. Criminal Practice and Practitioners' Works

13.04 To provide criminal defence work, a firm of solicitors must be a party to a contract with the Criminal Defence Service, which exists under the auspices of the Legal Services Commission. With restrictions on funding, the workload can be heavy and burdensome and therefore one of the main difficulties for the criminal practitioner is keeping abreast with legal research and development. This is ameliorated to a large extent by what are commonly referred to as "Practitioners' works". These are a yearly series (with regular updates) usually with two or three volumes that set out both the criminal law and criminal procedure within one simple manual to assist those who practice criminal law. They are invaluable in the sense that the hard work of legal research is done and they therefore provide a readily accessible means of identifying a principle of law. The works themselves are an ideal source for students as well as practitioners, for identifying relevant principles of law and they provide a useful analysis of the sources of law, the elements of the offence/defence and the procedural steps to be followed. In the magistrates' court it is "Stone's Justice Manuals", (Blue, three volumes) In the Crown Court it is either "Archbold—Criminal Practice" (Red, two volumes) or "Blackstone's Criminal Practice" (Blue, one volume).

5. The Jurisdiction of the Criminal Courts

13.05 For any criminal law student and those new to practice, it is important to be able to identify the hierarchy of the criminal courts and the relevant jurisdiction. What follows is a summary of the jurisdiction of each court, which is not designed to substitute the more detailed English legal system textbooks.

6. The Youth Court

13.06 The Youth Court forms part of the magistrates' court and operates within the same building complex. The Youth Court deals exclusively with defendants who are aged 10 to 17 years, and usually sits on separate days to the adult magistrate's court. Section 50 of the Children and Young Persons Act 1933 provides for the presumption in law that a child under 10 is incapable of committing a criminal offence and therefore, even if factually they have committed an offence they cannot be subject to any criminal proceedings. Section 37 of the Crime and Disorder Act 1998 sets out in statutory form the principal aim of the Youth Court as being the prevention of offending by children and young people. For this reason, it is important to note the jurisdictional differences of this court to that of the magistrates. All Youth Court hearings are held in private, except for legal representatives, parents or guardians, witness and the media.

A child (a person who is 10 to 13) and a young person (a person who is 14 to 17) will always be dealt with in the Youth Court, unless s.24 of the Magistrates' Court Act 1980 applies. The purpose for this is so far as possible to keep the young defendant away from the formality of the main court system and also from influential adult offenders. Accordingly, the Youth Court has greater powers of sentencing to that of the adult court. Under the Crime and Disorder Act 1998, the Youth Court can impose a detention and training order up to a maximum of two years. The Youth Court also has available specific non-custodial sentences for young defendants such as a supervision order and punishments for parents.

7. The Magistrates' Court (Court of First Instance, 95 per cent of All Criminal Cases Start and Finish in this Court)

13.07 Governed by the Magistrates' Courts Act 1980, the Courts Act 2003 and the Criminal Procedure Rules 2005, the magistrates' court is often referred to as the "jewel" in the criminal justice system on the basis that it deals with at least 95 per cent of all criminal cases (approx 1.5 million cases), that are brought by the Crown Prosecution Service. This makes the magistrates' court an effective court in terms of numbers, but also because it is cheap to run. On average a trial in the magistrates' court costs around £500, whereas in the Crown Court the figure is nearer to £15,000. The court itself has both a criminal and civil jurisdiction, it is a court of first instance only, this means that it deals exclusively with cases that appear for the first time in court from a decision of the Crown Prosecution Service to prosecute.

The criminal jurisdiction of the magistrates' court is to deal with all cases involving anyone aged 18 or over and who is charged with a summary only offence (See Pt 3 of the Criminal Jurisdiction and Procedure of the Courts Act 2003 which came into force on April 1, 2005) and/or a triable either way offence. This includes the conduct of summary trials for these offences in which the bench of magistrates, usually three, is both the tribunal of law and fact (see the Justice of the Peace (Size and Chairmanship of Bench) Rules 2005 (SI 2005/1553).

To ensure that they are properly informed and directed of the law, they are ably assisted by the Court Clerk. Indictable only offences are sent automatically to the Crown Court under s.51 of the Crime and Disorder Act 1998. Under s.78 of the Powers of Criminal Courts (Sentencing) Act 2000, the sentencing powers of the magistrates are restricted to six months' imprisonment, or 12 months aggregate and/or a £5,000 fine (s.154 of the CJA 2003 increases this to 12 months not yet in force). However, for certain specific regulatory offences the fine can be much higher, for instance under the Sea Fishing (Prohibition on the Removal of Shark Fins) Order 2007 (SI 2007/2554), any person found guilty of a relevant offence is liable on summary conviction to a fine not exceeding £50,000. The Marine Fisheries Agency would enforce these regulatory offences. In addition, the magistrates' court deals with a number of other important procedural issues, which are encountered on a daily basis by those who work in a criminal practice, and in that sense it is necessary for the student to have on awareness of these. The following is a list of the main procedural issues raised before the magistrates:

(i) Decide on a prosecution request to remand a defendant into custody (The magistrates would issue a "warrant of detention" under s.125 MCA 1980).

(ii) Hear an application of bail from the defence solicitor.

(iii) Grant or refuse an application to adjourn the proceedings.

(iv) Issue warrants of further detention.

(v) Determine sentence for a defendant who either pleads guilty or is subsequently found guilty after trial.

(vi) Sit as "examining justices" on either a s.6(1) or (2) committal hearing to determine that there exists sufficient evidence to show that there is a "case to answer". If so, the matter is then committed to the Crown Court. A "Certificate of Committal" is then issued. If not the matter will not proceed and the prosecution would have to consider the voluntary bill of indictment" procedure.

13.08 In addition to committal under s.6(1) and (2), the magistrates can further commit a defendant to the Crown Court under the following enactments:

(i) Section 3 of the Powers of Criminal Courts (Sentences) Act 2000 for sentence only.

(ii) Section 40 of the Criminal Justice Act 1988, trial of summary offence on indictment.

(iii) Section 41 of the Criminal Justice Act 1988, Committal for plea of summary offence arising out of the same set of circumstances of an either-way offence that is being committed to the Crown Court.

(iv) Section 56 Criminal Justice Act 1967, committal of summary offence.

(v) Section 40(3) Criminal Justice Act 1991, breach of unexpired sentence of previous offence together with the new offence.

(vi) Section 51 of the Crime and Disorder Act 1998, sending indictable only offences and related summary offences.

(vii) Section 4 of the Criminal Justice Act 1987, transfer of complex and serious fraud cases; and s.53 of the CJA 1991 in relation to violent and sexual offences.

The composition of the magistrates' court consists of lay magistrates (Justice of the Peace) (JP's) of which there are over 30,000 who are appointed not on the basis of legal qualifications, but competency. In addition there are also just over 100 District Judges who are legally and professionally qualified and paid, whereas JP's are unpaid volunteers of the local community. The emphasis here is to allow lay participation in the criminal justice system and for local justice to be dispensed by the local community members. However, the organisational structure of the magistrates' court has changed significantly with control moving away from petty sessions areas to England and Wales to being divided into local justices area under the auspices of a National Commission Area (see s.8 of the Courts Act 2003 and the Local Justice Areas Order 2005 (SI 2005/554). Inefficient courts are being closed and there is centralisation of the workload to busy city or town magistrates' courts that have seen heavy investment in new premises and technology (video link, special measures for vulnerable witnesses). The purpose of this sweeping change from localised justice to a centralised system is to give greater flexibility, in terms of allocating resources to demand and need without the previous restrictive administrative boundaries. Section 46 gives the magistrates a discretionary power to transfer a case to any other magistrates' court.

Lay magistrates, whilst not legally trained or qualified, often attend updates and professional development courses undertaken by the Local Bench Training and Development Committee. They are ably assisted by the Justices' Clerk who is legally and professionally qualified. The responsibility of the clerk, in terms of giving advice to the magistrates' is clearly delineated in Pt V.55 of the Criminal Practice Directions. Again, with the emphasis on saving costs and avoiding delay, the Justices' Clerk is taking on more of the preliminary matters that were once exclusively for the magistrates, such as issuing summonses and adjourning cases with the consent of parties. The full list of tasks that can be undertaken by the clerk are found in the Justices' Clerk Rules 2005 (SI 2005/545) which came into force on April 1, 2005.

8. The Crown Court (First Instance and Appeal Court)

13.09 Section 46 of the Supreme Court Act 1981 provides that all proceedings on indictment shall be brought before the Crown Court. This gives the Crown Court "exclusive jurisdiction" over trials on indictment (there are a total of 78 Crown Courts in England and Wales). This means offences that are classified as "indictable only", i.e. murder, manslaughter, rape, robbery, blackmail and perverting the course of justice, must proceed before the Crown Court. In addition "indictable either-way offences" can be heard in the Crown Court, which have been committed to the Crown Court from the magistrates' court under the "mode of trial procedure" set out in ss.17 to 25 of the Magistrates' Court Act 1980.

The indictment is a formal document, which is governed by Pt 14 of the CrPR 2005. It must be signed by the court and set out the following information, (i) defendant(s) name; (ii) the statement of the offence (sets out the definition and source of the offence); (iii) particulars of offence (brief summary of alleged offence). The indictment is an important document and close attention should be paid to its drafting. The prosecution draft the indictment, not the court, and it is vital to ensure that there are no fundamental errors which could be fatal to the prosecution's case. To refer incorrectly to the offence creating provision, a simple mistake perhaps, could lead to the proceedings being stayed, owing to the offence not being known to law. In addition, the indictment is one of the first documents that the jury will be referred to and consult during the trial.

The Crown Court is unique in the sense that it is the only criminal court to have a jury to determine guilt; the jury is often referred to as the "tribunal of fact", as are the magistrates when hearing a summary trial. This means that the jury's role is to assess the factual evidence and decide which evidence to accept or reject, and then determine if the prosecution has proved its case. Given that the magistrates deal with 95 per cent of cases, then the Crown Court only deals with about 5 per cent (approx 125,000 cases); around 85,000 of these will be for trial in which just over half (58 per cent) the defendant will probably change their plea to guilty. This, in effect, leaves just 1.2 per cent of all criminal cases to be tried by a jury. Although principally the Crown Court is a court of first instance dealing with those cases that have proceeded to it on indictment, it also has an appeal jurisdiction to determine appeals against conviction and/or sentence from the magistrates' court under s.111 of the Magistrates' Court Act 1980.

The Crown Court is administered by Her Majesty's Court Service, which is now an executive agency in the newly formed Ministry of Justice and is often located in combined court buildings, in the main cities throughout England and Wales. The country is divided into what are known as "circuits", for instance the North West circuit covers Cheshire, Merseyside, Manchester, Lancashire and Cumbria. Each circuit will have a leader who is responsible for the conduct of that circuit. The composition of the Crown Court consists of High Court Judges, Circuit Judges and Recorders/Assistant Recorders who are part-time. A significant development is the deployment of resources and to reduce costs and delay s.66 of the Courts Act 2003 provides that a High Court Judge, Circuit Judge and Recorder has the powers of a Justice of the Peace (District Judge) in relation to any criminal causes and matters.

9. The Divisional Court of the High Court (Appeal Court)

13.10 The criminal jurisdiction of the Divisional Court (Queen's Bench Division of the High Court) is to hear appeals exclusively by way of "case stated" on a point of law or jurisdiction from both the magistrates' court and the Crown Court or alternatively by way of judicial review, again from both the magistrates' and Crown Court, on the lawfulness of a decision made. The composition of the Divisional Court is a President who is head of the court with a Vice President and High Court Judges (often referred to as "Red" Judges due to the colour of their robes).

10. The Court of Appeal (Criminal Division)

13.11 The Court of Appeal, which is governed by the Supreme Court Act 1981, has exclusive jurisdiction to hear appeals lodged by the defendant against conviction, or sentence or both from the Crown Court under the Criminal Appeal Act 1968 as amended. Leave (permission) of the Court must first be applied for and be granted in order for the case to proceed to an appeal hearing before the full Court. The Court of Appeal also hears appeals raised by the prosecution on lenient sentences, opinions on a point of law and certain rulings by the trial judge. The composition of the Court is the Lord Chief Justice, who is head of the Court, together with Lord Justices of Appeal. Other judges, such as High Court judge can, if authorised to do so, sit on appeals in the Court of Appeal. Most appeals are heard at the Royal Courts of Justice in the Strand, however on occasions, appeals can be heard at other court centres. To be properly constituted three appeal judges must sit on an appeal against conviction, whereas for appeal against sentence two is sufficient (see *R. v Coates and Others* [2004] 1 W.L.R. 3043). However, if an important point of law is raised, then this can be five as occurred in *R. v James and Karimi* [2006] EWCA Crim 14, which involved an important point of precedent following the Privy Council's decision in *Holley*.

11. The House of Lords

13.12 The Judicial Committee of the House of Lords (to change its name to Supreme Court: see Constitutional Reform Act 2004), has exclusive jurisdiction to hear appeals against conviction or sentence or both from the Court of Appeal by either the defence or prosecution, but leave of the Court must first be applied for and the grounds of appeal must involve a point of law of general public importance. The House of Lords also hears appeals concerning rulings by the trial judge, lenient sentences and case stated/ judicial review appeals from the Divisional Court. The composition of the House of Lords is that of Lords of Appeal in Ordinary (Law Lords in short), usually five will determine an appeal but if a significant point of law is involved; this can be increased to seven or as in *Attorney-General for Jersey v Holley* [2005] 2 A.C. 351, where nine Law Lords heard the appeal in order to endeavour to return some certainty and consistency to the conflicting principles of law relating to the application of the partial defence of provocation to murder.

12. Diagram of the Criminal Courts

13.13

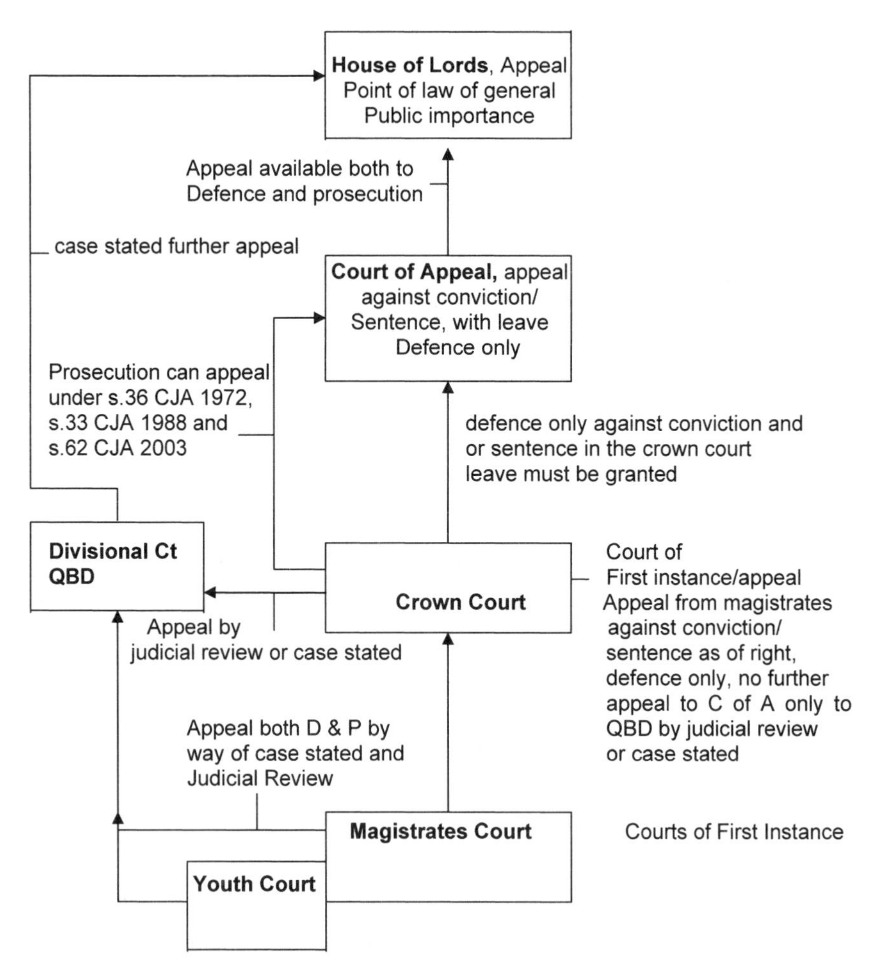

13. Safeguards in Criminal Procedure

13.14 The new CrPR 2005 and other statutory provisions exist also to safeguard the defendant against any risk of a miscarriage of justice and to ensure fairness for the prosecution, the complainant and the community. It is important that both the practitioner and student focus on these safeguards. The following, whilst not an exhaustive list, covers the main safeguards to be aware of:

(i) Independent Crown Prosecution Service.

(ii) Jury trial for the more serious offences.

(iii) Defendant not obliged to give evidence (subject to inferences being drawn.

(iv) Full and advance disclosure of prosecution case.

(v) Presumption of innocence.

(vi) Right to bail.

(vii) Strict rules of evidence, in terms of relevance, admissibility and weight of that evidence, in particular s.76 and s.78 of the Police and Criminal Evidence Act 1984.

(viii) Burden and standard of proof.

(ix) Publicly funded criminal defence service and court representation.

(x) Ability to appeal and the Criminal Cases Review Commission.

14. Discretionary Power of the Trial Judge

13.15 An especially important procedural issue to be aware of are the discretionary powers of the trial judge. Again these are an important method of safeguarding the integrity of the criminal justice system. From a defence point of view, they form part of the armoury to ensure that their client is not unfairly prejudiced, even if this means that a defendant is acquitted on what would have otherwise been a convincing case of guilt. The court must protect its integrity at all times against unfair practices or conduct by the parties involved. To do otherwise would lead to a loss of public confidence in the rule of law, the due process of the court and ultimately the criminal justice system as a whole. One of the roles of a trial judge is to ensure that the proceedings are conducted fairly; this includes having to make rulings on the admissibility of evidence, ensuring that the jury are properly directed both as to the law and their function as the tribunal of fact. Fundamentally, the trial judge must ensure that the defendant receives a fair trial, and therefore to ensure this, the trial judge has at his disposal the following discretionary powers, which can be subject to review on appeal:

(i) Stay of proceedings for an abuse of process.

(ii) Discretionary power of exclusion under s.78 of the Police and Criminal Evidence Act 1981.

(iii) Mandatory exclusion of a confession obtained by oppression or things said or done under s.76 of the Police and Criminal Evidence Act 1984.

(iv) A submission of no case to answer (usually at the conclusion of the prosecution case the defence may feel it appropriate to make a submission of no case to answer in that the prosecution have failed to prove the elements of the offence).

15. Classification of Offences

13.16 It is important for those studying and practising criminal law to be aware of and be able to identify the classification of criminal offences for two reasons. Firstly, to distinguish between the differing degrees (magnitude) of criminal culpability attached to each individual offence, and secondly, to ensure that the correct procedure is followed for that particular offence. Incorrect classification of the offence to which the client is charged could lead to the disastrous consequences of poor advice and procedural mistakes in case preparation All criminal offences are classified into three categories as set out in the Interpretation Act 1978, these are summary only offences, indictable either-way offences (sometimes referred to as triable either way) and indictable only offences.

16. Summary Only Offences

13.17 All summary offences are created by statute, no summary offences exist at common law. The descriptive word summary identifies that this type of offence can proceed by way of a summons, issued by the magistrates' court, to the defendant to appear at court on a given time and date to answer to the alleged offence(s) contained within the summons. For example, if stopped by the police for contravening a road traffic direction sign, then the officer, after caution, will advise the driver that they will be reported for the offence of failing to comply with a road direction sign. This means that the officer will send a report to the magistrates' court, which will include a copy of the officer's statement; if an offence is revealed on the evidence then the magistrates will issue a summons for the driver to appear before the court to answer the driving offence allegation.

The police have a power to arrest for some summary only offences and proceed by charging the defendant at the police station to appear at the magistrates at a later date, (an example would be s.5 of the Public Order Act 1986 which creates the summary only offence of causing harassment, alarm or distress, which has a power of arrest available to the constable after warnings, the offence is punishable by a fine only). The section creating the offence, like s.5, will state that the offence is a summary offence, a common statutory expression used for this is "on summary conviction the defendant is liable to a fine or imprisonment or both".

Another example is s.39 of the Criminal Justice Act 1988, which provides that both common assault and battery are summary only offences. Many of the road traffic construction and use offences are summary only offences, created by the Road Traffic Act 1988 and the regulations passed under it. On this basis, summary only offences are dealt with and concluded (unless, committed to the Crown Court) in the magistrates' court. It is accepted that these types of offences have a low degree of culpability and therefore punishment; this also determines the procedure to be followed for a summary only type of offence.

17. Indictable Either Way Offences (Also Known as Triable Either Way Offences)

13.18 All either-way offences are defined by statute; most either-way offences are listed in s.22 of the Magistrates' Court Act 1980 such as basic s.1 theft, s.47 and s.20 of the Offences against the Person Act 1861, and basic criminal damage. Alternatively, the offence creating provision will provide expressly the classification for the offence; for instance, s.3 of the Public Order Act 1986 provides that the offence of affray is an either-way offence. This means that the offence; dependant on the seriousness of it, can either be dealt with in the magistrates' court or alternatively, in the Crown Court on indictment. It is generally accepted that either-way offences are deemed to be intermediate in terms of seriousness. Such offences are more serious in nature than a summary only offence, but less serious than an indictable only offence.

18. Indictable Only Offences

13.19 Indictable only offences are those offences which must proceed by way of indictment. The defendant will make an appearance at the magistrates' court to resolve the initial matters of legal funding and possibly a bail application. The magistrates' court will follow the procedure set out in s.51 of the Crime and Disorder Act 1998 and send the case to the Crown Court. It is important to be aware that all offences which are classified as indictable only must be tried in the Crown Court. The magistrates' court has no jurisdiction to deal with indictable offences, other than to resolve the immediate preliminary matters of bail and funding. Indictable only offences exist both at common law and in statute. Common examples are murder and manslaughter, which are both common law offences and amount to indictable only crimes. Section 8 of the Theft Act 1968 provides expressly that the statutory offence of robbery is to be classified as indictable only. These offences, by their very nature, are serious and obviously need to be dealt with in the Crown Court.

19. Classification of Offences: An Example

13.20 Perhaps a clear example of a series of offences that show the differing degrees of culpability and therefore seriousness in terms of classification can be seen in the hierarchy of road traffic offences. Let's take a factual example: Tom Parker is a 25-year-old man who, whilst driving his Fiat Punto, decides to make a call on his mobile phone. In so doing he doesn't see that the car in front has stopped at the lights and collides with the rear of the vehicle. Later that afternoon, he picks up a couple of friends from college, when at a set of lights a Vauxhall Cora drives alongside him; when the lights change to green both drivers have a race, overtaking and undertaking each other, driving well above the speed limit and causing other road users to take evasive action. In the evening, Tom decides to take his girlfriend to the cinema, but is late, so he decides to drive at speed, fails to negotiate a sweeping right hand bend and collides with a car driven by Sylvia and Charles who were returning home from the daughter's house; both are killed. We shall now look at the various offences and the classification of each.

Summary Only Offences

13.21 The first potential summary only offence is that of using a mobile phone, which amounts to a summary only offence under the Construction and Use Regulations. Owing to this distraction, Tom collides with a car in front; this would amount to the offence of careless driving under s.3 of the Road Traffic Act 1988, and one that is expressly classified as summary only. If Tom refused to accept a fixed penalty, the police would give him notice of their intention to prosecute and request the magistrates' court to issue a summons to that effect. Tom, for these offences, will only be dealt with in the magistrates' court.

Indictable Either-Way Offences

13.22 On the facts, the deliberate racing by Tom with another car driver is clearly more serious than that which he had done previously. In this instance, the likely offence is to be that of dangerous driving under s.1 of the Road Traffic Act 1991. In accordance with the Road Traffic Offenders Act 1988, this offence is classified as an either-way offence, with six months' imprisonment and/or a fine in the magistrates' court; while on indictment to the Crown Court a maximum of two years' imprisonment and a unlimited fine. The decision on trial venue is determined by the magistrates' court at the "Mode of Trial" hearing, having heard representations from both the prosecution and the defence.

Indictable Only Offences

13.23 Causing the death of two other drivers is tragic and, if as in the case of Tom, the deaths were caused by his dangerous driving, then the offence will be that of causing death by dangerous driving contrary to s.1 of the Road Traffic Act 1991. This offence is classified as indictable only under the Road Traffic Offenders Act 1988, and if convicted carries a maximum of 14 years' imprisonment. If the driving is exceptionally dangerous and deliberate, the offence could be that of involuntary manslaughter. The difficulty with these cases is gathering sufficient evidence that would amount to an act of dangerousness and not carelessness. Ultimately establishing the degree of Tom's culpability depends upon this difficulty. For this reason and owing to public policy, Parliament has recently created an intermediate offence of "causing death by careless or inconsiderate driving". Under s.20 of the Road Safety Act 2006, this constitutes an either-way offence with a punishment of 12 months' imprisonment and/or a fine, while on indictment in the Crown Court five years imprisonment and or/ a fine.

It is important to note that the available and admissible evidence surrounding the allegation, usually determines a defendant's culpability. Although a defendant may be charged with an indictable only offence, it does not mean that they will be convicted of it. In many instances, either the prosecution or the judge, of his own motion, can leave obvious alternative offences to the jury or in the magistrates' court it is the magistrates themselves, who try the matter. Ultimately, the tribunal of fact determine on the evidence where the defendant's culpability lies and this may well differ between either the point of view of the prosecution or defence and from one offence to another.

20. Allocation of Business in the Crown Court

13.24 In all Crown Courts there is a "listings officer" who is responsible for ensuring that the court's resources are utilised efficiently and properly and that any wastage in terms of costs and court time is kept to a minimum. To assist in this role there is Pt III of the Consolidated Criminal Practice Direction, which places all criminal offences that appear before the Crown Court into one of three classes, in order of seriousness of the offence. The purpose of classifying offences in this way for the Crown Court is to ensure that the listings office can allocate the appropriate judge in terms of experience and that the correct court resources are available for that particular case. It is important not to confuse classification of offences for the purposes of court allocation and resources with the procedural classification of offences as explained above.

Offences for this specific purpose of court allocation fall into one of three categories as follows:

Class 1 (treason, murder, manslaughter)

Class 2 (sexual offences)

Class 3 (all other offences not listed in 1 or 2)

Class 1 offences must be allocated to a High Court Judge or Circuit Judge, authorised by the Lord Chief Justice to hear Class 1 offences. Class 2 and 3 offences, on the other hand, can be heard by a High Court Judge or more likely a Circuit Judge who deals regularly with such cases. For Class 3 offences, a Recorder can hear such cases.

21. Early Disposal of Certain Criminal Acts

13.25 It is important to be aware that not all criminal acts necessarily warrant prosecution; as an alternative to prosecution the police can either issue a fixed penalty or penalty notice for specified offences, or alternatively issue a caution. Both methods are a means of dispensing swift and efficient justice for low-level anti-social and nuisance offences.

22. Penalty Notice for Disorder and Other Offences (Came into Effect on August 8, 2002

13.26 Sections 1 to 11 of the Criminal Justice and Police Act 2001 (CJPA 2001), permits a constable who has reason to believe that a person aged 10 or over (this was originally 18 but was reduced to 10 on December 26, 2004) has committed a specific "penalty offence" may give that person a penalty notice for that offence. This can be issued on the spot (in public or private) or at a police station. The recipient then has the choice to pay and discharge their liability in order to avoid a conviction or alternatively, request a court hearing within 21 days. If the person is between 10 and 15, then the police must, within 28 days of the notice being issued, inform the parents of the penalty notice being issued to their child. If the alleged offence is a specific offence under the Anti-Social Behaviour Act 2003, then the minimum age for which a penalty notice can be issued is 16. Specified offences eligible for on the spot penalties are listed in the table to s.1 of the CJPA 2001. Section 1(2) gives the Secretary of State (Ministry of Justice) a discretionary power to make an order to add, if necessary, further offences to the list.

The listed offences in s.1 are:

(i) wasting Police Time;

(ii) Public Order Act 1986 s.5 causing harassment, alarm or distress);

(iii) throwing fireworks;

(iv) drunk and disorderly contrary to Criminal Justice Act 1967 s.91;

(v) drinking in a designated area (s.12 CJPA 2001);

(vi) dropping or throwing litter.

Originally, Parliament piloted the use of on the spot fines, which received positive feedback, especially from the police. Due to this success a further 10 offences, including criminal damage under £500 and retail theft under £200, are now eligible for a penalty notice. The CJPA 2001(Amendment) Order 2005 (SI 2005/1090) added the offences of buying or attempting to buy alcohol by a person under 18 and selling alcohol to a drunken person contrary to the Licensing Act 1964. In terms of the level of penalty the offender must pay, this will depend on which tier the offence falls. Presently there are two levels of penalty of either £80 or £40.

Section 24 of the Clean Neighbourhoods and Environment Act 2005 (CNEA 2005), together with s.97 of the Environmental Protection Act 1990, provides for certain environmental offences to be dealt with by way of a penalty notice. For instance, the offence of dropping litter can be dealt with by way of a penalty notice provided the offender consents to be dealt with that way, the amount being set by the Local Authority concerned. Other strict liability offences that can be disposed of by penalty notice include nuisance parking offences in ss.3 to 6 of the CNEA 2005, i.e. exposing a vehicle for sale on a road and abandoning a vehicle, breaching a "dog control order" (s.55), audible intruder alarms (s.71) and nuisance noise from premises (s.82). In some instances the relevant enforcement agency can issue a penalty notice of up to £300 (see s.45 of the CNEA 2005).

23. Reprimands, Final Warnings for Young Offenders

13.27 Section 65 of the Crime and Disorder Act 1998 introduced the option for the police to reprimand or warn a young offender (17 or under) where:

(i) there exists evidence of the commission of an offence such as to give a realistic prospect of a conviction, and

(ii) the offender admits the offence, and

(iii) the offender has not previously been convicted of an offence, and

(iv) the constable is satisfied that it would not be in the public interest for the offender to be prosecuted.

If so, the offender is reprimanded or given a final warning that next time it will be court; the offender is also referred to the Youth Offending Team in order to redirect them from further offending. In deciding whether to issue a reprimand or a final warning, the police have guidance issued by the Home Office. The police can, under s.56 of the Criminal Justice and Court Services Act 2000, grant bail whilst making a decision. To assist the police, the Ministry of Justice have produced guidance in terms of decision making and administering the warning or reprimand through a series of optional stages.

In addition, the police calculate an offence's specific gravity score with a final score of 4 meaning that they will always charge, with 2 requiring normally for a first offence a reprimand. In *U v Commissioner of Police* [2002] EWHC 2486, the claimant, who was 15, had admitted in the interview an offence of indecent assault, and then received a final warning and was then also required to register under the Sex Offenders Act 1997. The claimant contended in an application for judicial review that he had not expressly consented to such a procedure. The High Court ruled that, in the circumstances of this case, this breached art.6, since the claimant was denied a right to a fair trial at court and was declared guilty by an administrative process. The Court also observed that the scheme generally did not breach art.6, and that there must be "informed consent" by the offender, implied consent is not enough.

24. Conditional Cautions for Young Offenders Aged 16 to 17

13.28 Based on the principles of conditional cautions for offenders aged 18 or over, which have been in existence since July 2, 2005 (see para.13.26), s.48 and Sch.9 of the Criminal Justice and Immigration Act 2008 when in force, inserts a new s.66A and B into the CDA 1998. These provisions provide the police with the power, where there is sufficient evidence, to give a "youth conditional caution" (YCC) as an alternative to either a reprimand or final warning or commencing a prosecution. Before an YCC can be administered the police must be satisfied that the offender has no previous convictions for any offence and that each of the five specified requirements set out in s.66B are satisfied. These are the same as for an adult offender save with one difference; in regard to an offender aged 16 the explanation and warning must be given in the presence of an appropriate adult. As with adult conditional cautions a financial penalty can be attached, but this must not exceed £100. The same consequences arise as with adult cautions for failure to comply, but the prosecution can, with the consent of the offender, vary the conditions of the caution.

25. Conditional Cautions for Adult Offenders

13.29 Sections 22 and 23 of the Criminal Justice Act 2003 introduced a new regime applicable only to adult offenders. It allows the police to issue a caution subject to conditions; failure to comply without reasonable excuse may expose the offender to prosecution for the original offence. The conditions with may be attached to the caution must be directed to achieving one of the following objectives:

(i) facilitating the rehabilitation of the offender;

(ii) ensuring that they make reparation for the offence;

(iii) punishing the offender (inserted by s.17 of the Police and Justice Act 2006, yet to be brought into force).

Section 17(3) of the Police and Justice Act 2006 inserts a new subsection 3A and when in force will allow an authorised person (police, CPS) to attach a condition that the offender pay a financial penalty in relation to a prescribed offence (the penalty must not be more that one-third of the maximum fine after summary conviction or £250, whichever is the lower of the two. The amount of the fine must be decided by the CPS. The Secretary of State has a discretionary power to change these figures but this must be be approved by the affirmative resolution procedure) and or that the offender attend at a given place at specified times but not for more than 20 hours.

Before a conditional caution can be given five requirements contained in s.22 of the CJA 2003 must be satisfied:

(i) There is evidence to prove the person has committed an offence.

(ii) That the prosecutor (i.e. CPS) is satisfied there is sufficient evidence to charge and that a conditional caution is appropriate.

(iii) That the person admits their guilt.

(iv) The effect of the caution must be explained to the offender and a warning must be given that any failure to comply with the attached conditions may result in the commencement of a prosecution for the offence.

(v) That the offender signs a document that contains the details of the offence, a formal admission, their consent and the conditions of the caution.

Under s.24 any failure without reasonable excuse to meet any of the conditions attached to the caution may result in the commencement of criminal proceedings and the signed document will be admissible evidence at any subsequent proceedings. Section 18 of the Police and Justice Act 2006, which came into force on June 29, 2007 inserted a new s.24A in the CJA 2003 providing the police with a power to arrest without a warrant a person who they have reasonable grounds for believing has failed without reasonable excuse to comply with the conditions. Once a person is arrested, then there are three available methods of disposal:

(i) Charge the offender with the offence.

(ii) Release without charge and on bail pending a decision to be made as to whether or not to charge.

(iii) Release without charge or bail with or without any variations to the conditions of the caution. A person may be kept in police custody to enable the police to deal with their disposal and for as long as is necessary to investigate whether the failure to comply was with or without reasonable excuse. This is so as to avoid the consequences of what occurred in *G v Chief Constable of West Yorkshire* [2008] EWCA Civ 28 (see Chapter 14, para.14.34 on Police Powers in Criminal Procedure). The person arrested has all the relevant safeguards under PACE 1984.

To assist the police, the Ministry of Justice under s.25 of the CJA 2003 are required to produce a code of practice to assist in the effective and proper use of conditional cautions which came into effect on July 2, 2005.

In *Jones v Whalley* [2007] 1 A.C. 63, the House of Lords ruled, on an important point of law, that if the police in their discretion issue a conditional caution to an adult offender, then the complainant cannot, if feeling aggrieved by that decision, commence their own private prosecution. To allow the commencement of a private prosecution in these circumstances would undermine the system of cautioning and therefore amount to an abuse of process. It is to be noted that when brought into effect, ss.17 and 18 will extend the application of conditional cautions. In *DPP v Ara* [2001] EWHC 493, the High Court ruled that the police were under a duty to disclose the contents of a previous interview with the defendant, who was not legally represented, to a solicitor so that they could be in a position to give the defendant informed advise on whether to accept or refuse a caution. The Court further ruled that the magistrates were correct to stay the proceedings as an abuse of process, if in this situation the defendant did not accept the caution and proceeded to trial.

25. Summary

13.30 One of the important aspects of this chapter is the need to know and apply confidently the classification of offences, within the hierarchy of the criminal courts. Having mastered this, the rest of criminal procedure should slot in relatively easily. It would be impossible to know in depth all of the Criminal Procedure Rules 2005, a sound knowledge of the overriding objective and that of active case management is central to the operational application of the rest of the rules. It is important not to become overwhelmed by the rules, they exist as guidance and should a point of procedure arise, then the solution ought to be found quickly.

26. Classification of Offences Diagram

13.31

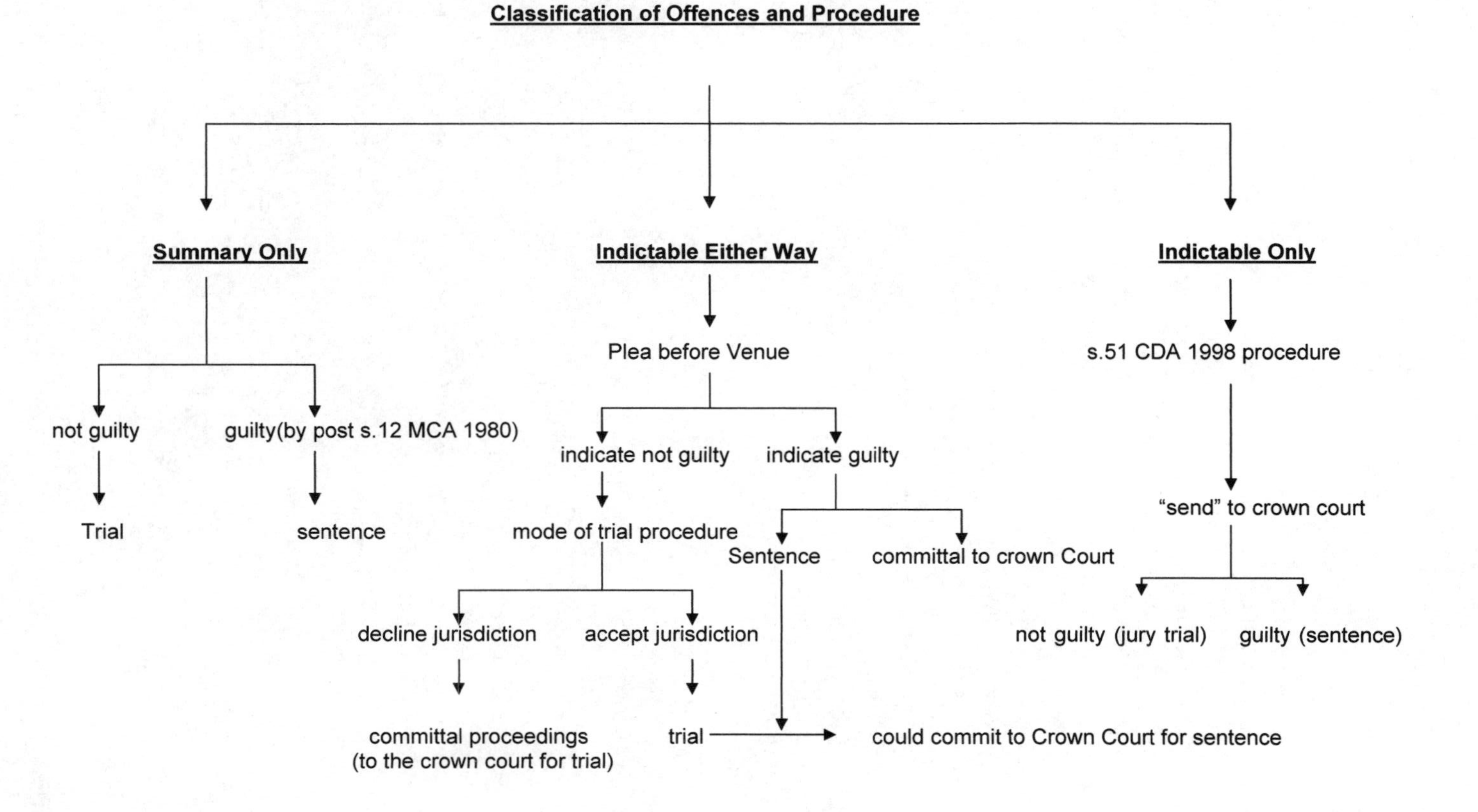

CHAPTER FOURTEEN

POLICE POWERS

1. POWERS OF THE POLICE: STRIKING A FAIR BALANCE

14.01 The main statutory powers of the police are to be found in the Police and Criminal Evidence Act 1984. The Police and Criminal Evidence Act 1984 (hereinafter PACE 1984) was passed based on the recommendations of the Royal Commission into Criminal Procedure 1981. One of the important aspects to be aware of was that PACE 1984 was designed to give the police the necessary powers needed to assist in the effective investigation and detection of crime, which must be balanced proportionately against the need to safeguard the individual rights of the suspect. The main powers of the police come within four categorises:

(i) Stop and search

(ii) Arrest and detention

(iii) Search of premises

(iv) Seizure of property

When considering the application and use of police powers, either as a student or defence advisor, it is important to be aware of the safeguards for the suspect and to ensure that the police have adhered to them properly. These safeguards do not exist to hinder the police, but to ensure that a fair balance is struck between the proper investigation and detection of crime and the protection of individual basic rights. However, since 1984 there has been extensive statutory reform and modification of police powers by Parliament, in the form of the Criminal Justice and Public Order Act 1992, the Crime and Disorder Act 1998, the Criminal Justice and Court Service Act 2000, the Criminal Justice and Police Act 2001, the Police Reform Act 2002, the Proceeds of Crime Act 2005, the Criminal Justice Act 2003, the Serious Organised Crime and Police Act 2005, the Drugs Act 2005 and the Police and Justice Act 2006. There exist also the substantive provisions relating to anti-social behaviour enshrined in the Anti-Social Behaviour Act 2005 and the amendments to it.

The weight of statutory intervention inevitably adjusts this delicate balance and therefore it is vital to always be aware of the changes. Always consider the impact of the Human Rights Act 1998 and check that Parliament does not act outside its "discretionary area of judgment" with an unjustifiable interference with certain basic rights. This sensitive issue of striking a fair balance between the competing interests can clearly be seen in the decision of the House of Lords in *R. (Gillan) v Commissioner of Police for the Metropolis* [2006] 2 W.L.R. 537, concerning the application of the stop and search powers in the Terrorism Act 2000. Lord Bingham, on the issue of the legality of those powers as a justifiable interference with human rights, observed that:

> "the lawfulness requirement in the Convention addresses supremely important features of the rule of law. The exercise of power by public officials, as it affects members of the public, must be governed by clear and publicly-accessible rules of law. The public must not be vulnerable to interference by public officials acting on any personal whim, caprice, malice, predilection or purpose other than that for which the power was conferred. This is the test which any interference with or derogation from a Convention right must meet if a violation is to be avoided."

From the outset, it is important to be aware of s.117 of PACE 1984 which allows the police, when necessary, to use reasonable force in the exercise of a power generally within the Act, but not in relation to a power which can only be exercised with the consent of the suspect.

2. PACE Codes of Practice, Codes A to H

14.02 Sections 66 and 67 of PACE 1984, as amended by s.11 of the Criminal Justice Act 2003, provide that the powers of the police must be accompanied by a code of practice issued by the Secretary of State for Justice, after a period of consultation and later approved by Parliament. The purpose of the codes is to give simple, clear guidance on the application of the complex statutory provisions that set out the powers of the police. The codes also regulate the use of such powers as against the safeguards and protection for the suspect.

It is important to be fully aware of the codes and to have a copy readily accessible, along with a copy of Michael Zander's comprehensive review of the Act, if undertaking police station work. Originally the codes consisted of six parts, but due to the number of statutory changes and modifications of police powers it was necessary to redraft the codes, in order to take into account these significant changes. This was achieved by the PACE 1984 (Codes of Practice) Order 2008 (SI 2008/167) which was approved by Parliament under the affirmative resolution procedure and which brought into effect the latest revised codes of practice on January 1, 2006. The revised codes of practice consisted of seven parts coded A to H:

Code A: deals with the power to stop and search.

Code B: deals with searches of premises and seizure of property.

Code C: deals with detention, treatment and questions of persons by the police.

Code D: deals with identification of persons.

Code E: deals with tape recorded interviews.

Code F: deals with visual recording with sound of interviews.

Code G: deals with police powers of arrest since the changes implemented by s.110 of the Serious Organised Crime and Police Act 2005.

Code H: deals with the requirements of the detention, treatment and questioning of suspects related to terrorism held in police custody (see the PACE (Code of Practice C and H) Order 2006 (SI 2006/1938) brought into effect on July 25, 2006).

The importance of the codes should not be ignored, since any breach of the codes is admissible in a criminal trial and could result in any cogent evidence obtained by the police in consequence of that breach being excluded by the trial judge, being inadmissible.

3. Powers of Stop and Search: Sections 1 to 3 of PACE 1984 and Code A

14.03 One of the most effective powers of the police in the prevention, investigation and detection of crime is the ability, dependant on the circumstances, to search persons and or vehicles. The power to stop and search does not require a warrant to be issued, it allows the police, provided the conditions of the power are satisfied, to search for certain specified items, which may then lead to arrest or if none are found, release. It is important to be aware that the detained person is not under arrest and they may or may not be a suspect for a particular crime. The detained person is held temporarily for the conduct of a search, dependant on what the search reveals a decision would then be made as to their arrest or release.

Sections 1 to 3 of PACE 1984 set out the main power of the police to stop and search, but is not the only power. Other statutory provisions such as the Misuse of Drugs Act 1971 also provide a specific power to stop and search for specific items in specific circumstances. Another example is s.37 of the Clean Neighbourhoods and Environment Act 2005 which gives a power to stop, search and seize any vehicle where there is a reasonable belief that controlled waste has been, is being or is about to be unlawfully transported. When considering this statutory power, it must also be read in conjunction with Code A of the Codes of Practice. First look at the breadth of the power itself and what it allows a police officer to do and then balance this against the safeguards and protection for the individual suspect. Albeit a vital and necessary power that is clearly justified in the need to prevent, investigate and detect crime, it is an intrusive power upon an individual's right of freedom of movement and liberty and especially so if the police abuse and use the power arbitrarily. For this reason, s.1 contains strict requirements and protective conditions that must be adhered to in its application.

4. Statutory Purpose of a Section 1 Stop and Search

14.04 Section 1 of PACE 1984 gives a constable (this includes an officer of all ranks) a power to search any person or vehicle and anything in or on that vehicle and detain either that person or vehicle in order to conduct such a search. This section also applies to a vessel, which includes any ship, boat, raft or other apparatus constructed or adapted for floating on water, including aircraft and hovercraft. It is clear therefore that this power is wide in its application as to what can be subjected to a search. Having considered what a constable can search, the next important point to be aware of is the actual purpose of the search. This is strictly limited to the specified items set out in s.1(2):

(i) Stolen goods (theft or handling stolen goods under the Theft Act 1968).

(ii) Prohibited articles. This is defined in subsection (7) and means any of the following:

(a) an offensive weapon (any article made or adapted for use in causing injury to persons or intended for such as set out in the Offences Weapons Act 1996). This includes a person who has committed, is committing, or is going to commit an offence under s.139 of the Criminal Justice Act 1988 (having an article in a public place which has a blade or is sharply pointed except a folding pocket knife if the cutting edge of the blade exceeds three inches);

(b) an article made, or adapted to be used in connection with the following offences: burglary, theft, taking a conveyance without consent contrary to s.12 of the Theft Act 1968 and an offence under the Fraud Act 2006;

(c) section 1 of the Criminal Justice Act 2003 amends the definition of prohibited article by inserting a paragraph (e) so as to include offences under s.1 of the Criminal Damage Act 1971 (came into force January 20, 2004).

(d) section 115 of the Serious Organised Crime and Police Act 2005 further amends the definition of prohibited article to include any firework set out in the "Fireworks Regulations 2004 (SI 2004/1836), under the Fireworks Act 2003. This creates offences for a person under 18 to possess prohibited fireworks in a public place.

5. Safeguards and the Protective Conditions for a Detained Person

14.05 Having reviewed the application and breath of the power to stop and search, it is now necessary to balance this power against the general safeguards contained in s.1 that exist to protect the detained person against the risk of the abuse and arbitrary exercise of this intrusive power. The protective safeguards are:

Public Place

14.06 The search, whilst it can be conducted at any time, can only be exercised in a place where the:

> "public or a section of the public have access, on payment or otherwise, as of right or by virtue of express or implied permission or in which people have ready access."

at the time of search, but it cannot be a dwelling. However, if the constable finds a suspect/vehicle in a garden or yard of a dwelling or land which is occupied as such, then they may exercise the search power, but only if they have reasonable grounds for believing that the suspect does not reside there, or does not have permission of the owner.

Information

14.07 If not in uniform, then the constable(s) must identify that they are a police officer and whether or not in uniform and in all circumstances, under s.2(2)(b), it shall be their duty to take reasonable steps before the search, to inform the suspect of the following:

(i) their name and police station,

(ii) the object and grounds for the search, and

(iii) make a record of the search, unless it is impracticable to do so

(iv) record, a copy should be made available within a period of 12 months.

The search cannot commence until the constable "has performed that duty". Under s.2(2)(b) this duty relates to "any other power" which means any other power of stop and search to be found in different legislation and this includes the power under s.60 of the Criminal Justice and Police Order Act 1994. The application of the protection found in s.2 in connection with a search conducted specifically under s.60, was addressed by the High Court in *Osman v Southwark Crown Court* [1999] 163 J.P. 725. The High Court, hearing a case stated appeal from the Crown Court, ruled that it was a breach of s.2(3) to search someone without the police officer first providing details of their names and station and that therefore the search was unlawful. The police were experiencing trouble at a local fair, authorisation had been given under s.60 to stop and search.

The defendant folded his arms and refused to be searched. The searching, who police officers had not given their names or station, then grabbed the defendant in order to conduct the search. His conviction for assaulting a constable in the execution of his duty was quashed. Sedley J. stated that on the clear wording of s.60, the statutory safeguards in s.2 applied to this provision. Section 2 provided expressly that the duty of disclosure applied to "any other power" and that non compliance with these requirements led to an officer not acting in the execution of his duty and therefore acting unlawfully. The decision in *Osman* was further applied in *Bonner v DPP* [2004] EWHC 2415, so that the safeguard in s.2 also applied to the conduct of a search under s.23 of the Misuse of Drugs Act 1971.

However a difficult issue arose in *DPP v Avery* [2001] EWCA Admin 748. The defendant had been demonstrating at Huntingdon Life Sciences and was wearing a skeleton mask, which she was told to remove. On refusal she assaulted the officer. The magistrates dismissed the charge on the basis that the officer when performing his power under s.60(4A) had to act in accordance with his duty under s.2(2) and that having failed to do so, the seizure of the mask was unlawful and he not acting in execution of his duty. The DPP appealed by way of case stated on a point of law, that the power of s.60(4) was not a search and that therefore s.2(2)(b) did not apply in these circumstances. The High Court allowed the appeal and Newman J. ruled that as a matter of statutory construction:

> "The exercise of power conferred by subs (4A) does not give rise to a search. No search is required. It is overt use of a mask, not its concealment or its detection, with which the sub-section is concerned. No power to search for a mask is conferred. If in the exercise of a lawful search a mask was discovered, it could not be seized unless the constable reasonably believed the person intended to wear it wholly or mainly for the purpose of concealing his identity (subs (4A) (b)). Subs (4A) is plainly not conferring upon a constable a power of search and is not within the powers regulated by Ss 2 & 3 of PACE."

Removal of Clothing

14.08 The power only allows the removal of an outer coat, jacket or gloves if in a public place. The police are not prevented from requiring other clothes to be removed, but if such a request is made, then the removal must take place in private (i.e. in back of police van).

Reasonable Grounds for Suspecting and Code A

14.09 A constable cannot exercise the power to stop and search unless they have *reasonable grounds for suspecting* they will find stolen goods or prohibited articles. Code A of the Codes of Practice requires the officer to use the power fairly and responsibly and that reasonable suspicion can never be supported on the basis of personal factors alone, without reliable supporting intelligence or information, or some other specific behaviour. Race, age, appearance or previous convictions cannot be used alone.

6. Other Stop and Search Powers

14.10 Section 23(3) of the Misuse of Drugs Act 1971 provides a specific power to stop and search for prohibited drugs. Similar powers exist in s.13 of the Aviation Security Act 1984 and s.47 of the Firearms Act 1968. Section 60 of the Criminal Justice and Public Order Act 1994 (as amended by s.8 of the Knives Act 1997, s.25 of the Crime and Disorder Act 1998, and s.94 of the Anti-Terrorism, Crime and Security Act 2001) gives a power to stop and search in anticipation of violence. If an officer of the rank of inspector or above believes that incidents involving serious violence may take place in any locality, they may give authorisation to allow the stopping of persons/vehicles for a period not exceeding 24 hours (which can be extended for a further six hours), but only if it is expedient to avoid occurrence of violence. The authorisation (which must be in writing and signed) allows any constable in uniform to:

(i) stop any pedestrian and search them or anything carried by them for offensive weapons or dangerous instruments they have in their possession without good reason;

(ii) stop and search any vehicle (includes a caravan), its driver and passenger for the same.

Subs (4A) as inserted by the Crime and Disorder Act 1998 gives a constable in uniform a power to:

(i) require any person to remove any item which they reasonably believe is being worn wholly or mainly for the purpose of concealing their identity;

(ii) seize any item which the constable reasonably believes that any person intends to be used for such purpose.

Under subsection(5) the constable can use this power as they think fit, without the need for any grounds of suspicion and seize any offensive weapon or dangerous instrument. A person who fails to stop when required to do so, or to remove an item worn by them when required to do so, commits a summary offence liable to one month's imprisonment or a fine.

Section 43 of the Terrorism Act 2000 provides a discretionary power for the police to stop and search a person or vehicle (s.116) whom they reasonably suspect to be a terrorist (defined in s.40 as a person who has committed certain specified offences within the Act, or who is or has been concerned in the commission, preparation or instigation of acts of terrorism) in order to discover whether that person has in their possession anything which may constitute evidence that they are a terrorist. Under s.116 if a person fails to stop their vehicle on request of an officer, then they commit a summary offence punishable with six months' imprisonment and/or a fine. Further, s.44 allows an officer of the rank of inspector (authorising officer) or above to give authorisation where it is *expedient* for the purposes of preventing acts of terrorism, for officers to stop and search vehicles and persons within vehicles and pedestrians, within a period of not more then 28 days in a certain geographical area. A second protective requirement to the exercise of the stop and search power is that the authorisation must then receive approval by the Secretary of State for Justice.

However, the authorisation remains lawful for up to 48 hours without such approval. If these conditions are satisfied, then the police can search for articles of a kind which could be used in connection with terrorism, whether or not there are grounds for suspecting the presence of such articles. If a person fails to stop when required to do so or wilfully obstructs a constable in the exercise of their power, then they commit a summary offence contrary to s.47. Section 45 removes the statutory safeguard of requiring the police to have reasonable grounds for suspecting the presence of articles for terrorism and gives the police the power to seize and retain articles found. However as with a s.1 search, the police cannot require the person stopped to remove any clothing in public other than headgear, footwear, an outer coat, jacket or gloves (see Home Office Circular 038/2004 for guidance on the use of this power by the police).

14.11 The extent of this power was reviewed by the House of Lords in *R. (Gillan and Another) v Commissioner of Police for the Metroplis* [2006] 2 W.L.R. 537. The appellant made a judicial review claim against being stopped and searched whilst being involved in a peaceful protest at an arms fair held in London. In dismissing the appeal, Lord Bingham, who gave one of the leading speeches, stated that whilst freedom of movement "is an old and cherished tradition of our country" which has been jealously guarded to such an extent that "it has almost become a constitutional principle", it is not an absolute rule and there exist statutory exceptions to it such as the Terrorism Act 2000.

Lord Bingham rejected the appellant's contention that the word "expedient" should be interpreted to mean that the power cannot be used unless there are reasonable grounds for considering the use of the power is necessary in all the circumstances. Expedient should be given a "meaning no wider than the context requires", namely that it is likely the use of the powers "will be of significant practical value and utility in seeking to achieve" the public need to prevent terrorism. On a second contention, Lord Bingham ruled that the authorisation and confirmation safeguards were followed properly and the stop and search lawful in accordance with the provisions of the Act. The third contention of the appellants, that the power unjustifiably interfered with a person's right to liberty under Art.5, was also dismissed.

The House of Lords further considered the ECHR decision in *Guzzardi v Italy* [1980] 3 E.H.R.R. 333, in which the Court drew a distinction between deprivation of and restriction upon liberty, based on "degree or intensity, and not one of nature or substance". In the instant case there was no deprivation of liberty. The detained person was simply prevented from proceeding or kept waiting for a short period and nothing more. Further contentions that the powers breached art.8: a right to a private life, or art.10: a right to freedom of expression and assembly, were also rejected in that the interference with those rights was justified as being no more than necessary for the legitimate aim of prevention of terrorism. Likewise, the powers satisfied the requirement that they were lawful in accordance with the "rule of law", since the powers were clearly defined and explained in Code A of the Codes of Practice, which amounted to a public document to which the public have access.

Under s.139B of the Criminal Justice Act 1988 the police have a specific power to enter schools and search for knives and offensive weapons where they have reasonable grounds for suspecting such weapons are being carried. Under ss.45, 46 and 47 of the Violent Crime and Reduction Act 2006 similar powers of search are given to authorised members of staff of a school or further education college or attendance centre.

7. Power of Arrest without a Warrant

14.12 Originally the power of arrest was found in s.24 for arrestable offences and s.25 for non arrestable offences of PACE 1984. However, both provisions had been extensively amended at various intervals, making it difficult for police officers to understand their actual powers of arrest. Accordingly, in a White Paper "Police: Modernising Police Powers to Meet Community Needs", it was felt that these existing powers should be replaced with a more simple consolidated provision. Section 110 of the Serious Organised Crime and Police Act 2005 (SOCP Act 2005) repeals both ss.24 and 25 of PACE and replaces them with one power of arrest as follows.

A constable (and designated officer under the Police Reform Act 2002) may arrest without a warrant, *anyone for an offence* who

(i) is about to

(ii) in the act of, or

(iii) they *have reasonable grounds* for suspecting to be about to or in act of, or

(iv) is guilty of such an offence, or

(v) if an offence has been committed anyone who is guilty of it or they have *reasonable grounds* for suspecting to be guilty of it.

This does not affect any other specified statutory power of arrest that may exist. For instance, under s.32 of the Anti-social Behaviour Act 2003, a constable has a specified power to arrest without warrant any person they reasonably suspect of breaching a dispersal direction. A similar power exists in s.5 of the Public Order Act 1986, but a warning must first be given to desist from conduct that is likely to cause harassment alarm or distress.

8. Protective Safeguards: Arrest Reasons

14.13 The above power of arrest can only be exercised if the constable *has reasonable grounds for believing* that one or more of six reasons listed exist and it is *necessary* to arrest the suspect. The arrest reasons are:

(a & b) to enable name and address to be ascertained;

(c) to prevent injury, damage or committing an act of public decency, or obstructing the highway;

(d) to protect a child or vulnerable person;

(e) to allow the prompt and effective investigation of the offence or the conduct of the person in question;

(f) to prevent hindrance of any prosecution by the person disappearing.

Section 31 also allows the police to arrest the detained suspect for other offences, should information come to light to provide the necessary reasonable suspicion for those new alleged offences.

9. Safeguard of "Reasonable Grounds for Suspecting" and Article 5

14.14 Article 5 of the European Convention of Human Rights provides that everyone has the right to liberty and security of person and that no one should be deprived of their liberty, unless lawfully arrested or detained in order to be brought before a court on reasonable suspicion of having committed an offence. In *Fox, Campbell and Hartley v UK* [1990] 13 E.H.R.R. 157, the ECHR stated that the requirement for reasonableness is an essential safeguard against the arbitrary use of the power of arrest and that reasonable suspicion:

> "presupposes the existence of facts or information which would satisfy an objective observer that the person concerned may have committed the offence. What may be regarded as 'reasonable' will however depend upon all the circumstances."

In *O'Hara v Chief Constable of the RUC* [1997] A.C. 286, the House of Lords stated that the test as to whether there are reasonable grounds for suspecting to justify an arrest is partly subjective, in that the arresting officer must have formed a genuine suspicion that the person being arrested was guilty of an offence and partly objective, in that there is objectively such reasonable suspicion. The House of Lords further observed that to have reasonable suspicion, the officer need not have evidence amounting to a prima facie case (a case sufficient to proceed to court). Since arrest is the preliminary stage of the investigation information derived from either an informer or indeed a tip off from a member of the public may be enough.

Likewise, hearsay evidence may be sufficient, in the sense that it may come from another officer. However, any such information that provides the suspicion must exist and be known to the arresting officer, at the time of arrest. Such grounds for suspicion can arise from information received anonymously, or in an emergency, even if subsequently that information proves to be wrong. In this situation:

> "the question whether it provided reasonable grounds for suspicion depends on the source of his information and its context, seen in the light of the whole surrounding circumstances."

In *O' Hara* the House of Lords ruled that an order given by a senior officer to another officer to arrest was in itself insufficient to give the arresting officer the reasonable suspicion to exercise his power of arrest. An arresting officer can never be a "mere conduit" for another officer. Accordingly, a police officer cannot solely rely on the instruction to arrest to form the necessary suspicion. Conversely in *Hough v Chief Constable of Staffordshire* [2001] EWCA Civ 39, the Court of Appeal stated that information obtained from the Police National Computer (PNC), "is likely to provide the objective justification". However, if there is no urgency and if:

> "in the light of the whole surrounding circumstances some further enquiry was clearly called for before suspicion could properly crystallise, then the entry alone will not suffice."

In the instant case, the PNC entry, which suggested that the men stopped in a routine vehicle check should not be approached as they might be armed with a firearm, provided sufficient objective justification for the arrest, even though subsequently no firearms were found, leading to the men's release from police custody.

10. Grounds for the Arrest

14.15 Section 28 of PACE 1984 provides that no arrest is lawful, unless the arrested person is informed of the ground for the arrest at the time of or as soon as is reasonably practicable after the arrest, even if that ground is obvious. The failure of a police officer to provide grounds for arrest, may render the arrest unlawful. This reflects the old common law principle found in *Christie v Leachinsky* [1947] A.C. 573. Likewise art.5 of the European Convention on Human Rights provides that everyone who is arrested shall be informed promptly in a language which they understand of the reasons for their arrest and any charge against them. In *Taylor v CC of Thames*

Valley Police [2004] EWCA Civ 858, a civil claim for wrongful arrest and false imprisonment, the Court of Appeal applied the judgment of the ECHR in *Fox, Campbell and Hartley* and stated that the question is:

> "whether, having regard to all the circumstances of the particular cases, the person arrested was told in simple, non-technical language that he could understand, the essential legal and factual grounds for his arrest."

In the instant case the claimant had been lawfully arrested, s.28 had been satisfied when the arresting officer had told him that he was being arrested on suspicion of violent disorder at a particular time and place. Conversely, the Court of Appeal in *Wilson v Chief Constable of Lancashire* [2000] Po. L.R. 367 took a different approach and allowed the claimant's claim for wrongful arrest, in that when he was arrested on suspicion of "theft of cheques" and nothing more, this did not satisfy the requirement of s.28, since the arresting officer had not informed the suspect of the name of the bank or branch in which the cheques were attempted to be cashed, such information which the officer knew and which formed the suspicion for arrest.

11. Administration of the Caution

14.16 It is critical that on arrest or alternatively, if questioning a person generally, but with a purpose to elicit facts relevant to the investigation of an alleged offence, the police officer must administer the caution concerning the suspect's rights about whether to provide answers. Part 10 of Code C provides that where there are grounds to suspect a person of an offence, they must be cautioned before asked any questions about the offence, or further questions, if initial answers provide a reasonable suspicion. A caution must be administered when being arrested, unless it is impracticable to do so by reason of their condition or behaviour. The caution is:

> "you do not have to say anything unless you wish to do so, but it may harm your defence if you do not mention when question something you later rely on in court, anything you do say may be given in evidence."

Clearly, if an officer is simply ascertaining general facts about a particular person or matter, then no caution need be given, at the same time no response can be expected. At the moment an officer asks questions directly or indirectly about an alleged offence, the caution must always be given. This is provided in Code C.10 which states that unless the questions are for other purposes, i.e. routine questions, then a suspect must be cautioned before any questions are put to him regarding his involvement or suspected involvement in that offence. If so, then this amounts to an interview requiring a caution. The distinction between routine questions and questions concerning an alleged offence was considered in *R. v Senior* [2004] EWCA Crim 454, in which Customs officers, having suspected two women of being involved in the importation of drugs had, unknown to them, detected drugs in a bag they were both in possession of, without informing the women of the discovery.

The Customs officers asked a series of questions regarding ownership of the bag and travel arrangements, but had neither cautioned nor formally arrested them. This, the court ruled, amounted to a breach of Code C, in that they should have been cautioned. This also amounted to a serious and significant breach regardless of the good faith of the officers, but did not cause any prejudice to justify exclusion of the answers given. The Court paid particular attention to the fact that such questions concerning ownership of a bag are routine questions regularly encountered by the travelling public and require no caution. If there is a objective formulation of suspicion, then those questions no longer constitute routine questions. A failure to administer a caution at the time of arrest or under questioning about an offence may render the arrest unlawful and any subsequent evidence could be ruled inadmissible at trial under s.78 of PACE 1984. Code C, para.11.1 provides that once a decision has been made to arrest the suspect then they must not be interviewed about the offence, until at the police station.

12. Arrest without Warrant: Other Persons (Citizen's Arrest)

14.17 Like the provisions of s.24, s.110 of the SOCP Act 2005 also provides for a power to be exercised by any person to arrest, without warrant, anyone who is in the act of or is guilty of, or they have reasonable grounds for suspecting to be committing, or is guilty of an *indictable offence*. This general power of arrest is more restrictive than that for a constable. By comparison, this power of arrest, unlike that of a constable, cannot be used until the alleged offender is committing or has committed the offence, or there is reasonable suspicion of guilt. Second, whilst a constable can arrest for any offence, any other person can only arrest for an indictable offence, namely indictable only or either-way offences, not summary offences. Quite how a ordinary person with no legal knowledge would be expected to be aware of these conditions, is unknown. This provision does not allow for the ordinary person to have easy access to the law and its powers.

13. Arrest without a Warrant of a "Terrorist"

14.18 Section 41 of the Terrorism Act 2000 provides the police with a specific power of arrest without warrant of a person whom the police reasonably suspects to be a terrorist. Unlike the general power of arrest, the police in this situation do not need to satisfy any arrest conditions, just that they have reasonable suspicion that the person they are wanting to arrest is a terrorist as defined in s.40.

14. Arrest Warrant

14.19 The police have wide powers to arrest without a warrant. A warrant of arrest usually arises in the following circumstances:

(i) Where a defendant fails to surrender to court having been granted bail then the court can issue a warrant for their immediate arrest, either backed with or without bail. If the warrant is backed for bail this means that upon arrest and detention at the police station the defendant is to be released on bail having been notified of the next court date. If it is not backed for bail then the defendant will be kept in police detention until the next available court date. The execution of a warrant of arrest is a matter for the police based very much on resources.

(ii) Non compliance with witness summons under the Criminal Procedure (Attendance of Witnesses) Act 1965. If a witness fails to answer a summons directing them to attend court or it is believed they will not attend, then the court can issue a warrant of arrest.

(iii) Warrant of committal. Although not strictly a warrant of arrest, if a person breaches a court order or acts in contempt of court, then the court can issue a warrant for that person to be committed to prison for a specified period.

(iv) European Arrest Warrant. Part 1 of the Extradition Act 2003 gives effect to the terms of the European Union Council Framework Directive (2002/548). The purpose of the Directive is to harmonise a simplified framework across the European Union for the detention and return to the requesting State a suspect currently resident in another Member State. The warrant can only be issued in respect of a sentence of four months or more imposed on the defendant who is unlawfully at large for an offence carrying imprisonment of 12 months or more (that the defendant deliberately absented themselves from their trial, s.20). The warrant in accordance with the Extradition Act 2003 (Multiple Offences) Order 2003 (SI 2003/3150), must particularise the sentence imposed and identify the specified extradition offence.

In *Pilecki v High Court of Justice* [2008] 1 W.L.R. 325, the House of Lords ruled unanimously that the provisions (ss.10, 11 and s.65(3)(c)) of the Extradition Act 2003 are consistent with the purpose of the Directive. In the case of multiple offences, it is the aggregate term of imprisonment which must be four months or over, not each individual offence. Accordingly, if the defendant is unlawfully at large for multiple offences which have a combination of sentences of less four months and more than four months, then provided the aggregate sentence is at least four months the warrant is valid for that purpose.

15. Police Detention and Procedure

14.20 Once a suspect is under police arrest, then in accordance with PACE 1984, the suspect must be taken to a "designated police station", a station that is equipped with a custody suite. Once a suspect is detained at a police station, the police, on the one hand, have extensive powers to take samples, photographs and interview in the investigation and detection of crime, whilst on the other there are clear safeguards for the treatment and interviewing of a suspect. It is important to be aware of both the powers and the safeguards for suspect and consider the delicate balance between them and to ensure that there is no arbitrary use of such powers to the detriment of the suspect's rights. The powers of the police in regard to a suspect's detention are contained in Pt IV of PACE 1984 and Code C of the Codes of Practice. From the point of view of a defence solicitor/advisor, there are two times that are essential and that need to be recorded on the "custody record" and monitored throughout the suspect's detention. These two times are:

(i) time of arrival at police station (start of the detention clock);

(ii) time detention was authorised by the custody officer (start of review clock).

It is important to note that depending on how busy the custody office is, these two times may only differ by a few minutes or there can be a significant difference, if the suspect is required to wait their turn to appear before the custody sergeant.

16. Duty of the Custody Officer

14.21 On arrival at the police station, the suspect is brought by the arresting officer before the custody sergeant or staff custody officer (created by s.120 of the SOCP Act 2005 which amends s.38 of the Police Reform Act 2002, the functions of a SCO are delineated in Schs 8 and 9 of the SOCPA 2005). The suspect appears before the "custody sergeant" who under s.36 is independent of the investigation and is responsible for the welfare of the suspect whilst in detention (see s.39). A suspect's detention must be authorised by the custody sergeant, the arresting officer outlines the circumstances of the arrest to the custody sergeant, who then, based on that information, decides whether or not to authorise that person's detention. The custody sergeant must apply a two-stage approach to this decision as set out in s.37 of PACE 1984:

(i) determine whether there is *"sufficient evidence"* to charge the person with the offence for which the person has been arrested. If there is then the suspect must be charged. If not then they,

(ii) are required to release the suspect without bail or with bail (including conditions can be arrested without warrant if breach conditions, s.46A) unless they have reasonable grounds for believing detention "is necessary in order to secure evidence whether by questioning or by other means". If so, the custody officer will authoris the suspect's detention.

On deciding to authorise a suspect's detention, the custody sergeant will then open a "custody record" in accordance with s.37(4) to (7) of PACE 1984. This is a prescribed pre-printed form. The first part of the form details the suspect; the next part is a full and detailed written entry of the conduct of the suspect's detention. Previous to s.8 of the Criminal Justice Act 2003, the custody sergeant was required under s.54 to record, bag and seal all items in the suspect's possession which would include things like a clothes button. This was time consuming and in many respects unnecessary. Section 8 of the CJA 2003 now removes this requirement. At this same time, the custody sergeant can authorise the suspect to be searched under s.54 and seize property that could cause injury, assist escape, or interfere with evidence (i.e. clothes from a rape or assault suspect). An essential requirement of the custody sergeant and an important safeguard of the detained person, is that the custody sergeant must inform the suspect of the three main rights whilst in police sdetention:

(i) to have someone informed of their arrest in accordance with s.56;

(ii) to have access to free legal advice in accordance with s.58;

(iii) to consult the Codes of Practice.

The custody sergeant must tell the detained person that they can exercise any of these rights now or at any time during their detention; they also give the suspect a leaflet explaining this. The custody sergeant also advises the suspect of the availability of help concerning drug dependency and the relevant agencies. If the detained person is a child (10 to 14) or a young person (15 to 17) then the custody officer has a duty, as soon as is practicable, to ascertain the identity of a person responsible for that person's welfare and inform them of their arrest and where they are detained. A responsible person is a parent/guardian or another person who has assumed responsibility.

17. Interviewing the Suspect, the Right to Silence and the "Genuine Reliance" of a Suspect on Legal Advice given in Good Faith

14.22 If the suspect exercises their right to free legal advice, then either the duty solicitor or the suspect's own solicitor will be called to attend at the police station. On arrival the solicitor will speak to the investigating officer, in order to obtain as much evidential disclosure of the allegation as possible.

The police have no statutory duty to disclose the evidence they possess at that time and there is criticism in some cases of deliberate drip feeding. However, to avoid a no comment interview, the police do generally and voluntarily make written disclosure (see *R. v Robb* [1997] Crim. L.R. 449). The solicitor will then have a private consultation with the suspect to take their instructions and give advice on the allegation generally and whether to answer questions in interview. The solicitor must warn the suspect of the effect of ss.34 to 37 of the Criminal Justice and Police Order Act 1994 in relation to the right to silence and the qualifications to it. It is not proposed to provide an in-depth analysis of the mass of case law that has developed around the application of this complex provision, simply to provide an explanatory overview.

In essence, ss.34 to 37 allow for the jury or magistrates to draw an inference of guilt in the following circumstances:

(i) Failure to mention facts later relied upon, which the defendant *could reasonably have been expected to mention* when earlier questioned under caution (s.34(1)(a)).

(ii) Failure to mention facts later relied on when charged or officially informed of prosecution (s.34(1(b)).

(iii) Failure or refusal to account to the police for objects, substances or marks. (s.36).

(iv) Failure or refusal to account to the police for the presence at a place at or about the time of the offence. The purpose of these provisions is to encourage suspects to disclose the nature of their defence at an early stage of the investigative process, and to reduce the number of "no comment" interviews and/or subsequent "ambush defences" at trial.

In *R. v B* [2003] EWCA Crim 3080, the Court of Appeal commented that this area of law is "a notorious minefield" and in *R. v Brizzalari* [2004] EWCA Crim 310, the Court of Appeal observed that the prosecution should be discouraged from too readily seeking to activate the provisions in s.34. In *R. v Birchall* [1999] Crim L.R. 311 the Court of Appeal ruled that a jury should only draw an inference if they have concluded that the case against the defendant is sufficiently compelling, otherwise there is a clear risk of injustice if logic and fairness are not observed. The development of this complex area of law and the considerable body of precedent in the Court of Appeal, was reviewed extensively by the House of Lords in *R. v Webber* [2004] 1 W.L.R. 404.

One of the significant developments with regard to the qualifications of the right to silence is whether or not a jury is still entitled to draw an inference from a suspect's refusal to answer police questions, where that suspect relied on the advice of the solicitor. Second, whether the drawing of such inferences breaches a suspect's right to a fair trial contained in art.6 of the European Convention on Human Rights. These issues where addressed by the European Court of Human Rights in *Beckles v UK* [2003] 36 E.H.R.R. 13, in which the Court held that the right to silence is not an absolute right under art.6 and that drawing inferences from a suspect's silence is not incompatible with that right. It would however be incompatible with the right to silence to base a conviction solely or mainly on the accused's silence:

> "in situations which clearly call for an explanation from him, from being taken into account in assessing the persuasiveness of the evidence adduced by the prosecution."

The Court further noted that whether or not the drawing of an adverse inference from the accused's silence breaches art.6 is to be determined as against all the circumstances of the case. In particular the court should consider the situations where an inference may be drawn, the strength of the evidence "and the degree of compulsion inherent in the situation". The Court further noted that the terms of the judge's direction to the jury are of clear relevance as to whether a defendant's right to a fair trial was breached.

As a consequence, in *R. v Beckles* [2004] EWCA Crim 2766, the Criminal Cases Review Commission referred the case back to the Court of Appeal. The Court of Appeal held that when a judge directed the jury that they may draw adverse interferences from a defendant's silence when interviewed by the police, they must also be directed that they should not draw such an inference if they considered that the defendant genuinely and reasonably relied on the advice of his solicitor to remain silent (see *R. v Hoare & Piece* [2004] EWCA Crim 784, and *R. v Betts & Hall* [2001] 2 Cr.App.R. 784). This the judge had failed to do and accordingly the appellant's conviction for attempted murder, robbery and false imprisonment was quashed as being unsafe due to that material misdirection of the judge.

18. The Judicial Studies Board "Section 34 Direction to the Jury"

14.23 Rather than trawl through the many different appeal decisions on the application and implications of s.34 in particular, it is perhaps better to refer to the Judicial Studies Board's guidance on the correct direction to be given to a jury concerning s.34. This provides when considering the application of s.34, the judge must decide whether a direction is appropriate. Such a direction is clearly appropriate, for instance, when the matter which the defendant failed to mention is the central feature in the case. It is important to be aware that the trial judge has the discretion whether or not to give a s.34 direction, regardless of the observations of counsel. If the interview is in breach of the Code of Practice, then there should be no s.34 direction (see *R. v Pointer* [1997] Crim. L.R. 676). The standard direction given to the jury takes the following steps:

(i) Before the interview the defendant was informed of their right to say nothing (silence). However they were also told that it might harm their defence if they did not mention when questioned something which they later relied on in court and anything they did say might be given in evidence.

(ii) The judge then tells the jury the facts the defendant rely upon, but that the prosecution say that they failed to mention other facts when interviewed. If the jury are sure about this then that failure may count against the defendant. This is because the jury can conclude that the defendant failed to answer because they believed that nothing would stand up to scrutiny, or has since invented or tailored their account to fit the prosecution's case.

(iii) If the jury draw that conclusion, they are then told that they must not convict wholly or mainly on the strength of it, but they may take it into account as some additional support to the prosecution's case and when deciding whether the defence evidence about these facts is true.

(iv) If the defendant remained silent based on legal advice then the jury are told, that it does not automatically prevent them from drawing any conclusions from the silence, since a defendant has a choice whether to accept or reject it. The question, taking into account the circumstances of the case, is: could the defendant have reasonably been expected to mention facts on which they now rely?

(v) If the defendant has or may have had an answer to give but genuinely relied on the legal advice to remain silent, the jury should not draw any conclusion against them. But if the defendant used the legal advice as a shield to hide behind because they had no answer, then the jury are entitled to draw a conclusion against the defendant.

The above direction is based on the "five essentials" of the application of s.34 listed in *R. v Cowan* [1995] 3 W.L.R. 818, *R. v Argent* [1997] 2 Cr.App.R. 27, *Murray v UK* [1996] 94 E.H.R.R. 193 and *Condron v UK* [2001] 31 E.H.R.R.

19. Conduct and Restrictions on Interviewing: Code C

14.24 When the investigating officer is ready to interview the suspect, the custody sergeant will release the suspect into the custody of the investigating officer and supply the officer with either two tapes or videos as required by ss.60 and 60A. The interview itself must be conducted in accordance with Code D of the Codes of Practice. This requires that the interview must either be taped or video recorded. In either case there is a master tape and a working tape. The master tape must be sealed, dated and signed, and returned to the custody sergeant, which is then handed over to the tape librarian and cannot be opened without a court order. The working copy is for the police officer and the defence solicitor, who will later request a copy. Whilst the police may interview a suspect on several occasions during their detention, Code C provides the following protection to a suspect so as to avoid the inappropriate use of interviewing:

(i) In any 24-hour period a continuous period of eight hours must be allowed for rest, free from questioning, where possible this should be at night.

(ii) The suspect should not be asked to stand during interview.

(iii) If seizing clothing for investigation, sufficient replacement clothing should be provided.

(iv) The interviewing officer should not try to obtain a confession by oppression (for the consequences of this see s.76 of PACE).

(v) The suspect should be given clean bedding and an exercise period.

It is especially important to note that Code C provides specific safeguards for a mentally disordered/vulnerable person or child or young person. Any of these persons must not be interviewed without an "appropriate adult" being present, unless the interview is urgent. An appropriate adult for a child or young person is a parent/guardian or if in care, a social worker or member of the youth offending team. For a vulnerable person it is a relative, guardian or other person responsible for their care. For foreign nationals a relevant interpreter would need to be present.

20. Right to Free Legal Advice and Someone to be Informed of Arrest

14.25 Section 58 of PACE 1984 provides a statutory right for a person in police custody to be entitled, if they so request, to consult a solicitor privately at any time. In *R. v Samuel* [1988] 2 W.L.R. 920, the Court of Appeal held that this right is of fundamental importance and that any refusal to allow such access would amount to a significant breach of PACE 1984. Any evidence obtained in such circumstances is deemed prejudicial to the defendant and ought not to be admitted at trial. Whilst the court in *Samuel* emphasised clearly the importance of this right, s.58 does allow a superintendent to delay access (up to a maximum of 36 hours) if a detained person is under arrest for a indictable offence and that there are reasonable grounds for believing that without such delay:

(i) it will lead to interference with or harm to evidence or injury to other persons;

(ii) it will lead to the alerting of other persons suspected of having committed such an offence, but who are not yet arrested;

(iii) it would hinder the recovery of any property obtained as a result of such an offence;

(iv) access may be delayed if the police have reasonable grounds to believe that the person arrested has benefited from their criminal conduct and the recovery of the value of the property constituting the benefit may be hindered.

If the superintendent authorises the delay, then the detained person must be notified of the reason for this and an entry made in the custody record. In *R. (Thompson) v Chief Constable of Northumbria Police* [2001] 1 W.L.R. 1342, the Court of Appeal allowed a judicial review claim against the decision of a senior police officer to refuse admission to a police station, to a particular representative. The Court placed great weight on the duty of the police to ensure that a person in custody has access to independent legal advice and it was the solicitor not the police who has the sole responsibility for the quality of advice to be given. Accordingly, this would not be a good reason to refuse admission and whether a probationary police station representative would hinder the investigation due to lack of experience had to be taken regarding each specific investigation and not, as in this case, a blanket policy of refusing access to all trainees.

21. Taking Samples in Accordance with ss.62, 63 and 64 of PACE 1984 as Amended

14.26 One of the important extensive powers of the police in the investigation and detection of crime is the ability to take and indeed retain samples from a detained suspect. Sections 62 to 64 contain the relevant powers and procedures and have been amended extensively through a series of later enactments. These amendments have systematically increased the power of the police to take samples, whilst at the same time weakening the important safeguards for a suspect against the arbitrary taking and retention of their samples. The procedural provisions are long and complex and are difficult to follow, given the many changes and amendments. PACE 1984 categorises samples into two types, namely "intimate" and "other samples" (non-intimate). Section 62 regulates the taking of intimate samples and provides that before any sample can be taken several conditions must be satisfied, namely:

(i) the suspect is in police detention;

(ii) for a recordable offence (generally, but not in all respects this means an offence that is imprisonable);

(iii) the suspect gives consent;

(iv) an inspector authorises the taking, but must have reasonable grounds for suspecting that person's involvement in the offence, and also believe that the sample when taken will tend to confirm or disprove such involvement.

Section 65 lists the following as intimate samples: blood, semen, any other tissue fluid, urine, pubic hair, dental impression, a swab taken from any person's genitals (including pubic hair) or from a person's body orifice other than the mouth, as added by s.119 SOCPA 2005. It is important to be aware that the suspect must consent to the taking of an intimate sample. Without such consent, the police have no power to take such a sample. Nevertheless, with that refusal the suspect will fall foul of s.65, which entitles the court to draw any inference from this failure to consent. Even if the suspect refuses to consent, then the police can take without consent a non-intimate sample.

It is this power that has been amended extensively by Parliament and whose use has increased significantly due to the unquestionable benefits derived from the retention of a suspect's sample, for the detection and investigation of crime. Sections 9 and 10 of the Criminal Justice Act 2003 further amended the provisions and provide that the police can take a non-intimate sample without the consent of the suspect, provided that the suspect is in police detention in consequence of his arrest for a recordable offence. This means that the police can now take a non-intimate sample from anybody they arrest for any recordable offence, even if they are never charged with any offence, or whether the sample is necessary to the proof of the alleged offence for which the suspect has been arrested.

14.27 Section 65 lists the following as non-intimate samples: hair (other than pubic), a sample from a nail or under a nail, a swab taken from any part of a person's body including mouth, but not any other body orifice, a swab taken from any part of a person's body other than a part from which a swab taken would be an intimate sample (added by s.119 SOCPA 2005), saliva, a skin impression. Once the sample is taken then the police have an discretion to retain that sample, even if the suspect is cleared, or not prosecuted for the alleged offence. In addition the police can, with the sample, conduct a speculative search on the DNA database. A suspect under s.64 can no longer demand that their sample be destroyed. It is now the policy of all Chief Constables to retain all samples from all suspects.

This absolute power to retain was as a direct result of the injustice highlighted in *Attorney-General's Reference (No.3 of 1999)* [2001] A.C. 91, in which the defendant had been arrested for but later acquitted of a burglary. At the time s.64 made it mandatory for the police to destroy the sample, however, the sample remained unlawfully on the database and later matched a semen sample taken from a brutal rape of a 66-year-old woman from whom money was stolen and who was then locked in a cupboard. The trial judge directed an acquittal for the serious sexual offence, since the evidence had been unlawfully obtained from a sample which s.64 forbid from being used as evidence when it should have been destroyed.

In *R. v Chief Constable of South Yorkshire Ex p. Marper* [2004] 1 W.L.R. 2196, the House of Lords ruled unanimously that s.64, as amended, was "objectively justified" and therefore did not violate either art.8 (right to a private life) or art.14 (a right not to be discriminated) of the European Convention on Human Rights. In addition, the "blanket policy" adopted by the Chief Constable of routinely retaining all samples taken was justified and perfectly lawful, even if as in this case, the sample was taken from an innocent person. The Forensic Science Service, an executive agency of the Ministry of Justice, is responsible for the DNA database. The Chief Scientist is the custodian of the national DNA database whose functional duties are contained within a memorandum of understanding with the Association of Chief Police Officers. On the other hand, the National DNA Database Board duties surround the operation and management of the system. This difference in managerial arrangements has led to criticism from the Joint Parliamentary Committee on Human Rights about who would be personally held legally accountable for any error made in the DNA database.

22. Taking Fingerprint Samples without Consent: Section 61

14.28 Section 61 gives the police the power to take fingerprints samples electronically (National Automated Fingerprint Identification System) without the suspect's consent if they have been arrested for a recordable offence or charged with such an offence. This power is the same as that for the taking of samples and therefore in the same way, the police have a blanket policy of retaining all fingerprints and conducting speculative searches on the database, as provided by s.63A. Section 27 of PACE 1984, as amended, provides the police with the power to require a person convicted of an offence to which they were not held in police detention, to attend at the police station within a period of no later than one month to have their fingerprints taken.

Section 61 is further radically amended by s.117 of the SOCPA 2005 by inserting a new s.61(6A), (6B) and (6C). The purpose of these amendments is to give the police a power to take fingerprints without consent, if the officer reasonably suspects that the person is committing or attempting to commit *an offence*, or has done either of these and one or both of the two conditions in (6B) are satisfied. The two conditions are:

(i) The name and address of the person is unknown and cannot be readily ascertained.

(ii) The officer has reasonable grounds for doubting that the name furnished is that person's real name. The prints can be checked against other fingerprints. Section 61(6C) makes it clear that when fingerprints are taken under this power this does not amount to taking them in the course of an investigation. If the police require fingerprints to assist in the investigation of an offence, they must take the fingerprints at a police station under s.61. Section 61A(8) provides the safeguard that once the fingerprints taken have fulfilled the purpose of ascertaining identity then they *must* be destroyed.

23. Impressions of Footwear without Consent: Section 61A Inserted by s.118 SOCPA 2005

14.29 The Forensic Science Service maintains two databases of footwear impressions, one being the "mark intelligence index" concerning impressions recovered from the scene of a crime whilst the other, the "national footwear reference collection", consists of impressions of newly manufactured footwear. To further develop and utilise this area of scientific evidence, which can amount to highly incriminating evidence without a viable reason for the presence of such evidence, s.118 of the SCOPA 2005 amends s.61 by the insertion of a new s.61A. The provision provides that a footwear impression cannot be taken without "appropriate consent", which must be in writing, unless the person is in police detention at a police station in consequence of their arrest for a recordable offence, or has been charged with such an offence, or that they will be reported for such an offence and they have not already given an impression, unless the impression was incomplete or of insufficient quality. The section provides for certain safeguards in the giving by the police of a notice to the person that the impression may be subject to a speculative search, the reason for which it is taken must be recorded and noted in the custody record.

24. Taking Photographs of Suspect without Consent: Section 64(A) Inserted by s.116 SOCPA 2005

14.30 Section 64A provides for the statutory power of the police to take a photograph of a person in police detention at a police station either with or without consent. This power is further extended by s.116 of SOCPA 2005, to allow the police to take a photograph (including a moving image) of a person, other than at a police station either with or without consent if one of six situations arise:

- (i) the person is under arrest for an offence;
- (ii) now in police custody having been arrested by another person not being a police officer;
- (iii) subject to a requirement to wait by a Community Support Officer in accordance with the CSO power contained in Sch.4 of the Police Reform Act 2002;
- (iv) given a penalty notice by an officer in uniform for a specified offence under Pt 1 of the Criminal Justice and Police Act 2001, an offence under s.444A of the Education Act 1996 or under s.54 of the Road Traffic Offenders Act 1988;
- (v) a penalty notice given by a designated CSO;

(vi) a penalty notice given by an accredited person in accordance with Sch.5 of the Police Reform Act 2002.

25. Request of a Sample for Ascertaining the Presence of Class A Drug

14.31 Section 57 of the Criminal Justice and Court Services Act 2000 (CJCSA 2000) amends s.63 of PACE 1984 and inserts a new s.63(B) and (C), which provides a power for the police to take a sample of urine or non-intimate sample from a person in police detention, in order to see if there is a presence of a specified class A drug in their body, provided three conditions are satisfied. The original conditions have been changed significantly by s.7 of the Drugs Act 2005 and a sample can only be taken if:

(i) Either the arrest condition or charge condition is met, (this means arrest/charge for "trigger offence" (Sch.6 of CJCSA 2000, as amended by the CJCSA 2000 (Amendment) Order 2004 (SI 2004/1892) and 2007 (SI 2007/2171) in respect of the new fraud offences) lists the specified trigger offences, examples are theft, robbery and burglary), or is arrested/charged with an offence which an inspector has reasonable grounds for suspecting that the misuse of drugs caused or contributed to the offence authorises (in writing and recorded) the sample to be taken).

(ii) Both the age condition (this means 18 if the arrest condition is satisfied, but reduces to 14 if the charge condition is satisfied) and request conditions are met. The request condition is that an officer has requested a sample and warned the suspect that if they fail without good cause to give a sample then they may be liable to prosecution for a summary offence (51 weeks' imprisonment or fine or both, see Sch.26 of the CJA 2003). If the suspect is under 17 then s.5 of the CJA 2003 provides that a sample and the failure warning must not occur except in the presence of an "appropriate adult", as defined in s.63(10). In regard to the age requirement, the Secretary of State can by statutory instrument amend the age.

(iii) Notification condition in accordance with subsection (4A) in that the Secretary of State has notified the Chief Officer that appropriate arrangements have been made for that police area.

Further changes include that if a sample is taken based on the arrest condition, then no other sample may be taken from during that same period of detention. If the charge condition is met during that period then the sample is treated as the same for that condition. A new subsection (5) (c) provides a power to take a sample from a person who is arrested initially for an offence (first offence) that meets the arrest condition and then is required to be released for that offence, but remains in police custody for another offence that does not satisfy the arrest condition. The sample for the first offence can still be taken, but only within a 24-hour period from form authorisation of detention for that offence. This is somewhat complicated, but simply means that if before the police manage to take a sample from the detained person, they no longer have the authority to keep that person in detention for that offence (i.e. evidence confirms that they are not the offender for that trigger offence) but the evidence still points to another offence for which they are now arrested which is not a trigger offence, then the police can still take the sample for the first offence.

It is important to note that only a prescribed person as set out in the PACE (Drug Testing of Persons in Police Detention) (Prescribed Persons) Regulations 2001 (SI 2001/2645) can take the necessary samples. Under subsection (7) any information obtained from the taking of the sample can be disclosed for four specified purposes: (i) decision concerning bail of the sampled person; (ii) the sampled person is in police detention or remanded in custody or on bail and a decision concerning their supervision; (iv) the sampled person is given the appropriate advice and treatment.

26. Section 54: General Search Power and Section 54A to Ascertain Identity

14.32 The police have two powers to search a detained person. The first is the general search power contained in s.54 and authorised at the time of the suspect's authorised detention. This power has since been extended by s.90 of the Anti-Terrorism, Crime and Security Act 2001 which inserts a new s.54A to provide a power to search in order to ascertain a detained person's identity. Section 54A provides that an inspector may authorise the search, or examination, or both of a person detained at a police station for the purposes of:

(i) ascertaining marks (subsection (12) defines mark so as to include features and injuries and an identifying mark includes any mark that facilities the ascertainment of that person's identity) that would tend to identify them as a person being:

(a) involved in the commission of an offence;

or

(b) facilitating the ascertainment of their identity.

The authorisation in relation to (i) above should only be given if the appropriate consent to the search, which would reveal the mark, is being withheld, or it is impracticable to obtain such consent. In other situations the authorisation may only be given if the detained person refuses to identify themselves, or the officer has reasonable grounds for suspecting that the detained person is not who they claims to be. This authorisation can be given orally but must be confirmed in writing as soon as practicable. Any mark found can under subsection (5) be photographed, (includes visual image) with or without consent of the detained person. Only a police constable can perform the search, and an officer of the same sex as the detained person must conduct it. An important point to note is the breadth of subsection (9), which allows the police, once the photograph of the mark is obtained from the detained person, to use or disclose it to any person for any purpose related to the prevention and detection or investigation of an offence, or the conduct of a prosecution and that once used for this purpose it may be retained for the same purpose.

27. Section 55: Intimate Searches

14.33 Section 55 allows an inspector to authorise an intimate search if they have reasonable grounds for believing that a person arrested and in police detention may have concealed on them anything which:

(i) could be used to cause physical injury, or

(ii) that such a person may have a class A drug concealed on him and was in possession of it with the appropriate criminal intent (subsection (17) defines a class A drug as that set out in s.2(1)(b) of the Misuse of Drugs Act 1971, and appropriate criminal intent relates to offences in s.5(3) of the Misuse of Drugs Act 1971 of possession with intent to supply or s.68(2) of the Customs and Excise Management Act 1979, with intent to evade a prohibition or restriction, i.e. drug trafficking), and

(iii) that such items cannot be found without the means of an intimate search.

This authorisation can be given orally, but must be later confirmed in writing. Only an officer of the same sex can conduct the search and the search must take place either at a police station, hospital or registered surgery. If the search is for an alleged drug offence only, then this cannot take place at a police station. The conduct of the search must be recorded in the custody record. Section 5 of the Drugs Act 2005 inserts into s.55 a new s.55A which allows for the taking of X-rays and ultrasound scans relating to the concealment of prohibited drugs. The conditions of authorisation of X-rays or ultrasound scans are virtually the same for intimate searches under s.55. The authorisation can only be given by an inspector or above who must have reasonable grounds for believing that the arrested person in police detention for an offence (i) may have swallowed a class A drug; and (ii) was in possession of it with the relevant criminal intent before their arrest.

It is important to note that neither an X-ray nor ultrasound scan can be taken without first obtaining the consent of the detained person. If the defendant refuses without good cause then subsection (9) allows an interference to be drawn by the magistrates' court or jury in determining whether the person is guilty of the offence charged, or in determining a submission of no case to answer, or an application for dismissal under s.51 for the Crime and Disorder Act 1998. If such an X-ray or ultrasound scan is requested, then an appropriate officer (constable, staff custody officer or detention officer) must inform the detained person of the authorisation and the grounds for it.

If the detained person gives the appropriate consent, then the X-ray or scan can only be taken by a suitably qualified person (registered medical practitioner or registered nurse) and can only be taken at a hospital or surgery. This must be entered in the custody record. Section 8 of the Drugs Act 2005 extends the power found in s.152 of the Criminal Justice Act 1988 which allows a magistrates' court to commit to prison a person charged with a s.5(2) offence under the Misuse of Drugs Act 1971 or drug trafficking offence and who had swallowed the drugs to conceal them for a period of up to 192 hours to allow for that vital evidence to be recovered. This power is extended to allow the police to have the same period, should a person swallow drugs on arrest.

28. Time Limitations on Detention without Charge (The detention Clock) and the Necessity Principle

14.34 To restrict the liberty of the person is a highly invasive power and must be strictly applied. It is for this reason that s.37 makes it clear that a person in police detention should only be kept in custody for as long "as is necessary" to either charge or secure evidence by way of questioning him. If it is no longer necessary, then the detained person must be released, bailed or charged. In *Fayed v Commissioner of the Metropolitan Police* [2004] EWCA Civ 1579, the Court of Appeal stated that the issue of necessity to detain is based on *Wednesbury reasonableness*. The Court cited with approval the observations of Beldam L.J. in *Wilding v Chief Constable of Lancashire* [1995] (unreported), that the court should ask itself the following questions:

> "whether the decision of the custody sergeant was unreasonable in the sense that no custody officer, acquainted with the ordinary use of language and applying his common sense to the competing considerations before him, could reasonably have reached that decision."

Further protection is found in s.34, which requires a custody sergeant to release immediately a detained person, if they become aware that the grounds for the detention cease to apply and there are no other grounds to justify detention. Under s.41 of PACE 1984 the "relevant time" for detention is 24 hours. This is calculated from time of arrival at the police station. If the person is arrested in one police area and is wanted in another then under subsection 2(3), the relevant time will run from the time they arrive at the police station in the other area, provided they are not questioned in the first police area about the offence.

Subsection (6) provides that if a detained person is taken to hospital, then that time is not discounted in the 24 hour calculation unless the police question them during this time, then this time must be discounted. If a person attends at the police station to answer police bail then the time runs from the time they arrive at the police station. It is important that the legal advisor, on arrival at the custody office, checks this time and records the length of custody time, since any detention beyond the time limits would amount to unlawful detention. The time of arrival of the arrested person is recorded in the custody record. The codes of practice allow the legal advisor to inspect the record.

29. Continuous Review of a Suspect's Detention

14.35 Under s.40 an inspector (known as the "review officer") who has not been directly involved in the investigation, must review periodically the continued detention of a suspect who is not charged in order to ensure it is still necessary to continue that person's detention in accordance with the two stage test as applied by the custody sergeant under s.37. The first review must take place within six hours of the time the detention was authorised and then subsequently every nine hours after that. A review may be postponed, if with regard to all the circumstances prevailing at the time, it is not practicable to carry out the review. Or at the time of the review, the detained person is being interviewed and the review officer is satisfied that to interrupt the interview in order to carry out the review would prejudice the investigation.

Subsection 12 provides that before making the decision on whether or not to authorise that person's continued detention, the review officer must give the detained person, (unless asleep) or the legal advisor, if available at the time of the review, the opportunity to make representations about the issue of detention, either orally or in writing. The review officer can refuse to consider representations from the detained person, if they consider the person is unfit to make such representations due to their condition or behaviour.

By virtue of s.73 of the Criminal Justice and Police Act 2001, as amended by s.6 of the Criminal Justice Act 2003, a detention review can be performed by telephone or by video conferencing facilities as set out in s.45A. If video conferencing can be used, then a telephone review does not apply. The review officer must direct a person at the police station to make the record of the review in the custody record and give the detained person or their legal advisor the opportunity to make representations. The purpose of these different methods of review is to utilise technology and to make better use of the resources of senior officers. Again it is important to record this time so as to ensure that your client's review of detention is conducted and ascertain whether you can make representations about your client's continued detention.

30. Extension of detention time by Superintendent

14.36 Parliament accepted the arguments made by the police that the 24-hour limitation on detention may hinder the proper and effective investigation of alleged offence(s) which did not constitute a "serious arrestable offences", and allowed the extension of detention. Accordingly s. 42, as amended by s.7 of CJA 2003, states that detention for an "indictable offence" can be extended for a further 12 hours (i.e. up to 36 hours) by a superintendent, provided they have reasonable grounds for believing:

(i) it is necessary to secure or preserve evidence by questioning; and

(ii) the investigation is being conduct *diligently* and *expeditiously*.

If the superintendent authorises a period less than 12 hours, then they supt can still later authorise the reminder of the time, provided the two conditions are still satisfied. Further, safeguards in the provision provide that the extended period of detention cannot be authorised if the 24-hour period has expired or before the second review of detention. Before authorising further detention, the superintendent must give the suspect or their solicitor an opportunity to make representations either orally or in writing opposing such authorisation. As with s.40, the superintendent can refuse to hear representations from the detained person if they are unfit. Moreover if the detained person has not yet exercised their right to have someone informed of their arrest or their right to free legal advice, then the superintendent must inform them of these rights, decide whether or not to delay them and make a record in the custody record.

31. Warrant of Further Detention granted by Magistrates Sections 43 and 44

14.37 An application must be made to the magistrates on oath supported with relevant information for a warrant to further extend the detention of the suspect. For the court to grant the warrant, it must be satisfied that there are reasonable grounds for believing that further detention is justified. For the extension to be justified the detention:

(i) must be necessary to secure or preserve evidence by questioning;

(ii) the offence must be an indictable offence;

(iii) the investigation must be conducted diligently and expeditiously.

The information presented to the court must state the nature of the offence, the general nature of the evidence, what further enquiries are proposed and the reasons for believing that it is necessary to extend the suspect's detention. The application can be made at any time before the expiry of the 36-hour period or after that period if it is not practicable for the magistrates' court to sit (i.e. late at night), but the court must sit during the six hours following the end of the 36-hour period. It is important to be aware that if an application is made by the police after the expiry of the 36-hour period and it appears to the court that it would have been reasonable for the police to make the application before the expiry time, then the court must dismiss the application. If the court is not satisfied that the extension of detention is justified, then it is the duty of the court to refuse the application; or alternatively adjourn the hearing to a time that does not exceed a period of 36 hours after the relevant time (i.e. the time the suspect arrived at the police station).

A further safeguard for the suspect is that the court cannot hear the application until the police have supplied the suspect with a copy of the supporting information to the application and also that the suspect appears at court in person to hear the application. Likewise the suspect is entitled to be legally represented at the application hearing. If the suspect appears unrepresented and the suspect now wishes to be represented, then the court must adjourn the hearing in order to allow the suspect to obtain that representation. During this time the suspect will be kept in police custody. If the magistrates grant the warrant of further detention, then this cannot be for a period greater than 36 hours. The court can grant a period as they think fit based on the evidence presented to the court (i.e. the period may be, for instance, 10 hours).

If the police are thinking of moving the suspect from one police area to another then the court must take the travelling time into account. It is important to note that if the magistrates refuse the application, then the suspect must be charged, released either with, or without bail and that no further application can be made, unless new evidence comes to light. If the first warrant of further detention is due to expire, and the police still need further time, then an application to extend that warrant of further detention can be made under s.44. Exactly the same procedure and protections must be adhered to as with the first application. If granted, then the further period can be for no longer than another 36 hours, until a maximum of 96 hours. On the expiry of this further period, no more applications can be made and the suspect must either be charged or released.

32. Detention and Treatment of a "Terrorist Suspect"

14.38 Section 41 of the Terrorism Act 2000 provides that if a person is arrested under that section, then the provisions of Sch.8 to the Act will apply in relation to their detention and treatment whilst in police custody. In addition the police can under s.41(3) keep a terrorist suspect in police detention for up to 48 hours. A warrant for further detention can be applied under para.29 of Sch.8 to extend the period of detention, (it is not intended to look at these previsions in depth, but simply to make the reader aware of them and the differences between the powers relating to a general suspect and that of a terrorist suspect).

Beyond the 48-hour period, a superintendent or above can apply to a senior District Judge or deputy for the detention period to be extended to 14 days, another 14 days can be applied (maximum 28 days) but this must be authorised by an High Court Judge, (s.23 of the Terrorism Act 2006). Schedule 7 deals specifically with detention at port and border controls. These provisions were considered by the House of Lords in *Ward v Police Service of Northern Ireland* [2007] 1 W.L.R. 3013, in which the House ruled that the relevant judicial authority can exclude the detained person or their representative from the hearing, if the judge wishes to be satisfied that the further detention is necessary to obtain evidence by way of questioning. Accordingly, there is no legal requirement for the police to reveal to the defence the precise questions they wish to put to the defence, as justification for the further detention.

33. Voluntary Attendance at Police Station

14.39 Section 29 provides that where a person voluntarily attends or accompanies a constable to a police station to assist with an investigation and is not under arrest, then in such circumstances the volunteer is entitled to leave at will, unless and until he is arrested to prevent him leaving. Although a volunteer is not under arrest the codes of practice provide that they must be informed of their rights whilst at the police station, the same rights as are explained to an arrested person.

34. Charge, Caution or Release with or without Police Bail before Charge or the decision to Charge

14.40 Once it is no longer necessary to keep the suspect in police detention, or the detention time is about to expire, the police must make a decision as to whether or not to charge the suspect or release them, with or without police bail. The discretion to charge a suspect with an offence(s) was the exclusive decision of the police. However, it was believed that the police had a tendency to over charge the suspect, based on an unrealistic assessment of the evidence. This would often lead to the suspect pleading not guilty and maintaining such a plea until nearer the trial date or on the day of the trial when an agreement was reached with the prosecution to offer a lesser offence in return for the defendant entering a guilty plea. This common practice would result in far too many "cracked trials" (see the Auld Report into Criminal Procedure). This practice does not encourage confidence in the justice system, nor does it achieve justice. It is financially wasteful and all parties involved have been put to considerable inconvenience, especially witnesses. It was felt therefore that if the appropriate charge was made at the police station, then this would encourage defendants to plead early and reduce the number of "cracked trials".

To this effect s.28 of the Criminal Justice Act 2003 and Sch.2 place the responsibility for decision to charge a suspect upon the CPS and not the police. The actual process of charging or releasing a suspect remains with the custody officer in accordance with s.37(7), but under s.37A the custody officer must have regard to guidance issued by the Director of Public Prosecutions (DPP) in terms of charging standards. A new option introduced by the Criminal Justice Act 2003 is for the custody officer to release the suspect on bail or keep them in police detention (s.11 of the Police and Justice Act 2006 since January 1, 2007) to enable the DPP to make a decision as to whether there is sufficient evidence to charge the suspect with an offence or instead administer a caution. The s.11 amendment arose as a response to the argument that any time spent in detention by a suspect while waiting a decision on the appropriate charge was unlawful. This was on the basis that if there is sufficient evidence to charge, then the custody officer must charge immediately or release on bail.

In determining whether or not there is sufficient evidence to charge, the custody sergeant must consider the "threshold test" (in all the circumstances there is at least a reasonable suspicion against the suspect of having committed an offence). If this test is met, then the custody sergeant must, as soon as is practicable, refer the case to a duty prosecutor. In limited circumstances the custody sergeant can make the decision to charge, such as if a prosecutor is not available. In these circumstances they must apply the "full code test" of a realistic prospect of securing a conviction. The custody officer must under s.37B provide the prosecutor with the necessary information contained in the guidance.

14.41 The new amendments were ruled to be inadequate in *G v Chief Constable of West Yorkshire* [2008] EWCA Civ 28, where the Court of Appeal held that s.37 did not provide any express authorisation to the custody sergeant to detain a suspect, pending a decision on appropriate charge from the CPS. Once the custody sergeant had sufficient evidence to charge, they must immediately proceed to charge, or bail the suspect. The guidance of the DPP cannot be taken to provide that necessary statutory authority. Accordingly the claimant's detention was unlawful, albeit this decision is now confined to its facts, since the coming into effect the amendment in s.11 of the Police and Justice Act 2006. The decision does nevertheless illustrate the oversight made due to the complexity of the amendments of important safeguards and principles made simply cannot be ignored. It also highlights the difficulties faced by those who have the task of ensuring the proper implication of the increasing and complex changes being made to the criminal process.

If the police have insufficient evidence to charge then they will have no option but to release the suspect. However they can under s.47 (known as Part 4 Bail) bail the suspect with or without conditions ("normal powers to impose conditions of bail") but in any event be in accordance with the provisions of the Bail Act 1976. The suspect can apply to the magistrates, court to have these conditions varied. The custody officer will advise the suspect that they must attend at the police station at a future date. If later, this is not necessary, the suspect must be notified in writing to this effect. If the suspect surrenders to police bail at the relevant time and is then arrested, then in terms of the detention clock, any time in police detention prior to the granting of the bail must be taken into account, (i.e. if a suspect was in police custody for six hours and then granted bail, if arrested having surrendered to bail that previous six hours forms part of the detention clock on his second arrest, meaning the police would have a maximum detention time of 18 hours) this includes being arrested under s.46A. If however, the suspect is arrested during the bail period then the detention clock for that arrest starts from 0 minutes.

Under s.46A a constable may arrest without warrant any person who fails to attend at the police station at the required time, or if the constable has reasonable grounds for suspecting that the bailed person has broken any of the conditions, the constable can arrest that person without warrant. Once arrested the person must be taken to the police station that they are required to surrender at. If arrested then the arrested person is deemed to have been arrested for the offence to which they where granted bail in the first instance. If the person is wanted at various police stations then they are deemed to have been arrested for all of them. It is important to note that a person who fails to attend or breaches conditions does not commit an offence in doing this, they are simply arrested for it and are deemed to have been arrested for the offence for which they were originally granted police bail.

35. Bail or Kept in Police Detention after Charge

14.42 Once a suspect has been charged with an offence(s) then the custody officer must decide whether to release the suspect on bail or to keep them in police custody to appear before the next available court for an early administrative hearing. Following a charge, s.38 of PACE 1984 requires the custody sergeant to release a person from detention unless certain criteria apply. These are listed in s.38(1), as amended by s.25 to 30 of the Criminal Justice Public Order Act 1994. It is important to note that these criteria apply to young offenders (10 to 17) as well as to adults:

(i) If charged with murder, manslaughter, rape or attempting these and they have a previous conviction for such an offence, then no bail is to be granted.

(ii) If name and address cannot be ascertained or custody officer had reasonable grounds for doubting details given.

(iii) If the custody officer has reasonable grounds for believing the suspect will fail to surrender into custody at court.

(iv) If the custody officer has reasonable grounds to believe that where he suspect is charged with an imprisonable offence, it is necessary to detain them to prevent them from committing further offences, interfering with the administration of justice or to protect the suspect.

(v) If the offence is not an imprisonable offence, then the charged person can only be detained if the custody officer has reasonable grounds for believing that it is necessary in order to prevent him from interfering with the administration of justice, or the investigation of an offence(s), or causing physical injury, loss or damage to property.

(vi) It is necessary to detain in order to enable a sample to be taken under s.63B.

(vii) If a young offender the custody officer has reasonable grounds for believing that detention is necessary for their own protection.

In making the decision on bail or custody, the custody officer must hear representations from both the investigating officer and the suspect or their legal advisor. They must also apply Pt.1 of Sch.1 of the Bail Act 1976. The custody officer can impose relevant bail conditions to the grant of bail if necessary, otherwise the suspect must be released on unconditional bail. If the custody officer grants bail then a written notice of this is made and given to the defendant. If the defendant is kept in police detention, the custody officer must make a written record for the decision in the presence of the suspect, unless they are incapable of understanding what is said, violent or likely to become so, or are in need of urgent medical attention.

Specifically, relating to the decision to keep an arrested juvenile in police custody, the custody officer must secure that this person is moved into local authority accommodation, unless it is certified that it is impracticable (Code C provides that neither the young person's behaviour or the nature of the offence amount to impracticability) to do so, or where the juvenile has attained the age of 12 and no secure accommodation is available and that other local authority accommodation would not provide sufficient protection to the public from serious harm (namely a violent or sexual offence).

36. Bail other than at a Police Station (Street Bail)

14.43 Section 4 of the CJA 2003 (which came into force on January 20, 2004) as amended and extended by s.10 and Sch.10 of the Police and Justice for Act 2006 (which came into effect on April 1, 2007) creates a new power for the police, in order to reduce unnecessary delay and inconvenience, to grant immediate bail to an arrested person for an offence, from the scene of the crime. Section 4 specifically inserts a new s.30A to D into s.30 of PACE 1984. In granting street bail, the officer may impose any conditions (but not surety, security or bail hostel requirement) that appear to the officer as necessary to secure that the person surrenders into custody, does not commit further offences while on bail, or interfere with administration of justice, or if under 17 for their own protection or welfare. The bailed person can later, if needed, request a relevant officer (custody officer) to vary or rescind those conditions, or impose further conditions (the same test as for granting bail on the street applies). If the conditions have been varied, or the officer refuses, or the request is not considered within a period of 48 hours, then the bailed person can make an application to the magistrates' court.

The officer who grants street bail must give the now bailed person written notice, before they are released, which must state the offence and the grounds of arrest, that they are required to attend at the police station on a specified date and time or may be informed later that this may change. If the detained person fails to attend when required, then the police have a power to arrest without warrant. Similarly if the police have reasonable grounds for suspecting the bailed person has broken any of the conditions then they have a power to arrest without warrant. In both arrest situations, the detained person must be taken to the police station as soon as practicable after arrest. In determining whether or not to grant street bail, the officer will need to take account of the nature of the offence committed, impact on the victim, would vital evidence be lost, the health of the person, whether correct details were given, whether they may commit further offences while on bail.

37. Power of Entry, Search of Property and Seizure

14.44 Within PACE 1984 the police have a wide range of powers relating to search and seizure relating to premises. In summary these are as follows:

(i) search warrants under s.8;

(ii) entry and search without a warrant under s.17;

(iii) entry and search after arrest under s.18;

(iv) seizure of property under s.19;

(v) retention of property under s.22.

Other powers exist in relation to the seizure and retention of motor vehicles (see s.152 of SOCPA 2005 and ss.59 and 60 of the Police Reform Act 2002).

38. Search Warrants Issued by a Justice of the Peace

14.45 Section 8 gives the police a power to apply to a Justice of the Peace for a search warrant. Before such a warrant can be granted the Justice of the Peace must be satisfied that there are reasonable grounds for believing that an *indictable offence* has been committed and there is material on the *premises* which is likely to be of substantial value to the investigation of the offence and the material is likely to be relevant evidence. Under s.8(d) this does not include items subject to (i) legal privilege; or (ii) excluded material (personal records held in confidence, journalistic material held in confidence); special procedure material (other information held in confidence); and one or more of four conditions apply as specified in s.8(3). The conditions are that it is not practicable to communicate with the person who can grant entry or if this is possible, it is not concerning the person who can authorise access to the evidence. Thirdly, that without a warrant, entry would not be possible and fourthly that without immediately securing the premises, the purpose of the search may be frustrated or seriously prejudiced.

An example of the application of s.8 would be where the police have information that a garage lockup contains stolen vehicles and parts. The suspects are known to the police and are put under surveillance in order to gather cogent evidence. At this stage it would be unwise to arrest the suspects, since the suspects may well have moved the property, or the property may not be there. Accordingly, when the time is right, the police will apply for a s.8 warrant to search the premises for stolen goods. If when executing the warrant the police find the vehicles they suspected would be there, then the suspects will be arrested.

It is important to note that the police have other search powers to search premises in other enactments, for instance s.23 of the Misuse of Drugs Act 1971 gives the police a power to apply for a search warrant specifically for the purpose of searching for prohibited drugs. Under the Protection of Children Act 1978, the police can apply for a search warrant specifically relating to the discovery of pornographic images. Under s.55 of the Clean Neighbourhoods and Environment Act 2005 a Justice of the Peace can issue a warrant to an authorised officer to enter premises with reasonable force to silence an intruder alarm. It is important also to be aware of the wide definition given to premises in s.23 of PACE 1984 which means any place and includes (i) any vehicle, vessel, aircraft or hovercraft; (ii) any offshore installation; and (iii) any tent or movable structure.

Further, it is important to consider the statutory power of entry and search together with Code B of the Codes of Practice. A specific and separate power for a search warrant can be granted by a Justice of the Peace under s.42 of the Terrorism Act 2000 to search specified premises, if the Justice of the Peace is satisfied that there are reasonable grounds for suspecting that a person who the police reasonably suspect to be a person involved in the commission, preparation or instigation of acts of terrorism is to be found there.

It is important not to simply pass off a search warrant as a mere formality, any non-compliance with the statutory requirements may render the warrant invalid and the search unlawful. This point is well illustrated in *Redknapp v City of London Police* [2008] EWHC 1177, in which the High Court lamented the "slipshod" approach taken by the police in completing the pro-forma application. In this case the form had failed to identify the relevant s.8(3) condition. The Court did nonetheless state that the police were justified to widely describe the subject matter of the search. (See also *C v Chief Constable of 'A' Police* [2006] EWHC 2352.)

39. Two Types of Section 8 Warrant

14.46 One of the difficulties for the police was that they had to specify the premises in question and therefore the warrant's authority was limited to those specified premises, which meant that in having executed that warrant other information led to other premises, then these could be searched without another warrant or by using s.18. For all purposes, this was not effective or practicable, so Parliament dealt with this problem by passing s.113 of the SOCPA 2005, which amends s.8 to create two types of search warrant:

(i) *Specified premises warrant* (applies to one or more sets of premises specified in the warrant);

(ii) *All premises warrant* (any premises occupied or controlled by the person specified in the application, if the premises are not specified, then an inspector must give written authorisation for them to be entered).

If the application is for an all premises warrant, then the Justice of the Peace must be satisfied that because of the particulars of the alleged offence, there are reasonable grounds for believing that it is necessary to search the premises which are not specified in the application and that it is not reasonably practicable to specify these premises that might need to be searched. Section 114 further amends s.8 to allow a Justice of the Peace to include in the warrant a provision for "multiple entries" (i.e. to search the premises on more than one occasion) but only if this will achieve the purpose for which the warrant is issued. The number of searches can either be unlimited or limited to a maximum number. In *Redknapp v City of London Police* [2008] EWHC 1177 the High Court observed that there is nothing in s.8 to prevent the magistrates from granting one warrant including both types.

40. Relevant Safeguards

14.47 Section 15 provides a number of safeguards to the individual to protect against the arbitrary use of this highly intrusive power. In the application the police are under a duty to:

(i) state the reasons and grounds for the warrant;

(ii) state the enactment under which the warrant is to be issued;

(iii) specify the premises which need to be searched; and

(iv) "so far as is practicable" identity the articles or persons to be sought. Under s.8(3) the application is made "ex parte", this means without notice to any other interested party, i.e. the owner of the premises, who will be unaware of the application, cannot attend the hearing. If having heard evidence given on oath by the police, a warrant is issued then the warrant must specify the following:

(a) the name of the person to whom it applies;
(b) the date on which it was issued;
(c) the enactment under which it was issued;
(d) the premises to be searched;
(e) so far as is practicable the articles or persons to be sought.

In *Hepburn v CC of Thames Valley* [2002] EWCA Civ 1841, the police in executing an entry and search warrant (Misuse of Drugs Act 1971) at a public house for "drugs and related paraphernalia", prevented the claimant from leaving the premises, he was forcibly detained and searched but not arrested. The Court of Appeal rejected an appeal by the Chief Constable and held that since the warrant did not state that the police could stop and search persons therein the claimant had been falsely imprisoned by the police by refusing to allow him to leave. The Court also stated that there is "no foundation in law" for the police to contend that the detention of the claimant was in order to ensure that he was under control and wouldn't pose a threat or to make sure he was not in possession of drugs. Sedley L.J. made it clear that:

> "It is a bedrock of our liberties that a citizen's freedom of person and movement is inviolable except where the law unequivocally gives the state power to restrict it . . . nobody is required in this country to satisfy a police officer that he or she is not committing an offence. The power to detain and search arises only where conditions prescribed by law, typically a reasonably founded suspicion, can be shown to exist."

It was accepted in this case that the officer in question at the initial stage of the search could not have formed such suspicion. The claimant was an innocent member of the public having a pub lunch and simply wished to leave the premises. In *DPP v Meadon* [2004] 1 W.L.R. 945, a case stated appeal against the magistrates' decision to rule that there was no case to answer on a charge of assaulting a constable in the execution of his duty during a premise search, the High Court ruled that the magistrates' reliance on *Hepburn* was misplaced. The two cases were clearly distinguishable on the basis that, in this case, unlike *Hepburn*, the warrant applied to both premises and persons and s.117 entitled the police to use reasonable force, if necessary to exercise their powers. Therefore, provided no more force than was necessary was used, the police could restrict the movement of occupants on the premises being searched. The decision received further approval by the Court of Appeal in *Connor v Chief Constable of Merseyside* [2006] EWCA Civ 1549 (see also the decision of the ECHR in *Keegan v UK* [2006] E.C.H.R. 764).

41. Execution of Warrant within Three Months and Power to Seize

14.48 Section 16 sets out the procedure for the execution of the warrant and states that the search can only be to the extent required for the purpose for which the warrant was issued. The relevant protection is that the warrant should be executed at a reasonable hour, unless it appears to the constable that to search at a reasonable hour would frustrate the very purpose of the search itself. Before the police actually enter the premises for the purposes of a search, the constable must identify themselves to the occupier and if not in uniform, produce evidence to confirm who they are. The police must produce and serve a copy of the warrant on the occupier. If they don't then the execution of the warrant will be invalid (see *Redknapp v City of London Police* [2008] EWHC 1177).

This same information must be given to a person who is present, but is not the actual occupier, who is not there at that time. If there is no person(s) present, then the police must leave a copy of the warrant in a prominent place. When on the premises, the police will generally conduct a thorough search. An officer will be assigned to record all seized articles, the police must then endorse the actual warrant stating whether they found the articles or person sought in the warrant and whether they sized other articles not stated in the warrant. The warrant, whether executed or not, must be returned to the court and retained for 12 months during which the occupier can inspect it. Originally, the warrant had to be executed within a month, however the SOCPA 2005 has now extended this to a period of three months.

Code B of the Codes of Practice provides that the police must, unless it is impracticable to do so, provide the occupier with a notice of powers and rights and that the police must allow either a friend, neighbour or other person to witness the search, unless there are reasonable grounds to believe that their presence would "seriously hinder the investigation or endanger the officers or others". Moreover, para.6.10 provides:

> "Searches must be conducted with due consideration for the property and privacy of the occupier and with no more disturbance than necessary. Reasonable force may be used only when necessary and proportionate because the cooperation of the occupier cannot be obtained or is insufficient for the purpose."

When searching the premises s.8(2) gives the police the power to seize and retain anything for which the search was authorised. In *McDonagh* [2008] EWHC 654 the High Court ruled that the power of retention in s.8(2) is not a stand alone power and is clearly subject to the requirement of necessity contained in s.22 (see para.14.57).

42. Items Subject to "Legal Privilege": Power to "Seize and Sift"

14.49 Section 10 provides that communications and items disclosed between a legal professional and client in connection with giving legal advice, or in contemplation of legal proceedings or advice, amount to items subject to legal privilege. Nonetheless s.10(2) makes it clear that items held with an intention of furthering a criminal purpose do not form part of legal privilege (see *R. v (Hallinan Blackburn Gittings & Nott (a firm) v Middlesex Crown Court* [2005] 1 W.L.R. 766. Section 10 was addressed by the Court of Appeal in *R. v Chesterfied Justices Ex p. Bramley* [2000] 2 W.L.R. 409, and given a restrictive application. The Court of Appeal held that it was unlawful to seize material from the suspect's car dealership, in order to sift through it later, since material seized could be outside the scope of the warrant or, as in this case, be legal privilege material. The decision received criticism in terms of effective police operational duties as it would make some searches where the information is stored in computer software and discs impossible to perform.

Sections 50 to 66 of the Criminal Justice and Police Act 2001 and Schs 1 and 2, which came into force on April 1, 2003, overturned this decision and provided that the police could seize material where it was not reasonably practicable, while on the premises, for them to sort through it, to the extent required, or to separate it out into seizable and non seizable elements. The provisions state that several factors must be taken into consideration in the determination of when it was not reasonably practicable. These include the amount of time and personnel needed, the use of special equipment, the risk of damaging computer software in trying to separate the material, with a potential loss of relevant material. Once the police have sifted and separated the material then s.54 provides that the police are then under a duty to return it, unless it is inextricably linked to other material which is seizable. When the police are considering the use of this extensive power strict adherence must be given to Code B paras 7.7 to 7.12.

43. The Meaning of "Excluded Material"

14.50 Section 11 defines excluded material to be (i) personal records that have been acquired or created in the course of any trade, business, profession or other occupation or any paid or unpaid office, which is held in confidence; (ii) human tissue or fluid taken for medical treatment or diagnoses which is held in confidence; (iii) journalistic material which consists of documents or records that are held in confidence provided it is held subject to a continuous undertaking (promise), restriction or obligation since the material was acquired or created for the purposes of journalism. In regard to non-journalistic material, i.e. personal records, the material must be held subject to either an expressed or implied undertaking to hold in confidence or there is a restriction on disclosure or a statutory secrecy obligation. Section 12 gives a meaning to what amounts to personal records as being "documentary and other records" about an individual whether living or dead and in which their identity is revealed; and relating to their (i) physical or mental health; (ii) spiritual/personal welfare, counselling or assistance. In s.12 journalistic material means only material that is created or acquired for the purposes of journalism, or where a third person intends the recipient to use such material for the purposes of journalism.

44. The Meaning of "Special Procedure Material"

14.51 Section 14 gives a meaning to special procedure material as being material other than legally privileged or excluded material held in confidence and is acquired or created in the same circumstances as that for legal privilege material (i.e. bank account details). Special procedure material also includes journalistic material that does not amount to excluded material, i.e. not held in confidence. Subsection (3) deals specifically with material acquired by an employee from an employer in the course of their employment and material acquired by a company from an associated company. Such material will not amount to special procedure material unless it constituted such material immediately before being acquired, i.e. business accounts. If an employee creates material during the course of employment, such material will only constitute special procedure material if it would gain such status had the employer created it. Subsection (4) creates similar rules for company and associated company arrangements.

45. Access to either Excluded Material or Special Procedure Material

14.52 Section 9 provides that the police can, in accordance with Sch.1 apply to a circuit judge to order the release/search of either excluded material or special procedure material, for the purposes of a criminal investigation. Legal professional privilege material is therefore immune and not subject to any form of disclosure to the police. Schedule 1 allows a circuit judge either to make an order for the material to be produced to the police or for them to have access in a period not more than seven days from the order being made, or alternatively, to issue a warrant giving the police the authority to enter and search premises for such material and seize or retain, authorised by a warrant. Before a circuit judge can order the production or access to such material, they must be satisfied that the "sets of access conditions" are fulfilled.

There exist two sets of access conditions. In the first set of conditions, the judge must having reasonable grounds for believing that:

(i) an indictable offence has been committed;

(ii) such material is likely to be of substantial value to the investigation;

(iii) it is likely to be relevant evidence;

(iv) other methods of obtaining the material have proved unsuccessful; and

(v) it is in the public interest having regard to the benefit to the investigation and the circumstances in which the material is in possession of the person in question. The second set of access conditions relates to previous powers of search for such material in which a warrant could have been issued, which have been abolished under s.9(2) (i.e. such as the Theft Act 1968).

Paragraphs 7 to 11 deal with the procedure for applying for such an order and provide that an application must be made with notice (inter partes) to the interested parties. This notice must be served on the other by delivering it, or by leaving it at their address, or by registered/recorded post. Once served with the notice, the person is under a duty not to conceal, destroy or alter or dispose of such material without permission of the police, leave of the court, or dismissal or abandonment of the application. In respect of an application for a search warrant, in addition to the same two sets of access conditions, four further conditions in subsection (14) must also be fulfilled, where it is not practicable to be able to communicate to the person who can gain entry to the premises. Any person to whom either the order or the warrant applies who refuses or fails to comply with its terms can be dealt with as if they committed a contempt of court. In terms of costs of the application the judge has a discretion as to which party should burden the cost or make a no costs order.

The special procedure provisions received an extensive review by the Court of Appeal in *R. v Central Criminal Court Ex p. The Guardian* [2000] (unreported), in the context of human rights and self incrimination. The Court, on an application of judicial review against the making of a production order, ruled that the provisions did not breach the right against self incrimination, as explained in *R. v Hertfordshire County Council Ex p. Green Environment Industries Ltd* [2000] 1 All E.R. 773, since the "Guardian" was not compelled to produce incriminating material, simply to allow access, in a passive sense.

46. Entry and Search Without a Search Warrant: Section 17

14.53 Section 17 gives a wide power to the police to enter and search any premises for any of the specified purposes listed in the section as follows:

(i) executing a warrant of arrest or a warrant of commitment under s.76 of the Magistrates' Court Act 1980;

(ii) arresting a person for a indictable offence;

(iii) arresting a person for an offence under s.1 of the Public Order Act 1936, as amended, or offences relating to entering and remaining on property contained in s.6 to 8 or 10 of the Criminal Law Act 1977;

(iv) arresting for an offence under s.4 of the Public Order Act 1986 (fear or provocation of violence);

(v) failure to stop under s.172 of the Road Traffic Act 1988;

(vi) s.76 of the Criminal Justice and Public Order Act 1994 (failure to comply with interim possession order;

(vii) to arrest a child or young person who has been remanded or committed to local authority accommodation under s.23 of the Children and Young Persons Act 1969;

(viii) recapturing a person unlawfully at large from custody or whom a constable is pursuing;

(viiii) of saving life or limb or preventing damage to property.

O'Loughlin v Chief Constable of Essex [1998] 1 W.L.R. 374, was a case in which the court was concerned with the striking of a balance between the triangulation of competing interests, namely the power of the police to enter and search premises, the public interest in effective policing and the right of privacy and security to the occupier. The Court of Appeal stated that before using reasonable force to enter premises under s.17, the police should, unless the circumstances made it impossible, impracticable or undesirable, give any occupant present at the time, even if the occupant is obnoxious, the source and reason for exercising that power of entry.

Further s.81 of the Terrorism Act 2000 gives the police a power to enter and search any premises (including a container) if they reasonably suspect that they are occupied by a terrorist (defined in s.40).

47. Entry and Search After Arrest: Section 18

14.54 Section 18 gives a constable a power to enter and search any premises occupied or controlled by a person who is under arrest for an indictable offence, provided the constable has reasonable grounds for suspecting that there is evidence on the premises relating to the offence the person was arrested for, or to some other indictable offence which is connected with or similar to that offence. The power can only be exercised to the extent that it is reasonably required, in order to discover such evidence. Another safeguard is that before a constable can exercise this power, the authorisation of an inspector must first be obtained in writing.

However, this power can be exercised without the authorisation of a senior officer if before the detained person is taken to a police station and their presence at the place to be searched is necessary for the effective investigation of the offence. If this part of the power is used, the officer must inform the inspector as soon as is practicable. Once on the premises, the police under subsection (2) may retain and seize any evidence permitted by the section. An example for the use of s.18 is where the police arrest a person on suspicion of theft and deception offences and their previous antecedents show that the person is an habitual thief. Before interview it would be appropriate for the police to search the premises of the arrested person, since there are reasonable grounds to believe that other stolen items might be found on those premises or evidence relating to similar offences.

The application of s.18 was considered in *Odewale v DPP* [2000] (Unreported). The High Court, by way of case stated, allowed the appeal and quashed the conviction for assaulting a constable in the execution of his duty. The police arrested the appellant then took him to his flat and conduced a s.18 search, during which it was alleged the appellant assaulted one of the officers. The High Court ruled, applying the reasoning in *Riley v DPP* [1989] J.P. 453, and distinguishing *Kynaston v DPP* [1988] 87 Cr.App.R. 200, that the magistrates were wrong to infer that the appellant had been lawfully arrested, without any evidence being presented to the court as to what the appellant was arrested for, the matters which caused the police to arrest the appellant.

Accordingly, due to the lack of evidence surrounding the circumstances of the arrest, the police could not exercise their power of search under s.18, since the appellant had not been lawfully arrested, a clear condition for the operation of s.18. On a separate point, the High Court confirmed that the justices were entitled to accept the oral evidence of the police that they had the written authority under s.18(4) and that it was produced on search, "the mere fact that the document was not put in evidence is not fatal to the prosecution's case". Support for this proposition is found in *Linehan v DPP* [2000] Crim. L.R. 861. Accordingly, the oral evidence of the police without any written evidence being available to the court was sufficient to confirm that the relevant senior officer's authority had been granted.

In *Khan v Metropolitan Police* [2008] *The Times,* June 16, the Court of Appeal adopted a literal construction to the expression "occupied or controlled" and that unless the arrested person either legally occupies or controls the premises, then any subsequent search under s.18 would be unlawful. The Court rejected without merit the contention of the police that such an interpretation would render the provision unworkable and irrational since the police can utilise s.18 in circumstances where they have sufficient knowledge of occupation or control. In this case the arrested person had falsely given the address of the claimant (Khan) as being his own.

48. General Power of Seizure: Section 19

14.55 Provided a constable is lawfully on any premises s.19 states that they may seize anything on those premises, if they have reasonable grounds for believing that the item(s) was:

(i) obtained in consequence of the commission of an offence, or that it is evidence in relation to an offence which they are investigating, or any other offence; and

(ii) that it is necessary to seize it in order to prevent it being concealed, lost, damaged, altered or destroyed.

The constable can also require that information contained in a computer is be produced in a form in which it can be taken away and in which it is visible and legible, provided the constable has the same reasonable grounds set out above. Under s.21 the police must provide a record of what was seized from the premises to either the occupier, or a person who had control or custody of the item immediately before it was seized. Subsection (2) relates to access and copying of anything seized under any enactment, a record of what was seized must be provided. Section 20 extends this general power of seizure to include information in a computer.

49. Meaning of "Premises"

14.56 Section 23 gives a wide definition of premises for the purposes of entry and search and means any place, which includes any vehicle, vessel, aircraft or hovercraft; any tent or movable structure; and offshore installation.

50. Retention of Property Seized

14.57 Section 22 allows the police to retain anything seized under s.19 or under any other power of seizure for "so long as is necessary in all the circumstances". If seized for the purposes of a criminal investigation, then the items can be retained:

(i) for use as evidence at trial for an offence; or

(ii) for forensic examination; or

(iii) for the investigation in connection with an offence.

Under subsection (4) nothing above can be retained, if a photograph or a copy would be sufficient for that purpose. It is clear that the police only have a transitory power of retention and that once it is no longer necessary to retain the seized items for the purposes of a criminal investigation, they must be immediately returned to the lawful owner, otherwise a claim could be made under the Police (Property) Act 1897. (See *Gough v Chief Constable of West Midlands Police* [2004] EWCA Civ 206.)

51. Powers of Police Civilians

14.58 Part 4 of the Police Reform Act 2002 allows Chief Constables to appoint designated persons who have been suitably trained to perform certain police functions. The Community Support Officer is such a person. Schedule 4 sets out the police powers that are exercisable by the designated person. This was further amended with additional powers by Schs 8 and 9 of the Serious Organised Crime and Police Act 2005. An example is the power to issue penalty notices for a range of anti-social and public disorder offences, such as dropping litter, throwing fireworks, or being drunk in a public highway. If the offender refuses to give relevant details, then the CSO can require that person to wait for up to 30 minutes. If they make off, then a summary offence is committed. Section 7 of the Police and Justice Act 2006, which came into force on April 7, 2007, amends the PRA 2002, to remove the confusion that has developed within different police forces, as to the designated powers. The Police Reform Act 2002 (Standard Powers and Duties of Community Support Officers) Order 2007 (SI 2007/3202) lists 20 standard powers that can now be exercised by a CSO across England and Wales. These powers relate to anti-social behaviour, alcohol and tobacco powers; enforcement powers; environmental powers; transport powers; and security powers.

CHAPTER FIFTEEN

COMMENCEMENT OF PROCEEDINGS AND LEGAL FUNDING OF CRIMINAL CASES

1. COMMENCEMENT OF PROCEEDINGS: CHARGE, WRITTEN CHARGE OR SUMMONS (PART 7 OF THE CRIMINAL PROCEDURE RULES 2005)

15.01 There are three ways in which criminal proceedings may be commenced:

(i) If the suspect was arrested and in police custody then they will be charged with the appropriate offence and presented to the next available magistrates' court.

(ii) If, on the other hand, the offence in question does not require arrest, then the police will inform the offender that they will be reported for the alleged offence in question. The officer will then lay an information before the magistrates, who will then send a summons to the suspect giving notice for them to attend at the magistrates' court. This method of commencing proceedings is most commonly used with minor offences, usually road traffic offences and where a penalty notice is inappropriate.

(iii) Section 29 of the Criminal Justice Act 2003 when fully in force will abolish the summons procedure set out in (ii) and replace it with a written charge and requisition procedure. At the moment s.29 is only partially in force and being piloted in 18 specified Magistrates Courts.

The preparation of the case files is undertaken by the CPS, (created by the Prosecution of Offences Act 1985 (POA 1985) together with the Criminal Justice Unit at the relevant police station for that area. If the offender is to be charged at the police station, then the decision on the appropriate offence(s) is for the Crown Prosecution Service (CPS) based on the Code for Crown Prosecutors issued under s.10 of the POA 1985, which contains a two stage test:

The Evidential Test

15.02 This provides that the CPS must be satisfied that there is enough evidence to provide a "realistic prospect of conviction". This is an objective test, which means that a jury or a bench of magistrates properly directed on the law is more likely than not to convict. The CPS must consider what the defence case may be and how it is likely to affect the prosecution's case. Other considerations are the reliability and admissibility of evidence.

In *R. v G* [2008] UKHL 37 the House of Lords by a majority of 3 to 2 ruled that the discretionary decision of the CPS to choose the offence(s) to be charged based on an assessment of the evidence available does not engage art.8 and therefore does not interfere with a defendant's right to a private life. If the decision to prosecute a particular offence is unduly harsh, then any unfairness from that should be remedied through the ordinary procedures of the criminal justice system, not human rights. In this case, the Court of Appeal had quashed the defendant's sentence of 12 months' detention and training order and substituted a conditional discharge. In a powerful dissenting judgment, Lord Hope felt that whilst the initial decision to charge the 15-year-old defendant with rape of a child under 13 contrary to s.5 of the Sexual Offences Act 2003 was appropriate; when the complainant later changed her evidence to suggest she had in fact consented and had falsely represented her age, the decision of the prosecution to continue with the s.5 offence and their refusal to substitute the more appropriate lesser offence found in s.13 which covers sexual offences committed by those under 18 was a choice that interfered with the defendant's right to a private life as being disproportionate to the actual unlawfulness of his conduct.

The Public Interest Test

15.03 This involves the CPS considering a number of "public interest" factors, either in favour for or against a prosecution. This includes taking into account the consequences of any decision for the complainant.

The CPS has essentially an unfettered discretion, subject to the principle of state immunity (see the State Immunity Act 1978 and *R. (Alamleyeseigha) v CPS* [2005] EWHC 2704 on whether or not to continue with a criminal prosecution, based on the public interest test). It is this unfettered discretion that has led to criticism of the CPS concerning the number (25,000 in 2006) of cases discontinued under the Prosecution of Offences Act 1985. For some offences, it is a statutory requirement that before a prosecution can be commencement the consent of the Director of Public Prosecutions (DPP) must first be obtained. Two notable examples are s.1(3) of the Protection of Children Act 1978 which requires the consent of the DPP for proceedings to be commenced in regard to an offence involving indecent photographs of children. Likewise s.7 of the Public Order Act 1986 provides that the consent of the DPP must be obtained before proceedings can be commenced for the offence of riot. In reality, this decision is taken by the Crown Prosecutor for the relevant area. However, if the case is of particular public importance then the DPP will make the decision. Neither the police, nor the CPS owes any duty of care to the victim of a crime when determining whether or not to prosecute. However, a claim can be made for judicial review of a decision not to prosecute based on *Wednesbury* reasonableness (see *R (DPP) Ex p. Manning* [2001] 1 Q.B. 330).

If the CPS decides not to prosecute, then a complainant can commence a private prosecution. In *R. (Charlson) v Guildford Magistrates' Court* [2006] EWHC 2318 the High Court ruled that the magistrates' decision to refuse to issue a summons for death by dangerous driving was flawed, having failed to apply the correct test and stating there had to be "special circumstances". In bringing a private prosecution, the informant, unlike the CPS, did not have to satisfy the evidential and public interest test. The criterion is much less onerous for a private prosecution. The magistrates should determine: (i) does the allegation reveal an offence known to law and if so was there prima facie evidence to establish the ingredients of the offence, (ii) is the summons out of time, (iii) does the court have jurisdiction, (iv) does the informant have the proper authority to prosecute? The Court further observed that the commentary in "Stones Justice Manual" on the test concerning private prosecutions needed to be reviewed in the light of this decision.

It is important to note that the decision to prosecute or discontinue with proceedings is the exclusive decision of the CPS. In *Attorney-General's Reference (No.2 of 2000)* [2001] 1 Cr.App.R. 503, the Court of Appeal gave the opinion on a point of law under s.36 of the CJA 1972, that the prosecution has a right to present its case to the jury. The judge has no power to intervene and withdraw the case before the evidence is presented. To have such a power would be to trespass upon the unfettered discretion of the CPS to bring proceedings. Only if there are defects in the indictment or there is an abuse of process can the case be stopped before being presented to the jury. Otherwise the jury have a right to form their own view of the evidence without the judge. Nonetheless, after the conclusion of the prosecution's case the defence may make a submission of no case to answer, for which the judge does have a power to withdraw the case in the interests of justice. Alternatively, if after arraignment the prosecution propose to offer no evidence, the court at its discretion can order that a not guilty verdict is entered without the need for the defendant being put in charge of the jury.

15.04 Alternatively, if the offender has not been arrested and is therefore not in police custody then the offender may be presented to the magistrates' court by the issuing of a summons. The police officer will inform the offender that they will be reported for the alleged offence and will in due course receive a summons in the post to that effect. To commence proceedings by way of summons the police officer will draft an "information" which is sent to the Clerk to the Justices at the local magistrates' court who must then decide whether the information discloses an offence known in law and check any time limitations. Section 1 of the Magistrates' Court Act 1980 and Pt 7 of the CrPR 2005 provide for the laying of an information before a Justice of the Peace, who may issue a summons directed to the defendant requiring them to appear before the magistrates' court to answer to the information (description of the offence(s)). If the Clerk to the Justices acknowledges that there is an answerable offence, then a signed summons will be issued which is served in accordance with Pt 4 of the CrPR 2005 upon the defendant by post, stating that they must attend court at a specified time.

Section 29 of the Criminal Justice Act 2003 which is at the moment only partially in force and being piloted in 18 specified Magistrates, Court (see The Criminal Justice Act 2003 (Commencement No.16) Order 2007 SI 1999 will abolish the summons procedure (except for private prosecutions) and replace this method of instituting criminal proceedings by giving a public prosecutor the authority to issue a document called a written charge, which sets out the offence(s) the accused is charged with. A public prosecutor is defined in s.29(5) and includes the police or a person authorised by them, the CPS and other prosecuting authorities, i.e. the Customs and Excise.

At the same time as issuing the written charge, the prosecutor must also issue a requisition which directs the accused to appear at a specified date and time at the relevant Magistrates' Court, to answer the written charge(s). Section 30 gives the power to make the necessary rules as to the form and content of the prescribed documents. Further, the s.29 procedure does not affect the power of a public prosecutor to lay information on oath before the Magistrates, in order to obtain a warrant of arrest to bring the accused suspected of offence before the court under s.1 of the Magistrates Court Act 1980. The method of issuing will be the same as currently for summons and the 6 month time limit for summary only offences will still apply. The purpose of the new procedure is to remove the administrative role of issuing proceedings from the Magistrates and giving the primary responsibility to the public prosecutor, who is more likely to bring the appropriate charge. Likewise, the new procedure simplifies matters together with the use of more straightforward and understandable terminology.

If service by post is not appropriate, then personal service can be used or service by substitution, whereby the summons is served on a third person who can pass the summons on to the defendant. Both methods amount to effective service of the summons, which will be deemed to have been served properly. It is important to be aware of s.127, which places a statutory time limitation on the issuing of a summons for a summary offence. This prevents the trial of an offence, unless the information was laid within six months from the time when the offence(s) was committed. To proceed to trial when a summons is out of time will clearly amount to an abuse of process and the proceedings will in consequence be stayed. (See also *Atkinson v DPP* [2005] 1 W.L.R. 96.)

The High Court in *DPP v Baker* [2004] EWHC 2797 ruled that if the offence involves a course of conduct, then for the purposes of the time limit, the last incident will be that from which the six-month limit is calculated. Once the time limit has elapsed, it would be an abuse to commence proceedings (see *R. v Ashton and Others* [2006] EWCA Crim 794). For further guidance see also *R. v Scunthorpe Justices Ex p. McPhee and Gallagher* [1998] 162 J.P. 635 and *R. v Thames Magistrates Ex p. Stevens* [2000] 164 J.P. 283. It is important to note that some offences can only be prosecuted within a specified statutory time, see for example s.19 of the Trade

Descriptions Act 1968 and *R. (Donnachie) v Cardiff Magistrates' Court* [2008] EWHC 1846.

Provided the magistrates' court is satisfied that a summons has been served properly (rule 4.2 of the CrPR 2005 provides that proof of service is by a solemn declaration made by the relevant person) on the person stated in it, then should the accused subsequently fail to attend at the magistrates' court as directed the court may in accordance with s.11 proceed in their absence, provided the prosecutor is in attendance. It is acceptable provided there is justification to do so for the defendant's solicitor to appear on behalf of the client.

15.05 Alternatively, the court can adjourn the proceedings and issue a warrant of arrest authoring the local police to execute the warrant by arresting the defendant. The warrant in these circumstances will either be "backed for bail", or without bail. If the warrant is backed for bail, this requires the police, having arrested the defendant, to release them on bail to appear at the magistrates' court at a specified time and date. If the warrant is not backed for bail, then the police are required to present the defendant to the magistrates in custody. If the warrant is executed in the day, then it may be possible for the defendant to be presented that day (including Saturday morning court). If however, the warrant is executed in the evening or at the weekend, then the defendant will have to remain in custody until the next available court (this includes bank holidays). In practice the legal adviser may get a call from the client who is wanted on a warrant, it is the solicitors' duty to advise the client that they must hand themselves in at the first opportunity to the police station, regardless of the time of day.

If the accused appears but the prosecutor does not, then s.15 gives the magistrates a discretionary power to dismiss the case against the accused. This point was considered in *DPP v Shuttleworth* [2002] EWHC 621, in which the defendant had attended in person for an offence of careless driving to which she intended to plead guilty. Although the prosecutor was in attendance the file was missing. The magistrates allowed a short adjournment for the file to be located, it was not, and the case was dismissed. The High Court ruled that that the words, "does not appear" include a situation where the prosecutor is present but is unable to proceed with the case. However, the magistrates were wrong to dismiss since there was sufficient information to proceed. Giving general observations, Evans J. acknowledged the frustration caused by a missing file and the unnecessary delay it may cause, but that the purpose of s.15 should not be used punitively or to discipline the CPS. The court should consider a costs order against the defaulting party and the legitimate expectations of the defendant had to be dealt with promptly. Section 123 of the MCA 1980 gives the prosecution a power to amend or withdraw the original charge, or alternatively to invite the magistrates to allow additional charges.

2. Pleading Guilty by Post: Section 12 of the Magistrates' Courts Act 1980

15.06 A quick and effective method of disposing of a uncontested adult summary case is giving the defendant the opportunity to plead guilty by post, without the need for attendance at the magistrates' court. The procedure is set out in s.12 of the Magistrates' Courts Act 1980 and provides that a guilty plea by post is permissible for offences, which do not have a sentence of more than three months imprisonment. Accordingly, it is not possible to plead guilty by post for theft, even if minor in terms of value, since the offence of theft carries a maximum of seven years' imprisonment. An example would be the offence of careless driving contrary to s.3 of the Road Traffic Act 1988, since the offence is punishable by way of a fine. Accordingly, for this offence, the offender can if they wish, plead guilty by post.

The procedure is as follows: a summons is served on the offender together with a statement of facts and another form, which both explains and enables the defendant to plead guilty and give a statement in mitigation. This is returned to the court within 14 days of the summons being issued, together with driving licence if appropriate. At this point the court can, under s.162 of the CJA 2003, make a "financial circumstances order". This requires the individual to give within a specified time a statement of their financial circumstances. Failure to do so without reasonable excuse amounts to a summary offence. On the listed date the statement of facts and mitigation are then read out to the court by the clerk, the prosecutor need not be present. The court can then accept the plea of guilty and impose sentence, or alternatively may adjourn the matter. The court can take into account any previous summary convictions of the defendant, but it may not pass a custodial sentence in the absence of the accused, nor impose any disqualifications, except after adjournment and the accused having been notified to attend.

3. Legal Funding of Criminal Cases

15.07 The funding of criminal cases is administered by the Criminal Defence Service (CDS) under the control of the Legal Services Commission (LSC). Only those firms that have a criminal contract (General Criminal Contract) with the LSC are eligible to seek funding of criminal work. In order to be granted a contract, the firm must first apply to the LSC, who will then consider whether the firm satisfactorily achieves a number of competency requirements. The unified contract consists of many standard terms and conditions, as with any contract. The statutory framework for the funding of criminal cases is found in the Access to Justice Act 1999 and the many regulations created under it. The funding of criminal cases arises in the following situations:

(i) police station advice and assistance court duty solicitor;

(ii) free initial advice;

(iii) representation in criminal proceedings (magistrates' court and Crown Court;

(iv) in very high cost cases;

(v) recovery of defence costs order;

(vi) appeal preparation in the Court of Appeal. It is not intended to give a detailed review of the funding requirements, but simply to explain the procedure for applying for funding.

At each stage of legal funding, the solicitor will need to complete the appropriate standard form which must be submitted to the CDS. It is worth noting that the current cost of criminal legal funding is around £1.9 billion a year, which has increased every year over the last 10 years. It is against this background the there is now in place a whole new framework of how funding for criminal cases is administrated. The Government first looked at a new approach by appointing Lord Carter to look into new ways of reducing costs and improving quality of service. This review led to the controversial report entitled "Legal Aid A Market Based Approach to Reform" which was published in July 2006. The foundations of the reforms to State procurement of legal funding are based on a market approach to ensuring better quality of service and value of money. The report made 62 recommendations which will result in a suggested saving of £100 million. The Department for Constitutional Affairs soon afterwards published in November 2006 its proposals in the command paper entitled Legal Aid Reform: the Way Ahead (Cm. 6993).

4. At the Police Station: Advice and Assistance and the Duty Solicitor Scheme

15.08 Section 58 of the Police and Criminal Evidence Act 1984 provides for the fundamental right of access to free legal advice and assistance whilst in police detention. To this effect, reg.4 of the Criminal Defence Service (General) (No.2) Regulations 2001 sets out the regulatory framework for the giving of advice and assistance at the police station. It is important to be aware that police station advice and assistance can be given either by the duty solicitor or the client's own solicitor, or a police station accreditation representative, (the PSAR can not assist a suspect who is under arrest for an indictable only offence).

The 2001 Regulations state that advice and assistance can be provided to a client who is (i) arrested and in custody at the police station, (ii) a volunteer or (iii) a member of the armed forces, (iv) detained under the Terrorism Act, (v) involved in a video identification parade. In the above circumstances, advice and assistance is available free and no issue of eligibility arises. In addition, advocacy assistance can be given in the magistrates' court in connection with an application for a warrant of further detention under ss.43 and 44 of PACE 1984 or under the Terrorism Act 2000. Police station advice and assistance is defined as (i) police station attendance, and (ii) police station telephone advice.

The administration for the giving of advice at the police station is governed by the duty solicitor scheme. The Duty Solicitor Arrangements 2001 provide for the selection and discipline of the duty solicitor and also the administration of the Duty Solicitor Scheme. All duty solicitors have to be accredited under stage 1 of the Law Society's Criminal Litigation Accreditation Scheme. All areas in England and Wales have local scheme arrangements with their own requirements, such as a limit on time travel to the police station. A solicitor can apply for membership of additional schemes. Since January 14, 2008, all requests by a detained person for legal advice must be allocated through the Defence Solicitor Call Centre (DSCC). Payment for police station advice and attendance is based on a localised standard fee relevant to that area's needs and requirements.

The client has a choice either to ask for the duty solicitor or alternatively, request their own regular solicitor, who will be paid under the duty scheme. If the DSCC can not make contact with the client's own solicitor within two hours, then the duty solicitor will be sent. Once a solicitor has been contacted concerning a client in custody, the initial steps are to first speak to the custody sergeant to establish what the alleged offence the client is in custody for and to record the time of arrest and time of detention. The next step is to speak to the client to determine the brief circumstances and to advise them to say nothing until they (the solicitor) arrive. Finally, the solicitor will against need to speak to the custody sergeant and request that the client is not interviewed until their attendance at the police station.

However, if the client is (i) detained for a non-imprisonable offence, (ii) arrested on a bench warrant (iii) arrested on suspicion for a drink driving offence, (iv) detained for breach of bail conditions, then only telephone advice can be given, unless one of several exceptions apply namely (i) the client complains of maltreatment or (ii) the "sufficient benefits" test is satisfied, i.e. the client would benefit from advice before and during interview, the client is a youth, or to advise on the implication of a caution. From April 21, 2008 all telephone only advice cases are to be forwarded to the CDS direct to provide the necessary advice. There also exists the Court Duty Scheme, which is available to a charged person who attends at the magistrates' court, without having previously had legal advice. They can if they wish, seek free advice from the duty solicitor.

5. Representation in Criminal Proceedings before the Criminal Courts (Part IV 38 CrPR 2005 and Part 76 Criminal Practice Directions)

15.09 The payment of advice and assistance at the police station is limited to those proceedings. Once the suspect is charged and appears before the magistrates as a defendant, the solicitor will now need to make an application for a representation order to cover proceedings, before the magistrates' court in the first instance. The issue that arises concerning representation in the magistrates' court, is whether a charged person is eligible for legal funding that will cover the whole of the proceeding. Section 21 of the Access of Justice Act 1999 defines "criminal proceedings" as:

(i) proceedings before any court for dealing with an individual accused of an offence, conviction of an offence, binding over for breach of the peace, or a criminal appeal contempt of court;

(ii) certain civil proceedings, i.e. proceedings under ss. 2, 5, 6 of the Anti-Social Behaviour Act 2003.

6. Eligibility for Funding in Criminal Proceedings

15.10 If the case falls within the meaning of "criminal proceedings", then under Regulation 3(2) of the Criminal Defence Service (General) (No.2) Regulations 2001 a client has right to representation, (a Representation Order) provided they are eligible to make such an application. Representation further extends to "any related bail proceedings and any preliminary or incidental proceedings". This will include the s.51 procedure of sending an indictable only offence to the Crown Court. A Representation Order will only be granted to a charged person if they are eligible. To be eligible, two sets of criteria must be satisfied:

The Interests of Justice Test (Merits Test)

15.11 This requires an assessment of whether it is in the interests of justice that this person should be granted a publicly funded representation order. This covers:

(a) the nature and seriousness of the offence;

(b) likely to lose liberty (does not include community sentence);

(c) likely to lose livelihood;

(d) likely to suffer serious damage to reputation;

(e) substantial question of law involved;

(f) unable to understand court proceedings or state their own case.

Means Test

15.12 Since the passing of the Criminal Defence Service Act 2006, which came into force on October 2nd, 2006, any applicant for criminal funding must also satisfy a means test based on income and capital. The means test is calculated to include the client to make a contribution to their legal costs. With the means test, government policy has gone full circle. It was originally abolished in order to speed up proceedings, given that the vast majority of criminal applicants had no or limited income. However, this led to applications being granted even to defendants with an income and did not result in any reduction in the public cost for legal funding. For this reason, the means test was re-introduced. Both tests must be satisfied before a Representation Order will be granted. However, the means test does not apply to defendants under 18 years (see The Criminal Defence Service (Financial Eligibility) Regulations 2006 (SI 2006/2492) and also SI 2007/2936 and 2937).

7. How is an Application Made and to Whom?

15.13 The applicant must complete form (CDS14) "Application for Legal Aid in Criminal Proceedings", which includes the interests of justice test. This form, together with the CDS 1 client details form and CDS 15 Financial Statement to Support (the applicant, i.e. client must sign the declaration of truth in the form), must then be submitted to the court. Any work undertaken by a solicitor before this application is submitted can be claimed under the "early cover" system. Since the Criminal Defence Service Act 2006, the responsibility for deciding whether or not to grant a representation order has been transferred to the Legal Service Commission from the court. It is promised that 90 per cent will be processed by 5pm on the date submitted, 99 per cent by the third day and 100 per cent within five days. The applicant can appeal against any refusal decision of the LSC.

8. The Representation Order and Fees

15.14 Once a Representation Order has been granted, it will cover the cost of the following types of legal work by the solicitor:

Preparation

15.15 Proper and full preparation of a client's case is vital if the client's case is to be presented properly before the court with all points and issues being fully explored and the prosecution's case being probed and scrutinised for consistency, accuracy and reliability. Preparation work therefore includes, taking instructions, interviewing witnesses, ascertaining the prosecution case, advising on plea and mode of trial and preparing and perusing documents. Also, dealing with letters and telephone calls, preparing for advocacy, instructing counsel and expert witnesses, conferences, consultations, reviews and work done in connection with advice on appeal or case stated. If an expert/medical report is required then before such work can be undertaken the solicitor must first obtain from the CDS "prior authority" to instruct the expert.

Advocacy

15.16 Just as important as preparation work, is advocacy, in terms of proper and effective presentation of the client's case in court. The representation order will cover work before the magistrates' court. If however the matter is either transferred or committed to the Crown Court, then the magistrates will grant a "Through Order" to cover the work in the Crown Court. The fees paid under a representation order in the magistrates court is paid on a standard fee basis. A standard fee is payable for "a case" which includes all work carried out in the magistrates' court. The fee is comprised of two elements (i) core costs, which covers all the work done by the solicitor, (ii) travel and waiting time. Standard fees fall into one of three categories dependent upon the stage the case reached, such as guilty pleas and cracked trials. Funding for cases before the Crown Court has radically changed based on a Litigators' Graduated Fee Scheme (LGFS) for solicitors, which came in to effect on January 14, 2008 (see the Criminal Defence Service (Funding) (Amendment) Order 2007 (SI 2007/3552 and SI 2007/1174).

Payment will be calculated against a number of variables based on (i) the nature of the offence, (ii) plea, (iii) length of trial, (iv) number of pages of prosecution evidence (PPE) and (v) number of defendants. Dependant on what happens, there is a tabular list of cuts offs for the number of PPE. Disbursements and travelling costs will be paid separately. The process of payment is done online through the Crown Court Litigator Fee online system. For barristers, there is a similar scheme in place. Certain matters attract a fixed rate such as an appeal against sentence from the magistrates' court is £340.43 whilst for appeal against sentence is £127.66. The payment reforms have abolished the previous system of being paid, based on a hourly rate to the complexity and volume of the case.

As part of the Carter Commission reforms restrictions have been placed on those criminal cases that may generate very high costs. A very High Cost case is defined in the Criminal Defence Service (General) (No.2) (Amendment No.3) Regulations 2007 (SI 2007/3550) which came into effect on January 14, 2008 as one which in the opinion of the Commission, if the matter proceeded to trial, would likely to last for more than 40 days, or if trial is likely to last between 25 and 40 days but the Commission considers it a case to be more suitably dealt with under the contractual arrangements of a high costs case.

Only solicitors who are members of the Very High Cost Case (Crime) Panel for the Crown Court can undertake the representation of a client for such cases. This would mean that a solicitor who represents a client at the police station but is not on the panel, would have to transfer the case to another firm who is. The purpose of the panel is to create a specialist pool of firms with experience of such cases, who by accepting a reduction in costs, would in return receive more cases. The LSC Complex Crime Unit is responsible for the arrangements under the scheme. A solicitor who granted a representation order must notify the unit as soon as it appears, (this will be based on all the factors in the case, i.e. nature of offence) that the case is likely to become a very high cost. A stage plan will then be drafted and agreed. The method of payment is based on a pre-event hourly rate calculation as opposed to a post event bill.

9. Advice and Assistance at the Office

15.17 The solicitor can claim for basic initial advice and assistance provided to a client at the office. This will cover the cost for two hours worth of work, such as taking instructions, drafting an initial letter and preparing the case in readiness for the next court appearance. This usually arises where a client simply walks in off the street, having been charged or reported for an offence. The solicitor will complete a standard form, with a simple means test based on disposable income. The client signs a declaration of truth on their earnings and that they have not previously had advice for the same legal point.

10. Recovery of Defence Costs (Part 77 of the Criminal Practice Directions)

15.18 In line with government policy to reduce the cost of legal funding, the court under s.17 of the Access to Justice Act 1999 and the Criminal Defence Service (Recovery of Defence Costs Orders) Regulations 2001, which came into force on April 2, 2001, now has a discretionary power to make the defendant pay some or all of the costs of any representation funded for them by the LSC.

11. The Public Defender Service

15.19 A further initiative to improve quality and a value for money criminal funding system, was the creation under the Access to Justice Act 1999 of the Public Defender Service, which is currently based in four locations. It is part of the Criminal Defence Service and is therefore a public state agency. The PDS consists of solicitors and accredited representatives who are directly employed by the LSC. The purpose of the PDS is to provide independent, high quality and value of money criminal defence services to the public. This means that a charged defendant rather than use the services of a private firm of solicitors, can approach the PDS directly for advice and representation. Accordingly, the State both prosecutes and also provides a defence service funded by the State with those who provide the service being employed by the State.

CHAPTER SIXTEEN

MAGISTRATES' AND YOUTH COURT PROCEDURE

1. RULES OF PROCEDURE AND THE GENERAL POWER OF ADJOURNMENT

16.01 The magistrates' court is an important court, in the sense that it deals with 95 per cent of all criminal cases. All defendants, regardless of the offence(s) they are charged with, will make at least one appearance at the magistrates' court. The procedural steps a defendant will take depend on the classification of offence, i.e. whether they are charged with a summary only, either way or indictable only offence. The magistrates' court itself is administered by the Magistrates' Courts Act 1980 (MCA 1980) and the Criminal Procedure Rules 2005 (CrPR 2005).

It is important also to be aware that the magistrates have assistance in the "Adult Court Bench Book", produced by the Judicial Studies Board and also sentencing guidance for the most common offences encountered by the magistrates' court (the guidance is currently being reviewed by the Sentencing Guideline Council). The guidance gives the magistrates an entry point for the appropriate sentence, i.e. custodial or non-custodial sentence. This is then either increased or decreased, taking into account a non-exhaustive list of aggravating and mitigating factors. These guidelines are especially important and useful when the magistrates are determining "allocation" for an either way offence, or for committal to the Crown Court for sentence. The case management procedure for the magistrates' court is set out clearly in Pt V.56 of the CrPR 2005 and it is advised that reference is made to the rules in their entirety as and where appropriate, as the case requires.

In order to administer their time and resources effectively, the magistrates have a general power to adjourn proceedings under s.10 of the MCA 1980. If the magistrates refuse to allow an application for an adjournment, by either party, then there is a risk of unfairness and a potential breach of natural justice and in particular a breach of art.6, a right to a fair trial, against the defendant. The court must always consider the "triangulation of interests." In *DPP v Abergavenny Justices* [2002] EWHC 206, the Divisional Court quashed a decision of the magistrates to refuse to allow an application by the CPS to adjourn the case and reviewed the main authorities as set out in *R. v Neath and Port Talbot* [2000] 1 W.L.R. 1376. Of particular importance is the observation of Lord Bingham in *R. v Hereford Magistrates' Court Ex p. Rowlands* [1997] 2 W.L.R. 854 that:

> "This court will only interfere with the exercise of the justices discretion whether to grant an adjournment in cases where it is plain that a refusal will cause substantial unfairness to one of the parties. Such unfairness may arise when a defendant is denied a full opportunity to present its case. But neither defendants nor their legal advisors should be permitted to frustrate the objective of a speedy trial without substantial grounds. Applications for adjournments must be subjected to rigorous scrutiny."

Similarly in *R. v Swansea Justices Ex. p. DPP* [1990] 154 J.P. 709 the Divisional Court stated:

> "In the context of adjournments the justices will, in order to maintain this balance of fairness, wish to take into account all the circumstances including the practicability to one side or the other of putting forward his or her case adequately if the adjournment is refused. The court will also want to consider questions such as the passage of time, also whether this is the first or only one of many occasions on which an indulgence by way of adjournment has been requested, and also whether the party asking for the adjournment is in fault in not being in a position to proceed at once. I emphasise in relation to the latter consideration that it is only one of the factors to be taken into account. The power to refuse an adjournment is not a disciplinary power to be exercised for the purpose of punishing slackness on the part of one of the participants in the trial. The power to adjourn is there so that they shall have the best opportunity of giving the fairest available hearing to the parties."

(see also the Court of Appeal ruling in *R. v Chaaban* [2003] EWCA Crim 1012.

It is important that the advocate should apply for an adjournment if the client's case is not ready to proceed to the next stage and base the adjournment on the need to ensure fairness for the defendant. However, it must be remembered that the court will not entertain an application where this would result in unnecessary delay, or for tactical reasons, such as to allow a fruitless fishing expedition, i.e. to locate unknown witnesses. Further, the High Court will not generally entertain an application to review a decision on adjournment, as explained in *Lauderdale v Mid Sussex Magistrates' Court* [2005] EWHC 2854.

2. Early Proceedings in the Magistrates' Court

16.02 Following an extensive review into the efficiency of proceedings in the magistrates' court by Martin Narey, the Crime and Disorder Act 1998 (CDA 1998) was passed and introduced a more effective early procedure system into the magistrates' court, increasing the power of the justices' clerk to act alone. One of the innovations was the creation under s.50 of the CDA 1998 of the Early Administrative Hearings (EAH) and the Early First Hearing (EFH), colloquially known as the "Narey court". Where the accused has been charged with an offence at the police station and makes their first appearance at the magistrates, they can be dealt with by either a single magistrate or a justices' clerk acting as a single justice. The matters to be dealt with at a EAH will be whether the accused wishes to receive legal funding and if so, eligibility of such funding will be determined.

A single justice can exercise any other powers they have when acting in a single capacity. Before concluding the EAH, the single justice may remand the accused either in custody or on bail. For a justices' clerk, they cannot remand in custody, but can remand on bail with conditions. Conversely, at a EFH the issue in question is whether the case is going to be a contested matter or not and to proceed, as far as possible with the case. Which ever hearing is used, the first step is to identify the defendant and then put the allegation to them. The next step is dependant upon the classification of the offence to which the defendant is alleged to have committed. An adjournment will usually follow, but it is quite possible, if the defendant pleads guilty, for example, to being drunk and disorderly for the court to impose a sentence, such as a conditional discharge, or a fine, bringing the matter to a quick and speedy conclusion.

3. Procedure where the Offence is Summary Only

16.03 If the offence is a summary only offence, then under s.9 of the MCA 1980, the defendant will be asked to enter a plea. If a plea of not guilty is entered, then the normal course would be for the magistrates to exercise their power under s.10 of the MCA 1980 and adjourn the matter for summary trial, or to a pre-trial review. If a guilty plea is entered, then under s.9(3), the magistrates would normally convict without hearing the evidence and proceed to sentence or if appropriate, adjourn to a later date. The prosecution is under no duty either at common law, or by statute, to disclose witness statements or other information of its case to the defence, in advance of trial. Nevertheless the prosecution are under a duty to disclose relevant material that in their opinion undermines the prosecution case, or assists the defence (primary disclosure).

However, a failure to disclose could lead to unfairness for the defence and a breach of Article 6, a right to a fair trial. In *R. v Stratford Justices Ex. p. Imbert* [1999] 2 Cr.App.R. 276, the Divisional Court ruled that there is no general right to advance information in summary only proceedings and that a failure to disclose does not breach art.6, since the magistrates can still ensure that the defendant receives a fair trial. The absolute right is to a fair trial; failure of pre-trial disclosure does not automatically render the proceedings unfair, so as to be an abuse of process. However the court stated obiter that disclosure ought to be made, unless there are good reasons not to do so.

4. The Procedure for an Indictable Either Way Offence

16.04 If the offence is an either way offence, then a different procedure will be followed to that for a summary offence. It is important for this reason to be sure that the offence the client is charged with is classified as an either way offence. Having made an appearance at the Narey Court the matter is usually adjourned for the next hearing, known as a "Plea before Venue" hearing (PBV) which, dependant on outcome at that hearing, will be followed by a "Mode of Trial" hearing. The creation of the PBV was another initiative designed to make the initial procedures more efficient in terms of cost and time and therefore reduce delay where possible.

5. Plea Before Venue Proceedings

16.05 If the defendant who has attained the age of 18 years old is charged with a either-way offence then the matter after the EAH will be to adjourn for the Plea before Venue procedure, introduced by s.49 of the Criminal Procedure and Investigations Act 1996, into ss.17 to 20 of the Magistrates' Courts Act 1980, which must be followed. The next stage is dependant on whether the defendant indicates a guilty or not guilty plea. The procedure is as follows:

Duty of the Clerk

16.06 The clerk will ask the defendant to indicate their plea if the matter were to proceed to trial. The defendant can either indicate they would plead guilty, or not guilty to this request or simply remain silent and refuse to give such an indication.

Defendant Indicates a "Guilty Plea" Proceed to Sentence

16.07 If the defendant indicates guilty, s.17A(6) provides that the magistrates must deal with the matter as if there had been a *"summary trial of the information"* from the outset. The court will then hear representations from the prosecution and the defence. The prosecution will outline the factual evidence of the case, the defence will then make a plea in mitigation. Having heard such representations, the court must determine whether or not they have sufficient powers to sentence, or alternatively commit the defendant to the Crown Court for sentence under s.3 of the Power of Criminal Courts (Sentencing) Act 2000. To assist in the determination of this decision, the court has access to sentence guidance produced by the Magistrates' Court Association, for the most commonly encountered offences.

Nevertheless, the guidelines are exactly that and both the magistrates and indeed the CPS and defence, must be alive to the fact of changes in sentencing policy. This is exactly what occurred in *R. (DPP) v Devizes Magistrates' Court* [2006] EWHC 1072. The High Court felt compelled to quash the sentencing decision of the magistrates who after the defendant had pleaded guilty to simple possession of heroin and cannabis, that had been found on him on his return to prison from temporary release, accepted jurisdiction to sentence. The DPP challenged this decision as being "truly astonishing" and irrational, given the clear sentencing guidance handed down by the Court of Appeal in *R. v Roberts* [1997] 2 Cr.App.R. (s) 187, in which 15 months was the appropriate length of sentence for this type of offence.

If the magistrates determine that they have sufficient powers to sentence, then they will either impose sentence or adjourn for reports to be prepared. The introduction of the PBV gives the defendant an early opportunity to admit guilt and have the matter dealt with quickly. Also, it is important as a practitioner to advise the defendant of the benefit of up to one-third reduction in sentence for pleading guilty. This is especially significant if the magistrates accept they have sufficient powers to sentence, since their powers of sentencing are limited to six months' imprisonment and/or a fine up to a maximum of £5,000 (subject to change in s.154 of the CJA 2003; yet to be brought into force).

Defendant Indicates a not Guilty Plea or Remains Silent

16.08 If, on the other hand, the defendant indicates a plea of not guilty, or remains silent, then s.17A(7) directs the magistrates to proceed in accordance with the mode of trial provisions set out in ss.18 and 19 of the MCA 1980. The court will usually adjourn to a later date for a mode of trial hearing.

Disorderly Conduct of the Defendant during Proceedings

16.09 Under s.17B of the MCA 1980, if because of the defendant's disorderly conduct it is not practicable for the PBV to be conducted in their presence, then provided the defendant is legally represented, the court can continue in their absence if it feels it should do. If the court decides to continue in the absence of the defendant, then the court must:

(i) cause the charge to be written down and read out;

(ii) ask the legal representative to give the indication of plea.

The remainder of the proceedings are exactly the same as if the defendant was present; as explained above.

6. Mode of Trial Procedure

16.10 The mode of trial procedure is used to determine the appropriate trial court, i.e. magistrates' or Crown Court to deal with the case. The procedure is as follows. It is important to be aware that the Mode of Trial procedure only arises if the defendant has pleaded not guilty at the PBV.

Step 1: Disclosure of Advance Information under Part 21 of the Criminal Procedure Rules 2005

16.11 Firstly, it will be considered by the court, if the prosecution have complied with Pt 21 of the CrPR 2005, formally the Magistrates' Courts (Advance Information) Rules. The magistrates may not proceed to determine the mode of trial, unless the defence have been given advance information, or they have waived their right to it. Prior to plea, the defence can request the prosecution to furnish them with Advance Disclosure under Pt 21.2 and 3, "as soon as practicable" of either:

(i) information provided in the form of copies of written statements; or

(ii) a summary of the facts, to which the prosecution proposes to adduce as evidence in the proceedings.

The prosecution can refuse to provide advance disclosure, if this would lead to any person being intimidated, or an interference with the administration of justice.

An important aspect of advance disclosure is to be aware that if a written statement refers to a "document" then under Pt 21.3 of the CrPR 2005, the prosecution must also furnish a copy of the document, or allow inspection of the document. By s.5A of the MCA 1980, as amended by s.47 of the CPIA 1996, a document means anything in which information of any description is recorded. In *R. v Calderdale Magistrates Ex p. Donahue* [2001] Crim. L.R. 141 the applicant was facing charges of theft and received advance information in the form of a case summary from the Crown, which made reference to a video which recorded them committing the offence. The defence applied to view the video. This was declined, as was an application for an adjournment. The defence sought judicial review of the decision not to adjourn the proceedings.

The Divisional Court concluded that the justices were in error in not granting an adjournment on the basis of fairness and further it was accepted that a video was a document within the meaning of s.5A that had been referred in the case summary. Conversely, in *DPP v Croydon Magistrates' Court* [2001] EWHC 552 the Divisional Court ruled that the magistrates had erred in requiring the prosecution to serve DNA evidence on the defence as part of the prosecution's advance disclosure and adjourned proceedings to enable the DNA evidence to be served. The Divisional Court distinguished the *Calderdale* authority on the basis that:

> "the prosecution were not obliged to provide further advance information beyond the case summary in the circumstances of this case because the advance information in the form of the case summary did not refer to a document upon which the prosecutor proposed to rely, within the meaning of rule 4(3) of the 1985 Rules(as amended). If it had done, there would have been an obligation on the prosecution to furnish a copy of the document or allow the defence to inspect it. However, the case summary in this case only referred to the offences being linked

to the defendant in most cases by DNA profiling from blood left at the scene. This is not referring to a document upon which the prosecutor proposes to rely."

16.12 Rule 21.6 of the CrPR 2005 provides that where a request for advance disclosure has not been complied with by the prosecution, then the court shall adjourn the proceedings, pending compliance with the requirement, unless the court is satisfied that the conduct of the case for the accused will not be substantially prejudiced by non-compliance with the requirement. If the magistrates decide not to adjourn, the reasons for such a decision must be recorded in the court register. It is essential to be aware of the purpose and importance of advance disclosure of the prosecution's case early in the proceedings at the magistrates' court. This is explained succinctly by the Divisional Court in *R. v Calderdale Magistrates Ex p. Donahue* [2001] Crim. L.R. 141 as follows:

> "It is common ground that one of the purposes of the prosecution providing such information is so that the defendant is able to make an informed choice as to his plea and mode of trial at a plea before venue hearing. He stands to gain by any early plea which he offers (discount in sentence). Moreover, it is clearly in the public interest that pleas of guilty, if they are to be forthcoming, are tender or indicated as soon as possible."

This is important for a defence solicitor since having considered the available evidence, they will be in a better position to properly advise the client on plea and the advantages and disadvantages of magistrates' court trial, to that of crown court trial. At the point the magistrates accept jurisdiction under the Mode of Trial Procedure for an either way offence, the client will then be given a choice as to whether they wish to consent to trial in the magistrates' court, or alternatively elect trial in the Crown Court. As a matter of professional conduct, the solicitor must be in a position to advise the client of the advantages and disadvantages of either trial in the magistrates court or alternatively in the Crown Court. The client can then make an informed choice as to where they wish to be tried. Failure to give this advice will be a breach of the professional conduct rules and potentially negligent. The following is a non-exhaustive list of the advantages and disadvantages of trial in each criminal court.

(1) Advantages of summary trial in the magistrates' court

- (i) less formal surroundings
- (ii) costs
- (iii) limitation on sentence
- (iv) quicker
- (v) tried by lay representatives
- (vi) right of appeal to crown court

(2) Disadvantages of summary trial in the magistrates' court

- (i) 70 per cent chance of being convicted

- (ii) magistrates can become "case hardened"
- (iii) tend to believe police evidence
- (iv) disparity in sentencing in different courts
- (v) magistrates not legally qualified

(3) Advantages of Crown Court trial

- (i) 40 per cent chance of being acquitted
- (ii) points of law can be argued before a professional judge
- (iii) represented by a barrister
- (iv) tried by a randomly selected jury
- (v) trial process is slower to take into account jury's understanding of evidence
- (vi) tactical decisions (i.e. witness may not attend or give unreliable evidence)

(4) Disadvantages of Crown Court trial

- (i) can be expensive
- (ii) longer waiting time to trial date (especially if remanded in custody) unlimited sentencing powers
- (iii) 60 per cent chance of conviction

Step 2: Suitability of Trial Venue, s.19 of the MCA 1980 and Pt V of the Consolidated Criminal Practice Directions

16.13 If no adjournment is necessary, the magistrates will proceed to hear representations from; first the prosecution and then the defendant, on suitability of trial venue. The representations of the defence will be to put before the court, the client's instructions as to their preference on trial venue, having taken advice on the advantages and disadvantages. The magistrates will usually retire to consider their decision on whether the case is more suitable for summary trial, or if not, then Crown Court trial. In considering the decision as to allocation the magistrates must make reference to s.19 of the MCA 1980 and the General Mode of Trial Considerations (see Pt V51.2 CCPD 2005), which states that they must have regard to the following points:

- (i) the nature of the case;
- (ii) whether the circumstances make the offence serious;
- (iii) adequacy of sentencing power. Section 78 of the Power of Criminal Courts (Sentencing) Act 2000 restricts the magistrates to impose a max sentence of six months. Section 133 empowers the magistrates to impose consecutive sentences and providing were there or two are more indictable offences involved, then the court has an extended power to impose consecutive sentences up to an aggregate term of 12 months. Sections 154, and 282 of the CJA 2003 increase the power of the magistrates to impose a 12-month sentence for a summary and

either way offence (this is not yet in force). Schedule 25 of the CJA 2003 lists summary offences that are no longer imprisonable and Sch.26 lists offences that have an increased sentence to 51 weeks;

(iv) hear representations about trial venue from both the prosecution and defence;

(v) Any other circumstances.

The magistrates will also be given access to the defendant's previous convictions found in the antecedents printout from the police. This is confirmed in the useful guidance for magistrates, when determining PBV and mode of trial proceedings found in the judgment of the High Court in *R. v Warley Magistrates' Court* [1999] 1 W.L.R. 216. The disclosure of a defendant's previous convictions, will form part of the new allocation procedure set out in Sch.3 of the CJA 2003 when brought into effect.

In addition, the magistrates must also consider the following general observations as listed in Pt V.51.3 of the CCPD 2005):

(i) The court should never make a decision on grounds of convenience or expedition. This is particularly important with regard to jointly charged defendants. In *R. v Ipswich Magistrates Ex p. Callaghan* [1995] 159 J.P. 748, where the Divisional Court allowed an application for judicial Review and quashed the magistrates' decision to decline jurisdiction, since they had taken into account the prospect of separate trials. The court ruled that it was impermissible for justices to base their decision upon a wish to avoid separate trials otherwise the right of election given to each accused individually would be defeated.

(ii) The court should assume that the prosecution's version of events are correct.

(iii) The fact that the offences are alleged to be specimen.

(vi) Does the case involve complex questions of fact or law and difficult issues of evidence disclosure (i.e. Public Interest Immunity applications).

(v) offence should be tried summarily, unless the offence consists of certain features outlined for specific offences.

To provide further assistance to the magistrates Pt V 54.4 to 54.18 contains guidelines relevant to the more common offences for theft, violent offences, public order offences, and criminal damage. The guidance states that for all the listed offences, the starting point is for the case to be dealt with summarily, unless one or more from a list of specified features to the offence exist and the general sentencing powers of the court are deemed to be insufficient. For example, the starting point for burglary of a dwelling house is for the matter to be tried summarily, unless the court considers one or more of a list of specified features exists and the sentencing powers of the court are insufficient.

These features include; entry in the daytime or evening with the occupier present, evidence of soiling, ransacking, damage or vandalism. Another commonly encountered offence in the magistrates is s.20 reckless wounding and s.47 assault occasioning actual bodily harm. For these two offences again the starting point is summary trial, unless a weapon is used or more than minor injury caused by head-butting or kicking, violence used against those working in a public service or having contact with the public. It is important to be aware that the PBV procedure has been significantly amended by s.41 of the Criminal Justice Act 2003 and Sch.3 to the Act, but the amendments have yet to be brought in to force.

It is also important to note that under s.23 of the MCA 1980 mode of trial proceedings can be conducted in the absence of the defendant, provided the defendant is represented; that the advocate informs the court of the defendant's consent to proceed in their absence and the court is satisfied there is good reason for doing so.

Step 3: Summary Trial more Suitable—Creation of a Right to Elect

16.14 If the magistrates decide that the case is more suitable for summary trial, then under s.20 of the MCA 1980, the defendant is told by the clerk that they now have a choice, either:

(i) accept (i.e. consent to summary trial) and that if they do consent, to be warned that the magistrates, if they are found guilty, have the power to commit them for sentence to the Crown Court trial. If the accused does consent, then matter will proceed to summary trial.

(ii) If the accused does not consent and elects trial in the Crown Court, then the case will generally be adjourned for "committal proceedings".

If and when Sch.3 of the CJA 2003 comes into effect, the defendant will be able to request the magistrates to give an indication of what sentence is likely to be imposed if they were to be trial summarily or plead guilty. If the court gives an indication, then the defendant is given the opportunity to reconsider their earlier indication of plea.

Step 4: Magistrates Decline Jurisdiction

16.15 If the magistrates decide that trial on indictment is more suitable and therefore decline jurisdiction, the defendant will, in accordance with s.21 of the MCA 1980, be informed of this and that the case will be adjourned for committal proceedings to the Crown Court.

7. Power to Change from Summary Trial to Committal Proceedings

16.16 Under s.25 of the MCA 1980, the magistrates have a discretionary power if they have begun to hear the matter summarily and to at any time before the conclusion of the prosecution case, discontinue the summary trial and adjourn the case for committal proceedings. In *Smith v Wigan Magistrates' Court* [2002] EWHC 2271 the Divisional Court gave the following guidance for the magistrates, when dealing with an application by a defendant to allow re-election of trial venue. Firstly, did the accused properly understand the nature and significance of the choice put to him; in determining this question it was ruled that:

> "There are two situations where the answer is likely to be clear and favourable to the accused. Firstly, when as in exp Hodgson and many other cases, the unrepresented accused has pleaded guilty and the justices have concluded that he should be allowed to change that plea to not guilty following the taking of legal advice that he has a good defence to the change in law. As McCullough J points out, the accused never applied his mind to the choice at all because he never intended to seek a trial. Secondly, cases where there were clear reasons why the unrepresented accused might not have understood the choice he was called to make, for example, because of obvious distress and a need for medical attention, or because of his youth."

In other situations the Court said:

> "it is necessary in these case to be clear about what the choice is, the nature and significance of which the accused person must understand. It cannot be the law that any misunderstanding of any kind about the differences between summary trial and trial in the Crown Court will result in an answer favourable to the accused wishing to re-elect."

If a defendant has been advised by a solicitor on the advantages and disadvantages of trial by jury, as opposed to trial by magistrates, even if that advice fails to be detailed or is inadequate; this will not amount to a lack understanding the choice to be made; namely that by electing summary trial they was depriving themselves of trial by jury.

Particular note should be made of the decision in *Revitt v DPP* [2006] 1 W.L.R. 3172 on the issue of the court permitting the withdrawal of a plea of guilty. The High Court in the judgment of the Lord Chief Justice, Lord Philips ruled that if the defendant entered an unequivocal plea of guilty which was accepted by the court, then the defendant is to be proved guilty according to law within the meaning of art.6.2. In these circumstances, the presumption of innocence no longer applied and the court could proceed to sentencing, the acceptance of a guilty plea being compatible with art.6. If however, the plea is deemed to be equivocal, then this must be treated as a not guilty plea. The court laid down several principles when determining between a unequivocal plea, as opposed to a equivocal one.

If it becomes apparent that the defendant did not appreciate the nature and elements to the offence, then justice would demand that an application (the onus of proof being on the defendant) to vacate the initial plea, should succeed. Nevertheless, the Court noted that this should be a rare occurrence given the availability of legal representation. To reduce such a situation arising, the magistrates need to make it clear to the defendant the nature of the offence before they enter a plea. Section 142 of the MCA 1980 can not be used to re-open a case in which a defendant has pleaded guilty, but now wishes to withdraw that plea given the dismissal of his co-accused (see *R. v Croydon Youth Court Ex p. DPP* [1997] 2 Cr.App.R. 415).

8. Section 22 of the MCA 1980: Special Procedure for Certain Offences

16.17 Section 17 of the MCA 1980 provides that the offences listed in Sch.1 to the Act are classified as either way offences. Included in this list is the offence of criminal damage contained in s.1(1) if the Criminal Damage Act 1971 (destroying or damaging property). Section 22 then states if the offence charged in the information is a "schedule offence", listed in Sch.2 to the Act, then before proceeding to mode of trial, the court shall consider (having heard representations from both the prosecution and defence) whether the value of the damage exceeds £5,000 in accordance with subsection (10) and the valuation criteria set out in Sch.2. If the value is calculated (appears to the court) not to exceed £5000, then in accordance with subsection (2) the court shall proceed "as if the offence were triable summary only". Alternatively, if the damage value exceeds £5,000 then under subsection (3) the court proceeds to determine mode of trial in the ordinary way for an EWO.

The offences in Sch.2 are:

(i) simple criminal damage in s.1(1) of the Criminal Damage Act 1971, not the more serious offence of either recklessly or intending to endanger the life of another;

(ii) accessory to the above, attempt, and incitement;

(iii) aggravated vehicle taking, involving damage to the vehicle and or other property under s.12A Theft Act 1968.

Under s.22(11), if a defendant is charged with more than one scheduled offence, the relevant value figure for the purposes of the special procedure is the aggregate value of the damage resulting from all the offences not the damage caused by any single offence.

The purpose behind the creation of the special procedure for certain offences is to reduce the minor commission of the most commonly encountered either way offences being heard in the Crown Court. Parliament has deliberately removed the right to elect trial by jury for these offences. However, this had led the Court of Appeal, having to address the classification of the special procedure offences and whether the Crown Court had jurisdiction to accept a lesser alternative offence. In *R. v Burt*

[1997] 161 J.P. 77, the Court of Appeal followed the ruling in *R. v Mearns* [1991] 1 Q.B. 82, and concluded that criminal damage valued under £5000 amounted to a summary only offence and that therefore the defendant's guilty plea to the lesser offence of basic criminal damage could not be accepted by the Crown Court, as not falling within the court's jurisdiction under s.6(3) of the Criminal Justice Act 1967. The Court was further persuaded that criminal damage under £5,000 amounted to a summary only offence since under s.40(3)(d) of the CJA 1988, it is a specified listed offence to which s.40 applies.

A similar problem arose in *R. v Bristol Justices Ex p. Edger* [1998] 1 Cr.App.R. 144, in relation to attempted criminal damage. The defendant had smashed a glass panel in a bus shelter that was valued well under £5,000. By judicial review to the High Court, he argued that, following *Burt*, the criminal damage offence was a summary only offence and therefore, given that under the Criminal Attempts Act 1981, the offence must be an indictable one; an attempt to commit a summary offence is an offence not recognised in law. Whilst accepting *Burt* has being decisive, the QBD held that in relation the Criminal Attempts Act 1981, Parliament could not have intended a procedural provision of which s.22 is, to create a situation where criminal damage cannot be attempted, based purely on a mathematical calculation of value.

The issue of whether or not s.22 had re-classified criminal damage as a summary offence if under £5,000, was finally resolved in *R. v Fennell* [2000] Cr.App.R. 318, the defendant had been indicted with racially aggravated criminal damage contrary to s.30 of the CDA 1998, which amounts to an either way offence, but as with *R v Brownless* and *R v Clifford*, no alternative simple criminal damage count had been added. Accordingly, the judge used s.6(3) and left such an offence for the jury's determination, who returned a guilty verdict. The defendant appealed, placing reliance on the *Burt* judgment. In rejecting the appeal, Rose L.J., whilst acknowledging that decisions of the Court of Appeal "enjoy respect", on this occasion they had misinterpreted the various statutory provisions, which resulted in a decision being given *per incurium*. His Lordship concluded that Parliament had never intended with the enactment of s.40 CJA 1988 to reclassify criminal damage and that s.17 of the Magistrates' Courts Act 1980, together with the Interpretation Act 1978, (neither of which were cited in *Burt*) clearly identify criminal damage as constituting an either way offence. Section 22 is simply a procedural provision to assist in the allocation of resources at mode of trial and no way affected or changed the classification of offences set out in other provisions.

9. Committal Proceedings: Sections 4 to 8 of the MCA 1980 and Part 10 of the CrPR 2005

16.18 Until Sch.3 of the CJA 2003 is fully implemented, which will abolish the need for committal proceedings, there are two ways in which committal to the crown court will be considered. First where the magistrates have decided that their powers are insufficient to deal with the either way offence under the "mode of trial" procedure and therefore declined jurisdiction. Secondly, where the magistrates accepted jurisdiction, but the defendant elects trial by jury. Once the case is adjourned for committal proceedings, the usual procedure of the Crown is to draft an indictment and put together a "committal bundle" which consists of witness statements or depositions and serve them upon the defence at the hearing.

This does not have to contain all the evidence, since further evidence can be served on the defence by way of "notice of additional evidence." In *R. v DPP Ex p. Lee* [1999] 163 J.P. 569, the High Court ruled that the disclosure procedure set out in the Criminal Procedure and Investigations Act 1996 of primary disclosure, defence statement and secondary disclosure, would in most cases, wait until after committal without prejudicing the defendant's right to a fair trial. The Act itself did not specifically deal with the period between arrest and committal. Nevertheless, the Court noted that a responsible prosecutor was under a duty to consider immediate disclosure in the interests of justice and fairness, particularly for an offence triable on indictment.

It is important to be aware that the purpose of committal proceedings is to determine whether or not there is a "case to answer", that ought to be put before a jury. If there is, then the case will be committed to the Crown Court for a Plea and Case Management Hearing. Conversely, if the magistrates accept there is no case to answer then they will dismiss the case. However, the prosecution could then proceed by using the "voluntary bill of indictment" procedure. Section 6 of the MCA 1980 sets out the relevant procedure and provides that there are two types of committal procedure known as:

(i) section 6(2), committal without consideration of evidence; and

(ii) section 6(1), committal with consideration of evidence. If the defendant is ill, then the solicitor can appear on his behalf at the committal hearing (s.4 MCA 1980).

16.19 Section 6(2) involves committal without the need to consider all of the evidence within the "committal bundle". The defence, having considered the evidence in the bundle accept that there is a case to answer and therefore do not intend to make a submission of a no case to answer therefore the matter can be committed to the Crown Court. The court must be informed that the evidence falls within the meaning of s.5 of the MCA 1980 for the purposes of committal. This is the most common procedure, where the defendant accepts that there is a case to answer at this stage. The hearing should take no more than five minutes. If, on the other hand, the defence having read the committal bundle disputes that there is a case to answer against them (i.e. weak ID evidence), then the matter will be listed for a s.6(1) committal hearing.

However, the CPIA 1996 and r.10.3 of the CrPR 2005 restricts the hearing to no more than a "read out" of the salient issue of evidence by the prosecution. No witnesses can be called and the prosecution simply set out their case in summary form. Statements can be read out if needed. Rule 10.3 of the CrPR2005 provides that the prosecution may give an outline of the case and the law and then tender any evidence which is only in written form as prescribed by s.5(A)(3) of the MCA 1980, without any oral evidence being given. The defence solicitor can only make a submission of no case to answer. They cannot call witnesses or cross-examine any witnesses. The magistrates will retire and make a decision as to whether there is a case to answer and commit the matter to the Crown Court or dismiss the case against the defendant. In *R. v Bedwellty Justices Ex p. Williams* [1996] 2 Cr.App.R. 594, the House of Lords unanimously held that a decision of the magistrates to commit where there is no admissible evidence presented to them, or that if there is admissible evidence but is incapable of establishing a prima facie case, will on a judicial review application be quashed. However, given that a decision to commit is not final there is not jurisdiction for the magistrates to state a case for the opinion of the High Court (see *Dewing v Cummings* [1971] R.T.R. 295).

It is also important to be aware that it is not permissible for the reporting of committal proceedings unless the defence, under s.8 of the MCA 1980, consents to the removal of this restriction. The reason for the reporting restrictions is that it may be prejudicial to the defendant, in the inaccuracy of reporting on the case against them at an early stage. Nevertheless, a defendant may wish to apply for an order removing the restrictions, in order that a potential defence witness might come to light, or other relevant evidence. The magistrates must decide whether the defendant remains on bail or in custody. If the accused is committed, then the magistrates' court must in accordance with r.10.5, serve as soon as is practicable after the committal (but not later than four days on the Crown Court) all the appropriate documents listed in r.10.5. This includes the committal evidence, exhibits, a certificate to confirm this, a copy of the decision on bail, statement that the committal was a s.6(2) without evidence and a copy of the representation order. A final point on committal is that s.25 allows the examining justices to revert to summary proceedings, provided the defendant consents.

10. Power to Commit for Sentencing to the Crown Court (Part V.52 of the Criminal Practice Directions)

16.20 Under ss.3 and 4 of the Powers of Criminal Courts (Sentencing) Act 2000, previously s.38 MCA 1980), a discretionary power exists for a magistrates' court, if they are of the opinion that the offence and those related to it are so serious to be beyond their sentencing powers to commit a defendant to the Crown Court for sentence. Until s.154 of the CJA 2003 is implemented, when sentencing an adult offender, the magistrates' court is restricted in the use of imprisonment to a maximum six months. Notwithstanding this, s.133

empowers the court to impose consecutive sentences and provided there are two or more indictable offences involved then the court has the extended power to impose consecutive sentences of up to an aggregate term of 12 months. It is worth noting that when Sch.3 is brought into force, para.22 will substitute a new s.3, and s.3A.

In *R. v North Sefton Magistrates' Court Ex p. Marsh* [1995] 16 Cr.App.R.(S) 401, the High Court approved the broad approach to s.38, stating that the magistrates have an "unfettered discretion" to commit for sentencing. Nevertheless, dependant on how the court explains matters to the defendant, there is a risk that they may create a "legitimate expectation" in favour of the defendant, that only the magistrates will sentence him on his return. If a defendant then returns to court for sentencing faced with a different bench of magistrates, who take a different view and decide instead to commit to the Crown Court. The issue is whether the first bench of magistrates have given the defendant a substantive lawful promise not to commit him for sentencing. This would tie the hands of the subsequent bench in that, to renege on that promise would be unfair and amount to an abuse of process. In *R. v Warley Justices* [1999] 1 Cr.App.R.(S) 156, the High Court gave helpful guidance to the magistrates on the proper approach to be taken as to adjournments for pre sentence reports. It is at this critical stage that the defendant it likely to gain a legitimate expectation and it is therefore vital for the magistrates to keep the option of committal open if it is their wish to avoid the risk of tying the hands of a subsequent bench.

In *R. v Norwich Magistrates Court Ex p. Elliot* [2000] 1 Cr.App.R.(S) 152, the Court of Appeal ruled that simply adjourning the case for pre-sentence reports, would never be enough to restrict the discretionary power of the court. More was necessary to create a promise of the kind that bound a court on jurisdiction. On this point, Lord Bingham in *R. v Nottingham Magistrates Court Ex p. Davidson* [2000] 1 Cr.App.R.(S) 167, said that the Court would, albeit reluctantly, intervene in circumstances where the magistrates had created an "unqualified promise" in the mind of the defendant as to a sentence, that was later reneged on by a different court. These instructive words of Lord Bingham C.J. were followed in *R. v Horseferry Road Magistrates Court Ex p. Rugless* [2000] 164 J.P. 311, where it was held by the Divisional Court that the magistrates, in giving an assurance to the defendant that all sentencing options remained open, except for committal to the Crown Court, created a promise sufficiently unqualified to restrict the sentencing power of the court.

Despite the guidance in *R. v South Worcestershire Magistrates Court Ex p. Roberts* [2000] (unreported), the High Court quashed the decision of the magistrates' court to commit, since the previous bench had fettered its discretion when they had in unequivocal language, told the defendant that their powers of sentencing were adequate to finalise the matter. Consequently, it is incumbent on the magistrates' court to use careful language. Since a waiver of the discretionary power is, likely to arise in respect of the words chosen and that neither mistake, inadvertence, nor the context used will avert the creation of an expectation. A point which could not be overlooked in *Rees v Feltham Justices* [2001] 2 Cr.App.R.(S) 1, where the Divisional Court held that although the magistrates had used the words "leaving all options", these had to be construed in the context in which they were used. Consequently, by taking representations on sentencing jurisdiction and then proceeding to invite the defence's mitigation, the appellant had been left with the impression that the magistrates' were leaving only summary sentencing options open. (See also *Dalzell v DPP* [2008] EWHC 1193.)

11. Power to Commit Summary Offences to the Crown Court

16.21 Section 40 of the Criminal Justice Act 1988 provides for joining in the same indictment summary offences as alternatives to indictable offences. Where a defendant is committed to the Crown Court for an "indictable offence," the prosecution may at the same time, also include in the indictment, an offence which would otherwise be triable only summarily, by virtue of s.22(2) of the MCA 1980, provided certain conditions are satisfied as follows:

(i) that the evidence discloses the summary offence;
(ii) that the summary offence either is (1) founded on the same facts or evidence as the indictable offence, or (2) forms with it a series of offences of the same or similar character.

Section 40 restricts the meaning of summary offence to include only the following offences for the purposes of inclusion:

(i) common assault;
(ii) assault on a prison custody officer;
(iii) taking a conveyance without consent;
(iv) driving whilst disqualified;
(v) criminal damage not exceeding £5,000.

If s.40 can not be used, then recourse can be made to s.41 of the Criminal Justice Act 1988, which gives power to the magistrates' court to commit an offender to the Crown Court to enter a plea to any summary offence where the defendant is committed for an *either way offence*, provided the summary offence arose out of circumstances which appeared to the court to be the same as, or connected with, those giving rise to one or more of the either way offences. It is important to be aware that the defendant will only enter a plea for these linked summary offences at the Crown Court.

For s.41 to operate, both the defendant and the Crown Court must be given notice. If the defendant pleads guilty, then they will be sentenced along with the other offences. But in relation to the summary offence committed, the sentencing power of the Crown Court is limited to that of the magistrates' court. If the defendant pleads not guilty, then the Crown Court ceases to have jurisdiction and the matter must, unless the prosecution offer no evidence, be returned to the magistrates' court. However, a significant development is s.66 of the Courts Act 2003, which allows either a High Court Judge, Circuit Judge or Recorder to exercise the powers of a Magistrate District Judge and so deal with the summary offence in that capacity, without the need to send it back to the magistrates' court (when Pt 2 of Sch.3 of the CJA 2003 comes into effect, s.41 will automatically be repealed).

16.22 The purpose of ss.40 and 41 is to bring together differently classified offences that would otherwise be tried separately, resulting in unnecessary costs, wastage of court resources, time and potential duplication. Difficulties have however arisen in the Crown Court, with regard to accepting a lesser alternative summary offence to an indictable either way offence. One such offence is that of common assault. The elements to the offence of common assault were reviewed by the House of Lords in *R. v Savage* [1991] 3 W.L.R. 914. Section 39 of the Criminal Justice Act 1988 provides that both common assault and battery constitute summary only offences and therefore fall only within the jurisdiction of the magistrates' court. In *R. v Mearns* [1991] 1 Q.B. 82, the Court of Appeal quashed the appellant's conviction for common assault on the ground that unless it is drafted as a separate count, then it cannot for the purposes of s.6(3) of the Criminal Justice Act 1967, come "within the jurisdiction of the court of trial" and therefore cannot amount to an alternative verdict to a s.47 assault occasioning actual bodily harm offence.

The decision in *Mearns* was later followed in *R. v Brownless* [2000] (unreported), and the Court of Appeal in *R. v Clifford* [2003] EWCA Crim 3630, which considered itself bound by the *Mearns* decision. In both cases, the defendant had been indicted with racially aggravated common assault, which under s.29 of the Crime and Disorder Act 1998 amounts to an either way offence. In neither case had ss.40 or 41 been utilised to include basic common assault, but the judge had still left common assault as an alternative offence, leading to both convictions having to be quashed, due to this procedural error. The Crown Court simply did not have the power to do so.

This glaring error continued to occur (see *R. v Savatori Disalvo* [2004] EWCA Crim 2051 and *R. v Health* [2004] EWCA Crim 3126). Consequently this caused Parliament to step in with a statutory amendment to s.6(3) of the CJA 1967 by virtue of s.11 of the Domestic Violence, Crime and Victims Act 2004 (which came into force on March 21, 2005 (SI 2005/579)). This inserts a new subsection (3A), which provides that, if a summary offence comes within the ambit of s.40 of the CJA 1988 and although not procedurally added as a separate count, the summary offence will still fall within the jurisdiction of the court of trial. Accordingly, s.11 will save the summary offence and any subsequent conviction from being quashed as a procedural irregularity.

In *R v Plant* [2008] EWCA Crim 960, the Court of Appeal ruled that it does not follow that if the indictable offence for the purposes of s.40 is withdrawn from the jury, then the summary offence must also be withdrawn. If this was the case, it would defeat the very purpose of s.40.

12. Indictable Only Offences: Sending to the Crown Court on Bail or in Custody

16.23 In 1997 a review was undertaken by Martin Narey into the causes of delay in the criminal justice system and proposed recommendations for reform. One such recommendation was to move the preliminary case management responsibility for indictable only offences from the magistrates' court to the Crown Court where the case would inevitably be concluded. The significance of this reform would be to reduce the need to prepare the case through to committal proceedings, the associated costs and unnecessary delay. Section 51 and Sch.3 came into force on January 15, 2002 and abolished committal proceedings for indictable only offences.

Section 51 of the Crime and Disorder Act 1998 provides where an adult appears before the magistrates' court charged with an indictable only offence, they "shall send him" and any co-accused, to the Crown Court together with any "related" either-way or summary offence that is punishable with imprisonment and/or disqualification from driving. An either way offence is related to an indictable only offence, provided it can be joined in the same indictment, whilst for a summary only offence, it must appear to arise:

> "out of the circumstances which are the same as or connected with those giving rise to the indictable only offence."

This need not happen at the same hearing, subsection(2) allows the court to send the defendant to the Crown Court for the related either way offence or summary offence, should the defendant make a subsequent appearance charged with those offences. If the co-accused is a child or young person then under subsection (5), the court, before sending them with the adult to the Crown Court, must consider whether "its necessary in the interests of justice to do so" The magistrates must decide whether to send the defendant to the Crown Court, either in custody, or on bail.

16.24 The procedure to be followed by the court in respect of s.51 of the CDA 1998 is set out in Sch.3 to the Act. Within that schedule is a residual power for the magistrates to summons any person who refuses to give a written statement, or produce a document or exhibit. This is providing that there is likely to be material evidence, for the purposes of proceedings for an offence for which a person has been sent for trial under s.51. The magistrates can also issue a warrant for the person's arrest. If the person in question "without just excuse" still refuses to give a statement, then the court can commit them to prison for a period not exceeding one month and/or a fine of up to £2,500.

This provision was considered by the High Court in *CPS v Bolton Magistrates' Court* [2003] EWHC 2697, which ruled that the proceedings are to be held in open court and therefore the magistrates were wrong to refuse the police to attend. On a second point, whilst a refusal on the grounds of a risk of self incrimination is a just excuse, the claim must be investigated properly and the magistrates should be satisfied from the nature of the evidence that there is real danger of incrimination, or other danger and not one of any imaginary insubstantial claim.

Paragraph 6 of Sch.3 sets out the power of the Crown Court to deal with summary offences sent with an indictable only offence. This states that if the court is satisfied that the summary offence is related to the offence that is triable only on indictment, or any offences that are *so triable*, then the defendant is asked to plead to the offence. If the defendant pleads guilty, the Crown Court will convict them and impose sentence, but this is limited to the sentencing powers of the magistrates' court. Alternatively, if the defendant pleads not guilty, then unless the prosecution offer no evidence, the case will be returned to the magistrates' court for trial. But as with s.41 of the CJA 1988, the Crown Court Judge under s.66 of the Courts Act 2003 can act in the capacity of a Magistrate District Judge on the summary offence.

16.25 Similarly Paragraph 7 deals with the situation where the defendant is sent for an indictable only offence, but the indictment is amended to reduce the offence to a lesser alternative, either way offence or the prosecution accept a guilty plea. The court initiates mode of trial proceedings, puts the new offence to the defendant and asks them to give an indication as to plea if the matter were to proceed to trial. If they plead guilty, the court will proceed to sentencing. On the other hand, if the defendant pleads not guilty, the Crown Court must consider whether the offence is more suitable for either summary trial or on indictment.

In *R. v Nembhard* [2002] EWCA Crim 134, the Court of Appeal ruled that the words "so triable" in para.6(2) include an either way offence, so that the appellant, who had originally been indicted with attempted robbery and pleaded instead to attempted theft, had been correctly convicted of assaulting a police officer in the execution of his duty, a summary only offence to which he had pleaded guilty. Paragraph 7 was further considered in *R. v Ashton & Others* [2006] EWCA Crim 794, in which the magistrates erroneously sent the defendant to the Crown Court under s.51 for burglary (an either way offence) believing incorrectly this was is third burglary and therefore s.111 of the Powers of Criminal Courts (Sentencing) Act 2000 applied, meaning that a minimum term of three years must be imposed, making the current burglary an indictable only offence.

Realising the error, the judge at the Crown Court proceeded, using para.7(3) mode of trial in the Crown Court. The defendant pleaded guilty, the Court imposed sentence, but did not prefer an indictment. The Court of Appeal, refusing the applicant's leave to appeal, concluded that although s.51 was used incorrectly, Parliament could not have intended the Crown Court to be deprived of its jurisdictional ability to deal with the applicant and that this procedural failure had not resulted in any prejudice or consequential injustice, especially given the applicant himself had consented to being dealt with in this way, which is a significant relevant factor.

13. Notice of Sending for Trial and Service of Prosecution Evidence

16.26 In accordance with Pt 12 of the CrPR 2005, the magistrates' court must within four days (this can be extended) from the date the defendant was sent to the Crown Court send the required notice and other associated documents listed in Pt 12, to the Crown Court Officer. On receipt, the Crown Court Officer shall cause the case to be listed in accordance with any directions given by the magistrates. The prosecution must also comply with The Crime and Disorder Act 1998 (Service of Prosecution Evidence) Regulations 2005 (SI 2005/902), which provide that when a person is sent for trial under s.51, copies of the documents containing the evidence shall:

(i) if the person is not in custody, be served on the defendant no later than 70 days from the date they were sent by the magistrates to the Crown Court;

(ii) if the person is in custody then 50 days.

The prosecution can make an oral application to the Crown Court for these time limits to be extended. Written notice of the application must be given to the court officer and the defendant, specifying the grounds for seeking an extension. The Regulations are silent on the consequences of non-compliance to the time limits, which led to the Court of Appeal having to address this issue in *Fehily, McCadden and Clarke* [2002] EWHC 1295, concerning an application for habeas corpus. The applicants were sent to the Crown Court for serious offences. In *Fehily and Clarke* the prosecution applied for an extension, but had breached the requirement to give the defendant three days' notice of the application, while in *McCadden*, the prosecution made an application for extension three days after the time limit. The applicant's claimed that the time limits were mandatory not merely directory, since the word "shall" is used.

The High Court rejected the applications and took a flexible approach to the interpretation of procedural time limits. Rose L.J. stated that rather than considering procedural time limits as either mandatory or directory (see *London Estates v Aberdeen DC* [1980] 1 W.L.R. 182, and *Ex p. Jeyeanthan* [2000] 1 W.L.R. 354), the correct approach was to consider the consequences of the non-compliance, taking into account the triangulation of interests. In this instance, Parliament could not have intended those who are charged with serious offences to have them dismissed for non-compliance, which was rectified earlier and dealt with the setting of a reasonable timetable and warnings of the proceedings being stayed in further breaches.

It is important to be aware of para.2 of Sch.3, which allows that a defendant who is sent for trial, may at any time after they are served with the evidence and before being arraigned, apply either orally, or in writing to a judge at the Crown Court, for the charge(s) to be dismissed and any counts quashed in the indictment. The test the judge must apply is whether it appears to them that the evidence against the applicant, would not be sufficient for a jury to properly convict them. If the application succeeds, the only course for the prosecution is to use the voluntary bill of indictment procedure, by applying to a High Court Judge for their consent to allow a new indictment to be preferred (s.2 of the Administration of Justice (Misc Provisions) Act 1933 and Pt IV.35 of the Practice Directions). The Court of Appeal in *R. v Thompson* [2006] EWCA Crim 2849, ruled that the prosecution is not permitted to circumvent this procedure by using s.58, since despite the wide breadth of appealing a ruling of a judge under s.58, the jurisdiction under that provision relates to a ruling that results in an acquittal, not a dismissal.

It is important to be aware that under s.4 of the Criminal Justice Act 1987, the magistrates can transfer to the Crown Court serious or complex fraud cases and under s.53 of the Criminal Justice Act 1991 cases of violent or serious sexual offences. Section 51 can still be used for these offences despite the separate provisions.

14. Pre-Trial Hearings (PTH)

16.27 Under s.8 of the MCA 1980 as amended by the Courts Act 2003, the magistrates have a discretionary power to hold a PTH before the summary trial of a not guilty defendant. A trial is deemed to have commenced, at the point the court begins to hear prosecution evidence. At a PTH the magistrates can, provided the defendant is represented or as been advised on the availability of legal funding, make a ruling on:

(i) any question of law relating to the admissibility of evidence;

(ii) any other question of law relating to the case.

A court can only proceed to make such a ruling if two conditions are met:

(i) it appears to the court to be in the interests of justice to do so; and

(ii) that the court as given both the prosecution and defence an opportunity to be heard.

Under s.8B any ruling has binding effect from the moment it is made until the case against the defendant is disposed of or if jointly charged, disposed of against all the defendants. A case is deemed to be disposed of in one of three ways; (i) the defendant is acquitted or convicted, (ii) the prosecution decide to discontinue, (iii) the case is dismissed. The court has a general power to discharge or vary a ruling provided the above same two conditions continue to be met.

15. Summary Trial Process: Part 37 of the Criminal Procedure Rules 2005

16.28 In accordance with the consolidated criminal practice directions, both the defence and prosecution must complete and comply with the directions in a case progression form. This includes directions relating to disclosure and admissibility of evidence and witnesses. Part 37 of the CPR 2005 provides in detail the relevant procedure to be followed for a summary trial. Section 121 MCA 1980 provides that a summary trial should be heard by at least two lay magistrates, the maximum being three. The procedure is as follows:

Step 1: Putting of the "Information"

16.29 A summary trial commences when the clerk puts the information (charge) to the accused, where they plead guilty or not guilty.

Step 2: Prosecution Case

16.30 The prosecution have a right to make an opening speech, if this is desirable and will then proceed to call its witnesses; and the following takes place:

(i) examination in chief (cannot ask leading questions);

(ii) cross examination by defence (can ask leading questions);

(iii) re-examination and any questions from the bench.

Step 3: Agreed Evidence and Formal Admissions

16.31 Section 9 of the Criminal Justice Act 1967 provides that written statements can be read out to the court provided that the statement is signed and contains a declaration of truth and notice of risk of prosecution if untrue and that the statement has been served on the other party. Section 10 of the CJA 1967 provides that either the defence or prosecution may personally admit any fact of which oral evidence may be given in criminal proceedings, i.e. a defendant admits that they were in a certain place, on such a date, at such a time. The purpose behind agreed evidence and formal admissions, is to save costs and time, since witnesses need not attend and the statement can be read out.

Step 4: Submission of No Case to Answer

16.32 At the close of the prosecution case, the defence may make a submission of no case to answer to the magistrates, stating that the prosecution have failed to establish that the defendant has committed the offence and that no competent bench of magistrates could convict on the evidence presented.

If the magistrates agree, then the defendant is found not guilty and is discharged. If they disagree then the trial continues. It is important to be aware that, as explained in *Khatibi v DPP* [2004] EWHC 83, the court does possess a general discretion to admit further prosecution evidence beyond that of rebuttal and mere formality, despite the prosecution closing their case against the defendant. Nevertheless, the High Court observed that the discretion ought to be exercised with great caution as against the strict rules of the adversarial trial.

In *Webb v Leadbetter* [1996] 1 W.L.R. 245, it was held that as a strict general rule no evidence can be received once the court had retired to consider its verdict. Only in special circumstances should evidence be admitted after retirement (see *Malcolm v DPP* [2007] 1 W.L.R. 1230, in which the High Court ruled that in deciding whether or not special circumstances existed, the Court also had to take into account the purpose of the overriding objective in the Criminal Procedure Rules in which the defence advocate had in her closing speech inappropriately raised the issue, that no warning under s.7 of the Road Traffic Act 1988 had been given. This it was agreed ought to have been raised before the close of the prosecution's case in accordance with r.3.3. Accordingly, the magistrates were right to allow the prosecution to call the police officer again).

Step 5: Defence Case

16.33 The defendant under the Criminal Evidence Act 1893 is not obliged to give evidence. However, under s.35 of the Criminal Justice and Public Order Act 1994, this may be the subject of an inference. The defence is not obliged to call any witnesses. This is part of the presumption of innocence, in that the prosecution bring the case and it is for them to prove the offence, not for the defendant to disprove it. In other words, the defence are putting the prosecution to proof. If however, the defence decides to call evidence, then the same formality applies with (i) examination in chief; (ii) cross-examination; (iii) re-examination. Under r.37.7 of the CrPR 2005, the prosecution can at the conclusion of the defence case call evidence to rebut that evidence.

Closing Speeches and Verdict

16.34 Part 37 allows for either party to address the court a second time. If so allowed, the prosecution make their address first, followed by the defence. The magistrates will retire and consider the verdict.

16. Trial or Sentence in the Absence of the Accused

16.35 Section 11 of the MCA 1980 gives the magistrates a general power to continue in the absence of the accused, or alternatively adjourn the proceedings provided the prosecutor is in attendance. Section 54 of the

Criminal Justice and Immigration Act 2008, when in force, will restrict this power and require the magistrates in the case of a defendant aged 18 or over to proceed with the trial in their absence, unless it appears to the court not in the interests of justice to do so. If the court decides not to continue in the defendant's absence, then the court must state in open court its reasons for not doing so. If the defendant was summoned to court as opposed to being charged, then before continuing in their absence, the court must be satisfied that the summons was properly issued and served, or that the court considers there to be an acceptable reason for the defendant lack of appearance (inserted by s.54(3) of the CJIA 2008). Nevertheless the court is under no duty to enquire into the reasons for the accused's failure to appear.

If the defendant fails to attend at the sentencing hearing, then the court, like with non appearance at trial, can continue and impose sentence in their absence. However, if the court imposes a custodial sentence, then the offender must be brought before the Court before being taken to prison. The purpose of the amendments are clear and designed to reduce unjustifiable delay or abuse by the defendant by placing a unequivocal duty on the court to continue with no general discretion to adjourn. For this reason the power to issue a warrant of arrest in s.13 of the MCA 1980 is abolished.

17. General Power to Vary or Rescind a Decision

16.36 Section 142 provides that the magistrates can, if it appears in the interests of justice to do so, order that the case in which the person was convicted, be heard again by a different court. There is no time restriction for the use of this power. It is often referred to as the "slip rule", in that its purpose, as described in the MCA 1980, is a power to rectify a mistake. The power cannot be used beyond a situation other than where the magistrates have made a mistake which needs rectifying. This will not include rulings in law, nor is it to be used as a substitute to an appeal (see *R. v Croydon Youth Court Ex p. DPP* [1997] 2 Cr. App. 411). Further as was held in *R. (D) V Sheffield Youth Court* [2008] EWHC 601 that s.142 does not empower the court to re-open a decision of an earlier court albeit by mistake to accept an unequivocal guilty plea and that the defendant does not wish to vacate his plea.

18. Youth Court Procedure

16.37 Section 163 of the Powers of Criminal Courts (Sentencing) Act 2000 defines a child to be one who has not yet reached the age of 14 and a young person to be one who is 14 but under 18. A young offender will always be first dealt with in the Youth Court. Only if the young person is charged with a grave offence, or jointly with an adult, will the matter proceed to the Crown Court. The Youth Court was introduced from October 1, 1992, when it replaced the Juvenile Court. The Youth Court is situated in the magistrates' court and sits on a separate day to that of the adult court, to avoid association with adult offenders. The re-offending rate of young offenders is about 75 per cent and one of the aims of youth justice is to reduce the entry and re-entry of young offenders into the criminal justice system. The emphasis is on pre-court intervention, with the use of reprimands, final warnings, referral orders, curfews and action plans. Also, a significant development is the law of anti-social behaviour legislation and parenting orders, together with youth inclusion schemes.

If a young offender does enter the criminal justice system, then the emphasis is on preventing delay (it now takes on average 60 to 65 days for a young offender to be dealt with from arrest to sentence. Previously it had been 142 days) and the use of restorative justice (i.e. reparation orders) and different sentencing aims and options, i.e. the detention and training order. This policy initiative came from the White Paper "No More Excuses—A New Approach to Tackling Youth Crime in England and Wales 1997" which led to the reforms found in the Crime and Disorder Act 1998 (CDA 1998) and the Youth Justice and Criminal Evidence Act 1999 (CJCEA 1999). The Youth Justice Board was created under the CDA 1998, a government agency, with responsibility for monitoring the operation of the youth justice system, making improvements and advising the Justice Minister. The board consists of various representatives within the justice system. Each Local Authority must have a youth offending team, together with a youth justice plan, with the purpose of co-ordinating a youth justice service for the area, (i.e. drafting pre-sentence reports).

Section 37 of the CDA 1998 sets out for the first time in statutory form the principal aim for youth justice, as being the prevention of offending by children and young people. This is to be achieved by the implantation of a number of specified objectives, one such objective is: "punishment proportionate to the seriousness and persistence of offending". Another important principle is found in s.44 of the Children and Young Persons Act 1933 (CYPA 1933), which provides that the court must have regard to the welfare of every child who appears before the court.

An important ruling is *T and V v UK* [1999] 30 E.H.R.R. 121 (the Bulgar case) in which the Human Court of Human Rights ruled that while the trial procedure of young defendant did not breach art.3 of inhuman or degrading treatment it did breach art.6 by preventing the defendant's a right to a fair trial. Further, the Court ruled that the home secretary's power in the CJA 1991, in setting a tariff higher than the one set by the trial judge, also breached art.6 since a court, not a member of the executive, should determine the sentence. This led to the a new procedure set out in s.82A of the Power of Criminal Courts (Sentencing) Act 2000, inserted by s.60 of the Criminal Justice and Court Services Act 2000, being applied together with a Practice Statement on the setting of a life sentence tariff being issued by the Lord Chief Justice and a Practice Direction (now found in Pt IV 39 of the CrPR 2005) setting out the principles to be adopted in the Crown Court for the trial of young defendants, i.e. all participants should be on the same level. Similarly, as with the adult court, the magistrates in the Youth Court have to hand, for assistance, "the Youth Justice Bench Book" and a clerk.

19. Composition of the Youth Court and Anonymity

16.38 Under s.50 of the Courts Act 2003, as amending the Children and Young Persons Act 1933, a Justice of the Peace (lay magistrates) may not sit in the Youth Court unless, they are authorised to do so by the Justice Minister. The Youth Courts (Constitution of Committees and Rights of Preside) Rules 2007 (SI 2007/1611), which came into effect on July 13, 2007, provides that for each local justice area there is to be a Youth Panel, which consists of youth justices and meets when necessary and at least twice a year. The function of the panel is to make recommendations on the development and pastoral care of the Youth Court. Rule 10 provides that a District Judge (Magistrates' Court) may sit alone in the Youth Court, if Youth Justices then there must not be more than three and be at least one male and one female Justice.

If for some unforeseen circumstance this composition is not possible, then the court may still be constituted, provided the other members of the court think it would be inexpedient in the interests of justice for there to be an adjournment. The chairman must be either a District Judge, or a Youth Justice on an approved list. The Youth Justices may appoint another justice to sit, if satisfied that they are suitability trained or undergoing training. Training of Youth Justices is undertaken by the local bench training and development committee which consists of six to nine justices, who must rotate by one-third in each year (see the Justices of Peace (Training Development and Committee) Rules 2007 (SI 2007/1609)).

Those who are qualified must be a member of the Youth Court panel. Under the CYPA 1933, no person other than those authorised by the court: members and officers of the court, parties to the case (parents/guardians) legal representatives, witnesses and the media, are allowed to be present. One of the difficulties encountered in the Youth Court and indeed in the Crown Court, is striking a fair balance between protecting the welfare of the young defendant against that of open justice and for the public to be informed of the administration of justice. In relation to the Youth Court, s.49 of the CYPA 1933 (amended by s.48 of the YJCEA 1999) sets out the general prohibition of the reporting of criminal proceedings, (starting at police investigation and court proceedings in the youth and adult court) which if published, reveals the name, address or school of the young defendant or witness. This also includes any particulars likely to lead to the identification of that person and any pictures.

In s.49(4A) of the CYPA 1933 there exists a limited exception in that a court has a discretionary power by order to dispense with the prohibition but only if the court is satisfied that it is in the public interest to do so and the young defendant has been convicted of an offence, or it is appropriate to do so, in order to avoid an injustice to the young defendant, or the defendant is unlawfully at large. Any publication in contravention amounts to a summary offence punishable by way of a fine.

Alternatively, more serious proceedings can be brought under the Contempt of Court Act 1981. In addition to s.49, there exists s.39 of the CYPA 1933, which gives all courts a discretionary power to impose reporting restrictions generally against the proceedings. In *T v St Albans Crown Court* [2002] EWHC 1129 it was stated that the principles are that the court must consider carefully the conflicting considerations and that there needs to be "good reason" for the lifting of reporting restrictions and that there is clearly a distinction between proceedings in the Youth Court and those in the Crown Court. In *Todd v DPP* [2003] EWHC 2408, the High Court concluded that the purpose of s.49 was not to provide protection to those who became adults in the course of the proceedings.

Another exception is s.141 of the Serious Organised Crime and Police Act 2005, which provides that the restriction in s.49 of the CYPA 1933 does not apply to proceedings relating to the application for an anti-social behaviour order. However, the operation of s.45 of the YJCEA 1999 does apply, but the court must given reasons. In *R. v Croydon Crown Court Ex p. Trinity Mirror Plc* [2008] EWCA Crim 50, the Court of Appeal held that the Crown Court had no statutory jurisdiction under s.45(4) of the Supreme Court Act 1981, nor did it have any inherent jurisdiction to issue injunctions. Accordingly, the judge was wrong to order the prohibition of the media in identifying the defendant convicted of downloading child pornography, in order to protect the interests of his innocent children. Judge L.J. noted the sad reality of a criminal prosecution that invariably those closest to the offender and innocent of all wrong doing, suffer shame and misery as a consequence. However, this should not be a qualification to the fundamental principle of open justice. Following the *Trinity* ruling the Divisional Court in *Crawford v DPP* [2008] *The Times*, February 20, 2008, has given similar guidance to the magistrates' court.

20. The Application of s.24 of the MCA 1980 and s.51A of the CDA 1998

16.39 As with the Adult Magistrates' Court, the same steps and rules of procedure on the serving of advance information by the prosecution on the defence, are equally applicable to proceedings in the Youth Court. One of the distinctions at the moment between the Youth Court and the Adult Magistrates Court is that in the Youth Court there is no Plea Before Venue, the court must consider s.24. This is clearly illustrated in *R(D) v Sheffield Youth Court* [2008] EWHC 601, when the defendant youth had appeared before the magistrates' court given he was charged jointly with an adult for drug offences. The Court in misunderstanding its powers under s.24 accepted the defendant's guilty plea and remitted the case to the Youth Court for sentencing. When the procedural mistake was realised the District Judge reopened the case under s.142 and proceeded to consider s.24 and committed the case to the Crown Court.

The High Court on a judicial review application held that s.142 did not give the power to the District Judge to vacate the guilty plea; that whilst there was a procedural error this did not invalidate the unequivocal guilty plea. It is important to note that when para.10 of Sch.3 of the Criminal Justice 2003 comes into force, a new s.24A will be inserted which will allow the court where the youth is either jointly charged with an adult of an indictable offence, or is charged with a grave offence, then before determining whether to send them to the Crown Court the Court must conduct a plea before venue hearing in exactly the same way as for adults by the youth giving an indication of their plea and the consequences flowing from that indication.

Concerning the application of s.24, the High Court In *CPS v Ghanbari* [2005] EWHC 2929, gave general guidance to the Youth Court on the determination of trial venue for young defendants. The Court recognised that the legislative policy is for a young defendant wherever possible, to be dealt with in the Youth Court. This is further recognised in ss.100 to 107 of the Powers of Criminal Courts (Sentencing) Act 2000, which gives the Youth Court a power to impose a detention and training order of up to a maximum of 24 months. If the young defendant is charged with murder or manslaughter, then the must be sent to the Crown Court for trial for all other offences s.24 is to be considered. Section 24 provides that where a person under the age of 18 appears, or is brought before a magistrates' court charged, with an *indictable offence*, other than homicide or certain firearms offences falling within the requirements of s.51A of the Firearms Act 1968 (s.42 of the CJA 2003 which came into force on January 22, 2004), they must be tried summarily unless the youth is charged with a:

(i) "grave offence" as defined in s.91(1) of the Powers of Criminal Courts (Sentencing) Act 2000, or

(ii) they are charged jointly with an adult and the court considers it necessary in the interests of justice, to commit them both for trial.

A "grave offence" means:

(i) an offence punishable with imprisonment of 14 years or more;

(ii) sexual assault on a woman or man.

Then, the court shall commit them for trial, if they are of the opinion that there is sufficient evidence or it has a power to commit without consideration of the evidence.

Difficulties have arisen in determining the correct test that the Youth Court ought to apply, when considering the application of s.24. This has led to a series of conflicting authorities in the High Court in judicial review proceedings, on the rationality of the decision of the Youth Court to either decline jurisdiction, or accept it. The decision on jurisdiction becomes especially difficult for cases that are borderline on two years' custody, such as assaults, sexual offences and robbery. Further, the only power of the Youth Court is to impose a detention and training order, which is only available for those 15 or over and those who are 12 to 14 must be deemed to be a persistent offender. In *C, D and N v Sheffield Youth Court* [2003] EWHC 35, the High Court reviewed the authorities and ruled in terms of precedent in order to reconcile the conflict of approach, following the most recent decision of Lord Woolf in *W v Southampton Youth Court* [2002] EWHC 1640, that there is a presumption against sending a young defendant to the Crown Court, unless they are satisfied that the offence is so serious that detention above two years is required:

> "or is one of those cases where they consider that the appropriate sentence is not only a custodial sentence, but a custodial sentence which is approaching the two year limit which is normally applicable to older offenders with whom they have to deal."

16.40 The High Court also stated that if an earlier observation of Lord Woolf was inconsistent with what was stated in *R. v Devices Youth Court Ex p. A* [2000] 164 J.P. 330, correctly stated, the requirement in s.24 is that if the conditions within the section are satisfied "the court shall commit the accused for trial." In essence, the test is whether the Youth Court considers that if the defendant is found guilty of the offence there is a real, not a vague or theoretical possibility of them receiving a sentence under s.91 of the PCC(S) Act 2000. In determining this question the Youth Court will need to assess the sentencing powers of the Crown Court, any sentencing guideline authorities and the aggravating and mitigating factors of the case.

On a final point, the High Court confirmed that in an application for judicial review of a decision taken under s.24, the test is to decide whether the decision was wrong. In *W v Thetford Youth Justices* [2002] EWHC 1252, Gage J. observed that for a young defendant under 15 who is not a persistent offender and therefore a detention and training order not available, then the punishment is one of a community sentence and that only in very exceptional circumstances should the youth court use s.91 to impose detention on these particularly young defendants. Despite the clarity of the developing test, the High Court has continued to deal with further challenges.

In order to reduce this and the citation of the previous authorities, the High Court in *R. (H and Others) v Southampton Youth Court* [2004] EWHC 2912, stated that the general policy of the legislature is that those under 18 and especially those under 15 should wherever possible, be dealt with in the Youth Court, in order to best meet their specific needs. The Crown Court, given its formalities should be reserved for only the most serious cases. Further, for offenders under 14, the use of detention is restricted and should only be used only for the exceptional cases. Leveson J. then stated:

> "in each case the court should ask itself whether there is a *real prospect*, having regard to his or her age, that this defendant whose case they are considering might require a sentence of, or in excess of, two years or, alternatively, whether although

the sentence might be less be less than two years, there is some unusual feature of the case which justifies declining jurisdiction, bearing in mind that the absence of a power to impose a detention and training order because the defendant is under 15 is not an unusual feature."

16.41 It is important for those who practice in the Youth Court to be familiar with the guidance of the correct test and be fully prepared to deal with mode of trial proceedings. If the offence is one that an older defendant would attract a substantial custodial sentence, could the same be said for a young offender, especially one under 15? This is well illustrated in the facts of *H and Others* in regard to a sexual assault arising out of essentially horseplay, but with serious consequences for the victim. Solicitors for the defence did not challenge the prosecution's contentions that the case should be treated as a grave crime, neither did they seek an adjournment to carefully consider the matter with better disclosure. Both the prosecution and the defence must be alive to the aggravating and mitigating factors in the case and any relevant sentencing guidelines/authorities.

Conversely, in *CPS v Redbridge Youth Court* [2005] EWHC 1390, the High Court ruled that the magistrates had taken a too strict application and incorrectly guided themselves, based on whether a sentence wuld be in excess of the two year threshold. The young defendant was charged with a series of offences including sexual assault on a child under 13 and malicious communications. There existed nine aggravating factors to the case. The High Court ruled that the magistrates were wrong to accept jurisdiction and quashed the decision.

It is to be noted that when brought into force, s.41 and Sch.3 to the CJA 2003, s.24 will be amended significantly with the insertion of a new s.24A to D. In addition, and to further complicate matters, Sch.3 introduces a new s.51A sending young defendant's to the Crown Court, to be inserted in s.51 of the CDA 1998. The current problem is this is only partially in force. Section 51A provides that if any of four conditions are satisfied, then the young defendant must be sent to the Crown Court. Condition D is currently the only one in force which provides that the offence is a specified violent (Pt 1 of Sch.15 lists 65 separate offences) or sexual offence (Pt 2 of Sch.15 lists 88 separate offences) within the meaning of s.224 of the CJA 2003 and that it appears to the court that if found guilty, the criteria for the imposition of a sentence under s.226(3) (detention for public protection from serious harm) or s.228(2) (extended sentence on licence) would be met.

16.42 These provisions came to be considered by the High Court in *R. v South East Surrey Youth Court and Ghanbari* [2005] EWHC 2929, and caused Rose L.J. to make the following observations concerning inconsistencies within the provisions, particularly that s.24, in its current form, is inconsistent with that of s.51A(d):

"so yet again, the courts are faced with a sample of the deeply confusing provisions of the Criminal Justice Act 2003, and the satellite Statutory Instruments to which it is giving stuttering birth. The most inviting course for this court to follow, would be for its members, having shaken their heads in despair to hold up their hands and say: 'the holy grail of rational interpretation is impossible to find'. But it is not for us to desert our judicial duty, however lamentably others have legislated. But we find little comfort or assistance in the historic cannons of construction for determining the will of Parliament which were fashioned in a more leisurely age and at a time when elegance and clarity of thought and language were to be found in legislation as a matter of course rather than exception."

His Lordship then provided guidance on the approach to the two sets of provisions, that:

(i) Wherever possible a young defendant should be tried in the Youth Court.

(ii) The guidance of the Court of Appeal in *R. v Lang* [2005] EWCA Crim 2864, when assessing significant risk should be considered.

(iii) The need of a pre-sentence report in determining a significant risk.

(iv) That assessment of significant risk will not be appropriate after conviction. If the criteria, is met, then commit the defendant for sentence.

(v) If jointly charged with adult, factors relevant to joint or separate trials will include age and maturity, culpability and previous convictions.

In this case, the High Court ruled that although the Youth Court was wrong not to consider s.51A(d), its decision to accept summary jurisdiction of a s.47 offence was unimpeachable.

It is important to note that as with the adult court, the Youth Court can under s.25(5), having commenced summary trial, discontinue the trial at any time before the conclusion of the prosecution's case and reconsider mode of trial. Conversely, if whilst acting as examining justices, it appears, that the s.24 criteria for summary jurisdiction is satisfied, then the court may proceed to summary trial. In *DPP v Camberwell Green Youth Court* [2003] EWHC 3217 the High Court by following a line of previous authority ruled that once a decision has been made as to mode of trial, that decision is irrevocable, unless the conditions in s.25 are satisfied.

The court does not have the power to make a decision as to venue and then before trial change its mind, due to new or additional factors which have emerged. The dicta in *R. v Newham Ex p. F* [1986] 1 W.L.R. 939, was disapproved. In *R. v Leeds Youth Court* [2001] 168 J.P. 694, the High Court stated that s.25 provides the court with a judicial discretionary power and must be based on some good, proper and relevant reason, in terms of seriousness of the offence. For instance, new evidential material may arise during the course of a trial, making the original decision on mode of trial now inappropriate. (see also *R. (C) v Grimsby Magistrates' Court* [2004] EWHC 2240.

21. Summary Trial of Young Offenders

16.43 The format of the trial of a young offender is the same for any other criminal trial. Other than to note that in Pt 38 of the CrPR 2005, if the defendant is not legally represented, the court must allow the guardian or parent or possibly relative to provide assistance in conducting the case. The court is under a duty to explain to the defendant the nature of the proceedings and the substance of the charge against them by using simple language only then can the court take the defendant's plea. Section 11 of the MCA 1980 (see para.16.35 above) equally applies to the Youth Court. However, s.54 of the CJIA 2008 when in force unlike with adult offender, gives the Court a greater discretionary power on whether or not to continue in their absence.

22. Power to Commit to the Crown Court for Sentence

16.44 In para.23 of Sch.3 of the CJA 2003 inserts after s.3 of the PCC(S) Act 2000, s.3C which provides that, if it appears to the court that the young defendant is a dangerous offender, within the meaning of s.226(3) and s.228(2), then the court must commit them either on bail, or in custody to the Crown Court for sentence. Section 5A then provides that the Crown Court can deal with the offender as if they had just been convicted on indictment.

23. Sentencing of Young Offenders

16.45 Like adults, the Youth Court or the Crown Court can impose a custodial or non custodial sentence. However, these differ in a number of respects to adult sentences as will become apparent in the following paragraphs. Section 9 of the Criminal Justice and Immigration Act 2008 sets out in statutory form the purpose in sentencing an offender under 18 by inserting a new s.142A into the CJA 2003, which provides that in addition to the principal aim of the youth justice system and the welfare of the offender (see para.16.37 above) the Court is also to have regard to principal purposes of sentencing similar to those for adult offenders. The four purposes are as follows:

(i) the punishment of offenders;

(ii) the reform and rehabilitation of offenders;

(iii) the protection of the public;

(iv) the making of reparation by offenders to persons affected by their offences.

The courts are not required to have regard to these purposes if the offence is murder, certain specified firearms offences (s.287 of the CJA 2003), offences of minding a weapon under s.29(6) of the Violent Crime Reduction Act 2006 and when determined to be a dangerous offender.

24. Sentences of Detention for Young Offenders

16.46 In regard to custodial sentences, it is important to be aware that s.89 of the PCC(S)A 2000 imposes a clear restriction on the use of imprisonment as a form of sentence by the court on a person aged under 21. Although yet to be brought into force s.61 of the Criminal Justice and Courts Services Act 2000 expressly abolishes s.89 in regard to offender's age between 18 and 21, for these offenders the court will impose a sentence of imprisonment and under subsection (5) may be detained either in a prison or a Young Offenders Institution. Nevertheless, for the moment a court in respect of a young offender can only impose a custodial sentence of detention. The court can impose the following sentences:

Custody for Life for Murder

16.47 Under s.93 of the PCC(S)A 2000, the court must impose a sentence of custody for life on conviction of murder. Section 269 of the CJA 2003 provides the statutory framework for the determination of the minimum term to be served before release can be considered. This is based on the seriousness of the offence by applying the general principles in Sch.21. This provides a starting point of 12 years for an offender under 18 at the time of the offence, dependant on a detailed assessment of the aggravating and mitigating factors. A non-exhaustive list is given in Sch.21 and the court can move up or down from the starting point.

Custody for Life for Other Certain Offences

16.48 Under s.94 of the PCC(S)A 2000, the court has a discretion to impose a sentence of custody for life, where the offence has a maximum sentence of life imprisonment, i.e. robbery.

Detention Under s.91 of the PCC(S) Act 2000 for a Grave Offence.

16.49 A grave offence is one that is punishable with 14 years or more imprisonment.

Detention and Training Order Under ss.100 to 107 of the PCC(S)Act 2000

16.50 This is split into half detention and the other half under trained supervision. The court must first be satisfied that the offence is so serious that only a DTO can be justified (consideration stage). The next step is to determine the appropriate length of the order, from a range of statutory specified terms of 4,6,8,10,12, 18 or 24 months (the determination stage). The court is under a positive duty to take into account in that determination, any time spent in custody (includes police detention and on remand) whilst on remand for that offence, or any other offence arising from the "same facts or evidence" (see *R. v Elsmore* [2001] EWCA Crim 943).

To impose an incorrect term would render the sentence unlawful (see *R. v Bancroft* [2001] EWCA 1545. Section 101(3) and (13) empowers the relevant court to impose a DTO to run consecutively "on the expiry of the term of any other DTO made by that or any other court". (see *R. v Norris* [2001] 164 J.P. 685). A sentencing court cannot under s.101(2) consider imposing a DTO on an offender, who at the time of conviction, was under the age of 15, "unless it is of the opinion that he is a persistent offender". There is no statutory definition of what is a persistent offender and therefore this will be purely a matter for the courts to determine in each individual case, (see *R. v Charlton* [2000] 164 J.P. 685). For offenders under 12 a DTO can only be imposed where there is no other adequate method of protecting the public

Detention for Life or Public Protection for being a Dangerous Offender

16.51 Chapter 5 of the CJA 2003 which came into effect on April 4, 2005, establishes a new range of mandatory sentences for certain specified violent, or sexual or serious offences, where the offender is deemed dangerous to the public. In relation to those under 18 on the date of conviction, s.226 provides that if they are convicted of a serious offence within the meaning of s.224(2) (i.e. a specified violent or sexual offence of which there are 153 offences listed in Sch.15, which is punishable with either life imprisonment or 10 years or more) and the court is for the opinion that there is a significant risk to the public of serious harm from further specified offences committed by the offender. In determining whether or not there is a significant risk, the court must under s.229 as amended by s.17 of the CJIA 2008 (see para.19.21) make an assessment of dangerousness, by considering the nature and circumstances of the offence, information and offender behaviour.

If the court is of this opinion and the offence is one in which the offender would, apart from this section, be liable to detention for life under s.91 of the PCC(S)A 2000 and the court considers that the seriousness of the offence and associated offences, is such as to justify such a detention, then the court must impose a sentence of detention for life under s.91. Alternatively, if the conditions of seriousness and the offence having a maximum sentence of life are not met and the use of an extended sentence is not appropriate to protecting the public, then as inserted by s.14 of the Criminal Justice and Immigration Act 2008, the court may impose a sentence of detention for public protection, if the notional minimum term is at least two years (see Chapter Nineteen, para.19.10).

The court, when determining the length of the detention which must be served before release can be considered, must ensure that it is proportionate to the offender's culpability. Section 236 of the CJA 2003 sets out the circumstances in which a sentence to detention can be converted into a sentence of imprisonment. Both the detention for life and detention for public protection constitute an indeterminate sentence, which means the release of the offender is subject to the parole board being satisfied they are no longer a risk. In other words, the offender does not know when they will be released if at all.

Extended Sentence of Detention

16.52 Under s.228 of the CJA 2003, if the offender (under 18 at date of conviction) is convicted of a specified violent or sexual offence and the court considers that there is a significant risk to the public of serious harm from future offending for further specified offences, the court may (once s.16 of the CJIA 2008 is in force) impose an extended sentence of detention. Before a court can impose an extended sentence of detention, the condition in subsection (2A) as inserted by s.16 of the CJIA 2008 must be met. The condition requires the court to be satisfied that, if it were to impose such a sentence, the appropriate custodial term would be at least four years. A new subsection (7) gives the Secretary of State a discretionary power to change the requirement of the condition. An extended sentence of detention will amount to an aggregate sentence consisting of the appropriate custodial term, which must not be less than 12 months and not exceeding the maximum for the offence and a further period of extension. This period of extension is where the offender is not in custody, but subject to licence conditions. The court has a discretion as to the length in terms of what it considers to be necessary for the protection of the public. For a specified violent offence, the length range must not exceed five years, whereas for a specified sexual offence, it is eight years.

25. Non-Custodial Sentences

16.53 The court has a extensive range of community and non custodial sentences at its disposal for young offenders. Imposition of some of these sentences very much depends on the age of the offender. The Criminal Justice Act 2003 created the Youth Community Order (YCO) in s.147 as a form of community punishment. However, barely three years later the Ministry of Justice has decided to repeal the YCO and replace it was a Youth Rehabilitation Order (YRO) contained in ss.1 to 8 of the Criminal Justice and Immigration Act 2008 (yet to be brought into force at the discretion of the Secretary of State). The YRO applies to any offender under 18 at the date of conviction. When making the Order, the court will have the power to impose one or more of 15 specified requirements, similar to those available to adult offenders contained in ss.199 to 213 of the CJA 2003. These requirements can be electronically monitored for compliance. The Order can also be made with intensive supervision and surveillance, or with fostering. The procedural requirements to the imposition of an YRO are contained in Schs 1 to 4. Schedule 1 which covers the material aspects of the YRO, has four parts to it and 36 sections. Until the YRO is brought into force the court will continue to impose the Youth Community Order.

26. Youth Community Order as a Community Sentence

16.54 Section 147, which came into effect on April 4, 2005, defines a youth community order and in essence encapsulates one or more of the following five orders:

(i) *a curfew order* as defined in s.163 of the PCC(S)A 2000

The court can, provided it does not interfere with religious beliefs or schooling, specify different places, periods and days of the curfew, not less than two hours or more than 12 in one day. If over 16, then a maximum of six months, if under 16 the court must first obtain a pre sentence report and consider information about family circumstances and the likely effect. The maximum length is three months. The court must explain the effects and consequences of the order and that it can be reviewed. The curfew can be monitored by electronic tagging.

(ii) an exclusion order under s.40A(1)

This provides that the court can prohibit the offender from entering a specified place, if under 16 the maximum is three months, if over 16 it is two years;

(iii) an attendance centre order defined in s.60

The offence must be one punishable with detention in which the offender must present themselves at an designated attendance centre for not less than 12 hours unless under 14. It can be increased to 24 hours for those under 16. For those youths over 16 but under 21 it is up to 36 hours. The court can impose a ACO even if the offender is currently subjected to one

(iv) a supervision order under s.63

This order can be up to a maximum of three years with a responsible officer designed to encourage and assist the offender to stop offending and protect the public)

(v) an action plan order under s.69(1)

If the offender is under 18 and the court is satisfied from the pre sentence report that an APO is desirable, in the interests of rehabilitation and prevent future offending. The offender is placed under supervision of responsible officer and must follow requirements in order and directions of the officer. The court cannot make an APO if one is already active.

In regard to a supervision order and action plan order, the court can under s.279 of the CJA 2003 and in accordance with the procedure set out in Sch.24, include a drug treatment and testing requirement as part of the order. The offender must be over 14 and consent to the inclusion. Further, the court must be satisfied that the offender is dependant on, or has a propensity to misuse drugs and this requires, or may be susceptible to treatment. The court must specify the period in which the offender must submit to treatment and the minimum number of samples for testing is to be arranged.

The youth community order is available for young offenders aged between 10 and 17. In passing a youth community order the court must under s.148(3) of the CJA 2003 be of the opinion that the terms of the order are the most suitable for the offender and any restrictions on liberty must be commensurate with the seriousness of the offence and any associated offences. If the offender breaches any of the orders, then in accordance with Sch.3, the court can revoke the order with or without the imposition of a new sentence (including fine) for the original offence.

27. Offenders Aged 16 or Over Community Sentence

16.55 Part 12 and Ch.2 of the CJA 2003 creates a new community order for disposal of criminal offences committed by those aged 16 or over. However, while the provisions are in force for adult offenders, the Ministry of Justice has decided to further delay the implementation date for 16 to 17 year olds until April 4, 2009. This had originally been April 4, 2007, but pressure generally within the criminal justice system has caused the further delay of two years, (see the CJA 2003 (Commencement No.8) Order 2005 (SI 2005/950)) as amended by SI 2007/291. As such, ss.41 to 58 and Schs 2 and 3 of the PCC(S) A 2000 will still apply for 16 to 17 year olds. The court therefore has four possible options of non-custody disposal as follows:

(i) Community Rehabilitation Order (CRO)

If the defendant is over 16 and found guilty of an offence for which the court is of the opinion that supervision by a responsible officer is desirable in the interests of securing rehabilitation of the offender, protecting the public or to prevent future offending, then the court can impose a CRO for a specified period not less than six months, but not more than three years.

(ii) Community Punishment Order (CPO)

Where the defendant is over 16 and is guilty of an offence which is punishable in the case of an adult with imprisonment then the court may make a CPO requiring the offender to perform unpaid work of not less than 40 hours or more than 240 hours.

(iii) Community Punishment and Rehabilitation Order (CPRO)

If the offender, aged 16 or over, is convicted of an offence punishable with imprisonment and the court is of the same opinion as for a CRO, the court may order that the offender is (i) placed under the supervision of a responsible officer for not less than 12 months or more than three years; and (ii) to perform unpaid work for not less than 40 hours, but not more than 100 hours. If the offender breaches any of the above orders without reasonable cause then the court will summons or issue a warrant for their arrest and either reinstate the original order, amend it or revoke and re-sentence the offender.

(iv) Drug Testing and Treatment Order (DTTO) (ss.52 to 47)

The DTTO is designed to reduce the amount of offences which are directly attributable to drug misuse. The testing requirement of the order will direct the offender to be the subject of a series of drug tests, in order to ascertain progress in being drug free. The treatment requirement will direct the offender to comply with a treatment programme. This will be based on individual need and can either be treatment as a resident at specified facility or treatment as a non resident. The order to be imposed requires the consent of the offender and if imposed, will be subject to periodical reviews by the court at intervals of one month. If necessary, the court can make amendments to the order. The duration of the order is to be not less than six months, but not more than three years.

In *R. v Belli* [2003] EWCA Crim 2752, the Court of Appeal, having reviewed the authorities, considered that it is important for the sentencing court to give proper consideration of the imposition of a DTTO, even if the offence committed or the scale of offending would, in all other circumstances, justify a custodial sentence. If the imposition of a DTTO gives a realistic prospect of reducing drug addition and therefore criminality, then a DTTO is a sensible option. Further guidance was provided in *R. v Woods and Collins* [2006] 1 Cr.App.R. 83. If the offender breaches the order, then the court will either issue an appearance summons, or issue a warrant of arrest. If the court is satisfied that the offender breached the order without reasonable excuse, then the court can impose a fine not exceeding £1,000, make a CSO, but not more than 60 hours, or revoke the order and sentence the offender as if they had just been convicted.

28. Other Methods of Disposal

16.56 The court also has the following options as an appropriate method of dealing with the offence:

(i) Reparation Order

In Pt IV of the PCC(S)A 2000, the court can impose a reparation order to a defendant under 18, requiring them to make reparation to a victim provided they consent, or to a person specified in the order, or to the community at large to undertake suitable work. The court must before making the order obtain a pre sentence report as to suitability and attitude of the offender. The offender will be monitored by a responsible officer. The maximum time that can be imposed is 24 hours of work and must not interfere with religious beliefs or schooling.

(ii) Fines

Under s.135 of the PCC(S)A 2000 the court has the power to impose a fine. In regard to 10 to 13 year olds, the maximum is £250, while for 14 to 17 year olds, it is £1,000. The court must consider the seriousness of the offence and the financial circumstances of the offender and their parent(s) must be taken into account, (an offence example could be evading a bus or train fare). Under s.137, the court can order the parent or guardian and this includes a Local Authority, if in care, to pay the fine. Section 39 of the Criminal Justice and Immigration Act 2008 and Sch.7, when in force, will allow the magistrates' court in respect of an offender under 18, instead of taking proceedings against the parent or guardian, to make a "Youth Default Order" compelling that person to undertake unpaid work, or be present at an attendance centre, or be subject to a curfew. The court has the power to postpone making the order and that if payment is received in full the order can be revoked or if only partial payment is made, then the order can be proportionately reduced.

(iii) Disqualification from driving

Under s.146 of the PCC(S)A 2000, the court has a general power to order the disqualification from driving of the offender, for such periods as the court thinks fit.

(iv) Anti-Social Behaviour Order

Under s.1C of the CDA 1998, the court can, if the offence is committed on or after April 1, 1999, make an ASBO to prohibit the offender from acting in a manner likely to cause harassment alarm or distress to one or more persons.

(v) Discharge

Sections 11 to 15 of the PCC(S)A 2000 provides for the court to impose a discharge, either conditionally or absolute.

(vi) Compensation Order

Under s.136 of the PCC(S)A 2000, the court can make an order that requires the offender to pay compensation to the complainant.

(vii) Ancillary Orders

These include forfeiture and destruction orders, notification requirements in the Sexual Offences Act 2003 and also sexual offences prevention orders and prosecution costs.

29. First Time Offenders: Referral Orders

16.57 Part 1 of the Youth Justice and Criminal Evidence Act 1999 created the "referral order", (now ss.20 to 28 and Sch.1 of the PCC(S)A 2000) designed specifically as mandatory disposal for those between 10 and 17 years, who have pleaded guilty and been convicted for the first time of an imprisonable offence. The requirement that the offender has never been bound over to keep the peace is to be removed by s.35 of the Criminal Justice and Immigration Act 2008 (CJIA 2008). The duration of the order is between three and 12 months, in which the young defendant is referred to the youth offender panel (YOP) as a form of restorative justice. The panel consists of a community member, an officer from the youth offending team, the victim if they agree to attend and anyone else who has a significant interest in the defendant. The purpose of the panel is to encourage the offender to consider directly the impact and consequences of their act, to ameliorate the harm caused and agree a contract for a programme to stop or reduce the risk of re-offending.

The Referral Orders (Amendment of Referral Conditions) Regulations 2003 (SI 2003/1605) removes the obligation to refer a first time offender for non-imprisonable minor or road traffic offences. If the panel believe that the offender is not complying or the parent/guardian fails to attend the meeting (added by Sch.34 of the CJA 2003), then a report must be sent to the court, where a summons will be issued requiring attendance and a warrant for arrest if necessary. If the court is satisfied on the findings in the report, the order can be revoked and the court can deal with the offender in any way in which the court could have for the offences, taking into account the circumstances of the referral back to the court and the extent of compliance with the contract. The offender can appeal to the Crown Court against this decision. In the alternative, the court can reinstate the original order, or discharge it if the contract time as expired. A parenting order can be made at the same time as a referral order. When ss.35 to 37 of the CJIA 2008 come into effect, the YOP will if the offender is making good progress and it is in the interests of justice refer the offender back to court with a view for the referral order to be revoked. Conversely, the YOP may apply for the referral order to be extended by up to a further three months but subject to a maximum of 12 months duration for the referral order.

30. Age of Offender at the Date of Sentence

16.58 A situation may arise where the offender reaches the age of 18 at or before the date of trial or sentence, but after the commission of the offence. How should the court now dispose of the case, in terms of whether the offender is now an adult, or despite the age change is still to be treated for the purposes of trial or sentence a young offender? In *R. v Ghafoor* [2003] Cr.App.R.(S) 428, the Court of Appeal considered the starting point to be that the offender is to be sentenced based on their age at the date of the commission of the offence. The appellant was charged with a number of serious public order offences that had occurred when he was 17. However, at the date of conviction when he pleaded guilty, he was 18. The Court of Appeal reduced his sentence of four and a half years' detention to that of 18 months DTO. Further, in *R. v M* [2003] Cr.App.R.(S) 26, the High Court quashed the DTO imposed, when the offender had turned 15 between the date the offence was committed and the date of conviction, (see also *R. v R* [2006] EWCA Crim 3184, in which it was held that a sentence of 18 DTO was wrong in principle when the offender had turned 15 after the date of the offence, but before the date of conviction. The Court substituted a supervision order).

31. For Parents

16.59 Relating specifically to parents of young offenders the court can impose:

Parenting Order

16.60 Under ss.8 and 9 of the Crime and Disorder Act 1998 which came into effect on September 1, 2000, the court can impose a parenting order, in circumstances where the court has made a child safety order, an ASBO or the young defendant has been convicted of an offence and the court is satisfied that it is desirable in the interests of preventing repetition of behaviour and future offending. A PSR will usually indicate to the court the need for parental intervention. If the offender is under 16 then the court is under a duty to make an order, unless it is not in the interests of preventing repetition or further offending.

The order consists of two elements, first a requirement for the parent to attend counselling or guidance sessions (up to three months) as directed by a responsible officer, the second element is at the discretion of the court and can include ensuring the proper care and control of the offender. The primary purpose of a PO is to provide support and help. Failure to comply without reasonable excuse after repeated warnings amounts to a summary offence punished by way of a £1,000 fine. The Anti-Social Behaviour Act 2005 and the Criminal Justice Act 2003, as from February 27, 2004, have further extended the availability of a parenting order, by giving the youth offending team a power to enter voluntarily into a parenting agreement and thereafter if the need arises, to make a free standing application to the magistrates' court for a parenting order, even if the young person is not required to attend court.

Parental Bind over Order and Child Safety Orders

16.61 Section 150 of the PCC(S)A 2000 provides that the court can bind over the parent(s) of an offender who is under 16 at date of sentencing, if the court is satisfied that in the circumstances of the case, it would be desirable in the interests of preventing the young defendant re-offending. The parent must consent to the bind over and enter into a recognizance with the court, not exceeding £1,000, to take proper care and control of the defendant. The bind over period must not exceed three years or until they are 18. If the parent unreasonably refuses, then court can order them to pay a fine of £1,000. This is treated as a court fine and the consequences for non payment or default will apply. It is impermissible to make a parental bind over order in conjunction with a referral order. Finally, for young children (under 10) who are at risk of offending, there is available a Child Safety Order under ss.11 and 12 of the Crime and Disorder Act 1998. This can be for a specified period in which the child is placed under the supervision of a responsible officer and can only be made by the Family Proceedings Court.

Parental Compensation Orders for Child Under 10

16.62 Section 144 and Sch.10 of the Serious Organised Crime and Police Act 2005, which came into force on July 26, 2006, but only in certain areas, provides that the magistrates' on hearing an application from a Local Authority, may make a Parental Compensation Order. In considering the application, the court must be satisfied on a balance of probabilities that (i) the child under 10 did a criminal act which resulted in the taking, causing loss of or damage to property (provided the child caused it, it matters not by whom), or (ii) acted in a manner that caused, or was likely to cause harassment, alarm or distress to one or more persons not of the same household as the child.

Once an Order is made it requires either the parent or guardian of the child (not a Local Authority), to pay an amount of compensation not exceeding £5,000 to a person(s) specified in the Order and when it must be paid. The Order is treated as if it were a fine imposed after a conviction for the purposes of collection and enforcement. When fixing the amount to be paid, the court must take into account the value of the property, any loss in consequence of the act of the child, whether compensation has already been paid or reparation has been made, the financial circumstances of the parents (the court will ask for an assessment) and any lack of care of the property owner. If property which was taken is returned undamaged then an order cannot be made. If a parent fails to comply with the terms of the order and are unable to show they had a reasonable excuse then they are guilty of a summary offence and liable to a fine not exceeding level 3 on the standard scale.

Chapter Seventeen

BAIL PROCEDURE

1. Meaning of Bail and Part 19 of the Criminal Procedure Rules 2005

17.01 Having been authorised to remain in police custody after being formally charged, a defendant will make a first appearance at the magistrates' court at the next sitting. Alternatively, the charged person will be released on police bail with or without conditions to attend at the magistrates' court at a specified date and time. If the defendant appears in custody, they will need to decide whether to make an application for bail. If they decide to apply for bail and the prosecution do not oppose such an application, bail with usually follow. If however the prosecution oppose bail, then the magistrates will hear representations from both parties and decide whether to remand the accused either on bail, or alternatively in custody.

In making this decision the magistrates must follow the provisions of the Bail Act 1976. The Bail Act 1976 itself has been extensively revised and amended by subsequent legislation, such as the Criminal Justice and Public Order Act 1994, the Crime and Disorder Act 1998, the Criminal Justice Act 2003 and now the Criminal Justice and Immigration Act 2008. To refer to the original 1976 Act would be misleading and indeed inaccurate with regard to certain aspects of bail. Parliament now needs to either codify or consolidate the existing provisions into a new comprehensive Bail Act to allow simple and easy access to an important part of criminal procedure.

Bail is in essence, the court authorising the accused person to be at liberty but subject to attendance at court when required to so do, i.e. surrender to custody of the court (s.2(2)). Under s.1 (6) of the Bail Act 1976, bail can be granted either "unconditionally" or "conditionally". The relevant procedure to be followed in relation to bail is delineated in Pt 19 of the CrPR 2005.

The provisions of the Bail Act 1976, apart from s.4, apply equally to extradition proceedings under the Extradition Act 2003. Whilst the general right to bail only covers substantive criminal proceedings, art.5 provides the necessary safeguard in extradition proceedings. This was confirmed in *R. (Raissi) v Secretary of State for the Home Department* [2008] EWCA Civ 72, where it was further observed that the prosecution are under a clear duty to disclose all material that is relevant to a bail application. Further, the court gave strong observations concerning the serious default by both the police and the CPS concerning the extradition proceedings brought against the claimant in the wake of the September 11th terrorist attacks, as being brought for an ulterior motive and that the continued opposition to bail, the claimant having been remanded into custody, was based on unsubstantiated assertions. This amounted to an abuse.

2. Section 4(1) General Right to Bail and Art.5 of the European Convention on Human Rights (Presumption of Unconditional Bail)

17.02 Section 4(1) of the Bail Act 1976 provides that a person who is accused of an offence and either appears before the magistrates' or the Crown Court in the course of, or in connection with proceedings for the offence, *shall* be granted bail. Under s.4(4) this applies also to persons who have been convicted and the case is to be adjourned for the completion of a pre-sentence report. Article 5 of the European Convention on Human Rights provides that everyone has the right to liberty and security of person and that no one shall be deprived of their liberty, unless "in accordance with the procedure prescribed by law". Under art.5(b) this includes the lawful arrest and detention of a person for non-compliance with a court order, or in order to secure that they fulfil any obligation prescribed by law. Further under art.5(c) the lawful arrest and detention of a person, in order to bring them before a competent legal authority on reasonable suspicion of having committed an offence, or alternatively where it is necessary reasonably to prevent further offences being committed or absconding, amounts to a legitimate interference with the right.

3. Limitation of "General Right to Bail" for Certain Offences

17.03 Whilst s.4 provides a general right to the granting of bail, s.25 of the Criminal Justice and Public Order Act 1994 places a clear limitation upon it. Section 25, as originally enacted, provided that bail shall only be granted to a person either charged with, or convicted of an offence of murder, attempted murder, manslaughter, rape and attempted rape and who has been convicted previously of one of these offences, *only if the court is satisfied that there are exceptional circumstances which justify it.* The unfortunate use of these words meant that the provision put the onus of proof upon the defendant to establish exceptional circumstances. In *Caballero v UK* [2000] 30 E.H.R.R. 643, the ECHR ruled that s.25 violated art.5, in that it did not allow for a consideration of all the relevant facts and in essence denied bail to any person who came within the limitation.

In consequence s.56 of the Crime and Disorder Act 1998 amended s.25 so that bail *shall be* granted to a person who is charged with or convicted of a qualifying offence, namely (i) murder; (ii) attempted murder; (iii) manslaughter; rape and other specified sexual offences under the Sexual Offences

Act 2003; (iv) attempted rape and who has previously been convicted of any such offence in a UK court, or of "culpable homicide" and in respect of manslaughter, was sentenced to a term of imprisonment, or in the case of a child/young person to long term detention. But *only if* the court, when considering the granting of bail is *satisfied* that there are exceptional circumstances which justify it. Conviction for this purpose includes a not guilty verdict by reason of insanity or fitness to plead.

The meaning of satisfied and exceptional circumstances was considered by the House of Lords in *O v Crown Court at Harrow* [2006] 3 W.L.R. 195. Their Lordships adopted a "reading down" approach to the literal meaning of these words, so as to ensure that under s.3 of the Human Rights Act 1998, the defendant's right to liberty contained in art.5 was not breached. For this reason the word "satisfied" imposes an evidential burden not a persuasive burden on the defendant to point to, or produce material which supports the existence of exceptional circumstances.

4. Primary Grounds (Exceptions) for Refusing Bail: Schedule 1 Part 1 Paragraph 2 for "Imprisonable Offence"

17.04 In regard to offences which are punishable with imprisonment (if the defendant is charged with several offences only one need be imprisonable), the court can refuse bail provided one or more of the statutory exceptions apply. However, when s.52 and Sch.12 of the Criminal Justice and Immigration Act 2008 comes into effect Pt 1 will not apply to any defendant including those under 18 who are charged with either a summary only imprisonable offence or an offence listed in Sch.2 of the Magistrates' Court Act 1980, namely criminal damage and aggravated criminal damage under £5,000. The court's starting point is always the general right to bail (presumption of bail) without attaching any conditions.

For these defendants, the court must consider the eight exceptions contained in a new Pt 1A. The eight exceptions are a combination of those found in Pt 1 and in Pt 2 for non imprisonable offences, with one new additional exception where the defendant if released on bail would commit an offence by engaging in conduct that would or is likely to cause physical or mental injury to any person or for that person to fear such injury. One of the important points to note concerning the new Pt 1A is that the test to be applied is simply that the court need not grant bail if it appears to the court that any of the eight exceptions is satisfied.

The statutory exceptions in Pt 1 para.2 are as follows:

(i) Bail may be refused if the court is *satisfied that there are substantial grounds for believing* that the defendant, if released on bail would:

- (a) fail to surrender to custody;
- (b) commit an offence while on bail;

(c) interfere with witnesses or otherwise obstruct the course of justice.

In the following situations the defendant need not be granted bail. It is important to be aware that the magistrates do not have to be satisfied that there are substantial grounds to believe, simply that certain specified circumstances exist to justify the refusal of bail.

(ii) Presumption against Bail

If a defendant is 18 years or over and *it appears* to the court that they were already on bail for another offence then the court may not grant bail *unless*, it is satisfied that there is no significant risk of them committing an offence whilst on bail. For those under 18 and on bail for another offence, there is no presumption against bail, but the court can give "particular weight" to this when deciding whether there are substantial grounds to believe that the young defendant may commit further offences (s.14 of the CJA 2003).

(iii) The court need not grant bail if it is satisfied that the defendant should be kept in custody for their own protection; or if a child, for their own welfare.

(iv) The defendant is already in custody serving a sentence.

This occurs where defendant is sentenced to custody for another offence, during the proceedings for the current offence. From the defence's point of view it may still be appropriate for a bail application to be made, since, if bail is not granted, the defendant will be remanded in custody for the offence. It is quite possible that the defendant may complete the term of their sentence, but on the date of release will have to stay in custody, now as a remand prisoner for the new offence. If the court does grant bail, then this is known as "technical bail", so that while serving the current sentence the defendant is on bail for the new offence in a technical sense. This becomes important at the release date, where the conditions of that bail will now apply and the defendant will be released from custody subject to that bail.

(v) It is not practicable at this stage to obtain sufficient information to make a decision.

Given the speed at which cases now appear before the courts from the police station, it may not be possible for either the defence or prosecution to have available sufficient information concerning the defendant, so as to allow the court to make an informed decision as to bail. From the defence's point of view, this becomes important especially with issues of residence, since to make an application for bail with insufficient information will almost certainly lead to the court refusing bail. This means that a bail application has been lost and the defence can only make two applications for bail, unless new information comes to light. Accordingly, it is better for the defendant to take what is known as a "lie down", so as to preserve the two bail applications.

(vi) The defendant is arrested under s.7 of Bail Act 1976 (amended by s.15 of the CJA 2003).

If a defendant over 18 is arrested under s.7 on suspicion of breaching their conditions of bail, or is arrested on a failure to attend warrant, then when brought before the court for this alleged breach, the court need not grant bail, unless it is satisfied that there is no significant risk that they would fail to surrender to custody, or that they had reasonable cause for the failure to attend. If however, it appears to the court that although the defendant had reasonable cause, they then failed to surrender as soon as is reasonably practicable after the appointed time, bail need not be granted.

If the defendant is under 18 then the court can give "particular weight" to the failure to surrender without reasonable cause to the decision whether there are substantial grounds to believe that if granted bail they would fail to appear, commit further offences or interfere with justice. For both defendants, the fact that the court did not give the defendant a copy of the bail decision, will not constitute a reasonable cause. Accordingly, the defendant cannot claim to have missed the court date, owing to the fact that the court had not given them a written recorded copy of the date. If the court refuses bail then the defendant will be remanded into custody for the duration of the proceedings.

5. Regard to Certain Considerations before Making a Decision on the above Grounds

17.05 When determining a decision on bail, the court must have regard to any of the following points as outlined in Sch.1:

(i) The nature and seriousness of the offence and probable method of disposal.

The more serious the offence, the more culpable the defendant, therefore the greater the punishment and the less likely they are to surrender to face these serious charges. Again, if the offence is serious, such as a sexual violent offence, then there is a greater risk that they will re-offend or interfere with justice and that there is a need to protect the public.

(ii) The character, antecedents, associations and community ties of defendant.

A defendant with hitherto impeccable character is less likely to offend on bail. Likewise, a defendant has strong ties with the community, such as marriage, home, job and family members living in the vicinity, then the more stable is that defendant's day to day life and they are therefore less likely to jeopardise this arrangement by failing to attend or offend. Both physical and mental health may be relevant. Conversely, a defendant with an unstable life and previous convictions for similar offences to the one charged, will show a propensity to offend. If the antecedents reveal bail offences and offending on bail this is clear evidence of a defendant who has a propensity not to surrender, commit offences while on bail or interfere with justice, the very exceptions to granting bail.

From the defence's point of view a client who has an appalling record of offending especially on bail or bail offences of dishonesty then the prospects of bail being granted are reduced dramatically. Nevertheless, this does not mean that a bail application should not be made, it may well be the defendant is determined to turn their life around and there is evidence to suggest this, i.e. a period of absence from offending and a more stable life. Only if it would be futile, should a decision not to make an application for bail be made.

(iii) The defendant's response to previous grants of bail.

This consideration naturally links into the previous consideration. If the defendant is shown from their antecedents to have not responded to previous warnings or sentences and continues to offend, this would suggest that they are less likely to attend at court, given that such previous convictions can be an aggravating factor in terms of sentencing for the current offence. Likewise, they are more likely to offend while on bail, undeterred by the prospects of yet another sentence. To mitigate, the defence will generally argue the same as under the previous considerations.

(iv) Strength of prosecution's evidence.

This consideration very much stands on its own, the stronger and more cogent the evidence against the defendant is, the less likely it is that they will attend at court to answer to the allegation, particularly if there is little or no prospect of a viable line of defence. Conversely, it can be argued that the defendant is eager to clear their name and put positively before a court their defence to the allegation, or to put the prosecution to proof. If, on the other hand, the prosecution's case at this stage is weak and circumstantial, i.e. unreliable identification evidence, which may later be ruled too weak to put before the court, or evidence is likely to be ruled inadmissible, then potentially it would be wrong to remand a defendant in custody and deprive them of their liberty, if the case against them may collapse later.

It is important to be aware that the considerations above are case specific and will invariably differ from case to case The examples given are mere illustrations, to assist the reader, many other arguments may arise both for and against the granting of bail.

6. Drug Users: Restriction on Bail: Section 19 of the Criminal Justice Act 2003

17.06 There is no doubt that for certain offences a casual link exists between the commission of those offences and the misuse of class A drugs. This is more acute if the offending is specifically for the purpose of funding habitual drug use. The purpose of s.19 is therefore to break this continuous cycle. Section 19 inserts further exceptions in Sch.1 to the general right to bail for drug users, provided the particular court area has as the assessment facilities (Drug Action Team). If a defendant who is over 18 has given a positive sample for a specified class A drug in the police station (s.63B), or under s.161 of the CJA 2003 pre sentence drug testing and either the alleged offence is that of simple possession, or possession with intent to supply (s.5(2) and (3) Misuse of Drugs Act 1971); then the court can refuse bail unless it is satisfied there is no significant risk of the defendant committing further offences.

Alternatively, if the court is satisfied that there are substantial grounds for believing that the misuse of the drug (i) caused or contributed to the offence; and (ii) even if it did not if the offence was motivated wholly, or partly by their intended misuse of that drug, bail will not be granted, if in such circumstances the defendant has been offered an assessment but refused, or consented but then refused to participate. If nevertheless the court is satisfied that there is no significant risk of offences being committed whilst on bail, then the court may still grant bail. Helpful guidance on the application of s.19 and the respective roles of the prosecution and defence has been published in the Ministry of Justice circular 1/2005.

7. Reasons for Granting Bail for Certain Offences: Section 5 and Rule 19.10 to 12 of the CrPR

17.07 If the court refuses to grant bail or grants bail with conditions, then under s.5(2) the court is required to ensure that the reasons and particulars are recorded and if requested that the defendant be given a copy. If the defendant wishes to challenge the decision in the Crown Court, a copy must be given. If the defendant is being sent or committed to Crown Court and the defendant is not legally represented, the court must explain that they can apply to a Judge in Chambers at the Crown Court for bail. The magistrates' court must issue a certificate that they have heard full argument on a bail application, or if this is a second bail application that it is satisfied that there is no change in circumstances or reasons for refusing bail. If a defendant is refused bail the court must provide a copy of the certificate to the defendant. Paragraph 9A of Sch.1 provides that if the court grants bail to a person charged with murder or attempted murder, manslaughter, rape or attempted rape, then the court must state the reasons for its decision and record those reasons, (see *(R.) Shergill v Harrow Crown Court* [2005] EWHC 2005).

8. Grounds for Refusing Bail for a Non-Imprisonable Offence: Schedule 1 Part 2

17.08 Where a defendant appears before the court charged or convicted of an offence which does not carry imprisonment as a penalty, the court can refuse to grant bail if and only if:

(i) it appears to the court that the defendant on a previous occasion been granted bail but failed to surrender to custody and that the court with this in mind believes that if released on bail they would again fail to surrender;

(ii) it is necessary to protect the defendant;

(iii) the defendant is already serving a sentence of the court;

(iv) the defendant was on bail but subsequently arrested under s.7 and the court is satisfied that there are substantial grounds to believe that if released with conditions or not they would fail to surrender, commit further offences, or interfere with justice (as amended by s.13 CJA 2003).

9. Duty to Surrender and Bail with Conditions

17.09 Under s.3 of the Bail Act 1976, a person granted bail is under a duty to surrender to custody to the court as directed. The defendant, once they have arrived at the court and informed the court official of their presence, are then in the control of the court, even if they are at liberty in the court building while waiting for the case to be heard (see *R. v Central Criminal Court Ex p. Guney* [1996] A.C. 616. To leave the court building could potentially amount to the offence of escaping from lawful custody.

Under s3.(6) the court has the general power to impose such requirements including the imposition of electronic monitoring (see s.3(6ZAA) as amended by s.51 and Sch.11 to the CJIA 2008) to the granting of bail as appear necessary to the court, to secure that the defendant (i) surrenders to custody; (ii) does not commit an offence while on bail; (iii) does not interfere with witnesses or otherwise obstruct the course of justice; (iv) makes himself available for the completion of reports; (v) attends appointments with legal representative; (vi) for his own protection or if under 18 for their own welfare or interests (added by s.13 CJA 2003). If a requirement under s.3 is to reside at "bail hostel", then s.6ZA provides that the defendant must comply with the rules of the hostel. If the defendant is charged with murder and the court decides to grant bail, then under s.6A it must impose as a condition of bail, if it has not already done so, that the defendant undergoes a medical examination by two medical practitioners and that they attend as directed.

If the court is satisfied that there are substantial grounds for believing that the defendant may fail to surrender, commit further offences or interfere with justice, then the question thereafter remains whether the prevention of these three situations from occurring can be only achieved by remanding the defendant into custody, or can bail with appropriate conditions be sufficient? In *R. v Mansfield Justices Ex p. Sharkey* [1985] Q.B. 613, Lord Lane L.J. explained succinctly the task of the court:

> "In the present circumstances the question the justices should ask themselves is a simple one: Is this condition necessary for the prevention of the commission of an offence by the defendant when on bail? They are not obliged to have substantial grounds. It is enough if they perceive a real and not a fanciful risk of an offence being committed. Thus s.3(6) and para 8 give the court a wider discretion to inquire whether the condition is necessary."

17.10 The following list covers the most commonly applied conditions used by the court to attach to a grant of bail:

(i) regular signing on at local police station;

(ii) residence at a particular place;

(iii) remain sober;

(iv) not to approach witnesses in case;

(v) not to enter a certain area other than to see legal representatives or attend court;

(vi) surrender passport;

(vii) curfew as the court thinks fit.

To ensure the compliance of a defendant with the curfew requirement, a common practice developed in some magistrates' courts that in conjunction with the curfew, an additional condition known as a "doorstep condition" would be imposed. This meant that as a condition of bail and to ensure compliance with the curfew, a defendant is required to present themselves at the door on the request of the police. Failure to do so would constitute reasonable grounds for believing that the defendant was in breach of bail and therefore liable to be arrested and a reconsideration of bail under s.5.

The use of this condition was challenged by judicial review in *CPS v Chorley Magistrates' Court* [2002] EWHC 2162, as being unlawful. The defendant appeared before the magistrates for a number of offences. The prosecution asked for a doorstep condition to be imposed. On the advice of the Clerk, the magistrates refused, having been told by the Director of Legal Services in a memorandum that it was unlawful. The CPS disagreed and applied for judicial review that the magistrates were wrong in law to accept that advice. The High Court agreed with the submissions of the CPS, the words of s.6(3) are straightforward and wide enough to give the magistrates a power to impose a doorstep condition.

The Court accepted that the imposition of a bail condition does engage art.8 and clearly interferes with the private and family life of the defendant. However, such interference is justified proportionately in the prevention of crime, a proper balance has been reached. The High Court granted a declaration in favour of the CPS as follows:

> "Where an accused in criminal proceedings is remanded on bail subject to condition, namely, that he reside at a particular address and remain at the address between specified times (that is, subject to a curfew), the court may impose a further condition requiring the accused during the hours of the curfew to prevent himself at the door of the premises if requested to do so by a police officer."

The Court then concluded that:

> "it is to be noted that the declaration is only intended to indicate that the justices have the power to do so. It will always remain a question, as I have already emphasised, as to whether or not that power should be exercised in the particular case. Although this case does not directly affect the powers of the police to grant bail, the construction of the statute which I favour leads to the same result in the case of police bail, namely that a police officer can, if he considers it necessary to do so, impose a doorstep condition. The relevant statutory provisions are identical in effect."

17.11 To ensure compliance with bail conditions, the court can, as already stated, impose an electronic monitoring requirement (EMR) under s.3(6ZAA), as amended by s.51 and Sch.11 of the CJIA 2008 when in force. Section 3(AA) sets out the conditions that the court must be satisfied are met before imposing EMR on a child or young person under 17. For those aged 17 and over s.2(AB) requires four conditions to be satisfied before a court can impose an EMR. One condition is that without the EMR, the offender would not be granted bail, another is that the Youth Offending Team (YOT) must have informed the Court that the offender is suitable for EMR.

If bail is granted with conditions, then it is essential that the defendant fully complies with them. Should their circumstances change, such as job changes which would cause them to be in breach of bail then an application under s.3 must be made in advance. Section 3(7) provides that where bail as been granted by a court, an application by the defence can be made to either the magistrates' court or Crown Court to vary the conditions of bail. If a client requests an application to vary bail conditions due to a change in circumstances, then the first step is to draft the application, send a copy to the CPS and obtain confirmation that they do not oppose the application. If there is no opposition then the application can be determined on the written application by the court without the need for the parties to attend. The client must be warned that until a court order had been received with the variation agreed, they must continue to comply with the existing conditions. If the CPS oppose the application, then an oral application will have to be made.

If the offence is an indictable or either way offence, then the prosecution can under s.5 apply to the court to vary the conditions of bail or impose conditions on bail either granted by the police or the court. However under s.5(3), no application for reconsideration of a decision to grant bail under this section can be made, unless it is based on information which was not available to the court or constable when the decision was taken. The procedural steps are set out more fully in rr.19.1 and 19.2 of the CrPR 2005. If an application is to vary police bail, then the application should be heard with 72 hours of the application being made.

Section 16 of the Criminal Justice Act 2003 allows either a defendant or the prosecution to appeal to the Crown Court against certain conditions, namely residence, surety or security, curfew or making no contact with another, which the magistrates had imposed on the granting of bail provided the bail was granted through adjournment (including s.52(5) of the CDA 1998, adjournment under s.51 procedure for indictable only offence, plea before venue mode of trial, or for medical examination under s.11 of the PCC(S) A 2000).

10. Surety and Security

17.12 These are not conditions for the purposes of bail, but a means by which the court can ensure attendance. Section 3(4) and (5) of the Bail Act 1976 allows the court at its discretion to accept either a surety or security in order to secure the defendant's surrender into custody as directed. A surety is where a third person promises the court that they will pay into court a sum of money, and promises to ensure that the defendant will appear at court later. This is known as a "recognizance". If the defendant fails to appear then the recognizance will be forfeited. A security on the other hand is where the defendant themselves enter in to an undertaking with the court for a fixed amount of money.

Before the court accepts either a proposed surety or a security it must under s.8 of the Bail Act 1976 determine the suitability of the proposal and consider (i) the surety's financial resources; (ii) their character and any previous convictions; (iii) their proximity, i.e. relationship, residence, to the defendant. The court can enlarge the amount later if this is required under s.129 of the MCA 1980. The relevant procedure is delineated in r.19.5 of the CrPR 2005, which provides that the court is required to issue a certificate setting out the terms of the undertaking. In *R. v Kent Crown Court Ex p. Jodka* [1997] 161 J.P. 638, it was stated that before a person accepts the surety's undertaking, it needs to be explained to them the obligations that arise and also warned of the consequences and possible imprisonment if forfeited.

Section 120(A) of the MCA 1980 sets out the enforcement procedure of a surety or security. First the court must declare that the recognizance is to be forfeited. The court will then issue an appearance summons to the person bound by the undertaking to show cause why they should not be adjudged to pay the sum (this is a means enquiry). If the summons was served correctly then the court can proceed in the absence of the person in question. The court can order the person to pay the whole amount, or part of it, or remit it. If required to pay then it can be enforced by the court as if it were a fine for a summary conviction of an imprisonable offence. The court can also make an order allowing the person time to ether pay the fine or the reconizance. If however, if it appears to the court that the person has insufficient means to pay, then the court can commit them to prison, if the amount is, for example, between £100,000 and £250,000 (three years), between £50,000 and £100,000 (two years) and between £20,000 and £50,000 (18 months).

The application of s.120 was considered in *R. v Leicester Magistrates Ex p. Kaur* [1999] 164 J.P. 127. Having reviewed the previous authorities, the High Court stated that s.120 provided the court with a wide discretion as to how to deal with a breach of surety. The court must have regard to the surety's assets in terms of what they could reasonably be expected to pay in full over a period of time. The assets of another cannot be considered, while the degree of culpability of the surety is not of itself a reason to forfeit or indeed remit. It may be a reason whereby the sum of the forfeiture can be reduced to take into account the efforts made by the surety to secure the attendance of the defendant.

The court should always be careful when asked to consider the value of the matrimonial home or shared home, so that the fixed sum does not exceed the personal equity of the surety. The surety needs to understand the risk of a sale of the house to satisfy the forfeiture, or if not a term of imprisonment. In *R. v Birmingham Crown Court Ex p. Ali* (1999) 163 J.P. 145, the High Court observed that it would be irresponsible, even professional misconduct for a legal advisor to tender a surety without having a reasonable believe that if a forfeiture order were to be made, they would financially be able to discharge that undertaking.

11. Breach of Bail under Section 7 and its Effect

17.13 Section 7 creates a power for a person released on bail and under a duty to surrender to custody, to be arrested for either failing to surrender at the appointed time, or breaching any bail conditions, to be brought before the court within 24 hours. In court the magistrates will then reconsider the granting or refusal of bail. Section 7(1) provides that where a person fails to surrender into the custody of the court when required to do so, the court may issue a warrant for their arrest, (in the Crown Court this is known as a "bench warrant"). In addition if a defendant attends court, but then absent themselves without leave of the court, the court may issue a warrant for their arrest.

Under s.7(3) where a person is released on bail and is under a duty to surrender into custody, then they can be arrested without a warrant by the police if and only if:

(i) the police have reasonable grounds for believing that they are not likely to surrender;

(ii) the police have reasonable grounds for believing they are likely to break any bail conditions or have reasonable grounds for suspecting that they have broken any conditions;

(iii) a surety informs the police in writing that they are unlikely to surrender and the surety wishes to be relieved of their obligations for this reason.

Upon arrest, the arrested person must under subsection (4) be brought as soon as is practicable and in any event within 24 hours after their arrest before a magistrate for that area (Christmas day, Good Friday or any Sunday are not included for this purpose). If they are arrested within 24 hours of the appointed time that they should have surrendered into custody, then they must be brought before the court they were required to surrender to.

The consequences for failing to surrender or breaching bail conditions are set out in s.7(5) under which the magistrates, if of the opinion that the defendant is not likely to surrender to custody, or has broken, or is likely to break any condition, can remand them in custody, or grant them bail as before, or with different conditions. If the defendant is a child then they will be remanded into secure accommodation of the Local Authority. Further, it is important to be aware that the court can proceed in the absence of the accused, which includes the trial.

17.14 In *R. v Havering Magistrates* [2001] 1 Cr.App.R. 2, the Divisional Court observed that s.7(5) involved a two stage approach, firstly, the court must decide whether or not there has been a breach of bail. The court must act fairly and give the defendant an opportunity to answer the allegation. Secondly, if the court is satisfied that there has been a breach, then they must reconsider the remand status of the defendant. At this stage the court will need to assess any reasonable excuse of the defendant. On the point of whether s.7 was incompatible with the art.5 right to liberty and art.6 right to a fair trial, the High Court ruled:

(i) Article 6(3) has no relevance to s.7 for alleged breach of bail condition or absconding as the proceedings are not criminal given that there is no sanction or penalty on the finding of a breach. Section 7 does not constitute an offence. It amounts to a procedural observation.

(ii) While s.7(5) must be compatible with art.5, the procedure of the two stage test is prescribed by law and is fair and proper and complies with the protection under art.5 deprivation of liberty. In the context of s.7 it does not require the proof of a breach to be to the criminal standard, or the strict rules of admissibility of evidence to be applied as set out in the *Liverpool Justices Case*, provided always the defendant is given a fair opportunity to respond to the allegation of a breach of a bail condition. Accordingly, a written statement of evidence can be received to determine whether there has been a breach. The prosecution are not required to call oral evidence to allow cross-examination.

In *R. v Teeside Magistrates Ex. p. Ellison* [2001] EWHC Admin 11, the magistrates wrongly committed a defendant who appeared before them in custody to the Crown Court which had previously granted bail to deal with the breach. The Divisional Court in the judgment of Woolf L.J. stated:

> "the idea of remanding in custody to the crown court a defendant who breaches a condition of his bail so that the crown court can then deal with bail thereafter is misconceived. The appropriate course for the magistrates' to take is to remand or commit the defendant to the crown court until his trial or further order. If the superior court wishes to grant bail, that can be done. Any order made by the superior court would then override the decision of the magistrates'. But the making of an order to a fixed date, (as was done in this case) was inappropriate."

If the defendant is brought to the magistrates relating to bail granted by the magistrates' court, then the consequences of that breach can be dealt with by them at that point. If the defendant is brought before the magistrates having breached Crown Court bail, then the magistrates should remand them in custody until trial. The defendant will then need to have the case listed "for mention" to deal with an application for renewed bail, or by application to a judge in chambers.

12. Offence of Failure to Surrender to Custody by Person Released on Bail: Section 6 of the Bail Act 1976, the "Bail Offence"

17.15 Section 6 provides that a defendant who is released on bail and fails, without reasonable cause, to surrender to custody, commits a summary offence. This offence can be committed in two ways as follows. The first offence is committed when a person is released on bail in criminal proceedings, fails without reasonable cause to surrender to custody and is therefore guilty of an offence. The second offence is committed where although it is shown that the bailed person does have reasonable cause for failing to surrender to custody at the appointed time, they still fail to surrender as soon after the appointed time as is reasonably practicable. It important to be aware that s.6(3) places a reverse burden of proof on the defendant, in that it is for the accused to prove that they had reasonable cause for their failure to surrender. Under subsection (4) a failure of a court to give a copy of the record of the decision does not amount to a reasonable cause.

Section 6(5) provides specifically that the court can deal with the offence in terms of punishment, either as (i) a summary conviction, or (ii) as if it were a contempt of court. Likewise under s.6(6) the magistrates, if they think the circumstances of the offence require greater punishment than they are able to inflict, or if they commit the defendant to the Crown Court for another offence and they think it more appropriate for them to be dealt with by that court, then they can either commit them in custody or on bail to the Crown Court for sentence. Under s.6(7) a person found guilty on summary conviction is liable to imprisonment not exceeding three months and or a £5,000 fine. A person committed to the Crown Court for sentence or to be dealt with as a contempt of court bail offence is liable to a sentence of imprisonment not exceeding 12 months and or a fine. Under s.6(8) a document purporting to be a copy of the part of the prescribed record, which relates to the appointed time and place for the accused to surrender and which is certified as a true copy, shall be evidence of the time and place. If the court proceeds to deal with the breach of bail as a contempt of court, then under s.13 of the Administration of Justice Act 1960, an appeal can be made to the High Court.

Part I(13) of the Consolidated Criminal Practice Directions 2005 sets out the relevant procedure for dealing with a bail offence. The rules make it clear that a failure to surrender causes delay, disruption to witness and victims and undermines generally the administration of justice. For this reason, r.13.4 provides that the common practice of postponing the disposal of a bail offence until the conclusion of the main proceedings, should no longer be followed, unless there is good reason to do so and that the court should deal with the offence as soon as is practicable. If deciding whether to deal with the bail offence now, the court will need to consider the seriousness of the offence, when the proceedings are likely to be concluded, the likely sentence of the bail offence and any other circumstances.

If the offence is unlikely to result in a custodial sentence, then the court may proceed with the trial in the absence of the defence. If it is police bail, then the bail offence is subject to the six-month time limit, whereas a breach of court bail is not. If in the meantime the offender commits further offences whilst missing in another court area, then the new court should deal with the bail offence. Proceedings can either be initiated by the CPS or by the court of its own motion, if so and the matter is contested, then evidence should be called. If convicted, then any sentence should, unless it is inappropriate, run consecutively to any other sentence imposed at the same time. On conviction of a bail offence, the court will need to review the remand status of the offender.

It is important to be aware that the Sentencing Guidelines Council have issued definitive guidelines to be applied from December 10, 2007 for bail offences. The guidelines invite the court to assess seriousness, in terms of culpability, harm, nature and seriousness of the original offence and any aggravating (i.e. repeat offending) and mitigating factors (i.e. prompt voluntary surrender). If the failure is deliberate, then the starting point in the magistrates' court is 14 days' imprisonment. While in the Crown Court it is a community order or up to 40 weeks in custody. If the failure is not deliberate, but negligent, then a fine applies in the magistrates' court while at the Crown Court, a fine to a community order. If surrender is late on the day, then a fine applies in both courts.

13. Prosecution Right to Appeal Against a Decision to Grant Bail

17.16 The Bail (Amendment) Act 1993, as amended by the CJA 2003, gives the prosecution a right to appeal against a decision of a magistrates' court to grant bail to a defendant charged with or convicted of an offence punishable by imprisonment. The prosecution may appeal to a judge at the Crown Court, if and only if they had opposed the initial bail application. The appeal is heard in chambers. If the prosecution wish to exercise this right, then they must give oral notice of the appeal to the magistrates at the conclusion of the proceedings and before the release of the person in custody (s.1(5)). On receiving the oral notice the court is required to remand the person in custody (s.1(6)). The prosecution must then give written notice, which must be served on both the court and the defendant within two hours of the conclusion of the proceedings. If they fail to do this, then the appeal is deemed to have been disposed of (s.1(7)). The appeal hearing before a Crown Court judge must be heard within 48 hours, excluding weekends and public bank holidays (s.1(8)).

In *R. v Middlesex Guildhall Crown Court Ex p. Okoli* [2001] Cr.App.R. 1, the High Court heard a judicial review application from the decision of a judge to hear the prosecution bail application three hours after the 48-hour time limit. The Court, dismissing the claim, ruled that the legislative intention when it used the words 48 hours "from the date on which notice of appeal is given", was not literally to mean from the actual time of that notice, but the day it was made. A similar approach was adopted in *Jeffery v Warwick Crown Court* [2002] EWHC 2469, in which High Court ruled that it was not the intention of Parliament to defeat an appeal against bail in circumstances where the prosecution had given itself sufficient time to serve notice on the defendant within the two-hour limit, but for reasons beyond their control it was served out of time (in this case three minutes out of time). Hooper J. was even prepared to insert the words "unless such failure was caused by circumstances outside the control of the prosecution and not due to any fault on its part" at the end of s.1(7). If the judge allows the prosecution's appeal and remands the defendant in custody, then, as stated in *R. v Governor of Pentonville Prison Ex p. Bone* [1994] 159 J.P. 111, as confirmed in *Houghton* [2003] EWHC 3096, the prosecution should invite the judge to stipulate the relevant period of remand, in accordance within s.128 of the MCA 1980.

14. Judge in Chambers "Bail Application" on Behalf of the Defendant

17.17 A defendant who is refused bail by the magistrates' court, or is granted bail with conditions, can make a further application to a judge in chambers at the Crown Court. Under r.19.18 of the Criminal Procedure Rules 2005, the defence are required to give the prosecution and the court at least 24 hours' written notice of their intention to make an application. Once the notice has been received, then the court will list the matter before the next available judge. The availability to a defendant to apply to the High Court against a refusal of bail, or to vary conditions has now been abolished by s.17 of the CJA 2003. However, this does not abolish the availability of challenging a decision on bail, either by judicial review or a writ of habeas corpus. Nevertheless, the High Court in *(R.) Wiggins v Harrow Crown Court* [2005] EWHC 882 ruled that a narrow approach is to be adopted to a judicial review application concerning bail. Only in exceptional cases would the court interfere with the decision on bail. The court would only do so if, in all the circumstances, the decision of the judge fell outside the "bounds of reasonableness", in terms of the *Wednesbury* test (see also *R. v Serumaga* [2005] EWCA Crim 370).

15. Periods of Remand and Limitation of Bail Applications

17.18 Since the decision of the Divisional Court in *R. v Nottingham Justices Ex p. Davies* [1981] 1 Q.B. 38 it is a settled principle that the defence is only entitled to two fully argued bail applications. Unless a significant change in circumstances arises, then the defendant will be remanded in custody for the duration of the proceedings. Under ss.128, s.128A and 129 of the Magistrates' Court Act 1980, the period of remand must not exceed eight clear days. Given that, the reappearance of the defendant is simply to confirm the continued remand. To reduce this regular procedure, the Criminal Justice Act 1982 inserted a new s.128A, which provides that the period of remand can be for 28 days, but only if the defendant consents to it.

16. Application of Custody Time Limits

17.19 Section 22 of the Prosecution of Offences Act 1985, as amended by the Crime and Disorder Act 1998, empowers the Secretary of State by regulations, to make provision as to the maximum period for which an accused person might be held in custody at different stages of the proceedings against them as follows:

(i) If the defendant is sent to the Crown Court under the s.51 procedure, then in accordance with the Prosecution of Offences (Custody Time

Limits) Regulations 2000 (SI 2004/3284) the maximum period of custody is a period of 182 days from being sent and the trial date.

(ii) If remanded in custody for trial in the magistrates' court, then the maximum period of custody is 56 days, from being remanded in custody to the trial date.

(iii) In relation to an either way offence, the remand time is 70 days from first appearance to "committal proceedings" and then 112 days to trial on indictment.

If it is unlikely that the trial will commence with the custody time limits, then the prosecution must, in advance, apply for an extension of the time limits, otherwise the defendant will be unlawfully held in custody and can apply for bail. This is a somewhat difficult area of law to apply and has resulted in a number of appeal decisions intended to determine the interpretation of the provisions. Section 22(3), as amended by s.43 of the Crime and Disorder Act 1998, provides that the prosecution can make an application to the court at any time before the expiry of the above limits, to extend, or further extend those times. The court shall not do so unless it is satisfied:

(i) that the need for extension is due to:

 (a) the illness or absence of the accused, a necessary witness, a judge, or a magistrate,
 (b) a postponement which is occasioned by the ordering by the court of separate trials, or
 (c) some other good and sufficient cause; and

(ii) that the prosecution has acted with all due diligence and expedition.

If the time limit is exceeded without an order for extension, then the defendant is entitled under reg.6 Prosecution of Offences (Custody Time Limits) Regulations 1987 (SI 1987/299) to bail under the Bail Act 1976, subject to s.25 of the CJPOA 1994. In *R. (O) v Harrow Crown Court* [2006] 1 W.L.R. 2756, the House of Lords ruled that s.25 still applied after the custody time limits had expired and was compatible with art.5(3).

The leading authority on the application of the custody time limits is *R. v Manchester Crown Court Ex p. McDonald* [1999] 1 Cr.App.R. 409, in which the Court of Appeal laid down a number of principles. The first is that the burden of proof is upon the prosecution to satisfy the court on a balance of probabilities that the two conditions for allowing the court to extend are met. If not, then the court has no discretion to extend. This requires the court to consider the matter fully and make an informed decision. Regarding whether the prosecution have acted with all due diligence and expedition, the court must consider this as against the standard of a:

> "competent prosecutor conscious of his duty to bring the case to trial as quickly as reasonably and fairly as possible."

17.20 In deciding whether or not the prosecution have exercised due diligence and expedition to the required standard, the court should have regard to the nature and complexity of the case, the level of preparation, the amount of co-operation from defence and that the time limits are a maximum not a target. In regard to good and sufficient cause, the Court stated that there are many reasons that may satisfy this condition and that this is a question for the court on an individual case basis, except that the seriousness of the offence cannot be a relevant factor. In all applications for extension, the court must have in mind the three overriding objectives of:

(i) ensuring that the time a defendant is in custody awaiting trial is as short as is reasonably and practically possible;

(ii) obliging the prosecution to prepare cases for trial with all due diligence and expedition; and

(iii) investing in the court a power to extend the time limits.

In *Gibson v Winchester Crown Court* [2004] EWHC 699, the High Court observed that in terms of due diligence, it is for the Crown:

> "to show that an extension is not sought because it has shown insufficient vigour in preparing the case for trial, the crown cannot prepare a case in a dilatory and negligent manner and then expect an extension in time."

However, if the prosecution are responsible for avoidable delay, but that did not impact on the trial date itself, then it would be an absurd outcome if the court was obliged to refuse an extension. The requirement of due diligence exists to protect the defendant, not to punish the prosecution. To this extent, as a matter of construction of the provisions, the conduct of the prosecution should be assessed by realistic, not impossible standards and the court should not refuse an extension, unless lack of due diligence and expedition had in fact delayed the trial date. Further, the Court held that the lack of resources, such as the availability of an appropriate judge, or court facilities, cannot be ignored, although for routine cases such problems should be overcome. The court should do its best to keep the proceedings within the time limits in terms of availability of resources although it is accepted that this may not always be possible. The Court also noted that when there is a challenge to a decision of a judge as to custody time limits by way of judicial review, then the court will only interfere if the decision was clearly decided wrongly.

17. Remanding Young Offenders into Secure Accommodation

17.21 A balance needs to be struck between the liberty and welfare of a young defendant, on the one hand, with that of the need to protect the public from repeat offenders and the offender absconding from unsecured care on the other. The relevant criteria is set out in s.23 of the Children and Young Persons Act 1969, as amended by the Crime and Disorder Act 1998, and further extended by ss.130 to 132 of the Criminal Justice and Police Act 2001. As with adult offenders, the court must decide on whether to remand the young defendant in custody or on bail. Section 23 allows the court to remand the defendant to Local Authority accommodation, secured or unsecured. Within s.23 there are several safeguards that must be satisfied by the court before exercising a power to remand to custody as follows:

(i) That the defendant has been charged with or convicted of, a specified violent or sexual offence, punishable in the case of an adult with 14 years' imprisonment, or secondly, the defendant must be charged with, or

(ii) convicted of an imprisonable offence(s) (includes previous convictions for similar offences) which shows a recent history of repeatedly committing imprisonable offences while on bail or in accommodation.

(iii) The court must be of the opinion that, having considered all other options (i.e. bail), that only remanding the defendant to secure accommodation (for 15 and 16 year olds, this can be a remand centre, prison or Local Authority accommodation with a security requirement) would be adequate to (i) protect the public from serious harm, or (ii) to prevent further imprisonable offences being committed by the defendant.

The provisions therefore make clear that only those young defendants who have been alleged to have committed serious offences, or continually offend when on bail or in unsecured accommodation are remanded into secure custody In *SR v Nottingham Magistrates' Court* [2001] EWHC 802, the High Court rejected an incompatibility claim that the remand provisions breached art.8, a right to a family life and art.14 as being discriminatory between boys and girls. The provisions were justifiably proportionate to achieving the legitimate aim of protecting the public from dangerous and repeat young offenders. Other options to the court are bail, (un)conditional, bail with support and supervision, or intensive supervision and surveillance with or without electronic monitoring.

18. Structure of a Bail Application

17.22 This following is a simple guide on the procedural steps to making an oral bail application in court:

Step 1 The court asks the defence solicitor if there is there an application for bail and then asks the prosecution if they intend to oppose the application. If the application for bail is unopposed, then the court will usually grant bail, if not then move to step 2.

Step 2 The prosecution must state the statutory grounds upon which bail is opposed.

Step 3 The prosecution must then address the court on the relevant facts, commenting, where appropriate, on the strength of the evidence against the defendant.

Step 4 Then where appropriate, produce and comment on the defendant's previous convictions and antecedents.

Step 5 Finally, the prosecution should relate the circumstances and any other matters relevant to support the grounds of objection.

Step 6 The defence solicitor then makes representations, together with any evidence that supports the general right to bail either with or without conditions.

CHAPTER EIGHTEEN

DISCLOSURE OF EVIDENCE AND CROWN COURT PROCEDURE

1. DISCLOSURE AND CATEGORISATION OF EVIDENCE

18.01 Disclosure, in terms of advance information for either way offences in the magistrates' court, has already been discussed in Chapter 16. The purpose of this chapter is to review the law relating to disclosure of evidence in the Crown Court, although this can be applied in certain situations in the magistrates' court. A thorough knowledge of the provisions on disclosure is essential, missing or incomplete evidence can have fatal consequences for the trial process. In *R. v H & C* [2004] 2 A.C. 134 Lord Bingham stated:

> "fairness ordinarily requires that any material held by the prosecution which weakens its case or strengthens that of the defendant, if not relied on as part of its formal case against the defendant, should be disclosed to the defence. Bitter experience has shown that miscarriages of justice occur where such material is withheld from disclosure. The *golden rule* is that of full disclosure of such material should be made."

Previously, the principles on disclosure were found in the common law. Given the importance of disclosure, the common law rules were abolished and replaced by Pt 1 of the Criminal Procedure and Investigations Act 1996 (CPIA 1996) which applies to offences for which criminal proceedings were commenced after April 1, 1997. Further extensive amendments were made in Pt 5 of the Criminal Justice Act 2003, ss.32 to 40. The difficulty with these provisions is that not all of them are in force and some only partially. Under s.25 of the CPIA 1996, the Ministry of Justice is required to publish a code of practice by statutory instrument under the affirmative resolution procedure.

The codes of practice deal with the practice to be followed by the police as to how they record, retain and reveal to the CPS relevant material obtained during a criminal investigation. In addition, the CPS has in conjunction with the codes of practice, a "disclosure manual" that provides practical guidance for the proper steps to be taken in terms of gathering, categorising and disclosing all evidence during the investigative and criminal process. To further improve the approach to disclosure of evidence in criminal proceedings, the Criminal Procedure Rules Committee have produced a Protocol for the Control and Management of Unused Material in the Crown Court, which came into effect on February 20, 2006. In the introduction of the Protocol it is said that (see also Pt 25 of the CrPR 2005):

> "disclosure is one of the most important, as well as one of the most abused-of all procedures relating to criminal trials."

In *R. v K* [2006] EWCA Crim 724, the Court of Appeal made it plain that the Protocol should be applied by trial judges, and that the prosecution and defence must familiarise themselves with it. It is essential therefore, that both the student and practitioner obtain a copy and have it to hand for reference. The disclosure of prosecution witness statements is mandatory in the Crown Court but is at the discretion of the prosecutor in the magistrates' court (advance information under Pt 21 CPR 2005), although to ensure fairness and standard procedure, the prosecution now, as a matter of course, disclose the relevant evidence in summary proceedings. Essentially, the prosecution will categorise the material evidence they have as the following:

(i) *Sensitive material;* this is material that the prosecution wish to withhold from the defence.

(ii) *Non sensitive material;* this is material that the prosecution intend to present at trial.

(iii) *Unused material;* this is material that the prosecution do not intend to use in the case.

18.02 It is important to be aware of and apply the different principles that apply to the disclosure of evidence, dependant upon when the investigation for the offence commenced. This is especially important when the prosecution concerns a "cold case" where the offence may have been committed many years ago, but due to advances in, for instance, DNA technology, there is sufficient evidence to bring the case to court. The three possibilities are as follows:

(i) For investigations prior to April 1, 1997 the common law rules in *R. v Keane* [1997] 99 Cr.App.R. 9 and *R. v Brown* [1995] 1 Cr.App.R. 191 in conjunction with the subsequent disclosure guidelines issued by the Attorney-General on November 29, 2000 will apply (these are not intended to be discussed.)

(ii) On or after April 1, 1997, but before April 4, 2005, the CPIA 1996 in its original form will apply.

(iii) For investigations on or after April 4, 2005 the CPIA 1996 as amended by the CJA 2003 will apply.

For proceedings to be fair and for convictions to be safe, disclosure of used and unused material must be made to the prosecution and to the defence, if the consequences in the conduct of the trial against Sally Clark (*R. v Clark* [2003] EWCA Crim 1020) are to never be repeated. In that instance, it was the non disclosure of both microbiological and biochemical analysis that, as fresh evidence on appeal, raised doubt about the death being unlawful and deliberate as opposed to being caused by an infection. To ensure that any expert instructed by the prosecution fulfils their overriding duty to the court, the Attorney-General published, as part of the Disclosure Manual, a guidance booklet for experts. This covers issues of retention and revelations. Likewise, it is essential for the defence team to review thoroughly all the unused material (see *R. v Adams* [2007] EWCA Crim 1).

2. Initial Test for Disclosure by the Prosecution

18.03 In accordance with s.3 of the CPIA 1996, as amended by the s.32 of the CJA 2003, the prosecution must disclose to the accused:

> "any prosecution material that has not previously been disclosed and which might reasonably be considered capable of undermining or of assisting the case for the accused."

Prosecution material is defined in s.3(2) of the CPIA 1996 as either material that came into the prosecutor's possession in connection with the case against the accused, or material that the prosecutor has inspected under the Code of Practice governing investigations under Pt 11 of the Act. However, one exception to this rule is that of "sensitive material". Under s.3(6) material that is deemed sensitive (this would be listed in the schedule of sensitive material) must not be disclosed, if so ordered by the court, which if disclosed would be contrary to the public interest. In these circumstances, the prosecution will need to make an application to the judge for a public interest immunity order, to prevent the disclosure of this material (see below).

In *R. v Alibhai* [2004] EWCA Crim 681, the Court of Appeal observed that the prosecution are only under a duty to obtain material from a third party, in circumstances where they have a reasonable suspicion that the information sought is of material use to the case. Even then, the prosecution are not obliged to disclose, they are able to exercise a "margin of appreciation". If criticism is to be made of the failure of the prosecution in securing third party disclosure, then it must be shown that such failure fell outside the Attorney-General's Guidelines. The Court did nonetheless acknowledge that in some extreme cases, it would be sufficiently unfair for the proceedings to continue in the absence of such material as being an abuse of process.

3. Defence Disclosure and the Proof of Evidence

18.04 Once the prosecution has complied with its duty of primary disclosure, the defence come under a statutory duty to serve, in accordance with s.5 CPIA, a "defence statement". This, in accordance with s.12 of the CPIA 1996 and the Defence Disclosure Time Limits Regulations 1997 (SI 1997/684), must be served on both the prosecution and court within 14 days of primary disclosure. Section 33 of the CJA 2003 inserts a new s.5A and when in force will require the defendant to also serve their own "defence statement" on any other co-accused, as specified by the court. Section 33(2) of the CJA creates a new s.6A of the CPIA 1996 which increase both the information and detail required in the defence statement and provides that the defence statement must be a written statement that contains the following:

(i) Sets out the *nature* of the accused's defence, including any particular defences the accused intends to rely on.

(ii) Indicates the matters of fact they take issue with the prosecution, and why they take such issue.

(iii) Fully sets out on each disputed point why they take issue with the prosecution. This when s.110 of the Criminal Justice and Immigration Act 2008 comes into effect will include particularising the facts on which the defendant intends to rely in their defence.

(iv) Indicates any point of law, including the admissibility of evidence which they wish to raise and any authorities in that respect they intend to rely on in support.

(v) If a defendant intends to rely on alibi evidence, then they must disclose this in their defence statement and must give the following particulars; (i) name, address and date of birth of any alibi witness or as many details as possible known to the defendant, (ii) any information in the accused's possession which might be of material assistance in identifying or finding such alibi witness.

For the purposes of the defence statement, alibi evidence under subsection (3) means evidence adduced by the defence in order to show that by reason of the presence of them at a particular place, or in a particular area at a particular time they were not, or was unlikely to have been, at the place where the offence is alleged to have been committed at the time of its alleged commission. Section 33(3) of the CJA 2003 when brought into force, will insert a new s.6B which will require the defendant, having served a defence statement in accordance with s.5 of the CPIA 1996, after a specified period to serve either a (i) updated defence statement (the contents must comply with s.6A, or (ii) a written statement stating that there are no changes.

The court may, under s.5A and s. 6B, either on its own motion or by application of any party order that the defence statement and update statement is served on any co-accused. This brings into statutory effect the principle derived from *R. v Cairns and Others* [2002] EWCA Crim 2838, in which the Court of Appeal distinguished the decision in *R. v Tibbs* [2000] 2 Cr.App.R. 309, concerning the application of s.5 and adopted a broad construction of the obligation of the prosecution under s.7 to make disclosure that if the test is satisfied for any evidence and in the context of this duty, this included any defence statement in their possession that would assist another co-accused (see also *R. v Mc Hugh* [2003] EWCA Crim 1766).

18.05 In order to reverse the decision of the Court of Appeal in *R. v Wheeler* [2001] 1 Cr.App.R. 150, that defence statement should be signed by the defendant personally so as to acknowledge its accuracy Section 36 of the CJA 2003 inserts a new s.6E which provides that if the solicitor serves a defence statement purportedly on behalf of the defendant, then unless the contrary is proved, it will be deemed to be given with the authority of the defendant. On this basis, any prejudice created by what was said in the proof of evidence, the defence statement and the evidence given at trial, will not as it did in *Wheeler* lead to any subsequent conviction being quashed (see also *R. (Sullivan v Crown Court at Maidstone* [2002] EWHC 967).

Section 34 of the CJA 2003 when brought into force will significantly increase the statutory duty of the defence to disclose specified details or information. A new s.6C provides that the accused must give notice to both the court and the prosecutor as to whether they intend to call other witnesses and give details of those witnesses. Should there be any changes to intended witnesses or new witnesses, then the accused must give a further amended notice. Likewise, a new s.6D provides that if the accused instructs a person with a view to them giving their expert opinion for possible use as evidence at trial, then they must give notice to the prosecution, stating their name and address, within a specified time. The purpose of s.6D is to reverse the ruling by the Court of Appeal in *R. v Davies* [2002] EWCA Crim 85, in which it was held that the defence were not required to disclose a psychiatric report that they did not intend to rely on at trial. Such communications between the expert and the defendant amounted to legal communications and were therefore legally privileged. Further, the Court ruled that such disclosure would breach the defendant's right against self (inadvertent) incrimination.

This extension of the disclosure duty of the defence is likely to have dramatic ramifications for the preparation of the defence's case, especially if the disputed issue in the case concerns a new and developing area of medicine or science that is yet to be universally agreed within the wider expert community. Section 40 of the CJA 2003 provides that the Secretary of State for Justice must produce a comprehensive Code of Practice, which gives guidance to the police on the arrangement and conduct of interviews with either alibi witnesses or other witnesses notified by the defence, who they intend to call to give oral evidence at trial. It is important to be aware that, on the one hand, the purpose of the increased duty on the defence to disclose the critical aspects of its case is to prevent the common occurrence of "ambush defences" and to allow the prosecution an opportunity to respond to any lines of the defence, While, on the other, as was said by Beldam L.J. in *R. v Tibbs* [2000] 2 Cr.App.R. 309 the provisions:

> "diminish the accused's right to silence and his privilege against self incrimination, they should be strictly applied."

Early in the preparation of the defence case, the legal representative will take from the defendant a full and detailed "proof of evidence". This is a statement setting out the defendant's own contentions and responses to each and every factual point raised by the prosecution that it intends to use to prove guilt, (instructions). This can be and often is, extremely labour intensive, in terms of making general observations on all the prosecution material (this can run into hundreds even thousands of pages, but each must be perused), and then raising these observations with the defendant.

Once drafted, the proof of evidence forms the factual basis of the defendant's case at trial. This is a living document, since as often happens, the prosecution will give notice and serve additional evidence which must be raised with the defendant and in the light of which, the proof of evidence can be amended. The proof of evidence is protected as legal professional privilege, and therefore there is no legal obligation to disclose it. However, what is said in the proof of evidence will form part of what is said in the defence statement, which must be disclosed, and once served, the defendant must not deviate from what is said in that statement, since to do so would bring into issue an inconsistency, which brings into question their reliability as a witness.

4. Draft Example of a Defence Statement

18.06 IN THE WOODLANDS CROWN COURT CALENDER No

BETWEEN

REGINA

-V-

JOHN SMITH

DEFENCE STATEMENT IN ACCORDANCE WITH S.5 OF THE CIPA 1996 AS AMENDED BY S.33(2) OF THE CJA 2003

---

1. The defendant is indicted with two counts,

   (i) Count 1: Unlawfully Wounding with Intent to do GBH contrary to s.18 of the OAPA 1861.

   (ii) Count 2: Unlawfully and Recklessly inflicts GBH contrary to s.20 of the OAPA 1861.

2. The defendant strenuously denies the allegation on which he is indicted, and disputes the contention for the prosecution that he did a deliberate and unprovoked act causing the complainant to suffer injury. The reason for this denial is that the defendant acted "lawfully" as set out in paragraph 4 or that the injuries was accidentally caused as set out in paragraph 5.

3. The defendant strenuously denies the contention of the prosecution that he formed the necessary mens rea of intent to cause the complainant serious bodily harm. The reason for this denial is that the defendant will claim he acted "lawfully" as set out at paragraph 4.

4. The defendant will say that he was attacked by the complainant. In response to this attack the defendant pushed the complainant away as he is statutorily entitled to do under s.3 of the Criminal Law Act 1967 by acting in self-defence. He honestly believed that it was necessary for him to defend himself, when he was confronted by the complainant, that he only used such force as he instinctively believed was reasonable and proportionate to the degree of threat of violence he was under from the complainant, in all the circumstances and in the prevention of a crime.

5. The defendant will also say that any injury sustained by the complainant was accidental and not a deliberate act. Such injuries were caused not by the defendant but by the complainant falling.

6. The defence put the Crown to strict proof as to the mens rea of specific intent and subjective recklessness and also to disprove beyond doubt the defendant's contention that he acted lawfully in self defence.

Signed .... Date ....

5. Faults in Defence Disclosure

18.07 Section 39 of the CJA 2003, which came into effect on April 4, 2005, inserts a new s.11 to replace the existing s.11 provision in the CPIA 1996 (subsections (4), (7) and (11) have not yet been brought into force). The new s.11 provides that failure to comply with any of the defences' duties of disclosure, including adequacy of the contents of the statement and serving the statement contrary to the time limit, or where the defendant puts forward a defence not mentioned, or is different to that in the defence statement, or calls an alibi witness in breach of the notice requirement, can lead to the following consequences:

(i) that the court or any other party (i.e. co-accused, but must have leave of the court) may make such comment as appears appropriate

(ii) that the court or jury may draw such inferences as appear proper in deciding whether the accused is guilty of the offence.

The same failures and consequences that flow from such failure apply in the same way in the magistrates' court, provided the defendant has served a defence statement. Section 6 of the CPIA 1996 provides that the service of a defence statement in the magistrates' court is not compulsory and is at the discretion of the defence. Nevertheless, serving a defence statement will trigger automatically the secondary duty of disclosure of the prosecution in response to the defence statement. As a safeguard, s.6E(2) (inserted by s.36 of the CJA 2003) provides that where it appears to a judge at a pre-trial hearing that the defendant has failed to comply and is now at risk of the consequences, the judge must warn the defendant of the risk. Further, the judge conducting the trial can either by their own motion, or on an application of any party, direct that the jury are given a copy or an edited copy, to remove any evidence that would be inadmissible.

The implication of the consequences of any failure in the disclosure can weaken the case for the defence dramatically as occurred in *R. v Moore* [2003] EWCA Crim 101, an appalling s.18 glassing case, in which the defendant, who had been previously tried twice for the offence, ran a defence of total denial relying on alibi evidence. However, at trial it was determined that the notice had been given late, leading to the prosecution to cross-examine the defendant as to why. On appeal it was revealed that in fact the notice had been served in time. The Court of Appeal, in quashing the conviction, given the directions of the judge on the adverse implications based on the late notice, gave warning that because of a number of unsatisfactory failings of the professionals involved in the conduct of the case, there was a real danger of damaging confidence in the administration of justice. This was a serious offence, with a victim who suffered significant injuries seeing justice being potentially denied to her due to these failings.

6. Continuing Duty of the Prosecution to Disclose

18.08 Section 37 of the CJA 2003 which came into effect on April 4, 2005, inserts a new s.7A into the CPIA 1996. This provides that once the prosecution has complied or purported to comply with the s.3 initial disclosure duty, then from that point onwards and at all times, it is under a continuing duty to keep under review whether there is any prosecution material, particularly in light of what the defence statement reveals, which satisfies the test for disclosure as applied by s.3. If such material comes to light, then the Crown must disclose it to the defence as soon as is reasonably practicable.

If, having received the defence statement, there is now further disclosure then the prosecution must serve this on the defence within the 14-day time limit set out in s.12 of the CPIA 1996. If there is no further duty of disclosure, then the prosecution must give a written statement to that effect to the defence. In *Murphy v DPP* [2006] EWHC 1753, the High Court, applying the decision of the House of Lords in *R. v Soneji* [2006] 1 A.C. 340 and also *DPP v Wood* [2005] EHWC 2986, ruled that it was never the intention of Parliament that if the defence served their defence statement just beyond the 14-day time limitation, it would be refused secondary disclosure by the prosecution of material that might assist the defence case or undermine that of the prosecution.

7. Application by the Defence for Disclosure

18.09 Even if the prosecution complies or purports to comply with its duty to review its evidence, in accordance with the test of disclosure in light of the information contained in the defence statement or indeed fails to comply with this duty the defence can still make an application under s.8 of the CPIA 1996 as amended by s.38 of the CJA 2003, which came into effect on April 4, 2005, to the court to make an order for further disclosure, if they have reasonable cause to believe that there is prosecution material which is required to be disclosed under the prosecution's continuing duty of disclosure (s.7A) but hitherto has not.

8. Third Party Disclosure

18.10 There is no provision to deal specifically with disclosure of material held by a third party such as files held by social services or a Local Authority. If a third party, on the grounds of confidentiality, refuses to disclose the material evidence (i.e. where for instance the defendant is facing criminal charges of child abuse or cruelty) then, in such circumstances, either the prosecution or the defence can apply for a witness summons for the material to be produced under s.2(2) of the Criminal Procedure (Attendance of Witnesses) Act 1965 in the Crown Court or s.97 of the Magistrates' Court Act 1980 in the magistrates' court. It is to be noted that the test differs between the two provisions.

In the magistrates' court, the applicant must satisfy the test that the documents are "likely to be material evidence", whereas under s.2(2) the burden shifts onto the third party to satisfy the court that the documents are not likely to be material evidence. Section 169 of the Serious Organised Crime and Police Act 2005 lowers the test for the issuing of a witness summons to the court, having only to be satisfied that the person will not voluntarily attend or produce the material, and it is in the interests of justice to issue a summons. In *R. v Brushett* [2001] Crim. L.R. 47, the Court of Appeal set out the central principles derived from the previous authorities as follows:

(i) The documents, to be material, must be both relevant and admissible in criminal proceedings.

(ii) If the documents sought are merely to be used as a tool in cross examination, they are not admissible in evidence for the purposes of s.97.

(iii) The applicant seeking disclosure must satisfy the magistrates with supporting evidence that there is a real possibility that the documents are likely to be material.

(iv) The procedure is not to be used as a fishing expedition, based on speculation as to what the third party might possess.

See also the comments of Longmore L.J. in *R. v Alibhai* [2004] EWCA Crim 681, concerning a number of unsatisfactory features about the disclosure of information held by a third party.

9. Disclosure of Prosecution Witness's Previous Convictions

18.11 The previous convictions of any witness will have an adverse impact on their credibility, in terms of how honest and accurate they are when giving evidence. For the defence, the non-disclosure of such relevant information can lead to any subsequent conviction being unsafe. The approach of the Court of Appeal is generally case specific. Bingham L.J., accepting that there is no simple or straightforward answer, stated in *R. v Ferrell* [1998] (unreported), as confirmed in *R. v Underwood* [2003] EWCA Crim 1500, "that the answer will depend on the weight of the evidence in the case". This will require the court to consider whether the evidence of the witness, whose conviction(s) have not been disclosed, is central to the case for the prosecution, and how this effects that witness's credibility and honesty:

> "The greater the weight of the other evidence the less significance, other things being equal, the non-disclosure is likely to have."

In *R. v Weaver* [2003] EWCA Crim 2214, the Court of Appeal did not hesitate in ruling the appellant's conviction for blackmail and burglary as unsafe, by the non-disclosure of the complainant's previous conviction which, had they been known, would have had a considerable effect on the jury in the cross-examination of the complainant. Conversely in *R. v Amber* [2003] EWCA Crim 2253, the Court of Appeal ruled that the appellant's conviction for indecent assault was still safe, despite the fact that the prosecution had failed to disclose the previous conviction of the father of the complainant.

10. Consequences of Non-Disclosure by the Prosecution on the Safety of Convictions

18.12 Any material that undermines the case for the prosecution that is not disclosed would lead potentially to a conviction being ruled unsafe in the Court of Appeal. In *R. v Higgins* [2002] EWCA Crim 336, the Court of Appeal quashed the defendant's conviction for robbery of a post office. At trial, the defence case was one of mistaken identity and alibi evidence. Quite reprehensibly, the investigating officer suppressed various statements made by a crucial prosecution witness that would have clearly assisted the defence's case. The Court expressed grave concern over the misconduct of the case, so much so that the Court directed a copy of the judgment be sent to the Chief Constable for action.

In *R. v Early* [2003] 1 Cr.App.R. 288, a VAT fraud case which involved some £35m that had not been paid on goods held and stored in bonded warehouses, the Court of Appeal quashed the defendant's conviction even though they had pleaded guilty. Subsequent to entering the guilty plea, it came to light that the prosecution had failed to make full disclosure concerning the involvement of Customs and Excise and deliberate lies to the court about the true status of an informant, who through the HM Customs and Excise investigation team, had encouraged the defendant's to take untaxed spirits out of bounded warehouses. Rose L.J. commented that:

> "if, in the course of a public interest immunity hearing or an abuse argument, whether on the *voir dire* or otherwise, prosecution witnesses .i.e. in evidence to the judge, it is expected that, if the judge knows of this, or this Court subsequently learns of it, an extremely serious view will be taken. It is likely that the prosecution case will be regarded as tainted beyond redemption, however strong the evidence against the may otherwise be."

A further example is *R. v Taylor and Taylor* [1994] 98 Cr.App.R. 361, in which two sisters were convicted of the murder of Alison Shaughnessy, the wife of the man with whom one of the sisters was having a sexual relationship. The prosecution case depended extensively on circumstantial evidence. Having served a year of a life sentence, the sisters had their convictions quashed by the Court of Appeal on the grounds that the Crown had failed to disclose vital information on a previous inconsistent description given by a crucial prosecution witness.

11. Public Interest Immunity (PII) and the Human Rights Act 1998 (Part 25 of the Criminal Practice Directions)

18.13 PII is a process used by the prosecution to seek an order from the court to withhold material that might undermine their case, on the grounds that to disclose it would create a serious risk of prejudice to the public interest. Examples of this type of sensitive material would include the identity of police informants, under-cover agents or the use of scientific or operational techniques or surveillance. To disclose this material would not be in the public interest since it could expose certain individuals to risk, or potentially jeopardise future investigations. Accordingly, a balance needs to be struck between, on the one hand, the public interest, in terms of secrecy of certain information as is necessary in the investigation and prevention of crime, whilst on the other hand ensuring that the defendant's right to a fair trial is not affected, under art.6.

It is important to be aware that art.6 does not prevent the investigation and prosecution of serious crime, (i.e. wholesale drug distribution) where evidence gained or obtained sensitively would jeopardise the prosecution's case if disclosed. What art.6 seeks to determine, as revealed in *Edwards v UK*

[1992] 15 E.H.R.R. 417, *Rowe v UK* [2000] 30 E.H.R.R. 1, *PG and JH v UK* [2002] Crim L.R. 308 and *Atlan v UK* [2001] 34 E.H.R.R. 833, is that there are in place sufficient safeguards to secure and protect the defendant's right to a fair trial and that it is also seen to be fair based on the application of the rule of law.

The House of Lords in *R. v H & C* [2004] 2 A.C. 134, having provided a detailed analysis of the jurisprudence of the European Court of Human Rights, gave authoritative guidance as to the proper approach to PII applications. Lord Bingham, at para.36, said that where in exceptional and rare cases the prosecution feel a need to depart from the golden rule of full disclosure, then the court must consider a series of questions as follows:

> "(1) What is the material which the prosecution seek to withhold?
>
> (2) Is the material such as may weaken the prosecution case or strength that of the defence? IF No, disclosure should not be ordered. If Yes, full disclosure should (subject to questions 3, 4, and 5) be ordered.
>
> (3) Is there a real risk of serious prejudice to an important public interest (and, if so, what) if full disclosure of the material is ordered? If no, full disclosure should be ordered.
>
> (4) If the answer to 2, and 3, is Yes, can the defendant's interest be protected without disclosure or disclosure be ordered to an extent or in a way which will give adequate protection to the public interest in question and also afford adequate protection to the interests of the defence?"

18.14 In regard to question 4, his Lordship stated that the court will need to consider the sensitive material in view of the facts of the case and whether limited disclosure is possible, with the preparation of summaries or extracts of evidence or documents either edited or kept anonymous, which would be sufficient in appropriate cases. Importantly, his Lordship approved the use in appropriate cases and if it is in the interests of justice (despite the delay which may be caused) of the appointment of an approved "Special Advocate" (neutral counsel), who can test the prosecution's contentions at the hearing and ensure that the defendant's right to a fair trial is protected (see para.22).

> "(5) Do the measures proposed in answer to (4) represent the minimum derogation necessary to protect the public interest in question? If No, the court should order such greater disclosure as will represent the minimum derogation from the golden rule of full disclosure.
>
> (6) If limited disclosure is ordered pursuant to (4) and (5), may the effect be to render the trial process, viewed as a whole, unfair to the defendant? If Yes, then fuller disclosure should be ordered even if this leads or may lead the prosecution to discontinue the proceedings so as to avoid having to make disclosure.
>
> (7) If the answer to (6) when first given is No, does that remain the correct answer as the trial unfolds, evidence is adduced and the defence advanced?
>
> It is important that the answer to (6) should not be treated as a final, once and for all, answer but as a provisional answer which the court must keep under review."

Following the ruling of the House of Lords in *R. v H*, the Court of Appeal in *R. v McDonald* [2004] EWCA Crim 2614 gave general guidance as to the conduct of an appeal against a PII ruling. In particular, it was stated that the Court of Appeal will need, before the main appeal hearing, to review all the material placed before the judge ex parte with the prosecution present. In *R. v BG* [2004] EWCA Crim 1368, an appeal against a ruling of a trial judge under s.9(11) of the Criminal Justice Act 1987, it was held that the judge was wrong to order that defence counsel must not disseminate sensitive material that had inadvertently been disclosed by the prosecution to any third party, including their clients. By applying the decision in *R. v Davis and Others* [1993] 97 Cr.App.R. 110, it would have been impossible for defence counsel "in the know", to conduct a professional relationship with his client. Preventing the communication of information in such circumstances would damage that relationship, with the client suspecting that his legal team are holding the interests of others in higher regard to theirs.

It is often the case, that in order to investigate properly and gather sufficient cogent evidence against those who are acting as street drug dealers, the police will need to use professionally trained, anonymous undercover police officers with recording/video devices, and become involved in the trade of drugs. The police must ensure that they do not become an agent provocateur and bring into issue entrapment evidence. The evidence from the recording devices will be of crucial importance to any prosecution case. The issue of disclosure will be the identity of the officer and the tapes of the recorded conversations. Based on Lord Bingham's guidance, limited disclosure can achieve fairness by allowing the defence to listen to the tapes at the police station, but ensuring this is done in privacy. Ultimately, in each case involving sensitive material, the issue of disclosure will be dependant on the facts of the case and the answers to the guidance, given by Lord Bingham.

12. Jurisdiction of the Crown Court

18.15 Section 46 of the Supreme Court Act 1981 provides that all proceedings on indictment shall be brought before the Crown Court. This gives the Crown Court "exclusive jurisdiction" over trials on indictment. This means offences that are classified as "indictable only", i.e. the common law offences of murder, manslaughter, perverting the course of justice and statutory offences such as robbery and blackmail, must proceed before the Crown Court. In addition, "indictable either-way" offences can be heard on indictment in the Crown Court. In the magistrates' court, the plea before venue and mode of trial procedure must be followed.

Having been committed by the magistrates, the defendant's first appearance at the Crown Court will be for what is now known as (since April 5, 2005) a "Plea and Case Management Hearing", formally known as a "Plea and Direction Hearing", which is heard in open court. If sent under the s.51 procedure for an indictable only offence, then the defendant's first appearance will either be a Preliminary Hearing if necessary; and then adjourned for a PCMH. As with the magistrates' court, the Crown Court can exercise a general power to adjourn proceedings, but must always ensure that the overriding objectives of the CrPR 2005 are complied with, taking into account the triangulation of interests. Only if a decision concerning an adjournment is unreasonable, will a court interfere by way of judicial review or case stated (see *R. v Chaaban* [2003] EWCA Crim 1012 and *R. (CPS) V Portsmouth Crown Court* [2003] EWHC 1079).

13. Instructing Counsel

18.16 Given that the matter is now in the Crown Court, the solicitor will need to instruct a barrister to present the case before the court. Nevertheless, there is a change of emphasis, with many of the larger criminal practices having their own specialist "solicitor-advocates" to represent clients before the Crown Court. The solicitor instructs a barrister by drafting what is called a "brief". This contains all the evidence and circumstances of the client's (defendant's) case and importantly, the client's instructions (these are set out in a "proof of evidence"). Having perused the brief, counsel will usually draft a "counsel Advice", which sets out what counsel believes must be done in order to ensure that the case is prepared properly for trial. Further, the solicitor will make arrangements to hold a "conference" at chambers with the client and the barrister present to discuss progress of the case. A simple example of a brief is as follows:

IN THE WOODLANDS CROWN COURT CALENDER No: T 2008/056

BETWEEN:

REGINA

V

JOHN SMITH

BRIEF FOR THE DEFENDANT

Counsel to find enclosed herewith;

1. Indictment
2. Prosecution case summary
3. List of witness statements
4. witness statements
5. List of Exhibits
6. Record of taped interview
7. Schedule of unused material

8. Representation Order
9. Prove of Evidence
10. Antecedents

INSTRUCTING SOLICITORS represent the defendant John Smith who is indicted on two counts; count 1 s.18 wounding with intent and s.20 reckless wounding in the alternative. This matter was sent to the Crown Court by the Forest Magistrates Court under the s.51 procedure on *(date)* when the defendant was granted conditional bail. The PCMH is listed for *(date)*. Those who instruct have had an opportunity to take instructions from the defendant who intends to plead not guilty and raise the defence of self defence. Primary disclosure has been served and those who instruct have taken the liberty to draft the defence statement and ask counsel for his observations.

The Prosecution Case

The Crown will allege that on *(date)* the defendant who was drinking in the same pub (The King's Arms) as the complainant, launched a deliberate, unprovoked and sustained attack on the complainant who suffered a serious head wound, along with cuts and bruising around the head and body. The Crown will call a number of eye witnesses, including the bar attendant to support its case. The police attended and the defendant was arrested by PC Withers and conveyed to Forest Police Station

The Defence Case

The defendant does not deny being the person who was involved in an altercation with the complainant, he denies absolutely forming any intent to cause serious bodily harm. The defendant states that the complainant has for some time manifested a grievance with him over a previous girlfriend. The defendant will say that whilst in the King's Arms the complainant was making gestures and started to come towards the defendant. Fearing attack the defendant put his hands up to prevent any punches, the complainant made a punch at him which hit his forearm, the defendant then instinctively pushed the complainant away, who then stumbled and fell. The defendant will say that the injuries sustained by the complainant must have occurred as a consequence of the fall.

Counsel is respectfully requested to attend at the PCMH on the *(date)* to advise in conference and thereafter represent the defendant at trial.

Instructing Solicitors trust the above is sufficient for counsel's purposes but should he require any further information then he ought not to hesitate in contacting John Brown of Instructing Solicitors.

14. Case Progression: Active Case Management (Part IV.41 of the CrPR 2005)

18.17 Once the magistrates have committed the case to the Crown Court or have sent it under the s.51 procedure, the clerk must, in accordance with the Criminal Practice Directions complete a "case progression form", for either a Preliminary Hearing (PH) or for a Plea and Case Management Hearing (PCMH). The progression form for the PCMH contains "directions" to both the prosecution and the defence, which must be complied with. One direction is for the defence to serve a "defence statement" within the time limit. The progression form is sent to the "case progression officer" at the Crown Court, who at that point, will take control of the progress of the case through the Crown Court. The magistrates' court will determine the date for the hearings in the Crown Court. A Preliminary Hearing is likely to be held, either where the defendant is likely to plead guilty, or there are other pressing directions to be ordered by the judge; for instance to resolve issues of bail and disclosure prior to the PCMH. This hearing should be listed to be held within 14 days of either being committed or sent to the Crown Court.

At the PCMH, the defendant will be arraigned; the count(s) in the indictment will be read out to them and they will be asked to enter a plea. Both counsel for the defence and prosecution are required to complete in advance and submit to the court a "Plea and Case Management Hearing in the Crown Court" form (a tick box and brief explanation form), which identifies any key issues, such as any points of law, i.e. admissibility of evidence, witness requirements and any special arrangements for vulnerable witnesses, estimated length of trial, disclosure of evidence, any human rights arguments, exhibits, and custody time limits issues (see r.3.10). Rule 3.8(3) provides that the Crown Court must conduct a PCMH, unless the circumstances of the case make it unnecessary to do so.

The judge can, if necessary, give directions relevant to the effective management of the case. Under r.3.10 this requires the court to establish the disputed issues the parties intend to explore at trial. Further, the court can require a party to identify witnesses they intend to call to give oral evidence (this is especially important if the prosecution seek to use the bad character provisions). In *R. (Kelly) v Warley Magistrates' Court* [2008] 1 Cr.App.R. 14, the order of the District Judge requiring the defence to disclose their witness details under r.3.10 breached the right of legal privilege, on the basis that there was no regulatory regime in place to support the rules of procedure. In consequence of this decision, the Criminal Procedure (Amendment No.3) Rules 2007 (SI 2007/3662), which came into effect in April 2008, insert a new r.3.5 which gives the court the necessary enforcement measures to deal with a party who fails to comply with either a rule or a direction. The three enforcement measures are: (i) re-set an hearing date, (ii) make a cost order and (iii) impose any other sanction deemed appropriate.

Other matters could include ensuring, for instance, an agreement between the prosecution and defence as to summary/editing of police interview within 21 days. The judge will then set down a trial date. This date must be maintained. If either the defence or the prosecution cannot have their case ready to start on that date, for reasons such as witness availability difficulties, then the matter must be listed for mention to vacate. Ultimately, the judge will need to balance the public interest with that of the need to avoid delay (especially if the defendant is in custody) and for the matter to be finalised, when deciding whether or not to grant a new trial date. A judge will not look favourably on a party who requests the vacation due to lack of diligence or expedition. The PCMH should be held within 14 weeks after sending or committal, if defendant is in custody, or 17 weeks if on bail.

15. The Indictment

18.18 The indictment is the formal document that sets out the following information, in accordance with s.3 of the Indictments Act 1915 and rr.4, 5 and 6 of the Indictment Rules 1971:

(i) defendant(s);

(ii) statement of the offence (this sets out the offence(s) either under statute or common law. Each offence is known as a count in the indictment);

(iii) particulars of the offence (must disclose the essential elements of the alleged offence, unless this would prejudice or embarrass the defence. If there is a victim then the name should be included).

The responsibility of drafting the indictment lies with the CPS and under Rule 14(2) of the CrPR 2005 can include more than one count for any offence provided each offence is "founded on the same facts or form or are part of a series of offences of the same or similar character" (the joinder rule). In *R. v Barrell and Wilson* [1979] 69 Cr. App.R. 250, the Court of Appeal adopted a wide construction to the expression "founded on the same facts" by stating that: "it does not mean that for charges to be properly joined in the same indictment, the facts to the respective charges must be identical in substance or virtually contemporaneous. The test is whether the charges have a common factual origin" (see also *R. v Roberts* [2008] EWCA Crim 304).

The indictment can also include what is called "specimen or sample counts", which means that the prosecution place in the indictment a manageable number counts that are indicative of a substantial level of offending, which is impossible to indict. For instance, it is revealed that A has committed over 200 separate, but in exactly the same way, offences of Social Security Benefit fraud. It would be unrealistic to frame a 200 count indictment; in such circumstances, the prosecution draft specimen count(s) and list the others in a schedule. Part IV r.3.3 of the Consolidated Practice Directions provides that a large count indictment would not be in the interests of effective case management.

It is possible in such a situation for the court to utilise the provisions of ss.17 to 21 of the Domestic Violence, Crime and Victims Act 2004, so that in multiple offending cases, the jury try certain counts and if found guilty, the judge alone tries the remainder of the associated counts. Alternatively, a prosecutor can indict on a single count that has "multiple incidents" contained in it of the same offence (see r.14.2 and Part IV 34.8 of Practice Direction). Rule 34.2 allows for there to be in existence more than one indictment. This can occur where the defendant has been sent or committed to the Crown Court for offence A, and is later sent or committed for offence B; if offence B is connected with offence A, then the prosecution will need to consider joining the indictments or choosing which of the two to proceed with.

Part 14 of the CPR 2005 provides that the prosecution must prefer (draft) a bill of indictment within 28 days from when the defendant was committed or sent to the Crown Court Officer. This may, on written application to a judge, before expiry, be extended. Section 2 of the Administration of Justice Act 1933 allows at committal or being sent under the s.51 procedure for the draft bill of indictment to have additional counts to be added or substituted for the counts charging the offence, provided such counts are founded on facts or evidence disclosed to the magistrates' court. For the bill to become an indictment s.2 directs the court officer to sign the bill, if satisfied that it meets the contents requirements.

18.19 In *R. v Clarke* [2008] 1 W.L.R. 338, the House of Lords ruled that the Court of Appeal in *R. v Ashton* [2006] All E.R. (D) 62 was wrong to distinguish the decision in *R. v Morais* [1988] 87 Cr.App.R. 9, which was clearly binding upon it and instead adopt a liberal approach to s.2, by ruling that an indictment not properly signed is not rendered automatically invalid. All their Lordships recognised the laudable and pragmatic approach taken when there is no prejudice; a procedural failure does not mandatorily nullify the proceedings. This is all the more acute if the offences are serious. However, Lord Bingham, having reviewed the historical background to bills of indictment, concluded that the intention of Parliament is inescapable on the clear wording of s.2; a preferred bill of indictment does not become an indictment until and unless signed. The Court is duty bound to apply the law even if this is distasteful and contradictory to justice. Referring to the decisions in *Sekhon and Soneji* as being "valuable and salutary", Lord Bingham observed:

> "the sea change which they wrought has been exaggerated and they do not warrant a wholesale jettisoning of all the rules affecting procedure irrespective of their legal effect."

The effect of the House of Lords ruling is clear; if the indictment is not properly signed, this is not a simple administrative error, it will remain a bill and therefore the proceedings will be a nullity. Any conviction in consequence must be quashed, as were the serious convictions of s.18 wounding in *Clarke* (other similar cases on this point are *R. v Thompson* [1975] 1 W.L.R. 1425 and *R. v Newland* [1988] Q.B. 402). Formality, within certain respects of the procedural rules is of importance in order to ensure due process, and lawful authority and fairness. This cannot be undermined by saying that despite such failures there is no prejudice. A similar approach was taken by the House of Lords in *R. v J* [2005] 1 A.C. 562 concerning a clear reading of the 12-month time limitation for commencing proceedings for unlawful sexual intercourse with a girl under 16, contrary to s.6 of the now repealed Sexual Offences Act 1956, Parliament had intended to prevent prosecution of events that have become stale. For this reason it was impermissible for the prosecution to instead bring proceedings of indecent assault for a s.6 offence. Lord Bingham noted that:

> "if a statutory provision is clear and unambiguous, the court may not decline to give effect to it on the ground that its rationale is anachronistic, or discredited or unconvincing."

Further, s.5(1) of the Indictments Act 1915 provides the court with the power to amend a defective indictment as the court thinks necessary, to meet the circumstances of the case. In *R. v Mehmet* [2002] EWCA Crim 514, the Court of Appeal followed the earlier decision in *Osieh* [1996] 2 Cr.App.R. 145, that the meaning of defective can include the amending of an indictment by adding a count for an offence that had not been committed, by the magistrates' court. The question of whether the addition should be permitted, is whether the defendant would suffer any injustice, s.2 of the Administration of Justice Act 1933 does not prevent this.

18.20 It is essential that the indictment is drafted correctly if the prosecution are to avoid the fatal consequences that occurred in *R. v Hadi* [2001] EWCA Crim 2534. The Court of Appeal quashed the appellant's (an Iraqi shopkeeper) conviction, despite pleading guilty to conspiracy to assist asylum claimants. The substantive offence to the conspiracy is that contained in s.25 of the Immigration Act 1971 as amended by s.25 of the Asylum and Immigration Act 1996. The precise offence being "any person knowingly concerned in making or carrying out arrangements for securing or facilitating the entry into the UK of anyone they know or has reasonable cause for believing to be an illegal entrant". The count as drafted made no reference to the illegal "entry" which is the very purpose of the substantive offence. There are many lawful ways of assisting an asylum claimant. For this reason, the indictment was fundamentally defective, the defendant having pleaded guilty to an offence not known to law. Laws L.J. stated:

> "there are some areas of the law in which technicalities are rightly out of date. But for the protection of the individual's liberty the courts jealously guard the need for care and accuracy in matters such as the terms of an indictment. The difference between a fundamental error and a correctable error, which in other spheres may be regard as arid, in this area remains of great importance."

In *R. v Drayton* [2005] EWCA Crim 2013, the Court of Appeal stated obiter that whilst it is not mandatory for an indictment to specify arson when the count alleges criminal damage by fire, it is desirable to use the word arson to denote the statutory offence alleged. The Court felt that was a matter that required classification in another case, since this case involved a charge in the magistrates' court and was valid in that context.

Similarly, the framing of inchoate offence counts can fall foul of the strict requirements of rr.4 to 6 of the Indictment Rules 1971. This can be seen with the offences of basic and aggravated criminal damage, including arson. To frame the particulars of a conspiracy to incite count as A and B did "unlawfully incite persons unknown to commit criminal damage, contrary to s.1(1) plus (3) of the Criminal Damage Act 1971", was ruled to be bad for duplicity in *R. v Booth and Others* [1998] (unreported) applying the decision in *R. v Roberts* [1998] 1 Cr.App.R. 441. The principle against duplicity is contained in r.4(2) of the Indictment Rules 1971, which provides that each count should allege just one offence, if a count alleges several offences, then this is said to be bad for duplicity and the indictment should be quashed.

18.21 This point of principle is confirmed in *R. v Thompson* [1914] 9 Cr.App.R. 252, but it was also ruled that this would not automatically result in a conviction being quashed. In *R. v Marchese* [2008] EWCA Crim 389 the Court of Appeal, accepted that the count containing the threats to kill offence (s.16 of the OAPA 1861) was duplicitous having alleged multiple threats, each should have been treated as separate offence. Applying the decision in *R. v Greenfield* [1973] 1 W.L.R. 1151, the Court observed that duplicity was concerned not with substantive law but with form (drafting). Distinguishing the decision of the House of Lords in *R. v Clarke* [2008] 1 W.L.R. 338, the Court held that the decision in *Thompson* remained good law and had not been indirectly overruled by *Clarke*. However, such a strict application of the rule can lead to the overloading of the indictment with many counts.

In *DPP v Merriman* [1973] A.C. 584, the House of Lords applied common sense and stated that:

> "it will often be legitimate to bring a single charge in respect of what might be called one activity even though that activity may involve more than one act."

So if A punches B several times, then this can be framed in one count of ABH, as opposed to three separate counts and not offend the duplicity principle. At the same time, the prosecution will be aware that it is in the public interest to ensure that the defendant is answerable for all their culpability. So, if A hits B twice but on consecutive days, then such conduct would be better framed as two separate count offences, unless of course, it is treated as one continuing act. Further, the Court also ruled that is it perfectly proper to charge more than one defendant jointly in the same indictment or together on the same or some of the counts. In *R. v Smith & Tovey* [2005] 2 Cr.App.R. (S) 100, the Court of Appeal observed that the prosecution need to be mindful, when drafting the indictment for multi offending, to provide sufficient examples of the offending behaviour to enable the court to impose a sentence that reflects the defendant's culpability properly.

Similar sentiments were expressed by the Court of Appeal in *R. v French* [1982] 4 Cr.App.R. (S) 57, relating to the need to reflect the degree of culpability concerning the offence of robbery, in which a firearm was used in its commission, by including a separate count of the s.17 Firearms Act 1968 offence; a failure to do so would mean that the judge could only sentence on the factual basis of the robbery alone, having to ignore the use of a firearm as an aggravating feature. The Court of Appeal considered itself bound by the previous decision in *Faulkner* [1972] 56 Cr.App.R. 594 and disapproved of two other Court of Appeal decisions to the contrary, which had been decided *per incuriam*, having not had the benefit of the decision in *Faulkner*.

18.22 The Court ruled that an indictment should always be kept as brief and as uncomplicated as possible; normally one count is adequate, unless there is very good reason to add more counts. In relation to the offence of possessing a firearm with intent to injure, resist arrest or to commit an indictable offence, then for sentencing purposes there is a need to add a separate count to the indictment. Further, to not include a separate count might be argued to be a concession by the prosecution to accept that no firearm was used. Finally and importantly, if the defendant admits the substantive offence but denies the use of a firearm, then the defendant is entitled to the verdict of the jury without a separate count. The defendant will not have been determined to have been convicted of the firearms offence and the sentencing court can only sentence on convicted facts, either found by the jury or if admitted by the defendant.

It is important to note also that it is not duplicitous for the prosecution to state in the particulars that the offence(s) occurred during or over a particular period of time. This can often arise for old offences such as sexual offences, where the victim is unable to remember the precise date but can remember the period in which it is alleged to have committed (see *R. v Wallwork* [1958] 42 Cr.App.R. 153, and *Hodgetts v Chiltern DC* [1983] 2 A.C. 120). Nevertheless, the prosecution will need to bear in mind that the greater the time in which the offence is alleged to have taken place the greater the uncertainty of the offence will become, leaving the defendant in a difficult position when it comes to answering the allegation. Given that the issue of duplicity is concerned with the form in which it is drafted it does not affect how the evidence is presented at court. In *R. v Mintern* [2004] EWCA Crim 7, the Court of Appeal dismissed the appeal and ruled that if a conspiracy count alleges one conspiracy but the evidence later reveals another conspiracy to the one already alleged in the count, it does not necessarily become bad for duplicity, provided a reasonably minded jury could still convict the defendants of the conspiracy charged. Only if the evidence reveals a separate conspiracy to the one charged, should a judge allow a submission of no case to answer.

Likewise, where the offence requires the prosecution to prove various states of mind, such as s.20 of the OAPA 1861, which has a mens rea of intentionally or recklessly, it is common practice to frame the statement of offence as simply "Unlawful wounding, contrary to s.20 of the OAPA 1861". The particulars would then dependant on the case be "A on (or about or between) the . . . day of . . . unlawfully and maliciously wounded (or inflicted) GBH on V." If it comes to light that the indictment is defective, then s.5(1) of the Indictments Act 1915 provides a power for the Crown Court, either before trial or at any stage of a trial, to make an order allowing for the amendment of an indictment, if it appears to the Court to be defective and the Court thinks that the amendment is necessary in order to meet the circumstances of the case, unless such an amendment would lead to an injustice. In *R. v Palmer* [2002] Crim. L.R. 973, Rose L.J. stated that the term "defective" encapsulates the concept of "lack" and "want" and therefore, was wide enough to allow a judge to add a new co-accused, provided there is no injustice.

18.23 The whole emphasis of the need to have a clear and simply framed indictment is so that the defendant knows exactly what is being alleged against them and build their defence case on that. If the offence is unknown to law or the count does not make it clear what and how many offences the defendant is alleged to have committed, then the defence cannot properly prepare its case and that would clearly amount to an injustice. This is exactly the purpose behind s.5(3) of the Indictments Act 1915, which gives the court a power to sever the counts in the indictment and order separate trials, if the court is of the opinion that the defendant may be prejudiced or embarrassed in their defence, if they were tried on the one indictment.

There is no requirement for a judge to order separate trials if the counts in the indictment do not support each other evidentially, provided that it is made clear to the jury that they must consider each count separately and independently of the other (see *R. v Cannan* [1991] 92 Cr.App.R. 16). This problem is particularly acute when a defendant is charged with separate, but distinct sexual offences involving different victims and over a period of time and the evidence is not cross-admissible. Allowing the separate counts to remain in the single indictment could prejudice the defendant in the minds of the jury (see *R. v Christou* [1997] A.C. 117 and *R. v Thomas* [2006] EWCA Crim 2442).

In *R. v Hayter* [2005] 1 W.L.R. 605, the House of Lords made it clear that there are strong public policy grounds for joint offences to be tried jointly. Although avoiding delay, reducing costs and ensuring convenience are considerations, the main reason is the perception that a just outcome is more likely to be reached in a joint trial, as opposed to severing an indictment and having separate trials. Subject only to the discretion of the judge to order separate trials as being in the interests of justice, it is always in the interests of the public to have joint trials of those it is alleged acted jointly in the commission of a criminal offence. It is important to bear in mind that whilst defendants are tried jointly, there are in effect, separate trials and that the jury must be directed that the prosecution must prove all the elements of the offence individually against each defendant.

16. Alternative Counts and Compromise Verdicts

18.24 It is for the CPS and not the courts to determine who should stand trial and upon what charges, but s.6 of the Criminal Justice Act 1967 provides the Crown Court with a discretion to place a lesser, alternative charge before the jury. The previous authorities on leaving alternative offences had purposively provided trial judges with only broad guidance, ensuring that their discretion was not restricted (see *R. v Fairbanks* [1986] 1 W.L.R. 1202) but with the consequence that similar cases could be decided differently. The House of Lords in *R. v Coutts* [2006] 1 W.L.R. 2154 has reduced these risks and set out in clear terms the duty and responsibility of any trial judge when faced with the task of leaving alternative offences regardless of the wishes of both counsel. Section 6(2) of the CJA 1967 relates specifically to an indictment of murder and provides the trial court with the discretionary power of leaving either manslaughter (both voluntary and involuntary) or causing GBH with intent or attempted murder as alternative offences. Section 6(3), on the other hand, allows a jury to bring a guilty verdict for another indictable offence, if that offence comes within the allegation of the indicted offence, either expressly or by implication.

Both s.6(2) and (3) come into play where the prosecution have chosen not to put alternative lesser offences as separate counts on the indictment and instead run an "all or nothing" case. This can place a defendant, who is contesting their guilt, in an invidious position. If they propose the inclusion of an alternative offence, they risks being convicted of it; if they do not, they risk being convicted of what may be a more serious offence than their conduct and culpability deserve. Therefore, responsibility for this must rest with trial judges, in accordance with the principles now laid down in *Coutts*. In *R. v Coutts* [2006] 1 W.L.R. 2154, the defendant had, with the victim's consent, engaged in sexual asphyxiation using tights, which resulted in the victim's death.

The prosecution based their case on a single count of murder, saying that such an act was nothing other than a deliberate intent to kill. The defence claimed the death was a tragic accident. Both counsel and trial judge agreed that there would be no manslaughter alternative. The defendant was convicted and appealed on the grounds that the trial judge should have left a manslaughter verdict to the jury. The Court of Appeal dismissed the appeal on the basis that there existed no risk of the jury reaching an improper verdict, and secondly, given the nature and presentation of the prosecution's case, leaving an alternative offence would have complicated matters unnecessarily and therefore not served the interests of justice.

18.25 However, the House of Lords reversed the Court of Appeal's decision. Approving the principle of law stated by Lord Clyde in the Privy Council decision of *Von Starck v The Queen* [2000] 1 W.L.R. 1270 at p.1275, concerning the functions and responsibility of the trial judge, Lord Bingham, with whose opinion the other Law Lords concurred, set out at para.23 a new test to be applied when dealing with the issue of alternative offences:

> "the public interest in the administration of justice, is best served if, in any *trial on indictment*, the trial Judge leaves to the jury, subject to any appropriate caution or warning, but irrespective of the wishes of trial counsel, *any obvious* alternative offence which there is evidence to support."

Any obvious alternative offences would, according to his Lordship, amount to those:

> "which should suggest themselves to the mind of any ordinarily knowledgeable and alert criminal judge" but "excluding alternatives which ingenious counsel may identify through diligent research after trial."

His Lordship further confined the rule to trial on indictment and not summary proceedings, since the public interest was not affected to the same degree.

Agreeing with Lord Bingham, Lord Rodger took the view that a failure by a judge to leave a viable alternative offence of manslaughter, based on a reasonable view of the facts, would be to "misrepresent the position by making the law seem more rigid and less nuanced than it actually is" and that the jury should be made aware of the "intermediate position" regardless of the wishes of counsel so that they may reach a decision "in light of a complete understanding of the law applicable to them". Both Lord Hutton and Lord Rodger expressly disapproved of Lord Ackner's approach in *R. v Maxwell* [1990] 1 W.L.R. 401, that a conviction should only be quashed if a jury is found to have convicted "out of reluctance to see the defendant get clean away" with disgraceful conduct, as amounting to an unsatisfactory principle.

18.26 Referring to the Australian authorities of *Gilbert v The Queen* [2000] 201 C.L.R. 414, and *Gillard v The Queen* [2003] 219 C.L.R. 1, Lord Hutton acknowledged that he has been a member of the Privy Council that decided the case of *Hunter and Moodie v The Queen* [2003] UKPC 69, which approved the *Maxwell* approach but now accepted that it was unworkable since "it appears to oblige the appellate court to engage in speculation as to factors which may have influenced the jury's decision" and that therefore,

> "save in exceptional circumstances, an appellate court should quash a conviction, whether for murder or for a lesser offence, as constituting a serious miscarriage of justice where the judge has erred in failing to leave a lesser alternative verdict, obviously raised by the evidence".

Section 1(1) of the Criminal Attempts Act 1981 requires the prosecution to prove that a defendant did an act which is more than merely preparatory to the commission of an offence and that they did so "with intent to commit" the indictable offence alleged. In *R. v Morrison* [2003] 2 Cr.App.R. 37, the Court of Appeal had to address the issue of whether an indictment containing a single count of "attempted murder", expressly or impliedly amounted to or included an allegation of attempted GBH with intent. Giving the leading judgment of the court, Lord Woolf ruled, in applying s.6(3) CJA 1967 and referring to the judgment of Hutchinson L.J. in *R. v Adebayo*, that it did, despite the fact that certain conduct, such as putting a ligature around a person's neck, would point to a single offence of attempted murder. Without hesitation and with a "degree of relief" his Lordship concluded "that there can be no intention to kill someone without the intention also to cause GBH".

In *R. v Foster and Others* [2007] EWCA Crim 2869, the Court of Appeal considered the application of the principle in *Coutts*. In dismissing the appeal, the Court of Appeal ruled that within the principle of *Coutts*, the judge must consider, as a legal question, whether the alternative offence is in terms of proportionality trivial or insubstantial to the real issues presented in the case. As a matter of law, the judge is not required always to leave an alternative lesser admitted offence to the jury, even if that is part of the defence case.

18.27 Provided the judge has considered all the evidence and the issue of fairness, there is no obligation to leave a lesser alternative offence, if it is remote from the real issues and the jury are not put in a position to have to make a stark choice between conviction of a serious offence and that of acquittal of a defendant who admits a degree of culpability and would be unfairly disadvantaged by it. Further, the Court stated that the principle in *Coutts* does not extend beyond the ambit of s.6(3) and that it would in such circumstances be undesirable for a judge to be obliged at the end of the presentation of evidence to consider amending the indictment specifically to include alternative counts. This would lead to confusion and would not only complicate matters for the jury, but would also complicate the summing up of the judge (see also *R. v Banton* [2007] EWCA Crim 1847).

The cases establish a number of principles in relation to the application of s.6(3) of the CLA 1967, within the offence range of the Offences Against the Persons Act 1861. In *R. v Mandair* [1994] 99 Cr.App.R. 250, the House of Lords confirmed unanimously that an indictment containing a single s.18 count of causing GBH with intent also *by implication* included an allegation of the lesser offence under s.20 and therefore such an alternative should have been left for the jury's determination when assessing the mental culpability of the appellant. Likewise, in *R. v Wilson* [1984] A.C. 242, it was held by the House of Lords that the jury were entitled to consider s.47 as an alternative offence to s20.

More recently, in *R. v Lahaye* [2005] EWCA Crim 2847, the Court of Appeal ruled that the defendant had not suffered any unfairness when the trial judge had left an alternative s.20 offence to a single s.18 count indictment, which resulted in a conviction for the former. Sir Igor Judge observed that the court was "troubled" by the lack of a s.20 count and that, "the authorities established beyond doubt that a verdict under s.20 is normally available when a s.18 is alleged".

18.28 His Lordship further observed that there was no advantage in a single s.18 count indictment, neither was there any disadvantage to the Crown if a s.20 charge was made available, since they could present their evidence accordingly. The jury, according to his Lordship:

> "should be trusted to reach the appropriate verdict according to the evidence," and that if as a matter of law a s.20 by virtue of s.6(3) is a viable alternative then "we consider that it would be better practice for the s.20 count to be included on the face of the indictment."

Conversely, in *R. v Griffiths* [2005] EWCA Crim 237, the Court of Appeal, whilst acknowledging that s.20 is as a matter of law a viable alternative to s.18, determined that in this instance the defendant was prejudged unfairly by the judge when without consulting counsel he decided to leave an alternative verdict to the jury during the summing up. This deprived the defence both of a reasonable opportunity to consider an alternative verdict and of addressing the jury about it and therefore amounted to an irregularity, rendering the conviction unsafe.

Section 1 of the Road Traffic Act 1991 created the offence of causing death by dangerous driving, s.3 of the RTA 1988, as amended by s.1(2) Road Traffic Act 1991 creates the offence of careless or inconsiderate driving. In *R. v Luckie* [2004] EWCA Crim 1223, the Court of Appeal had to determine whether the judge was wrong in refusing to leave careless driving as an alternative offence to the more serious death by dangerous driving offence. Scott Baker L.J. ruled that the same legal principles applied to motoring offences. In upholding the appellant's conviction for death by dangerous driving, the Appeal Court concluded there was no basis for believing that the jury did not adhere to their oath and simply convicted him to ensure he was answerable for his reprehensible conduct. Secondly, there existed no evidence to support an alternative careless driving offence, had this been the case then the Court may have been able to interfere with the judge's discretion.

A similar conclusion was reached in *R. v Dunne* [2003] EWCA Crim 2975, whilst in *R. v Hart* [2003] EWCA Crim 1268 the Court of Appeal simply refused to interfere with the judge's discretion given that there was no indication of the judge actually misdirecting himself as to the relevant law. In *R. v Hussain* [2004] EWCA Crim 325, however, the Court of Appeal, although dismissing the appeal, accepted that different judges and even differently constituted Appeal Courts, might have concluded differently on refusing to leave careless driving as an alternative. Applying the principle in *Coutts*, these decisions would appear to be wrong and that alternative lesser motoring offences ought now be left to the jury.

Further, the Court of Appeal in *R. v Phillips* [2007] EWCA Crim 485, distinguished the decisions in *R. v J* [2005] 1 A.C. 562, and *R. v WR* [2005] EWCA Crim 1907 on the impermissibility of charging indecent assault as an alternative to consensual sexual intercourse with a girl under 16 as being procedurally time barred. In *Phillips*, the Court held, following the decision in *R. v Timmins* [2006] 1 Cr.App.R.(S) 18, that the main count alleging rape was maintained throughout the trial by the prosecution and that indecent assault which can include penetration was a viable alternative. It is important that these authorities are read in light of the changes made by ss.9 and 13 of the Sexual Offences Act 2003.

17. Sample Draft of an "Indictment"

INDICTMENT **18.29**

IN THE CROWN COURT AT WOODLANDS

REGINA

-V-

JOHN SMITH, DAVID HOOK, PATRICK O'CONNOR

JOHN SMITH, DAVID HOOK, and PATRICK O'CONNOR are charged as follows;

Count 1

STATEMENT OF OFFENCE

CAUSING GRIEVOUS BODILY HARM WITH INTENT, contrary to Section 18 of the Offences Against the Persons Act 1861.

PARTICULARS OF THE OFFENCE

JOHN SMITH, DAVID HOOK and Patrick O' CONNOR on the 10th day of July 2008 unlawfully caused grievous bodily harm to Mark Bowland with intent to do him grievous bodily harm.

Count 2

STATEMENT OF OFFENCE

UNLAWFUL WOUNDING, contrary to Section 20 of the Offences Against the Persons Act 1861.

PARTICULARS OF THE OFFENCE

JOHN SMITH, DAVID HOOK, and Patrick O' CONNOR on the 10th day of July 2008 unlawfully and recklessly wounded Mark Bowland.

Count 3

STATEMENT OF OFFENCE

DAMAGING PROPERTY, contrary to Section 1(1) of the Criminal Damage Act 1971

PARTICULARS OF THE OFFENCE

DAVID HOOK and PATRICK O'CONNOR, on the 10th day of July 2008 without lawful excuse damaged a Ford Escort belonging to Mark Bowland, intending to destroy or damage such property or being reckless as to whether such property would be destroyed or damaged.

Signed by Crown Court Officer

18. Preparatory Hearings Under the Criminal Procedure and Investigation Act 1996 (Part 15 of the Criminal Practice Directions)

18.30 Prior to the commencement of the trial, i.e. before a jury is sworn, a preparatory hearing can be held in order to assist in expediting the management of the case, involving questions relating to, i.e. admissibility of evidence or points of law. The purpose of such pre-trial reviews is to eliminate delay and inconvenience during the trial (jury and witnesses waiting while points of law are argued before presentation of evidence) and indeed reduce the possibly of a later appeal. The issue is argued before the judge who will then make a ruling on the question raised. In outline, statute provides three possible situations in which the Crown Court may make rulings as to questions of law and/or the admissibility of evidence prior to the swearing of the jury:

(i) serious or complex fraud: ss.7 to 10 of the CJA1987;

(ii) other serious, long or complex cases: ss.28 to 38 of the CPIA 1996;

(iii) pre-Trial hearing under s.39 to 43 of the CPIA 1996.

The procedure for other non-fraud cases is set out in ss.28 to 38 of the CPIA 1996, and corresponds essentially with those for fraud cases. Before a judge orders that a preparatory hearing is to be held, it must first appear to them that the evidence reveals a serious complex case of fraud or other serious offence and that the holding of such an hearing before a jury is sworn, results in a substantial benefit in terms of:

(i) identifying issues material to the verdict of the jury;

(ii) assisting the jury's comprehension of such issues;

(iii) expediting the proceedings before the jury; or

(iv) assisting in the case management of he trial.

It is important to note that if a judge does order a preparatory hearing, then this forms part of the trial. The trial therefore will be deemed to begin with that hearing and the defendant is to be arraigned if not already done so (see s.8 CJA 1988 and s.30 CPIA 1996).

Section 7 of the CJA 1987 and s.31 of the CPIA 1996 provide the judge with the power to determine (i) any question as to the admissibility of evidence and (ii) other questions of law relating to the case. Section 310 of the CJA 2003 amends this and inserts a further question as to severance or joinder of charges as falling within the ambit of a preparatory hearing (this removes the narrow interpretation taken by the court in *Moore* [1991] unreported and *R. v Hedworth* [1997] 1 Cr.App.R. 421). If necessary, the judge can adjourn the hearing. Additionally, the judge can order the prosecution to produce a "case statement", revealing the principal facts of the case, witnesses, any exhibits and any propositions of law they intend to rely on. A preparatory hearing can be at the request of either the prosecution or defence, or of the court's own motion. An appeal lies to the Court of Appeal against the ruling of a judge in relation to either or both of these questions provided leave is granted by a single judge.

18.31 Difficulties, however, have arisen in terms of jurisdiction to deal with, at the same time, other issues that may arise in relation to the management of the case and whether a ruling on these matters can be appealed. In *R. v Claydon and Others* [2004] 1 W.L.R. 1575 the Court of Appeal held that whilst the court had jurisdiction to hear an appeal from a preparatory hearing concerning a ruling under s.78 of PACE 1984 to exclude evidence, since this fell within the purpose of s.29(2) expediting the proceedings before the jury, the court could not hear an appeal relating to a ruling on a point of an abuse of process, as ruled in *Re Gunarwardena* [1990] 1 W.L.R. 703 since an application to stay proceedings does not fall within the ambit of when a preparatory hearing can be held and therefore no availability to appeal such a ruling exists.

In *R. v H* [2007] 2 A.C. 270 Lord Mance, having referred to the Roskell Report that led to the passing of the CJA 1987, stated obiter that the power of the judge to make rulings at a preparatory hearing in the context of questions of law includes any other application challenging the validity of the proceedings or inviting the termination of a trial or amending the indictment. On the point in issue in *H*, their Lordships ruled unanimously that once a preparatory hearing has been ordered validly, a judge could deal with other relevant rulings that do not necessarily fall within the ambit of s.9 (and indeed s.31) questions. However, for such rulings there is leave to appeal.

As a matter of construction, a question of disclosure of evidence does not amount to or involve a question of law. The current language of the statute does not permit such a finding. Nevertheless, Lord Mance noted particularly that with long trials allowing a possible appeal from a ruling on disclosure may have advantages and therefore should be looked at by the Law Commission and others. It should be noted that if the ruling is subject to appeal, leave must first be granted and that the Court of Appeal will only interfere with a discretionary power of a trial judge where that decision is clearly wrong.

18.32 A clear example of this is *R. v A* [2001] 1 W.L.R. 1546, where before the trial of the defendant, a preparatory hearing was held to determine the effect of s.41 of the Youth Justice and Criminal Evidence Act 1999, on whether the defendant could adduce evidence as to his recent consensual sexual activity with the complainant. The trial judge ruled not. The defendant appealed to the to the House of Lords which held that s.41 was not compatible with a right to a fair trial and that such evidence could be presented to the jury if that ensured that the defendant received a fair trial. In *Re Kanaris* [2003] 1 W.L.R. 443, while the House of Lords held that it was perfectly proper for a judge to hold separate preparatory hearings in respect of a jointly charged defendant, it was important to be aware that the safeguards of the custody time limits were not circumvented.

A preparatory hearing forms part of the trial and so the custody time limits cease to apply at the point a preparatory hearing is held, Although a judge can adjourn the preparatory hearing and vacate the trial date thereafter, this would mean that a defendant is held in custody beyond their time limit, when they should be granted bail. If this situation arises then the defendant ought to make an application for bail and the judge must take into account in that decision, the actual expiry of the time limit. Further, if a preparatory hearing is to be ordered, this should be held when it is realistic for the trial to commence immediately or soon afterwards.

The procedure for appeal against the ruling at a preparatory hearing is contained in Pt 66 of the CrPR 2005. This follows a similar format as with other types of appeal, namely an appeal notice, oral or written application (no more than two days after the ruling) for permission to appeal and response notice with representations. The prescribed forms must be used as per the *Practice Direction (Criminal Appeals: Forms)* [2007] 1 W.L.R. 2607. An important point of precedent was resolved in *R. v M and Others (No.2)* [2007] 2 Cr.App.R. 17, in which the original ruling by the judge on the application of the offence in s.57 of the Terrorism Act 2000, to that of s.58 in the context of the meaning of "article", was overturned on appeal. However, in a later subsequent appeal decision in *R. v Rowe* [2007] 2 Cr.App.R. 14, it was ruled that the decision in the first appeal of *M* (see *R. v M* [2007] EWCA Crim 218 by the Court of Appeal was given *per incuriam*, based on false assumptions of the differences in the statutory context used. At *M's* trial, therefore the judge maintained his original ruling, based on the decision in *Rowe*, *M* appealed again against this ruling. The Court of Appeal, in the second appeal, ruled that as a matter of precedent, the judge was bound to follow the later decision in *Rowe*, since it would be in the interests of justice to do so, as this now represented the law.

Section 39 of the CPIA 1996 provides for the judge to hold a "pre-trial hearing" (PTH) for any matter which relates to "trial on indictment" and which may take place at any time after the defendant has been committed or sent to the Crown Court from the magistrates' court, but before the start of the trial (i.e. when the jury is sworn in). At a PTH, the judge may make a ruling on any question concerning the admissibility of evidence and or any questions relating to the case generally. An application to hold a PTH can be made by either party, or by the court on its own motion. Any ruling given by the judge will be binding throughout the proceedings until the case is disposed of, either by acquittal or conviction, or discontinuance. At any time on an application by either party or on the court's own motion, a judge may vary or discharge any ruling if it appears to them that it is in the interests of justice to do so. However, this power can only be exercised if there has been any material change of circumstances since the initial ruling. There is no availability of appeal against such a ruling, unless s.58 of the CJA 2003 is satisfied. If a ruling is detrimental to the defendant, then if convicted, the defendant will need to apply for leave to appeal against conviction.

19. Prosecution Appeal Against Evidentiary Ruling

18.33 Under ss.62 to 67 of the CJA 2003 (not yet brought into force) the prosecution have a right to appeal to the Court of Appeal against a qualifying evidentiary ruling (this means a ruling on admissibility or exclusion of prosecution evidence) made by the judge at any time but before the opening of the defence's case. The ruling must relate to a specific offence listed in Pt 1 of Sch.4 such as s.18 wounding with intent but does not include other lesser assault offences.

The prosecution must inform the court before the opening of the defence's case of its intention to appeal. Leave to appeal will only be given by the Court of Appeal if the condition in s.63 that the ruling significantly weakens the prosecution's case in relation to the specified offence(s) is satisfied. Section 64 provides for the appeal to be expedited if necessary and/or the case adjourned or the jury discharged. Section 65 allows for any part of the trial not connected with the appeal to continue. Under s.66 the Court of Appeal can affirm, reverse or vary any ruling made, but only if that ruling was wrong in law or in error or principle, or the ruling was unreasonable. If so the Court can either order for the trial to resume, or a fresh trial, or for the defendant to be acquitted. Section 68 preserves the right of leave to appeal to the House of Lords. Costs of any appeal are to be met out of central funds. It is important to be aware of s.70 which amends the Prosecution of Offences Act 1985 and provides that any adjournment time will not affect the defendant's custody time limit, where the appeal arises before the commencement of the trial.

20. Prosecution Right of Appeal Against General Rulings by the Judge

18.34 The trial judge has a duty to ensure a fair trial; the judge can, if they feel it is in the interests of justice, terminate the proceedings in one of two ways:

(i) accepting that there is "no case to answer" against the defendant;

(ii) stay the proceedings as an abuse of process (in that it would be unfair and wrong for the court to allow a prosecution to continue.

Although the commentary in relation to s.58 refers to the prosecution having a right to appeal against a "terminating ruling" of a trial judge, this is not an expression used in the CJA 2003 or in the provision itself and, as the Court of Appeal has said, while the expression "terminating ruling" might be a convenient use of shorthand, it is best avoided as a matter of statutory construction, particularly in regard to a jurisdictional question.

Section 58 of the CJA 2003 gives the prosecution a general right to appeal to the Court of Appeal, against any ruling of the judge in relation to a trial on indictment, which relates to an offence(s) contained in the indictment made at any time up to the summing up of the jury (the "applicable time"). Always consider whether the proceedings are concerned with a trial on indictment and the ruling given by the judge relates to an offence in the indictment. The prosecution must under s.58(4) inform the court that it intends to appeal or alternatively, request an adjournment to consider whether or not to appeal (r.67(2) states that the general rule is not to require a decision there and then but until the next business day).

However, before or at the time of giving notice the prosecution must under s.58(8) agree to accept the acquittal of the defendant (acquittal agreement) if either (i) leave to appeal is not granted, or (ii) the appeal is abandoned. This clearly amounts to ensuring that a balance is struck since s.58 is exclusive only to the prosecution and it would clearly be unfair to allow the prosecution to continue with the proceedings if unsuccessful in pursuing their appeal. In *R. v R* [2008] EWCA Crim 370, the Court of Appeal ruled that provided the "acquittal agreement" is made by the prosecution in good faith and not for some improper motive then the decision to enter into an acquittal agreement is the sole the responsibility of the prosecution based on the public interest. It is the price the prosecution must pay if it wishes to appeal against a ruling under s.58.

18.35 Section 58 is clear and unqualified and is in stark contrast to the test in s.62 which creates an objective test for the court to determine based on whether the ruling of the judge significantly weakens the case for the prosecution. No such test is inserted into s.58, had Parliament intended such an objective assessment to apply to s.58 then it would have expressly done so. In referring to the decision in *R. v Y* [2008] EWCA Crim 10 (see below) the Court ruled that there is no statutory power for a court when applying s.58 to consider the merits of the prosecution decision in terms of whether it was objectively justified to enter into an acquittal agreement. Parliament has entrusted the prosecution to act both competently and conscientiously in the public interest as to whether they bind themselves into an acquittal agreement. The Court nevertheless went on to refuse leave to appeal against the ruling of the judge who under r.24.3 of the CrPR 2005 had refused to grant leave to the prosecution to adduce expert evidence. There were a number of failures by the prosecution in obtaining and serving expert evidence. This was deplorable and constituted a serious failure by them to comply with the overriding objective of the rules. The decision of the judge was reasonable and was not, as the prosecution claimed, perverse.

Further, s.58 (7) provides that where the ruling relates to no case to answer and the prosecution informs the court of their intention to appeal then the prosecution can also nominate one or more other rulings by the judge (in relation to trial on indictment and which relate to the offence(s) subject to the appeal) to run "piggy back" with the no case to answer challenge. A clear example of this would be where a judge excludes prosecution evidence under s.78 of PACE 1984 and then due to the absence of such evidence finds that there is now no case to answer.

In *R. v Y* [2008] EWCA Crim 10, the Court of Appeal, having considered the piggy back provision, ruled that while s.58(1) must be construed strictly it was wide enough to cover a ruling as to the admissibility of evidence, even though such a ruling would also qualify under s.62. The ruling of the judge and any consequences flowing from it will have no effect while the proceedings of appeal are being pursued. In terms of what is meant by a "ruling" s.74 defines it so as to include "a decision, determination, direction, finding, notice, order, refusal, rejection or requirement". The decision in *R. v Y* was approved in *R. v O and Others* [2008] EWCA Crim 463, as binding authority that a ruling of a judge as to the admissibility of evidence which may lead to the collapse of the case can be subject to appeal under s.58 provided the statutory conditions are met.

18.36 Taking into account the wide breadth of the meaning of ruling, the Court of Appeal in *R. v Clarke* [2007] EWCA Crim 2532 held that a case management decision such as refusing an adjournment could constitute a ruling for the purposes of s.58 if the effect of the refusal would terminate the case, by the prosecution having to offer no evidence. On the facts, the judge's decision to refuse an adjournment to allow the prosecution to trace an untraceable witness who was unlikely to attend was reasonable.

Although the language of s.58 is broad the Court of Appeal in *R. v Thompson* [2007] 1 Cr.App.R. 15 ruled that it was concerned only with rulings resulting in an acquittal and therefore did not extend to the dismissal of a charge or indictment under the Sch.3 procedure in relation to the sending of a case to the Crown Court before arraignment took place. In this situation the prosecution will need to pursue the voluntary bill of indictment procedure. In *R. v JG* [2006] EWCA Crim 3276, the Court of Appeal observed that a judge should only grant leave to appeal a ruling if it is merited, in that there is a real prospect of success, otherwise leave should be refused and application to the Court of Appeal should be made, where a combined hearing of leave and the disputed ruling could take place.

Further, the Court noted that it was wrong for the judge to announce their ruling in the presence of the jury, since had the appeal been allowed a fresh trial would have had to be ordered, instead of continuing with the existing jury. For a clear example of s.58 see *R. v R; sub nom. Re Prosecution Right of Appeal (No.23 of 2007)* [2007] EWCA Crim 3312, in which the Court of Appeal allowed an appeal by the prosecution against the ruling of the judge that there was no case to answer. The judge was wrong to conclude that leather gloves with a padding of lead and sand, designed to be used for self defence did not amount to offensive weapon.

The Court of Appeal can under s.61 confirm, reverse, or vary any ruling to which the appeal relates. If the Court confirms the ruling, the defendant must be acquitted. If it reverses or varies the ruling, then the Court can either:

(i) order the resumption of the case;

(ii) order a fresh trial; or

(iii) order the defendant to be acquitted.

18.37 In respect of (i) and (ii), if the Court of Appeal allow the prosecution appeal before making either of the two orders it must be satisfied that it is necessary in the interests of justice to do so. Section 44 of the CJIA 2008, when it comes into force, amends this test as to whether the court considers that the defendant would receive a fair trial. As with s.62 above the proceedings can, if necessary, be expedited by the judge and adjourned, or discharge the jury, or continue the proceedings not connected to the appeal. Costs and custody time limits are the same as with s.62 above. If and when a point of law arises during the trial which requires the judge to make a ruling, then a *voire dire* (often referred to as a "trial within a trial") is held in the absence of the jury, so that the trial advocates can make their legal submissions about the disputed point of law.

Section 71 of the CJA 2003 sets out the general restrictions on the publication of the appeal proceedings against a ruling of a judge. Section 71(8) allows for certain specified information to be published, such as the identity of the court and the name of the judge. Anything not falling in subsection (8) is prohibited, The judge will make the initial decision on whether, and to what extent other prohibited information can be published, subject to an application to the Court of Appeal and further to the House of Lords to have the restriction wholly or partly lifted. Any contravention of the reporting restrictions constitutes a summary only offence under s.72 and is punishable by way of a maximum fine of £5,000.

The procedure to be followed in an appeal under s.58(2) is contained in Pt 67 of the CrPR 2005. The prosecution must serve an appeal notice, which must comply with the contents requirements set out in r.67.4 (i.e. identify the grounds, summary of facts, relevant arguments and authorities and transcripts and be served the following day, if appealed expedited or five days if not. In seeking permission to appeal, the prosecution can either make an application orally with reasons immediately after the ruling or in writing, served on the court and defendant after the next day. In *R. v O and Others* [2008] EWCA Crim 463, the Court of Appeal ruled on the particular events in the case that a decision of the judge to allow the prosecution to consider his ruling overnight and two hours on the following day was sufficiently immediate to satisfy the rules. The Crown Court must allow the defence to make representations. If the prosecution wish the matter to be expedited then they must provide reasons for this request. The defendant may serve a "response notice", but must do so if they wish to make representations or the court so directs. Both the appeal and response notice must be in the form as set out in the Criminal Practice Directions.

21. Trial in Absence of the Defendant and Direction of not Guilty or to Convict

18.38 Article 6 ensures that a defendant must receive a fair trial, including the proceedings, at all times. However, in *R. v Jones* [2003] 1 A.C. 1, the House of Lords ruled that in clear circumstances where a defendant has voluntary absented themselves, then the judge can order that the trial is to commence in their absence and any subsequent conviction will have been obtained fairly. As Lord Bingham said:

> "anyone who voluntarily chooses not to exercise a right cannot be heard to complain that he has lost the benefits which he might have expected to enjoy had he exercised it ... If he voluntarily chooses not to exercise his right to appear, he cannot impugn the fairness of the trial on the ground that it followed a course different from that which it would have followed had he been present and represented."

Nevertheless, the discretion:

> "should be exercised with the utmost care and caution. If the absence of the defendant is attributable to involuntary illness or incapacity it would very rarely, if ever be right to exercise the discretion in favour of commencing the trial, at any rate unless the defendant is represented and asks that the trial should begin."

If the judge decides to exercise their discretion, then they must ensure that the proceedings are conducted fairly and invite solicitors and counsel to continue to do as best as they can for the defendant. If a defendant changes their plea to guilty during a trial, then the procedure generally is for the judge to discharge the jury and direct them to appoint a foreman and formally return a verdict of guilty. Section 17 of the CJA 1967, on the other hand, provides a trial judge with a discretionary power to direct a jury to return a not guilty verdict if the case against the defendant collapses evidentially. This power exists to ensure that the judge does not allow a weak case to be put to a jury, in order to safeguard against a serious risk of a wrongful conviction.

In *R. v Brown* [2002] 1 Cr.App.R. 46, the Court of Appeal ruled that a judge can withdraw the case from the jury at any time, even at the end of the defence's case, if at that point there is insufficient evidence. Nevertheless, in *R. v Brown* [2001] EWCA Crim 961, the Court of Appeal stated that the power to acquit should be "very sparingly exercised and only if the judge really is satisfied that no reasonable jury, properly directed, could on the evidence safely convict".

In *R. v Kemp* [1995] 1 Cr.App.R.(S) 151, it was held that the judge should not direct an acquittal simply if this would cause the defendant to have a sense of grievance if convicted, whether this was justifiable or not. One particular difficulty for a judge is how to direct a jury if, on the evidence, the defendant has no defence in law and therefore the case is proven. In *R. v Wang* [2005] EWCA Crim 9, the House of Lords, applying the ruling of the majority in *DPP v Stonehouse* [1978] A.C. 55, held unanimously, allowing the appeal against conviction for possessing an offensive weapon in a public place, that there can be no circumstances which allow a judge to direct a jury specifically to return a guilty verdict. It is not the function of the judge to assess guilt factually, it is a matter for the jury. If the case against the defendant is overwhelming or the judge has ruled that a legal defence does not exist, they must still direct the jury to consider the factual evidence within the legal principles and decide a verdict. If a judge does this, they will not fall foul of the decision in *Wang* (see *R. v Kelleher* [2003] EWCA 3525 and *R. v Caley-Knowles* [2006] EWCA Crim 1611).

22. Outline of Trial Procedure in the Crown Court (Part 39 of the Criminal Practice Directions)

18.39 A trial in the Crown Court itself will usually consist of the following format:

1. Jury sworn and challenging of any of the jury panel.
2. Opening speech for the prosecution.
3. Prosecution call witnesses, followed by examination in chief; (during examination in chief, advocate is prohibited from asking "leading questions", a question which tends to suggest the answer, i.e. you saw the defendant hit the complainant) cross-examination by defence (can ask leading question in cross-examinations); re-examination for clarification if needed.
4. Prosecution closes its case. The defence can, if appropriate, make a submission of no case to answer. The court does have a general discretion beyond the two well-established exceptions of rebuttal and mere formality to allow, if the interests of justice test is satisfied, for the prosecution to call further evidence even though they have closed the case, but before the jury retire (see *R. v Francis* [1990] 91 Cr.App.R. 271 and *Khatibi v DPP* [2004] EWHC 83 in the magistrates' court). Only if there are special circumstances should a court allow the reception of evidence after the jury have retired (see *Webb v Leadbetter* [1996] 1 W.L.R. 245).
5. Defence opens case by calling witnesses, examination in chief, cross-examination and re-examination.
6. Closing speeches.
7. Judge's summing up.
8. Jury Bailiff sworn to ensure safe keeping of jury.
9. Jury retire to deliberate verdict.
10. Jury foreman pronounces the verdict of the jury in open court (unanimous, majority 11–1, 10–2: Juries Act 1974).
11. If defendant is found not guilty, then they are formally acquitted and free to leave the court. If convicted, then the judge will proceed to impose sentence. Usually, sentencing will be adjourned for the preparation of pre-sentence reports, psychiatric reports).

12. If the defendant believes that they have been wrongly convicted or received a long sentence they can within 28 days apply for leave to appeal against conviction/sentence, to the Court of Appeal.

23. The Jury: Juries Act 1974 (JA 1974) as Amended

18.40 The jury in itself is a detailed subject, what follows is an assessment of the main principles. The jury is independent (see *Bushels Case* [1670] 124 E.R. 1006) from the judge and both the prosecution and the defence. A jury in a criminal trial must consist of 12 persons, although should a juror die or be discharged, i.e. for ill health or conflict, the trial may continue in accordance with s.16 of the Juries Act 1974. This provides that the jury remains properly constituted, provided the number does not fall below nine. In a trial for murder, consent must be obtained from the prosecution and defence. Section 2 of the Juries Act 1974 provides that the Ministry of Justice is responsible for summoning jurors to attend for jury service.

This is now carried out centrally in London, in order to avoid regional differences in the selection of jurors. The details of persons summoned are taken at random from the electoral register and the average period for jury service is two weeks. A panel of those summoned is prepared which the parties involved can inspect. Usually, more persons are summoned then are actually needed. In *R. v Sheffield Crown Court Ex p. Brownlow* [1980] 2 W.L.R. 892, the Court of Appeal disapproved of jury vetting of eligible potential jurors as being unconstitutional and offending the requirement of randomness and fairness. If a juror fails to answer the summons, this amounts to a contempt of court with a fine usually imposed if proven (see *R. v Dodds* [2003] 1 Cr.App.R. 60)

However, should there be a short fall, there exists a power in s.6 of the Juries Act for the court to summons any person in the vicinity of the court who is eligible to sit. Section 321 and Sch.33 of the CJA 2003 provides that every person is qualified to serve as a juror and is liable to attend for jury service when summoned, provided they are:

(i) on the electoral register;

(ii) over 18;

(iii) not mentally disordered; and

(iv) not disqualified. These are people who have been sentenced to life imprisonment, imprisonment for public protection, to an extended sentence, or within the last 10 years to five years or more imprisonment, suspended sentence, community order and DTTO. Any person currently subjected to bail in criminal proceedings is also disqualified. The court in the form of an appropriate officer, does have available under s.9(2) of the JA 1974 a general power to grant an excusal or deferral.

18.41 Section 321 incorporates the intention of Parliament to increase the availability of persons to sit on a jury and to entrust that those who are selected observe impeccably the important duty of being a juror. This policy of jury selection came to be considered by the House of Lords in *R. v Abdroikof and Others* [2007] 1 W.L.R. 2679. By a majority of three to two it was held that when applying the test of apparent bias found in *Magill v Weeks* [2002] 2 W.L.R. 37, that the test was "whether the fair-minded and informed observer having all the facts, would conclude that there was a real possibility that the tribunal/jury was biased".

In relation to either a police officer or long serving employee of the CPS, there is a real possibility of bias with justice not being seen to be done (see *R. v Sussex Justices Ex p. McCarthy* [1924] 1 K.B. 256).

Whilst it is recognised that all potential jurors have their own ordinary prejudices and predilections, these are as far as possible neutralised by the safeguards in place to protect the impartiality of the jury, such as directions and warnings of the judge, secrecy and immunity from personal liability. However, applying the apparent bias test no neutrality can be achieved in regard to a police officer who works in the area and where the case involves an assault on another police officer, which is disputed by the defence. Likewise, a fair-minded and informed observer would assume the same lack of apparent impartiality in regard to an employee of the CPS. Lord Bingham concluded that:

> "it cannot be supposed that Parliament intended to infringe the rule in the *Sussex Case*, still less to do so without express language . . . if its metal is flawed a bell will not ring true. It is of the utmost importance that juries ring true, and be generally recognised to do so."

Lord Roger, in the minority, felt that while a fair-minded and informed observer would see the possibility of a police officer or CPS employee being biased, this does not mean they were incapable of following the directions of the judge and assessing the evidence impartially. Without more, these professional persons' mere presence on the jury would not give rise to any real possibility of bias. In *R. v Khan and Others* [2008] EWCA Crim 531, the Court of Appeal dismissed three appeals against conviction on the grounds of apparent bias of a juror as either being a police officer, prison officer or CPS employee. Lord Phillips, who gave the leading speech, observed that there was clearly a difference between partiality to a defendant, on the one hand, and that of choosing whether or not to accept or reject the evidence of a witness, on the other.

18.42 His Lordship, whilst finding it difficult to adduce clear principles from the decision of the House of Lords in *Abdroikof* concerning a police officer juror, affirmed that there is no principle which disqualifies automatically a police officer juror on the basis of lacking impartiality. The issue is not one of eligibility, as Parliament had made clear in relaxing the rules on disqualification in s.321, but whether their presence would render the trial unfair. Further, whilst it would be over ambitious for the Court to produce guidance for court officials, it was undesirable for appeals on grounds relating to juror bias and particularly undesirable for a conviction to be quashed and a re-trial ordered. This point is firmly recognised in the dismissal of the *Lewthwaite* appeal against conviction for an appalling s.18 wounding, where there was other strong evidence to link the appellant to the assault and that the test of bias in relation to a police juror had not been satisfied. To avoid the potential for appeals the issue of partiality should be identified before the trial starts and that if there is identified any risk of bias the juror could be stood down. It is essential that a juror in waiting is identified as falling into one of the previous disqualified categories of a police officer, prison officer or an employee of the CPS by completing the appropriate form and that the judge is informed of jurors' occupational status.

It is important to contrast the ruling reached in *Abdroikof* with that in *R. v Mirza and Connor* [2005] 1 A.C. 1118 (post conviction a juror had in each case sent a letter expressing concern about possible bias) where, by a majority, the House of Lords upheld the common law rule that jury deliberations are to remain secret. Any evidence which may reveal any impartiality on the part of the jury is always inadmissible no matter how compelling the evidence may be and regardless of the gravity in the circumstances of the lack of impartiality.

To relax this rule would cause a real risk of a jury feeling unable to deliberate freely on the evidence, due to possible future enquiry and would have the potential to destroy the integrity of the jury system, even if that raised possible doubts about a conviction. The House of Lords did nonetheless agree that a limited exception existed to the sacrosanct rule, if and only if, the evidence was extrinsic to the actual deliberations. An example is *R. v Young* [1995] Q.B. 324, where the Court of Appeal ruled that it could consider evidence of the jury using a Ouija Board outside of the jury room, or as in *R. v Brandon* [1969] 53 Cr.App.R. 466, where the jury bailiff informing the jury of the defendant's previous convictions amounted to a grave irregularity.

18.43 Further, s.8 of the Contempt of Court Act 1984 prohibits any investigation into jury deliberations and any such investigation is punishable as a contempt of court (see *Attorney-General v Scotcher* [2005] 2 Cr.App.R. 573). Nevertheless, in *Miza*, the House of Lords also ruled that this prohibition does not have the effect of preventing a judge from conducting a investigation into irregularities that may have occurred in the jury room; if and only if, this was appropriate. Accordingly, if a member of a jury raises concerns about the conduct of other members of the jury during the deliberations, the court may investigate.

In *R. v Smith* [2005] UKHL 12, unlike what occurred in *Mirza*, an individual juror sent a letter of concern to the judge before returning a verdict. The House of Lords ruled that the judge was not, as a matter of law, obliged to make enquires of the jury about possible irregularities or lack of adherence to the jury oath and legal directions by other members of the jury. In such circumstances, the judge could either discharge the jury or give further directions, but it was,"incumbent upon the judge to ensure that they were apposite, clear and as emphatic as the situation required". (see also *R. v Karakaya* [2005] EWCA Crim 346).

However, if a jury foreman returns incorrect verdicts agreed by the jury and the other members of the jury raise concerns about the mistake, the judge ought to reconvene the jury to correct the mistake. If the judge fails then limitedly, as occurred in *R. v Charnley* [2007] EWCA Crim 1354, the Court of Appeal can rule that the conviction reached by the non-verdict was unsafe.

24. Empanelment and Challenging a Jury

18.44 The next stage is to empanel a jury, in which a selection is made from the panel (jury in waiting). Section 11 of the JA 1974 requires the jury to be elected by ballot in open court. The clerk, who calls out the names of those randomly selected, carries out the ballot. He will explain to the defendant that they have a right to challenge, and that this challenge is to be made after the names of the jurors, who are to try him, have been called. However, in certain circumstances where there is a risk of interference, the names may be withheld (see *R. v Comerford* [1998] 1 W.L.R. 191). Unless there is impropriety the random selection of the jury is essential for fairness to be achieved.

The judge cannot interfere with this process, or change the composition in order to average it out on grounds of gender or culture or ethnicity (see *R. v Ford* [1989] 89 Cr.App.R. 278 and *R. v Smith* [2003] EWCA Crim 283). Under s.12 of the Juries Act 1974 the defendant has a statutory right to challenge up to all the jurors on the panel by showing cause. The challenge procedurally is made at the point the name of the juror in waiting is called by the clerk. Beforehand, the defence are entitled under s.5 (3) of the Juries Act 1974 to inspect the panel of names "from which the jurors are or will be drawn". Section 21(5) of the Juries Act 1974 preserves expressly all enactments and rules of law relating to jury trials.

Accordingly, the causes for which a defendant can challenge a juror under common law still remain and are as follows:

(i) privilege of peerage;

(ii) past criminal convictions;

(iii) lack of requisite qualifications; to be a juror;

(iv) presumed or actual bias; this would include having a connection with the case, knowledge of the defendant's character, general hostility.

18.45 The burden is upon the defendant to provide evidence to support the reason (cause) for the challenge on a balance of probabilities. Prior to 1988, the defendant had, under s.12 of the Juries Act 1974, a right to make what was known as a peremptory challenge, on up to three jurors. This was a challenge without cause, in that the defendant did not need to give a reason for not wanting that particular juror to sit. However, this became controversial after the *Cyprus Spy Trial* [1985] (see [1988] Crim L.R. 731) in which seven defendants all used the peremptory challenge to the full. This resulted in a jury consisting of all male and young people, who acquitted the defendants. The practice was seen as an abuse and affront to the proper administration of justice and was therefore abolished by s.118 of the Criminal Justice Act 1988.

Notwithstanding this, the defendant can challenge all the jurors on the grounds of Array by arguing that the person responsible for summoning the jurors in question is biased or has acted improperly. The position is different for the prosecution; like the defendant, the prosecution can also challenge the entire jury panel with cause. However, what is more controversial is that the prosecution have a common law power to "stand by" any juror and if necessary, it can stand by the entire panel. This common law power is derived from *Mansell v The Queen* [1857] 8 E. & B. 54 and later confirmed in *R. v Mason* [1980] 3 W.L.R. 617. This right to stand by any member of the jury can be exercised without the need to show any provable valid objection until such time as the panel is exhausted.

In effect, this is just like the prosecution having a peremptory challenge on the whole panel if necessary, and therefore creates a lack of equality, since the defendants' right to make a peremptory challenge has been abolished. For this reason, the practice became very controversial and led to the Attorney-General giving guidelines on its use in practice. These guidelines (see the *Attorney-General's Guidelines: Jury Checks* [1989] 88 Cr.App.R. 123) which state in the main that the prosecution should only use its right to stand by sparingly and in exceptional circumstances, i.e. terrorist or national security cases or where a juror is manifestly unsuitable.

25. Duty of the Judge and Function of the Jury (Part IV.42 of the CrPR 2005)

18.46 Once the jury is empanelled, each juror must give an oath or affirmation to decide the case and give a true verdict according to the evidence. In a trial on indictment, the basic function of the jury is to consider questions of fact, the role of the judge at the conclusion of the presentation of all the evidence for the prosecution and defence is as follows:

(i) To summarise the evidence presented during the trial and in particular to put the case for the defence.

(ii) To summarise the relevant law and the ingredients of the particular offence in question.

(iii) To explain the burden and standard of proof.

In the case of *R. v Hancock* [1986] A.C. 455, Lord Scarman described the traditional course of summing up as follows:

> "He [The Judge] must explain the nature of the offence charged, give directions as to the law applicable to the particular facts of the case, explain the incidence and burden of proof, put both sides' cases making especially sure that the defence is put; he should offer help in understanding and weighing up all the evidence and should make certain that the jury understand that whereas the law is for him the facts are for them to decide."

It is the function of the jury to decide the innocence or guilt of the accused. To convict, they must be sure that the prosecution has proved its case beyond all reasonable doubt (this is known as the standard of proof). The respective role of judge and jury was further explained eloquently by Lord Bingham in *R. v Wang* [2005] 1 W.L.R. 661:

> "Thus the trial is by judge and jury working together, although as judges routinely explain, their functions are different. The judge directs, or instructs, the jury on the law relevant to the counts in the indictment and makes clear that the jury must accept and follow his legal rulings. But he also directs the jury that the decision of all factual questions, including the application of the law as expounded to the facts as they find them to be, is a matter for them alone. And he makes plain that whatever views he may express or be thought to express, it for them and not him to decide whether, on each count in the indictment, the defendant is guilty or not guilty."

Whilst in *R. v Soames-Waring* [1999] Crim. L.R. 89, the Court of Appeal endorsed what was said in *R. v Cutin* [1996] (unreported) that:

> "it is a judge's duty, in summing up to a jury to give directions about the relevant law, to refer to the salient pieces of evidence, to identify and focus attention upon the issues, and in each of those respects to do so succinctly as the case permits. It follows that as part of this duty a judge must identify the defence."

In terms of the jury's responsibility as to the oath and to avoid bias or pressure, the judge will always, in their summing up, give a *Watson Direction*, explained by Lord Lane in *R. v Watson* [1988] Q.B. 690:

> "Each of you has taken an oath to return a true verdict according to the evidence. No one must be false to that oath, but you have a duty not only as individuals but collectively. That is the strength of the jury system. Each of you takes into the jury box with you your individual experience of wisdom. Your task is to pool that experience and wisdom. You do that by giving your views and listening to the views of others. There must necessarily be discussion, argument and give and take within the scope of your oath. That is the way in which agreement is reached. If unhappily (10 of) you cannot reach agreement you must say so."

18.47 The judge is under a duty, as explained in *R. v Kritz* [1949] 33 Cr.App.R. 169, to direct the jury that they must not return a verdict of guilty until they are satisfied, so that they feel sure, and that the onus of proof is upon the prosecution at all times and not the defence. It is not the particular formula of words used but the effect of them in the context of summing up that is important. A failure of a judge to emphasise the standard and burden of proof will constitute a serious defect resulting in an unsafe conviction (see *R. v Edwards* [1983] Cr.App.R. 5. The judge is further required to follow the guidance given in *R. v Oliver* [1996] 2 Cr.App.R. 514 and direct the jury:

(i) that they must only consider the evidence presented in court;

(ii) that they should not seek to find further evidence or information of any sort;

(iii) that they must not talk to anyone or allow anyone to talk to them about the case other than in the jury room with all the other jurors present;

(iv) that outside of court they should put the matter to one side until they return to court to deliberate.

If it comes to the attention of the judge that there is dissent or internal pressure amongst the jury, then in accordance with the guidance in *R. v Orgles* [1993] 4 All E.R. 533, the judge should inquire of the whole jury through the foreman in open court, to ascertain whether as a body they can fulfil the oath that they have given (see *R. v Marron* [2006] EWCA Crim 3304).

Undoubtedly the determination of factual guilt or innocence by a jury in a criminal trial is the cornerstone of the justice system and the fairest possible method. However, both the justice and the jury system are not without weaknesses, as clearly identified in *R. v Thompson* [2001] EWCA Crim 468, in which the Court of Appeal quashed the appellant's conviction for rape on the exceptional facts of the case. The complainant, who had been a virgin, met the defendant in a night club and went back to a friend's house, where they had sex. The crucial issue was one of consent. The defendant, who already had a pregnant partner, after sex took place left the house without saying goodbye. This unchivalrous act with respect to a young girl who was a virgin may have impacted on the jury's verdict, as having a particular distaste for the defendant morally.

18.48 Combining this with the fact that the verdict was reached by a majority after some seven hours of deliberations, an unfortunate summing up, concerns raised by prosecution counsel about the safety of the verdict and the analogy by defence counsel during the trial to a Mills and Boon encounter, could only have inflamed the jury so as to make the conviction unsafe. The Court made it clear that its decision was based on the exceptional facts of the case. A jury hear the evidence and see the witnesses and determine factual guilt. In such circumstances, the court must be reluctant to intervene unless and only if the conviction is unsafe.

Likewise, as explained in *R. v Marr* [1990] 90 Cr.App.R. 154, the judge must give an unbalanced summing up of the defence case. Lord Lance commented that it is:

> "an inherent principle of our system of trial that however laughable his defence, he is nevertheless entitled to have his case fairly presented to the jury both by counsel and by the judge. Indeed it is probably true to say that it is just in those cases where the cards seem to be stacked most heavily against the defendant that the judge should be most scrupulous to ensure that nothing untoward takes place which might exacerbate the defendant's difficulties."

In *R. v Spenser and Snalls* [1986] 2 All E.R. 928, it was stated that the judge must fairly, properly and adequately put the defence to the jury, as being an overriding requirement of fairness, Nevertheless, the judge is not under an obligation to rehearse the evidence and arguments in their summing up. As Lord Lowry said in *McGreevy* [198] 57 Cr.App.R. 424:

> "It is not essential that a judge should make every point that can be made for the defence. ... The fundamental requirements are correct directions in points of law, an accurate review of the main facts and alleged facts and a general impression of fairness."

In *R. v Amado-Taylor* [2000] 2 Cr.App.R. 194, the Court of Appeal made the point that in a trial lasting several days or more, the judge should assist the jury by summarising the factual issues which are not disputed and those where there are significant dispute. The judge should explain the evidence which is in conflict and the points in issue that they must resolve. The summing up must consist of more than just a rehearsal of the evidence, otherwise this would be unsatisfactory and inadequate.

In *R. v Farr* [1998] 163 J.P. 193, Rose L.J. observed that:

> "brevity in summing up, as in examination or cross-examination of witnesses and in counsel's speeches, is a virtue not a vice."

18.49 Nevertheless, his Lordship affirmed that in a short and simple trial there is no need for the judge to recite the facts, such as where there are only two witnesses in a one-day trial. If the jury seek clarification from the judge as to why a defendant had not called a particular witness or evidence, then they must again remind them of the burden of proof and exercise caution in making any adverse comments (see *R. v Whitton* [1998] Crim. L.R. 492 and *R. v RG* [2002] EWCA Crim 1056). If the defendant answers questions in police interview but decides not to give evidence at trial, then the judge, as explained in *R. v Akhtar* [2001] (unreported) and *Bagga* [2002] EWCA Crim 1049, must in their summing up summarise the main points made in the interview, to simply tell the jury to take into account the interview is not enough and invariably leads to the conviction being unsafe. Likewise, if the jury pose further questions having retired then the judge should avoid speculation as to what has prompted the questions. The judge will need to state the communication from the jury in open court and discuss them with counsel and give additional directions if necessary, but make it plain that these directions must be taken together with the earlier directions (see *R. v Wright* [2000] Crim. L.R. 510 and *R. v Forsyth* [1997] 2 Cr.App.R. 299).

In *R. v Thornton* [1989] 98 Cr.App.R. 54, it was held that a judge must never been seen to be exerting pressure on a jury to reach a verdict before they are ready to do so. If a jury cannot reach a verdict and there is no prospect of them doing so, then the jury must be discharged as a hung jury and the prosecution will need to seek a re-trial. Neither is it the duty of the judge to act as an advocate, and the judge should only intervene rarely in examination in chief or cross-examination by posing questions to witnesses (see *R. v Cameron* [2001] EWCA Crim 562. Likewise, a judge should never show inappropriate personal animosity toward defence counsel since this would undoubtedly damage the defendant's confidence in the fair administration of justice (see *R. v Lashley* [2005] EWCA Crim 2016 and *R. v Hare and Sullivan* [2004] EWCA Crim 3324).

Even if the judge is somewhat frustrated the matter of examination should be left to counsel (see *R. v Uddin* [2003] EWCA Crim 2321). If the judge deliberately interrupts and intervenes in the proper presentation of the defence case then, as stated in *R. v Matthews* [1984] Cr.App.R. 23, this might lead to any conviction being unsafe. Neither should the judge be seen to be taking responsibility for the institution of proceedings. In *DPP v Humphrys* [1977] A.C. 1 Lord Salmon also made the point that:

> "nor has he any power to refuse to allow a prosecution to proceed merely because he considers that, as a matter of policy, it ought not to have been brought. It is only if the prosecution amounts to an abuse of process of the court and is oppressive and vexatious that the judge had the power to intervene."

If there is a case to answer, then the judge, no matter how weak the prosecution's case, must leave it with the jury. He can of course identify those weaknesses in his summing up but in such circumstances he must not direct them to acquit. If, during the summing up, it comes to the attention of both prosecution and defence counsel that the directions on the law or evidence are potentially inadequate, then once aware of the error, both have a duty to intervene and provide assistance and advice to correct the mistake.

26. Jury Nobbling and the Majority Verdict (Part IV.46 of the CrPR 2005)

18.50 In order to find someone guilty before 1967, there had to be a unanimous verdict. However, it became apparent that a juror could be threatened or bribed into refusing to convict. Accordingly, the Criminal Justice Act 1967 (now s.17 of the JA 1974) provides for verdicts by majority of 11 to one, or 10 to two. The judge directs the jury to reach a unanimous verdict. If however, after at least two hours of deliberations the jury have still not reached a unanimous verdict, the judge may then, depending on the seriousness and complexity of the case, give a majority direction. It would be a material irregularity for a judge to accept a majority verdict returned in under two hours, even if the irregularity was an oversight as occurred in *R. v Black* [2008] EWCA Crim 344 (see also *R. v Pigg* [1983] 1 W.L.R. 6 and *R. v*

Barry [1975] 1 W.L.R. 1190). If there are only 11 jurors, then it can only be 10 to one, while if the jury consists of just 10 then the majority verdict can only be 9 to one.

In *R. v Barry* [1975] 1 W.L.R. 1190, the Court of Appeal indicated that s.17(3) of the JA 1974 required that a court should not accept a majority verdict of guilty unless the foreman of the jury had stated in open court the number of jurors who respectively agreed to and dissented from the verdict and that as the statutory provisions had not been complied with, the conviction would have to been quashed. Section 51 of the Criminal Justice and Public Order Act 1994 provides for two offences of intimidating, harming or threatening to harm a juror or a witness assisting in the investigation of offence.

27. Trials on Indictment without a Jury

18.51 The CJA 2003 makes significant changes as to when an application can be made for certain trials to be heard without a jury. Section 43 of the CJA 2003 allows the prosecution to make an application to a judge of the Crown Court for certain fraud cases to be conducted without a jury. No order can be made unless the Court is satisfied that the conditions of complexity or length of trial would be such as to be likely to be burdensome to a jury and the interests of justice demand consideration of such an order. A further safeguard is that the judge must seek the approval of the Lord Chief Justice before an order can be made. However, in order to ensure the safe passage of the Bill in the House of Lords the Home Office had to compromise and include in the provisions that s.43 could only take effect by statutory instrument affirmed by both Houses of Parliament. Since then the House of Lords have been unwilling to give their approval. To circumvent this the Home Office tried without success to push through the controversial Fraud (Trials without a Jury) Bill so as to allow s.43 to be implemented by negative resolution (for a critical discussion of this see Liberty's briefing issued in March 2007 at http://www.liberty.co.uk).

Similarly, s.44 (which came into effect on July 24, 2006) allows the prosecution to apply to a judge for a trial on indictment to be conducted without a jury. No order must be made unless the judge is satisfied of two conditions: (i) if there is evidence of a real and present danger that jury tampering would take place, and (ii) that the risk, despite police protection, of tampering is so substantial that it is in the interests of justice to do so. Subsection (6) provides specific examples of potential tampering such as (i) where there is a retrial having arisen from the discharge of a previous jury because of tampering, or (ii) tampering has taken place in a previous trial of the defendant, or (iii) where there has been intimidation or attempted intimidation of any person who is likely to be a witness. The expression "has been" suggests that such intimidation has in fact occurred, suspicion that it may occur would seem to be insufficient.

Section 45 sets out the procedure to be followed if the prosecution wish to make an application. If notice of an application is made, then the matter must be determined at a preparatory hearing and the parties given an opportunity to make representations. The remainder of the provisions makes the necessary amendments to s.7 of the CJA 1988 and also the CPIA 1996. Leave to appeal may be made to the Court of Appeal against the ruling of a judge.

28. Discharge of Jury

18.52 The judge has a discretionary power to discharge a juror or a jury if it is in the interests of justice to do so. Under s.46 of the CJA 2003 (which came into effect on July 24, 2006), a judge, if minded to discharge a jury during a trial on indictment on the basis that it appears to them that there has been jury tampering, must first inform the parties of this and the grounds for the appearance of tampering. The judge must allow the parties an opportunity to make representations. If the judge decides to discharge the jury, they can make an order for the trial to continue without a jury, but only if they are satisfied that (i) jury tampering has taken place, and (ii) continuing with the trial would not be fair to the defendant.

If it is necessary in the interests of justice the judge must terminate the trial and order a re-trial without a jury under s.44 provided the relevant conditions are likely to be fulfilled. Section 47 provides for a right to appeal to the Court of Appeal from a ruling under s.46. Leave must be obtained from either the judge or the Court of Appeal. The Court of Appeal has the power to confirm or revoke the order of the judge. A further appeal can be made to the House of Lords. The time limits for making an appeal are the same as for any other appeal to either the Court of Appeal or House of Lords. The initial order does not take effect during the process of an appeal.

Section 48 provides generally that if a trial is conducted or continued without a jury, then the court can exercise all the powers, authority and jurisdiction the court would enjoy if the trial was by jury. Instead of a finding or verdict of a jury, it is that of the court. If the court convicts the defendant, then the court must give a judgment which states the reasons, as soon as is reasonably practicable after the conviction was pronounced. As with any conviction, the defendant has the same routes of appeal.

Chapter Nineteen

SENTENCING PROCEDURE

1. Sentencing Procedure and Culpability

19.01 Once the defendant is convicted either after trial or having entered a guilty plea, the court will proceed to a sentencing hearing and determine the appropriate sentence that reflects the seriousness of the offence. The court will then pronounce in open court the imposition of sentence. Sentencing policy and its development is sensitive and complex and is becoming more controversial with increasing political interference and intervention. It is felt that such interference challenges unjustifiably the independence and integrity of the judiciary. The courts, when determining sentence, now face greater restrictions, having lost much of the discretion the court had in terms of choice, upon the feelings and knowledge of the judge who has sat throughout the proceedings, heard the evidence and observed the witnesses. Such is this interference that some judges have been prepared to break their silence and speak openly about their views on this highly charged and controversial area of procedure. Much of the new sentencing framework is found in the Criminal Justice Act 2003 and follows the recommendations of the Halliday Report of a Review of the Sentencing Framework for England and Wales.

It is not the purpose of this chapter to review the controversy but to expostulate in simple terms the principles and procedure of the imposition of sentence. Sentencing principles are ever more detailed and complex, much of it now set out in large volumes of statutory provisions. This alone could warrant a complex book. The application of the proceeds of crime in respect of confiscation orders is now generating an ever increasing volume of statutory construction and case authority. It is not proposed to review in any depth these authorities, this being left to other more specific textbooks on the subject.

It has already been emphasised that criminal liability is based on the culpability of the acts of the defendant. The more serious the offence, the more culpable the defendant is for their acts. The sentencing court can only impose a sentence that reflects properly the gravity of the offence as reflected in the defendant's culpability. This is well illustrated in the sentencing guidelines for manslaughter by provocation. For instance, in *R. v Eubank*

[2002] 1 Cr.App.R.(S) 4, the Court of Appeal ruled that if the prosecution, in accepting a guilty plea to a robbery on a shop, allege also that it was committed with a firearm, which the defendant disputes, then the prosecution must make this a separate count on the indictment, otherwise the judge can only sentence on the culpable facts of the robbery, unless the defendant admits to the possession of a firearm. Nevertheless, in *R. v Lydiate* [2004] EWCA Crim 245, the Court of Appeal ruled, distinguishing the decision in *Eubank*, that it would be a nonsense and wholly artificial to add separate counts where the commission of the substantive offence in the indictment involved the commission of other offences in order to reflect the defendant's overall culpability so as to ensure an appropriate sentence. As Sir Edwin Jowitt highlighted it could only complicate matters to suggest that where a defendant is charged with rape by drugging their victim that this factual part of the Crown's case was to be ignored for sentencing purposes, if there was no separate count of administering an noxious substance. The same applies when a conspiracy is charged regarding which the Court concluded that:

> "so long as the other offences constitute the means chosen to work out the conspiracy or conspiracies the court is entitled, after conviction, to take them into account in deciding what is the appropriate sentence, without there being any need to complicate the indictment by including counts for those offences."

There are three main categories of sentence available to a judge:

(i) a custodial sentence, or

(ii) a community sentence, or

(iii) other penalties and orders.

The principles relating to sentencing for the purposes of this chapter are found in:

(i) Criminal Justice Act 2003 (Part 12) (CJA 2003);

(ii) Power of Criminal Courts (Sentencing) Act 2000 (PCC(S)A 2000);

(iii) Sentencing guideline case authorities;

(iv) Sentence Advisory Panel (SAP);

(v) Sentences Guidelines Council (SGC).

2. General Provisions about Sentencing

19.02 Part 12 of the Criminal Justice Act 2003 changes radically the principles relating to sentencing, especially for serious offences. Section 142 of the CJA 2003 provides that any court when sentencing an offender must have regard to the five purposes of sentencing:

(i) punishment of offenders;

(ii) reduction in crime (including its reduction by deterrence);

(iii) reform and rehabilitation of offenders;

(iv) protection of the public; and

(v) the making of reparation of offenders to persons affected by their offences.

These have been aims of sentencing for some time, but now for the first time, they are set out clearly in a statutory context. In particular, one of the new aims of sentencing is the reduction in crime. This is a new concept which the court must now take into account. Similarly, reparation is a concept that is used extensively with young offenders but is now also being applied to adult offenders. While the aims of sentencing are of general application s.142(2) provides expressly that they do not apply to offences of murder or offenders under 18, since s.37 of the Crime and Disorder Act 1998 applies to young offenders, or certain minimum terms for firearms offences (s.51A(2) of the Firearms Act 1968 as set out in ss.110 and 111 of the PCC(S)A 2000). Neither do they apply to the sentencing provisions of ss.225 to 228 of the CJA 2003 in regard to dangerous offenders, or those to whom an Hospital Order is to be imposed under the Mental Health Act 1983. In *R. v Trigger and Others* [2007] Cr.App.R.(S) 69, Philips L.C.J. emphasised that:

> "unless imprisonment is necessary for the protection of the public the court should always give consideration to the question of whether the aims of rehabilitation and thus the reduction of crime cannot be better achieved by a fine or community sentence rather than imprisonment and whether punishment cannot be adequately be achieved by such a sentence."

See also the judgment in *Attorney-General's Reference (No.104 of 2001)* [2001] EWCA Crim 3069 about the need to balance, on the one hand, the need to rehabilitate and reduce re-offending against, on the other, the need to punish.

3. The Seriousness of the Offence: Aggravating and Mitigating Factors

19.03 The seriousness of the offence will be an important determinate feature in the type of sentence a court will impose. The seriousness of the offence will be the determinate factor that the court will use in its decision whether to impose either a custodial, or non custodial sentence. Section 143 of the CJA 2003 sets out in statutory form what the court must consider when formulating an opinion of the seriousness of the offence:

Culpability and Harm Caused

19.04 This requires the court to assess the state of mind for which the defendant was convicted, i.e. a mens rea of intention which creates a more culpable mind than that of a reckless mind. The court must also consider the harm caused by the offence in the context of whether it intended, or might reasonably have been caused. The courts also recognise and take account of the fact that culpability for an attempted crime is less than what would otherwise be the case if the offence had been completed (see *Attorney-General's Reference (No.3 of 2008)* [2008] EWCA Crim 790 concerning attempted GBH with intent).

Previous Convictions of the Offender

19.05 The court must treat each previous conviction (including any conviction inside and outside the UK) as an aggravating factor provided the court considers it reasonable to treat it as aggravating the current offence, having regard to (i) the nature and relevance of the previous offence to the current offence, (ii) the age of the previous conviction.

Offence Committed Whilst on Bail

19.06 If the current offence is committed while on bail, then the court must treat this as an aggravating factor in terms of the seriousness of the current offence.

Section 152 of the CJA 2003 provides that the court when determining any offence punishable by imprisonment, other than murder, s.51A of the Firearms Act 1968, or dangerous offenders, must not impose a custodial sentence, unless it is of the opinion that the offence, or the combination of the offence with other associated offences, was so serious that neither a fine alone, or a community sentence can be justified. If a community order is justified but the offender refuses to comply or the offender refuses to comply with a pre-sentence drug testing order, then the court can impose a custodial sentence, if justified. In regard to the imposition of a community sentence the test is set out in s.148 which provides that the court must not pass a community sentence unless it is of the opinion that the offence or the combination of that offence with other associated offences was serious enough to warrant such a sentence.

Section 10 of the Criminal Justice and Immigration Act 2008, when in force, makes it clear that even if the offence is serious enough for the imposition of a community sentence, the court has a discretion whether or not to impose such a sentence. Nevertheless, s.150 of the CJA 2003 restricts the court's discretion and provides that a community sentence cannot be imposed for murder, certain specified firearms offences under s.287, repeat burglary and drug offences, and serious, specified offences in ss.225 to 228. Section 11 of the Criminal Justice and Immigration Act 2008 (CJIA 2008), when in force, inserts a new s.150A and further restricts the use of a community order to offences punishable with imprisonment, or under s.151.

Section 151 of the CJA 2003 (as amended by s.13 of the CJIA 2008) allows the court to impose a Community Order on an offender, even if the current offence is non-imprisonable or imprisonable, but is not serious enough to justify an order, provided they have been fined on at least three previous occasions (known as a persistent offender previously fined).

It is important to be aware that the two tests are similar but not the same. For a custodial sentence it must be so serious as to be *justified* whereas for a community sentence it must be serious enough to *warrant* it. It is also important to be aware that in addition to the specific seriousness factors above, the court when assessing the tests for a custodial and non custodial sentence must also under s.156 of the CJA 2003 consider all relevant information about the circumstances of the offence, including any aggravating or mitigating factors. This requires the court to give adequate weight to the all the various aggravating and mitigating factors that are made available to the court at the time.

4. Statutory and Case Specific Aggravating Factors

19.07 If there exist any aggravating factors in the case then, such factors will be deemed by the court to aggravate the current offence that the defendant is to be sentenced for and therefore increase the seriousness of the offence, which could result in the imposition of a greater punishment. The statutory aggravating factors are as follows:

Section 143 of the CJA 2003: Seriousness of the offence (as above); section 145 of the CJA 2003: Racial or religious aggravated offences.

19.08 This does not apply to the specific racial or religious offences found in the Crime and Disorder Act 1998 and the Racial and Religious Hatred Act 2006, since these offences already have longer sentences available. This applies to any other offence in which the offence was racially or religiously aggravated, in the context of the meaning within the CDA 1998 and if established this must be treated by the court as an aggravating factor. The court must state this in open court. This potentially has significant implications in that a offender may be charged with s.20 racially aggravated reckless wounding, and be found not guilty of this, but guilty of s.20 simpliciter, only to find that the court could still treat the racial evidence as an aggravating factor. Whether this would this be permissible on a finding of not guilty by a jury of the racial element, is an issue to be resolved. The writer thinks not, but it could apply if the defendant pleads guilty to the standard s.20 offence. Section 29 of the Violent Crime Reduction Act 2006 provides that where an offender is convicted of the offence of using another person to mind a dangerous weapon, then if the minder is under 18 this must be treated as an aggravating factor.

Section 146 of the CJA 2003: sexual orientation and disability hostility directed at the victim.

19.09 This provides that if the offender at the time of the offence or immediately before, or after doing so, demonstrated towards the victim sexual orientation or (presumed) disability hostility (disability means any physical or mental impairment), or the offence is wholly or partly motivated by such hostility, then the court must treat this as an aggravating factor and so state in open court.

General Aggravating Factors

19.10 The following is a non-exhaustive list of case specific factors that can amount to aggravating factors. The court will analyse the nature of the offence by considering: (i) offending behaviour, (ii) degree of preparation, (iii) multiple offences, (iv) impact on victim, (v) lavish lifestyle, (vi) repetition, (vii) breach of trust, (viii) weapon used, (iv) sophistication, (x) deliberate/ premeditated, (xi) use of children to commit crime (see *R. v Ball* [2002] EWCA Crim 2777)

Offences Taken into Consideration Offences (TIC's)

19.11 The defendant can, if they expressly agree, ask the court to take into consideration other non-prosecuted offences which they admit to committing. The advantage to the offender is that they will not be prosecuted for these offences and therefore this allows the offender to wipe the slate clean. The disadvantage, of course, is that explained in *R. v Miles* [2006] EWCA Crim 256, whereby any TIC's offences are relevant to the offender's overall criminality and therefore this must be reflected in the overall sentence to be imposed.

Victim Personal Statements (VPS) (Part III.28 of the CrPR 2005)

19.12 Victim personal statements (VPS) have been in use since October 1, 2001, and the procedure is now set out in Pt III(28) of the Consolidation Criminal Practice Direction. This provides that the making of VPS is entirely a decision for the victim, if a statement is given then it must be in the form of a formal witness statement (see s.9 of the CJA 1967) and be served on the defence. If the court is presented with a VPS, then the rules require the court, before passing sentence, to consider and take into account the statement, but it must not make assumptions unsupported by evidence. Importantly, the court must impose a sentence that is proportionate to the seriousness of the offence, taking into account, so far as the court considers it appropriate, the consequences of the offence on the victim. Nevertheless, any opinions as to what the sentence ought to be are irrelevant and must not be taken into account. The court may, if it is desirable, make reference to the evidence of the victim in the sentencing remarks (see *R. v Perks* [2001] 1 Cr.App.R. 66).

5. Mitigating Factors

19.13 On the other hand, the sentencing court, while determining the seriousness of the offence and taking into account all the relevant aggravating factors, must balance these against any mitigating factors that would justify a reduction in the actual sentence. The defence advocate must therefore as far as possible emphasise to the court the strength and weight of the mitigating factors and invite the court to impose the least possible sentence in all the circumstances. The following is a non-exhaustive list of commonly encountered factors that may mitigate the seriousness of the offence:

(i) background of offender (usually explained in the Pre-Sentence Report (PSR));

(ii) good character (offence committed wholly out of character), employment;

(iii) family history;

(iv) health (mental, depression, personality disorder);

(v) state of mind (intention, recklessness, carelessness);

(vi) impulse crime;

(vii) remorseful/embarrassed, not likely to reoffend;

(viii) pre-sentence report;

(ix) voluntary payment of compensation;

(x) youth and immaturity (i.e. reduced intellectual and social function abilities).

In *Attorney–General's Reference (No. 126 of 2006)* [2007] 1 All E.R. 1254, the Court of Appeal reiterated the long established principle that in terms of responsibility the degree of culpability of a young offender is likely to be, but might not necessarily, lower than that of an adult offender (see also the important observations of Judge L.J. in *R. v Peters and Others* [2005] 2 Cr.App.R.(S) 101.

6. Indication of Sentence and Reduction in Sentence for a Guilty Plea

19.14 A significant mitigating factor which undoubtedly acts as a real incentive to many defendants is the potential to see a reduction in the sentence that would otherwise be imposed if the defendant decides to run a trial and is convicted as opposed to entering a guilty plea. In an attempt to reduce the number of cracked trials (this occurs where the defendant changes plea, either near to or on the morning of the start of the trial) and to quickly process those who wish to admit their guilt, instead of simply putting the prosecution to proof for tactical reasons. It is accepted and one must take a pragmatic approach that in order to encourage a guilty plea there must be in return an incentive or benefit to the offender. This comes in the form of s.144 of the CJA 2003 which provides that the court must take into account: (i) the stage in the proceedings the offender indicated their intention to plead guilty; and (ii) the circumstances in which the indication was given. This does not compel the court to give a reduction in sentence, the court retains a discretionary power. Section 144 simply demands that the court considers at what point in the proceedings the defendant pleaded guilty and where appropriate give credit for it.

The Sentencing Guidelines Council on January 10, 2005 issued its definitive guidelines "Reduction in Sentences for a Guilty Plea". These state that the level of reduction should be a proportion of the total sentence based on the stage in the proceedings the plea is entered and a sliding scale of reduction. The maximum reduction should be one-third where the guilty plea was entered at the first reasonable opportunity. This is reduced to one-quarter if a trial date has been set and further down to one-tenth if the plea is entered on the day of the trial. Even if the offender was effectively caught red handed, the reduction sliding scale should still apply. However, the Court of Appeal in *Attorney-General's Reference (Nos 14 and 15)* of 2006); *R. v French and Webster* [2006] EWCA Crim 1335, concerning an unduly lenient sentence referral, followed the guidelines unhappily and refused to interfere with the one-third reduction given by the sentencing judge. The Court agreed that the discount was excessive based on the fact that the evidence against the defendants was so overwhelming that they had no alternative other than to plead guilty. Given that the case involved extreme deprived sexual acts on a child, the Court stated that this was a matter in urgent need of re-consideration by the SGC.

In light of the recommendations of Lord Justice Auld in Chapter 10 of his one-man review of the criminal justice system that the principle in *R. v Turner* [1970] 2 W.L.R. 1093, should relaxed so as to allow the court in advance of the imposition of sentence to give an indication to the defendant of the likely sentence that would be imposed if they pleaded guilty, the Court of Appeal in *R. v Goodyear* [2005] EWCA Crim 888 ruled that there has been a change in practice and policy since *Turner* was decided and it should no longer be followed strictly. The Court laid down a series of guidelines; first the court should not give an indication on its own motion, but only if the defence invites it to do so. Secondly, the court retains an unfettered discretion to refuse to give one or postpone the giving of an indication. Once an indication is given, then this becomes binding on the judge and any other judge who may hear the case. Before an indication is invited there should be an agreed written basis of plea between the prosecution and defence, to avoid any prospect of the judge becoming involved in negotiations, or plea bargaining.

The defence advocate must ensure that the defendant appreciates that they should not plead guilty, unless they are guilty; that any indications do not prevent the Attorney-General making an unduly lenient referral (see *Attorney–General's References (Nos 86 and 87 of 1999); Webb and Simpson* [2001] Cr.App.R(S) 141, nor does it affect the defendant's entitlement to appeal, if the judge has given insufficient weight to the mitigation. Further, the indication applies at that time and if a guilty plea is not tendered, then the indication will cease to have effect. In respect of the prosecution advocate, if no factual plea can be reached, they must remind the judge that until there is such agreement, an indication should not be given. If an indication is sought, then the prosecution should ensure that the judge has all the evidence, i.e. antecedents in their possession. The prosecution should remain neutral in all respects of the sentence indicated. To do otherwise may create a legitimate expectation of the defendant and bind the Attorney-General in seeking a possible unduly lenient sentence review under s.36 of the CJA 1988 (see *Attorney–General's Reference (No.44 of 2000); (Peverett)* [2001] 1 Cr.App.R.(S) 416). The Court fully recognised the benefits to be gained in permitting advance indication of sentence particularly to the defendant, victim, witnesses and the efficiency and effectiveness of the justice system generally.

7. Reduction in Sentence for Assistance Provided by the Offender

19.15 Sections 71 to 75 of the Serious Organised Crime and Police Act 2005 create a new statutory framework for allowing a reduction in sentence for offenders who provide assistance. The purpose behind the provisions is to remove the difficulties with the common law and provide a simple procedure that gives the incentive of a lesser sentence to serious offenders in return for information and assistance that helps in the apprehension and possible conviction of others, who would otherwise escape justice. In *R. v Blackburn* [2007] EWCA Crim 2290, Sir Ivor Judge stated that whilst there can never be any enthusiasm for such a procedure, "like the process which provides for a reduced sentence following a guilty plea, this is a longstanding and entirely pragmatic convention".

Section 71 allows for a specified prosecutor (DPP), where it is appropriate in relation to any investigation, or prosecution of any offence, to make an offer of immunity from prosecution (immunity notice) to any person. This will cease to have effect if the person fails to comply with any conditions of the offer. Likewise, s.72 allows for the specified prosecutor to offer an undertaking (a restricted use undertaking) to any person that certain information will not be used in evidence in any criminal proceedings against them (including Pt 5 of the Proceeds of Crime Act 2002).

This undertaking ceases to have effect if the person fails to comply with the conditions of the undertaking. Importantly, s.73 allows for the court to take into account the extent and nature of the assistance given, or offered by the defendant, but only if the defendant has pleaded guilty to an an offence in the Crown Court, or is committed for sentence and has entered into a written agreement with the specified prosecutor to provide assistance and does, or offers such assistance with regard to the offence they were convicted of, or any other offence. Unless it would not be in the public interest to do so, the court must state in open court that it has given a discount and what the sentence would have been had that discount not been given. Of significance is s.73(5) which provides that in giving a discount, the court is not restricted by other provisions which set minimum terms, neither does it restrict the court in taking into account any other matter relevant to determining sentence, i.e. reduction for guilty plea and mitigating and aggravating factors.

19.16 Section 74 provides for any discounted sentence to be reviewed in three situations;

(i) if the offender having offered assistance knowingly fails to give, to any extent, such assistance in accordance with the agreement;

(ii) subsequent to a discounted sentence already received, they provide further assistance; and

(iii) they receive the appropriate sentence, but then later enter into an agreement to give assistance and do so.

If one of these situations arises, then the specified prosecutor can at any time refer the case back to the original sentencing court, but only if the person is still serving their sentence and it is in the interests of justice to do so. In situation (i) the court can substitute any sentence that would have been given for that offence without the discount, while in (ii) and (iii) the court can give a discount for the assistance provided. Both the offender and the specified prosecutor can under s.74(8) appeal against the decision of the Crown Court to the Court of Appeal and then if necessary to the House of Lords. Leave (permission) to appeal must first be obtained from the Court of Appeal or the House of Lords. The details of the appeal procedure are set out in the SOCPA 2005 (Appeals under s.74) Order 2006 (SI 2006/2135), which came into effect on August 28, 2006.

Section 75 amounts to an exception to the open justice principle by allowing the court to exclude any person, other than advocates and court officials, from the proceedings and prohibit any reporting of the proceedings. In *R. v Blackburn* [2007] EWCA Crim 2290, the Court of Appeal gave generalised guidance on the correct amount of discount that could be given, since the Act itself is silent. The Court made it clear that there are no hard and fast rules that can be laid down. If the offender admits all of their criminal conduct, then concurrent sentences ought to be imposed. The Court was unable to envisage a situation where no sentence can be given, since "a effective sentence remains a basic characteristic of the process". Dependant on the quality and quantity of the material assistance, such as being willing to give Queen's evidence, a reduction of between one-half and two-thirds would be the normal level of discount, as previously stated, under the common law. A reduction that exceeds three-quarters should only be given in the most exceptional case that would merit such a reduction.

8. Determining the Length of Sentence to be imposed (Part 46 of the Criminal Practice Directions)

19.17 If the court, having determined the seriousness of the offence, is of the opinion that only a custodial sentence can be justified, or a community sentence, then the next step to be determined by the court is the appropriate length of the sentence. It is important to be aware that all offences, expect murder which is fixed in law, have a maximum and for certain offences a minimum sentence is available. Section 153 of the CJA 2003 provides that unless the offence is murder, or a s.50A firearms offence or a dangerous offender, then the length of the sentence must be for the shortest term, that in the opinion of the court is *commensurate* to the seriousness of the offence or the combination of offences. In *R. v Kefford* [2002] 2 Cr.App.R.(S) 495, it was observed that the court needs to take into account the grave crisis of prison overcrowding.

Likewise, in *R. v Mills* [2002] EWCA Crim 26, the Court of Appeal stated that where the offender is a young mother of previous good character and is unlikely to re-offend, then it is wrong in principle to impose a custodial sentence where the offence is non-violent and is of relatively low financial loss. The appropriate sentence would be a Community Punishment Order. If the offence justified prison then this should be as short as possible a "clang of the prison door" type sentence. In *R. v Trigger and Others* [2007] Cr.App.R.(S) 69, Philips L.C.J. made no apology for repeating the need for the court to be mindful of the prison overcrowding problem and that:

> "particular care should be exercised before imposing a custodial sentence on a first offender. Association with seasoned criminals may make-reoffending more likely rather than deter it, particularly where the offender is young. A clean record can be important personal mitigation and may make a custodial sentence inappropriate, notwithstanding that the custody threshold is crossed."

In *R. v Martin* [2007] Cr.App.R.(S) 3 Judge L.J. made the important point that the sentencing judge carries an heavy responsibility when determining the appropriate sentence, since this requires a balanced analysis of both justice and mercy to be made in each case. Whilst mathematics may provide an appropriate solution to a mathematical problem, the sentencing decision is:

> "infinitely more complex and refined. The objective of the sentencing decision is an outcome which is within the appropriate range or bracket of sentence, given all the circumstances of the case. Mathematics does not supply to this most sensitive and difficult of judicial responsibilities."

His Lordship acknowledged that whilst there clearly needs to be consistency of approach, sentencing guidelines remained guidelines and not a definitive precise formula. Such difficult sentencing decisions are often encountered when there is little violence used but results in grave consequences, such as what can be termed "one punch manslaughter" where violence breaks out in which the defendant punches his victim once but that is enough for that person to fall and suffer a fatal injury in consequence of it. The general sentencing indications are found in *R. v Coleman* [1992] 13 Cr.App.R.(S) 508, *R. v Moreby* [1994] 15 Cr.App.R.(S) 53, and *R. v Rumbol* [2001] 2 Cr.App.R.(S) 299.

As observed in *R. v McNeill* [2008] EWCA Crim 553, prosecution counsel is under a duty to assist the judge in determining the appropriate sentence so as to avoid the judge falling into error by imposing an unlawful sentence. The mistakes made in this case were based on a lack of appreciation that for a summary only offence an aggregate maximum could be imposed. Similarly, in *Attorney-General's Reference (No.113 of 2007)* [2008] EWCA Crim 22, the Court of Appeal noted that the sentencing judge was not ably assisted by prosecution counsel who had not referred any sentencing authorities to aid the judge. The Court further recognised the difficulty that can be encountered by a sentencing judge who is striving to strike a marked balance between, on the one hand, protection of the public and punishment, while on the other personal mitigation.

9. Maximum and Minimum Sentences

19.18 All statutory and common law offences have a maximum sentence which the court can impose. For instance, s.1 basic theft is seven years, while domestic burglary is 14 years and robbery discretionary life imprisonment. The greater the public abhorrence of a particular offence, the greater the punishment will be. A clear example of this change in public sentencing policy is the driving offence of causing death by dangerous driving. This offence originally had a maximum sentence of five years' imprisonment, but in 1993 this was increased to 10 years' imprisonment and then under s.285 of the CJA 2003, to reflect the public distaste for this offence, it was increased further to a maximum of 14 years (see *R. v Gray* [2006] 1 Cr.App.R.(S) 126. There are two types of life sentence:

(i) Mandatory life imprisonment fixed by law, currently the only offence for which there is a fixed life sentence is murder.

(ii) Discretionary life imprisonment, concerning offences that carry a maximum sentence of life imprisonment but where the court can exercise a wide discretion of sentencing power, based on the seriousness of the offence. The sentencing range is from conditional discharge up to life imprisonment. Offences such as attempted murder, manslaughter, robbery and rape all carry discretionary life sentences.

Chapter 7 (including Schs 21 and 22) of Pt 12 of the CJA 2003 promulgates the basic framework for the determination of the specified minimum period to be served for murder. In determining the minimum term of the life sentence the court must take into account what it considers appropriate based on the seriousness of the offence, including combined and associated offences. When considering the seriousness of the offence the court must have regard to the general principles in Sch.21. This provides that if the seriousness of the offence is "exceptionally high" and the offender was 21 or over at the date of commission of the offence, the starting point is an "whole life order" (i.e. murder of two or more persons involving abduction, sexual or sadistic conduct, high level of preparation, children, political or similar cause, previously committed murder).

If the seriousness is "particularly high" and the offender was over 18, then the starting point is 30 years (i.e. murder of a police/prison officer, use of firearms/explosives, done for gain robbery, sexual or sadistic, aggravated by sexual/racial/religious orientation). If neither of these starting points applies and the offender was 18 at the date of the commission of the offence then the starting point is 15 years. If under 18, then the starting point is 12 years. Once the court has chosen a starting point, it must then take into account any relevant aggravating and mitigating factors, they may lead to the court either deducting from the starting point or increasing up to a whole life order.

19.19 Schedule 21 lists seven aggravating (i.e. significant planning, concealment of body, vulnerable victim, abuse of trust, victim public service employee) and mitigating factors (lack of intent to kill or premeditation, provocation, mental disability, self defence, act of mercy killing, age). This provision came into effect on April 4, 2005, any offence committed before that date will be dealt with under the previous provisions in the PCC(S)A 2000. Only when the offender has served the minimum term can they apply to the parole board for release. In *R. v Bouhaddou* [2006] EWCA Crim 3190, the Court of Appeal stated that a murder which was committed during the commission of a burglary in order to facilitate escape will generally fall in the particularly high category with a starting point of 30 years.

Section 284 and Sch.28 of the CJA 2003 which came into effect on January 29, 2004 increase the length of imprisonment from five years to 14 years for the offences of producing, supplying to another, supplying with intent and the control of premises, and other drug related offences involving a class C drug. This change was made necessary to avoid the lower sentences by the downgrading of cannabis from class B to Class C status (note, Ministry of Justice has indicated its intention to upgrade Cannabis back to Class B). Section 285 (which came into effect on February 27, 2004) and s.286 (which came into effect on January 29, 2004) increase the length of imprisonment for certain driving related offences, namely aggravated vehicle taking from five years to 14 years, and death by dangerous driving/careless driving under the influence of drink or drugs from 10 years to 14 years. Sections 287, 288, 289, 291, which came into effect on January 22, 2004, set the minimum sentence a court can impose for various firearms offences (possessing or distributing) contained in s.5 of the Firearms Act 1968. If the offender is over 18 when the offence is committed, then under s.51A(4)(a)(i) a sentence of at least five years' imprisonment must be imposed.

However, this provision conflicted directly with the plain meaning of s.89 of the PCC(S)A 2000 which prohibits the imposition of a sentence of imprisonment on an offender under 21. In *R. v Campbell* [2006] 2 Cr.App.R.(S) 96, the Court of Appeal, given that this was a penal statute, adopted a strict interpretation and refused to read into the provision the relevant words to give it effect. In particular, the Court noted the wide discretionary power of the Secretary of State in s.333 to make supplementary, consequential and transitional provisions to the Act but the Secretary of State had failed to utilise them. As a consequence, the Firearms (Sentencing) (Transitory Provisions) Order 2007 (SI 2007/1324) came into force on May 28, 2007 and inserted the necessary words "sentence of detention" for those offenders aged 18 but under 21, to give it legal effect.

19.20 The Ministry of Justice accepted that s.287 have been drafted on the assumption that s.61 of the CJCSA 2000 would have been brought in to force to repeal s.89. If 16 or over but under 18, then a minimum custodial sentence of three years must be imposed. In both situations the court need not impose the mandatory minimum sentence, if it is of the opinion that there are exceptional circumstances relating to the offender or the offence to justify it. The limited discretionary power of the court to avoid imposing the statutory minimum by finding exceptional circumstances has received criticism for being too readily applied (see *The Times*, March 25, 2008). Section 293 increases the length of sentence from five years to seven years for offences relating to the importation of any weapon or ammunition.

Section 29 of the Violent Crime Reduction Act 2006 requires the court to impose a minimum term of five years if offender is 18 or over, and three years minimum if under 18, where the offender is convicted of the offence contained in s.28 of using another person to mind a dangerous firearms weapon, an offence which carries a maximum sentence of 10 years for an offender aged 16 or over. Under the same Act and in response to the growing concern about the carrying of offensive weapons contrary to s.139 of the Criminal Justice Act 1988, s.42 increases the sentence from two to four years imprisonment.

Sections 110 and 111 of the PCC(S) Act 2000 sets out minimum sentences for those who commit the same offence more than once (three strikes and you're out policy). Section 110 requires the court to impose a minimum prison sentence of at least seven years on a person who is convicted of a class A drug trafficking offence within the meaning of the Proceeds of Crime Act 2002, who at the time of the offence was 18 and had two or more previous convictions for similar offences, unless the court is of the opinion that is would be unjust to do so. Section 11 requires the court to impose a minimum three-year sentence for domestic burglary committed after November 30, 1999 (an attempted burglary does not amount to a qualifying offence, see *R. v Maguire* [2003] 2 Cr.App.R.(S) 40) provided the offender was 18 at the time and has two separate previous convictions, unless it would be unjust to do so (see *R. v McInerney* [2003] 1 Cr.App.R. 627).

Section 280 of the CJA 2003, when brought in to force, alters the penalties for summary offences specified in Sch.25 which abolishes imprisonment as a sentence. For the summary only offences listed in Sch.26 that had a sentence of four months or less, the sentence of imprisonment is increased to 51 weeks. Section 282 increases the penalty for any either way offence (listed in Sch.1 or so classified by the offence creating provision) which is dealt with by summary conviction in the magistrates' court from six months to 12 months, provided the offence is punishable with imprisonment on summary conviction. Of particular note, are ss.281 and 283 which gives the Secretary of State a wide discretionary power to change by negative resolution any penalty for any summary or either way offence not already altered.

It is important to note that the court will rarely impose the maximum sentence for an offence as the Court of Appeal in *R. v Bright* [2008] EWCA Crim 462, observed:

> "the maximum sentence permitted by statute is, of course very rarely imposed, and nowadays when there has been a guilty plea, effectively never. Such sentences should be reserved for those cases which, at the end of the trial and within the statutory context, can fairly be regarded as crimes of the utmost gravity."

The test is one of utmost gravity and not as may have been suggested previously the worst possible case that realistically can be conceived (see also *R. v Butt* [2006] 2 Cr.App.R.(S) 364). On a different but similar point, it is recognised that in situations where the defendant is convicted of an offence, the facts of which can also amount to another offence with a lower maximum sentence, then the sentencing court should have regard to this lower sentence. This point is well illustrated in *R. v Blair* [1996] 1 Cr.App.R.(S) 336, in relation to the old offence of indecent assault, which would be charged owing to the expiry of the 12 month statutory time limit to bring a prosecution for unlawful sexual intercourse, the offence that ought to have been charged. For indecent assault the maximum was 10 years, whereas for unlawful sexual intercourse it is two years. A similar approach was taken in *R. v Bourgass* [2006] EWCA Crim 3397, where the appellant was convicted of conspiracy to cause a public nuisance which carried an open sentence at the court's discretion. On the facts, the defendant had committed an offence under s.113 of the Anti-Terrorism Crime and Security Act 2001 of the use of obnoxious substances which endangered the lives of others, as a form of intimidation. This particular offence carries a maximum of 14 years, the defendant for the nuisance offence had received 17 years.

The Court, did however, having considered the decision of the House of Lords in *R. v Rimmington* [2006] 1 A.C. 459, mention that this only amounted to guidance and was not to be treated as being prescriptive. Such sentiments were applied in *R. v Bright* [2008] EWCA Crim 462, when the Court of Appeal refused to interfere with the appellant's sentence of seven years for conspiracy to defraud relating to the collapse of the Independent Insurance Group with a loss of £1 billion. The maximum for conspiracy to defraud is 10 years, whereas for the offence of fraudulent trading under the Companies Act 1985 it is seven years. The appellant had claimed that given that his conduct fell squarely within this offence the sentence was set too high. The Court of Appeal, rejecting this argument, ruled that the seriousness of the appellant's conduct was reflected properly in the conspiracy to defraud count. Even if the appellant was right, there is nothing to prevent a court imposing the maximum sentence if this is rightly deserved.

10. Life Imprisonment or Imprisonment for Public Protection for Offenders deemed to be Dangerous (Indeterminate Sentences)

19.21 As explained with regard to young offenders, Ch.5 of the CJA 2003, which came into effect on April 4, 2005, establishes a new range of mandatory sentences for certain specified violent or sexual offences, or serious offences and where the offender is deemed dangerous to the public. As a side point, although these provisions are a new phase in strong Parliamentary penal policy, they are in no real sense new policy. As far back as 1908 and the Prevention of Crime Act of that year, the courts had a power to impose a term of preventative detention for habitual criminals.

Concerning the CJA 2003 provisions in relation to those over 18, s.225 provides that if they are convicted of a serious offence within the meaning of s.224(2) (i.e. a specified violent or sexual offence of which there are 153 offences listed in Sch.15 but only those offences that have a punishment of 10 years or more including life) and the court is for the opinion that there is a significant risk to the public of serious harm from further specified offences being committed by the offender, then the court must impose an indeterminate sentence. In determining whether or not there is a significant risk the court under s.229, as amended by s.17 of the CJIA 2008 (when in force), has a duty to make an assessment of dangerousness. In making this assessment the court must have regard to:

(i) the nature and circumstances of the current offence and any other convicted offences anywhere in the world;

(ii) any appropriate information, including information about pattern of behaviour;

(iii) any information about the offender. If an offender is assessed as dangerous based on a previous offence, which is then subsequently quashed, the offender can appeal to the Court of Appeal against the sentence under s.231. For the purposes of assessing the dangerousness of the offender, if the offence is committed over a period of two or more days, then s.234 states that the offence is deemed to have been committed on the last of those days for the assessment of dangerousness.

To assist the court in its determination of significant risk, Rose L.J. in *R. v Lang* [2006] 2 Cr.App.R(S) 13 outlined nine factors that the court should bear in mind (see para.17). In particular his Lordship noted that while the offence may be serious, this not mean there is a significant risk of serious harm, the offence of robbery being such an example of an offence that can be committed in a variety of ways. Currently under s.229(3) if the offender has a previous conviction of a relevant specified offence, then the court must assume that they are dangerous, unless such a conclusion would be unreasonable (this will be repealed by s.18 of the CJIA 2008 when in force).

19.22 If the court is of this opinion and considers that the seriousness of the offence (the offence being one that has a maximum sentence of life imprisonment) or those associated with it justifies a life sentence then the court must impose a sentence of life imprisonment. Under s.225(3), as amended by s.13 of the Criminal Justice and Immigration Act 2008, if the serious offence has a maximum of 10 years or more or has a sentence of life imprisonment but such a sentence is not justified, then the court *may* impose a sentence of imprisonment for public protection provided either of two conditions are satisfied. The first condition is that the offender at the time of committing the serious offence has a previous conviction for a specified offence listed in Sch.15A. This lists 23 various violent and sexual offences. The second condition is that the notional minimum term is at least two years (see *R. v Lang* [2006] 2 Cr.App.R.(S) 13 below)

A sentence of imprisonment for public protection amounts to an indeterminate sentence subject to the release and licence provisions in Pt 2 of the Crime (Sentences) Act 1997. Nevertheless, in *Lang* Rose L.J. noted that:

> "repetitive violent or sexual offending at a relatively low level without serious harm does not of itself give rise to a significant risk of serious harm in the future. There may, in such cases, be some risk of future victims being more adversely affected than past victims but, of itself, does not give raise to significant risk of serious harm."

Importantly, Parliament, according to his Lordship, could not have intended relatively minor offences to be punished with indeterminate sentences. Assessing the degree of risk is no doubt a difficult task and may lead to an appeal as occurred in *R. v Terrell* [2007] EWCA Crim 3079, in which the Court of Appeal quashed the defendant's sentence of imprisonment for public protection having pleaded guilty to four offences of making indecent photographs of children with 36 other offences being taken into consideration. The Court ruled that for the purposes of public protection the link between the unlawful act of downloading images and the potential harm that might be done to a child in the production of the images is too remote to satisfy the requirement of significant harm. The risk of the appellant re-offending would be indirect and a small contribution to the harm that a child might or might not suffer. The Court stated:

> "the imprisonment for public protection provisions of the CJA do not apply in circumstances here, where simply as a matter of generalization, a small, uncertain and indirect contribution to harm may be made by a repeat of this offender's offending. No significant risk of serious harm of the requisite gravity, occasioned by a repetition of the offending in this case by this offender can reasonably be said to exist."

Similarly, in *R. v Xhelollari* [2007] EWCA Crim 2052, the Court of Appeal concluded that the refusal of the defendant to accept guilt and the perceived vulnerability of the complainant alone were not sufficient to make a finding of a significant risk so as to justify the imposition of imprisonment for public protection.

In either situation the court must under s.82A of the PCC(S)A 2000 fix a determinate (specified) term of imprisonment to be served which is commensurate with the seriousness of the offence. This therefore means that having served the fixed term the offender's release from custody falls to be considered by the parole board. This means that they will only be released if they not longer pose a risk to the public. On release from a life sentence the offender will in accordance with Sch.18 be subject to licence conditions until death. For sentences imposed for the protection of the public the offender again will be subject to release licence conditions until death but may after the qualifying period of 10 years apply to the parole board to recommend to the Justice Minister that the licence be revoked. These provisions came into effect on April 4, 2005, any offence committed before that date will mean that the offender will be subject to the previous framework in the PCC(S)A 2000 of discretionary life sentences, longer than commensurate sentences and extended sentences.

19.23 In *R. v Lang* [2005] EWCA Crim 2864, the Court of Appeal stated that in fixing the minimum term to be served for the now indeterminate sentence, the court is required to apply s.82A and consider the seriousness of the offence and any associated offences. The court must then consider what the "notional determinate" sentence (NDS) would have been had this offence not warranted a life sentence or imprisonment for public protection. This must not exceed the maximum for the offence in question. The court should then take as the calculation for the minimum term half of the NDS less any time to be deducted for time spent on remand, in accordance with s.240 of the CJA 2003. The Court acknowledged, that in exceptional circumstances the court could conclude that more than half of the NDS should be the calculation where the offender would serve no longer time in custody, due to having already served a determinate sentence, the indeterminate tariff cannot be consecutive to an determinate sentence. (see *R. v Szczerba* [2002] 2 Cr.App.R.(S) 387).

This point is now recognised in s.19 of the CJIA 2008 which amends s.82A to give the court a wider discretionary power in regard to two specified cases known as A and B to reduce the NDS from less than half to nil. In case A if the offence attracts a discretionary life sentence and is deemed exceptionally serious but not so serious so as to justify a life tariff and the court is of the opinion that to halve the NDS would not adequately reflect the seriousness of the offence, then the court can impose a NDS from one half to nil. Case B preserves the ruling in *Lang* to depart from taking half of the NDS above and that in such a situations, the court can reduce the NDS but not by less than one-third.

If the court determines that a life sentence or a sentence is required for public protection, then under s.174 the court must give reasons and identify the information they have taken into account in reaching that decision. In *R. v Mayo* [2007] EWCA Crim 2173, the Court of Appeal observed that:

> "Sentences of imprisonment for public protection have serious consequences for defendants over and above an ordinary custodial sentence. It is both right in the interests of fairness and an important discipline for judges their reasons for imposing such a sentence be set out with some specificity."

In *R. v Johnston* [2007] 1 Cr.App.R.(S) 112, the Court of Appeal made it clear that the appeal court will only interfere with the conclusions reached by the sentencing judge if the sentence itself was either wrong in law or manifestly excessive. The procedure for the imposition of life sentences is found in Part IV.49 of the Practice Direction to which reference should be made as appropriate, but this will not be discussed here.

19.24 Of notable interest is the decision in *R. (Brooke) v Parole Board* [2008] EWCA Civ 29, in which the Court of Appeal affirmed the decision of the High Court that the present arrangement of the Parole Board did not secure the necessary independence, either apparent or actual of its judicial function from the influence of the Secretary of State (Executive). Section 239 of the CJA 2003 establishes the Board as having the status of a Executive Non-Department Public Body, but that its critical function is inextricably linked to the National Offender Management Service (NOMS) and it is therefore not seen to be independent of the Executive.

Moreover, in *R. (Walker) v Secretary of State for Justice* [2008] EWCA Civ 30, the Court of Appeal declared that the Secretary of State had acted unlawfully in his policy for the treatment and management of life sentence prisoners operated by NOMS by failing to put in place sufficient resources to ensure that measures exist to allow and encourage prisoners to demonstrate their suitability for release by the Parole Board, so that a prisoner who has served their tariff is not unlawfully detained. However, this did not breach art.5, since a post-tariff prisoner's detention is subject to continued review and is justified is they are assessed as still being dangerous. On this important point, Lord Phillips observed that the purpose of this sentencing regime is primarily to protect the public and not to rehabilitate the offender and that only when this no longer be necessary, or there is no continued review, would the detention become disproportionate and arbitrary; in breach of art.5. His Lordship then stated:

> "Failure to comply with the obligations of Article 5(4) will not, of itself, result in infringement of Article 5(1)(a). Nor will delay in the provision of rehabilitative treatment necessary to obviate the risk that they would pose to the public if released."

11. Extended Sentences for Adult Offenders

19.25 If the offence is not a serious offence but a specified violent or sexual offence (all 153 offences listed in Sch.15), then under s.227 of the CJA 2003 as amended by s.15 of the Criminal Justice and Immigration Act 2008 (CJIA 2008) (when in force), the court may impose an "extended" sentence on persons 18 or over, provided the court considers that there is a significant risk (assessment of dangerousness under s.229, same as for indeterminate sentences, but the assumption of dangerousness being for a specified offence, see para. 19.21) to the public of serious harm by the offender of further offences. Before imposing an extended sentence, the court needs to be satisfied that either of two conditions as inserted by s.15 of the CIJA 2008 (when in force) are met. The first condition is that at the time of the current offence the offender has a previous conviction for an offence specified in Sch.15A. The second condition is that the court considers the appropriate custodial term of the sentence would be a least four years. A new subsection (6) gives the Secretary of State a discretionary power to change the requirement of the second condition. An extended sentence means a sentence of imprisonment, the term of which is equal to the aggregate of:

(i) the appropriate custodial term; and

(ii) a further period (the extension period) for which the offender is to be subject to a licence, the length of which the court considers necessary for protecting the public.

In regard to a specified violent offence the extension period must not exceed five years, while for a specified sexual offence, not more than eight years. In terms of release, s.247 provides that the offender must serve a minimum of half of the custodial period, release then being subject to the decision of the Parole Board based on the protection of the public. The offender must be released at the end of the custodial period. In *R. v S and Others* [2005] EWCA Crim 3616, the Court of Appeal, albeit tentatively, held that the extended period commences at the end of the custodial period, and not when the offender is released at the half way point. For example, the court imposes a four-year term of imprisonment followed by a two-and-a-half year extension period. The parole board direct the offender's release at the two-year point, the extension period will only start to run in another two years, i.e. at the end of four years.

12. Distinguishing between "Serious Offence" and "Specified Offence" and the Correction of a Mistake

19.26 The new sentencing provisions are challenging and have caused the courts problems in following the correct statutory approach, a point amplified in *R. v Reynolds* [2007] 2 Cr.App.R.(S) 87. It will be of no surprise that others' including practitioners and students' will feel the same frustration with the lack of ease in decoding the complexity of the provisions. A basic approach therefore to take is:

(i) Consider the offence, if this is a serious offence and the criteria of significant risk (dangerousness) is met, then the court must impose an indeterminate sentence. If the serious offence carries life imprisonment, the court must impose life. If the serious offence does not carry life but a sentence of 10 years or more, or the offence does carry life, but the court considers the seriousness of the offence not to justify life imprisonment, then provided the criteria of dangerousness (the court can use the guidance in *Lang* and *Johnston*) is still met, then the court may impose imprisonment for public protection.

(ii) If the offence is not a serious offence but specified violent or sexual offence (this means all the 153 offences listed in Sch.15) and the criteria of dangerousness is satisfied, then the court must impose a extended sentence.

(iii) If the offence is neither a serious offence nor a specified violent or sexual offence, or if the offence is either or both a serious or specified offence but the criteria of dangerousness is not satisfied then the court will impose a determinate fixed sentence in the normal way.

If the sentencing court falls into error in distinguishing between the meaning of a serious offence and a specified offence and therefore imposes either a indeterminate or extended sentence when the criteria are not satisfied, can the mistake be rectified? The problem becomes more acute if the judge imposed an extended sentence when in fact they had a duty to impose a indeterminate sentence. To rectify this mistake would require the sentence to be increased. These difficulties were addressed in *R. v Reynolds* [2007] 2 Cr.App.R.(S) 87, in which the Court of Appeal ruled that only if the mistake was identified within 28 days from the date of sentence could the court utilise s.155 of the PCC(S)A 2000 which allows the Crown Court to vary or rescind the sentence and this includes increasing the sentence as well as reducing.

Following the decision in *Annesley* [1976] 62 Cr.App.R. 113, and *Gordon* [2007] Cr.App.R.(S) 66, provided the judge rescinds the original sentence within the 28-day period the court has the power to adjourn sentence to a later day, beyond the 28 days. If the 28-day period has elapsed when the mistake is discovered and the mistake is to the disadvantage of the defendant (i.e. receiving an indeterminate sentence when they should have received an extended sentence, or indeed a determinate sentence) then this can be corrected on appeal by the defendant as being wrong in law or manifestly excessive. However, if the mistake is to the defendant's advantage (i.e. received a extended sentence for a serious offence when they should have received a indeterminate sentence), the Court of Appeal is constrained by s.11(3) of the Criminal Appeal Act 1968 (CAA 1968) which provides that while the court can quash any sentence and replace it with any such sentence as the court thinks appropriate for the offence they cannot be more severely dealt with than they were in the Crown Court.

The appeal court cannot therefore impose a mandatory indeterminate sentence to correct a mistake of the imposition of an extended sentence for a serious offence. The only power the Court of Appeal has at its discretion to increase sentence is that contained in s.36 of the CJA 1988 on a reference by the Attorney-General against an unduly lenient sentence. Although s.11 of the CAA 1968 does not sit easily with the new dangerous sentencing framework, the Court is bound by s.11 of the Act which created it. Although an incorrect sentence imposed may be unlawful it still remains a valid sentence until varied or quashed, as explained in *Cain* [1985] 1 A.C. 45. The Court reinforced the need, as underlined in *R. v Cain* [2006] EWCA Crim 3233, of the importance for both prosecution and defence to be fully aware of the impact of the new provisions in Ch. 5 of the CJA 2003 so as to avoid the many mistakes that are being made.

Further problems arose in *R. v Howe* [2006] EWCA Crim 3147, and *R. v Harries* [2007] EWCA Crim 1622, concerning offences that were committed over a period that straddled the commencement date of the dangerousness provisions on April 4, 2005. In both cases the Court took the tentative view that neither s.234 nor the transitional periods in para.5(3) of Sch.2 to the CJA 2003 (Commencement Order) 2005 (SI 2005/950) empower the Court to impose a new sentence on an offender whom it is alleged committed the offence during a period before and after April 4, 2005. The Court must construe the CJA 2003 strictly in favour of the defendant and not an overpressed draftsman.

13. Prison Sentences of less than 12 Months

19.27 Section 181 of the CJA 2003 (which came into effect on January 26, 2004) provides that if the sentence is for 12 months or less, then the term of imprisonment must be:

(i) expressed in weeks;

(ii) must be at least 28 weeks;

(iii) must not be more than 51 weeks in respect of any one offence; and

(iv) must not exceed the maximum for the offence.

When passing sentence the court must specify the "custodial period" which must be at least two weeks and not more than 13 weeks, and from which the offender will be released on licence. Secondly, the "licence period" with the imposition of any of eight specified conditions set out in s.182, will be known as the "custody plus order" for the remainder of the term which must be at least 26 weeks in length. The specified licensed conditions are the same as the requirements that a court can impose in a community order, i.e. unpaid work, activity requirement. If the court decides to impose two consecutive sentences, then the overall sentence must not exceed 65 weeks and the custody period not more than 26 weeks. Section 20 of the CJIA 2008 provides that when calculating the overall sentence for the purposes of consecutive sentences not exceeding 65 weeks the court aggregates the custodial period, but then only with the longest of the licence periods.

14. Use of Suspended Sentences and Intermittent Custody (Part 47 of the Practice Directions)

19.28 Sections 189 to 194 restrict the use of suspending a sentence of imprisonment to that of prison sentences of less than 12 months. Section 10 of the Criminal Justice and Immigration Act 2008 inserts a new subsection (1A) into s.189 and prohibits the use of a suspended sentence for summary only offences. However, this restriction does not apply if the summary only offence is to be sentenced at the same time as an indictable offence. If imposing a suspended sentence, the court first determines the period of imprisonment of between 28 weeks and 51 weeks. The court can then either make a "supervision order" with one or more of the same 11 requirements as are available for a community order and then state that the sentence of imprisonment does not take effect unless the offender breaches the supervision order or commits another offence during the operational period. The supervision and operational order must be at least six months but not more than two years. If during this time the offender breaches the order or commits another offence, then the court can order that the offender serve the custodial period.

The court can make an order for periodical reviews of the supervision part under ss.191 and 192. If the offender breaches any of the community requirements of the suspension then Sch.12 will apply. This is effectively the same procedure to be followed as for breach of a community order, save that the court can deal with the offender by activating the original custodial period or a lesser period, or amend the community requirements with more onerous requirements and extend the supervision and suspension periods. However, since being introduced the Home Office has recognised such a sentence to be unworkable and has therefore withdrawn the use of such sentences for the foreseeable future.

Section 183 created the ability of the court to impose a sentence of imprisonment in which the offender is temporarily released during part of the week subject to license conditions set out in s.185 and remains in custody for the other part. However, the use of intermittent custody is restricted to sentences of not more than 51 weeks for an offence. The minimum custody is 14 days and must not be more than 90. A court cannot impose such a sentence unless the offender has expressed a wilingess to serve the custodial part. Under s.264A, as amended by s.20 of the CJIA 2008, the court can impose consecutive terms of intermittent custody in which the offender must serve all of the custody periods and complete all of the licence periods as well.

15. Sentencing Advisory Panel and Sentencing Guidelines Council

19.29 The Sentencing Advisory Panel (SAP) was created under s.81 of the Crime and Disorder Act 1998 and is formally preserved by s.169 of the CJA 2003. The constitution of the SAP is solely at the discretion of the Justice Minister after relevant consultation with the Lord Chief Justice. Section 171 sets out the function of the SAP which in essence is to issue proposed sentencing guidelines for certain offences to the Sentencing Guidelines Council (SGC), or if the SAP receives notification from the SGC that they wish to frame guidelines, then the SAP must obtain and consider the views of all relevant persons after consultation with the Secretary of State. Section 167 creates the Sentencing Guidelines Council which consists of the Lord Chief Justice, together with seven other judicial members and four non-judicial members (i.e. police, barrister or solicitor).

Having received a proposal from the SAP or the Secretary of State, the SGC must first consider whether to frame sentencing guidelines, having regard to the need to promote consistency, costs and effectiveness, promoting public confidence and the views of the SAP. If it decides not to, then that's the end of the matter. If alternatively, it decides to frame relevant guidelines from a proposal or of its own initiative then the SGC must draft and publish the guidelines for consultation. After the process of consultation the SGC can adopt or amend the guidelines and then issue them as "definitive" guidelines. To assist practitioners, the SGC periodically produce a "Guideline Judgments Case Compendium" which brings together as a collection in a summary format all the relevant guideline case authorities.

Section 172 provides that the sentencing court must have regard to the guidelines as far as they are relevant to the case. If no specific guidelines exist, then the Court of Appeal itself can provide general sentencing guidance to the lower courts. A notable example is *R. v Page* [2005] 2 Cr.App.R.(S) 37, in which the Court of Appeal provided guidance for shoplifting and stated that custody would be the sentence of last resort for a first offence, and that a community penalty would be more appropriate, an adult persistent offender on a minor scale would justify a three-month sentence, if violence is used, then a sentence in excess of four years would be appropriate. In *R. v Rees and Others* [2006] 2 Cr.App.R.(S) 20, the Court of Appeal stated that offences of violent disorder committed by young people who had been binge drinking caused real anxiety and distress to the public. Those offenders, even of exemplary character, could expect to receive substantial sentences, usually three years. Nonetheless, it is important to bear in mind the comments of Rose L.J. in *R. v Lyon* [2005] EWCA Crim 1365:

> "one or two decisions of this Court, which are neither guideline cases nor expressed to be of general application, are unlikely to be a reliable guide to the appropriate sentencing bracket for a particular type of offence, because the facts and circumstances of cases vary infinitely. That is why, generally, this Court is, and will continue to be, reluctant in sentence appeals to look at cases which are merely illustrative of the sentence appropriate on particular facts."

In *Attorney–General's Reference (Nos 24 to 29 of 2006)* [2007] EWCA Crim 2217 the Court of Appeal, on a unduly lenient sentence reference concerning offences of robbery and conspiracy to rob train passengers by a gang of hooded youths, considered the SGC guidance for robbery and concluded that the judge had failed to give sufficient weight to the aggravating features and the need to reflect the elements of punishment and deterrence. In respect of sexual offences, the Court of Appeal issued what is deemed to be "non-prescriptive guidance" in *R. v Corran* [2005] Cr.App.R. 404 in relation to the various sexual offences in the Sexual Offences Act 2003. In *R. v Taylor* [2008] EWCA Crim 465, the Court of Appeal, whilst accepting that guidelines should not be applied in a straightjacketed fashion, it was unfortunate that the judge had failed to make reference to the SGC's definitive guidelines on robbery published in July 2006 given that s.172 of the CJA 2003 imposes a duty on a court to have regard to such guidelines.

16. Credit for Time Spent in Custody on Remand

19.30 Section 240(3), which came into effect on April 4, 2005 (offences before this date must be dealt with under s.67 of the CJA 1967) provides that the judge must in open court state that the number of days spent in custody by the offender for the offence or a related offence is to count as time served by them as part of the sentence. Section 242 defines remand in custody narrowly to mean that ordered by the court and therefore does not include time spent in police custody. Under the Remand in Custody (Effect of Concurrent and Consecutive Sentences of Imprisonment) Rules 2005 (SI 2005/2054), any days spent on remand for the current offence at the same time as serving a sentence of imprisonment for an unrelated offence will not be credited. If the defendant is being sentenced for an offence before April 4, 2005 and an offence subsequent to that date, then the remand time can only be counted towards the old offence. Further, the court has a new discretion (unlike the old s.67 of the CJA 1967) not to discount all or part of the remand time, if it considers it just in all the circumstances. If the judge exercises this discretion, then they should inform defence counsel so as to give them an opportunity to address the court that no such circumstances exist. Defence counsel should be alive to the possibility of departing from the normal practice, and seek clarification from the judge (see *R. v Barber* [2006] 2 Cr.App.R.(S) 81).

Section 21 of the CJIA 2008 and Sch.6 inserts a new s.240A which will allow the court to take into account time spent on bail as time served. The provision states that the offence must be a qualifying offence which means that it must have been committed on or after April 4, 2005 and that the offender for that offence was remanded on bail with an electronically monitored curfew condition of nine hours or more each day after the commencement of the provision. The court must, unless it is of the opinion that it is just in all the circumstances not to, give a direction to credit the remand time. In considering its opinion, the court must take into account whether or not the offender has breached the curfew conditions, or such rules introduced by the Secretary of State disallow the crediting of bail time. If not of this opinion, then the court must direct in open court that the bail time credit period counts towards the sentence based on half a day for each full bailed curfew day. If the court decides not to give a direction, it may still give a direction that a period of days, albeit less that the full credit period, can count towards time served.

In *R. v Gordon* [2007] Cr.App.R.(S) 66, the Court of Appeal had to address the issue of a calculation mistake in the amount of time served to be credited. The Court of Appeal made it plain that once a judge has informed the defendant that the time served will be discounted from the actual sentence, then a short adjournment can be directed to allow the accurate calculation of the time with written representations or a short oral hearing should there be any disputes. A misstatement of the number of days will, according to the Court, invariably amount to an administrative error. Practically, there is nothing wrong with a judge stating that on the current information available X number of days will be discounted as time served but should this later be revealed as a mistake, then this can be corrected with an amended order, the first order being temporary in nature. It is to be noted that Judge L.J., who gave the leading speech, expressed the view that the statutory provisions "are convoluted yet have practical consequences for defendants, and they can be easily overlooked or misapplied by advocates and sentencers".

However, this will not necessarily eliminate the practical problems as can be seen in *R. v Norman* [2006] EWCA Crim 1792. If a judge imposes an incorrect term of imprisonment as a result of miscalculation of time spent in custody, then s.155 of the PCC(S)A 2000 allows for the court to correct the mistake within 28 days. If the mistake comes to light after 28 days, then if detrimental to the defendant, the defendant will need to apply for leave to appeal to be extended. If the miscalculation is however, favourable to the defendant, then the court can do nothing in such circumstances. For this reason the Court emphasised the need for care to be taken in the sentencing process (see para.19.26).

17. Concurrent and Consecutive Sentences and the Principle of Totality

19.31 If an offender is convicted of several offences, then the court most impose a separate penalty for each offence. The issue that arises for the court will be whether to order that part or some run, either concurrently or consecutively to each other. If the court orders them to run concurrently this means that the offender will serve one sentence for al the offences. For example; Offender A is convicted of s.20 reckless wounding and s.47 assault occasioning ABH. In respect of the s.20 the court imposes a two-year sentence of imprisonment and one year for the s.47 to run concurrently. This means that although the offender received three years, their sentence is two years in total, the one year for the ABH will run together with the two-year sentence but they cannot be released until the expiry of the longest term (see s.263 of the CJA 2003 which further provides that if the sentences were imposed at different times, the offender is not to be released until the expiry of the last sentence).

Alternatively, the court can order that each sentence be served consecutively so that each sentence will run one after the other. So in the above example, if the two sentences were ordered to run consecutively then the offender will serve an aggregate term of three years, the one-year sentence for the ABH will only run on the expiry of the two-year sentence for the s.20 offence (see further s.264 of the CJA 2003). If the court is deciding on ordering the sentences to run consecutively, then close attention must be given to the principle of totality which requires the court not to impose an overall sentence which is manifestly disproportionate to the culpability (totality) of the offending. In *R. v Greaves* [2004] 2 Cr.App.R.(S) 41, Lord Woolf stated that if a weapon is used in the commission of a robbery, then the proper policy is to impose consecutive sentences for the robbery offence and the weapon offence, particularly if the weapon is a firearm. The purpose of the policy is to send out a clear message that those who commit robbery with the use of a weapon, can expect to receive an additional sentence (see also *R. v French* [1982] 4 Cr.App.R.(S) 57).

A particular problem that the Court of Appeal has had to address is whether the sentencing court should impose an indeterminate sentence on an offender who is currently serving a determinate sentence. In *R. v C and Others* [2007] EWCA Crim 680, Latham L.J. noted that it is not unlawful for a court to impose concurrent or consecutive sentences for either determinate or indeterminate sentences provided it was justified and did not result in a sentence being manifestly excessive, otherwise this may cause administrative problems.

His Lordship did however state that:

> "judges should try to avoid consecutive sentences if that is at all possible and adjust the custodial term or minimum period within concurrent sentences to reflect the overall criminality if that is possible within other sentencing constraints."

If consecutive sentences are necessary then the determinate sentence should be imposed first, followed by the extended sentence or for public protection (see also *R. v Ashes* [2007] EWCA Crim 1848).

18. The Newton Hearing

19.32 A *Newton* Hearing, derived from the decision in *R. v Newton* [1982] 77 Cr.App.R. 13, is held where a defendant has pleaded guilty to an offence(s) but disputes the factual version of events claimed by the prosecution which may, for instance, suggest that the offence is more serious than the defendant is prepared to admit. In this instance the judge will hold a *Newton*

Hearing where these issues are argued and the judge must make a decision as to which are the true facts surrounding the actual commission of the offence. The court can hold a *Newton* Hearing of its own motion, even where the prosecution and defence have agreed a basis of plea. Further guidance on the utility of a *Newton* Hearing in such circumstances encapsulated neatly in *R. v Underwood* [2005] 1 Cr.App.R. 178, of particular importance is that the court must impose a sentence that is based as far as is possible on an accurate reflection of the facts in the case. If the prosecution disputes the facts as against those admitted by the defendant, then the prosecution is as stated in *McGrath and Casey* [1983] 5 Cr.App.R.(S) 460, required to prove this.

Also it was held in *Gillan v DPP* [2007] EWHC 380 that on the clear wording of s.5(1) of the PCC(S)A 2000 (which imposes a duty on the Crown Court to "enquire into the circumstances of the case") the Crown Court does have jurisdiction to hold a *Newton* Hearing on a committal for sentence from the magistrates' court who themselves had conducted a *Newton* Hearing. However, this is a discretionary power, and a Crown Court should not exercise it unless the defendant can point to some significant development or matter since the magistrates' findings of fact.

It is important to be aware of the decision in *R. v Eubank* [2002] 1 Cr.App.R. 11, in which the Court of Appeal held that in a situation where the defendant had admitted robbery but denied the possession of a firearm, it was wrong to hold a *Newton* Hearing to determine whether or not the defendant had possession of a firearm. To be convicted of such a grave offence the defendant is rightly entitled to the verdict of a jury and so if the prosecution wishes to pursue the firearms allegation, they must add it as a separate count to the indictment and proceed to trial, unless it is not in the public interest to do so. Lord Woolf, who gave the leading judgment, made note of the practical importance of a *Newton* Hearing within the sentence process has being an effective method of resolving issues of facts in order that the court can impose the proper sentence.

19. Release from Fixed Term Sentences

19.33 Section 244 of the CJA 2003, which is only partially in force, provides that an offender who is serving a sentence of 12 months or more will be released at the half way point (requisite custodial period) of the sentence. However, under s.249 the offender will remain on licence until the expiry of the whole sentence. This means that they will be subject to the standard licence conditions under s.250 and any prescribed conditions (see The CJA (Sentencing) (Licence Conditions) Order 2005 (SI 2005/648)). Section 246 preserves the availability of the home detention curfew, which allows the offender (provided sentence not less than 12 weeks and they have served a minimum of four weeks and at least 14 days of the sentence must remain) to be released early by up to a period of 135 days. The offender will be subject automatically to an electronic curfew under s.255. Once released the offender is always at risk of being recalled back to prison, if they either commit further offences or breach any of the licence conditions. Those who are serving a sentence imposed before March 7, 2005 will still be subject to the old regime in the CJA 1991.

20. Community Penalties (Part 48 of the Criminal Practice Directions)

19.34 The court has a range of community type penalties available, should a custodial sentence not be appropriate. Section 177 of the CJA 2003 came into effect on April 4, 2005 and creates a new "community order" which encompasses all the previous community penalties into one order. A court may impose a community order on a person aged 16 or over who is convicted of an offence which imposes on them one or more of the following requirements:

Unpaid Work

19.35 This is set out is ss.199 and 200 and requires the offender to perform at the direction of the responsible officer (defined in s.197) unpaid work of not less than 40 but not more than 300 hours (even if consecutive terms are ordered). The court must be satisfied by the probation officer that the offender is a suitable person.

An Activity Requirement

19.36 This is set out in s.201 and requires the offender to present themselves to a relevant person and place (i.e. Community Rehabilitation Centre) for up to a maximum of 60 days in order to become involved in activities such as reparation for the victim, who must consent. The court must consult the probation service and be satisfied that it is feasible to secure compliance.

A Programme Requirement

19.37 This is set out in s.202 and requires the offender to participate in an accredited programme that entails a systematic set of activities for "such number of days as may be so specified". It must have been recommended to the court that the accredited programme is suitable for the offender.

A Prohibited Activity Requirement

19.38 This is set out in s.203 and requires the offender to refrain from participating in such activities as are specified and on such days or for such periods as are specified. The court must first consult the probation service.

A Curfew Requirement

19.39 This is set out in s.204 and requires the offender to remain for a period of not less than two hours or more than 12 hours in any day for such periods (not more than six months) at such places as specified. The court must obtain and consider relevant information.

An Exclusion Requirement

19.40 This is set out in s.205 and makes provision for the offender to be excluded from entering a specified place (includes area) for such days and periods as specified but for not more than two years.

A Residence Requirement

19.41 This is set out in s.206 and requires the offender to reside at a specified place for such periods as ordered. The court must first consider the home surroundings of the offender, if the place is a hostel or other institution, then the court must first seek recommendation from the probation service.

A Mental Health Requirement

19.42 This is set out in ss.207 and 208 and requires the offender, in order to improve their mental condition, to submit to specified treatment from either a GP or psychologist for such periods as are specified.

A Drug Rehabilitation Requirement

19.43 This is set out is s.209 and requires the offender to submit to treatment by a an appropriately qualified person for a period of at least six months (known as the treatment and testing period) so as to reduce or eliminate their dependency/propensity to use drugs. The court must first be satisfied that that the offender is drug dependant or has a propensity to misuse them. The offender will be required to provide samples when directed. If the period is for more than 12 months, the court must (if under 12 months may) provide for the requirement to be reviewed periodically in accordance with s.211.

An Alcohol Treatment Requirement

19.44 This is set out in s.212 and requires the offender to submit to treatment with a qualified person so as to reduce their alcohol dependency for such periods as are specified but not less than six months. Before an order can be made the court must first be satisfied of the offenders' dependency on alcohol.

A Supervision Requirement

19.45 This is set out in s.213 and requires the offender to attend at appointments as specified with a relevant person so as to promote their rehabilitation.

Attendance Centre Requirement

19.46 This is set out in s.214 and requires that if the offender is under 25, then they must attend at a specified attendance centre for not less than 12 hours or more than 36 hours. The court must first be satisfied that the attendance centre is reasonably accessible to the offender in terms of mode of transport and any other circumstances (i.e. disability).

With any of the requirements the court can order that such requirements be monitored electronically in accordance with s.215. The community order must specify a date, not more than three years after the date of the order, by which all the requirements in it must have been complied with. If the order consists of two or more requirements, then the court can impose an earlier date for completion of a particular requirement.

If the offender fails to comply with the community order then Sch.8 will apply. This requires the responsible officer to give the offender a warning of the consequences, if the officer is of the opinion that they have without reasonable excuse failed to comply. If within a period of 12 months from the date of the warning the responsible officer is of the opinion that the offender has without reasonable excused breached the order, then they must lay an information before the magistrates or the Crown Court if there is no direction for the magistrates to deal with breach of an order from the Crown Court.

The court (this means either the magistrates' or Crown Court) may then either issue a summons for the offender to appear at court or if the information is in writing and on oath, then issue a warrant of arrest. If the offender does not answer to the summons, then the court will issue a warrant for their arrest in any event. If the court, having heard the evidence, is satisfied that the offender has without reasonable excuse breached the order, then the court can deal with them in one of three ways:

(i) Amend the community order imposing more onerous requirements (if the order did not previously contain an unpaid work requirement and the court now wishes to impose one, then under s.38 of the CJIA 2008 the minimum period is reduced from 40 to 20 hours.

(ii) Revoke the order and re-sentence the offender.

(iii) If the offence is non-imprisonable and the offender is 18 or over and it is proved that the offender willfully and persistently breached the order, then the court can impose a sentence of up to 51 weeks' imprisonment. It is important to note the decision in *West Yorkshire Probation Service v Boulter* [2005] EWHC 2342, in which the High Court ruled that it is for the prosecutor to prove the breach of a community order to the criminal standard of beyond reasonable doubt; where facts are disputed in the sentencing process the criminal standard must be applied, since they are criminal proceedings for that purpose. Over 121,000 community orders are issued each year, with the probation service costing around £807 million a year.

21. Deferment of Sentence (Part 45 of the Criminal Practice Directions)

19.47 Section 278 and Sch.23 of the CJA 2003 enable the court to defer the passing of sentence in order to allow the court to have regard in dealing with the defendant to their (i) conduct after conviction, (ii) any change in circumstances. The court can only defer imposing sentence if (i) the defendant consents, and (ii) agrees to comply with any requirements as to their conduct. The court can only defer for a period not more than six months, if the offender commits an offence during the deferment period, then they can be dealt with for the original offence.

22. Pre-Sentence Reports (PSR) and Drug Testing

19.48 For a court to make a proper determination of the appropriate sentence, all relevant information needs to be at the court's disposal, such as the circumstances surrounding the offence and the offender's behaviour and attitude towards the offence. Accordingly, pre-sentence reports are a vital part of the sentencing process. Section 156 provides that a court must take into account all such information as is available to it about the circumstances of the offence, including any aggravating and mitigating factors. The court must obtain and consider a PSR in the case of a custodial or community punishment, unless the court is of the opinion that such a PSR is not necessary. Section 159 provides for the PSR to be disclosed to the offender and prosecutor. A new addition is s.161 which will allow the court in respect of either a community order or suspended sentence to order that the offender provide a sample of any description so as to identify whether they have any class A drugs in their body. However, this is not yet in force.

Section 12 of the CJIA 2008 when in force will allow a PSR to be given orally, unless the offender is under 18 and a written report is required under s.153(3)(a) of the CJA 2003.

23. Other Penalties and Orders

19.49 The court also has the following further penalties available as an appropriate method of disposal of the matter:

Fines (Part 51 and 52 of the Criminal Practice Directions)

19.50 The court has a discretionary power to impose a fine, which can be, but rarely is imposed in conjunction with a sentence of imprisonment. In the magistrates' court this is based on a sliding scale up to a maximum of £5,000. The MCA 1980 provides for five levels of fines as follows, level 1 = £200, level 2 = £500, level 3 = £1,000, level 4 = £2,500, and level 5 = £5,000. Section 163 of the CJA 2003 gives the Crown Court a general power to impose a fine instead of, or in addition to dealing with the offender in any other way, except if they are sentenced under ss.225 to 228 of the CJA 2003 or ss.110(2) or 11(2) of the PCC(S)A 2000. The court in determining the level of fine to be imposed must first under s.164 of the CJA 2003 inquire into the offender's financial circumstances. The court can under s.162 make a financial circumstances order, which requires the offender to produce to the court a statement of their finances. If the offender fails to do so without reasonable excuse then they commit a summary offence punishable by a fine at level 3. If they produce a statement that they know is false or is reckless as to that falsity, or knowingly fail to disclose a relevant fact, then they commit a summary offence punishable by a fine at level 4.

In fixing the amount of fine, the court must calculate an amount that, in the court's opinion, reflects the seriousness of the offence, taking into account all the circumstances of the case. If the offender fails to attend or fails to cooperate with the court's inquiry into their financial circumstances, then provided the court has insufficient information to determine the fine, it can a make such a determination regardless. If subsequent to fixing a fine under s.164, the court is satisfied that had at its disposal the financial information, now being made available, the court can remit the whole or part of the fine. If the offender defaults on payment of the fine, then the court can under s.139 of the PCC(S)A 2000 for the Crown Court and s. 82 of the MCA 1980 in relation to the magistrates' court allow more time to pay, direct different installment terms, or fix a specified term of imprisonment as set out in the table set out in s.139(4) (i.e. fine between £501 and £1,000 amounts to 28 days' imprisonment).

If the financial circumstances of the offender later change and would have resulted in the fixing of a smaller sum or no fine at all, then the court can under s.129 of the PCC(S)A 2000 remit the whole or any part of the fine. While the enforcement of fines is a judicial matter, the collection of fines is an administrative task for the Fines Officer under Sch.5 of the Courts Act 2003 and the Fines Collection Regulations 2006 (SI 2006/501). There are various methods of collection, such as Attachment of Earnings Order, a Deduction from Benefits Order, discharge by performing unpaid work, clamping of vehicles, and warrant of distress. Furthermore, ss.92 to 97 of the Access to Justice Act 1999 allow for the court to employ civilian enforcement officers or approved private enforcement agencies to execute warrants. When in force Pt 6 of the Criminal Justice and Immigration Act 2008 will implement greater cooperation between European Member States of the enforcement and transfer of financial penalties (includes fines, costs and compensation). Part 6 will give effect to the European Council Framework Decision and give the magistrates' court the power to issue a transfer certificate where the defaulter now resides in another State or has property or income in that State, for the relevant State to enforce the outstanding financial penalty.

Lord Philips in *R. v Trigger* [2007] 1 Cr.App.R.(S) 69, said that where appropriate the court should make greater use of fines and observed that:

> "we believe that there may have been a reluctance to impose fines because fines were often not enforced. Enforcement of fines is now rigorous and effective and, where the offender has the means, a heavy fine can often be an adequate punishment. If so, the 2003 Act requires a fine to be imposed rather than a community sentence."

As an alternative to committing a fine defaulter to prison, s.300 of the CJA 2003 allows for the magistrates' court, as against an offender over 16, to make a "default order" which can require the offender to comply with an unpaid work condition or a curfew requirement or if under 25 an attendance centre requirement (s.40 of the CJIA 2008). Section 301 gives the magistrates' court the power to disqualify the fine defaulter from driving for a period not exceeding 12 months.

At the moment the Ministry of Justice is currently piloting Sch.6 of the Courts Act 2003 relating to fine payment work or the conversion of fines into work. This provides the court with the power to allow an offender who was sentenced to a fine to discharge their financial liability in regard to outstanding fines or fixed penalties but not compensation, costs or confiscation orders, by undertaking unpaid work. In exercising the power, it must first appear to the court that the amount owing cannot be collected by any of the other available methods of enforcement. If the court decides to exercise this power then it can make the appropriate order known as a "work order". Currently, the order is only available to offenders aged 18 or over, who must also consent to the making of the order. If the pilots are evaluated to be a success then the measure is likely to be rolled out nationally. The purpose behind the new order is to promote confidence in fines as being a credible punishment.

Discharge (Part III.31 of the CrPR 2005 and Part 54 of the Practice Directions)

19.51 If the judge takes the view that it is not necessary to impose a punishment, then the court can, under s.12 of the PCC(S)A 2000, determine that the offender, either be given an absolute discharge which means that they are discharged absolutely with nothing more to do. Alternatively, the court can if it thinks fit, impose a conditional discharge, which means that the defendant is discharged, subject to the condition that they must commit no further offences during a period not exceeding three years set by the court. Section 13 provides that a conditional discharge can only be breached if during the fixed period the defendant is convicted of an offence during that period. A discharge cannot be used for breach of an ASBO. Section 14 further provides that the imposition of a discharge means that the offender does not have a disclosable conviction unless re-sentenced.

Compensation (Part 53 of the Criminal Practice Directions)

19.52 Both the Crown Court and the magistrates' court have a general power under s.130 of the PCC(S)A 2000 to make a compensation order instead of or in addition to any other sentence. This requires the convicted person to pay to the complainant compensation for the loss or damage (this includes recovered property, i.e. stolen or damaged car), or injury suffered (including any funeral expenses). The amount of compensation is at the discretion of the court (in the magistrates' court this must not exceed £5,000), taking into account any evidence and representations and the financial means of the offender. The court is required to give preference to making a compensation order as against imposing a fine, if the offender has insufficient means to pay both. At any time the compensation order can be reviewed in terms of reduction or discharge, or to be paid in installments. If the court decides not to make a compensation order, then when passing sentence it must state its reasons for not doing so. It is important to be aware that the complainant may wish to make a claim to the Criminal Injuries Compensation Scheme, either way the compensation from one will be off set against the other.

Binding Over (Part III.31 of the CrPR 2005)

19.53 In relation to the magistrates' court, a power to bind over an offender is an ancient power to be found in the Justice of the Peace Act 1361 and also in s.115 of the MCA 1980. The Crown Court possesses the same power. A bind over is often utilised for minor drunken and disorder offences, it is not that dissimilar to a conditional discharge with can be alternatively be used. A bind over means that the offender promises, subject to the forfeiture of a fixed sum (usually £100), to keep the peace for a specified period. A bind over can be given whether or not the offender is charged with an offence and therefore no conviction arises. An appeal lies to the Crown Court under the Magistrates' Courts (Appeals from Binding Over Orders) Act 1956. An important ruling is that of the European Court of Human Rights in *Hashman and Harrup v UK* [1999] 30 E.H.R.R. 241, in which the European Court held by 16 votes to 1 that the English common law power to bind over "to be of good behaviour" in circumstances where the person's behaviour is deemed to be *"contra bonos mores"* (this means "conduct which has the property of being wrong rather than right in the judgment of the majority of contemporary fellow citizens", see the judgment of Glidewell L.J. in *Hughes v Holley* [1988] 86 Cr.App.R. 139) and no more, breached art.10 for lack of sufficient precision.

Confiscation Order under the Proceeds of Crime Act 2002 (Parts 56 to 62 of the Criminal Practice Directions)

19.54 Part 2 of the Proceeds of Crime Act 2002 sets out the procedure to be followed in the Crown Court for the imposition of a confiscation order. This is a substantive piece of legislation of some complexity. The power to make a confiscation order is limited to the Crown Court for an offence of which the defendant is convicted or committed for sentence and the prosecution invites the court to proceed to consider an order. The court must determine whether the defendant had a criminal lifestyle. Section 10 allows the Court, having determined that the defendant has a criminal lifestyle, to make four assumptions for the purpose of deciding whether they have benefited from their general criminal conduct. If these conditions are satisfied then the court must decide on the recoverable amount and make a confiscation order to that effect.

The recoverable amount is an amount equal to defendant's benefit from their criminal conduct. The Court has a power to postpone proceedings for a confiscation order. Under s.16 the prosecution are required to submit a statement of information, a copy of which is served on the defence. The Court may order the defence to indicate to what extent they accept the contents of the statement or order the defence to supply information specified by the court in an order (the defence will be required to serve an affidavit). If the defendant defaults on payment despite the use of other enforcement measures, then exactly as with default of fines the same conversion table as in s.139(4) applies. So if a confiscation order is made for £60,000 and the defendant defaults, the term of imprisonment will be two years. Importantly, under s.38 of the PCA 2002, the serving of a sentence does not discharge the confiscation order, which the offender will still remain liable to pay.

If the prosecution or other law enforcement agencies are intending to seek a confiscation order, then they must do so with a reasonable time, as required by art.6.1 and avoid any unnecessary and disproportionate delay. In *Lloyd v Bow Street Magistrates' Court* [2003] EWHC 2294, the High Court, on a judicial review application, ruled that what amounted to a reasonable time is determined by all the circumstances of the case and the diligence of those involved. In this instance a delay of two and a half years was inexcusable and unacceptable and the proceedings should have been stayed.

Deprivation or Forfeiture and Restitution Orders

19.55 Section 143 of the PCC(S)A 2000 gives the court a general power to order the forfeiture of any property by the convicted defendant provided the court is satisfied that the property (including a vehicle for certain traffic offences) has been lawfully seized from them including property which was in their possession, or control (lawfully or unlawfully) at the time when they where apprehended for the offence. Further, it must be shown that the property was used for the purpose of committing, or facilitating, or was intended to be used in the commission of any offence. In determining whether or not to make an order the court must have regard to the value of the property and the likely financial and other effects upon the defendant.

The effect of the order is to deprive the defendant of any rights (if they have any) in the property which will be held by the police, subject to the Police (Property) Act 1897. Any lawful owner will then need to make a civil claim against the police for the release of the property within six months of the deprivation order being made, that they neither consented to, or knew of the offender's use of the property. Under s.145 the court can order that any proceeds from the sale of the property be paid as compensation to the complainant. Other specific powers exist in the Misuse of Drugs Act 1971, the Firearms Act 1968 and the Prevention of Crime Act 1951 in respect of possessing an offensive weapon in public place, and s.7 forfeiture orders in relation to a s.6 offence or s.23 in relation to offences contained in ss.15 to 18 of the Terrorism Act 2000.

Under s.148 of the PCC(S)A 2000 the court has a wide discretionary power, where goods have been stolen and the defendant has been convicted of a theft offence to order the restoration of the goods or other goods directly or indirectly representing the stolen goods to the person entitled to them. Alternatively, the court can order restoration of a sum from any money in the offender's possession at the time of apprehension to the value of the goods.

Under s.60 of the Sexual Offences Act 2003, as amended by Sch.4 of the Violent Crime Reduction Act 2006, the court can, if a defendant is convicted of the trafficking of person into or within the UK for a sexual exploitation offence contained in ss.57 to 59, order the forfeiture of a land vehicle, ship or aircraft which was used or intended to be used in connection with the offence and which the offender owned, was in possession of, or used it during the commission of the offence.

Disqualification from Driving and Working with Children

19.56 Section 146 of the Powers of Criminal Courts (Sentencing) Act 2000 provides that a court has a discretion to disqualify an offender who is convicted of an offence from driving (either from holding or obtaining a licence), instead of, or in addition to any sentence for the offence and for such period as the court thinks fit. Nevertheless, s.146(3) restricted the use of this power by the court until such time as they had been notified by Secretary of State that it could be used. This notification was not given January 1, 2004, some four years after the provision was created and had to a large extent been forgotten. Section 28 of the Criminal Justice and Courts Services Act 2000 gives the court a power to order that the offender is to be disqualified from working with children.

Prevention Orders and Notification Requirements (Part 50 of the Criminal Practice Directions)

19.57 Under s.104 of the Sexual Offences Act 2003 the court can, if satisfied that the defendant's behaviour since being convicted or cautioned for a specified listed sexual offence contained Sch.3 or 5 before or after the commencement of the 2003 Act makes it necessary for a Sexual Offences Prevention Order (SOPO) to be made, make such an order. The necessity must be to protect the public from serious sexual harm which includes physical and psychological as well as death or serious personal injury (see *R. v Collard* [2005] 1 Cr.App.R.(S) 34). In *R. v Richards* [2007] 1 W.L.R. 847, the Court of Appeal ruled that:

> "it is not a pre-condition to the making of a SOPO that the judge should be satisfied that the offender would also qualify for an extended sentence or a sentence of life imprisonment or for protection of the public."

The Court noted that while the two sentencing regimes have similarities in the need to protect the public and that there may well be potential overlap requiring close attention; the two regimes are distinct in application and therefore:

> "the ambit of the court's discretion to make a SOPO is prescribed by the provisions which created it, without reference to s. 224–229 of the CJA 2003."

The Sexual Offences Act 2003 does not make express or implied reference to the dangerousness provisions in the CJA 2003. If Parliament had intended to restrict the use of SOPO in this way it would have said so. The threshold of dangerousness in the CJA 2003 is higher than public protection for a SOPO (see also *R. v Rampley* [2006] EWCA Crim 2203). A SOPO can be drafted in wide terms to prohibit the defendant from doing anything, so as to reduce the risk to the public. The duration of the order must be fixed, and not be less than five years or until further order. The order can be varied or discharged. One important aspect of this is that the police can make a direct application to the court for such an order.

Part 2 of the Sexual Offences Act 2003 sets out the procedure for the imposition of notification requirements on an offender who is convicted or cautioned for a specified offence listed in Sch.3. Section 82 sets out the relevant notification period, if the offender is sentenced to 30 months or more imprisonment, then the period is indefinite, under 30 months but not less than six months it is 10 years, under six months, seven years. If the offender is under 18, then the above periods are halved. Sections 83 to 87 set out the information that the offender must provide to the police, including travel arrangements. A breach of these requirements constitutes under s.92 an either way offence with the same punishment as for a SOPO, unless the offender has a reasonable excuse. Section 57 of the Violent Crime Reduction Act 2006 ensures that if the offender is given a sentence of imprisonment for public protection, then they will still remain subject to the notification requirement regime for an indefinite period. Further, s.58 provides for the police to apply to the magistrates' court for a warrant to authorise them to enter and search the home of an offender who is subject to the notification requirements for the purpose of making an assessment as to the risk they may pose to the local community.

19.58 Part 1 of the Serious Crime Act 2007 delineates corresponding powers for the Crown Court to make, in addition to any other sentence, a Serious Crime Prevention Order against a defendant over 18 who is convicted of a specified serious offence listed in Pt 1 of Sch.1 or one that the court considers sufficiently serious to be a specified offence. A relevant safeguard is that no order can be made unless the court has reasonable grounds to believe that such an order would protect the public by preventing, restricting, or disrupting involvement by the person in serious crime. The duration of the order must not exceed five years and can be varied or discharged. Under s.24 the defendant can appeal to the Court of Appeal in relation to the order. If the defendant breaches the order without reasonable excuse, then under s.25 they commit an either way offence which on summary conviction is punishable with 12 months' imprisonment and or a £5,000 fine, while on conviction on indictment a sentence of up to five years and or a fine. With this offence the burden of proof would seem to be on the defendant to show they have a reasonable excuse. The issue will be whether this amounts to an evidential or a legally persuasive burden.

Continuing with this theme and in response to the consultation paper "Rebalancing the Criminal Justice System in Favour of the Law-abiding Majority" (July 2006), s.98 of the Criminal Justice and Immigration Act 2008, when in force, will allow the police to apply to the magistrates' court for a Violent Offender Order (VOO) against a qualifying offender for a specified offence. A specified offence means manslaughter, soliciting murder, s.18 wounding/causing GBH with intent, s.20 malicious wounding/infliction of GBH, attempted murder or conspiracy to murder. A qualifying offender is a person who has a previous conviction for a specified offence and received at least 12 months' imprisonment. In making a VOO or an interim order the court has an discretion to impose any prohibitions, restrictions or conditions that are necessary for protecting the public from the risk of serious violent harm including both physical or psychological harm caused by the offender. The order must, unless varied or discharged, be for at least two years.

Section 99 requires the court before making an order to be satisfied that the person is a qualifying offender and since conviction has acted in such a way as to make in necessary to make a VOO. Under s.100, the court is given the power to vary, renew or discharge the order. A person who is subjected to VOO can appeal to the Crown Court against the making of such an order. If the offender is under 17, then the order must be reviewed periodically by the police. The court can also attach notification requirements to the order, similar to those under the Sexual Offences Act 2003. The Secretary of State under s.108 is given a discretionary power to make regulations in respect of travelling outside the UK. For those offenders under 18, the court can order that the notification obligations are instead imposed on the parents. Any breach without reasonable excuse of a VOO or any of the notification requirements amounts to an either way offence with a possible sentence of five years' imprisonment if convicted on indictment.

Banning Orders

19.59 In accordance with the provisions of the Football Spectators Act 1989, as amended by the Football (Disorder) Act 2000, the court can impose a banning order in relation to a regulated domestic and international football match of a person who is convicted of one or more of 18 specified offences. The court must be satisfied that the order would help prevent violence or disorder at or in connection with a regulated football match. The duration of the order is set out in s.14F. The court can order the surrender of the offender's passport. A failure to comply with the order amounts to an imprisonable summary offence. The compatibility of football banning orders with freedom of movement was considered extensively by the Court of Appeal in *Gough v Chief Constable of Derbyshire* [2002] Q.B. 1213. In *R (White) v Crown Court at Blackfriars* [2008] EWHC 510, the High Court observed that whilst the starting point before an order is made requires the court to be convinced that the individual has a propensity to football violence, it is also proportionate and benefical for it to be known that an isolated assault on an official will merit the making of an order.

Similarly, in Pt 1 of the Violent Crime Reduction Act 2006, if a person aged 16 or over is convicted of an offence which was committed whilst they were under the influence of alcohol, the court can make a "drink banning order" including an interim order provided the court is satisfied that the offender has engaged in drunken criminal or disorderly conduct and that it is necessary to protect others from further drunken conduct by them. The court may impose any prohibition that is necessary to secure the protection of others, which can include access to and from certain premises (i.e. off-licence). The duration of an order must not be less than two months and not more than two years and be subject to the satisfactory completion of an approved course. The court can vary or discharge the order and a right of appeal lies to the Crown Court. Any breach of the order without reasonable excuse amounts to a summary offence punishable by way of a fine at level 4. The court cannot under s.11(4) impose a conditional discharge for a breach.

This is linked to other similar powers, such as those in s.15 which allows the Secretary of State to make regulations to give power to Local Authorities to create an "alcohol disorder zone" and charge a monthly levy on licensed premises within the zone. Under s.21 the police are given the power to apply to the licensing authority to review and take any necessary steps against the licence holder where in the opinion of the police the premises are associated with serious crime or disorder or both. Finally, s.23 creates a new summary offence of persistently selling alcohol to persons under 18 on three or more occasions with a maximum fine of £10,000. This creates strict liability in which the defendant must prove that they had reasonable grounds to believe the person to whom alcohol was sold was 18 or over. On conviction the court can order that the premises' licence be suspended for a period not exceeding three months. If there is sufficient evidence to secure a conviction under s.23, then the licensing authority can make a closure notice prohibiting the sale of alcohol for up to 48 hours.

Deportation Order

19.60 The court can, if the continued stay of the offender in UK is because of their offending behavour, not conducive to the public good order that they be deported to their country of origin (see *R. v Bennabas* [2005] EWCA Crim 2113).

Costs Order

19.61 If the defendant is acquitted, then dependant on how they funded their defence the court has a discretionary power to make a "defence costs order" under s.16 of the Prosecution of Offences Act 1985 for all or some of the defence costs to be paid out of central funds. Conversely, if the defendant is convicted, then the court can in the same way order that the prosecution costs be paid out of central funds under s.17, or under s.18 that the defendant pays such an amount to the prosecution as the court considers just and reasonable.

24. Procedure Followed at a Sentencing Hearing

19.62 The following is a basic and simple step by step guide to the procedural steps usually taken during the sentencing process:

Step 1 Adjournment for Pre-Sentence Report (PSR)

On conviction the court will proceed to sentence. First, the court will consider the need for PSR's. If so, the matter will be adjourned for the completion of such reports. The adjournment time for the submission of the report will depend on whether the defendant is in custody or not.

Step 2 Aggravating Factors and Antecedents

On return to court the prosecution will assist the court with what might be considered to be the aggravating factors in the case and refer the court to the defendant's antecedents of previous offending behaviour that may aggravate the current offence and also inform the court of any taken into consideration offences. The prosecution must not influence the actual sentence to be imposed, that is a matter for the judge, the prosecution's duty is simply to assist the court. Although in *R. v Pepper and Others* [2005] 1 Cr.App.R.(S) 20 the Court of Appeal stated that it is the duty of prosecution counsel where appropriate to draw to the court's attention to any relevant statutory provisions or sentencing guidelines which might assist the court.

Step 3: Plea in Mitigation

The defence advocate will now make a plea in mitigation, focusing the court's attention on the mitigating factors generally and on those identified in the PSR that reduce the seriousness of the offence. The defence advocate will, if the report is favourable, refer the court to those aspects of the PSR. Ultimately, the defence advocate is seeking to avoid the imposition of a custodial sentence. If, however, a custodial sentence is inevitable then, the defence will need to persuade the court to impose the shortest possible term for that offence.

Step 4: Judge imposes sentence

Usually the judge will retire and consider the sentence and then return to impose sentence, by making "sentencing remarks". In accordance with s.174 of the CJA 2003 the judge must state in open court and use ordinary language to explain the reasons for the sentence. Section 174(1)(b) and (2) provides a long and arduous list of what the judge must explain or comply with, dependant on the sentence to be imposed. This led Mitting J. to despair in *R. v HMP Drake Hall and Minister of State for Justice* [2008] EWHC 207, especially with regard to a legislative failure to make the law accessible in accordance with the Rule of Law, which was unacceptable.

Each case will be dependant on its own particular facts, but the judge will need to structure their sentencing remarks properly and explain how they reached the sentence to be imposed. Within their sentencing remarks the judge, in general, needs to:

(i) give close attention to the overall criminality/culpability based on the facts proved;

(ii) identify and give reasons for taking into account any aggravating factors;

(iii) where appropriate give credit for a guilty plea;

(iv) identify and take into account such mitigation as is available and so far as possible make allowance for it;

(v) make reference to and acknowledge any statutory criteria, provision, or sentencing guideline, or case authority;

(vi) the judge must also in accordance with s.174 of the CJA 2003 inform the offender of the length of time they will spend in custody, or the purpose and effect of a community order. In *R. v McNeill* [2008] EWCA Crim 553, the Court of Appeal observed that the judge's sentencing remarks were brief in the extreme and lacked the degree of detail necessary for a complicated sentencing case such as that over which he presided.

Chapter Twenty

APPEAL PROCEDURE

1. Introduction

20.01 The availability of an appeal procedure is fundamental to preserving confidence in the justice system by ensuring that any mistakes or errors in the lower court are corrected by the Appeal Courts. A practical problem is the time it can take for an appeal to be determined. Another point to be aware of are the jurisdictional differences between an appeal from the magistrates' court and that from the Crown Court. Further, the defendant may decide that they wish to appeal against either conviction on the grounds that it is unsafe or sentence on the grounds that it is wrong in law or manifestly excessive or both. In each case the defendant will become the appellant and must have sufficient grounds to justify the appeal and state these in the written grounds of appeal. Legal funding is available for legal representation on appeal, this will need to be granted by the Court of Appeal, if appealing from the Crown Court. A representation order will cover the funding of an appeal from the magistrates' court. Further the representation order will cover the funding for Counsel's advice on the prospects of an appeal from the Crown Court. Looking first at the magistrates' court and Youth Court, there are several possible routes of appeal:

(i) to the Crown Court;

(ii) to the High Court by case stated;

(iii) to the High Court on a judicial review challenge.

2. To the Crown Court "as of right" by Defence Only: Part 63 of the CrPR 2005

20.02 Section 108 of the Magistrates' Court Act 1980 gives a defendant an absolute right of appeal against conviction or sentence in the Crown Court. This means that the defendant does not need to first seek leave (permission) to appeal and can appeal regardless of the merits or strength of the grounds of appeal. In accordance with r.63.2 the defendant must first give notice of their intention to appeal to the magistrates' court and the CPS within the prescribed period of 21 days after the date of conviction and if different the date of sentence. The written notice must state the grounds of appeal (see draft example below). The appellant may at any time abandon the appeal by giving written notice to all parties. At the Crown Court the appeal is a full retrial taking evidence by examination and attendance of witnesses.

The appeal must be heard before a circuit judge or Recorder and two lay magistrates. The requirement of two lay magistrates can be dispensed with if it appears to the judge that it would cause unreasonable delay. The appeal can then be heard with just one lay magistrate. If the appeal is initially heard by two lay magistrates, the court can continue with hearing the appeal if one magistrate has withdrawn or is absent for any reason. Of importance, is that a lay magistrate is disqualified from hearing an appeal they adjudicated on in the magistrates' court. The Crown Court can allow or dismiss the appeal. If the appeal is against sentence then the court can only increase it to what the magistrates could have given. It is important to be aware that if the appeal is dismissed there is no further appeal to the Court of Appeal. The only possible appeal is to the High Court by way of judicial review on the grounds that the decision of the Crown Court was unlawful.

3. Draft Example of an Appeal Notice in the Magistrates' Court

20.03 IN THE FORREST CROWN COURT

BETWEEN

REGINA

-V-

JOHN SMITH APPLICANT

NOTICE OF APPEAL AGAINST CONVICTION AND SENTENCE

Take notice that the Applicant John Smith in accordance with s.108 of the Magistrates' Court Act 1980, intends to exercise his right to appeal to the Crown Court against conviction and sentence from Wayford Magistrates Court.

On 10 December 2007 the Wayford Magistrates after trial convicted the defendant of Theft and imposed a custodial sentence of 4 months.

The grounds of appeal against conviction are as follows:

(i) That the conviction is unsafe under s.1 of Criminal Appeal Act 1968.

(ii) That the stop and search performed by PC Brown was unlawful in that he failed to provided that required statutory information in accordance with s1 of the Police and Criminal Evidence Act 1984 and that therefore any evidence obtained in consequence should have been ruled inadmissible at trial as being prejudicial to the applicant to admit it.

The grounds of appeal against sentence are as follows:

(i) that the sentence of 4 months' imprisonment was in all the circumstances "manifestly excessive" in that that it was disproportionate to the culpability of the applicant and that the magistrates did not follow s.153 and impose the shortest possible sentence that is commensurate to the seriousness of the offence.

(ii) The magistrates failed to give sufficient weight to the mitigating factors.

(iii) That the magistrates failed to properly follow the sentencing guidelines contained in the judgment of the court of appeal in *R. v Page* [2005] 2 Cr.App.R.(S) 37

Signed. .... Date. ....

4. To the High Court "by way of case stated": Part 64 of the CrPR 2005

20.04 Under s.111 of the Magistrates' Court Act 1980, either the prosecution or the defence can challenge a decision of the magistrates' court on the ground that (i) it was wrong in law, or (ii) in excess of jurisdiction. The applicant must in writing identify the question or questions for the opinion of the High Court on the points of law or jurisdiction involved. If the particular question concerns a finding of fact by the magistrates that cannot be supported by the evidence, this must be stated in the application.

The application must be sent to the magistrates whose decision is being questioned. On receipt of the application the clerk must within 21 days send a draft case stated to the applicant and the respondent. The contents of the draft case must include a statement of facts found by the court, the question(s) of law or jurisdiction for the opinion of the High Court, or whether the finding of fact by the magistrates cannot be supported by the evidence. Within a further 21 days, both the applicant and respondent can make written representations which must be signed. The magistrates then consider whether or not there is sufficient merit in the application to state a case. If there is not, a certificate setting out the reasons must be served on the defence or prosecution, who can then apply directly to the High Court for an order compelling the magistrates to state a case. On giving its opinion the High Court can (i) reverse, (ii) affirm, or (iii) amend the magistrates' decision or remit the matter back to the magistrates with its opinion therein, or it may make any order it thinks fit, such as costs. A further appeal lies to the House of Lords under the Administration of Justice 1960, provided the High Court certifies that a point of law of general public importance is involved and leave is either granted by the High Court or directly from the House of Lords. It is important to note the decision in *R. v Rochford Justices Ex p. Buck* [1978] 68 Cr.App.R. 114 (see below at para.20.05) that the magistrates do not have jurisdiction to state a case until the proceedings are finalised. However, in *R. (Donnachie) v Cardiff Magistrates' Court* [2007] 1 W.L.R. 3085, the High Court ruled that a decision as to jurisdiction on a time limitation on the commencement of proceedings under the Trade Descriptions Act 1968 amounted to a preliminary decision which was final on that point and which could therefore properly be challenged by either case stated or judicial review. The Court also pointed out that a refusal to state a case can itself be challenged by judicial review.

A case stated appeal by the defendant on the grounds that the magistrates' decision was wrong in law is illustrated by *DPP v Rose* [2006] 2 Cr.App.R. 29 in which the defendant was found guilty at the magistrates' court after trial for the common law offence of committing an act of outraging public decency. The defendant had an act of oral sex performed on him in the foyer of a bank at 1 a.m. Unknown to the appellant this was recorded by 24 hour CCTV and the manageress in the morning witnessed the act on replaying the video. The defendant contended at trial that what he did could not have outraged public decency, the District Judge ruled that since he knew or ought to have known that his act would be a public nuisance, he had the mens rea for the offence, and the manageress was a sufficient witness to the act to satisfy the requirements of the offence.

The defendant appealed by way of case stated for the opinion of the High Court on the grounds that the District Judge was wrong in law to find that the one witness to the act satisfied the requirements of the offence. The High Court quashed the defendant's conviction and applied the previous authorities of *Watson* [1847] 2 Cox C.C. 376 and *Webb* [1848] 1 Den. 338 which confirmed that an essential element of the actus reus of the offence cosnsists of having to prove that more than one person either actually saw or could have seen the act complained of. In *R. v Hamilton* [2008] 1 Cr.App.R. 13 the Court of Appeal, having reviewed the previous authorities, stated that whilst the prosecution are required to prove the presence of two or more persons, it is not required to prove that they actually saw the lewd, obscene or disgusting act, only that it was capable of being seen. This is likely to be the subject of an appeal to the House of Lords for clarification on the elements of the offence.

Conversely, an appeal by case stated by the prosecution on the grounds that the decision of the magistrates was wrong in law can be seen in *DPP v Mullally* [2006] EWHC 3448, in which the DPP appealed by way of case stated against the decision of the magistrates to acquit the defendant of drink driving contrary to s.5 of the Road Traffic Act 1988 on the basis that the prosecution had failed to disprove the defence of duress. The High Court ruled that the magistrates were wrong in law to conclude that a defence of duress was available to the defendant (see Chapter nine para.9.16).

5. Challenge by "Judicial Review" to the Administrative Court in the High Court

20.05 Either the prosecution or the defence may apply under s.29 of the Supreme Court Act 1981 to the High Court for a judicial review hearing challenging the lawfulness of a decision, action, or failure of magistrates' court on one or more of three possible grounds: (i) illegality, (ii) irrationality and (iii) procedural irregularity. The usual claims that fall within the three main grounds, challenging the decision of a magistrates' court in this way are: (i) the court exceeds its power, (ii) commits an error of law, (iii) commits a breach of nature justice (bias), (iv) reaches a decision which no reasonable court could have reached, or (v) abuses its powers. In *R. v Highgate Justices Ex p. Riley* [1996] R.T.R. 150, the High Court quashed the defendant's conviction for driving whilst disqualified on the grounds that the chair of the bench, having intervened in the defence's cross-examination of a police witness and then saying that "it is not the practice to call police officers liars in this court", had displayed a real danger of bias.

It is important to note that this may not be the appropriate route to challenge a sentence that is manifestly excessive. The power to challenge a sentencing decision by the magistrates' is contained in s.43 of the Supreme Court Act 1981 but the court can only interfere with the sentence passed if it was in excess of jurisdiction, or wrong in law. In *R. v DPP Ex p. McGeary* [1999] 2 Cr.App.R.(S) 263, this was held to mean that there existed a:

> "departure of the sentencing court from the normal standards or levels of practice of sentencing must be so great as to constitute an excess of jurisdiction or an error of law."

If the Court is satisfied that the sentence was in excess of jurisdiction or wrong in law (a excessive sentence alone will not come within these two grounds), then the Court can amend it by substituting a sentence with one that magistrates had the power to impose. In *Allen v West Yorkshire Probation Service* [2001] 165 J.P. 313, the High Court observed that, unless there are clear and substantial reasons for pursuing the case stated or for taking judicial review route the appropriate and proper course in relation to a wrongful sentence is to appeal to the Crown Court.

The procedure to be followed is that set out in Pt 54 of the Civil Procedure Rules 2006. The question for the court is did the magistrates depart from the normal standards or levels of practice so as to constitute a error of law or an excess of jurisdiction? Permission must first be sought from the High Court, within three months, identifying that there is an arguable case. If the claimant shows on a balance of probabilities that one of the above grounds has occurred, then the Court can grant one of the following remedies, which are known as Prerogative Orders:

(i) *Mandatory Order*, which compels the magistrates' to whom this order is addressed to comply with the terms set out in the order.

(ii) *Quashing Order*, which directs the original decision to be abrogated and if necessary replaced with a new decision.

(iii) *Prohibiting Order*, this prevents the magistrates from performing or doing certain acts or making certain decision.

20.06 In *R. v Hereford Magistrates' Ex p. Rowlands* [1997] 2 W.L.R. 854, Bingham L.C.J. in the High Court on a challenge against the decision of the magistrates to refuse an adjournment ruled that the decision in *R. v Peterborough magistrates' Court Ex p. Dowler* [1997] 2 W.L.R. 843, was decided correctly on the facts. It was never authority to deny access to the judicial review procedure until having exhausted all alternative routes of appeal:

> "So to hold would be to emasculate the long-established supervisory jurisdiction of this court over magistrates' court which have over the years proved an invaluable guarantee of the integrity of proceedings in those courts."

However, his Lordship noted that:

> "the court should be respectful of the discretionary decisions of magistrates' court as of all other courts. This court should be slow to intervene, and should do so only where good (or arguably good) grounds for doing so are shown."

Nevertheless, in *R. v Rochford Justices Ex p. Buck* [1978] 68 Cr.App.R. 114, the High Court ruled, concerning its own jurisdiction, that the obligation of the High Court is not to interfere or consider any decision made by the lower court until the proceedings in the magistrates are concluded. Only then should an aggrieved party commence proceedings, preferably by way of case stated. In *Hillman v Richmond Magistrates' Court* [2004] EWCA Crim 751, the High Court, whilst disagreeing with Kennedy L.J. in *Hoar-Stevens v Richmond Magistrates' Court* [2003] EWHC 2660, that the decision in *Buck* is binding, agreed with the practicality of avoiding unnecessary delay since:

> "it would require some gross and extraordinary feature in the Magistrates, Court to justify this court interfering before the conclusion of the proceedings below."

An example of a judicial review challenge would be where one bench of magistrates gives the defendant an "unqualified promise" and therefore a legitimate expectation before adjourning for a pre-sentence report that they will be sentenced in the magistrates' court, but the defendant later appears before a different bench for sentence who then renege on that earlier promise and commit the defendant to the Crown Court for sentence. In such circumstances the decision would challengeable by way of judicial review (see *R. v Nottingham Magistrates' Court Ex p. Davison* [2000] 1 Cr.App.R.(S) 167. Another example is where that magistrates have either shown actual or perceived bias in their decision making, which gives rise to a breach of the rules of natural justice (see *R. v Gough* [1993] A.C. 646 and *Magill v Weeks* [2002] 2 W.L.R. 37).

6. Appeal Procedure from the Crown Court

20.07 There exist various routes of appeal from the Crown Court to either the Court of Appeal (Criminal Division) or the High Court. Some routes are exclusive to either the defence or the prosecution while others are available to both. We will consider each route of appeal separately. The statutory provisions relating to appeal procedure are found in the Criminal Appeal Act 1968 (CJA 1968) as amended by the Criminal Appeal Act 1995. As with the magistrates' court, both the prosecution and the defendant can under s.28 of the Supreme Court Act 1981, if the Crown Court by any order, judgment or other decision has acted in excess of jurisdiction or wrongly in law, request the Court to state a case for the opinion of the High Court.

In *Hardcastle v Chelmsford Crown Court* [2003] EWHC 3356, the High Court heard a judicial review application against the dismissal by the Crown Court of applicant's appeal against his speeding conviction in the magistrates' court. In refusing permission Thomas L.J. stated that the High Court could only intervene if it was established that the Crown Court had based its decision on an error of law or "some demonstrable lack of rationality". The Court cannot consider questions relating to weight of evidence or any matters of fact or degree, unless they are shown to be wrong in law or unreasonable.

There is also available the ability to challenge the lawfulness of a decision of the Crown Court by way of judicial review. In relation to challenging a sentencing decision s.43 of the Supreme Court Act 1981 applies in exactly the same way as with the magistrates' court. It is important to note the observation made by the High Court in *R. (White) v Crown Court at Blackfriars* [2008] EWHC 510 that the Court would be slow to entertain a judicial review application as an alternative to a case stated appeal owing to the applicant being time barred.

An interesting example of a case stated appeal from the Crown Court to the High Court is *DPP v Glendinning* [2005] EWHC 2333. The defendant was convicted in the magistrates' court of the offence of obstructing a police officer in the execution of his duty, when he was driving his lorry and waved in order to warn oncoming motorists in advance of a police speed gun. He appealed as of right to the Crown Court under s.108 of the MCA 1980 and at a re-hearing the Court allowed the appeal and quashed the defendant's conviction. The prosecution then appealed by way of case stated for the opinion of the High Court on a point of law. The High Court followed its previous decision in *Bastable v Little* [1907] 1 K.B. 59, and ruled that a motorist who warned other motorists in advance of a speed trap did not commit the offence of obstructing a police officer in the execution of his duty. A distinction exists between warning those who are not at the time committing any offence with a warning to those who are and who therefore desist from the act. The Court was not persuaded by the prosecution's argument that the later decision in *Green v Moore* was critical of the *Bastable* authority.

The procedure to be followed for a judicial review application against the decision of the Crown Court is the same as with the magistrates' court. However, this must be considered carefully, since s.29(3) of the Supreme Court Act 1981 provides that the High Court has no jurisdiction to make a quashing order in relation to the jurisdiction of the Crown Court in "matters relating to trial on indictment". The generally accepted purpose of this expression is avoid the consequences of satellite litigation (i.e. where there is a potential for a settled principle of law to needlessly generate supplementary cases that hover around it like a satellite orbiting a planet) and appeals which would unduly delay criminal proceedings causing chaos for the Crown Court in pending cases. In *R. v (CPS) Crown Court at Guildford* [2007] 1 W.L.R. 2886, the High Court rejected an application to review a decision as to the sentence imposed by the judge in the Crown Court. The judge had fallen into error and imposed an extended sentence on the defendant when he should have imposed an indeterminate sentence for the offence of rape. Lord Phillips, applying the decision of the House of Lords in *Re Smalley* [1985] A.C. 622, stated that if after conviction a judge in the Crown Court falls into error as to the extent of their jurisdictional powers of sentencing this is clearly a matter relating to trial on indictment and therefore the High Court has no power to review a decision on sentencing.

Given the lack of clarity on what is meant precisely by matters relating to trial on indictment and the different routes available to challenge the decision of the Crown Court, in the High Court, the Law Commission are currently reviewing the jurisdiction of the High Court in criminal proceedings (see Consultation Paper No.184) with a view to the possible streamlining of appeals to the Court of Appeal.

7. Appeal to the Court of Appeal (Criminal Division) Defence Only

20.08 A defendant, having appeared before the Crown Court, can under ss.1 and 2 of the Criminal Appeal Act 1968, as amended by the Criminal Appeal Act 1995, appeal to the Court of Appeal (Criminal Division) (provided there exist grounds on which to appeal):

(i) against conviction on the ground that it is "unsafe" under s.1 of the CAA 1995; and/or

(ii) against sentence under s.9 of the Criminal Appeal 1968 on either or both of the following grounds (i) it is wrong in law, (ii) it is manifestly excessive.

The procedure to be followed is set out in Pts 65 to 68 of the CrPR 2005 and Pt 2 of the Consolidated Criminal Practice Directions. The defendant must first obtain leave to appeal from a single judge by submitting within a period of 28 days the prescribed form attaching the grounds of appeal. These documents must in the first instance be sent to the Appeal Officer at the

Crown Court and not directly to the Court of Appeal. Within the prescribed form the appellant will need to apply for the Court of Appeal to grant legal funding and bail if relevant. Alternatively, the trial judge may within 28 days (added by s.47 and Sch.8 of the CJIA 2008) from the verdict or sentence issue a certificate under ss.11 and 12 of the Criminal Appeal Act 1968 that the case is fit for appeal, at the end of the proceedings in the Crown Court. Often, a defendant who may be in custody can have real difficulties in complying with the 28-day time limit. This is recognised in the Criminal Appeal Act 1968 which allows the defendant to apply for leave out of time and for the court to grant an extension of time to appeal (under r.65.4 of the CrPR the defendant must give reasons). This can be many years after the conviction, especially if fresh evidence comes to light. Usually, the single judge will consider both the extension of time and whether or not to grant leave. If the single judge refuses to grant leave, then the defendant can make a renewed application for leave to the full court. This means that the arguments for leave will be heard orally before three appeal judges, who can refuse or grant leave. Legal funding may not be available and if not, this does not breach art.6 (see *R. v Oates* [2002] EWCA Crim 1071).

The appeal procedure is subject to the same case management objectives as for any other case under the CrPR 2005, the appeal hearing itself must be held in public, unless the court orders otherwise. Rule 68.11 gives the appellant a right to be produced, if in custody, at the hearing, unless this is incidental to the main hearing. Rule 65.8 deals with the obtaining of transcriptions from the Crown Court and the preservation of any exhibits. If the appellant wishes to abandon all or part of the appeal, then a notice of abandonment must be sent to the Registrar.

One particularly important point to be aware of is that when advising a defendant on the possibility of an appeal it must be made plain to them that the Court of Appeal in s.29 of the CAA 1968 have a power to order that either all or part of the time spent in custody after sentence and up to the appeal will not count as a discount to their sentence. In *R. v Hart and Others* [2007] 1 Cr.App.R. 31, the Court of Appeal stated that if the application to appeal is totally without merit then the Court is more likely to exercise its discretion, especially if leave has been refused by the single judge, but an application is still made to the full court.

8. Meaning of Unsafe and Unfairness

20.09 Section 2(1) of the CAA 1968 provides that the only ground of appeal against conviction is that it is unsafe. If the Court of Appeal concludes that the conviction is unsafe, then the appeal against conviction must be allowed. The issue of safety may arise from procedural irregularities such as non-disclosure of evidence, material misdirection by the judge, witnesses later proven to have lied; or the defendant did not receive a fair trial, wrongful admission of evidence, a ruling of the judge on the legal meaning of a word or expression in an Act, or distinguishing a previous authority. The CCA

1968 deliberately provides no definition for the meaning of the word unsafe so as to avoid any prescriptive application. In *R. v CCRC Ex p. Pearson* [2000] 1 Cr.App.R. 141, Lord Bingham gave observed that while the word unsafe is a somewhat imprecise term, the issue of unsafety is obvious in cases:

(i) where it appears that someone other than the appellant committed the crime and the appellant did not, or

(ii) where the appellant has been convicted of an act that was not in law a crime, or

(iii) where the conviction is shown to be vitiated by serious unfairness in the conduct of the trial or by a significant misdirection.

Lord Bingham at the same time acknowledged that the issue of unsafety becomes much less obvious in other cases, in which the Court is not in any way persuaded of the appellant's innocence, but that there is (i) some lurking doubt, or (ii) uneasiness about whether an injustice has been done. Lord Bingham then pointed out that the role of the Court of Appeal in this situation is:

> "If on consideration of all the facts and the circumstances of the case before it, the court entertains real doubts whether the appellant was guilty of the offence, the court will consider the conviction to be unsafe. The court is only concerned with the safety of the conviction. A conviction can never be safe if there is doubt about guilt. However, the converse is not true. A conviction may be unsafe even where there is no doubt about guilt but the trial process has been "vitiated by serious unfairness or a significant legal misdirection."

In *R. v Chalkley and Jefferies* [1998] 2 All E.R. 155, the defendants pleaded guilty in consequence of the trial judge having ruled that taped recordings of conversations involving the defendants that had been obtained covertly by making a copy of the defendant's car key which had been seized, were admissible evidence. The two appellants then appealed against conviction on the ground that the tape recordings should have been excluded, in that it was highly prejudicial and unfair to admit them, given the manner in which they were obtained. The Court of Appeal rejected the appeal and applied a narrower test, stating that were there is a change of plea founded upon a ruling of the trial judge, then a conviction will only be unsafe where the effect of an incorrect ruling of law on admitted facts was to leave the accused with no legal escape from a verdict of guilty on those facts. In this instance a conviction was potentially deemed to be safe where as a result of a ruling by a judge on the admissibility of evidence they changed their plea to guilty in direct consequence of the ruling, their defence being rendered hopeless. The Court of Appeal will only interfere if the ruling of the judge was clearly wrong. The change of plea by the defendants was an acknowledgement by them of the truth of the facts constituting the offence.

Conversely, a wider approach to the Court's determination of unsafe was taken in *R. v Mullen* [1999] 2 Cr.App.R. 143, in which the appellant had been deported to this country without the proper recourse to extradition procedures. The appellant appealed on the ground that owing to the prosecution's abuse of process, no trial should have taken place. The Court of Appeal quashed the appellant's conviction as being unsafe because of the abuse of process. The unsafety of the appellant's conviction in this instance was not based on innocence, but for the very reason that the Court cannot uphold convictions that have been obtained by unlawful means employed by the prosecution which fundamentally abuse the criminal process. The Court of Appeal in *R. v Togher* [2001] 1 Cr.App.R. 457 preferred the wider approach adopted in *Mullen* to that taken in *Charkley and Jeffries*. Lord Woolf, who gave the leading speech, stated that fairness is not an "abstract concept" nor is it "concerned with technicalities", it is a principle of great importance. The general test is that if the defendant did not receive a fair trial, then the conviction is likely to be held unsafe. His Lordship stated:

> "if a defendant has not had a fair trial and as a result of that injustice has occurred, it would be extremely unsatisfactory if the powers of this court were not wide enough to rectify that injustice."

20.10 In *R. v Dundon* [2004] EWCA Crim 621, Rose L.J. provided some general assistance, stating that:

> "in every case the outcome depends on the kind of breach and the nature and quality of the evidence in the case. Just and proportionate satisfaction may, in an appropriate case, be provided, for example, by a declaration of breach or a reduction in sentence, rather than quashing of a conviction. Breach arising from delay may be such a consequence. (See *Attorney-General's Ref (No 2 of 2003)* [2004] 2 WLR 1). And there may be other exceptional cases in which a conviction may not be unsafe, for example if there has been unfairness because of a legal misdirection but the evidence is overwhelming (see *Lambert* [2002] 2 AC 545) or, possibly, if the trial is unfair because of inadequate prosecution disclosure on a peripheral issue but compelling evidence of guilt makes the conviction safe."

Ultimately, not every breach of Art.6, which gives a right to a fair trial, will lead to automatically a conviction being unsafe. Each case will depend on an assessment of the severity of the breach and any impact that it had on the fairness of the proceedings, taking into account public policy. In *R. v Craven* [2001] 2 Cr.App.R. 12, the appellant's conviction for murder of a young girl in a glassing attack in a night club was held to be safe. Although, a fingerprint on the weapon, which did not match that of the appellant, was not disclosed, there was other strong evidence to prove that he was the offender. Likewise, in *R. v Lewis* [2005] Crim. L.R. 796, the Court of Appeal refused to interfere with the safety of the appellant's conviction for counterfeiting offences. Although the ECHR had ruled that he did not receive a fair hearing due to entrapment, his conviction was still safe given that he had pleaded guilty and had admitted that he was tempted to commit the offences due to his financial difficulties.

A similar approach was taken when the High Court in *Dowsett v Criminal*

Cases Review Commission [2007] EWHC 1923 dismissed a challenge by the applicant to the decision of the CCRC refusing to refer his conviction back to the Court of Appeal. While the European Court of Human Rights had determined that non-disclosure of evidence by the prosecution violated his right to a fair trial the nature of the non-disclosed evidence did not impact on the safety of his conviction. In *R. v Dundon* [2004] EWCA Crim 621, the Court Martial Appeals Court quashed the appellant's conviction as unsafe in the light of the decision of the ECHR in *Grieves v UK*. The lack of an independent and impartial tribunal in the form of a Judge Advocate presiding over a Court Martial case, who at the same time was a serving officer, resulted in significant unfairness and in any subsequent conviction being unsafe (see also *Millar v Dickson* [2002] 1 W.L.R. 1615, and *R. v Spear* [2003] 1 A.C. 734). This led to Parliament passing the Naval Discipline Act 1957 (Remedial) Order 2004 (SI 2004/66) under s.10 of the Human Rights Act 1998 so as to rectify this incompatibility.

9. Material Irregularities and Unsafe Conviction

20.11 In *Randell v R.* [2002] 1 W.L.R. 2237 19, a Privy Council decision, Lord Bingham made the important observation that a breach of procedure does not in all instances result in a trial being unfair, especially if it is isolated and does not undermine the integrity of the trial process, by way of correction through relevant legal directions, such as warnings to the jury. It would damage confidence in the criminal process if an unrealistic and unattainable level of perfection was demanded. Nevertheless, the defendant is entitled to a fair trial and that his Lordship readily accepted:

> "there will come a point when the departure from good practice is so gross, or so persistent, or so prejudicial, or so irremediable that an appellate court will have no choice but to condemn a trial as unfair and quash a conviction as unsafe, however strong the grounds for believing the defendant to be guilty. The right to a fair trial is one to be enjoyed by the guilty as well as the innocent, for a defendant is presumed to be innocent until proved to be otherwise in a fairly conducted trial."

There is clearly a distinction to be drawn between new evidence which casts doubt on a conviction and a procedural flaw that taints the trial process and its effect on a conviction, otherwise obtained by strong evidence. In respect of the impact of a misdirection of the law or non-direction taken by the trial judge on the safety of a conviction obtained, the Court of Appeal in *R. v Williams* [2001] EWCA Crim 932, took the view that not every misdirection will automatically render a conviction unsafe. The misdirection must be significant in nature, if the misdirection or a breach of art.6 has an insignificant impact on the conviction, then it will be safe. Both common law and procedural fairness requirements are evolving concepts and irrespective of when the trial took place, the issue of fairness is assessed against current standards; as are any changes in the common law, even though these changes could not reasonably have been applied at the time. In *R. v Bentley*

[2001] 1 Cr.App.R. 307, the Court of Appeal posthumously allowed the appeal of Derek Bentley, who had been convicted on the murder of a police officer in a joint enterprise. The direction of the judge on the burden of proof was flawed, as was his direction suggesting that police witnesses are assumed to be accurate. Conversely, in *R. v Ellis* [2003] EWCA Crim 3556, the Court of Appeal dismissed the appeal against conviction for murder as the trial judge had applied the common law principles relating to provocation correctly.

Regardless of the evidence, a failure to adhere to due process can lead to a conviction being ruled unsafe. In *R. v Cordingley* [2007] EWCA Crim 2174, the Court of Appeal quashed the appellant's conviction for handling a stolen car radio. The trial judge had behaved inappropriately and to such an extent that Laws L.J. observed that the judge should be ashamed. The Court stated that every defendant is entitled to be treated fairly which includes courtesy and full regard for the presumption of innocence.

10. Developments in the Common Law Since Conviction

20.12 Difficult issues arise when the law was correct at the time of conviction is subsequently changed so that, which doubt is now cast on the conviction. Accordingly, if there is a development in the common law post conviction can the defendant now be allowed, regardless of lapse of time between the conviction and the development, be granted leave to appeal on the grounds of the change, in order to argue that their conviction in now unsafe? The problem that arises is the need for finality in criminal law, to avoid having to reconsider old convictions. There exists no problem with changes in the law made by statute, since an Act of Parliament, unless expressly stated, only takes effect when commenced formally by Parliament.

However, changes in the common law apply retrospectively, this is because judicial decisions form part of the "declaratory theory of the common law", which provides that the principle in the decision is a declaration of what the law is and has been since "time immemorial". This theory of the common law was discussed in some detail and received approval by the House of Lords in *Benson v Lincoln City Council* [1999] 2 A.C. 349 (see in particular the judgment of Lord Goff). The theory was also applied in the criminal law by the Court of Appeal in *R. v Bentley* [2001] 1 Cr.App.R. 307. Lord Bingham stated:

> "Where between conviction and appeal there have been significant changes in the common law (as opposed to changes affected by statute) or in standards of fairness, the approach indicated requires the court to apply legal rules and procedural criteria which were not and could not reasonably have been applied at the time."

Likewise, in *R. v Kansal* [2001] EWCA Crim 1260, Rose L.J. referring to this passage, stated:

> "Accordingly, an appellant, once the court by virtue of a reference, is entitled to have his conviction quashed as unsafe in the light of authoritive decisions since his trial."

Although his Lordship was less than enthusiastic, it was accepted that once a reference has been made by the CCRC, the Court of Appeal is obliged, regardless of the age of the conviction, to declare it unsafe if a change in the law now makes it unsafe. In *R. v Foster* [2007] EWCA Crim 2869 the Court of Appeal, despite the change in the law made by the House of Lords in *R. v Coutts* concerning the leaving of alternative verdicts, dismissed the appeal on the basis that the facts of the case came within the exception approved by their Lordships. It is clear that any proposition of law approved and stated in judicial decisions under the declaratory theory, has retrospective effect. This has led to an unhappy relationship between the CCRC and the Court of Appeal (see para.20.18 below). As a consequence of this s.42 of the Criminal Justice and Immigration 2008, when brought into force; gives the Court of Appeal a discretionary power to disregard any developments in the law since the date of conviction, provided that it is appropriate to do so in all the circumstances of the case.

11. Reception of Fresh Evidence, the "Jury Impact" Test and Unsafe Convictions

20.13 When considering an appeal against conviction and or sentence, s.23(2) of the Criminal Appeal Act 1968 gives the Court of Appeal a discretionary power to receive new evidence, if the Court thinks it is necessary or expedient in the interests of justice. In deciding whether or not to receive this evidence, the Court must have regard to:

(i) does it appear credible and would it have been admissible at trial?

(ii) does it appear to afford any ground for allowing the appeal?

(iii) does there exist a reasonable explanation for failure to adduce it at the original trial?

The Court has a power to order the production of any document, exhibit or other thing connected to the proceedings and which appears to the Court to be necessary for the determination of the appeal. Further the Court can; when s.47 and para.10 of Sch.8 of the CJIA 2008 is in force, order that such information be produced to the Court, appellant or respondent. The Court can order any witness to attend for examination whether or not they were a witness in the original trial and receive the evidence of that witness.

The House of Lords in *R. v Pendleton* [2002] 1 W.L.R. 73 set out the approach to be adopted by the Court of Appeal when exercising the power on whether to accept or reject fresh evidence and if accepted its impact of the safety of a conviction. Lord Bingham approved the previous test stated in

Stafford v DPP [1974] A.C. 878 and made it plain that the Court of Appeal should not encroach upon the task of the jury, who unlike the appeal court, had the opportunity to test and evaluate the witness evidence. The Court will need to assess the new fresh evidence but it is at a clear disadvantage, given its inability to relate this new material to the rest of the evidence. His Lordship observed:

> "for these reasons it will usually be wise for the Court of Appeal, in the case of any difficulty, to test their own provisional view by asking whether the evidence, if given at the trial, might reasonably have affected the decision of the trial jury to convict. If it might, the conviction must be thought to be unsafe."

The test adopted by Lord Bingham was approved by Lord Brown in *Dial and Another v State of Trinidad and Tobago* [2005] 1 W.L.R. 1660, (see paras 31 and 32 of the judgment). The Court of Appeal in *R. v Neaven* [2006] EWCA Crim 955, having reviewed the authorities on diminished responsibility and provocation, outlined the relevant guidance to be followed in deciding whether or not to receive fresh evidence. The Court observed that a defendant must advance their defences at trial and that the Court will treat will real scepticism any tactical decision not to run a defence to be used later on appeal. Only in exceptional cases will it be in the interests of justice to admit and give effect to fresh evidence relating to diminished responsibility which was not relied upon at court and where the defendant does not object to it.

However, each case must be viewed against its own facts and that if the new evidence of mental illness or substantial impairment is clear and undisputed, then it may be in the interests of justice to admit it. If the fresh evidence of diminished responsibility is revealed post conviction, then this is of little weight, unless there is unanimity in the new expert evidence as to the existence at the time of the offence of the elements of the defence. In *R. v Martin* [2002] 1 Cr.App.R. 27, (Norfolk Farmer Case) the Court of Appeal received new credible psychiatric evidence that was not available at trial and quashed the appellant's conviction for murder and substituted one of manslaughter by way of diminished responsibility.

20.14 In contrast, the Court of Appeal in *R. v Andrews* [2003] EWCA Crim 2750 refused to admit additional psychiatric evidence obtained post conviction of previous child abuse suffered by the appellant, which if it had been available at trial, it was contended, would have strengthened the defence of diminished responsibility, which the jury may have accepted. The Court, in confirming the murder conviction, stated that as with almost every criminal case, the defendant was given a fair and proper opportunity to advance any defence at trial and should not generally be allowed to advance new evidence on appeal, which should and could have been advanced at trial, for tactical reasons. If fresh evidence is admitted, then the court is required the assess the value and quality of the fresh evidence and consider what impact, if any, that new evidence would have had on the jury, had they been aware of it.

In *R. v Hakala* [2002] EWCA Crim 730, Judge L.J., having referred to

Pendleton, made the interesting point that fresh evidence may have the opposite effect and:

> "serve to confirm rather than undermine the safety of the conviction." [Whilst the court must evaluate the fresh evidence], "the essential question, and ultimately the only question for this court, is whether, in the light of the fresh evidence, the convictions are unsafe."

The Court of Appeal took a similar approach in *R. v Hanratty* [2002] EWCA Crim 1141, when allowing and considering new DNA evidence under s.23 presented by the prosecution which proved that the appellant's conviction for an appalling murder in 1961 was safe.

On the other hand, in *R. v Maloney* [2003] EWCA Crim 1373, the Court of Appeal refused to receive new evidence in the form of an expert witness in an accident investigation as adding nothing to the jury's task of considering the plausibility of the appellant's claim that he had accidently ran over his wife when entering the driveway of the family home (see also the judgment in the appeal of Barry George and the difficulties with the Firearms Discharge Residue evidence, *R. v George* [2007] EWCA Crim 2722).

12. Ordering a Retrial or Substitution of an Alternative Offence

20.15 If the Court of Appeal quashes the conviction, then the Court can, if it is in the interests of justice under s.7 of the CAA 1968, order that the appellant is to be retried for the offence of which they where convicted at the original trial, or an offence to which they could have been convicted in the alternative to the original offence. Section 8 of the CAA 1968 provides that if a retrial is ordered, then a fresh indictment must be preferred by direction of the Court of Appeal. Further, the defendant must be arraigned (i.e. enter a plea) within two months of the date of the retrial order. If not, then the prosecution cannot proceed without leave of the Court of Appeal. Should the defendant be convicted after a retrial then s.8(4) and Sch.2 provide that the new sentence must not be of greater severity than that passed on the original conviction and that the sentence is deemed to begin to run from the date of the original sentence (in terms of sentence the defendant will be no better or no worse off).

Under s.4, as amended by s.47 and Sch.8 of the CJIA 2008 when in force, if the Court of Appeal partially allow an appeal against conviction, on some counts in the indictment but not others, then the Court has a discretionary power to re-sentence the appellant for the "related offences" of which they remain convicted as the Court thinks proper. This is to ensure that the remaining culpability of the defendant is reflected properly in the sentence. A related offence means one for which they were sentenced on the same day as the other offences, or sentences passed on different days but treated as substantially one sentence, or which form counts in the same indictment. These amendments are to ensure that if the Court allows an appeal against an indeterminate sentence, the defendant's overall culpability is reflected properly in the remaining determinate sentence.

Likewise, if the defendant is a young offender, but in the meantime crosses the age threshold the Court is limited to imposing a sentence as if they were still a young offender. The purpose of these provisions is plain, they are designed to ensure that a defendant has their conviction or sentence reviewed on appeal, but if this fails they should not be punished by having an heavier sentence imposed. In *Attorney-General's Reference (No.82a of 2000)* [2002] EWCA Crim 215, the Court of Appeal ruled that it was not the intention of Parliament to allow the Attorney-General to refer the sentence received at a second trial, if that would result in a sentence of greater severity than the first, the only possible way is for the Attorney-General to make the unduly lenient sentence reference before the appeal is heard and if increased under s.36 of the CJA 1988, and the conviction subsequently quashed, this would raise the sentence cap if convicted after the retrial. If the Court of Appeal decides to order a retrial, then a decision on bail will need to be made.

If the Court of Appeal decides that it is not in the interests of justice to order a retrial, then under s.3 of the CCA 1968 the Court has a discretionary power to substitute an alternative offence provided the jury could on the facts have convicted for the alternative offence. For instance, where the appellant is convicted of a s.18 wounding with intent, but this is then quashed due to a misdirection on the mens rea of intention, the Appeal Court could substitute a s.20 conviction based on the fact that the jury must have found them guilty of reckless wounding. If the Court substitutes an alternative offence, then it must impose a sentence based on the appellant's culpability for that offence.

13. Appeal from the Court of Appeal (Criminal Division) to the House of Lords (Supreme Court)

20.16 On determination of the appeal by the Court of Appeal, either the defence or the prosecution can, under s.33 of the CCA 1968, appeal to the House of Lords, subject to leave being granted by either the Court of Appeal or the House of Lords and the Court of Appeal has certified that there is a point of law of general public importance. The statutory time limits for making an application are set out clearly in s.34, as amended by the Courts Act 2003, which provides that this must be done first to the Court of Appeal within 28 days from the "relevant date". (date of decision or reasons, if different). Should this be refused, then under s.2 of the Administration of Justice Act 1960 application is made to the House of Lords for leave to appeal within the period of 28 days beginning with the date on which the application to the Court of Appeal was refused (prior to April 1, 2005 the time limit was 14 days, but s.88 of the Courts Act 2003 changed this to 28 days).

Often, the defendant, who may be in custody, can have real difficulties in complying with the 28-day time limit. This is recognised in s.33(2), which allows, on application by the defendant only, for an extension of time. The prosecution does not have this luxury and the time limits will be applied strictly, as can be seen in *R. v Weir* [2001] W.L.R. 421, when the House of Lords refused to grant leave to appeal to the DPP who had lodged the application a day late. The Court is powerless to act once the time limit has expired for the prosecution, even if the prosecution first apply within the time limit but then later abandon the appeal, as occurred in *R. v Palmer* [2002] EWCA Crim 2675. In such circumstances only if the abandonment is declared a nullity, in accordance with the principle in *R. v Medway* [1976] 62 Cr.App.R. 85, will the Court of Appeal consider certification. For the defence, the extension is indefinite.

If the prosecution is appealing against the ruling of the Court of Appeal quashing the appellant's conviction, the Court has a discretion under s.37 to order that the defendant remains in custody or be released on bail. However, s.47 and para.13 of Sch.8 of the CJIA 2008 amend s.37 by removing the Court's discretion, and providing that the Court must make an order detaining the defendant, or grant bail, or release without bail but only if the Court thinks it is in the interests of justice to do so given the likely outcome of the appeal.

14. Appeals Available Exclusively to the Prosecution

20.17 The prosecution has two exclusive appeal options open to them from the Crown Court. Their availability is very much dependant on the circumstances. Strictly speaking, these are not appeals in the normal sense, they are reviews of either an unduly lenient sentence or a ruling of a judge on a point of law that resulted in the acquittal of the defendant.

15. Review of Unduly Lenient Sentence

20.18 Sections 35 and 36 of the Criminal Justice Act 1988 allow the Attorney-General to refer an "unduly lenient" sentence imposed at the Crown Court for an indictable only offence, or an offence specified by statutory instrument (see the CJA 1988 (Reviews of Sentencing) order 1994 (SI 1994/119, 2006/1116). The Court of Appeal will review the sentence with regard to current sentencing guidelines and the aggravating and mitigating factors. The Court of Appeal can, at its discretion, quash the original sentence and instead pass a sentence that it in all the circumstances of the case thinks appropriate after giving a discount on account of "double jeopardy" (i.e. that the offender is effectively being sentenced twice). The power to increase an unduly lenient sentence was as a direct result of the appalling acts committed in the Ealing Vicarage Rape case and the public abhorrence of the sentences imposed in that case.

Shortly after the power came into effect on February 1, 1989 the then Lord Chief Justice, Lord Lane, felt it necessary in *Attorney-General's*

Reference (No.4 of 1989) [1989] 11 Cr.App.R.(S) 517 to clarify the proper approach to be adopted in dealing with a s.36 reference. First, the purpose of the provision was never meant to deal with a sentence of mere leniency. For a sentence to be treated as being manifestly lenient it must, according to his Lordship, be one that fell "outside the range of sentences which the judge, applying his mind to all the relevant factors, could reasonably consider appropriate", bearing in mind the relevant sentencing guideline authorities. His Lordship further noted that s.36 provides the Court with a discretionary power and one which the Court can refuse to exercise, even if it considered the sentence to be one that should be increased but justifiable circumstances now existed to suggest otherwise.

Similarly, should the Court grant leave for a reference, there is at the same time no restriction, in his Lordship's view, on the Court's power to decrease a sentence. These safeguards against an unwarranted departure from a sentence imposed were outlined in *Attorney-General's Reference (No.14 of 2003); Sheppard* [2003] EWCA Crim 1459, when Kay L.J. noted that the Attorney-General himself has a discretion having considered all the circumstances, whether or not refer a sentence that they believe to be unduly lenient, and that the Court has a discretionary power as to whether or not to grant leave, which is not to be assumed as being granted automatically.

It is important to be aware that if the Court of Appeal accepts that the sentence is unduly lenient, then when determining whether or not to increase the sentence the practice of the Court, as confirmed in *Attorney–General's Reference (Nos 14 and 15 of 2006) (French and Webster)* [2006] EWCA Crim 1335, is to take into account the principle of "double jeopardy" which requires the Court to have regard to the fact that the procedure will subject the defendant to some degree of distress and anxiety in having to be sentenced twice and that this should be reflected in some discount from the sentence that would have otherwise been imposed. The discount is typically between 12 per cent and 30 per cent. In the *French and Webster* reference, the Court of Appeal rejected the contention made by the Attorney-General that the double jeopardy rule should not be considered in a case where the defendant was sentenced to a long term of imprisonment but which still did not reflect the gravity of the offence. Lord Philips, in response; stated "so to hold would constitute an unwarranted interference with the discretion of the court when determining a sentence".

Nevertheless his Lordship did accept:

> "that in such circumstances the principle is of limited application and that there will be occasions where a judge can properly decline to make any discount for double jeopardy."

Section 272 of the CJA 2003 inserts a new subsection (3A) in s.36 and prohibits the Court of Appeal expressly from making any allowance for double jeopardy where the Court is reviewing the minimum term set by the judge to be served for the life sentence for murder under s.269. This restriction does not apply to discretionary life sentences and in *French and*

Webster Lord Philips observed that Parliament has left it open to the Court to decide on whether or not to allow some reduction for double jeopardy in any review of a minimum term set for a discretionary life sentence, and that this will very much depend on the individual circumstances of the case. Nevertheless, the concession should not be of an amount which would cancel out the increased part of the total sentence. Section 46 of the Criminal Justice and Immigration Act 2008, when in force, will reverse the decision in *French and Webster* and prevent the Court of Appeal from taking into account double jeopardy when reviewing any indeterminate sentence (life sentence or imprisonment for public protection and the equivalent detention provisions for offenders under 21) as being unduly lenient.

16. Review of Point of Law Ruling

20.19 If a defendant is acquitted on the direction of the judge in consequence of a legal ruling as to a point of law, this would set a precedent and prevent further prosecutions without having the point of law considered by the Appeal Court (see now s.58 of the CJA 2003). Section 36 of the Criminal Justice Act 1972 allows the Attorney-General to refer a case to the Court of Appeal for the Court's opinion on the correctness of the ruling which led to the defendant's acquittal. In *Attorney-General's Reference (No.3 of 1994)* [1997] 3 W.L.R. 421 the Attorney-General asked for the House of Lords' opinion on whether in law a foetus was an integral part of the mother or a separate entity and, if a separate entity, could the doctrine of "transferred malice" apply. A further exclusive power of appeal in respect of the prosecution is also found under s.14A(5A) of the Football Spectators Act 1989.

17. Prosecution Appeal Procedure

20.20 The procedure to be followed in respect of an unduly lenient sentence or an opinion on a point of law is contained in Pt 70 of the CrPR 2005. This provides that if the Attorney-General intends to seek permission to make a reference concerning an unduly lenient sentence this must be done by giving notice to the Registrar within 28 days from the date of sentence. Rule 70.3 requires the Attorney-General in either reference to state the grounds and indicate the opinion that is being sought concerning a point of law or why the sentence is unduly lenient, together with relevant authorities and a summary of the facts. The Registrar must then serve on the defendant a notice of the Attorney-General's application, who may serve in response a "Respondent's Notice" and must do so, if intending to make representations before the Court. This must be served on the Court and the Attorney-General within 28 days of receiving notice in respect of a point of law and 14 days, if a reference concerning sentence. The notice must set out the defendant's arguments in opposition to those of the Attorney-General. Of importance is r.70.8 which, in regard to a point of law referral, is the preservation of the defendant's anonymity during those proceedings, unless the defendant gives permission.

18. The Criminal Cases Review Commission (CCRC)

20.21 A number of well-publicised and appalling miscarriages of justice that occurred during the 1970s and 1980s led to the creation of a Royal Commission on Criminal Justice. One of the recommendations made was to remove the exclusive power of the Home Secretary to refer cases back to the Court of Appeal and place this responsibility with an independent body, now in the form of the CCRC created by the CAA 1995. The CCRC is based in Birmingham and is composed of appointed Commissioners and case workers who have the responsibility to investigate and determine any application where it is claimed that either the conviction or sentence is wrong. Section 9 of the CAA 1995 gives the CCRC a discretionary power to refer either the conviction or sentence to the Court of Appeal, subject to the conditions contained in s.13. This provision provides that the CCRC shall not make a reference to the Court of Appeal unless there is a real possibility that the conviction or sentence would not be upheld were the reference to be made. The meaning of real possibility and the proper approach to this test is now well established by *R. v CCRC Ex p. Pearson* [2000] 1 Cr.App.R. 141, where Lord Bingham stated that the test is whether there:

> "is more than an outside chance or a bare possibility but which may be less than a probability or a likelihood or a racing certainty. The Commission must judge that there is a least a reasonable prospect of a conviction, if referred, not being upheld."

It is important to note that the decision on whether or not to refer is that of the Commission alone, based on its judgment of the evidence or legal developments. The Commission will not entertain an application unless the defendant has appealed previously and the appeal was dismissed or leave was refused and only if there are new legal arguments or fresh evidence. If these criteria are not met then only in exceptional circumstances will the Commission consider an application. When the Commission receives an application, it is first reviewed by a Commissioner who will determine whether the above criteria are met and publish a preliminary statement of reasons. If there is merit in the application, then priority is given to those in custody. The case is allocated initially to a case worker, dependant on complexity, who will undertake the initial steps of information gathering.

The case is then allocated to a case review manager who will draft a statement of reasons which is then placed before three Commissioners who make the decision on whether or not to refer the case. Even if the Commission is satisfied that there exists a real possibility, it may still decline to exercise its discretion to refer. If the Commission decides to refer, then the Court of Appeal must consider the appeal based only on the grounds as outlined in the statement of reasons. Section 315 of the CJA 2003 amends s.14 of the CAA 1995 and limits the grounds of appeal to those that are related to any reason given by the Commission. This means that the defendant cannot raise any new unrelated grounds and overturns the decision in *R. v Smith* [2003] Crim. L.R. 398.

In *R. v Siddall & Brooke* [2006] EWCA Crim 1353, the Court of Appeal stated that a referral from the CCRC should be listed to be heard within six months, unless there was good reason not to do so. Further, a timetable should be adopted for the presentation and pagination of documents; any breach of the timetable or delay could be punished by a wasted costs order. Recently, in *Cottrell and Fletcher* [2007] EWCA Crim 2016, the Court of Appeal reviewed the approach that should be taken in change of law referral cases. The Court of Appeal emphasised that when the CCRC is considering making a referral of a conviction based on a subsequent change in the law which makes the conviction unsafe, it should not ignore the policy approach of the Court of Appeal, if it was determining whether or not to allow an extension of time to appeal. This policy is set out in the judgment of the Court of Appeal in *R. v Ramzan* [2007] 1 Cr.App.R. 150, as being:

> "the very well established practice of this court, in a case where the conviction was entirely proper under the law as it stood at the time of trial, to grant leave to appeal against conviction out of time only where substantial injustice would otherwise be done to the defendant."

This means that the defendant must signify something more than just the change or development in the law.

Part III

CRIMINAL EVIDENCE

Chapter Twenty One

INTRODUCTION TO CRIMINAL EVIDENCE AND PROOF

1. Introduction to Criminal Evidence

21.01 On the alleged commission of an offence, the police have a duty to investigate the factual circumstances and gather all the available evidence in whatever form. This may be documentary, scientific, witness statements, video, visual, background of parties involved, motive, or whether there is a pattern to this and any other offence. All the evidence gathered by the police will be processed into an MG file of evidence and passed to the CPS. The CPS will then assess the evidence against the code for Crown prosecutors. This is a continuing assessment, since it is usual during the course of criminal proceedings for "additional" evidence to become available. When assessing the evidence disclosed, a useful starting point, which ought to be applied to that evidence on a continual basis, is to consider whether that evidence is:

Relevant

21.02 Does the evidence in whatever form prove or disprove an essential element to the offence? Accordingly, before evidence can be adduced at trial it must be relevant to an issue in the case, namely a definitional part of the offence, or as stated by Lord Steyn in *R. v A* [2001] 2 W.L.R. 1546:

> "relevance and sufficiency of proof are different things. The fact that the accused a week before an alleged murder threatened to kill the deceased does not prove intent to kill on the day in question. But it is logically relevant to that issue. After all, to be relevant the evidence need merely have some tendency in logic and common sense to advance the proposition in issue."

If the evidence is significantly remote to the material aspects of the case, then it is potentially irrelevant and inadmissible. Ultimately the question is one of degree as to the usefulness of the evidence in terms of proof of a fact in issue, or as to what bearing it would have on proving that fact. If the evidence has probative value, then the question of relevance is less difficult to determine.

On the other hand, if it has only a marginal significance, then the need to strike a fair balance is all the more important.

Admissible

21.03 If the evidence is irrelevant then it is also inadmissible. If the evidence is relevant, then the question is whether it ought to be admitted in the trial. Since the Criminal Justice Act 2003 and sweeping changes to the reception of bad character/hearsay evidence, the general rule has now shifted from that of an exclusionary principle to an inclusive one. This means that the general test the court applies is to admit the evidence, unless the prejudicial effect of that evidence so outweighs its probative value in terms of proof that it ought not to be admitted. This test requires the court to strike a fair balance, ensuring that the defendant's right to a fair trial is not endangered and that the presumption of innocence is maintained. This can often be a difficult and sensitive decision, which is well illustrated by the admissibility of previous sexual behaviour.

Whilst art.6 guarantees an absolute right to a fair trial, there is no express qualification concerning the admissibility of evidence at trial and therefore the European Court in *Schenk v Switzerland* [1988] 13 E.H.R.R. 242 held that the rules governing the reception of evidence are "primarily a matter of regulation under national law".

Probative Value or Weight

21.04 If the evidence is both relevant and admissible, the final analysis is to consider its strength and support of the case. This raises questions in respect of both its credibility and reliability in terms of honesty and accuracy. Can the evidence be impugned, does the evidence simply diminish credibility or does it also show through the lack of credibility guilt as an issue in the case? In *R. v Boardman* [1975] A.C. 421 Lord Hailsham commented generally that:

> "It is helpful to remind oneself that what is not to be admitted is a *chain of reasoning* and not necessarily a state of facts. If the inadmissible chain of reason is the only purpose for which the evidence is adduced as a matter of law, the evidence itself is not admissible. If there is some other relevant, probative purpose, than for the forbidden type of reasoning, the evidence is admitted, but should be made subject to a warning from the judge that the jury must eschew the forbidden reasoning."

What is meant by the forbidden chain of reasoning is that if the evidence, i.e. previous misconduct, is adduced at trial it may influence the jury not to assess the quality of the factual evidence but reason instead that if the defendant has done something similar in the past, then they must have committed the current alleged offence.

2. Burden of Proof: A General Rule

21.05 Enshrined both in the common law and art.6(2) of the European Convention on Human Rights is the presumption of innocence. This is a legal presumption, the rebuttal of which, as a burden, is placed upon the prosecution. In *Woolmington v DPP* [1935] A.C. 462, Lord Sankey encapulated the fundamental importance of this principle in the following well-rehearsed statement:

> "Throughout the web of English criminal law one golden thread is always to be seen, that it is the duty of the Prosecution to prove the prisoner's guilt subject to what I have already said as to the defence of insanity and subject to any statutory exception."

The operation of this principle was well illustrated in *Kingsnorth v DPP* [2003] EWHC 768, an appeal by way of case stated concerning the proof of one of the ingredients of the offence of driving whilst disqualified (s.103 (1)(b) of the Road Traffic Act 1988). The issue focused on whether it could be proved that the defendant was, at the relevant time of driving, a disqualified driver. The Divisional Court ruled that a magistrates' court cannot, if the prosecution fail to adduce the material evidence, consult their own computorised records in order to satisfy themselves that the essential element of disqualification to the offence is proved. Mitchell J. stated:

> "First and foremost, it is the prosecution's responsibility, and no one else's, to provide prima facie evidence of each ingredient of the offence it is alleged a defendant committed. It is the duty of the court in the event of a submission of no case being made to decide whether there is prima facie evidence to each ingredient of the offence. If there is not, ordinarily it will dismiss the case."

3. Proving all Elements of the Offence: Brown Direction

21.06 Whatever offence(s) the prosecution allege, then as outlined in *More* [1988] 86 Cr.App.R. 234, it is their duty to prove all the necessary ingredients to that offence(s) as set out in the indictment or summons. The prosecution need to make it clear from the outset which factual basis they intend to rely on in order to present their case before the jury, so that in the alternative, the defence can build their case to challenge those facts. But where in relation to a single count there are various pieces of factual evidence to prove a particular ingredient to the offence, then the trial judge will need to consider whether to give a "Brown Direction", derived from *R. v Brown* [1984] 79 Cr.App.R. 115. This requires the judge to direct the jury that they must all be agreed, .i.e. unanimous upon same factual evidence for which they find the ingredient of the offence proven.

Otherwise, it is possible that some jurors will rely on one piece of evidence, while others may rely on a separate piece of evidence but all agree the ingredient to be proved. For example a s.18 GBH offence can be committed either by wounding or causing. The prosecution will need to specify what ingredient they are relying on, it must be proved that the defendant did an act which caused GBH with the necessary intent. If this arises in a pub brawl, then the defendant may have used weapons, his fists, kicking, head butting or glassing.

If the prosecution present their case so that any one of these caused the serious injury, then the jury may need to be directed that all of them must be agreed on which fact caused the injury. If they are not, the verdict is not guilty. Similar problems can occur with public order offences, where there are a series of incidents with short interludes and the jury have to decide which incident proves the offence.

Each case will depend on its own individual facts, but the judge must be conscious not to unnecessarily over burden the task of the jury (see *R. v Mitchell* [1994] Crim.L.R. 66 and *R. v Carr* [2000] 2 Cr.App.R. 149, where the Court of Appeal quashed the appellant's conviction for manslaughter on the basis that a Brown Direction wasn't given in regard to the two separate factual issues of whether it was a kick or a punch that delivered the blow that caused the death. These were two separate forms of assault to which the defendant had raised separate defences).

Nevertheless, as ruled in *R. v Giannetto* [1997] 1 Cr.App.R. 1, if a number of defendants are charged as a joint enterprise or as a principal or accessory, then a Brown Direction is unnecessary, since whilst there are different ingredients to be proved, whether it be as the principal or accessory they are equally liable for the same offence, even though it was committed in different ways.

4. Classification of the Burden of Proof

21.07 Having established that the burden of proof rests with the prosecution, the question then arises as to what the extent of the burden is and in what circumstances if at all it can be passed partly or wholly to the defence. The burden of proof for this purpose is often classified in one of two categories, as follows:

The Legal Burden on the Prosecution

21.08 This is where the law requires or places an obligation on a party (in criminal cases the prosecution) to prove its case by adducing before the tribunal of fact admissible evidence in order to satisfy all the required ingredients of the offence alleged. The defence, in turn, can take issue with any of the facts presented by the prosecution.

The Persuasive (Legal) Burden and Raising a Defence

21.09 A persuasive burden effectively reverses or removes the burden of proof from the prosecution by transferring it to the defendant. In these circumstances, the defendant is now required to adduce evidence to prove on a balance of probabilities (standard of proof to be reached) a particular fact that is essential in determining their innocence or a defence to the offence. Conversely, an evidential burden seeks only to place upon the defendant the need to adduce sufficient evidence in defence to the alleged offence. This is uncontroversial and is not a burden in the strict sense. The starting point is that the prosecution bring the case. It is for them to rebut the presumption of innocence. The defendant is not legally compelled to answer police questions or give or bring evidence to court.

The defendant, if they wish, can put the prosecution to strict proof of the ingredients to the offence, "you bring the case you prove it". This becomes more of a tactical and pragmatic decision. Whilst the defendant is entitled to remain silent throughout, they are also vulnerable to inferences being drawn, lack of secondary disclosure by the prosecution and the jury forging a forbidden chain of reasoning. If the defendant takes issue with the factual evidence of the prosecution, then they may if they wish present evidence to conflict with and/or cast doubt on the evidence raised by the prosecution. If this is a burden at all, then it is one that simply requires the defendant to raise evidence in their defence (see para.1 of Lord Bingham's judgment in *DPP v Shaldrake* [2004] UKHL 43). In respect of only an evidential burden being placed on the defendant, clear examples can be found when raising the defences of self-defence, provocation and duress. It is for the prosecution to prove beyond doubt that the defence does not arise on the facts.

5. Exceptions to the General Rule

21.10 As stated earlier, the general rule is that the burden of proof rests firmly with the prosecution, subject to the defence of insanity and subject to any statutory exception. In the case of insanity, the legal burden is affected by the presumption of sanity as ruled in the *M'Naghten* case (see also the judgment of Viscount Kilmuir in *Bratty v Att.-Gen. of Northern Ireland* [1963] A.C. 386 at 407). It is for the defendant on a balance of probabilities to rebut the presumption, by adducing evidence to satisfy the legal ingredients of insanity.

6. Statutory Exceptions: Reverse Burden of Proof Cases

21.11 As illustrated in Chapter Two, the courts will apply the presumption of mens rea to all criminal offences, unless Parliament has chosen either expressly, or through necessary implication to exclude it (see the discussion of *B v DPP* [2000] 2 W.L.R. 452 in Chapter Two at para.2.44). Whilst the court will show deferrence to the will of Parliament, Parliament should not legislate outside its discretionary area of judgment (Parliament is able to work within a margin of appreciation to make reasonable adjustments to the law) and if it does by breaching the right to a fair trial, the court will interfere to correct this unfairness by utilising the principle of legality as a rule of statutory construction within s.3 of the Human Rights Act 1998.

The principle of legality was explained by Lord Hoffmann in *R. v Home Secretary Ex p. Simms* [2000] 3 W.L.R. 328 as meaning that "Parliament must squarely confront what is it doing and accept the political cost", if a statutory provision interferes unjustifiably with a basic human right (see also *R. v Hunt* [1987] 1 A.C. 352). This clear conflict has received great attention in terms of whether Parliament has not only placed a burden on the defendant, but whether, when Parliament chooses expressions such as "the defendant must prove, or most show", this amounts to a persuasive burden, or an evidential one; and under either burden, is the defendant's right to a fair trial affected disproportionately?

The main European authority is *Salabiaku v France* [1988] 13 E.H.R.R. 379 whereby the ECHR recognised the existence of domestic presumptions of law and fact, provided they are defined within reasonable limits, taking "into account the importance of what is at stake and maintain the rights of the defence". Parliament can therefore reverse statutorily the burden of proof and in doing so will not offend art.6, provided the defendant's right to fair trial is maintained. In *Brown v Stott* [2001] Lord Bingham acknowledged the absolute right to a fair trial in art.6, but said that:

> "the constituent rights comprised whether expressly or implicitly with Art 6 are not themselves absolute. Limited qualification of these rights is acceptable if reasonably directed by national authorities towards a clear and proper public objective and if representing no greater qualification then the situation calls for."

21.12 It is for the court to determine whether a statutorily reversed burden of proof is disproportionate (unjustifiable) to the legitimate aim, by ensuring that a fair balance is struck within the triangulation of interests. In such a situation the court will need to decide:

(i) is the burden necessary;

(ii) is a legal burden justified or unjustified; and

(iii) if not is a evidential burden justified? In making this determination the court has a choice either to resort to s.3 of the Human Rights Act 1998 and take an interpretive read down approach to the words so as to ensure compatibility, or alternatively, use s.4 and make a declaration of incapability.

In *R. v A (No.2)* [2002] 1 A.C. 45, *R. v Lambert* [2002] 2 A.C. 545, *R. v Shayler* [2001] 1 W.L.R. 2206 and *Ghaidan v Godin-Mendoza* [2004] 3 W.L.R. 113, the House of Lords have given divided opinions as to the correct approach to be taken when the court is considering using s.3. The more flexible approach of Lord Steyn is to "read down" or imply a meaning into the provisions, so as to make it Convention compatible, whereas for Lord Hope, a more narrow approach should be adopted so that the courts do not act as legislators. But what is clear is that if Parliament wishes to interfere with the presumption of innocence, the court will need to be satisfied that such interference is justified and proportionate to the triangulation of interests and is no greater than necessary, in achieving the legitimate aim of the offence in question.

In *DPP v Sheldrake* [2005] 1 A.C. 264 Lord Bingham was not prepared to endorse the guidance given by the Court of Appeal in *Attorney-General's Reference (No.1 of 2004)* [2004] EWCA Crim 1025 and observed that:

> "the task of the court is never to decide whether a reverse burden should be imposed on a defendant, but always to assess whether a burden enacted by Parliament unjustifiably infringes the presumption of innocence. It may nonetheless be questioned whether (as the Court of Appeal ruled in para 52D) 'the assumption should be that Parliament would not have made an exception without good reason'. Such an approach may lead the court to give too much weight to the enactment under review and too little to the presumption of innocence and the obligation imposed on it by section 3."

In *Sheldrake*, the House of Lords ruled that the statutory defence under s.5(2) to the offence of being in charge of a motor vehicle on a road or other public place while over the prescribed limit imposed a legal persuasive burden on the defence. It is for the defendant to prove on a balance of probabilities that there was no likelihood of them driving. On a second appeal by the Attorney-General, in respect of the offence under s.11 of Terrorism Act 2000, belonging to and professing to belong to a proscribed organisation, the House of Lords, reversing the decision of the Court of Appeal, ruled that the word "prove" in the defence contained in s.11(2) that the organisation was not proscribed and that they had not taken part in any of its activities, imposed only an evidential burden.

21.13 Similarly, in *R. v Lambert* [2002] 2 A.C. 545, the House of Lords had to address the ambit of the statutory defence in s.28 of Misuse of Drugs Act 1971. This provides that it shall be a defence for the accused when charged with either simple possession, or possession with intent to supply, *to prove* that they neither *knew* of, *nor suspected*, nor *had any reason to suspect* the existence of some fact, alleged by the prosecution, which is necessary for the prosecution to prove in order to convict. The House of Lords ruled that the word "prove" imposes only a evidential burden, not a legal one on the defendant. To impose a legal burden would be disproportionate in the circumstances of the offence (i.e. the severity of punishment). An evidential burden will not lead to unwarranted acquittals, since the defendant cannot be acquitted by reason only of being mistaken as to the particular drug they were in possession of. The defendant must prove evidentially that they neither believed, nor suspected, nor had reason to suspect, that the substance or product was in fact a controlled drug.

In *R. v Davies* [2002] EWCA Crim 2949, the Court of Appeal, in regard to the more technical offences under the Health and Safety at Work Act 1974, ruled that the statutory defence contained in s.33 imposed a legal burden as being proportionate to the need to ensure a high level of responsibility for public safety and in the public interest. In *R. v Johnstone* [2003] 1 W.L.R. 1736, the House of Lords adopted a similar approach to the offence in s.92 of the Trade Marks Act 1994 and that the reasonable belief defence imposed a legal burden on the defendant. In *R. v Drummond* [2002] EWCA Crim 527, the Court of Appeal ruled that s.15 of the Road Traffic Offenders Act 1988 imposed a legal burden on the defendant in relation to the offence of causing death by careless driving, not being fit through drink or drugs. Section 15 allows for the defendant to displace the assumption that the proportion of alcohol in their body at the time of the alleged offence was not less than the specimen given, provided they can prove the "hipflask" defence namely, having ceased driving they took alcohol and that had they not done so, they would have at the time of the offence, been under the limit.

L v DPP [2001] 166 J.P. 113 involved the offence of possessing in a public place an article "which has a blade or is sharply pointed except a folding pocket knife" (s.139 of the CJA 1988). Subsection (4) provides a defence to the defendant "to prove" that he had good reason or lawful authority for the possession, or that one of the specific lawful reasons contained in subsection (5) applies. The High Court ruled that it was justified to impose a legal burden to prove the statutory defence. Once possession is proved, it is for the defendant to prove on a balance of probabilities the statutory defence. This decision was further approved in *Matthews* [2003] EWCA Crim 813 (see also *R. v Daniel* [2003] 1 Cr.App.R. 99, in which the statutory defence contained in s.352 of the Insolvency Act 1986 imposed a legal burden).

In *R. v Keogh* [2007] 1 W.L.R. 1500, the Court of Appeal, applying the guidance, concluded that the statutory defence contained in ss.2 and 3 of the Official Secrets Act 1989 only imposed an evidential burden on the defendant. Section 2 of the 1989 Act creates the offence of making a damaging disclosure of any information, document, or other article relating to the defence of the realm, without lawful authority. It is a defence to this offence for the defendant to prove that they did not know and had no reasonable cause to believe that such disclosure would be damaging. The Court of Appeal observed that it would be both disproportionate and unjustified to impose a legal burden on the defence. It would breach the presumption of innocence on the basis that the defendant would have to disprove a state of mind which formed a substantial ingredient to the offence. It is unnecessary in the legitimate aim of protecting state security to impose a legal burden, since the prosecution can still pursue the case by adducing evidence to show knowledge or belief.

Similarly in *R. (Griffin) v Richmond Magistrates' Court* [2008] *The Times*, March 31, 2008, the Divisional Court ruled that the statutory defence of showing no intent to defraud to an offence under s.208 of the Insolvency Act 1986 of failing to deliver the accounts of a company in winding up proceedings, placed a legal persuasive burden of proof upon the defendant.

7. Statutory Exceptions to Summary Offences and Offences Generally

21.14 Section 101 of the Magistrates' Courts Act 1980 provides that if the defendant intends to rely on any exception, exemption, proviso, excuse or qualification to a summary offence, then the burden of proof falls upon them to prove it. This provision, in its previous statutory context, was considered in *R. v Edwards* [1975] Q.B. 27, in which the Court of Appeal ruled that the provision was re-stating a common law principle and ruled that it applied to all criminal offences, where the defence relies on such a ground of exoneration. The burden is upon them, on a balance of probabilities, to establish it before the court.

In *Edwards*, the issue was selling alcohol without a licence in the context of a trial on indictment. The burden is upon the prosecution to prove the offence of not having a licence. It is for the defendant to prove that they had one by producing it at court. This is clearly sensible and fair, it would be unrealistic to burden the prosecution with having to establish that the defendant does not have a licence. If on request by the police or other enforcement agency, the defendant cannot produce a licence, then this amounts to evidence to prove the offence and it is for the defendant to either produce the licence, or alternatively establish an exception or exemption from having a licence.

This point of general application in regard to offences that prohibit an act or an omission, subject to a ground of exoneration, was subsequently affirmed in *R. v Hunt* [1987] 1 A.C. 352, in the context of the requirement for an offence of simple possession of morphine, combined with other inert ingredients, to have a minimum content of at least 0.2 per cent of morphine. However, the House of Lords ruled that this formed part of one of the essential ingredients of the offence and that therefore the burden was upon the prosecution to prove that ingredient of the offence. It was not for the defendant to prove otherwise, since they would be assisting the prosecution in its case against them.

8. Direction to the Jury on Reverse Burden of Proof

21.15 It is conceptually difficult and can lead to confusion, for a jury to appreciate the distinction between the legal and evidential burden. For this reason the Court of Appeal in *R. v M* [2007] EWCA Crim 3228 recognised the good sense in the practice that has developed in consequence of the decision in *Lambert*, whereby counsel for the defence would invite the judge to rule that the defendant has raised sufficient evidence on lack of belief, or suspicion of possessing the drug. If so, then the judge simply had to leave the question to the jury as to whether the prosecution have proved that the defendant did believe or suspect that the drug found in their possession was a controlled drug. If the judge is not satisfied that the defendant has discharged the evidential burden, then the jury will, in such circumstances, have to be given careful directions as to the differences in the legal, as opposed to evidential burden, as well as the different standards of proof required for each. Due to the lack of a careful and comprehensive direction, the Court of Appeal quashed the appellant's conviction for possessing a drug with intent to supply.

CHAPTER TWENTY TWO

WITNESS EVIDENCE PART 1: COMPETENCE AND COMPELLABILITY

1. THE STATUTORY TEST FOR COMPETENCY TO GIVE EVIDENCE

22.01 To ensure that those who are a witness to the commission of a criminal offence can give evidence safely and in security, without infringing the defendant's right to a fair trial, a series of new special measures were created in Pt II of the Youth Justice and Criminal Evidence Act 1999 (YJCEA 1999). The Act itself was enacted following the proposals in the Home Office report "Speaking up for Justice", which was published in June 1998. Against this background, Ch. V of the Act seeks to simplify the competency and the capacity of child to give sworn evidence. The issue of competency is simply whether a particular person is capable of giving evidence.

Section 53 provides that, at every stage in criminal proceedings, all persons are, regardless of age, competent to give evidence. The starting point is that all persons are competent witnesses. Subsections (3) and (4) set out the exceptions to general competency. The use of the expression "all persons" means that the accused is competent just like any other person. The accused is treated no differently than any other competent witness. However, if the accused is incompetent then that may raise issues of fitness to plead. Under s.53(3) a person is not competent if it appears to the court that they are a person who is unable to:

(i) understand questions to be put to them as a witness; and

(ii) give answers to them which can be understood.

Lack of competency is a matter for the court either on its own motion, or by being invited to rule on competency by the defence or prosecution. In determining the issue of competency, under s.54, it is for the party wishing to call the witness to satisfy the court on a balance of probabilities that the witness is indeed competent. The court must consider competency as against the availability of a special measures direction. The determination proceedings must be held in the absence of the jury and if appropriate, medical evidence can be relied on.

Under s.53(4) a person who is charged in criminal proceedings, either alone or jointly with others, is not competent to give evidence for the prosecution. This does not, however, include a person for whom it is no longer possible to be convicted of any offence, whether by pleading guilty, being found guilty, or discontinue of proceedings. Accordingly, if the prosecution have the situation of a multi-handed trial and one of the defendants is prepared to give evidence against any co-accused, then in order to do so, the prosecution will either have to withdraw the charges or accept a guilty plea to the offence, or a lesser offence.

2. Giving of Evidence on Oath by a Competent Witness

22.02 Section 55 sets out the test to be applied by the court as to whether the reception of the evidence by a competent witness can be given unsworn, or must be given on oath. This is generally applicable to young witnesses, but can include adult witnesses as well. The question of giving sworn evidence can be raised by either the defence, or the prosecution, or by the court of its own motion. Section 55(2) sets out two conditions that must be satisfied before the giving of sworn evidence. The first condition is that the witness must be at least 14 years old and secondly, be able to have a sufficient appreciation of the solemnity of the proceedings, of the need to tell the truth and the importance of this in terms of the oath.

Subsection (3) creates the presumption of sufficient appreciation if the person is capable of giving "intelligible testimony". A person is deemed to be capable of giving intelligible testimony if they are able to understand questions put to them and give answers to them. If this is disputed by either the prosecution or defence, then evidence will need to be produced to rebut the presumption. Medical evidence can be received to either support the presumption or rebut it. The determination of whether evidence is to be given sworn or unsworn is for the court and must be considered in the absence of the jury.

Accordingly, unless and in circumstances where the witness is 14 or over and has a sufficient appreciation of the solemnity of the proceedings, such evidence may not be given as a sworn testimony. The word "may" means the court has a discretion to decide on the matter against the particular circumstances of the witness. If the witness is over 14, but lacks sufficient appreciation, then their evidence may be received as unsworn evidence. Section 56 gives authority to accept unsworn evidence, if either the age or sufficient appreciation requirement are not met, this includes unsworn written depositions. If the court orders the evidence to be given as a sworn testimony, then like any other witness, the oath is given in accordance with the Oaths Act 1978, either on the Bible or other religious book. If the witness does not have any religious belief, the evidence will be sworn by affirmation to tell the truth.

3. Compellability of a Witness

22.03 If a witness is competent, then generally they can be compelled to give evidence. If a witness refuses to give evidence, then either the defence or the prosecution can invite the court to issue a witness summons. If the witness fails to attend or give evidence this can be treated as a contempt of court. If a witness attends but gives evidence unfavourable to the party who called them, that party may seek the permission of the court to treat them as a hostile witness.

However, the spouse of the accused is treated differently in terms of compellability. Section 80 of the Police and Criminal Evidence Act 1984, as amended by Sch.4 of the YJCEA 1999, provides that the spouse of the person charged is compellable to give evidence on behalf of that person, unless they themselves are charged with an offence.

Subsection 2(A) further provides that the spouse of a person charged is compellable to give evidence:

(i) for the prosecution, or

(ii) on behalf of any other person charged in the proceedings.

In both situations, however, the spouse only becomes compellable if their partner to whom they are married, or any person who is charged in those proceedings, is charged with a specified offence. A specified offence for this purpose is deemed to be one that:

(i) involves an assault on, or injury or a threat of injury to, the spouse or a person under 16 at the time of the offence;

(ii) is a sexual offence against a person under 16 at time of allegation; or

(iii) being an accessory, to the specified offence, or attempting, conspiring, or inciting it.

22.04 Accordingly, if a husband is charged with a sexual offence against a person under 16, then even if the wife supports and believes the husband, the prosecution could compel her to give evidence against him. If the spouse is not charged with a specified offence, the prosecution cannot compel the other spouse to give evidence against their partner. In neither of these circumstances can the failure of a spouse to give evidence on behalf of their partner be made the subject of any comment by the prosecution. This is an important safeguard, since the prosecution cannot in their closing speech seek to take advantage of the fact that the defendant's spouse has not given evidence, by asserting why that is. However, whether a breach of this clear prohibition leads to a unsafe conviction will depend on the particular circumstances of the case (see *R. v Whitton* [1998] Crim. L.R. 492).

In *R. v Pearce* [2002] 1 Cr.App.R. 551, the appellant had in tragic circumstances killed his brother. The prosecution had sought successfully to treat his partner and daughter as hostile witnesses, based on previous statements they had made. The appellant contended that s.80 prevented the compellability of his partner and daughter and treating them as compellable had breached his right to a family life under art.8. The Court of Appeal rejected this in its entirety, s.80 was limited to husband and wife and did not include unmarried partners. The interference with family life in these circumstances was necessary and justified. In relation to the daughter, she was clearly compellable. It would require Parliament by legislation to bring children into the s.80 concession, if there was to be a change in the intention of Parliament.

Conversely, in *R. (CPS) v Registrar General of Births, Deaths and Marriages* [2003] 2 W.L.R. 504, the prosecution's attempt to circumvent the plain application of s.80 was rejected. The defendant was charged with murder, his partner had made several statements in connection with the allegation. Whilst in custody on remand, the defendant applied to the prison governor for permission to marry his partner, which was granted and the couple then gave notice to the local registrar. Despite the representations of CPS, the Registrar considered that under the Marriage Act that there were no public policy grounds for refusing to allow the marriage to take place.

The CPS sought to challenge this decision by way of judicial review. The Court of Appeal, in dismissing the claim, ruled that Parliament must have had in mind the very situation that arose, the words in the provision were plain. If a defendant seeks to take advantage of the non-compellability principle in s.80 by marrying his partner, this is neither unlawful, nor contrary to public policy. The Registrar has an unfettered duty to issue a marriage certificate. It would be going too far to impose a duty on the Registrar or a vicar to postpone the marriage in order to make such enquires. A change of this significance required the intervention of Parliament. Although a spouse is not compellable to give evidence against their married partner, unless charged with a specified offence, the husband or wife can waive that right, but in order to ensure fair proceedings and that the waiver is made by informed consent, it is usual for the judge to warn the spouse that they are not compelled to give evidence and if they are aware of this, that it is their decision whether to give evidence (see *R. v Acaster* [1912] Cr.App.R. 187).

4. Calling and Securing Witness Attendance

22.05 If a witness is compellable, then if they refuse or fail to attend at court to give evidence, the court can, if it is in the interests of justice to do so, issue a summons under s.2 of the Criminal Procedure (Attendance of Witnesses) Act 1965, as amended by s.169 of the Serious Organised Crime and Police Act 2005. If there is no just excuse, then the witness will be in contempt of court and liable to be punished for such. Under s.4, a High Court Justice can, having heard evidence on oath that the witness is unlikely to comply with the summons already issued, issue a warrant of arrest and have the witness brought before the court where they are required to attend. Under s.4(2) the trial court can, if the witness fails to attend at the specified time, either issue a notice requiring them to attend or alternatively, if there are reasonable grounds for believing they do not have a just excuse, issue a warrant of arrest. The importance of credible witness evidence being given at trial as clearly being in the public interest, was emphasised in *R. v Yusef* [2003] EWCA Crim 1488.

The police will obtain statements from all potential witnesses. The prosecution will call those who support their case. Statements they do not intend to rely upon ought to be disclosed as part of unused material to the defence, as confirmed by the House of Lords in *R. v Mills and Poole* [1998] 1 Cr.App.R. 43. The prosecution is not compelled to call witnesses. In *R. v Russell-Jones* [1995] 1 Cr.App.R. 538, the Court of Appeal laid down general guidance for the prosecution:

(i) If the witness is on the witness list then, if the defence give notice of requiring all or some of the witnesses in the list to attend, those witnesses ought to be called to attend.

(ii) The prosecution have a discretion whether to call witnesses to testify.

(iii) The discretion is qualified in that it must be exercised in the interests of justice.

(iv) In determining whether to call a witness, the prosecution can consider the credibility of the witness, or whether they are unworthy of belief. In making this decision the prosecution are not obliged to proffer a witness merely in order to give the defendant material with which to discredit other prosecution witnesses.

5. Accused Calling and Giving Evidence

22.06 Prior to s.1 of the Criminal Evidence Act 1898, a defendant was not allowed to give evidence in his own defence. Since the Act a defendant has a choice. It is the Crown who bring the case and it is for the Crown to prove to the criminal standard the definitional elements of the offence. This common law principle together with the right to a fair trial contained art.6 safeguards fiercely the "presumption of innocence". Accordingly, a defendant does not have to prove their innocence, they is fully entitled to put the Crown "to proof": "prove your case, I am not going to give evidence in my defence", and any failure to give evidence cannot be held against him. In this situation, as in *R. v Bathurst* [1968] 2 Q.B. 99, the trial judge has to direct the jury not to draw any assumptions of guilt from the absence of the defendant from the witness box.

However, although the accused cannot be compelled to give evidence, this safeguard must be read subject to ss.34 to 38 of the Criminal Justice and Public Order Act 1994, which has qualified this once absolute right of the defendant. This provision provides that at the close of the prosecution case, the judge must inform the defendant that they have a voluntary choice whether or not to give evidence themselves, in the presentation of their defence. The defendant must then be warned that if they choose not to give evidence, or having been sworn, refuse to give evidence without good cause, it will be permissible, either for the court or jury as it appears to them, to draw inferences from the defendant's failure to give evidence. No comment should be made if the defendant's physical or mental condition makes it undesirable to do so.

To assist judges in the proper application of the provision, the Judicial Studies Board has produced a specimen direction. This explains that the defendant is not compelled to give evidence. But if the jury accept on that evidence there is a case to answer and no other sensible explanation for the failure, other then the defendant having no answer to the case against him or none that could conceivably stand up to cross-examination, then the jury are entitled to hold this failure against the defendant, but only if they decide that it would be fair to do in the circumstances. This direction was approved as being fair and balanced by the Court of Appeal in *R. v Cowan* [1996] Q.B. 373.

This was further approved and confirmed as being sufficiently fair to defendants by the House of Lords in *R. v Becourarn* [2005] 1 W.L.R. 2589. If a defendant fails deliberately to give evidence, so as to avoid the risk of their previous bad character being admitted this does not amount to a good cause. To allow this failure to be a good cause would be potentially misleading to the jury, particularly as their decision very much depends on assessing the credibility of both the prosecution witnesses and the defendant. Further, it would be quite wrong to allow a defendant to avoid having legitimate comment being made upon his failure, simply by refusing to give evidence. The JSB direction is fair and requires no modification as contended by the appellant to the extent of requiring the judge to explain to the jury other possible reasons why a defendant may not wish to give evidence and not to hold this against them.

CHAPTER TWENTY THREE

WITNESS EVIDENCE PART 2: EXAMINATION AND PROTECTION

1. WITNESS EXAMINATION AND THE BEST EVIDENCE RULE

23.01 In a criminal trial the advocate for both the prosecution and defence will each examine their own witnesses and cross-examine the others. This will involve the probing, testing and weakening of the reliability of the evidence adduced by the other party, with the purpose of casting sufficient doubt in the minds the jury of that particular witnesses' honesty and the accuracy of the evidence they gave. The best evidence rule provides that witness evidence should be given first hand, orally on oath at trial, so as to allow the defendant to look the accuser in the eye and hear them tell the court their version of events. Similarly, with documentary evidence, the original should be presented to the court, not a copy. Further cross-examination is used to highlight any weaknesses or inconsistencies in the strength or weight of that evidence.

In an important and unanimous ruling of the House of Lords in *R. v Davis* [2008] UKHL 36, Lord Bingham confirmed that:

> "It is a long established principle of the English common law that subject to certain exceptions *(i.e. dying declarations and the Res Gestae principle)* and statutory qualifications *(i.e. special measure protection)*, the defendant in a criminal trial should be confronted by his accusers in order that he may cross examine them and challenge their evidence."

It was further stated that the policy of open justice required the defendant to know the identity of his accusers and that by allowing these witnesses to give evidence shrouded in anonymity such as withholding identification, giving evidence under a pseudonym or behind a screen, or using voice distortion, would render the trial unfair in circumstances where the presentation of the defence case is unjustifiably impeded or the evidence to be protected is the "sole or decisive basis" on which alone the defendant could be convicted (see Lord Mance at para.96). The Court whilst fully recognising the contention for the prosecution that without such protection the interest of justice in the investigation and prosecution of serious crime would be greatly undermined, felt that given the important issues involved, it is clearly a matter for Parliament to bring reform, not the courts to create an exception.

In respect of defence counsel, the code of conduct for barristers sets out the duty of the defence barrister and provides that they:

> "must promote and protect fearlessly and by all proper and lawful means the lay client's best interests and do so without regards to his own interests or to any consequences to himself or to any other person."

This means that they must not be "flagrantly incompetent" in the conduct of presenting the defendant's case so as to be prejudicial, see *R. v Clinton* (1993) 1 W.L.R. 1181. At the same time they need to exercise an independent discretion in the preparation, conduct and management of the case, taking full account of the client's instructions and the need to ensure the efficient management of the court service resources. Notwithstanding this, ss.27(2A) and 28(2A) of the Courts and Legal Services Act 1999, as inserted by s42 of the Access to Justice Act 1999, places upon the advocate an overriding duty to the court and the administration of justice. This means that the advocate must not mislead the court dishonestly or otherwise in the furtherance of their client's interests, neither must they waste time on irrelevancies, even if the clients thinks that they are important.

In order to ensure that cases for the prosecution are prepared properly and that the advocate is fully aware of their duties as a "minister of justice", there are in place the "Farquharson Guidelines" which set out the role and responsibilities of the prosecution advocate in terms of pre-trial matters and sentencing. In addition, the CPS also has in place the "National Standards of Advocacy" which state:

> "The art of good advocacy is based on a sound understanding of the law and procedure, thorough preparation and the ability to present one's case in a cohesive, structured and persuasive manner, having mastered the facts and understand the issues to be decided in the case."

Particular note should be taken of the decision in *R. v Momodou (Practice Note)* [2005] 1 W.L.R. 3442, in which it is made clear that any form of witness training or coaching in relation to criminal proceedings, whether by the prosecution or defence, is not permitted. To conduct such training can led to the discussion between witnesses of their evidence which is not permitted, neither is the disclosure of witness statements to other witnesses. This can lead to the very real dangers of a witness concentrating on a particular emphasis of their evidence, there is also the inherent risk of contamination and collusion. The Court did, however, state that this rule of practice does not prevent the familiarisation of witness in pre-trial arrangements with the layout of the court, the procedure that is followed and the different roles of the various participants. Indeed the Court welcomed such a practice on the basis that a witness should not be disadvantaged by ignorance.

2. Examination in Chief and Re-Examination

23.02 Evidence to be adduced at trial is generally in the form of witness statements (depositions) taken by the police. Where that evidence is important to the case, then the witness generally attends at court to give oral evidence. The advocate will use the contents of the statement as previously given and effectively take the witness through it. Provided a witness stays generally within the thrust of what they said previously then, as a witness, they have come up to proof. If, on the other hand, they show confusion, vagueness or inconsistency, then their evidence is potentially undermined and more likely to be rejected rather than accepted.

To ensure that the witness gives a free account of their evidence, the rules of evidence provide that a person who calls a witness to give oral testimony is prohibited from asking leading questions, i.e. a question that tends to suggest the answer before it is given. The witness cannot be led in this way during examination in chief. The advocate must ask open ended questions, for example "On the 3rd June can you explain where you were and what you were doing at about 8 pm on the particular evening?" Re-examination occurs after the witness has been cross-examined, it is at discretion of the party who called the witness and is limited to simply clarifying any matters raised by cross-examination but no more.

3. Hostile Witness Exception

23.03 A problem can arise when a principal witness unexpectedly retracts their statement or refuses now to give evidence in accordance with their statement or tell the truth in respect of the person who wishes to call them. In such circumstances, the party who called the witness can with leave of the court ask leading questions of the witness or cross-examine them (see *R. v Honeyghon and Sayles* [1999] Crim. L.R. 221).

Section 3 of the Criminal Procedure Act 1865 (CPA 1865) allows for the judge to grant leave to cross-examine an adverse witness called about previous statements they have made, which are now inconsistent with their oral evidence. In such circumstances, the witness must be asked whether or not they made such a statement. Accordingly, under this section it is possible to cross-examine a witness declared hostile on their previous inconsistent statement(s). However, any cross-examination can only go to the witnesses' creditability, not to an issue of fact in the case, since out of court statements are, as a general rule, not treated as evidence of facts. To allow cross-examination is at the discretion of the court and can be refused if such cross-examination is considered to be unfair or prejudicial (see *R. v Booth* [1982] 74 Cr.App.R. 123).

Should a witness for the prosecution become favourable to the defence then the Crown can wait until this witness is called by the defence and utilise s.4 of the Criminal Procedure Act 1865. This provides along with s.5 (written statements) that a witness may be asked under cross-examination about a previous inconsistent statement provided it is relevant to the subject-matter of the indictment or procedure and is inconsistent with their present testimony.

If the witness denies making the statement then the prosecution can produce it to prove that they did. If faced with a potential hostile witness, the judge should consider whether they are just unwilling to participate and remind them that a refusal to answer questions can amount to a contempt of court, which may involve punishment (see *R. v Darby* [1989] Crim. L.R 817 also *R. v Jones (Kerry Marvin)* [1998] Crim. L.R 579).

Note also the change made by s.119 of the Criminal Justice Act 2003 which allows an out of court inconsistent statement to be admissible evidence. Accordingly, if a witness does not come up to proof or becomes uncooperative, then the statement can be produced for the jury to assess and jury decide where the truth lies. In all circumstances the judge will need to consider whether there is a risk of an unsafe conviction and exclude the statement under s.78 of PACE 1984, or direct an acquittal. The weight given to the evidence in the statement will be a matter for the jury and the judge will need to direct the jury that it is a matter for them what amount of weight they attach to it and that they are not obliged to accept it and must reject it, if they dismiss it as untruthful (see para. 23.08 below).

4. Cross-Examination, Impugning Credibility and the "Finality Rule"

23.04 In *R. v Baldwin* (1955) 18 Cr.App.R. 175 Lord Hewart stated that the purpose of cross-examination is that "What is wanted from the witness is answers to questions of fact. In order to achieve this, the advocate is entitled to ask leading questions of the witness".

When assessing the credibility of the witnesses by cross-examination, those witnesses' knowledge, veracity and confidence is being tested for their honesty and accuracy. If the evidence of a witness is contaminated by implausibility, inconsistency and illogicality, then the less are they an honest and/or accurate witness. The jury can accept or reject any evidence based on this assessment. However, there are clear limitations on the extent to which cross-examination can be pursued. In *R. v Funderburk* [1990] 90 Cr.App.R. 466, the Court of Appeal give general guidance that if the question posed goes solely to the witnesses' creditability, or to facts that are merely collateral to the main disputed issue then:

> "the general rule is that answers given to such questions are final and cannot be contradicted by rebutting evidence. This is because of the requirement to avoid multiplicity of issues in the overall interests of justice".

This means that whatever answer the witness gives to the question this must be treated as the final answer to it. There does exist a number of exceptions to the requirement of finality, in which after the answer is given counsel cross-examining the witness are fully entitled to produce contradictory evidence and ask further questions in response. These exceptions are as follows:

(i) goes to an issue in the case (that is obvious);

(ii) shows that the witness made a previous inconsistent statement relating to an issue in the case (s.4 CPA 1865);

(iii) shows bias in the witness (*Philips* [1936] 26 Cr.App.R. 17;

(iv) shows that the police are prepared to go to improper lengths to secure a conviction.

In *Busby* [1982] 75 Cr.App.R. 79, it was held that the defence should have been allowed to question a witness about police officers threatening him so that he would not give evidence for the defence, since it was central to the issue of the alleged admissions made by the defendant to the police (i.e. fabrication) and the reliability of the officers.

If police officers are under investigation for corruption and malpractice, by fabricating and planting evidence such as drugs, or committing assaults on suspects, or even stealing the proceeds of the offender's crimes then the defence can, at the discretion of the judge, cross-examine on these matters. This is providing that this impacts upon, or impugns the reliability of those police witnesses and is not just unsubstantiated innuendo, or attempts to smear unfairly and does not concern un-concluded internal investigations (see *R. v Edwards* [1991] 1 W.L.R. 207). If the police officers in question have either at the time, or post conviction, been discredited, then if the evidence becomes tainted by a suspicion of perjury, a conviction may be ruled unsafe, if that, evidence was central to the prosecution case. It would now be impossible to be confident that, had the jury known of the misconduct, they would have still been bound to convict.

This has led to a number of appeals against the safety of convictions for serious offences, arising from the lamentable tactics used by officers at Stoke Newington Police station and the disbanded West Midlands Serious Crime Unit (see *R. v Twitchell* [2000] 1 Cr.App.R. 373, *R. v Maxine Edwards* [1996] 2 Cr.App.R. 345, 207, *R. v Malik* [2000] 2 Cr.App.R. 8 and *R. v Guney* [1998] 2 Cr.App.R. 242).

(v) proving the witness has previous convictions. Under s.6(1) of the Criminal Procedure Act 1865, a witness can be questioned as to previous convictions and if they deny this or refuse to answer, then "it shall be lawful for the cross-examining party to prove such a conviction". Under s.73 of PACE 1984, this can be proved by the production of a "certificate of conviction" signed by the court clerk;

(vi) shows that the witness has a general reputation for untruthfulness, see *R. v Nagrecha* [1997] 2 Cr.App.R. 401.

Whilst the interests of justice test is the guiding principle, when the question is directed to creditability, then the finality rule applies, unless one of the above recognisable exceptions exists. The distinction between creditability and a factual issue, especially in a disputed consent sexual offence case, can be reduced to vanishing point. The truth of what happened is very much based on witness creditability, if there are the only two main witnesses. In *R. v Nagrecha* [1997] 2 Cr.App.R. 401, the complainant alleged that she had been indecently assaulted by her employer on one occasion. The defence had a statement from a witness who knew her well and who said that she had also previously made similar complaints against him and others. The witness claimed that she had told her work colleagues that she had been sexually assaulted by a taxi driver and by building workers. The trial judge refused to allow questioning of the complainant in regard to this statement. The defence had wanted to rebut the complainant's denial that she had made complaints against others. Rose L.J. stated:

> "by failing to permit such evidence, the judge's ruling was unfair to the defendant. The issue in the case because the outcome turned on the word of the complainant and the appellant as to whether there had been an indecent assault-was essentially the complainant's credit. Had the jury been aware of the matters about the contents of the statement, they might well have looked at the matter in a different way."

In *R. v Summers* [1999] Crim. L.R. 745, the Court of Appeal affirmed the finality rule as being a general rule that states that evidence is not admissible to contradict answers given by a witness to questions put in cross-examination concerning "collateral matters". These are such matters which only concern the credibility of the witness and are otherwise irrelevant to the central issues disputed in the case. The Court did recognise the various exceptions to the general rule and the blurred distinction between an issue of consent and credibility in sexual cases. Accordingly, dependant on each individual case, the court will need to adopt a somewhat flexible approach to the general rule in order to ensure fairness.

5. Oath Helpers and Good Character of Prosecution Witness

23.05 The general rule, as set out in *R. v Beard* [1998] Crim. L.R. 585, and *Robinson* [1994] 98 Cr.App.R. 370, is that evidence is not admissible to show that a prosecution witness has good character, in the sense that they are generally a truthful person who should be believed. The reason for the rule against admissibility is that whether the witness is a truthful person or not is a matter for the jury to determine, without assistance from what are sometimes referred to as "oath helpers". The reason behind the inadmissibility of evidence to bolster a prosecution witness is that it adds no probative value to the material disputed issues in the trial.

As part of this general rule, the prosecution cannot use the occupation of the witness to bolster their credibility, although it is normal practice for a witness at the beginning of their evidence to be asked their occupation. In *R. v DS* [1999] Crim. L.R. 911, the Court of Appeal ruled that the appellant's conviction was safe, even though the witness had stated his occupation to be that of a clergyman. The prosecution did not call any evidence to bolster the credibility of the witness and the judge gave adequate warnings to the jury not to accept the evidence simply because he was a clergyman. In *R. v Amado-Taylor* [2001] EWCA Crim 1898, the Court of Appeal ruled that under the common law the complainant's attitudes and religious beliefs that intercourse before marriage was wrong could be relevant and admissible with regard to determining the issue of consent, although such evidence could at the same time go to bolster the complainant's credibility.

Likewise, the Court of Appeal in *R. v Tobin* [2003] EWCA Crim 190 stated that, as a matter of principle, it is permissible in sexual offence cases to allow the prosecution to adduce evidence of the complainant's background and characteristics. In the instant case the Court concluded that the judge was right to allow the prosecution to call the complainant's mother to describe her daughter's general approach to life. This decision takes a liberal approach to the inadmissibility of oath helpers, by side stepping the rule and determining the evidence as going loosely to an issue in the trial. It is to be noted that the defendant can call character references and that in this case the defendant gave evidence that he was a married man.

6. Reliability Affected by a Disability

23.06 If, however, either the prosecution or defence wish to challenge the reliability of a witnesses' general reputation on the basis of a medical condition, then this is permitted as an exception to the general rule under the principle enunciated in *Toohey v Metropolitan Police Commissioner* [1965] A.C. 595 in which Lord Pearce said:

> "Human evidence shares the frailties of those who give it. It is subject to many crosscurrents such as partiality, prejudice, self-interest and, above all imagination and inaccuracy. Those are matters with which the jury, helped by cross-examination and common sense, must do their best. But when a witness through physical (in which I include mental) disease or abnormality is not capable of giving a true reliable account to the jury, it must surely be allowable for medical science to reveal this vital hidden fact to them. If a witness purported to give evidence of something which he believed that he had seen at a distance of fifty yards, it must surely be possible to call the evidence of an oculist to the effect that the witness could not possibly see anything at a greater distance than twenty yards, or the evidence of a surgeon who had removed a cataract from which the witness was suffering at the material time which would have presented him from seeing what he thought he saw. So, too, must it be allowable to call medical evidence of mental illness which makes a witness incapable of giving reliable evidence, whether through the existence of delusions or otherwise. It is obviously in the interest of justice that such evidence should be available."

7. Reputation for Untruthfulness and Lack of Credibility

23.07 Further, in *Richardson and Longman* 52 Cr.App.R. 317, the Court of Appeal observed that it is permissible to call a witness to impeach the credibility of another witnesses' reputation to tell the truth and state whether such a person in their opinion, based on personal knowledge, can be believed on oath. The impeaching witness may not give reasons for their belief, unless in answer to questions by the other party. For instance, in an assault case where the defence is one of acting in self defence, the defence may use this exception to adduce evidence establishing that the complainant, who claims to have been assaulted by the defendant, is in fact a person with a violent disposition and that it is due to this violent temper that the defendant had to act in self defence.

8. Previous Inconsistent Statements and Self Serving Statements

23.08 During the police investigation of an alleged offence, statements will be taken from witnesses. Those witnesses may make amended statements or retract them. If that witness comes to court then during cross-examination states something which does not correspond with what they have said previously, then that goes directly to the witnesses' credibility as being honest and accurate. Further, it could go to an issue in the trial, i.e. consent, or identification. The law governing cross-examination in regard to the statements of a witness which are deemed to be inconsistent is found in the old Criminal Procedure Act 1865 (CPA 1865) (known as Lord Denman's Act).

If a witness during cross-examination makes a statement that is inconsistent, or different to a previous statement, (whether oral or written) that is relevant to an issue in the trial, then s.4 of the CPA 1865 allows the advocate to adduce the statement as proof of its existence. But before doing so, s.4 provides that the advocate must first mention the existence of the statement to the witness and ask whether or not they made such a statement. If the witness admits making it then no proof is required.

Section 5 further allows the cross-examination of a witness on previous statements in writing, or reduced into writing, that are relevant to an issue in the trial, without needing to show the statement to them. However, if it is intended to contradict what they had said on oath at trial, then the advocate must bring to the witnesses' attention those parts of the statement they wish to focus on as contradictory proof. A proviso to such cross-examination is that the judge has a discretionary power to require its production for their inspection and make such use of it as they think fit (i.e. show it to the jury).

If the witness denies making the statement and this cannot be proved by the advocate wishing to focus on an inconsistency, then the previous statement, being made out of court, would amount to hearsay and is generally inadmissible. However, s.119 of the Criminal Justice Act 2003 removes this difficulty and provides that if the witness admits making the previous inconsistent statement, or it is proved under ss.4 and 5 of the CPA

1865, then the statement is admissible regarding any matter stated of which oral evidence by them would be admissible. It is important to be aware of what is meant by "statement" and "any matter stated". These two expressions are defined in s.115, a statement amounts to any representation (this can be in a sketch, photofit or other pictorial form) of fact or opinion, by a person by whatever means. A matter stated relates to something that appears to the court to have been made by a witness as having the purpose of causing another to believe the matter, or to cause that person to act or a machine to operate on the basis of that matter.

23.09 In *R. v Beattie* [1989] 89 Cr.App.R. 302, the Court of Appeal confirmed the well-known general rule of evidence, as stated in *R. v Oyesiku* [1972] 56 Cr.App.R. 240 that it is inadmissible for the party calling the witness to put to them the previous statements made by them that are consistent with the trial testimony, in order to add weight to what they are saying now. In *Oyesiku* [1972] Cr.App.R. 240 the Court, referring to *Coll* [1889] 25 L.R.Ir 522, stated that even if the witness has been impeached by the advocate cross-examining them under s.5 as to a previous inconsistent statement, the general rule still applies and the party who called the witness cannot in re-examination adduce other statements that are in fact consistent with what they have said on oath (see *R. v Weekes* [1988] Crim. L.R. 244).

Although this general rule has not been abolished by the Criminal Justice Act 2003, it is apparent that it will need to be applied as being subject to s.124(3) of the CJA 2003 (which came into effect on January 29, 2004). This allows the court to permit a party to lead additional evidence, as specified by the court, for the purpose of denying or answering the allegation. This would seem to mean that if s.124(1)(a) admission of an out of court statement is applied on its own and not subject to the s.124(1)(b) requirement that the witness has not given oral evidence in connection to the subject matter then if the defence prove and admit a previous inconsistent statement, the prosecution, with leave of the court, can under s.124(3) admit a previous consistent statement to bolster the witnesses' credibility, in the light of the inconsistency revealed.

There are nevertheless three recognisable exceptions to the general rule where a previous consistent statement can be admitted. These are as follows:

(1) Recent invention or fabrication: s.120 of the CJA 2003

If it is suggested to the witness in cross-examination that their account is a recent invention or fabrication, even if not deliberate or dishonest, then in re-examination, as a matter of fairness, a previous consistent statement can be adduced to demonstrate that there is no invention or fabrication. Section 120(2) of the CJA 2003 provides that the statement used to impute fabrication of the witness, although amounting to an out of court statement, is admissible for the purpose of allowing the jury to assess and attach such weight as they feel appropriate to it.

(2) Recent complainant evidence in sexual offences

The prosecution can adduce evidence, where the complainant of a sexual offence was seen either in a distressed state, or made a complaint soon after the event, to show consistency as to what they are saying at trial (see *R. v Islam* [1999] 1 Cr.App.R. 22) (this is discussed in greater detail with corroboration evidence).

Section 120(4) provides that a previous statement of a witness is admissible evidence so long as that evidence would be admissible if given orally. Before the evidence becomes admissible, any of three conditions must be satisfied and the witness, when giving oral evidence, indicates that to the best of their belief, they made the statement and that it states the truth. The three conditions are:

(i) the statement identifies or describes a person, object or place;
(ii) the statement was made soon after the event when the matters were fresh in the maker's mind, and the witness cannot now, giving oral evidence, reasonably be expected to remember what they said;
(iii) to satisfy the third condition, six requirements must be satisfied:

(a) the witness claims to be the complainant of an offence(s);
(b) the offence in question forms part of the proceedings;
(c) the contents of the statement must consist of a complaint made by them of the alleged offence to any person and what they said, if proved, must constitute an element of the offence;
(d) the complaint must have been made as soon could be reasonably expected after the alleged offence;
(e) the complaint must not have been made as a result of a threat or indeed a promise; and
(f) the witness must give oral evidence in connection with the offence before the statement can be adduced in evidence.

It is clear that the three conditions act as safeguards before such an out of court statement can be adduced as evidence in the trial.

In *R. v Xhabri* [2006] 1 Cr.App.R. 26, the Court of Appeal ruled that all six requirements had been, or were likely to be satisfied, in respect of complaints made by the complainant to her mother, father and another person, supporting the truthfulness in her complaint that she was being held against her will, forced to work as a prostitute and raped by the defendant.

(3) The *Res Gestae* Rule

This principle as an exception to the general rule is confirmed in *Qyesiku* [1972] 56 Cr.App.R. 240 and allows in evidence a statement made spontaneously or contemporaneously with the event at the material time, so as to form an "integral part" of the act itself. It therefore ought to be admitted in order to provide a sensible understanding of the events surrounding the act.

Accordingly, the principle of *res gestae* allows evidence to be given of events (a narrative) as they unfold and includes spontaneous comments made by those who were involved, but had no opportunity, either for concoction by them of what occurred, or distortion of their account of what occurred.

9. Restrictions on Cross-Examination of Certain Vulnerable Witnesses

23.10 The main statutory restrictions on the cross-examination of vulnerable witnesses who are at risk of intimidation or humiliation, or that are frightened embarrassed, or suffer from a physical, mental disability or who are young, are to be found in the Youth Justice and Criminal Evidence Act 1999.

10. Previous Sexual Behaviour: *R. v A (No.2)* [2001]

23.11 Sections 41 to 43 of the Youth Justice and Criminal Evidence 1999 impose wide restrictions on evidence and the method of questioning a complainant about her previous sexual behaviour for certain specified sexual offences. The purpose of the restrictions was, first to avoid the humiliation and accusations suffered by victims at trial that are clearly irrelevant to the issues in dispute. And secondly, to dispel the *twin myths* often deployed by the defence to show that a woman who has previous sexual experience is by that reason more likely to have consented on the occasion in dispute and that owing to such previous sexual experience, she lacks credibility in terms of being believed as a witness.

In *R. v Cartwright* [2007] EWCA Crim 2581, the Court of Appeal, in giving an important judgment on statutory construction, ruled that s.41 is a procedural and evidential provision and not part of the substantive law, unlike the decision in *R. v C* [2006] 1 Cr.App.R. 433. Therefore it had not been repealed, disapplied, nor amended by the subsequent codification of sexual offences in the Sexual Offences Act 2003, it remained fully in force. The Court did accept on a literal interpretation that s.41 ceased to apply to the new sexual offences, given the failure of the Secretary of State to make the necessary amendment. However, to apply such an interpretation would create an extraordinary absurdity (see *IncoEurope Ltd v First Choice* [2000] 1 W.L.R. 586, for the principles to be applied when dealing with legislative absurdities) and produce a result that could only restrict the intentions of Parliament and defeat the very purpose of s.41. It would mean that a defendant charged with rape in one count before May 1, 2004 would not be restricted by s.41, although it was in force at the time, whilst in another count, the rape occurring after May 1, 2004 would be governed by s.41.

Section 41 is a long and complex provision and therefore it would be good practice to have a copy of it.

In *R. v A (No.2)* 2 W.L.R. 1546, the House of Lords was called upon to decide whether the legal effect of s.41 on the admissibility in evidence of the previous sexual behaviour of the complainant was compatible with the Convention right to a fair trial in art.6. Lord Steyn was in no doubt about the restrictive nature of the statutory expression contained in s.43(3)(c) "that the similarity cannot be reasonably be explained as a coincidence" as being disproportionate to the legislative aim of the section.

The ordinary rules of interpretation could not, according to his Lordship:

> "cure the problem of the excessive breath of s.41 read as a whole". [In these circumstances the court must apply s.3 of the Human Rights Act 1998 which] "requires the court to subordinate the niceties of the language of s.41" [by reading the provisions of the section as being,] "subject to the implied provision that evidence or questioning which is required to ensure a fair trial ... should not be treated as inadmissible."

The court must strike a fair balance between the protected rights of the defendant as against the public interest, taking into account the familiar triangulation of interests of the accused, the victim and society.

Whilst their Lordships all recognised the laudable approach taken by Parliament in passing s.41 in order to remove the "twin myths" in sexual offences and rebalance the notion of a fair trial, it had on this occasion stepped beyond the legal boundaries of the concept of proportionality, in striving to achieve that fair balance on which the, "court is qualified to make its own judgment and must do so". Whilst the courts will show deference to the will of Parliament, Parliament itself can only act within it discretionary area of judgment when choosing the ordinary words to be used to strike the fair balance.

11. General Rule of Inadmissibility and Limited Exceptions

23.12 Section 41 prohibits the questioning or adducing evidence "about any sexual behaviour of the complainant" with the defendant or a third party, except with leave of the court and provides that one of the two qualifying subsections apply. Subsection (5) provides for allowing the defence to rebut evidence adduced by the Crown about the sexual behaviour of the complainant (i.e. that the complainant is a virgin) (see *R. v Singh* [2003] EWCA Crim 485). Under subsection (3), the second qualification is restricted to issue and consent and similarity. For subsection (3) to apply, the question or evidence must be relevant to an issue in the case, namely a definitional part of the offence.

The defence must make an application in advance for leave to be granted by the court. The court will not grant leave to question unless it is satisfied on two conditions:

(i) that either or both subsection (3) or (5) apply; and

(ii) to refuse leave might render a conclusion on any issue falling to be proved in the trial by the prosecution or the defence unsafe.

Part 36 of the CrPR 2005 contains the relevant procedural steps to be taken and provides that an application for leave by the defendant must be in writing and received by the Court Officer within 28 days of committal or s.51 sending for trial, or such period as the court determines appropriate in the case. If the CPS oppose the application or the application is received within 14 days of the trial date, then the application must be determined by a Crown Court judge.

12. Impugning the Credibility of the Witness Impermissible

23.13 Under s.41(4) what would clearly not be a relevant issue is that *the purpose* of the question or evidence to be adduced would have the sole effect of impugning the credibility of the complainant as a witness. Having satisfied the threshold test of a relevant issue in the case, the issue itself is then further restricted to the following four situations.

(i) Section 41(3)(a) an issue not of consent. In *R. v A* [2001] 1 W.L.R. 1546 Lord Hope described the issues which would fall into this particular category on the basis that sexual behaviour was being adduced for specific reasons:

(a) The defence of honest belief, namely that the accused may honestly but mistakenly (but not necessarily reasonably) have believed that the complainant was consenting to the sexual act (see *R. v Satnam & Kewal* [1984] Cr.App.R. 149).

(b) That the complainant was biased against the accused or had a motive to fabricate evidence.

(c) That there is an alternative explanation for the physical conditions on which the Crown relies to establish that intercourse took place.

(ii) Section 41(3)(b) or if the issue is one of consent, then the sexual behaviour of the complainant can only be that which is alleged to have taken place "*at or about the same time as the event which is the subject matter of the charge against the accused*". In *R. v A* Lord Hope stated that the words "*or about*" give some flexibility: "around a matter that has to be determined according to facts and the circumstances of each case".

(iii) Section 41(3)(c)(i) or is "in any respect so similar" to that which "took place as part of the event which is the subject matter of the charge".

(iv) Section 41(3)(c)(ii) or that which "took place at or about the same time as that event and the *similarity* cannot reasonably be explained as *a coincidence*.

Lord Steyn in *R. v A* stated obiter that the overall purpose of provision:

> "deals sensibly and fairly with questioning and evidence about the complainant's sexual experience with other men" [as being] "almost always irrelevant to the issue whether the complainant consented to sexual intercourse on the occasion alleged in the indictment or to her credibility."

but that:

> "the blanket exclusion of prior sexual history between the complainant and an accused in section 41, subject to narrow categories of exception in the remainder of s41, poses an acute problem of proportionality."

According to his Lordship, the restrictive nature of s.41 as to the exclusion in evidence or questioning of a sexual relationship between the victim and the accused shortly before the alleged offence breaches the defendant's right to a fair trial contained in art.6, by potentially denying the accused the right to put forward a full and complete defence by advancing truly probative evidence as to the issue of consent or their honest and reasonable belief that there was consent. Accordingly, s.3 of the Human rights Act 1998 was employed to "read down" the wide breath of the section.

Lord Steyn confirmed that the task of the trial judge in difficult cases involving the application of s.41 is as follows:

> "It is of supreme importance that the effect of the speeches today should be clear to trial judges who have to deal with problems of the admissibility of questioning and evidence on alleged prior sexual experience between an accused and a complainant. The effect of the decision today is that under s41(3)(c) of the 1999 Act, construed where necessary by applying the interpretive obligation under s.3 of the HRA1998, and due regard always being paid to the importance of seeking to protect the complainant from the indignity and from humiliating questions, *the test of admissibility is whether the evidence (and questioning in relation to it) is nevertheless so relevant to the issue of consent that to exclude it would endanger the fairness of the trial under Art 6 of the convention. If this test is satisfied the evidence should not be excluded.*"

In *R. v Beedall* [2007] EWCA Crim 27, the Court of Appeal ruled that the s.41 protection applied equally to a male rape complainant and that there was no relevant distinction between asking questions of a female complainant concerning her sexual activities in order to suggest that she was more likely to consent, than asking a similar question of a male complainant on whether he was engaged in homosexuality or had practiced anal sex and therefore more likely to consent. Both are plainly prohibited under s.41.

13. Meaning of "About any Sexual Behaviour", "Relevant Issue in the Case" and "Issue of Consent"

23.14 Section 42 provides a meaning for the application of the above statutory expressions:

(i) "Relevant issue in the case", means any issue falling to be proved by the prosecution or defence in the trial of the accused.

(ii) "Issue of consent" means any issue as to whether the complainant in fact consented to the conduct constituting the offence of which the accused is charged (and accordingly does not include any issue as to the belief of the accused that the complainant so consented).

(iii) "Sexual behaviour" means any sexual behaviour or other sexual experience, whether or not involving any accused or other person, but excluding (except in s.41(3)(c)(i) and (5)(a)) anything alleged to have taken place as part of the event which is the subject matter of the charge against the accused.

14. Distinguishing between Credibility and Issue

23.15 The distinction between a permitted question going to an issue and one going to credibility and therefore prohibited, is not an easy one to draw for the trial judge. This has led to a number of appeal decisions on the correctness of such rulings by the court. *R. v T and H* [2002] 1 W.L.R. 632 involved two separate appeals against the ruling of the trial judge at a preparatory hearing under s.35 of the Criminal Procedure and Investigations Act 1996. In *T* the defence sought to question the complainant about her failure to utilise several opportunities on which she could have mentioned the alleged indecent assaults and rape by her uncle. In *H* the defence sought to question the complainant about lies she had allegedly told to others about being raped, i.e. false complaints.

In each case the Court of Appeal allowed the appeal. In considering the cases of *Nagrecha* and *Funderburk* and relying on the judgment of Lord Hope in *R. v A*, who indicated at para.79 that questions about the sexual behaviour of a complainant could be admissible, if they went to show that the complainant had a motive for fabricating the evidence, despite the prohibition contained in s.41. The Court, in the judgment of Keene L.J., concluded that:

> "It seems to this court that normally questions or evidence about false statements in the past by the complainant about sexual assaults or such questions or evidence about a failure to complain about the alleged assault which is the subject matter of the charge, while complaining about other sexual assaults, are not ones 'about' any sexual behaviour of the complainant. They relate not to her sexual behaviour but to her statements in the past or to her failure to complain."

On this basis and applying a purposive approach to the interpretation of s.41, the Court of Appeal ruled that s.41 does not automatically exclude questions proposed to be asked by each defendant, even if such questions relate principally to credibility. Acknowledging the "triangulation of interests" and the right of the victim under art.8 to a private life and therefore privacy regarding her sexual past, Keene L.J. felt that:

> "A balancing exercise would be required. But in the present cases the balancing exercise must recognise the gravity of the charges faced by these two defendants and the serious consequences which they face if convicted."

The court, before granting leave, should consider whether the defence have a proper evidential basis and that in the case of previous statements can show that such statements were made and that the questions are concerned with lies told in them, not about sexual behaviour. The court must be convinced that the defence's proposed questions do not simply form part of a fishing expedition (see *R. v SK* [2002] EWCA Crim 1319). If the questions go to the issue of whether the rape took place, then s.41 does not prohibit questions for this purpose. This is essentially a matter for the judge to decide and one which the Court of Appeal will not usurp unless clearly wrong (see further *R. v Cooper and Betts* [2003] EWCA Crim 29, *R. v Davies* [2004] EWCA Crim 1389).

In *R. v Winter* [2008] EWCA Crim 3, the Court of Appeal ruled that the judge was correct under s.41 to refuse to allow the defence to question the complainant about her admission that she was having a sexual relationship with a man, and having said in an earlier statement she was in a loving and devoted relationship with her boyfriend was a lie. The Court of Appeal ruled that such questions, albeit sought to impinge on falsity, would elicit information about the complainant's sexual behaviour with another man. In any event the complaint's assertion could not be adjudged a lie simply because she was involved in another sexual relationship.

15. Other Restrictions on Cross-Examination

23.16 The general rule of the common law is that an accused has the right to cross-examine prosecution witnesses, to give evidence and call evidence. In relation to trial on indictment a defendant's right to call evidence is contained in s.2 of the Criminal Procedure Act 1865, s.9 of the Magistrates' Courts Act 1980 covers summary trials.

The Youth Justice and Criminal Evidence Act 1999 formed part of a strategy to provide improved protection for the victim within the criminal process. This includes the prohibition on a defendant to cross-examine an adult witness in sexual cases under s.34 which can be extended to others under s.36 if the quality of the witness evidence is likely to be diminished. This particular restriction was due to the shocking conduct of the defendant in *R. v Brown* [1998] 2 Cr.App.R. 364. Under s.35 a defendant is prohibited from cross-examining a protected chid witness in certain specified sexual offences. The procedure to be followed is that contained in Pt 31 of the CrPR 2005, which requires the court to explain to the defendant that they are personally prohibited from cross-examining the witness and where necessary, for the appointment of legal representation.

16. Special Measures Provisions

23.17 Part II of the YJCEA 1999 contains eight special measure directions, each designed to allow a vulnerable or intimidated witness to give evidence in a particular way at trial, so as to improve the quality of their evidence, by reducing the inevitable stress that is often encountered by these witnesses, or those who have difficulty in giving evidence. To have access to one of the special measures, the court must be satisfied that the witness is eligible under ss.16 or 17. Before a special measure provision can be admitted by the court, s.18(2) of the Act requires the Secretary of State to have given notification that it is available for that area. The special measure provisions have come into effect on different dates and through piloting schemes. In the Crown Court most of them came into use on July 24, 2002, whilst in the magistrates' court it was the June 3, 2004.

However, in *R. v Rochester* [2008] EWCA Crim 678, the Court of Appeal had to address the acute difficulties created by the effect of s.18(2) on whether or not pre-recorded evidence could be tendered even though s.27 had been brought in by commencement order, but where the Crown Court at Chelmsford had not received notification from the Secretary of State as required by s.18(2). The case involved a serious offence of marital rape, in which the complainant's evidence was adduced by pre-recorded video. Without this evidence, the prosecution could not prove the offence. The appellant contended on appeal against his conviction that given the lack of notification, the evidence was wrongly admitted and therefore his conviction was unsafe. The Court of Appeal rejected this in its entirety on two clear grounds; firstly:

> "under our constitution, unless Parliament has by very clear language conferred powers on the executive, it is Parliament which decides whether the substantive law should be changed, not the executive. Unless there was very clear language (which cannot be found in s.18(2)) we cannot accept that, Parliament would give power to a Secretary of State to decide by administrative action and not by Statutory Instrument whether to implement legislation, in the light of the Secretary of State's subsequent evaluation of the legislation subsequent to passage of an Act. The commencement of legislation by Commencement Order is subject to various safeguards and ensures that it is public. It is a central element of control over legislation by Parliament and of its duty to make laws passed publicly known and accessible."

The second ground that the Court adopted was based on the important principle that the application of the substantive criminal law must apply to all citizens within the jurisdiction of England and Wales. It would be wholly wrong to implement laws on a geographical basis and on the say so of the Executive. Accordingly, the Court concluded that the s.27 special measure applied to all Crown Courts from the date of the Commencement Order, not from when given notification from the Secretary of State. Applying the decision of the House of Lords in *R. v Clarke* [2008] 1 W.L.R. 338, Parliament could not be taken to have intended to invalidate the implementation of the special measures provisions due to the lack of notification under s.18(2). The Court went further and stated that even if they were wrong on this point, Parliament could not have intended the evidence wrongly received to be inadmissible.

17. Child or Vulnerable Adult Witnesses

23.18 Section 16 provides that an eligible witness other than the accused is (i) a person under 17 at the time of the hearing, or (ii) a witness, the court considers, whose quality of evidence is likely to be diminished, owing to them suffering mental or physical disability. Subsection (5) refers to quality of evidence as meaning completeness, coherence (ability to answering questions) and accuracy.

18. Witnesses in Fear or Distress or Intimidation

23.19 Section 17 provides the same protection to a witness where the court is satisfied that the quality of their evidence is likely to be diminished, owing to fear of or distress in testifying. Subsection (2) directs the court to take into account such matters as the nature of the offence, age, background and beliefs of the witness and also any views expressed by the witness. The court must also consider any behaviour towards the witness by the accused or a member of their family or associates.

19. Improvement in Quality of Evidence: Section 19

23.20 Once the court has determined that the witness is eligible, before a special measure can be ordered the court must under s.19 be of the opinion that the placement of such a measure would be likely to improve the quality of that witnesses' evidence. If of this opinion, the court must then decide which measure (or combination of measures) is in its opinion likely to maximise the quality of the evidence, so far as is practicable. In so deciding, the court must consider all the circumstances of the case, including the views of the witness and whether such a direction might tend to inhibit the effective testing and probing of the evidence. Once a direction is made, it becomes binding. However, the court does have a discretionary power to discharge or vary such a direction, if it appears to be in the interests of justice to do so.

An application by one of the parties for a discharge, or variation, can only be made if there has been a material change of circumstances.

20. Primary Rule for Child Witnesses

23.21 Section 21 sets out the specific requirements relating to a child witness who is either under 17, or is deemed to be in need of special protection (s.35(3)), if the offence is a certain specified sexual offence, including kidnapping, child abduction, cruelty to a child or any offence which involves an assault on, injury or threat of injury to any person. Where that child witness has given evidence in an interview to the police by video recording, the court must provide for that to be admitted under s.27 as video recorded evidence in chief, or if this is not possible then evidence must be given by live video link, including cross-examination. This is deemed to be a primary rule (a presumption, an irrebutable one in regard to a child in need of special protection) which is subject to certain limitations such as it is not in the interests of justice to do so, or it is not likely to maximise the child's evidence, who is not in need of special protection.

In *R. (DPP) v Camberwell Green Youth Court* [2005] 1 W.L.R. 810, the House of Lords ruled unanimously that the presumption that child evidence be given by video recording does not offend art.6(3)(d) nor do the provisions create an inequality of arms between an accused to whom the provisions do not apply and other witnesses. In respect of art.6(3)(d), which gives the accused a right to examine witnesses against them, their Lordships applied the ruling in *Kostovski v Netherlands* [1989] 12 E.H.R.R. 434 which requires all evidence to be produced in the presence of the accused at a public hearing, with a view to adversarial argument, but that pre-trial statements can be admitted. This is not inconsistent with art.6(3)(d). To ensure fairness:

> "the accused should be given an adequate and proper opportunity to challenge and question a witness against him, either at the time the witness was making his statement or at some later stage of the proceedings."

The House of Lords further stated that the power of the court to discharge or vary a special measure direction in s.21(3) should not be used to frustrate the policy of the legislation, by making a direction as required for a child witness to give video recorded evidence and then immediately discharge it based on the nature of the case, or age of the defendant. Provided all the evidence, in whatever form, is presented at trial and the defendant with legal representation can have the opportunity to challenge it appropriately then there is no unfairness.

On the equality of arms point, the House of Lords recognised the criticisms in certain cases such as gang violence, that the special measures protection will apply to certain witnesses (such as those involved who decide to give the Queen's evidence) but other participants such as the accused do not qualify for protection. However, their Lordships felt that the court should not be deprived of the "best evidence" available from the other witnesses just because the special measures do not apply to the accused. There are practical difficulties to be overcome in allowing the special measures to apply to the accused, such as who would conduct the interview. To ensure a fair trial, the court has available its inherent powers, such as allowing them to give their best evidence, or allow an interpreter to assist with communication difficulties, or allowing a written statement to be read out, or even allowing leading questions.

Nonetheless, the House of Lords recognised, but left open, the issue of whether the decision in *R. (S) v Waltham Forest Youth Court* [2004] EWHC 715, which stated the court had no power to allow a child defendant to give evidence by live video link, could lead to a unfair trial where a young child defendant fears or is intimidated by a co-defendant.

21. The Special Measure Directions

23.22 The special measures themselves are contained in ss.23 to 30 and are as follows:

(i) Section 23: Screening the witness from the accused. This must not prevent the witness seeing or being seen by the judge/magistrates or legal representatives.

(ii) Section 24: Evidence by live link. To give evidence in this manner it must appear to the court to be in the interests of justice to do so. If the particular magistrates' court does not have the facilities, the case can be moved to a place with such facilities. Once a direction is given, the witness cannot give evidence in any other way without the permission of the court. Note also s.32(1)(a) of the Criminal Justice Act 1988, which came into effect on September 1, 2004 (see CJA 1988 (Commencement Order (SI 2004/19) which allows a court to order that a person other than the accused give evidence by live television link, relating to trial on indictment and appeals, if that witness is situated outside the UK. The relevant procedural steps for the reception of live link evidence of a non-vulnerable witness are contained in Pt 30 of the CrPR.

(iii) Section 25: Evidence given in private. This allows the court to order that all persons, other than the defendant and their legal representatives, that be excluded while the evidence is given. This is an exception to the important principle of open justice, but is justified in the interests of justice.

(iv) Section 26: Removal of wigs and gowns: This is only relevant to the Crown Court.

(v) Section 27: Video recorded evidence in chief. Before such a direction can be given, the court must be of the opinion that the admission of evidence, or part of it, in this manner, having regard to all the circumstances, is in the interests of justice. Of importance is subsection (3), which provides that the court, when considering whether the evidence, or part of it, should not be admitted, must consider whether any prejudice to the accused which might result if that part of the evidence is admitted, is outweighed by the desirability of showing the whole, or substantially the whole recorded interview. This is to allow the court to consider the method and conduct of the interview by the police and any questions or answers that are highly prejudicial, or inadmissible and should not be shown to the jury.

In *R. v K* [2006] 2 Cr.App.R. 10, the Court of Appeal approved the test of admissibility given in *R. v Hanton* [2005] EWCA Crim 2009, that despite any inducements to the child, could a reasonable jury with proper directions be sure that the child witness had given a credible and accurate account on the tape?

;Further, once a direction is made, the witness must not give evidence in any other way as to any matter that had been dealt with adequately in the recorded testimony, or without the permission of the court. The witness must be called by the prosecution unless it is agreed with the defence that they be cross-examined by live video link. If the witness cannot attend for cross-examination, then the court can direct the recorded testimony in chief not be admitted.

(vi) Section 28: Video recorded cross examination or re-examination. If a s.27 direction is given, then the court may also direct that the cross-examination of the witness is video recorded in the absence of the defendant, who is able to see and hear the cross-examination elsewhere.

(vii) Section 29: Examination through an intermediary. This allows for the examination in chief and cross-examination of a witness to be conducted through an interpreter or other approved person.

(viii) Section 30: Aids to communication. This allows for various communication aids to be used to enable the questions and answers to be communicated, regardless of an disability or impairment.

22. Warning to the Jury

23.23 Section 32 provides that if evidence has been given by way of a special measure in respect of a trial on indictment then the judge must give, if necessary, a warning to the jury that the special measure does not prejudice the accused.

23. Request by Jury to Review Video Recorded Evidence after Retiring

23.24 Difficulties may arise when evidence of examination in chief is given by video recording to the jury who have requested again to see it, having retired. No evidence can be given once the jury have retired to consider their verdict. It is often the case and no objection is generally raised, for the jury to take away with them the relevant exhibits, unless such exhibits may cause unpleasantness or prejudice the defendant. If the jury subsequently request to see additional exhibits then, as stated in *R. v Shankly* [2004] EWCA Crim 1224, the request should be discussed in open court and counsel given an opportunity to make representations.

The leading authority dealing with a request to see again evidence by video recording is *Rawlings and Broadbent* [1995] 2 Cr.App.R. 222. The Court of Appeal ruled that the judge had a discretionary power whether or not to grant the request, but must guard against any possible unfairness to the defendant by the jury seeing the examination in chief and no other evidence. If the request cannot be met by the judge giving directions from his written notes of what the witness said, rather the jury wishing to see how it was said, then the judge must comply with three requirements:

(i) the replay must be in court with the judge and both counsel present;

(ii) the judge must warn the jury against giving any disproportionate weight to the repeated evidence and to consider all the other evidence given;

(iii) after the replay the judge should remind the jury of what the witness had said from his notes.

In *R. v Mullen* [2004] EWCA Crim 602, the Court of Appeal ruled that allowing the jury to see a replay of the video recorded evidence is not restricted to the complainant and can apply to any supporting child witness providing that the guidance in *Rawlings and Broadbent* is followed. The Court further ruled that the special measure provisions do not provide a power to the judge to order the video recording of evidence given by live link on the possibility that the jury may request to see it again.

If the judge fails to follow the guidance in *Rawlings and Boardbent*, then as occurred in *R. v Y* [2004] EWCA Crim 157, this can amount to a material irregularity and render a conviction unsafe (see in contrast *R. v Collins* [2003] EWCA Crim 2643). In *R. v Welstead* [1996] 1 Cr.App.R. 59, the Court of Appeal ruled it to be permissible for the jury to have a copy of the transcript of the interview whilst they where watching the video if this would assist them in following the evidence. The judge must warn the jury that the transcript should only be used for that purpose and for them to concentrate on the oral evidence. In *R. v Mc Quiston* [1998] 1 Cr.App.R. 139, the Court of Appeal ruled that should the judge refuse to allow the jury to see the video recording again, then he should remind them of what that witness said from his notes and warn them not to give disproportionate weight to this evidence as against all the other evidence.

24. Part 29 of the Criminal Procedure Rules

23.25 Part 29 of the CrPR 2005 sets out in some detail the procedural steps to be taken if an application for a special measures direction is to be requested. This provides that the party must (except in the event of a later application under r.29.3 which can be made orally) complete the prescribed form to be sent to the Court Officer and to all other parties. If in the Youth Court this should be within 28 days from the date the defendant makes their first appearance or is brought before the court for the alleged offence. In the magistrates' court this is 14 days from the date the defendant indicates that they intend to plead not guilty and in respect of the Crown Court within 28 days of committal, or s.51 sending procedure (all subject to an application for extension of time).

The other parties can, if they wish, oppose the application, but must do so in writing within 14 days of the application being served on them. If the application is opposed, then the matter must be listed for a hearing. If unopposed, this can be done on the papers. The court must within three days of making its decision notify the parties involved. The remainder of Pt 29 deals with each particular special measure as set out in the legislation. Part 29 must be read in conjunction with Pt III.29 and Pt IV. 40 of the Criminal Practice Directions concerning support of witnesses giving evidence by live link and video recorded evidence in chief.

25. Ability of a Witness to Refresh their Memory

23.26 The principles of law that provide for a witness to be allowed to refresh their memory at trial as to what they may have written earlier, are to be found in s.139 of the Criminal Justice Act 2003 and two common law authorities. Section 139 provides for a witness who, when giving oral evidence about any matter and at any stage to be allowed to refresh their memory from a document previously made by them. This is provided (i) they confirm that the document records their recollection; and (ii) this recollection, when recorded earlier, is likely to have been significantly better than when now giving oral evidence.

Initially under the common law, the earlier statement had to have been made "*contemporaneously*". In *R. v Da Silva* [1990] 90 Cr.App.R. 233, the Court of Appeal stated that the trial judge has a discretionary power in the interests of justice to permit a witness, who has embarked upon giving evidence, to refresh their memory from a previous statement made at or near the relevant time, even if not done contemporaneously. This is subject to a number of specified conditions:

(i) that they cannot remember the events because of lapse of time;

(ii) that when they made the statement it represented their recollection at the time;

(iii) that they have not read the statement before coming into the witness box;

(iv) that they wish to read the statement before continuing with their evidence;

(v) that having read the statement they should then continue giving their evidence without further reference to it.

If the statement had been made contemporaneously, then the witness may use the statement to refresh their memory whilst giving evidence. In *R. v South Ribble Magistrates Court Ex p. Cochrane* [1996] 2 Cr.App.R. 544, the Divisional Court felt that the Court of Appeal in *Da Silva* had not intended the strict satisfaction of the first four conditions, before the court could exercise its discretionary power in respect of non-contemporaneous statements. It is much wider in that respect, so that the judge, when deciding whether to exercise his discretionary power, should apply the requirements of fairness and justice.

Section 137 of the Criminal Justice Act 2003 extends and relaxes the method by which witness evidence can be presented at court, by allowing the court to direct any evidence previously video recorded to be admitted as evidence in chief of the witness. This is available to both prosecution and defence witnesses, but not the defendant (s.137(1)(3a)). Subsection (2) states expressly that if the witness asserts that what they said in the recording is the truth, then that will be treated as part of their evidence in court and will not constitute hearsay evidence. Before a court makes a direction to allow the reception of the recorded evidence, it must appear to the court that the recollection of the witness in that recording is likely to be significantly better than their evidence if given orally and it is in the interests of justice to do so. In looking at the interests of justice, the court must have regard to the lapse of time, any issues of reliability, the quality of the recording itself and the views expressed by the witness.

Under s.138, if the recording is admitted, the witness may not give oral evidence of any matter which in the opinion of the court has been dealt with adequately in the recording. In terms of what can be admitted, the court has a discretion to allow all the recording or part of it to be read to the court, taking account of any possible risk of prejudice to the defendant. When considering the risk of prejudice, the court will need to balance this against the interests of justice in terms of it being desirable to show all, or substantially all of the recorded evidence.

Chapter Twenty Four

IDENTIFICATION AND EXPERT EVIDENCE

1. Introduction

24.01 When an alleged offence is reported to the police for investigation naturally the primary purpose of the police is to identify the offender(s). This can be achieved in a variety of ways:

(i) Visual identification, description, ID parade (including recognition evidence and CCTV).

(ii) Forensic identification, DNA/fingerprint samples, marks, and impressions, trace and contact evidence, explosives, documentary, fire, firearms, toxicology.

(iii) Facial mapping (see *R. v Stockwell* [1993] 97 Cr.App.R. 260)

(iv) Voice identification (See *R. v Hersey* [1998] Crim. L.R. 281, *R. v Robb* [1991] 93 Cr.App.R. 160).

(v) Written identification.

(vi) Ear identification.

The issue involved when such evidence is to be adduced is the weight/quality to be attached, in terms of probative value/prejudice. If this is compelling, then for the defence the issue will be one of human fallibility, incorrect lifting and logging of samples, multiple identities and breaks in continuity. In *Paterson v DPP* [1970] R.T.R. 329, the Divisional Court ruled that the police had failed to follow the correct procedure so as to ensure continuity of proof. There was no direct evidence to show continuity between the specimen container being sent by the police for testing and that which was examined at the laboratory. This gap in the prosecution's evidence could not be overcome by drawing an inference of continuity.

To avoid this gap appearing and the possibility of cross-contamination, the prosecution will need to obtain a statement from every person who handled the sample, at every stage. Nevertheless, the High Court in *Khatibi v DPP* [2004] EWHC 83 distinguished *Paterson* and ruled that a reasonable inference could be drawn from the fact that the placing of the label on the sample container had occurred at the material time when the sample was taken, although the prosecution had no evidence to show who or how and in what circumstances the label had been placed.

If the identification is scientific, then it is likely an expert opinion will be required to explain the methodology used and the analysis. In this instance, it is necessary to consider whether this forms part of an established field of expertise and whether scientific opinion within that field is united or divided. These issues are clearly of concern in regard to so-called identification by way of ear print on a glass panel (see *R. v Kempster* [2003] EWCA Crim 3555, below at para.24.25).

2. Visual Identification

24.02 If a prosecution case is based substantially on the visual identification of the defendant, then there is a real risk, should a conviction follow, of a miscarriage of justice, owing to the inherent weakness of such evidence, namely that of mistake. The defence, in rebuttal of such evidence, will generally challenge it by claiming either:

(i) mistaken identity (I was never there, it was not me, you have made a mistake), or

(ii) yes I was there (but I was never involved in the incident in question, you have seen me and mistaken me for the offender).

Both of these issues, for the prosecution, will be based on the "quality" of the identification.

3. The "Turnbull Direction"

24.03 Where visual identification is in dispute, then in order to avoid the risk of a miscarriage of justice, the jury need to take real care when assessing that evidence. To this effect, a court is required to give a "*Turnbull* Direction", as set out in *R. v Turnbull* [1977] 63 Cr.App.R. 132.

4. Starting Point and Submission of No Case to Answer

24.04 Under *Turnbull*, if the quality of the visual identification is poor, particularly where it is a "fleeting glance or a longer observation made in difficult conditions", then the judge should in these circumstances withdraw the case from the jury and direct an acquittal (see s.17 of the Criminal Justice Act 1967), unless there is other supporting evidence of the identification. Usually, the defence will approach the issue of identification in one of two ways: either make an application to have the evidence excluded before the commencement of the trial under s.78 of PACE 1984, or alternatively, wait and see how the case for the prosecution develops and at the conclusion of their case make a submission of no case to answer.

5. Special Need for Caution and Dangers of Identification Evidence with Reasons Warning

24.05 If the case for the prosecution is based wholly or substantially on visual identification evidence then fundamental to the *Turnbull* Direction is the duty of the judge to warn the jury of the special need for caution, before convicting on that evidence. The judge is then required to explain to the jury the reason for the need for such caution. This reason is that a convincing and credible witness, or witnesses, can still be mistaken. At this point the judge will need to consider whether it is necessary to give a full warning to the jury. In *R. v Bentley* [1994] 95 Cr.App.R. 342, the Court of Appeal stated that, for a full warning, there must be a warning as to the *dangers* of identification evidence and the reasons for those dangers existing, namely the courts' experience of miscarriages of justice based on mistaken identification.

Having given the warning, the judge should direct the jury to assess carefully the circumstances in which the identification is said to have taken place. Importantly, the judge must point to and remind the jury of any specific weaknesses in the identification evidence. Not only that, the judge must do so in a coherent fashion. In *R. v Fergus* [1994] 98 Cr.App.R. 313, Steyn L.J. observed (see also *R. v Pattinson & Exley* [1996] 1 Cr.App.R. 51 and *R. v Keene* 65 Cr.App.R. 247):

> "In a case dependent on visual identification and particularly where that is the only evidence, Turnbull makes it clear that it is incumbent on the trial judge to place before the jury any specific weaknesses which can arguably be said to have been exposed in the evidence. And it is not sufficient for the judge to invite the jury to take into account what counsel for the defence says about the specific weaknesses. Needless to say the judge must deal with the specific weaknesses in a coherent manner so that the cumulative impact of those specific weaknesses is fairly placed before the jury."

Likewise, the judge is required to point to and remind the jury of, evidence which supports the identification. Finally, if the case involves recognition evidence, then the judge must direct the jury that those who say they recognise the person, even close friends or relatives, can be mistaken. It is incumbent on the judge to follow the crucial elements in *Turnbull*, although the choice of words to emphasise the "full impact" of the direction is left to the judge. Each case will depend on its own particular facts, but the judge must explain the warning and the specific weaknesses otherwise, as occurred in *R. v Nash* [2004] EWCA Crim 2696, a conviction may be unsafe. In *R. v Davies* [2004] EWCA Crim 2521, the Court of Appeal accepted that in respect of voice identification, the judge will need to take greater care than even that for visual identification, but that for both types of identification the Turnbull direction applies.

In *R. v Hersey* [1998] Crim. L.R. 281, the Court of Appeal approved the use of a voice identification parade of 12 recorded voices listened to by the witness, who had had a 15-minute conversation with one of the offenders in a robbery. The Court further agreed with the trial judge's refusal to allow the defence to call expert evidence, but did state that some cases may require such evidence in order to assist, but that this should not be allowed to descend into a proliferation of expert evidence and any issues could be dealt with adequately in closing speeches and the summing up (see also *R. v Gummerson & Steadman* [1999] Crim. L.R. 680.

6. Border Line Cases

24.06 Invariably the trial judge is going to encounter cases where the difficult decision has to be made whether or not to accept a submission of no case to answer or allow the case to proceed and let the jury assess the weight of the evidence. This becomes all the more difficult in cases that involve serious offences. This point is well highlighted in *R. v Ryan (Shaun Joseph)* [2000] (unreported), in which the defendant was convicted of five counts of robbery of shops. The case for the prosecution rested heavily on visual identification together with seized clothing that similar to descriptions of the stolen items and weapons, and the defendent also lived in the vicinity. The Crown adduced the video image evidence of an expert analyst who confirmed that two of the robberies were committed by the same person who had certain facial features, but without reference to an eye witness who said that the robber had a burnt or scarred face.

The defence claimed mistaken identity on the ground that he was not responsible, but a man called Adams was. He was arrested for a similar robbery the day after the defendant had been arrested. Likewise, the defendant had similar features to another offender who had recently been released from an eight-year sentence for robbery. The defence made a submission of no case to answer; this was rejected by the judge. The defendant appealed. The Court of Appeal agreed with the trial judge on the basis that there was positive identification and expert evidence, but did say it was a case "close to the line".

Even though the identification evidence on its own is weak and therefore the case should be withdrawn for the jury, if there is other evidence to support that, albeit weak evidence, then the case could go before the jury. In *R. v George* [2003] Crim. L.R. 282, the Court of Appeal ruled that a qualified identification (this is where the witness sees the offender, gives a description but then fails to make a positive identification at an identification parade) can still be admitted, but that the prosecution cannot through careful questioning make it an unqualified one. Provided this evidence is relevant and probative in that it supports or is consistent with other evidence, or where it may assist in showing that the other evidence of the witness is correct, it is a matter for the judge to weigh up the probative value against its prejudicial effect. A defendant cannot be convicted on qualified identification evidence alone. This principle of law was later applied and confirmed by the Court of Appeal in *R. v Rose* [2006] EWCA Crim 1720.

7. Present at the Scene but deny participation (Innocent Presence)

24.07 If the defendant does not deny being at the scene, but denies participation then the judge may still as a matter of fairness, give a *Turnbull* Direction. This point is well highlighted and enunciated in *R. v Slater* [1995] 1 Cr.App.R. 584 where the Court of Appeal ruled that if the defendant did not deny that he was present at the scene, but denied involvement, then a *Turnbull* Direction is not automatic. Each case will depend on its own particular facts as to whether such a direction should be given. The Court concluded that:

> "It will be necessary (to given a Turnbull Direction) where, on the evidence, the possibility exists that a witness may have mistaken one person for another, for example, because of similarities in face, build, or clothing between two or more people present. In the present case the defendant had unusual features he was 6ft 6inchs tall and of heavy weight".

In contrast, the Court of Appeal in *R. v Thornton* [1995] 1 Cr.App.R. 578, held that a *Turnbull* Direction should have been given where the defendant had admitted being at a wedding reception and also present in the garden where the victim was assaulted by two men, but denied participation. The defendant was picked out at an ID parade both by the victim and a neighbour who witnessed the attack. Given that mistake as to participation was the sole contention of the defence, this was the only issue for the jury to decide; a *Turnbull* Direction was needed to ensure fairness (see also *R v O'Leary and Lloyd* [2002] EWCA Crim 2055.

8. Recognition Evidence by Police Officers

24.08 Even an honest witness can mistake someone whom they thought they recognised. A difficult issue arises when a police officer recognises someone committing an offence with whom they have had previous dealings. The following two cases highlight the point. In *R. v Caldwell and Dixon* [1994] 99 Cr.App.R. 73, four men were filmed robbing an off licence. The film was shown to a number of police officers, three of which recognised the defendants. At trial the Crown adduced identification evidence from the victims who had identified the defendants at an ID parade and secondly, the recognition evidence of the police officers.

The defence contended, relying on the authority of *Fowden and White*

[1982] Crim. L.R. 588, that this recognition evidence should be excluded on the ground that its prejudicial effect far outweighed its probative value. The Court of Appeal rejected this and stated that *Fowden and White* was not of general application given its own limited facts. On the issue of recognition of police officers the Court concluded that:

> "The plain fact is that recognition evidence of this kind is, subject always to the discretion of the trial judge to exclude it, prima facie admissible. Had the identifying police officers actually been present in the shop at the time of the robbery, plainly no one would have sought to question the admissibility of their evidence, whatever difficulties they might have faced in making their recognition. Recognition, all would surely agree, is generally more reliable than identification of a stranger and accordingly it ordinarily deserves greater evidential weight.
>
> The mere fact that police officers' knowledge of an accused comes from the accused's previous criminal activities cannot operate to bar the admissibility of their recognition evidence-any such approach would unfairly advantage those with criminal records."

To overcome the potential difficulties in challenging the officer's knowledge, they (the officer giving evidence) should avoid making any reference in evidence to any convictions or criminal associations.

24.09 More recently in *Attorney-General's Reference (No.2 of 2002)* (2002) EWCA Crim 2373, the Attorney-General made a reference under s.36 of the CJA 1972 for an opinion from the Court of Appeal on when and in what circumstances does recognition evidence become admissible? At the trial of G for violent disorder, the judge ruled that identification evidence by the camera operator who spent a considerable amount of time viewing the various films, becoming familiar with the appearance of G and where a police officer who had known G for about five years recognised him in the film, was inadmissible and directed an acquittal.

The Court of Appeal, approving the decision in *Caldwell* and other established authorities, ruled in its opinion on the law as follows:

> "In our judgement, on the authorities, there are, as it seems to us (at least four circumstances in which, subject to the judicial discretion to exclude, evidence is admissible to show and, subject to appropriate directions in the summing up) a jury can be invited to conclude, that the defendant committed the offence on the basis of a photographic image from the scene of the crime;
>
> (i) where the photographic image is sufficiently clear, the jury can compare it with the defendant sitting in the dock (*Dodson & Williams* 79 Cr App R 220)
>
> (ii) where a witness knows the defendant sufficiently well to recognise him as the offender depicted in the photographic image, he can give evidence of this (*Fowden & White* [1982] Crim LR 588, *Kajala v Noble* (1982) 75 Cr. App. R. 149, *Caldwell & Dixon* and *Blenkinsop* 1 Cr App R (S) 7); and this may be so even if the photographic image is no longer available for the jury (*Taylor v The Chief Constable of Chester* 84 Cr App R 191).
>
> (iii) where a witness who does not know the defendant spends substantial time viewing and analysing photographic images from the scene, thereby acquiring special knowledge which the jury does not have, he can give evidence of identification based on a comparison between those images and

a reasonably contemporary photograph of the defendant, provided that the images and the photograph are available to the jury. (*Clare & Peach* [1995] 2 Cr App R 333)

(iv) a suitably qualified expert with facial mapping skills can give opinion evidence of identification based on a comparison between images from the scene,(whether expertly enhanced or not and a reasonably contemporary photograph of the defendant, provided the images and the photograph are available for the jury (*Stockwell* 97 Cr App R 260, *Clarke* [1995] 2 Cr App R 425 and *Hookway* [1999] Crim LR 750).

Accordingly, the Court of Appeal ruled in regard to the specific questions raised that evidence from a witness not at the scene, but who recognises the defendant from a video, is admissible, even though the video is available for the jury to make their own assessment of its quality. Likewise, it is not a requirement of law for the witness to have a special skill, ability or any particular experience.

It is important to bear this very much in mind, when faced with a case in which not only is there video or filmed evidence, but also evidence from a witness who has viewed the video several or indeed many times and makes a positive identification. In such a case thorough and careful analysis will need to be made as to the quality of the video footage and the possibility of a mistaken identification, even if the witness states that they recognise the defendant. The quality of the footage is very much down to the equipment used, such as footage from a mobile phone which will have varying degrees of quality.

9. DNA/fingerprint Samples: Admissibility in Evidence at Trial

24.10 DNA or Deoxyribonucleic Acid is concerned with the genetic information derived from cells that contain chromosomes, given by our parents, i.e. male and female gametes. In giving evidence at court, the forensic expert will give a frequency of the genotype by calculations, using the accepted STR (Short Tandem Repeats). The difficulty for the defence and the court is what proper weight a jury ought to give to such evidence. In *R. v Doheny and Adams* [1997] 1 Cr.App.R. 369, the Court of Appeal set out the procedures which should be adopted when DNA evidence is adduced. Philips L.J. stated:

> "The prosecutor's fallacy can be simply demonstrated. If one person in a million has a DNA profile which matches that obtained from the crime stain, then the suspect will be one of perhaps 26 men in the UK who share that characteristic. If no fact is known about the defendant, other than that he was in the UK at the time of the crime, the DNA evidence tells us no more than that there is a statistical probability that he was the criminal of one in 26."

His Lordship went on to say:

> "When the scientist gives evidence it is important that he should not over step the line which separates his province from that of the jury. He will properly explain to the jury the nature of the match (the matching DNA characteristics) between the

> DNA in the crime stain and the DNA in the blood sample taken from the defendant. He will properly, on the basis of empirical statistical data, give the jury the random occurrence ratio-the frequency with which the matching DNA characteristics are likely to be found in the population at large. Provided that he has the necessary data, and the statistical expertise, it may be appropriate for him then to say how many people with the matching characteristics are likely to be found in the UK-or perhaps in a more limited relevant sub-group, such as, for instance, the Caucasian sexually active males in the Manchester area.
>
> This will often be the limit of the evidence which he can properly and usually give. It will then be for the jury to decide, having regard to all the relevant evidence, whether they are sure that it was the defendant who left the crime stain, or whether it is possible that it was left by some one else with the same matching DNA characteristics. The scientist should not be asked his opinion on the likelihood that it was the defendant who left the crime stain, nor when giving evidence should he use terminology which may lead the jury to believe that he is expressing such an opinion."

In *Pringle v The Queen* [2003] UKPC 9, Lord Hope, having referred to the helpful guidance given by Phillips L.J. to trial judges on how to manage DNA evidence in *R. v Doheny* [1997] 1 Cr.App.R. 369 stated:

> "the cogency of this evidence makes it particularly important that DNA testing is rigorously conducted so as to obviate the risk of contamination in the laboratory and the method of analysis and the basis of the statistical calculation should be transparent to the defence so far as possible."

In *R. v Mitchell* [2004] EWCA 1928, the Court of Appeal quashed the appellant's conviction of kidnapping, rape and indecent assault of a 16-year old-girl, on the basis that the judge was wrong to direct the jury that DNA evidence in the form of a male profile obtained from the victim, which did not implicate the appellant, could not assist the defence case one way or another and neither supported or detracted from each case. Given the possibility of contamination, it was neutral evidence, since expert evidence showed that it could not be ruled out that the profile was entirely innocent and may have belonged to the offender. Rix L.J., giving the leading judgment, stated that trial judges should exercise great care when considering the value of scientific evidence for the benefit of the jury and should guard against the raising of scientific speculative possibilities that could distract the jury's concentration from evidence that genuinely supports the defence case.

24.11 In a comprehensive review on the use of DNA the Australian Law Reform Commission (Discussion paper 66 on "Protection of Human Genetic Information" (2002) Chs 34 to 39) proposed the giving of a standard direction to juries, highlighting the need for caution, both when evaluating and considering the statistical calculations of DNA evidence. In particular, within the direction, the judge should highlight the potential unreliability of such evidence, and the need to avoid misunderstanding the "prosecution fallacy" and to weigh the forensic evidence against all the other relevant evidence. In *R. v Watters* [2000] (unreported) the Court of Appeal held, on the particular facts of the case, that the DNA evidence presented to the jury alone, without other corroborating evidence, was insufficient to sustain a conviction.

Advances in the techniques of abstracting DNA samples have led to the use of Low Copy Number (LCN) as a method of DNA testing in which microscopic particles of DNA are amplified to produce a larger sample. However, its continued use and reliability has been brought into question in *R. v Hoey* [2007] (trial at first instance in Northern Ireland), in which Justice Weir ruled inadmissible not so much the reliability of the evidence but the risks of contamination during the collection and storage of the minute samples, in the instant case being "thoughtless" and "slapdash" .

Simply touching a cup will leave enough cells to allow the LCN extraction which had occurred in *Hoey*, in which the LCD matched not only the defendant, but also a 15-year-boy from Sussex who had never been to Northern Ireland. Accordingly, it was impossible for the defendant to have a fair trial for the mass killing in the Omagh bombing. Given the greater use and strength of DNA evidence and the wider powers of the police to take and retain such samples the Nuffield Council of Bioethics have recently produced a detailed report with recommendations into the ethical, social and legal impact in the use of bioinformation for forensic purposes (see http://www.nuffieldbioethics.org).

10. Admissibility of Fingerprint Evidence

24.12 The issues surrounding the accuracy and precision of fingerprint analysis and its admissibility, were determined by the Court of Appeal in *R. v Buckley* [1999] 163 J.P. 561. The Court of Appeal, in reviewing the historical development of fingerprinting, ruled:

> "Fingerprint evidence, like any other evidence, is admissible as a matter of law, if it tends to prove guilt of the accused. It may so tend, even if there are only a few similar ridge characteristics but it may, in such a case, have little weight. It may be excluded in the exercise of judicial discretion, if its prejudicial effect outweighs its probative value. When the prosecution seek to rely on fingerprint evidence, it will usually be necessary to consider two questions: the first, a question of fact, is whether the control print from the accused has ridge characteristics, and if so how many, similar to those of the print on the item relied on. The second, a question of expert opinion, is whether the print on the item relied on was made by the accused. This opinion will usually be based on the number of similar ridge characteristics in the context of other findings made on comparison of the two prints."

The Court then gave the following guidance:

> "If there are fewer than eight similar ridge characteristics, it is highly unlikely that a judge will exercise his discretion to admit such evidence and, save in wholly exceptional circumstances, the prosecution should not seek to adduce such evidence. If there are eight or more similar ridge characteristics, a judge may or may not exercise his or her discretion in favour of admitting the evidence. How the discretion is exercised will depend on all the circumstances of the case, including in particular:

(i) the experience and expertise of the witness;
(ii) the number of similar ridge characteristics
(iii) whether there are dissimilar characteristics
(iv) the size of the print relied on, in that the same number of similar ridge characteristics may be more compelling in fragment of print than in an entire print; and
(v) the quality and clarity of the print on the item relied upon, which may involve, for example, consideration of possible injury to the person who left the print, as well as factors such as smearing or contamination.

In every case where fingerprint evidence is admitted, it will generally be necessary, as in relation to all expert evidence, for the judge to warn the jury that it is evidence opinion only, that the expert's opinion is not conclusive and that it is for the jury to determine whether guilt is proved in the light of all the evidence."

The evidence of fingerprints is gathered at the scene by the scenes of crime officer, who will take a lift from possible items where the suspect may have left a print. If this is matched to the defendant, then it can amount to powerful evidence to establish their presence at the scene. To challenge this evidence a defendant will need a legitimate explanation as to why their prints were found at the scene. As with DNA evidence, the defence will be one of (i) innocent (i.e. was at the scene innocently and lawfully, (ii) it was planted, (iii) quality of the sample and (iv) contamination, (see *R. v McNamara* [2004] EWCA Crim 2818).

11. Identification Procedure

24.13 If a witness provides a description of a suspect, the police must make a note of this and in the case where a suspect's identity is not known, may take the witness to the particular neigbourhood or place to see if they can identify the suspect. The procedure relating to the identification of a suspect is found in the Codes of Practice, Code D3(2). In *K v DPP* [2003] EWHC 351, the High Court ruled that where the police had taken the defendant to the window of a police car in which the victim was sat for identification, this was in clear breach of Code D3(2)(b) which provides that such a procedure can only be used when the suspect's identity is not known. In this case the defendant was clearly known. Once the suspect's identity is known, then one of the identification procedures, namely (i) video and ID parade, (ii) group identification and (iii) confrontation, must be considered.

Conversely, in *B v DPP* [2006] EWHC 660, the High Court distinguished *K v DPP*, ruling that although the police had driven the victim past a bus stop for a second time, having identified the suspect on the first time, this was one continuous procedure and therefore the suspect was not known to the police until the second drive past and therefore this did not breach Code D3(2)(b) in terms of procedure once the suspect was known.

12. Showing Photographs of Suspect: Annex E of Code D

24.14 It is important to note that if from the description the suspect is known to the police, then a witness must not be shown photographs. Only one witness must be shown photographs at any one time. The witness must be shown at least 12 photographs and be told that the suspect may or may not be in the photographs. If a witness makes a positive ID, then no other witness must be shown photographs. The responsibility of showing photographs is that of a sergeant. The Code does not prevent or restrict the showing of films or photographs to the public through the media locally or nationally and to other police officers. However, the Code makes it clear that when showing them to potential witnesses this must be done on an individual basis in order to avoid the risk of collusion.

13. Requirements to Hold an Identification Procedure

24.15 If the suspect disputes an identification or purported identification made by a witness, then an identification procedure must be held unless it is not practicable, or it would not serve any useful purpose in proving or disproving the suspect's involvement in the alleged offence. If it is proposed to hold an Identification Procedure (ID), then the suspect must at first be initially offered a video or a parade ID procedure, unless neither are practicable and a group ID is more suitable. In all circumstances, the police have a discretion to hold an ID procedure, if it would be useful.

14. Safeguards

24.16 If the police are to hold either a video or ID procedure then the following safeguards must be adhered to:

(i) The arrangements for and conduct of the ID procedure must be the responsibility of an inspector, who is not involved with the investigation (the identification officer).

(ii) A suspect must consent to the procedure and shall be asked to state their reasons if they don't consent (not needed for a group identification or confrontation).

(iii) It must be explained to the suspect the purposes of the ID procedure (unless covert group identification), their entitlement to free legal advice and to have a friend or solicitor present, in regard to a vulnerable suspect an appropriate adult.

(iv) All unauthorised persons must be excluded, including any investigating officer.

(v) The witness must not be able to see, or be reminded of any previous identification, i.e. photograph or image or any description.

(vi) The suspect is entitled to be provided with any descriptions given by witnesses.

(vii) Written records must be made.

15. Consequences of a Suspect Refusing or Failing to Take Part

24.17 If the suspect refuses to take part in a video or ID parade, then the consequences of refusing or failing to take part are that the Identification Officer has a discretion to make arrangements for a either a covert video, or group identification. In addition, the reasons for refusing or failing to take part are admissible evidence at any subsequent trial. If none of these procedures are practicable, then the ID Officer can arrange for a confrontation, which does not require the suspect's consent. The ID Officer must supply the suspect a written notice explaining their rights and the procedure. If a suspect changes their appearance prior to the parade in order to avoid being identified, then this may be adduced as evidence or that an alternative method of identification is used.

16. Video Identification: Annex A of Code D

24.18 There must be at least eight other people in the images in addition to the suspect. Those shown must resemble the suspect in age, height, general appearance and stance. The suspect or their solicitor must be given a reasonable opportunity to see the images and object if necessary. Before showing the images, the suspect/solicitor must be supplied with details of the first description. Only one witness at a time should be shown the images, and must view them at least twice and then be asked to state the number of the suspect if identified. A record must be made of those participating and of the outcome.

In *R. v Marcus* [2004] EWCA Crim 3387, the appellant was alleged to have committed six street robberies by knife point at cash machines. The complainants described the offender as black, 30 to 40, with greying hair on the temples and a grey goatee beard. The defendant matched the description, but denied any involvement. He consented to a video ID procedure. However, there were insufficient numbers of volunteers of similar appearance to the defendant. An inspector searched two databases and selected what he thought were the best images, but these did not sufficiently match the defendant. Accordingly, he arranged for the images to "masked" that is, marks to be superimposed, but identification from such images is known to be low.

For this reason and on the advice of the CPS the police, unknown to the defendant, made two parallel unmasked compilations (none of which was similar to the defendant) with the intention of showing the to complainants who could not make an identification from the masked images. Four complainants made an identification from these images. The defendant was convicted and appealed on the basis that such a procedure was unfair and in breach of the codes of practice. The Court of Appeal quashed his conviction and held that it was quite extraordinary that the police did not inform the defendant and that this amounted to a deliberate device to evade the provisions of the Code and that such conduct must be condemned by the Court. Therefore the trial judge was wrong not to exclude the evidence under s.78 of PACE 1984.

17. Parade Identification: Annex B of Code D

24.19 The suspect must first be cautioned. The identification parade must consist of at least eight persons in addition to the suspect, who as far as practicable resemble the suspect in age, height, and general appearance. The suspect has a right to change position. The witness must be told that the suspect may or may not be present. There should be only one witness at a time and the witness must walk along the parade at least twice. The witness may ask for a person in the parade to speak or gesture. If the witness cannot make a positive ID, then they must say so (this can include the witness asking for a hat to be removed). Once the witness has left, the suspect will be asked if they wish to make any comment.

In *R. v Marrin* [2002] EWCA Crim 251, it was stated that it was not a breach of the code or indeed objectionable or unfair to use some facial colouring or dye to give similar features to the suspect. Conversely, in *R. v Quinn* [1995] 1 Cr.App.R. 480, the police in a number of respects breached the basic procedure to be followed. The Court of Appeal stated that the police are legally required to follow and observe the statutory code and not substitute it with their own procedure or rules. Whilst the judge may have been right to admit the ID evidence, he failed to make specific reference adequately to the breaches of the code and leave it the jury to assess the discrepancies in identification, in the light of the breaches.

18. Group Identification: Annex C of Code D

24.20 A group identification is when the witness sees the suspect in an informal group of people. These can be held with the suspect's consent or covertly without their consent. The location of the group identification is a matter for the identification officer taking into account any representations. The place should be where other people are either passing by or waiting around informally, in groups so as the suspect is able to join them and be capable of being seen by the witness at the same time as the others in the group. If covertly (i.e. without the suspect's knowledge) then the location will need to be somewhere where the suspect travels regularly. The witness is asked to observe the group and to look at each person in the group at least twice and point out any person they saw previously. The suspect should be allowed to take what position they wish in the group and the length of observation is at the discretion of the ID Officer.

19. Confrontations: Annex D of Code D

24.21 This is where the witness confronts the alleged suspect. The witness is told that the person they saw on an earlier specified occasion may or may not be the person they are about to confront. Force cannot be used to make the suspect's face visible. The witness must be asked "Is this the person?" Confrontation ought to take place in the police station. It is important to note that the use of a confrontation as a means of identification is to be used as a last resort and only if no other procedure is practicable. In *R. v McCulloch* [1999] (unreported) the Court of Appeal quashed the appellant's conviction owing to significant breaches of Code D when a Customs officer had identified the appellant by confronting him at his arrest. In such circumstances, a identification or video film parade should have been by which the officer could have identified the suspect (see also *R. v Kensett* [1993] 157 J.P. 1116).

20. Failure to Hold ID Parade under Code D and the "Forbes Direction"

24.22 Code D3.12 states that if a suspect disputes a identification, then an identification procedure shall be held. This led to several conflicting decisions in the Court of Appeal (see *R. v Popat (No.2)* [2000] 1 Cr.App.R. 387 as to whether in the context of the codes of practice the word "shall" was either mandatory or directory. This conflict was resolved by the House of Lords in *R. v Forbes* [2001] 1 A.C. 473. If the suspect consents or requests an identification procedure, but the police refuse to hold one, then a "Forbes Direction" ought to be given. In *R. v Forbes* [2001] 1 A.C. 473, the House of Lords held that:

> "In any case where a breach of Code D has been established but the trial judge has rejected an application to exclude evidence to which the defence objected because of that breach, the trial judge should in the course of summing up to the jury
>
> (a) explain that there has been a breach of the code and how it has arisen, and
> (b) invite the jury to consider the possible effect of the breach.
>
> The terms of the appropriate direction will vary from case to case and breach to breach. But if the breach is a failure to hold an identification parade when required by D2.3, the jury should ordinarily be told that an identification parade enables a suspect to put the reliability of an eye witness's identification to the test, that the suspect has lost the benefit of that safeguard and that the jury should take account of that fact in its assessment of the whole case, giving such weight as it thinks fair.

In cases where there had been an ID parade with the consent of the suspect, and the eye- witness has identified the suspect, in circumstances involving no breach of the code, the trial judge will ordinarily tell the jury that they can view the identification at the parade as strengthening the prosecution case but may also wish to alert the jury to the possible risk that the eye-witness may have identified not the culprit who committed the crime but the suspect identified by the same witness on the earlier occasion."

In *R. v Haynes* [2004] EWCA Crim 390, the Court of Appeal, having considered the decision in *Forbes*, observed that the Code must not be applied too rigidly and that if a ID parade is not held in breach of Code D, then the issue becomes one of fairness, bearing in mind the purpose of the Code D. It is also important to note that Code D3.12 makes it clear that an ID procedure does not have to be followed if it would be impracticable, or to do so would serve no useful purpose in proving one way or the other the suspect's involvement, i.e. where the suspect is well known to the complainant or witness.

21. Reception of Expert Evidence

24.23 The use of expert evidence in a criminal trial generally becomes necessary where, without such evidence, the jury and the court would not be able to assess properly the quality and weight of either other evidence or the findings of the expert themselves (see *R. v Turner* [1974] 60 Cr.App.R. 80 and the judgment of Lawton L.J.). It is an exception to the fundamental rule that a witness in giving oral evidence can only recall what they saw or did, or personally heard and that they are not to give their opinion.

In a murder trial the prosecution will call a pathologist to explain the cause of death, which will assist the jury in deciding whether this was due to an unlawful act caused by the defendant. Recently, however, the reliance on expert evidence alone has led to a number of unsafe convictions. This becomes especially more acute where there is no consensus of opinion within that field of expertise, see *R. v Cannings, R. v Patal* and *R. v Sally Clark* [2003] EWCA Crim 1020, concerning the flawed evidence of Dr Meadows' statistical analysis to show that the death of a child by the mother was unlawful and not medical. See also *R. v George* [2007] EWCA Crim 2722, concerning the quality and strength of a single particle (11.5 microns, 1:100th of a millimetre) of firearm discharge residue to support a conviction of murder. And *R. v Jenkins* [2004] EWCA Crim 2047, concerning the disputed expert examination of fine blood splatter found on the defendant from a dying person.

The principle found in *Turner* has been approved in several authorities including *R. v Stockwell* [1993] 97 Cr.App.R. 260 and *R. v Clarke* [1995] 2 Cr.App.R. 425. In *R. v Robb* [1991] 93 Cr.App.R. 161, Bingham L.J. set out the principles to be adopted on the reception of expert evidence as follows:

> "the two relevant questions are whether study and experience will give a witness's opinion an authority which the opinion of one not so qualified will lack, and (if so) whether the witness in question is skilled and has adequate knowledge. If these conditions are met the evidence of the witness is in law admissible, although the weight to be attached to his opinion must of course be assessed by the tribunal of fact."

For the court to allow to the reception of an opinion the court must be satisfied that the expert has the necessary learning and experience. This test is important in order to avoid and ensure that the defendant is not faced with some enthusiastic amateur or a person who is considered to be a charlatan. Nevertheless, a well-respected expert can become a formidable witness whose expert opinion is seen as almost infallible or incontrovertible, as can be seen in *R. v Sally Clerk*. It is important to be aware that, as stated in *R. v Stockwell*, the judge must direct the jury and make it clear to them that they are not bound to accept the opinion of an expert witness and that it is for them to consider it and either accept, or reject wholly, or partly, such evidence. A failure to give this direction would lead to a conviction being ruled unsafe.

It can often be the case that in trials for the possession of a prohibited drug with intent to supply, the defendant will claim that it was for personal use only and therefore no intent to supply. To refute this contention, the Court of Appeal ruled in *R. v Hodges v Walker* [2003] 2 Cr.App.R. 15 that evidence in the form of the expert opinion of an experienced police officer in the field of drug supply, methods, costs and quantity can be received and admitted for this purpose. The reception of this evidence is required to give assistance to a jury on matters which fall outside their common knowledge and experience. Conversely in *Edwards* [2001] EWCA Crim 2185, the Court of Appeal ruled that expert opinion on the tolerance to ecstasy was inadmissible where the person called lacked the necessary medical and toxicology qualifications.

22. Admissibility of a New or Developing Science

24.24 If either the prosecution or the defence seek to adduce evidence from an expert in a new or developing science, then the issue of admissibility becomes more difficult. In *R. v Clarke* [1995] 2 Cr.App.R. 425, the Court of Appeal ruled on the admissibility of facial mapping techniques, whereby images taken from CCTV footage of the crime were made into stills and then superimposed onto photographs of the alleged offender. The Court observed, referring to *Stockwell* [1993] 97 Cr.App.R. 260, that new and developing techniques for the prevention and detection of crime could not be ignored by the courts and, "that it would be entirely wrong to deny the law of evidence he advantages to be gained from new techniques and new advances in science".

If that evidence provides the jury with relevant information and assistance that themselves do not possess, then the evidence ought to be admitted. This will be case specific and the question of admissibility on whether such evidence can be tendered is for the trial judge to determine. Nevertheless, the court will need to adopt a cautionary approach to the issue of weight and admissibility of yet to be substantiated scientific evidence. In *R. v Gilfoyle* [2001] 2 Cr.App.R. 57, the appellant contended that he had no involvement in his wife's death, which he claimed was suicide by hanging. The Court of Appeal refused to accept fresh psychiatric evidence in the form of a "psychological autopsy" on what state of mind of the victim would have been in, in a potential stressful situation, as amounting to an, "unstructured and speculative conclusion" resulting in "little or no help to the jury". The Court held, approving the approach in *R. v Studwick and Murry* [1998] 99 Cr.App.R. 326, that evidence derived from a new or developing branch of science or medicine was inadmissible unless adopted or accepted by the "scientific community as being able to provide accurate and reliable opinion" (see also *R. v Weightman* [1991] 92 Cr.App.R. 291).

This is exactly the difficult issue surrounding the quality of making comparisons with a human ear print found on a glass panel at the scene of the crime to that of the suspect's. In *R. v Dallagher* [2003] 1 Cr App R 12, the Court of Appeal quashed the appellant's conviction for an appalling murder of an elderly lady and ordered a re-trial. The court received fresh evidence and was concerned with the reliability of ear print identification given as a new technique, but lacking a clear range of expert opinion. Further, new evidence suggested the technique used by the expert for the prosecution, a Mr Van Der Lugt (a Dutch Police Officer), had real and potential flaws in its findings. Nevertheless, in applying the decision in *Gilfoyle* [2001] 2 Cr.App.R. 57, the Court stated that the question of admissibility is very much dependant on whether that particular body of scientific expertise was now considered to be sufficiently well established to satisfy the tests of relevance and reliability ordinarily and generally applied to evidence. There is no reason or justification to have an enhanced test of admissibility of such evidence.

24.25 In *R. v Kempster* [2003] EWCA Crim 3555, the appellant was convicted of a series of appalling burglaries on properties occupied by elderly resident. His conviction was based on ear print identification of which he sought on appeal to challenge its reliability in light of the *Dallagher* decision. The Court of Appeal distinguished *Dallagher* as being materially factually different. In *Dallagher* there was a complete denial, whereas the appellant admitted that it may have been his ear print and that it was there for a legitimate reason of previously doing some work at the property. Given other supporting evidence in the case, the fresh expert evidence presented by the appellant on appeal would not had affected the outcome of the case.

In a renewed appeal referred by the CCRC based on fresh evidence, the Court of Appeal in *R. v Kempster* [2008] EWCA Crim 975 confirmed that a positive identification is capable by ear print comparison. The issue in each case will be based on comparison reliability, surrounding the uneven structure of the ear itself and the amount of pressure exerted which can distort the ear at variable points.

Applying the ordinary tests of relevance and reliability, the Court of Appeal, in *R. v Luttrell and Others* [2004] EWCA Crim 1344, dismissed the appellant's appeal against conviction for conspiracy to handle stolen goods and ruled that lip reading expert evidence (auditory perception) of non-audible CCTV footage was admissible, even though such evidence can lack perfection. For this reason if lip reading evidence is admitted, the judge must give a "special warning" as to its limitations and the inherent dangers from it and the special need for caution. The precise terms of the warning will be fact dependent, but in most cases the judge will need to put emphasis on the risk of mistakes as to the words indicated to have been used by the lip reader, the reasons for such potential mistakes and the fact that even a convincing authoritative and truthful witness can still be a mistaken witness.

In *R. v Robb* [1991] 93 Cr.App.R. 161, the Court of Appeal ruled that the judge was right to admit evidence from a phonetics expert as identifying the appellant from a tape recording, by auditory analysis alone, even though this technique only represented a minority view within the field of linguistics. The fact that he preferred this method and given that such a method was not discredited or wrong the appellant had not been unfairly prejudiced. However, in *R. v O'Doherty* [2003] 1 Cr.App.R. 5 the Court of Appeal of Northern Ireland distinguished the decision in *Robb* and ruled that unlike a fingerprint, which is unchangeable and unique, a person's voice is variable, therefore auditory analysis alone is insufficient. Auditory analysis can only reveal that samples have the same accent and a similar voice quality.

To improve the quality and reliability of such evidence, it will need to be supported by quantitative acoustic analysis to reveal whether the voice is that of the same person. Listening alone would not produce a high positive match. The Court did nonetheless recognise three exceptions to the general requirement of quantitative analysis, namely:

(i) where the voice is known;

(ii) a voice with rare characteristics; and

(iii) the issue of identification was related to accent or dialect.

24.26 To ensure a fair trial and to safeguard against prejudice, the Court ruled that the jury should be allowed to listen to the tape recording from which the identification was made and the judge in summing up should warn of the dangers of relying on their listening observations, since they neither have the training or equipment.

Additionally, the judge will need to balance out the strengths and weakness of the material in the case, and to remind the jury that the quality of such evidence may be impaired by the lighting, the angle of the view of the suspect talking, the distance involved, other possible interferences with the observation, the language spoken and the expert's familiarity with it. They should also consider use of single syllable words, the context of the speech and the probative value of the analysis in terms of certain words or phrases or long passages of conversation. This warning is very similar to that found in *Turnbull* for visual identification and whilst each direction will need to be tailored to the particular facts a failure by the judge to follow the general thrust of the warning may lead to a conviction being ruled unsafe.

In *R. v Barnes* [2005] EWCA Crim 1158, the appellant sought to rely on the expert opinion of arboriculturalist to establish that his fingerprint could not have been obtained from the door at the scene of the crime, based on the type of wood grain. The Court of Appeal ruled that the fresh evidence of this expert was of limited relevance, given that he was not qualified nor experienced to evaluate and compare a fingerprint lift from a door. The Court concluded that if such evidence had been available to the jury, it would not have impacted upon the guilty verdict.

23. Probative Value of Expert Evidence and Lack of Certainty

24.27 It must always be remembered that a conviction is secured on legal proof, not medical proof. The prosecution must prove all legal elements to the offence. If there is any doubt, then the jury ought to acquit, or at the insistence of the judge withdraw the case from the jury. In *R. v Bracewell* [1979] 68 Cr.App.R. 44, the Court of Appeal approved the direction of the trial judge on his approach to the problematic issue of needing to draw a distinction between scientific proof as opposed to necessity of legal proof, in order to found a conviction. If the expert is unable to give scientific/medical certainty to their findings then there will arise other possibilities and the expert will need to make concessions to these possibilities.

It is these other possibilities that will be pursued vigorously in cross-examination, by inviting the expert witness to consider them and pose the question "can you exclude the possibility?" If the expert findings cannot exclude other possibilities, then the answer must be no. The issue will then become one of remoteness in the sense of realistic likelihood of other possibilities being a factor. In other words can such possibilities, although in existence, be for all practical purposes, so unlikely that they can now safely ignored (see also *R. v Dawson and Others* [1985] 81 Cr.App.R. 150, *R. v Williams* [2003] EWCA Crim 2960). Where there exists a clear divided opinion between experts within the same field, then in some instances concern will be raised about the strength of the case against the defendant and whether it should be withdrawn from the jury, or if following conviction, new fresh evidence can be received to challenge further that divided opinion.

This dilemma for the law is well illustrated in cases involving the unexplained death of an infant child where there are no identifiable physical injuries, but the child suffers an apparent life threatening event. If the allegation is murder or manslaughter, then it is for the prosecution to prove an unlawful and deliberate act, or an infliction of violence. If the defence claim that the cause of death was not these, they may suggest that it can only be explained by natural or other possible causes such as infection, or that it simply cannot be explained by the known causes of infant death, i.e. organ defect. Medically, this is generally called Sudden Infant Death Syndrome and was explored in a long judgment by the Court of Appeal in *R. v Cannings* [2004] 2 Cr.App.R. 7.

24.28 Paragraph 178 contains the premise of the Court's decision to quash the appellant's conviction for murdering two of her children by suffocation, the defence having contended cot death. The Court ruled that in cases where there are two or more unexplained infant deaths in the same family, which is rare (there is unequivocal disagreement amongst the reputable experts on the explanation for the cause of death, leading to an inability to exclude as reasonable and not a fanciful possibility death by natural causes) the death could have been from natural causes, either explained or unexplained.

In such circumstances the starting point is that the prosecution of a parent(s) ought not to be commenced or discontinued unless there is other convincing evidence independent from the expert evidence, which tends to support the allegation of deliberate harm. No trial should proceed on strongly divided or conflicting medical opinion alone, which is currently the position regarding the sudden and unexpected death of a child, despite the known fact that mothers do smother their infant child(ren). Such deaths will remain unexplained, until medial opinion changes. It is unsafe to draw inferences of guilt from the coincidence of other infant deaths in the family. This decision had the potential to have wide ranging implications for the reception of prosecution expert evidence where there is divided opinion. However, the Court of Appeal in *R. v Kai–Whitewind* [2005] EWCA Crim 1092 observed that the ruling is to only apply in the particular context of the uncertainly of two or more unexplained infant death situations where:

> "in the absence of any other cogent evidence beyond the inferences drawn from coincidence, the jury would lack any reasoned basis for preferring the opinions of one reputable set of experts to the other in an area where the true knowledge, even of the experts themselves, is necessarily limited."

Dismissing the appellant's appeal against her conviction for the deliberate killing of an infant, the Court of Appeal distinguished *Cannings*, stating on the facts that it had no application. There was no risk given the evidence of the jury drawing adverse inferences from coincidence. *Cannings*, according to the Court, is not authority for creating a general proposition of law. If there is conflicting expert opinion, then the evidence for the prosecution is neutralised automatically. In consequence of the decision in *Cannings* the Attorney-General appointed an interdepartmental party working group to consider previous cases for possible wrongful convictions (several hundred have been reviewed).

This led to the appeal in *R. v Harris and Others* [2006] 1 Cr.App.R. 5, concerning the uncertainty surrounding shaken baby syndrome or non-accidental head injury (NAHI). Prosecutions where based on proof of a triad of intracranial injuries to establish unlawful and deliberate infliction of violence as opposed to accident or just rough play. The critical question for the jury is to decide what degree, if any, of force was applied to the child and the gravity of the injury suffered. However, the infallibility of the triad has been doubted by a team of reputable doctors. The Court of Appeal, in considering the principle in *Cannings*, ruled that prosecutions of NAHI cases are fact specific, to be determined on the individual facts of each case.

The Court was not prepared to give any further guidance on the reception of expert evidence other than to approve and confirm the current principles found in *Clarke* [1995] 2 Cr.App.R. 425 and the obligations of an expert witness as summarised by Cresswell J. in *Ikarian Reefer* [1993] 2 Lloyds Rep. 68 at 81 as being equally applicable in criminal cases. Nevertheless, in *R. v B(T)* [2006] 2 Cr.App.R. 3, the Court of Appeal stated that in addition to the obligations set out by Cresswell J. the expert report must contain the following:

(i) Details of qualifications, experience, and accreditation and any limitations of expertise.

(ii) Statement setting out the instructions received and any material or documents supplied.

(iii) Information about any others involved in testing and the methodology used.

(iv) A summary of the range of opinions and the reasons in support and any points that can fairly be made against the expert's opinion.

(v) Any relevant other literature in the field of expertise.

(vi) A declaration that the expert has complied with their overriding duty to assist the court independently, by way of objective, unbiased opinion and provision of any updates.

It is important that reliance on a particular expert is not treated as a presumption of skill and quality in all cases, since to do so can lead to an unsafe conviction and the lack of justice for the complainant. This point is well illustrated in *R. v Savva* [2003] EWCA Crim 3434, in which it came to light that the evidence of Dr Harrow, a facial mapping expert, had been discredited due to him having given an opinion that the defendant was the offender in a robbery, to which the real offender later confessed.

24. Reception of Psychological Evidence and Confessional Evidence

24.29 In cases such as diminished responsibility, insanity, or duress where the defendant brings into issue their mental condition or other abnormality, there will be a need to adduce evidence from either a psychiatrist or psychologist. In *R. v O'Brian and Hall* [2000] Crim. L.R. 676, the Court of Appeal, in a case involving the reliability of a confession, concluded that psychiatric evidence was admissible to assist the jury in deciding whether or not the defendant was suffering from either a mental illness or a personality disorder.

But in the context of a unreliable confession, the abnormality must be of a type that might cause such a confession to be unreliable. Therefore those who suffer a personality disorder are not necessarily compulsive liars or fantasists such that would make any admissible unreliable (see also *R. v Smith* [2003] EWCA Crim 927, in which the appellant was assessed to be "abnormally suggestable and compliant" and therefore his confession, being the sole evidence against him for two serious offences, was unreliable and his conviction was unsafe). In *R. v Tipu Sultan* [2008] EWCA Crim 6, the Court of Appeal admitted new fresh psychiatric evidence. Unknown at the time of the alleged rape of his estranged wife the defendant was suffering from Asperger's syndrome (a development disorder) and was therefore liable to misunderstand the signs and straightforward indications given by others. The Court accepted that the expert evidence was capable of belief and such evidence would have affected the jury's decision as to the issue of consent. A re-trial was therefore ordered.

25. Parts 24 and 33 of the Criminal Procedure Rules

24.30 Part 33 of the CrPR 2005 sets out the basic procedure to be followed, when a party intends to rely on expert evidence at trial, r.33.2 ensures that the duty of the expert is to help the court to meet the overriding objectives of the rules by giving an objective, unbiased opinion on matters that come within the field of expertise. It ensures that this duty overrides that to the party providing the instructions. Rule 33.3 sets out the required contents of the report as per the judgment in *R. v Harris* [2006] 1 Cr.App.R. 5. Rule 33.5 deals with the situation where more than one party wishes to produce expert evidence. In this instance the court may direct the experts in question to discuss matters and prepare a statement on what they agree and disagree, with reasons why. A failure to do so will lead to the evidence not being admitted without the court's permission.

Similar to the Civil Procedure Rules, rr.33.7 and 8 give the court a power to direct that if more than one defendant seeks the opinion of an expert, then only one expert is to be instructed to give an opinion on that disputed issue. If the parties cannot agree, the court will on its own motion select an expert for that purpose. If the parties agree they both must give the instructions.

Part 24 deals with the issue of disclosing any expert evidence which requires the party intending to adduce expert evidence to furnish a written statement setting out the findings to the other parties and the court as soon as is practicable. This is unless there are reasonable grounds to believe that disclosing this might lead to the (attempted) intimidation of the expert. Failure to disclose in accordance with Pt 24 will result in that evidence not being admitted at trial, without leave of the court to do so.

Chapter Twenty Five

CHARACTER EVIDENCE

1. Purpose of Character Evidence

25.01 To justify the admissibility of evidence in a criminal trial, fairness demands that it must have some relevance to an issue that concerns the offence alleged and that the probative value of such evidence must outweigh any potential prejudice against the defendant, should it be admitted. The concepts of justice and fairness require that the court is presented with the necessary information about the characters involved and the background to the current allegation so as to be able to determine the truth of what happened. Both character and background evidence for the commission of an offence may be informative, but where it discloses past misconduct, it can be unduly prejudicial.

A balance must, therefore be struck. The relevant law is now found in Ch. 1 of Pt II of the Criminal Justice Act 2003, which came into effect on December 15, 2005 (S1 2004/3033) and which was based on extensive research undertaken by the Law Commission. More or less from the outset, by bringing the provisions into effect impetuously, judicial criticism followed. In *R. v Bradley* [2005] 1 Cr.App.R. 397, for instance, the Court of Appeal stated that bringing the provisions into force without first ensuring that the judiciary had received proper training in dealing with the complex provisions, led to wasting otherwise valuable court time. The Court of Appeal in *Bradley* ruled that the expression "criminal proceedings" for the purposes of the bad character and hearsay provisions means a trial where the issues of fact are to be determined and not the whole process. Accordingly, the provisions applied to trials commencing after December 15, 2004, regardless of the date of the indictment.

2. Admissibility of Bad Character of the Defendant: The Statutory Gateways

25.02 Chapter 1 of Pt 11 of the Act sets out the statutory provisions that govern the admissibility of evidence of bad character which under s.98 is defined as being evidence relating to the defendant's "disposition towards misconduct" on his part, but does not include evidence which either has "to do with alleged facts of the offence" or "is evidence of misconduct in connection with the investigation or prosecution of the offence".

This provision provides a wide definition of what amounts to bad character in that under s.112(1) it covers all types of misconduct that relate to, "the commission of an offence or other reprehensible behaviour", other than the two limited exclusions which, it is suggested, would still be governed by common law rules. For misconduct falling within s.98, the common law rules of admissibility have been abolished under s.99 and have been replaced by s.101.

In *R. v Tirnaveanu* [2007] EWCA Crim 1239, the Court of Appeal observed that the expression "to do with", which forms part of the exception to the application of the bad character provisions, requires there to be identified a link in time between the alleged offence and the misconduct evidence that the prosecution seek to adduce. If the misconduct evidence is such as to embrace both the exception "has to do with the alleged facts" and also amounts to explanatory evidence under the s.101(1)(c) gateway, then either of those routes of admission can be taken without any legal implications. A clear example of the exception would be where a prisoner is accused of assaulting another inmate, or supplying drugs in prison. Their bad character of being in prison forms part of the alleged offence. The jury need not be told the offence which led them to being in prison.

Whether the evidence amounts to misconduct will be a fact specific question, but this is developing invariably into a pool of judicial determinations of what is and what is not misconduct. In *R. v Saleem* [2007] EWCA Crim 1923, for instance, the Court of Appeal ruled that evidence of the defendant possessing violent images and writing rap lyrics with a view to committing a violent assault, amounted misconduct in the form of reprehensible behaviour (see also *R. v Leslie B* [2006] EWCA Crim 2150). Under s.101 bad character evidence of the defendant becomes admissible if and only if, one or more of the seven statutory "gateways" is unlocked, without any need for judicial leave. The seven gateways are as follows:

(a) All parties agree to the evidence being admissible.

If both prosecution and defence agree to the evidence being admitted, then no issue arises as to the question of admissibility for the judge.

(b) Evidence is adduced by the defendant or is given as an answer under cross-examination.

If the defendant of their own volition, when giving evidence, decides to inform the jury that they have bad character, again no issue of resolving admissibility will arise.

(c) It is important explanatory evidence as set out in s.102.

To unlock the gateway the court must be satisfied that without such evidence either "the court or the jury will find it impossible or difficult properly to understand other evidence in the case", or secondly, the value of the evidence is substantial to understanding the whole case. The type of evidence the prosecution will adduce through this gateway is that of background evidence, which is evidence of previous misconduct that is said to form the relevant history and to be necessary for a proper appreciation of the current offence.

25.03 Before the 2003 Act the law was firmly established in the unreported decision of Purchas L. J. in *R. v Pettman* [1985], which was approved by Lord Bingham in *R. v Sawoniuk* [2000] 2 Cr.App.R. 220, where evidence of eye witnesses adduced at the defendant's trial under the War Crimes Act for murder, was admissible not only to show that he was a local policeman in Nazi occupied Poland, but was also prepared to use violence in kill and search operations. His Lordship stated:

> "Criminal charges cannot be fairly judged in a factual vacuum. In order to make a rational assessment of evidence directly relating to a charge it may often be necessary for a jury to receive evidence describing perhaps in some detail, the context and circumstances in which the offences are said to have been committed."

Admissibility is therefore dependant upon an assessment of whether the jury would be left with an "incomplete or incomprehensible" account of the alleged offence, if such background evidence was not admitted. The risk, of course, in allowing such evidence to be adduced is that the jury may divert their attention away, or be distracted from the actual offence itself and may place more emphasis on the past conduct of those involved. Where this risk is too great, the prejudicial effect of the evidence will outweigh its probative value and fairness will demand its exclusion.

In *R. v Phillips* [2003] 2 Cr.App.R. 35, the defendant appealed against his conviction for murder of his wife by drowning in a bath, on the ground that evidence relating to the history of his marriage was inadmissible as being too remote in time. The prosecution claimed that such evidence was necessary to show motive and background and to rebut the defence's claim that the marriage was a happy one. In dismissing the appeal Dyson L.J., giving the leading judgment of the Court, referred to the House of Lords decision in *R. v Ball* [1911] A.C. 47, and the proposition postulated by Lord Atkinson in relation to a charge of murder that:

> "you can give in evidence the enmity of the accused towards the deceased to prove that the accused took the deceased's life. Evidence of motive necessarily goes to prove the fact of the homicide by the accused as well as his malice aforethought in as much it is probable that men are killed by those who have some motive for killing them than by those who have not."

and held that this remained good law. His Lordship therefore removed any doubt cast on this proposition by an earlier Court of Appeal in *R. v Berry* [1986] 83 Cr.App.R. 165, where it was ruled that background evidence of the defendant's relationship with the victim was to remote in time to be allowed to support the prosecution's case of murder. In *R. v Dolan* [2002] EWCA Crim 1859, the Court of Appeal, whilst not doubting the *Pettman* principle, warned against the admissibility of background evidence being used as a method of:

> "smuggling in otherwise inadmissible evidence for less than adequate reason, relevance and necessity are the touchstones of the principle."

In this instance, evidence that the defendant was quick tempered towards inanimate objects was both irrelevant and unnecessary for the jury to be made aware of it, since it was prejudicial and would have distracted them from the very serious issue of whether this defendant and not his partner, had killed their child.

25.04 In relation to background evidence, the question arises whether it actually amounts to bad character at all and instead comes within the first limitation that it is evidence which relates to the alleged facts of the offence. In *R. v McLean and Others* [2005] EWCA Crim 3244, the Court of Appeal made some general observations regarding the provisions of the CJA 2003. The Court accepted that whilst difficult questions will arise under s.98 on whether background evidence amounts to bad character, its application should not be overlooked. If the exclusions in s.98 apply then according to the Court, "the evidence will be admissible without more ado". Nevertheless, it is submitted that issues of relevance, necessity and fairness under s.78 of PACE 1984 will need to be considered and determined by the trial judge (see also *R. v Watson* [2006] EWCA Crim 2308, *R. v Edwards* [2006] EWCA Crim 3244).

(d) It is relevant to an important matter in issue between the defendant and the prosecution, supplemented by s.103.

Under s.112(1) an important matter means that, in the context of the whole case, the matter is one of substantial importance. To open this gateway therefore, the defendant must be shown to have a propensity to commit offences of a kind with which they are charged, but does not include such a propensity which factually makes it no more likely that they are guilty. This could be argued to amount to general propensity evidence, the admission of which is more controversial. For instance, possessing incriminating articles (i.e. animal rights or other similar propaganda) or a person with a particular disposition, .i.e. homosexuality shows that they do have a propensity to a certain activity, but by itself provides no probative value to proving, for instance, criminal damage or sexual assault.

The previous law was found in *R. v Wright* [1990] 90 Cr.App.R. 325, concerning a guide for homosexuals visiting Paris and *R. v B (RA)* [1997] 2 Cr.App.R. 88, in which evidence concerning the defendant's sexual proclivities and possession of homosexual pornography were ruled inadmissible (see *R. v Simons* [2005] EWCA Crim 1284). Similar issues arise with evidence of life style and large quantities of cash and other drug paraphernalia (see *R. v Yalman* [1998] 2 Cr.App.R. 269 and *R. v Guney* [1998] 2 Cr.App.R. 242).

However, if such evidence is to be used not to rebut a defence of simple denial, but more specifically to rebut a defence of innocence explanation or accident, for instance, then such evidence gains strength in probative value in order to be admissible. In *R. v West* [1996] 2 Cr.App.R. 374, concerning the events that occurred at 25 Cromwell Street, evidence of the defendant having certain sexual desires was admitted to negate a claim of innocent explanation. Subsection (2) provides that a defendant's propensity can be established by previous convictions of the same description (where the statement of offence in the indictment is drafted in the same terms of the previous offence) or of the same category prescribed offences (see CJA 2003 (Categories of Offences) Order 2004 (SI 2004/3346)). In *R. v Hanson* [2005] 2 Cr.App.R. 824, Rose L.J. posed three questions on propensity arising from previous convictions as follows:

(i) Looking at the history of convictions, is there established a propensity to commit offences of the *kind* charged?

(ii) Did the propensity make it more likely that the defendant committed the offence alleged?

(iii) Would it be unjust to allow the prosecution to rely on previous convictions of the same description or class and if such convictions were admitted, would this make the proceedings unfair?

Rose L.J. commented that a particular problem with bad character evidence (i.e. general propensity) is that it can be weak and therefore by its nature brings to trial on its own a real danger of unfairness. Thus, it is important for the judge to determine the bad character evidence the prosecution wish to adduce, in light of the strength of all the other admissible evidence. Of importance is the ruling of the Court of Appeal in *R. v Kordansinki* [2006] EWCA Crim 2984, in which evidence of previous convictions of the defendant committed in Poland obtained in accordance with ss.7 and 8 of the Crime (International Co-operation) Act 2003 were admissible under s.101(d) and (g) and under s.7 of the Evidence Act 1851 (not having been repealed by the CJA 2003 which makes it permissible to prove foreign court proceedings properly authenticated by seal of the foreign court).

25.05 Alternatively, any evidence is inadmissible which goes to show that the defendant has a tendency to be an untruthful person, except where it is not suggested that the defendant's case is untruthful in any respect. On this point the Court of Appeal in *R. v Campbell* [2007] EWCA Crim 1472 felt that it would rarely be appropriate in cases where the defendant's contention is one of denial, for the admission of evidence showing the defendant to be untruthful and for the judge to direct the jury that a person with previous convictions is less likely to tell the truth. Lack of truthfulness of the defendant only becomes an important issue and therefore useful to the jury, if the offence requires the prosecution to prove lies as an element of the offence.

This would seem to mean dishonesty type offences, but not others. If the trial is based on different versions of events in direct conflict with each other, the jury ultimately have to decide which is true and which are therefore lies. If as in *Campbell*, the prosecution seek to adduce evidence of previous violence as showing a propensity towards committing violent offences, then the jury may find this supportive of the complainant's version of events and therefore will therefore be convinced, when assessed against all the other evidence in the case, that the complainant is telling the truth. It is important to note the decision of the Court of Appeal in *R. v Lamaletie* [2008] EWCA Crim 314 (see also under gateway (g) below) in which it was held that there exists no rule or principle which makes it necessary for the prosecution to provide full details of previous convictions. It was accepted that it would be good practice to do so, but this does not prevent the prosecution seeking to use gateway (d) to establish a propensity, whether such details are necessary in ensuring that the jury fairly assess the relevance of those convictions as demonstrating propensity will depend on the particular facts of each case. In *Lamaletie*, the simple fact that the defendant had six previous convictions for violence without more detail was sufficient for the jury to draw the conclusion that he was a violent man who did not act in self defence but unlawfully assaulted the complainant.

If the defence strategy is one of claiming either accident, innocent association or explanation, then the prosecution can use this gateway to adduce evidence in rebuttal and show otherwise. In *R. v Saleem* [2007] EWCA Crim 1923, evidence in the form of possessing violent images and written rap lyrics was relevant evidence to rebut the defendant's claim of innocent presence at the scene of an appalling assault. If the defence is one of denial that the alleged act(s) in question never happened, then this would not necessarily open the gateway for that purpose alone (see *R. v Campbell* [2007] EWCA Crim 1472).

25.06 Although based on its own particular facts, the decision in *R. v McKenzie* [2008] EWCA Crim 758 highlights the difficulty with the possibility of over complicating a trial with collateral issues, as against ensuring a fair trial and the prosecution being able to rely on propensity evidence to support their case on an important disputed issue. In this case the offence was causing death by dangerous driving. The prosecution have always had the problem of having to limit their case to the standard of driving of the defendant at or just before the fatal crash, so as to satisfy the objective test of dangerousness (see *DPP v Milton* [2006] R.T.R. 21). The appellant, it was claimed, had taken a right turn and pulled directly into the path of a motorcyclist, resulting in the rider's death. The prosecution wished to strengthen their case by relying on past incidents of dangerous risk-taking manoeuvres with evidence in the form of a previous driving instructor and previous girlfriend. Although, dismissing the appeal, the Court of Appeal ruled that the judge was wrong to admit the evidence of the driving instructor, since this concerned disputed isolated events that occurred some four to five years earlier, which were as such irrelevant.

(e) It had substantial probative value to an important issue between the defendant and a co-defendant, supplemented by s.104.

To open this gateway, it is suggested that the defendant has a propensity to be untruthful and any evidence to suggest this must be relevant and only becomes admissible if the nature or conduct of the defence goes to undermine the defence of a co-accused. Only evidence which is adduced by the co-defendant, or evidence which a witness is invited to give during cross-examination by the co-defendant, is admissible under this gateway.

Substantial probative value means evidence which is both relevant and true, if it is not true then it has no probative value. This gateway was considered in *R. v Musone* [2007] 2 Cr.App.R. 29, in which the Court of Appeal held that the judge was entitled to rule that a confession of a co-defendant, relating to a murder of which he had been acquitted some 12 years earlier, was of substantial probative value. Both the appellant and his co-accused were found guilty of the murder by stabbing of another prisoner in his cell of which they had both entered. Each blamed the other, running a "cut-throat" defence, the confession therefore, claimed that it was the co-accused who was the murderer. Further, the confession under s.104 also showed that the co-accused, having been acquitted of a previous murder to which he later confessed, was a person as having a propensity to be untruthful. This is clearly seen in the previous law ruled upon by the House of Lords in *R. v Randall* [2004] 1 Cr.App.R. 26, where it was held that in a case of serious violence in which several defendants blamed each other for the fatal blow(s), then previous convictions for violence of a co-accused can be adduced by another co-accused as evidence which is relevant to impugning their credibility, but also showing they had a propensity to violence and were more likely to be the attacker.

25.07 Of particular importance, the Court of Appeal in *Musane*, having observed that the exclusionary rule in s.103 does not apply to gateway (e), nor does s.78 of PACE 1984, since it is not evidence upon which the prosecution intend to rely, considered the issue of a fair trial in art.6. It was held that art.6 could not be deployed in this case and there was no need to read down the provision. Once the court had ruled the evidence to be of substantial probative value, then in those circumstances it would be difficult to envisage such evidence of that quality being unfair. Accordingly, the Court concluded that admissibility under gateway (e) is dependant solely on the judge making an assessment of the quality of the evidence. Once this standard is reached, the judge had no power to then exclude the evidence as being unfair.

In *R. v Lawson* [2007] 1 Cr.App.R. 11, the Court of Appeal ruled that the judge had admitted correctly the s.20 GBH previous conviction as being of substantial probative value to an important matter of whether a disputed incriminating conversation, alleged by the co-accused, had taken place. The judge had ruled correctly that the evidence did not go to propensity to commit manslaughter but did go to showing an propensity to be untruthful. The Court observed that a defendant who disputes evidence of a co-accused that undermines their defence, has a right to adduce relevant evidence that goes to show the co-accused as being unreliable or unscrupulous.

In distinguishing *Hanson*, the Court ruled that showing unreliability is not limited necessarily to offences of untruthfulness, but is capable of being shown by a wide range of misconduct from drug offences to theft and violent offences. Further, the caution that is applied in relation to when the prosecution seek to undermine truthfulness, i.e. the risk a jury might subconsciously use the evidence instead as that of propensity to commit the offence charged, should not be applied in this situation. Whether the previous conviction(s) amount to substantial probative value is a matter for the judge.

25.08 Although in this case it was absolutely wrong that defence counsel sought to cross-examine the co-accused on his previous conviction as amounting lamentably to an ambush defence, the conviction was still safe. If a defendant intends to rely on gateway (e) they should without exception alert the other co-defendant of this intention, which then allows them to raise objections with the judge, and for the judge to make a ruling on the matter having heard representations from both parties. This, according to the Court, is not a substitute for the required notice under the CrPR 2005, but forms part of the practice to be observed for all cases, where the notice requirement has not or could not be given. The Court further reiterated what was said in *Renda* that the Court of Appeal is not likely to interfere with the discretionary decision of the judge, unless they were plainly wrong to rule as they did or demonstrated *Wednesbury* [1948] 1 K.B. 223 unreasonableness.

(f) it is evidence that challenges a false impression given by the defendant, as set out in s.105.

To open this gateway the defendant, it is suggested, had made an express or implied assertion and in doing so gave the court or the jury a false or misleading impression about them. The false statement can be made at pre-trial under caution, in the proceedings generally, by the calling of a character witness, through the questioning of a witness or by an out of court statement by another. Only if the defendant withdraws the assertion or disassociates themselves from it, will they not be responsible for it. If it appears to the court that the defendant by their conduct intends (includes appearance or dress) to give the court or the jury a false impression, the court can treat the defendant has being responsible for such conduct.

The prosecution in this situation will seek permission to adduce probative evidence that must be proportionate for the purpose of correcting the inbalance for which the defendant is responsible.

(g) the defendant has attacked the character of another person, as set out in s.106.

To open this gateway the defendant, it is suggested, has intended to attack the character of another in one of three ways:

(i) by adducing evidence to this effect, or

(ii) by way of cross-examination they ask questions that are intended to elicit such evidence or are likely to do so, and

(iii) casting an imputation on another when questioned under caution or on being charged.

The gateway will only open if it is shown that the alleged evidence used to attack the character of another was to highlight that they have committed offences or have behaved, or are disposed to behave, in a reprehensible way, An imputation about the other person means a statement to that effect. In *R. v Lamaletie* [2008] EWCA Crim 314, the Court of Appeal accepted that because of the peculiar history of the case reference to the pre-2003 Act case authorities may be useful in determining whether or not this gateway is opened, otherwise such a practice is redundant. In affirming the appellant's conviction for a s.20 offence, the Court held that the appellant's claim in a police interview that the complainant was the aggressor, who instigated the violence, was clearly an attack on that person's character, despite the appellant's claim of self defence. Accordingly, the judge was correct in allowing the prosecution to read out six previous convictions for violent offences commited by the appellant.

Further, the Court noted that by the judge stating that he would only allow the previous convictions to be relevant to credibility was favourable to the appellant. Considering the previous authority of *R. v McLeod* [19940 1 W.L.R. 1500 and the observations of Lord Woolf at para.10 in *R. v Highton* [2006] 1 Cr.App.R. 7, it was held that such previous convictions under gateway (g) can be deployed properly to show a propensity to violence, it was not limited to credibility and that no restriction of this kind as a principle was established in *R. v Meyer* [2006] EWCA Crim 1126. Further, the Court also rejected the defence's contention that merely reading out the list of previous convictions without more detail was unfair. On this point Underhill J. noted that the word "character" in the context of the 2003 Act is to be viewed in its broad general sense and therefore it was both unnecessary and indeed potentially distracting to consider the details of the bad character evidence raised. The jury were entitled to consider the appellant's significant record of violence in the determination of who they believed started the violence.

3. Similar Fact and Contaminated Evidence

25.09 Similar fact evidence is used by the prosecution so as to invite the jury to draw inferences from facts of similar misconduct of the defendant as being highly relevant to proving the current offence, or offences. It would be an affront to common sense to disregard it. In *R. v Weir and Others* [2005] EWCA Crim 2866, the Court of Appeal held that the existing test of admissibility of similar fact evidence of enhanced probative value in *DPP v*

P [1990] 2 A.C. 447, was obsolete and that s.101(d) and (3) governed admissibility of this type of evidence (see in particular paras 33 to 37 of the judgment of Kennedy L.J.).

However, difficulties still arise in the prosecution of defendants charged with sexual offences against different complainants in the same indictment, with the risk of collusion and unconscious influence, or innocent contamination from one count from another, although these are required to be treated as separate incidents. If after the close of the prosecution case, the judge is satisfied that the evidence is contaminated to such an extent as may lead to an unsafe conviction, then the judge must either, direct the jury to acquit or discharge the jury and order a re-trial.

Evidence becomes contaminated for the purposes of bad character under s.107 if a witness either discusses, or hears of other evidence in the case and that evidence amounts to being false, misleading, or changes in nature had it not been for the other influential evidence. In *R. v Card* [2006] Cr.App.R. 28, the Court of Appeal quashed the appellant's conviction for sexual offences against his step children, when it became apparent that the evidence of the child complainant had been influenced unequivocally by what their mother had told them to say. The Court also noted that if the prosecution seek to adduce the bad character of the defendant, whilst at the same time defence counsel seek to raise issues of contaminated evidence, then in such circumstances the judge ought to postpone a decision of the bad character question until the suggested contamination evidence had been examined in the trial. This would then allow the judge to make an informed decision on the actual evidence as opposed to forming a view on anticipated evidence.

In *R. v Lamb* [2007] EWCA Crim 1766, the Court of Appeal, applying the ruling in *R. v Chopra* [2006] EWCA Crim 2133, stated that evidence from multiple complainants is cross-admissible if, but only if, it is relevant under s.101(d) as an important issue in dispute. This would clearly be so if the evidence indicates in the defendant a propensity to commit offences of a similar kind and in a similar way or method. Alternatively, if the jury find the defendant guilty on one count they can then use that guilt as propensity evidence, when determining the other counts. If there exist no relevant similarities, then each count must be tried separately with no cross-admissibility (an argument may be raised to sever the indictment, leading to separate trials). The Court of Appeal, in quashing the appellant's conviction, stated that a failure of a judge to give a necessary warning to the jury about the dangers of innocent contamination through cross-admissibility constitutes a material misdirection. The Court noted that with similar fact evidence the critical test surrounded the issue of whether from the evidence there was a likelihood or unlikelihood of innocent coincidence. In summing up, it is important for the judge to first outline the similarities and then:

> "give a balance and accurate account of them, so far as they evidence a propensity which makes it more likely that a defendant has committed an offence."

Section 112(2) provides that if a defendant is indicted on several counts, then each count or offence in the indictment is for the purposes of the bad character provisions, to be treated as if being tried separately. In *R. v Wallace* [2007] 2 Cr.App.R. 30 the Court of Appeal held that circumstantial evidence (common features) forming part of one count of robbery was relevant and admissible to prove the defendant's involvement in the other offences of robbery and was not adduced as being of bad character. The defendant claimed that, taken individually, there was insufficient evidence to establish guilt. This amounted to circumstantial evidence and the test of admissibility was probative value assessed against prejudicial effect. In any event, the Court ruled that such evidence, although coming technically within the wide definition of bad character, could be admitted under s.101(1)(d). The appellant had suffered no injustice and for the reasons such evidence was admitted there was no requirement for a direction on bad character evidence to the jury.

4. Exclusion of Bad Character

25.10 It is important to be aware that both gateways (d) and (g) are subject to s.101(3) which requires the court not to admit the evidence if, on a defence application, it appears to the court that such evidence would have an adverse effect on the fairness of the proceedings, it ought therefore not to be admitted. Likewise, under subsection (4) the court must consider the length of time between the evidence itself and that of the alleged offence (see *R. v Doncaster* [2008] EWCA Crim 5). In relation to the other gateways, reliance will need to be placed on s.78 of PACE 1984 to prevent unfairness, as well as the danger of a breach of art.6. However, this does not apply to gateway (e), as confirmed in the judgment of the Court of Appeal in *R. v Musone* [2007] 2 Cr.App.R. 29 (see above).

5. Application of s.78 and the Weight to be Attached to any Evidence Admitted Through the Gateways

25.11 On the issue of whether s.78 is applicable to the bad character provisions, Woolf L.C.J., at para. 13 in *R. v Highton* [2005] EWCA 1985, whilst not proposing, "to express any concluded view as to the relevance of s78", without the benefit of full legal argument, was inclined "to say that s78 provides an additional protection to a defendant". Similarly, in *R. v Weir* [2005] EWCA Crim 2866, Kennedy L.J. saw "no reason to doubt that s78 of the 1984 Act should be considered" when this gateway is relied upon.

In *R. v Smith* [2006] 2 Cr.App.R. 4, the Court of Appeal applied the ruling of the House of Lords in *R. v Z* [2005] 2 A.C. 483 and allowed the evidence relating to three separate sexual offences that had been stayed on the indictment, as an abuse of process, to support other offences. This was evidence of propensity under s.101 of the Criminal Justice Act 2003. The weight to be attached to this evidence was a matter for the jury, not the court. Scott Baker L.J., giving the leading judgment, recognised that both s.101(3) and s.78 of PACE 1984 gave the judge a discretionary power whether or not to allow the reception of evidence, based on the circumstances of the case and the potential adverse effect such evidence, if admitted, would have on the fairness of the proceedings.

Importantly, his Lordship commented that whilst the judge will need to assess the weight of such evidence, "it is not his job to usurp the jury's function of deciding what evidence is accepted and what is rejected" but if such evidence is "inherently incredible" then that would be a strong factor for exclusion. His Lordship then referred to the cautionary words of Rose L.J. in *R. v Bovell* [2005] EWCA Crim 1091 of the "undesirability of descending into satellite litigation". The role of the trial judge "is to police the gateway not embark on the jury's job of evaluating the evidence".

25.12 Similarly, in *R. v Ngyuen* [2008] EWCA Crim 585, the Court of Appeal dismissed the appeal against conviction for murder. The appellant had contended that it was unfair for the prosecution to be allowed to adduce bad character in the form of an alleged assault by the appellant with a glass in a pub which had taken place three weeks prior to the brutal attack on the deceased pub landlord. Both incidents involved the use of a broken glass as a weapon. The appellant had argued that this incident should have been the subject of a separate charge and trial. A refusal by the prosecution to charge and instead adduce the evidence tactically of that particular assault to show that the appellant had a propensity to violence, placed the appellant at a significant disadvantage at his murder trial. It is possible that he could have been acquitted of the uncharged assault, had there been a separate trial, with the consequence that no bad character could have been used.

Relying on the judgment in *Smith* [2006] 2 Cr.App.R. 4, the Court of Appeal rejected this in its entirety and ruled that the reasoning in that case applied with equal force to a situation where the prosecution decide at their discretion not to prosecute and instead rely on that evidence as bad character in relation to another serious allegation against the defendant. If the evidence is relevant and admissible, then the mere fact that the Crown make a choice not to prosecute and adduce the evidence of an earlier offence as bad character, does not adversely effect the fairness of a subsequent trial for another similar serious offence.

In summary, based on the judgment in *Smith*, it would seem that three determinative steps are taken in relation to bad character evidence:

Relevance of Evidence

25.13 The judge must first consider whether the evidence sought to be adduced by the prosecution is relevant, in seeking to prove an element to the offence. The general assessment of logically probative will be applied to the evidence, as with all evidence. Section 109 provides that, unless it appears otherwise to the court, the assumption is that evidence which is relevant and with probative value is true. In *R. v Bullen* [2008] EWCA Crim 4, the Court of Appeal, whilst acknowledging the provisions in the CJA 2003, abolished the previous common law principles. It should not be overlooked that the test of relevance still remains and the question of propensity in regard to s.101(d) must be relevant to an important matter in issue. The Court of Appeal, on the facts of the case, ruled that the judge was wrong to allow the appellant's previous convictions for only basic intent offences of violence, as these were not relevant to the crucial but limited issue at his trial for murder of a specific intent to kill or do GBH.

The defendant had admitted unlawful and dangerous manslaughter, which was not accepted by the Crown, and relied on self induced intoxication as his defence to murder. In the circumstances of the case it would be unjust to allow the non-specific intent convictions to be admitted as posing no significant relevance to establishing that the appellant had a propensity for serious specific intent violence. Further, the judge had failed in his direction to the jury to give a clear explanation as to why they had been informed of the appellant's previous convictions.

Admissibility of Evidence

25.14 The duty of the judge is to consider the admissibility of the evidence under the statutory gateways and any question of exclusion, either within the Act itself (s.98) or under s.78 of PACE 1984. It is the duty of the judge only to assess the weight of the evidence in terms of whether the defendant would receive a fair trial.

Assessment of the Evidence in terms of Weight

25.15 Once such evidence is admitted, then it is for the jury to assess the weight to be given to that evidence, subject to the judge's power to stop the case under s.107, if the evidence is found to be contaminated, and any directions from the judge to the jury on relevance and other matters, as explained in the important guidance cases of *R. v Hanson* [2005] 2 Cr.App.R. 21, and *R. v Highton* [2005] 1 W.L.R. 3472. The thrust of the guidance is that any summing up to the jury must contain a clear warning, "against placing undue relevance on previous convictions" and that "propensity is only one relevant factor". In giving the leading judgment in *Hanson* Rose L.J. made an important general observation that, "evidence of bad character cannot be used simply to bolster a weak case, or to prejudice the minds of a jury against a defendant".

This is especially important when assessing the purpose and quality of both general propensity and background evidence and the potential risks to the defendant. Such risks can be identified in the *Dolan*. It will be interesting to see whether the evidence that was wrongly admitted in *Dolan* would now be admitted under s.101(c), bearing in mind Rose L.J.'s observation on prejudice. To ensure fairness the judge's direction would need to be impeccable and follow the general guidance in paras 17 and 18 of Rose L.J.'s speech in *Hanson* if a miscarriage of justice is to be avoided, especially when it was stated in *Mclean and Others* that, "the feel of the trial judge is very important and this court will only interfere where the conviction is unsafe".

An important ruling of the Court of Appeal in *R. v Highton* (2005) EWCA 1985 provides that where bad character evidence is admitted under s101(g) it, "may depending on the particular facts, be relevant not only to credibility but also propensity to commit offences of the kind with which the defendant is charged". Giving the leading judgment, Woolf L.C.J. concluded that a distinction must be drawn between the gateway of *admissibility* and the *use* of the evidence once admitted. The use of such evidence is not restricted to the specific statutory gateway, but can be used for any issue that is relevant.

Despite the relative clarity of the guidance given by the Court in *Hanson* this created the risk of an increase in appeals, making complaints that where a judge does not adhere strictly to the guidance this amounts to a material misdirection. The Court of Appeal in *R. v Edwards* [2005] EWCA Crim 1813 and in *R. v Campbell* [2007] EWCA Crim 1472 disapproved of this developing state of affairs. Simplicity is important and provided a direction contains a clear warning about attaching too much weight to previous convictions, an explanation as to why the evidence was admitted and its particular relevance, this will help the jury in their determination of the facts. Then the form used is very much at the discretion of the judge, tailored to meet the needs of the facts of the case (see *R. v Chohan* [2005] EWCA Crim 1813 for an impeccable summing up).

In *R. v Campbell* [2007] EWCA Crim 1472, the Court of Appeal questioned the desirability of the judge informing the jury as through which particular gateway the evidence had been admitted. This would be apparent in the overall explanation given by the judge. In *R. v Lowe* [2007] EWCA Crim 3047, the Court of Appeal quashed the appellant's conviction for rape on the grounds that the judge had provided insufficient guidance on the relevant of bad character evidence in the form of background evidence. The judge should have directed the jury to consider each background incident and whether the prosecution had proved to the criminal standard those incidents. If not proved then they have no significance. If proved then they can help the jury on the issue of consent.

6. Interference with the Discretion of the Judge

25.16 The bad character provisions in the CJA 2003 can be a critical factor to the outcome of a particular case in terms of guilt or innocence. The decision of the judge as to whether wholly or partly the defendant's bad character is to be admitted, requires the balance to be strict so as to ensure that this critical factor is fair to all. In *R. v Renda and Others* [2005] EWCA Crim 2826, the Court of Appeal observed that this determination is very much fact specific in the particular context of the case. The power of the Appeal Court to interfere is limited to decisions in which the judge erred unreasonably in their assessment, since the judge, unlike the Appeal Court, has a contextual feel for the dynamics of the case:

> "The creation and subsequent citation from a vast body of so-called "authority", in reality representing no more than observations on a fact specific decision of the judge in the Crown Court, is unnecessary and may well be counterproductive ... The principles have been considered by this court on a number of occasions. The responsibility for their application is not for this court but for trial judges."

In *R. v Heffernan* [2006] EWCA Crim 2033, the Court of Appeal observed that the judgment in *Hanson* provides useful guidance for trial judges, but does not form part of the CJA 2003 and it was not in any way intended by that Court to be "followed slavishly". Judges should tailor their directions in accordance with the particular facts and issues in the case.

7. Admissibility of Bad Character of Persons Other than the Defendant

25.17 Section 100, if satisfied, and where leave of the court is given, allows a party to adduce evidence of bad character of other witnesses who give evidence at the defendant's trial. This will include all the witnesses called for the prosecution and defence. In contrast to s.101, s.100 only has three possible gateways as to admissibility of bad character:

(i) It is important explanatory evidence (has the same meaning as that relating the bad character of the defendant).

(ii) It has substantial probative value to (a) matter in issue and (b) is deemed to be of substantial importance in the context of the whole case.

(iii) All interested parties consent by agreement to the evidence being admitted.

In relation to assessing whether the bad character evidence has substantial probative value, the court must have regard to a number of specified factors but can take into account any other factors the court deems relevant. The specified factors are:

(i) the nature and number of events or any other things the evidence relate to;

(ii) the material time when those events took placed or existed;

(iii) if the probative value of misconduct is based on similarities in other alleged misconduct, then the court must have regard to the nature and extent of the suggested similarities and any dissimilarities between the alleged instances of misconduct;

(iv) the evidence of the person's misconduct is to be used to suggest that this person is responsible for the alleged offence which the defendant disputes and the extent to which that evidence shows or tends to show that the same person is responsible each time.

8. Rehabilitation of Offenders and "Spent" Convictions

25.18 Section 108 abolishes the rule contained in s.16 of the Children and Young Persons Act 1963, that offences committed by a defendant under 14 were to be disregarded as evidence amounting to previous convictions. Under subsection (2) in relation to a defendant aged 21 or over at the time of the alleged commission of the offence, evidence of previous offending that occurred when they where under 14 is inadmissible as bad character unless the current offence and previous under 14 offence amount to indictable only offences and the court in such circumstances is satisfied that it would be in the interests of justice to rule the evidence admissible.

Section 1 of the Rehabilitation of Offenders Act 1974 provides that a person whose conviction is not excluded under the Act (i.e. life sentence or over 30 months) and is deemed to be spent shall be a rehabilitated person. Section 4(1) provides that subject to subsections (7) and (8) a rehabilitated person is to be treated in law "as person who has not committed or been charged with or prosecuted for or convicted of or sentenced for the offence(s) which were the subject of that conviction".

Under s.4(1)(a) no evidence shall be admissible in judicial proceedings to prove the conviction, charge or sentence, for any offence which was the subject of a spent conviction. Likewise, under s.4(1)(b) a person if asked, shall not be required to answer any questions relating to those spent convictions. Importantly, s.7(2)(a) provides that nothing in s.4 above shall affect the determination of any issue, or prevent the admission or requirement of any evidence, relating to a person's previous convictions, or circumstances, ancillary to any criminal proceedings before a court in Great Britain (including any appeal or reference in a criminal matter).

Reference should be made to the *Practice Direction (Crime: Spent Convictions)* [1975] 1 W.L.R. 1065 issued by Lord Widgery L.J. In particular, para.4 makes the recommendation that both court and counsel should give effect to the general intention of Parliament by never referring to spent convictions when such can be reasonably avoided. Paragraph 6 further provides that no one should refer in open court to a spent conviction without the authority of the judge and then only if it is in the interests of justice to do so.

9. Proof of Previous Convictions

25.19 If the prosecution intends to rely on the previous convictions of the defendant as part of their bad character, or alternatively, to prove an essential element of the offence, then they will need to prove that those convictions belong properly to the defendant. Section 73 provides that any conviction of the defendant in the UK is admissible in evidence. To prove the conviction s.73 requires the prosecution:

(i) to produce a certificate of conviction; and

(ii) prove to the criminal standard that the certificate relates to the defendant.

In respect of the offence of disqualified driving proving that the defendant is actually disqualified has led to a number of challenges against conviction. In *R. v Burns* [2006] EWCA Crim 617, the Court of Appeal, applying the decision of the High Court in *Pattison v DPP* [2005] EWHC 2938, ruled that essentially it was a question of fact and degree, based on the individual facts of each case as to whether the name and date of birth appearing in the certificate (memorandum) of conviction is prima facie evidence that those convictions relate to the defendant.

In *R. v Derwentside Justices Ex p. Heaviside* [1996] R.T.R. 384, it was stated that evidentially there were three possible ways to prove that the conviction belongs to the defendant, namely:

(i) an admission by the defendant;

(ii) fingerprint/DNA evidence;

(iii) a person who was present in court when the defendant was convicted.

If none of these are available then the prosecution will have to rely on proof by coincidence. As stated in *Olakunori v DPP* [1998] C.O.D. 443, if the defendant has a common name which does not precisely match that on the certificate, together with the date of birth, then this may prove insufficient due to the risk of mistake. However, if the defendant has an unusual name consisting of different components, it may be unnecessary to have an identical date of birth.

Further, if the coincidence of name and date of birth are sufficient to establish a prima facie case and, in the circumstances, the defendant refuses to give evidence, then the court can, provided it is fair, take that failure into account by drawing an appropriate inference under s.35 of the CJPO Act 1994, that the identity is proved and no danger of mistake can arise, given that the defendant has decided not to adduce evidence to suggest such a mistake. In *Burns*, the Court of Appeal ruled that the judge was correct to direct the jury on four previous convictions as belonging to the defendant, with two precisely matching, whilst the other two, not giving an identical match, had sufficient similarity to be proved and were therefore admissible to indicate the defendant as having a propensity to commit burglary.

It is also worth noting s.132 of the Supreme Court Act 1981, which provides that a document purporting to be sealed or stamped by the Supreme Court can be received in evidence without further proof.

10. Procedural Requirements

25.20 Part 35 of the CrPR 2005 and s.111 of the CJA 2003 delineates the procedure to be followed if a party intends to make an application to adduce evidence of bad character. For an application to adduce the bad character evidence of a non-defendant, r.35.2 provides that the application must be made in the prescribed form and served on the court and all other parties, not more than 14 days after primary disclosure of the prosecution under the CPIA 1996 or as soon as is reasonably practicable, if the person is being called on behalf of the defendant. This application can be opposed by any party, who must give notice in writing to the court and all other parties of their objection not more than 14 days after receiving the application notice.

Where the prosecution wishes to adduce the bad character evidence of the defendant in accordance with s.101, then under r.35.4, they must give notice in the prescribed form. If the case is being tried in the magistrates' court, this notice must be given at the same time as primary disclosure. Alternatively, if trial in the Crown Court, then not more then 14 days after (i) committal proceedings, (ii) transfer of fraud case under s.4 of the CJA 1987, or (iii) s.51 procedure in the CDA 1998.

If a co-defendant wishes to adduce the bad character evidence of another co-defendant, then the notice in the prescribed form must be given not more than 14 days after prosecution's primary disclosure. If the defendant wishes to apply to the judge to have their bad character excluded, then the prescribed form will need to be completed and notice of it given to all parties within seven days of receiving notice from either the prosecution, or another co-defendant, or both of their application to seek to adduce their bad character evidence.

In all situations the service of the notice can be by fax or other electronic communication if the other parties consent to such a method. The court has a discretionary power to allow the notice to be given in a different form, or orally, or if necessary, either shorten, or extend a time limit. A defendant can at their discretion waive their right to receive written notice by informing the other relevant parties. In *R. v Hanson* [2005] EWCA Crim 824, the Court of Appeal stated that practitioners must be fully aware and alive to the fact that it is especially important that they assist the court with active case management. The application must state the previous convictions and the circumstances and manner in which the applicant intends to use them. Where possible the nature and facts of any previous convictions should generally be capable of being agreed and therefore adduced by way of a formal admission under s.10 of the Criminal Justice Act 1967.

All parties must comply fully with the overriding objectives of the Criminal Procedure Rules 2005; non compliance with the notice requirements, can at the court's discretion, be dealt with by imposing one of three possible enforcement measures contained in r.3.5. Further, in *R. v Musone* [2007] 2 Cr.App.R. 29, the Court of Appeal observed that where there has been a breach of the procedure rules, then if the evidence in question is of substantial probative value, it will be rare for such evidence to be excluded. Indeed it was emphasised that a court should be most reluctant to sanction a breach of the rules by excluding evidence of high quality. Nevertheless, even if the test in s.101 is satisfied, if the evidence is improbable and there has occurred a breach of the rules, then in such circumstances the court can take this into account and if necessary exclude the evidence, if as a consequence of the procedural breach the defendant would not receive a fair trial. If the breach is shown to be a deliberate manipulation in order to avoid the rules and has been done so as to ambush another party, then that would be a strong factor for excluding the evidence.

11. Good Character Direction

25.21 A defendant who has no previous convictions or previous misconduct and enjoys good character, can call good character witnesses, usually persons who themselves have standing and respect. By the defendant stating to the jury that they are a person of hitherto good character, they are presenting themselves as a person for that reason, who would not commit the alleged offence. If a defendant is of impeccable character, then they are entitled to a "good character direction". The principles of law relating to the giving of a good character direction are explained clearly in the guidance given by Lord Taylor in *R. v Vye* [1993] 1 W.L.R. 471. The decision establishes that where a defendant is of good character, or is to be treated as such, then the judge should direct the jury to take account of such good character in terms of (i) credibility and (ii) propensity.

12. First Limb of direction on Credibility

25.22 His Lordship ruled that the first limb of the direction as to good character, namely credibility, must be given where a defendant testifies. A non-testifying defendant is only entitled to a first limb direction when, according to his Lordship:

> "the defendant has not given evidence at trial but relies on exculpatory statements made to the police or others, the judge should direct the jury to have regard to the defendants good character when considering the credibility of those statements."

The judge would be entitled to point out to the jury that such statements were not given on oath. If the defendant does not give evidence and has not given any pre-trial statement, then no direction is required. The justification for such a first limb direction is that a jury, when assessing the truthfulness of a defendant's evidence, would consider the fact that a person, being of good character, is more likely to be believed and to tell the truth than someone who is not.

13. Second Limb of direction on Propensity

25.23 Lord Taylor ruled further that a defendant with good character, whether they have testified or not, should be given a second limb direction as to propensity. This requires the judge to direct the jury that a person who presents themselves as a person of good character, is for that reason less likely to commit crime and the offence alleged.

Each defendant, if of good character, is entitled to a *Vye* good character direction, even if charged jointly with others who are less so. The giving of a good character direction is at the discretion of the judge and the precise wording is a matter for judge, tailored to the particular circumstances of the case. On this point, Lord Taylor referred to the situation where a defendant is charged with murder, but admits manslaughter, which is not accepted by the Crown. It might be thought that in such a case a direction on propensity would be of little help to the jury. There is still an argument that if the issue is one of intent, then the defendant could contend that they had never shown any intent to commit murder before. In such a case his Lordship felt that a judge might:

> "wish ... to stress the very limited help the jury may feel they can get from the absence of any propensity to violence in the defendant's history. Provided that the judge indicates to the jury the two respects in which good character may be relevant, i.e. credibility and propensity, this court will be slow to criticise any qualifying remarks he may make based on the facts of the individual case."

14. Residual Discretionary Power of the Judge

25.24 In *R. v Aziz* [1996] 1 A.C. 41, the House of Lords ruled that not in every case, even if the defendant has no previous convictions, should a good character direction be necessarily given, such as where the guilt of the defendant is compelling and beyond doubt. In such situations, whilst the judge does enjoy a residual discretion on the appropriateness of when to give or dispense with a direction, it would be an affront to common sense to give such a direction. The discretion is limited to those cases in which a direction would not be justified. The starting point, as confirmed in *R. v Gray* [2004] EWCA Crim 1074, is if the defendant is of previous good character, then they are entitled to a full two limb character direction being given to the jury. If his credibility is in issue at trial, then the second limb only need be given.

15. Blemished Character

25.25 The issue of directing the jury in the complex situation where the defendant has a blemished character and whether they lose the benefit of a good character direction, was addressed by the House of Lords in *R. v Aziz* [1996] 1 A.C. 41 and endorsed by the Court of Appeal in *R. v Howell & Lamont* [2001] EWCA Crim 2862. Lord Steyn, giving the judgment of the House of Lords in *Aziz*, stated that a trial judge has a residual discretion as to whether, in the circumstances, a good character direction is appropriate. It is not appropriate to give meaningless directions, especially in a situation where the defendant's claim to good character is doubtful.

It is quite proper for a judge to give the general thrust of a *Vye* direction and then if necessary, qualify it by explaining the defendant is not completely impeccable in the light of other criminal conduct (such as telling lies or admitting other disreputable conduct connected to the alleged offence) that has arisen. Lord Steyn made it plain, as have the Court of Appeal in *R. v Gray* [2004] EWCA Crim 1074, that whether or not a direction should be given and the formula used, should be left to the good sense of the trial judge, with counsel being given full opportunity to make their own observations (see also *R. v Metcalfe* [2005] EWCA Crim 1814). If the defendant seeks to admit into trial his good character either by way of examination in chief or by character witness, the prosecution are entitled to rebut such a contention of good character, bearing in mind the purpose and importance of rehabilitation and "spent convictions" under the Rehabilitation of Offenders Act 1974 (see *R. v Gray* [2004] EWCA Crim 1074).

CHAPTER TWENTY SIX

HEARSAY EVIDENCE

1. ADMISSIBILITY OF HEARSAY EVIDENCE

26.01 Evidence which is given otherwise than orally at court by the maker of the statement amounts to hearsay evidence. All out of court statements regardless of who made them and in what circumstances another may have received them, constitute hearsay evidence. If the police take a statement from an eye witness to an offence, at that stage in the proceedings, the evidence is hearsay and will remain so, until such time as that witness comes to court to give their evidence. The reception of "orality of evidence" in a criminal trial is important to ensuring a fair trial, since it allows all parties to challenge robustly the accuracy and honesty of that evidence in the presentation of their case.

If the evidence is received in other forms, i.e. written statements, this would reduce the effectiveness of such a challenge and lead potentially to an unfair trial taking place. Nevertheless, the triangulation of interests must balance this detrimental impact on the interest of the party in question, against the need to ensure the effective prosecution of crime as being in the public interest, together with that of the complainant, balancing all three interests to ensure that justice is achieved.

The previous common law rule as set out in *R. v Blastland* [1986] A.C. 41 was that any evidence which constituted hearsay was generally inadmissible, unless a recognised exception was satisfied. The reason for this general inadmissibility was due to two potential dangers that risked the fairness of the trial:

Inability to Cross-examine the Maker of the Statement

26.02 If a witness were allowed to give evidence regarding what another person said either in writing, orally or by assertions (i.e. gestures) on a previous occasion, then in such circumstances, the defence would be deprived of a fair trial. The unfairness would be the inability to test and probe the truthfulness and accuracy of the person who spoke those words or statements, as to what they may have witnessed, through cross-examination.

Distortion of the Truth and a Risk of Concoction

26.03 To allow the repetition in court of what was said by the person who witnessed at first hand the offence through a chain of other persons, would create the inherent danger of error and distortion of what in fact actually and truthfully happened at the time.

Following the recommendations of the Law Commission Ch. 2 of the Criminal Justice 2003 provides for a wholesale reform of the previous common law principles that governed the admissibility of hearsay evidence. Section 114 of the CJA 2003 is the main provision and sets out the statutory test of admissibility for hearsay evidence, available both to the prosecution and the defence. This provides that a statement which is not made orally is admissible as amounting to evidence to prove what its contents assert, but only if one of four situations arise:

(i) Either the provisions of the CJA 2003 or any other statutory provision allow it to be admissible. In *R. v Lynch* [2007] EWCA Crim 3035, the Court of Appeal ruled that an answer given to the standard question "What exactly did you see this person do?" which followed a positive identification at the police station, could not be admitted under ss.66 and 67 of PACE 1984 (as being any other statutory provision). These simply authorise the issuing of a code of practice. The question asked did not form part of that, only the ID procedure itself. This was different to what occurred in *McCay* [1990] Crim. L.R. 340. Nevertheless, the Court did rule that such evidence would be admitted, under (iv) the interests of justice test or alternatively under s.139 to aid in refreshing the memory.

(ii) A rule of law preserved under s.118.

(iii) Consent of all parties to it being admissible.

(iv) It is in the interests of justice to do so, of which the court must be satisfied. The court in determining the interests of justice test for admissibility must under s.114 (2) have regard to eight specified statutory factors and any other factors the court deems relevant. The eight (non-exhaustive) factors are:

  (a) probative value of the statement in relation to a matter in issue or to assist in the understanding of other evidence;
  (b) other evidence which has been or can be given on the matter, or evidence in factor (i);
  (c) the importance of the evidence or matter in factor (i) in the context of the case as a whole;
  (d) the circumstances in which the statement was made;
  (e) the reliability of the maker of the statement as it appears to the court;
  (f) the reliability of the evidence in the statement as it appears to the court;

(g) can oral evidence be given by the witness of the matter stated, if not why not;
(h) the amount of difficulty faced by the defendant in challenging the statement and the likely prejudice faced in surmounting that difficulty.

2. Meaning of Statement and Matter Stated for the purposes of Hearsay Evidence

26.04 Section 115 provides statutory assistance by explaining that the expression "statement", in relation to hearsay, means a representation of fact or opinion made by a person in any form which can include a sketch, photofit or other pictorial form. This is important, since a still from a photograph or an image from CCTV or a video recording, do not amount to hearsay evidence, but constitute real evidence and are admissible for that reason. Further, evidence generated from a computer, which when information is imputed in performs a specified task and produces a print out, does not amount to hearsay evidence but an item of real evidence. Section 60 of the YJCEA 1999 abolished the requirement in s.69 of PACE 1984 that a party wishing to rely on such evidence had to adduce evidence in the form of a certificate to prove that the computer was operating properly at the relevant time. For a "matter stated" to fall within the provisions the purpose(s) of the persons making it must appear to the court to have been to:

(i) cause another person to believe the matter, or

(ii) cause that other person to act or a machine to operate on the basis that the matter is as stated (implied assertions).

3. Application of s.114

26.05 In *R. v Taylor* [2006] 2 Cr.App.R. 14, the Court of Appeal, in dismissing the appeal for an appalling s.18 wounding, ruled that the judge had applied s.114 correctly, when refusing to edit out video evidence by two witnesses. This was hearsay evidence, that they had been informed by another of the appellant's active participation in the assault, so as to rebut his claim of innocent presence. The Court determined that the expression "must have regard" to the eight factors, does not impose an obligation on the judge to embark on an investigation in order to reach a specific conclusion on each factor. The provision requires the judge to give consideration to each identifiable factor and any others that they consider relevant. Next, the judge will need to assess the significance of those factors in terms of individual weight and in relation to each other. Finally, they must reach a conclusion on the admissibility of the evidence. Accordingly, if as in this case, the judge cannot form a conclusive view as to a specific factor such as reliability of the evidence, this does not lead to the evidence being inadmissible.

In *R. v Xhabri* [2006] 1 Cr.App.R. 26, the Court of Appeal ruled that s.114 is not incompatible with the requirement in art.6 that for there to be a fair trial, the defendant has a right to cross-examine witnesses against them. The Court ruled that the discretionary power contained in s.114 is not limited to hearsay statements made by a person who is not available for cross-examination. In any event the court does have a power to exclude the evidence under s.126 if to admit it would infringe the right to a fair trial in art.6. Further, neither is there, contrary to European Law, inequality of arms between the prosecution and defence, since the provisions apply to both parties.

In *R. v Y* [2008] EWCA Crim 10, the prosecution sought to have admitted a confession made by one defendant, who had pleaded guilty to murder which implicated the appellant in the murder, which he had denied. The judge ruled that s.118(5) prevented the admission of the hearsay statement in the confession for this purpose. The Court of Appeal allowed the interlocutory appeal of the prosecution under s.58 on the grounds that, as a matter of statutory construction, s.118(5) did not qualify the application of s.114(d). The Court observed that it is important to identify who is making to application for the hearsay evidence to be admitted since the assessment for the interests of justice test is not necessarily the same and may be applied differently in respect of an application on behalf of the defence to that of the prosecution. The court will need to consider the prejudice to the person faced with challenging the evidence if admitted and that:

> "since the burden of proving the case is upon the Crown and to the high criminal standard, very considerable care will need to be taken in any case in which the Crown seeks to rely upon an out-of-court statement as supplying it was a case against the defendant when otherwise it would have none. In such a case if there is genuine difficulty in the defendant challenging, and the jury evaluating, the evidence, the potential damage to the defendant from that difficulty is very large."

In *R. v Finch* [207] 1 W.L.R. 1645, it was observed that if the witness is available, even if compelled, then unless it is clearly not in the interests of justice to do so, the evidence ought to be received in oral form.

4. Admissibility of Implied Assertions

26.06 Under the previous common law, if a person made a general statement or gesture without intending to assert a specific fact from what they said or did, then it would be wrong to allow a jury to draw inferences from what was said to establish a crucial fact by implying something which they did not directly say, but could have meant. In other words, although they did not expressly say it, it is clear impliedly that they intended it to mean that fact. The leading authority had been *R. v Kearley* [1992] 2 A.C. 228, in which the defendant was indicted with possession of a controlled drug, with intent to supply. Having been arrested by the police and taken into custody, 11 telephone calls were made to the flat during the search, in which only a small quantity of drugs was seized by the police. Each caller asked for the defendant and about drugs. In addition seven people called personally at the house and asked for the defendant, offering to buy drugs for cash. At trial none of these callers gave evidence, instead the judge, despite objections from the defence, allowed the prosecution to call the police officers to give evidence of the visits and what was said by them. The defendant was convicted and appealed against conviction on the basis that the evidence of the police officers was hearsay.

The House of Lords by a three to two majority ruled, in applying the long established principle in *Wright v Doe d. Tatham* [1837] 7 Ad & E 313, that it is admissible to adduce in evidence the hearsay statement of another for the sole purpose of inviting a jury to draw an inference from that statement of an unintentional implied statement (assertion), as evidence of the truth of what they meant when they made that statement. In this case this was the belief of the callers (although not intentionally and expressly said by them) that the defendant would supply them with drugs and that there was therefore evidence to show he had the relevant intent to supply others, not simple possession. For the majority, putting aside the issue of admissibility, the evidence of the police officers was irrelevant as not going to a direct issue of the state of mind of the defendant. It only went to show the state of mind of the person making the request and therefore was not relevant and thus inadmissible on that point.

The dissenting view of the minority of their Lordships was that such evidence went to establishing the state of mind of the defendant, revealed in their spoken words, that they would be supplied with drugs by the defendant and that this was a permissible inference to be drawn. To support this view, assistance was derived from *Ratten v The Queen* [1972] A.C. 378, on the admissibility of evidence from the receiver of a telephone call as to what the caller had said to them, so as to explain the acts of the third party. In other words, the minority view was that such evidence was not hearsay, although those who made the statement naturally refused to give evidence. It amounted to direct evidence, given the number of enquiries, to prove that the defendant had the necessary intent to supply prohibited drugs.

In *R. v Singh* [2006] 1 W.L.R. 1564, the Court of Appeal confirmed that although the mutual application of s.114 and s.115 is "deeply obscure" it is clear that by reference to s.118, the common law rules on the inadmissibility of hearsay evidence, save for those expressly preserved, have been abolished. Accordingly, the new test in s.114 does not extend to implied assertions, which for that reason do not constitute hearsay evidence and will be admissible, as the minority contended in *Kealey*, as amounting to direct evidence to prove the mens rea for the offence, in that case an intent to supply others. Accordingly, the Court of Appeal in *Singh* ruled that evidence from the mobile phones of those accused in a conspiracy to kidnap where they were in contact with the appellant at the time the kidnapping took place, was direct evidence to prove that he was part of that conspiracy.

5. Statutory Admissibility of Out of Court Statements: Section 116 First Hand Hearsay

26.07 As already stated, s.114 provides for four situations in which a statement not made in oral evidence can be admitted as evidence of any matter stated. The first situation is any provision of Ch. 2 which makes it admissible. The main provisions are s.116 and s.117 (ss.119 and 120 has been covered in Chapter Twenty-two at para. 22.08).

Section 116, which replaces ss.23 to 26 of the Criminal Justice Act 1988, provides that the starting point is to admit a statement not being part of the oral evidence of any matter stated, provided:

(i) if it could be given orally it would still be admissible evidence;

(ii) the court is satisfied of the identity of the person who made the statement, deemed to be the "relevant person", and

(iii) any one of five conditions are satisfied in regard to the relevant person.

The statutory specified conditions are that the maker of the statement is:

(i) dead (this will include a dying declaration, as was admitted in *R. v Musone* [2007] 2 Cr.App.R. 29, in which an inmate named the defendant as the person who had stabbed him to another prisoner, for this evidence to be excluded the defence would need to deploy s.78 of PACE 1984);

(ii) unfit because of bodily or mental condition;

(iii) located outside the UK and it is not reasonably practicable to secure their attendance at court;

(iv) missing and despite all reasonably practicable efforts being made they cannot be found;

(v) in fear in giving oral evidence and the court grants leave for their statement to be given as evidence.

In regard to the condition relating to fear, the meaning of fear under subsection (3) is to be construed widely by the court and can include fear of the death or injury of another, or of financial loss. Before granting the required leave under condition (v) the court must consider it to be in the interests of justice that the statement ought to be admitted having regard to:

(i) the actual contents of the statement;

(ii) the risk of unfairness, either by admitting it or excluding it for any party, paying particular attention to the difficulty of challenging the statement, if the relevant person does not give oral evidence;

(iii) the availability of a special measure direction under s.19 of the Youth Justice and Criminal Evidence 1999;

(iv) any other relevant circumstances.

As a safeguard against the risk of fabrication, s.116(5) provides that even if any of five conditions are satisfied they are not to be treated as satisfied and therefore the evidence will not be read. If it is shown that the circumstances of the condition are caused either by:

(i) the person who seeks to adduce that evidence in support of their case; or

(ii) by a person who, acting on their behalf, seeks to prevent the relevant person from giving oral evidence.

The application of s.116 requires the trial judge to perform a balancing exercise between two inherently polarised risks of unfairness. On the one hand; there is the inherent risk of unfairness to the defendant, if evidence is read, of not being able to challenge that evidence robustly. Whilst on the other hand, if the evidence is refused, then the prosecution will suffer a similar inherent unfairness, by not being able to adduce important relevant evidence to the jury. In *R. v Doherty* [2006] EWCA Crim 1410, the Court of Appeal observed that this balancing test is evaluative and fact sensitive and for this reason, the appeal court will only interfere with a ruling if, as was said in *CPS v CE* [2006] EWCA Crim 1410, it is satisfied that the ruling was obviously wrong as being perverse or unreasonable.

6. Section 116 and Article 6(3)(d)

26.08 Article 6 provides that everyone subject to a criminal charge is:

> "entitled to a fair and public hearing within a reasonable time by an independent and impartial tribunal established by law."

Paragraph 3 of art.6 sets out the minimum rights of those charged with a criminal offence. One of those rights is contained in subparagraph (d) which states:

> "to examine or have examined witnesses against him and to obtain the attendance and examination of witnesses on his behalf under the same conditions as witnesses against him."

In *Brown v Scott* [2001] 2 W.L.R. 817, Lord Bingham, sitting in the Privy Council, reviewed the jurisprudence of the Court of Human Rights and observed that one of the fundamental requirements for ensuring a fair trial is that between the prosecution and defence there maintained an equality of arms. This principle dictates that there must be a right to an adversarial trial, in which all parties and in particular, the defence, have a full opportunity to probe and challenge the evidence the prosecution adduce at trial, in order to prove the offence. This opportunity is reduced if the prosecution are allowed to read out a statement under s.116.

In *R. v Sellick and Sellick* [2005] EWCA Crim 651, the Court of Appeal reviewed the jurisprudence of the European Court of Human Rights in the context of the provisions of ss.23 to s26 of CJA 1988 and extracted the following four propositions:

(i) The admissibility of evidence is primarily a matter for the national law of each domestic State.

(ii) It is a general requirement that evidence is adduced at a public hearing at which the defendant is to be given a proper and adequate opportunity to challenge and question witnesses.

(iii) Article 6 does not prohibit the reading out of a statement (deposition) even if the defendant has not had the opportunity in the proceedings to actually question the witness. Article 6(3)(d) is illustrative of what a judge must achieve in striking a fair balance in order to ensure a fair trial.

(iv) Relevant to the exercise in striking a fair balance, is an assessment of the quality and inherent reliability of the evidence against the need to take a cautionary approach to placing reliance upon it in those circumstances.

The Court of Appeal then went on to consider whether there is a fifth proposition, which prohibits as being unfair the admission of written evidence not tested by the defence through questioning the witness. If that evidence is the sole or decisive evidence against the defendant, this fifth proposition is particularly troubling in the context of drive by gang related shootings, or violence where the evidence of witnesses either to the incident or association is crucial to securing a conviction. But that witness either is in fear or fear is exerted on them directly or indirectly (see *Luca v Italy* App. 33354/96 and *PS v Germany* App. 33900/96). In its determination on this proposition, the Court referred to the decision in *R. v Martin* [2003] EWCA Crim 357, which had cited with approval the dictum found in *R. v Harvey* [1998] (unreported) that:

> "The fact there is no ability to cross-examine, that the witness who is absent is the only evidence against the accused and that his evidence is identification evidence is not sufficient to render the admission of written evidence from that witness contrary to the interests of justice or unfair to the defendant per se. "[What matters in our judgment, is the content of the statement and the circumstance of the particular case bearing in mind the considerations which s26 require the judge to have in mind.]" (per Lord Taylor in *R. v Dragic* [1996] 2 Cr.App.R. 232 at 237)

Waller L.J. then referred with approval to the observations made at para.30 in the judgment of the Court of Appeal in *R. v Arnold* [2004] EWCA Crim 1293, that care must be taken in ensuring that the Convention right of a fair trial is not infringed or that the court should be too readily persuaded by the prosecution that it is in the interests of justice to admit the evidence. However, his Lordship then adopted a caveat to the fifth proposition, being that if the defendant is shown to have kept the witness away by invoking fear, then in such circumstances, there is no question of any infringement of art.6(3)(d): "since he is the author of his inability to examine the witness".

If there is an allegation of intimidation of a witness, then the court must examine the circumstances of this suggestion with care, looking at matters such as are they in genuine fear and are they being kept away from court. Is this as a result of the defendant either directly or indirectly; and can any other steps be taken to ensure the attendance of the witness with the necessary protection? The court must always consider the quality and reliability of the evidence against the need to ensure a fair trial. In *R. v Kelly* [2007] EWCA Crim 1715, a case similar to that of *Sellick* which involved a violent gang related killing and fearful witnesses, the Court of Appeal endorsed the caveat devised by Waller L.J., stating that it formed part of the circumstances of the case which also includes the contents and coherence of the statement the process by which the statement came to be in existence and whether it was supported by other eye witness evidence (see paras 20 and 21 in the judgment of Calvert-Smith J. in *R. v Campbell* [2005] EWCA Crim 2078.

7. Admissibility of Documentary Evidence

26.09 Section 117 is broadly representative of the provisions on the admissibility of documents in s.24 of the CJA 1988. Section 117 provides that a statement in a document is admissible in criminal proceedings as evidence of any matter stated if (i) the evidence was be admissible if orally given and (ii) one of three conditions is satisfied:

(i) The document was created or received by a person in the course of a trade, business, profession or other occupation, or as the holder of a paid or unpaid office.

(ii) The person who supplied the information, deemed the "relevant person", had or may reasonably be supposed to have had, personal knowledge of the matters dealt with

(iii) Each person (if any) to whom the information was passed from the relevant person and then by them to the person in (i) above also received the information as part of a trade, business, profession or other occupation or in an (un)paid office.

The person referred to in (i) and (ii) can be the same person

If the statement has been prepared for the purpose of either (i) pending, or (ii) contemplated criminal proceedings, or (iii) for a criminal investigation, (excluding a request for overseas evidence pursuant to s.7 of the Crime (International Co-Operation) Act 2003 or para.6 of Sch.13 to the CJA 1888), then a further two conditions must be satisfied: (i) that any of the five conditions relating to the admissibility of first hand hearsay from a person who is absent under s.116 are met and (ii) the relevant person has no recollection of the matters contained in the statement, nor can they reasonably be expected to have such recollection. When assessing this condition, the court must have regard to the length of statement, when the statement was supplied and all other circumstances.

A relevant safeguard against the admission of documentary evidence under this provision is that if, having assessed the statement, the court is satisfied that its evidential reliability is doubtful when viewed in terms of contents, source of information and method by which the information was supplied or received.

For the purposes of this provision s.134 defines document as meaning anything in which information of any description is recorded. In *R. v Humphris* [2005] EWCA Crim 2030, the Court of Appeal observed that the fact of previous convictions can be admitted under s.117 or alternatively under s.73 of PACE 1984. However, police information stored on a computer as to the method used to commit those previous offences does not come within the ambit of admissibility under s.117. The relevant person in this instance who would have had personal knowledge of the offence was the complainant, but the description of the method used was inserted by a police officer and was therefore not within (ii) above. The Court further observed that if the prosecution wish to rely on greater detail surrounding a previous offence than the simple fact of its commission, therefore falling outside of s.73 of PACE 1984, they must ensure that they possess the relevant supporting evidence. In a case of this nature involving previous sexual offences, then the prosecution will need either the availability of:

(i) a statement taken from the complainant to the previous offence, or

(ii) that complainant to give oral evidence at trial.

In *Wellington v DPP* [2007] EWHC 1061 the High Court dismissed the appeal by case stated against conviction for driving whilst disqualified. The High Court distinguished the decision in *Humphris* and ruled that a standard PNC print out, which contained several aliases used by the appellant, came inescapably within the ambit of s.117 in that the actual police officers who imputed the information had themselves personal knowledge of the fact that the appellant used aliases. Neither, according to the Court, did the lack of opportunity to cross-examine the actual officers who imputed the information render the information unreliable or in breach of art.6(3)(d) given that the personal information involved was of a routine nature contained properly in an official record.

8. Inadmissibility of Multiple Hearsay Evidence

26.10 Multiple hearsay evidence arises in a situation where, for instance, A witnesses an offence, describes what they saw to B, who then informs C. Both B and C are only in possession of second hand hearsay, put simply the source of evidence of the matter in issue has multiplied from the original source of the evidence. Each witness is simply proving what was said by another to them. The inherent dangers in the reception of such evidence at a criminal trial are obvious and based on the risk of unreliability. For this reason s.121 provides that such evidence is inadmissible unless either of the hearsay statements are admissible under s.117, forming part of a business document, under s.119, forming part of a previous inconsistent statement, and s.120, forming part of statements admissible for a given statutory purpose.

9. Capability in Making the Statement

26.11 Section 123 of the CJA 2003 makes is clear that an out of court statement will not be admissible under ss.116, 117 119, or 120 if the maker at the time of making the statement did not have the required capability to do so. For a person to have the required capability, it must be shown they are capable of understanding the questions put to them and the answers they give to them. Any issue as to capability must be determined by the judge in the absence of the jury and then if needed, the court can receive expert evidence and any evidence from the person who took the statement. The provision makes it clear that the burden of proof lies on the party who seeks to have the statement admitted and the standard which must be reached is on the balance of probability.

This would now cover the difficulty encountered in *R. v D(H)* [2002] EWCA Crim 990, under the previous s.23 provision, it which the Court of Appeal agreed with the trial judge that the video evidence obtained by the police from the complainant taken 10 days after the alleged incident, was admitted correctly. The complainant, a, 81-year-old lady, had been subjected to appalling sexual acts but at the time was suffering from delusions and early Altzheimer's disease. The complainant was not fit to give live evidence at trial. The appellant, despite not having an opportunity to cross-examine the complainant, still received a fair trial, since he was able to call medical evidence to challenge the capacity of the victim to remember, understand and say what happened and the defence was able to point out that they have been unable to cross-examine her. Accordingly, the Court felt that it would be possible for the defendant to contradict the statement of the victim and that it would therefore not be unfair. Further, given the seriousness of the allegation it was clearly in the interests of justice to admit the video, leaving the jury to assess, with the aid of expert evidence, the accuracy and honesty of the witness.

10. Adducing Evidence to Impugn Credibility

26.12 The purpose of s.124 is to re-balance any detriment to the party against which hearsay evidence is admitted, in terms of the loss of oral cross-examination. If necessary and with leave of the court, that party can introduce evidence that is relevant to impugning the credibility of the maker of the out of court statement. This can include any previous inconsistent statement that is contradictory to the current out of court statement. In response, the party calling the now impugned out of court statement can, with the court's permission, lead additional evidence specified by the court to either deny the alleged discreditable evidence or alternatively to bolster the credibility of the maker.

11. Safeguard against Unsafe Convictions and Exclusion of Evidence

26.13 Section 125 of the CJA 2003 provides a very important safeguard against the risk of a miscarriage of justice occurring due to the admission of hearsay evidence. The provision provides that at a trial on indictment (therefore this does not apply to trial in the magistrates' court) and at the close of the prosecution's case the court is satisfied of two matters, namely:

(i) the case against the defendant is based wholly or party on an out of court statement; and

(ii) proportionately the weight of this evidence to the case against the defendant is so unconvincing that a conviction obtained in consequence of it would be unsafe.

Then in such circumstances the court can take one of two steps either:

(i) direct the jury to acquit the defendant, or

(ii) discharge the jury and order a re-trial.

If the judge directs an acquittal on the indicted offence, then under s.125(2) if circumstances allow, the defendant could be found guilty of that alternative offence, unless like the other offence, the alternative offence is tainted by the same unconvincing evidence.

Section 126 brings into effect a similar provision to s.78 of PACE 1984 but in respect of out of court statements. The provision provides that a court has a discretionary power to refuse to admit an out of court statement, provided that the court is satisfied that the case for excluding it substantially outweighs the case for admitting it. In determining this issue of proportionality, the court is required to take into account the danger in admitting it and the resultant undue waste of time, balanced against the value of the evidence in terms of admitting it.

12. Statutory Preservation of Certain Specified Common Law Rules

26.14 Section 118 specifies lists the preservation of a number of common law rules which allow for reception of hearsay evidence and which were created as exceptions to the general rule that prima facie hearsay evidence is inadmissible. The preserved rules are:

(i) The rule that published works of a public nature, i.e. maps histories, scientific works and dictionaries are admissible.

(ii) Public documents, i.e. public registers and returns kept under public authority which are of a public interest are deemed admissible as evidence of the facts stated in them.

(iii) Other record, i.e. records of certain courts, treaties, grants and pardons are admissible as evidence of the facts stated in them.

(iv) Evidence relating to age and date or place of birth.

(v) The rules on the admissibility of evidence relating to reputation or character.

A further rule that is preserved is any rule relating to the admissibility of confessions, or of a mixed statement that includes an admission. The common law rule was limited in that a confession could only be admitted against the person who made it. However, in *R. v Y* [2008] EWCA Crim 10, the Court of Appeal ruled that this limitation does not restrict the application of s.114(d) (see above). An out of court statement which contains or includes a confession is admissible under s.114(d) which is not in any way qualified by s.118 (5). Nevertheless, the court emphasised that the judge had to be sure that all the factors contained in s.114 (2) are satisfied and considered properly, with a genuine need for the statement to be admitted as being in the interests of justice. The Court emphasised that it would not generally be in the interests of justice for a police interview to be admitted in the case of a defendant, other than the person who was interviewed. Section 114(1)(d) should not be considered as allowing routinely the admission of police interviews for this purpose.

Although allowing the prosecution's appeal against the ruling of the judge against the admission of a confession by one defendant which implicated the appellant in the appalling murder of a young man, the Court of Appeal emphasised that in a case of this nature, the interests of justice test requires an assessment of the reliability of the guilty person's confession and the circumstances in which it was made. In the absence of any inducement, mental in stability or incentive to protect another, a confession is likely to be reliable, given the unliklihood of a person confessing to a serious crime. However, the maker of the implicating confession may have a possible motive to blame another wrongly as apart of their own self interest in order to secure a beneficial outcome for themselves.

Other rules that are preserved are those relating to the admissibility of a statement made by a party to a joint enterprise, as proving any matter stated against another party to the common venture. A further rule of which remains is that which allows an expert witness to refer to evidence from within a relevant body of expertise.

13. The *Res Gestae* Principle

26.15 The *res gestae* principle provides that if a person makes a spontaneous or contemporaneous statement, so that what they said naturally becomes an "integral part" of what they were doing, then the statement ought to be admitted in order to provide the jury with a sensible understanding of the events surrounding the offence.

In a broader sense, the principle of *res gestae* allows evidence to be given of any events (narrative) as as they unfold and includes spontaneous comments made by those who are involved, who could not have had any opportunity to concoct or distort their account of what they witnessed or of what in fact occurred. The test of admissibility is based on the relevance of the statement and whether what was said was said in circumstances of such intensity and pressure that this evidence can be regarded as an accurate reflection of the events as they unfolded or occurred. Only if the statement is detached from the overall event ought it to be excluded, given the inherent dangers of concoction or distortion.

In *Ratten v R.* [1972] A.C. 378, an appeal to the Privy Council from Australia, the defendant was convicted of killing his wife with a shotgun. At trial, he claimed the death was accidental on the basis that whilst he was cleaning the gun, he accidentally discharged it. The Crown, in order to rebut this defence of accident, called evidence from the telephone operator who stated that shortly before the shooting she had received a call from the deceased's address. The operator stated that the call was from a female who was voice sobbing and becoming hysterical and who said "get me the police please" and gave the address, but then hung up.

26.16 The defence objected to the admission of this evidence on the grounds that it was hearsay. The judge rejected this and admitted the evidence. On this point the Privy Council stated that the evidence did not amount to hearsay, but was admissible as evidence of the fact of the telephone call and its surrounding circumstances, where the defendant denied that the call had been made. The evidence from the telephone call was both closely and intimately connected to and interwoven with the shooting that occurred very shortly after it was made and that:

> "The way in which the statement came to be made (in a call for the police) and the tone of the voice used, showed intrinsically that the statement was being forced from the deceased by an overwhelming pressure of contemporary event. It carried its own stamp of spontaneity and this was endorsed by the proved time sequence and the proved proximity of the deceased to the accused with his gun. Even on the assumption that there was an element of hearsay in the words used, they were safely admitted. The jury was additionally, directed with great care as to the use to

which they might be put. On the counts, therefore, their Lordships' can find no error in law in the admission of the evidence."

In this case the evidence of the telephone call to the police did not raise an issue of hearsay, but was relevant evidence adduced in order to rebut the appellant's claim that the killing was not a deliberate act but a tragic and unfortunate accident. In *R. v Andrews* [1987] 84 Cr.App.R. 382, the House of Lords approved and adopted the reasoning of the Privy Council in *Ratten* as forming the correct basis of English law. Lord Ackner recognised the difficulties they may confront a judge when faced with an application to admit evidence claimed to be *res gestae* and offered general guidance as follows:

(i) Is there a potential risk of concoction or distortion or can this be disregarded?

(ii) In determining this potential risk the judge will need to consider the circumstances in which the statement was made and whether the event in question had such an impact on the witness that what they said or uttered to another was nothing less than an instinctive reaction to an event so overwhelming so as to dominate their mind.

(iii) Can it be safely concluded that the statement made had sufficient spontaneity so as to leave no real opportunity for reflection contaminated by concoction or distortion of the truth?

(iv) The fact that the statement was made in response to a question asked of them is but one factor the judge must take into account in the assessment.

26.17 In *R. v Newport* [1998] Crim. L.R. 581, the appellant was indicted and convicted of the murder of his wife, which had occurred following an argument between them. The wife had left the house, hotly pursued by the appellant, who then stabbed her with a knife which he had earlier been using to make a sandwich. The appellant had claimed this was a tragic accident. Evidence was adduced of a telephone call made by the deceased to a friend about 20 minutes before her death, in which the deceased it was claimed, was agitated and sounded frightened and asked if the friend if she could come to her house as she, (the deceased) had to flee the house in a hurry. The deceased had also stated during the telephone call that the appellant had slashed her dress. The judge had allowed evidence of the telephone call under the *res gestae* principle.

Allowing the appeal on this point, the Court of Appeal accepted that whilst in the majority of cases the *res gestae* statement is made in the immediate aftermath of a violent event, they can, as concluded in *Ratten*, the principle can apply equally to statements prior to the event. The Court found the integral approach to admissibility as somewhat uncertain, owing to the difficulties of defining its limitations, but that proximity of time and place are relevant issues to take into account. On the facts of the case the Court held that the telephone call lacked all the essential elements of spontaneity or immediacy to an impending emergency, given a 20-minute lapse and the appellant not being present when the long phone call was made. For these reasons, the evidence was admitted wrongly as forming part of the *res gestae* principle. However, because of other compelling evidence from the pathologist as to the stab wound entry point showing a clear deliberate act, the conviction was ruled as being safe.

Equally, in *R. v Harris* [2002] EWCA Crim 1597, the Court of Appeal ruled that the judge was wrong to admit in evidence a telephone conversation by an eight-year-old girl with the police operator as to a fight between the appellant and another man that had started in her mother's house. It was the mother who told the girl to call the police from a neighbour's house. Given that others may have intervened, this may have influenced the girl's appreciation of what was happening and of who in fact was the aggressor, as well as what her mother told her to say to the police. For these reasons the risk of concoction or distortion was too great to ignore.

26.18 In *R. v Gilfoyle* [1996] 1 Cr.App.R. 302, the appellant was convicted of the murder of his wife, which at first was taken to be a straight forward case of suicide by hanging. On further investigation, evidence was gathered to suggest that the defendant was at the time and with the knowledge of the deceased having an affair. He had killed his wife and then tried to make it look like suicide. One aspect of the evidence against the appellant was that the victim had, whilst at work, told several friends that the appellant had asked her to write a suicide note, based on a course about that he was doing at work. This, according to those witnesses, frightened the deceased, that the defendant had asked her in the first place and that he had also told her what to write and later took her to the garage to show her how to use the rope. Although these statements were excluded at trial as being hearsay, the defendant was still convicted. On appeal, the appellant wished to adduce new fresh expert evidence.

In considering the discretion to receive fresh evidence under s.23 of the Criminal Appeal Act 1968, the Court of Appeal felt that a miscarriage of justice can arise from the acquittal of the guilty, as well as a conviction of the innocent. For this reason the Court held that it was entitled to receive the witness statements in evidence, (although they had been ruled inadmissible at trial) and take them into account when considering whether the appellant's conviction is unsafe.

The Court, on the issue of admissibility, referred to the authorities of *Subramaniam v Pubic Prosecutor* [1956] 1 W.L.R. 965 and *Blastland* [1985] 81 Cr.App.R. 266 and confirmed that evidence which goes to prove the state of mind of the maker, in respect of a fact in issue, is an exception to the general rule of inadmissibility. In the instant case, the statements showed that the deceased was not depressed or worried to the point of suicide, but wrote the note in the mistaken belief that she was helping the defendant and that therefore the statements of the friends were relevant and admissible. They went to prove that the appellant had instructed her to write the suicide note, provided that what the deceased had said to the friends was said soon after the writing of the note.

The Court of Appeal reviewed the *res gestae* principle and ruled that the statements contained evidence which related to events that at that time were still dominating the deceased's mind. The statement was made the morning after the note was written so that the risk of concoction or distortion could be discounted. In rejecting the contention of the appellant that the statements were highly prejudicial, Beldam L.J. ruled that the circumstances in which the statements were made amounted to a "circumstantial guarantee of trustworthiness", which meant that the statement was made in circumstances which rendered it most improbable that it was concocted or unreliable.

14. Section 9 of the Criminal Justice Act 1967

26.19 Section 9 of the CJA 1967 is an important provision and is often used for the efficient management of criminal cases. The provision allows for a witness statement, properly signed, to be admitted in the proceedings without the need for the maker of the statement to attend court. The maker of the statement, by signing the statement, does so in order to assert the contents are true to the best of that person's knowledge and belief and that they are aware that if the statement is tendered in evidence they would be liable to prosecution if they wilfully stated anything which they knew to be false or did not believe to be true. Both the prosecution and defence must agree to the statement being "read out".

Section 9 is used commonly for the admission of a statement with which the other party it is tendered against does not take issue as to anything in its contents and is happy for it to be read out to the court in in full knowledge they take no issue with it. In these circumstances, it would be a waste of money and time for the witness to attend. To ensure proper case management and the efficient use of court resources, s.9 statements ought to be agreed at the earliest opportunity.

15. Procedural Steps

26.20 If a party wishes to adduce hearsay evidence, then the procedure set out in Pt 34 of the Criminal Procedure Rules must be complied with. This is exactly the same as that relating to an application for bad character evidence, (see para.24.09). It is important to note that the High Court ruled in *CPS v City of London Magistrates' Court* [2006] EWHC 1153 that the notification requirements in Pt 34 do not apply to committal proceedings, but only to summary trials or trials on indictment.

Chapter Twenty Seven

CORROBORATION AND CIRCUMSTANTIAL EVIDENCE

1. Introduction

27.01 The general rule is that the unimpeached evidence of a single witness is sufficient for a conviction in a criminal trial to be sustained and accepted. The issue of reliability and credit are matters for the jury to decide, having listened to the evidence presented. In *R. v Muktarr* [2001] EWCA Crim 1850, the Court of Appeal quashed the conviction of the defendant for making threats to kill and abusive behaviour, for which he was sentenced to three years' imprisonment. A police officer claimed that the defendant had been verbally abusive towards him. There was no corroborative evidence, despite others being present. The defendant denied this. The same officer was due to give evidence in a separate trial for violent disorder against four men. Again, his evidence was uncorroborated. A video was seized of the incident that rebutted the officer's version of events and therefore his reliability. Corroboration evidence is evidence that tends to confirm, support or strengthen other evidence, making that evidence more probable or creditworthy (see *R. v Hester* [1973] A.C. 296 and *R. v Kilbourne* [1973] A.C. 729).

2. Admissibility of Corroboration

27.02 The legal test on the admissibility of corroborative evidence can be found in *R. v Baskerville* [1916] 2 K.B. 658 and the judgment of Reading L.C.J. as follows:

> "evidence in corroboration must be independent testimony which affects the accused by connecting or tending to connect him with the crime. In other words it must be evidence which implicates him, that is, which confirms in some material particular not only the evidence that the crime has been committed, but also that the prisoner committed it."

The justification for a corroboration warning was to safeguard the accused against wrongful conviction.

3. Abolition of the "Full Warning" for a Limited Class of Persons

27.03 Prior to the passing of Criminal Justice and Public Order Act 1994, the common law had developed so that as a matter of law, a full warning as to the dangers of convicting on uncorroborated evidence had to be given in certain classes of case, where it was felt that the reliability of the witness was suspect, owing to issues of motivation of self-interest or a purpose of their own. Alternatively, such persons were likely to be vindictive, or the truth might be distorted by immaturity, suggestibility, imagination, fallibility, embarrassment, remorse, regret and fabrication.

The classes of person for which a full warning had to be given were:

(i) unsworn evidence of children;

(ii) accomplice evidence; and

(iii) complainants in sexual offences (see *Davies v DPP* [1954] A.C. 378). In *R. v Thompson* [2001] EWCA Crim 468, a case decided on it own exceptional facts, the Court of Appeal quashed the appellant's conviction for rape on the basis that the complainant's version of events was uncorroborated and that there was some indication to particular aspects of the critical times, that the complainant was not telling the truth.

In all other cases it was at the discretion of the judge as to whether a full warning should be given or that of a special need for caution. In *R. v Spencer* [1987] A.C. 128, the House of Lords held that a warning ought to be given in respect of witnesses outside the recognised categories by reason of their mental condition and criminal history. In *R. v Becks* [1982] 1 W.L.R. 461, the Court of Appeal ruled that in respect of other "suspect" witnesses, a warning must be given, but with a discretion for the judge as to the precise wording of the warning.

One of the particular problems with the common law principles was the lack of consistency in application, since in respect of the recognised categories, if the complainant's evidence was uncorroborated, then the judge had, as a matter of law, to direct the jury that it was dangerous to convict on the evidence of the victim alone. Whereas if a accomplice ran a "cut-throat defence", then according to the Court of Appeal in *R. v Prater* [1960] 2 Q.B. 464, it was simply desirable to give a warning as a matter of practice. This approach was criticised for being indiscriminate, since it applied to all accomplices regardless of the circumstances of the case, or the risk to the accomplice themselves.

Further, it was illogical in that it was not mandatory if the accomplice gave evidence on their own behalf. In all other appropriate cases it was at the discretion of judge who simply had to warn the jury of the "special need for caution", based on the *Turnbull* Direction. In respect of sexual offences, the mandatory requirement of giving a full warning was a necessary safeguard against the risk of false accusations. This was criticised for treating woman less favourably than, say mental patients where a warning is not required, or for presuming that they are fabricators and prepared to lie on oath.

27.04 As well as the inflexible nature of the rules, another difficulty was the complexity of rules faced by the judge and jury. This was well illustrated in *R. v Willoughby* [1988] 88 Cr.App.R. 91 as follows:

> "It is settled law that it is for the judge to identify to the jury the evidence which (if they accept it) can amount in law to corroboration . . . It is the function of the jury not only to decide whether or not they accept the evidence, but also whether or not they regard the evidence legally capable of amounting to corroboration as in fact doing so in the circumstances of the case."

The reason for this was to prevent the judge usurping the function of the jury in considering the value of evidence which in law cannot be corroboration. This led to difficulties in that the jury was told that they could convict on uncorroborated evidence, but would then be given a full warning on the dangers of doing so and that they had next to decide whether the evidence amounted to corroboration, based on what the judge stated might amount to such.

In direct response to these real and perceived difficulties Parliament inserted s.32 into the Criminal Justice and Public Order Act 1994. The effect of s.32 was to abolish the requirement in law to give a corroboration warning, in respect of an alleged accomplice, or a complainant of a sexual offence. The question remained whether the provision, by using the words "merely because", left intact a discretion for the judge to give where appropriate a warning in a particular case. In *R. v Makanjuola* [1995] Cr.App.R. 469, the Court of Appeal confirmed that s.32 did not affect the judge's discretionary power to issue a warning when necessary. The case concerned indecent assault and on behalf of the defendant it was argued that the judge ought to have given a warning to the jury. This was rejected, but Taylor L.J. gave the following guidance:

> "The circumstances and evidence in criminal cases are infinitely variable and it is impossible to categorise how a judge should deal with them. But it is clear that to carry on giving "discretionary" warnings generally and in the same terms as were previously obligatory would be contrary to policy and purpose of the 1994 Act. Whether, as a matter of discretion, a judge should give any warning and if so its strength and terms must depend upon the content and manner of the witness's evidence, the circumstances of the case and the issued raised. The judge will often consider that no special warning is required at all.
>
> Where, however, the witness has been shown to be unreliable, he or she may consider it necessary to *urge caution*. In a more extreme case, if the witness is shown to have lied, to have previous false complaints, or to bear the defendant some grudge, a *stronger warning may be thought appropriate* and the judge may suggest it would be wise to look for some supporting material before acting on the impugned witness's evidence. We *stress* that these observations are merely illustrative of some, not all, of the factors which judges may take into account in measuring where a witness stands in the scale of reliability and what response they should make at that level in their directions to the jury. We also *stress* that judges

are not required to confirm to any formula and this court would be slow to interfere with the exercise of the discretion by a trial judge who has had the advantage of assessing the manner of a witness's evidence as well as its context."

4. Warning in Respect of Accomplice and Cell Confession Evidence

27.05 In respect of a accomplice who is running a cut-throat defence and by doing so may clearly have a purpose of their own to serve, then as stated in *R. v Francom* [2001] 1 Cr.App.R. 237, the jury need to be warned that they ought to approach such evidence with caution. However, there is no obligation on the judge to direct the jury that if the evidence is blaming directly another co-accused, that in such circumstances they should reject it. The Court approved the decision in *R. v Cheema* [1994] 98 Cr.App.R. 195, as to the general approach on the desirability of given an appropriate warning.

On the basis that the mandatory requirement of a corroboration warning has been abolished, it then becomes plain that the central disputed issues in any individual case will for the jury to assess as a matter of credibility and reliability. In any contested case, there will arise a conflict of evidence as to what did or did not happen. This is a matter for the jury who can accept the defence case or, alternatively reject it, having been convinced by the prosecution.

In all cases, the judge will need to approach counsel for both the prosecution and defence to discuss and agree on the appropriate direction, if any. Only if the decision of a judge is unreasonable would an appeal court feel inclined to intervene. The same approach is taken where, whilst in prison, a cell mate claims that the defendant admitted to them during conversations that they were guilty, but the defendant denies that any such conversations took place. The prosecution then call that prisoner as a witness to the conversation. The judge in this situation should advise the jury to treat such evidence with a degree of scepticism and caution, when considering its accuracy and honesty. In *Pringle v The Queen* [2003] All E.R. (D) 236, Lord Hope in the Privy Council, on the issue of cell confessions, stated that it was not possible to lay down any fixed rules for the giving of a direction. The may be cases where the prisoner can be treated simply as an ordinary witness, i.e. assault on another prisoner:

> "but a judge must always be alert to the possibility that the evidence by one prisoner against another is tainted by an improper motive. The possibility that this may be so has to be regarded with particular care where a prisoner who has yet to face trial gives evidence that the other prisoner has confessed to the very crime which he is being held in custody. It is common knowledge that, for various reasons, a prisoner may wish to ingratiate himself with the authorities in the hope that he will receive favourable treatment from them."

5. Reception of Distress or Recent Complaint Evidence

27.06 As a general rule, distress evidence cannot amount to corroboration since it lacks independence. In *Whitehead*, it was stated that a rape victim cannot corroborate herself, since if she could than it would only be necessary for her to repeat her story 25 times in order to gain 25 corroborations of it. Nevertheless in *Redpath* [1962] 46 Cr.App.R. 319 and *Chauhan* [1981] 73 Cr.App.R. 319, the Court of Appeal held that where the complainant is unaware of their being observed in a distressed state, then that is independent from the complaint and is therefore admissible evidence. On the point of law as to what weight should be attached to distress evidence, the Court of Appeal in *R. v Romeo* [2003] EWCA Crim 2844, approved the observations of the Court in *R. v Chauhan* [1981] 73 Cr.App.R. 232 as follows:

> "in normal cases, however, the weight to be given to distress varies infinitely, and juries should be warned that, although it may amount to corroboration, they must be fully satisfied that there is no question of it having been feigned."

6. Enhancing Witness Credibility

27.07 A general principle of evidence is that previous consistent statements or "self-serving" statements are inadmissible at trial. An exception to this general principle is the admissibility of recent complaint evidence. Such statements can only be adduced to show consistency, not the truthfulness of what the victim is saying, or if consent is in issue to show that their conduct was inconsistent with their consent. In *R. v Islam* [1999] 1 Cr.App.R. 22, the defendant was a doctor convicted of indecent assault on female patients. Recent complaint evidence was adduced at trial. The defendant appealed on the ground that the judge had failed to properly direct the jury on recent complaint evidence in terms of their evidential status. Allowing the appeal, Buxton L.J. approved the dicta of Lord Goddard in *Wallwork* [1958] 42 Cr.App.R. 153 on the evidential value of recent complaint evidence:

> "the evidence may be given only for a particular purpose not as evidence of the fact complained of ... (but) for the purpose of showing consistency in her conduct and consistency with the evidence she has given in the box". His Lordship then confirmed the Judicial Studies Board standard direction which provides "the evidence may possibly help you to decide whether she has told you the truth. It can not be independent confirmation of X's evidence since it does not come from a source independent of her."

Since recent complaint evidence is not corroborative, the obligation of the judge remains unaffected by s.32 of CJPO Act 1994. The Court made it plain that, as a matter of law, it was essential for the trial judge to direct the jury on the limited effect of recent complaint evidence as going only to credibility, not as proof of a disputed issue. His Lordship then stated that:

> "without such discretion, there is every danger of the jury thinking, as on one view might be a commonsense reaction, that such evidence is indeed further evidence of the truth of the complaints, rather that being of, limited assistance in assessing the veracity of the complainer."

Provided the recent complaint is sufficiently consistent to be admissible, then it is, according to the Court of Appeal in *R. v Spooner* [2004] EWCA Crim 1320, irrelevant that the alleged event occurred some time ago. It is for the jury to assess the weight to be attached to such evidence as to whether it supports or enhances in terms of consistency the credibility of the complainant. Even if it was recent after the event, it does not have to be shown that the complainant availed themselves of the first opportunity to complain. In such circumstances the complaint can still be relevant and admissible but as confirmed in *R. v Birks* [2002] EWCA Crim 3091, each case will be dependant on its own particular facts (see also *R. v Valentine* [1996] 2 Cr.App.R. 213).

In *R. v Archibold* [2002] EWCA Crim 858, the Court of Appeal rejected the defences' contention that before a third party can give evidence of a recent complaint, the victim themselves must have given evidence of such complaint to the third party. In this case the victim had given evidence of it by videotape. Recent complaint evidence was therefore admissible. This must, however, be contrasted with *R. v Wallwork* [1958] 42 Cr.App.R. 153, in which the Court of Appeal held that since the purpose of recent complaint evidence was to show consistency in the complainant's evidence and conduct, then if the complainant herself gave no evidence, such consistency could not be shown and therefore any recent complaint is inadmissible. In this case the child complainant did not give evidence, but the Crown was allowed wrongly by the judge to adduce recent complaint evidence from the grandmother to whom the child had complained that the defendant (father) had sex with her. Conversely in *White v The Queen* [1999] 1 A.C. 210 the Privy Counsel ruled that if the recipients of the complaint do not themselves give evidence, then the complainant's own evidence that they made a complaint to another cannot be used to show either consistency or negate consent in a sexual offence.

7. Inferring Guilt from Lies Told: The Purpose of a Lucas Direction

27.08 When a defendant tells lies, then the prosecution will seek to use such lies as supporting the case against the defendant who told them and such lies are indicative that the defendant is not telling the truth and is therefore unreliable. In such instances, the common law may require the trial judge to give what is known as a "*Lucas* Direction". This is derived from the case of *R. v Lucas* [1981] 73 Cr.App.R. 159, when the trial judge directed the jury that lies told by the defendant in the witness box could constitute corroboration of an accomplices' evidence. On this point the Court stated:

> "To be capable of amounting to corroboration the lie told out of Court must first of all be deliberate. Secondly it must relate to a material issue. Thirdly the motive

for the lie must be a realisation of guilt and a fear of the truth. The jury should in appropriate cases be reminded that people sometimes lie, for example, in an attempt to bolster up a just cause, or out of shame or out of a wish to conceal disgraceful behaviour from their family. Fourthly the statement must be clearly shown to be a lie by evidence other than that of the accomplice who is to be corroborated, that is to say by admission or by evidence from an independent witness. As a matter of good sense it is difficult to see why, subject to the same safeguards, lies proved to have been told in court by a defendant should not equally be capable of providing corroboration. In other common law jurisdictions they are so treated..."

Despite the relative simplicity of the *Lucas* guidance, difficulties have arisen as to when a judge ought to give a *Lucas* Direction. This has led to number of appeals on the issue.

The purpose of a *Lucas* Direction is clear. It is designed to ensure that the defendant is not prejudiced, in the sense that it is given to prevent the jury embarking upon a forbidden chain of reasoning. This, potentially, occurs where the jury infer improperly that if the defendant told lies this is indicative of guilt. If however, there is no such risk or the prosecution do not rely on lies to support their case, then in such circumstances, it will be unnecessary to give a *Lucas* Direction, since to do so would only serve to add further complexity and do more harm than good to the defendant. Accordingly, deciding whether or not to give a *Lucas* direction is a discretionary power for the judge, but the judge would need to consult counsel for their observations on such a direction. Only if the judge exercised their discretionary power unreasonably so as to render a conviction unsafe, would the Court of Appeal intervene and a deficient summing up does not automatically render a conviction unsafe (see *R. v Bain* [2004] EWCA Crim 525).

In *R. v Burge and Pegg* [1996] 1 Cr.App.R. 163, the two defendants told lies in their police interviews which were later inconsistent with their evidence at trial. The judge gave a *Lucas* Direction which the defendants complained was inadequate. The Court of Appeal declined to quash the convictions and stated that it is not appropriate to give a *Lucas* Direction in every case when the prosecution suggest the defendant is lying. Kennedy L.J. noted that there was a growing number of appeals on the grounds that either the judge had failed to give a direction, or that the direction given was inadequate. To reduce the chance of an appeal, the Court stated that there were four categories in which a direction should be given:

(i) Where the defence relies on a false alibi.

In some situations a defendant may decide to invent an alibi in order to add strength to a genuine defence contended by them. Accordingly, a false but innocently relied upon alibi is not probative of guilt. In *R. v Lesley* [1996] Cr.App.R. 39, the Court of Appeal stated that whilst an alibi direction "should routinely be given" telling the jury that the prosecution must disprove the alibi, a failure to do so will not automatically render the conviction unsafe. This will depend on the facts and strength of the evidence. In *R. v Keene* [1977] 65 Cr.App.R. 247, the Court observed that:

> "the jury must be told that they can rely on a false alibi as supporting identification only if they are satisfied that the sole reason for the fabrication was to deceive them on the issue of identification."

(see also *Broadhurst v The Queen* [1964] A.C. 441)

(ii) Where the judge considers it desirable or necessary to suggest that the jury should look for support or corroboration of one piece of evidence from other evidence in the case and that other evidence draws attention to lies told, or allegedly told, by the defendant.

(iii) Where the prosecution seek to show that something said, either in or out of court, in relation to a separate and distinct issue, was a lie and to rely on that lie as evidence of guilt in relation to the charge which is sought to be proved.

(iv) Where although the prosecution have not adopted the approach in point (iii), the judge envisages reasonably that there is a real danger that the jury may take the view that the lies told equate to guilt.

8. The Contents of a Lucas Direction

27.09 If a direction is deemed necessary, based on the particular facts of the case, then the judge in their summing up will need to make several essential, but basic points to the jury:

(i) The lie in question must either have been admitted by the defendant, or proved to be a lie by the prosecution to the criminal standard of beyond all reasonable doubt.

(ii) Whilst the defendant did lie, this does not constitute evidence of guilt, since a defendant may lie for a number of innocent reasons. If the jury are satisfied of the innocent reasons for the lies told, then they must ignore them.

(iii) Only if the jury are satisfied that the defendant did not lie for whatever innocent reasons, can the evidence of a lie or lies support the case for the prosecution.

(iv) If the alleged offence is murder and the defence is provocation, then, in accordance with *R. v Richens* [1994] 98 Cr.App.R. 43, if the defendant has told lies, it would be wrong to direct the jury that such lies, told without innocent reason, are probative of them committing murder. It is an incontestable fact that a person who has killed will have the same strong reasons to conceal their act of killing whether that be by deliberate murder, or by loss of self control.

In *R. v Bullen* [2008] EWCA Crim 4, the Court of Appeal observed that the particular facts of the case highlighted a *Lucas* Direction, like many others in evidence, should be tailored to the specific circumstances of the case being tried, as being of more valuable to, "a formulaic repetition of a necessarily standard and general exemplar". In this case the judge had failed to explain to the jury that one possibility of the defendant lying to the police about the use of a broken glass used to assault the deceased, was that he may have tried to distance himself from the death. Fear of admitting liability in terms of manslaughter as a lesser offence, may stand as an innocent reason behind the lies not one proving intent to kill.

9. Lies Told in Court Giving Evidence

27.10 In *R. v Middleton* [2001] Crim. L.R. 251, Judge L.J. addressed the issue of whether a *Lucas* Direction should be given in a situation where the lie is told by the defendant in evidence during the trial. His Lordship observed that where the jury reject the evidence of the defendant given at trial, then they might feel the defendant has lied to them. In this situation, it would generally be inappropriate for the judge to give a *Lucas* Direction. This would be covered sufficiently and dealt with by a clear direction on the burden and standard of proof, it would be insufficient to give a *Lucas* Direction and would be "circular and confusing in its effect" (see also *R. v Jefford* [2003] EWCA Crim 1987). Accordingly, if the defendant denies the allegation against them, which the jury reject, this would mean the defendant must have lied. In this obvious situation there is no requirement for a *Lucas* Direction, but it is important to be aware that each case must always be considered against its own individual facts.

10. Lucas Direction and the Offence of Handling Stolen Goods

27.11 In *R. v Barnett (Richard Dean)* [2002] EWCA Crim 454, the defendant was convicted of handling a stolen painting called "The Hawking Party" worth £40,000, that was found by the police under his bed, in the course of executing a search warrant. When questioned and to asked to explain how he was in possession of the painting, the defendant gave three different stories, each inconsistent with the other, one being that he found it in a wood whilst walking the dog, which he later in evidence said was a joke. The second explanation was that he met a friend in a pub with whom he had previous dealings and who asked him to store the painting. Later the friend asked the defendant to retrieve the painting as he had a potential purchaser for it. The defendant claimed that he had believed that the painting belonged to his friend's family.

The defendant again gave a different slant on his second explanation whilst giving evidence. The issue at trial was whether the defendant *knew or believed* that the painting was stolen. In summing up the judge told the jury that the prosecution contended that he knew or believed it to be stolen, since by giving three inconsistent explanations this indicated that he was "not telling the truth as" to what was "blindly obvious". The judge did not give a *Lucas* Direction.

The defendant appealed against conviction on the grounds that not giving a *Lucas* Direction was a fatal omission by the judge in his summing up. This was rejected by the Court of Appeal on the basis, as said in *R. v Taylor* [1994] Crim. L.R. 680, that the fact that inconsistent statements are made does not itself call for a *Lucas* Direction, where there was no issue of alibi, corroboration or identification. The Crown did not rely on a specific lie, but on the defendants's:

> "constant changes of story, or at least as part of the evidence, that he was trying to escape from the obvious inference, namely that he must have realised that the painting was stolen."

Jackson J. then stated obiter:

> "In almost every contested handling case the defendant denies knowing or believing that the relevant goods are stolen, and the prosecution assert that that evidence is a lie. It would be absurd to suggest that every handling case requires a Lucas direction."

11. Similar-Fact as Corroborative Evidence

27.12 In *R. v H* [1995] 2 W.L.R. 737, the defendant was tried and convicted of several sexual offences committed against his adopted daughter and step-daughter. Both gave similar accounts of the offences committed against them. The defendant claimed that that they had collaborated in order to concoct a false story.

The House of Lords held that if the evidence is admissible as similar-fact, applying the test set out in *DPP v P* [1991] 2 A.C. 447, then unless it is determined that no reasonable jury could accept the evidence as free from collusion, such evidence can be corroborative as being independent. But if the question raised by the defence is one of collusion, then the judge should draw the importance of collusion to the jury's attention and direct them that it is for them to consider and assess the issue of collusion and the weight to be attached. If they are not satisfied of a lack of collusion, then the judge must tell them that they cannot rely upon it as corroboration.

12. Circumstantial Evidence

27.13 As previously stated, for evidence to be relevant, it must be logically probative of some issue or matter in dispute which requires proof in order to sustain a conviction. If the evidence is relevant, then the judge has a discretion whether or not to admit it at trial. This requires the judge to strike a balance between the probative value of the relevant evidence as against its prejudicial effect upon the defendant's right to a fair trial. If its prejudicial effect outweighs its probative value, then the judge has a discretionary power contained in s.78 of PACE 1984 to exclude the evidence for that reason. Circumstantial evidence amounts to a fact, or series of facts, that taken individual or collectively, do not directly prove guilt alone. But a jury can, in assessing the cumulative effect of this indirect evidence, infer properly from it a fact or facts, which prove an essential or crucial part of the prosecution's case.

In *R. v Moore* [1992] (unreported), Steyn L.J. observed that a jury can apply their common sense to a particular piece of evidence and draw properly inferences from that evidence. However, his Lordship indicated that if a case is based solely on circumstantial evidence, then when determining the issue of admissibility or a submission of no case to answer:

> "it may be helpful for the judge to address specifically the question whether the crude facts are such that they exclude every reasonable inference from them save for the one sought to be drawn by the prosecution. If the proved facts do not exclude all other reasonable inferences, then there must be a doubt whether the inference sought to be drawn is correct."

However, in *R. v Van Bokkum and Others* [2000] (unreported), the Court of Appeal stated that Steyn L.J. comments should not be read literally and that whilst what his Lordship said was perhaps right when considering a single piece of circumstantial evidence, it did not necessarily follow that there was a combination of circumstantial facts. This issue will be one of considering the totality of the circumstantial evidence and deciding whether it would still be unsafe to allow the case to be put before a jury, based on the test adumbrated in *R. v Galbraith* [1981] 73 Cr.App.R. 124.

In *Mc Greevy v DPP* [1973] 1 W.L.R. 276, the House of Lords ruled that it would be both unnecessary and undesirable to impose an obligation on a judge to give a special direction to a jury, if the prosecution's case was dependant solely on circumstantial evidence. It is for the jury to assess all the evidence in terms of the weight to attach to it and either wholly or party reject it. The judge is not required to classify evidence as direct or indirect circumstantial evidence, as Lord Morris noted, "the mental element in a crime can rarely be proved by direct evidence". Circumstantial evidence is no different to any other relevant and admissible evidence, to convict the jury must be satisfied so that they are sure beyond all doubt that the evidence for the prosecution proves all the elements to the offence.

In *R. v Jonathan Jones* [1998] 2 Cr.App.R. 53, the Court of Appeal quashed the appellant's conviction for the murder of his parents-in-law, a case which was presented by the prosecution based on circumstantial evidence, motive and alibi lies. The Court of Appeal ruled that the judge was wrong to admit evidence of a previous burglary at the farm at which the murders took place and of a shotgun being stolen, as it was irrelevant and could not support an inference that the appellant was the thief.

Chapter Twenty Eight

CONFESSIONAL EVIDENCE AND THE DISCRETIONARY POWER OF THE TRIAL JUDGE

1. Introduction

28.01 In certain circumstances, the police may adopt somewhat unorthodox methods of investigation, that may infringe on the rights (under art.6 a right to a fair trial and right against self incrimination) of the suspect and therefore any evidence gathered may be excluded at trial, on the ground that it would be unfair to admit it. Alternatively, there may have been an abuse of process of the court's procedure resulting again in evidence being excluded.

2. Admission and Meaning of a Confession

28.02 A full and frank admission of guilt is compelling evidence and is undoubtedly powerful evidence against the defendant, if they later retract or deny the admission. Previous police interrogation techniques were focused on obtaining a confession from the suspect. This practice led to an appalling series of miscarriages of justice during the 1990s (the Guildford Four and the Birmingham Six) and the subsequent creation of the Royal Commission on Criminal Justice. Section 82 of the Police and Criminal Evidence Act 1984 (PACE 1984) defines a confession as including any statement in words or otherwise, wholly or partly adverse to the maker, whether made to a person in authority or not.

In *R. v Z* [2005] 2 A.C. 467, the House of Lords held, approving the Court of Appeal decision in *R. v Sat-Bhambra* [1988] 88 Cr.App.R. 55, that a statement made by the defendant, which was intended to be purely exculpatory or neutral, if later used at trial by the prosecution to either discredit or to show inconsistency in what the defendant is claiming or to demonstrate prevarication on his part does not fall within the meaning of a confession. Lord Steyn felt that s.82 gives a plain meaning to what is meant by a confession and that the Court of Appeal were wrong to adopt s.3 of the Human Rights Act 1998 to give it a strained meaning, due to a misplaced reliance on the decision in *Saunders v UK* [1996] 23 E.H.R.R. 313, a case concerning statements made under compulsion.

There is nothing in the statutory provisions to demand that such an approach to be taken. It would be inconceivable on policy grounds to do so. Their Lordships were fortified in their decision by the fact that s.78 provides the necessary safeguard so as to avoid any injustice from such statements being used to the advantage of the prosecution. Accordingly, ss.76 and 82 are compatible with art.6. This decision of the House of Lords relates specifically to pure exculpatory statements. If the statement is mixed, one containing both innocence and adverse comments, then on the plain meaning in s.82 this would amount to a confession (see *R. v Park* [1993] 99 Cr.App.R. 270).

Section 76 of PACE 1984 governs the admissibility of a confession at trial and provides that a confession may be given in evidence, so far as it is relevant to any matter in issue in the proceedings. The defence, if contesting the admissibility of a confession, will need to raise the matter with the trial judge and seek to convince the court that the confession ought to be excluded. Once a judge has ruled on admitting a confession as evidence before the jury and it is subsequently revealed by fresh evidence that this decision was wrong, then they are powerless to act under s.76, since the provision applies only to confessions the prosecution propose to rely on before the trial. In such circumstances, the judge can utilise s. 82 (3) to give an appropriate direction to the jury or if the prejudice is inescapable discharge the jury.

Section 76(2) provides that a confession must be excluded as a matter of law if one or both of two grounds exist, where the confession:

(i) was obtained by oppression, or

(ii) in consequence of anything said or done which was likely to render it unreliable.

Once the issue of the admissibility of a confession is raised and the judge is willing to entertain the application, then it is for the prosecution to disprove beyond all reasonable doubt that the confession was obtained oppressively or unreliably. If they fail to discharge this burden, the confession, as a matter of law, must be excluded.

3. Meaning of Oppression and the Right against Self Incrimination

28.03 In regard to oppression s.76(8) states that it includes any torture, inhuman or degrading treatment and the use or threat of violence. Although this provides a partial statutory definition, the Court of Appeal in *R. v Fulling* [1987] 85 Cr.App.R. 136, stated that the oppression should be given its ordinary dictionary meaning, reference being made to the Oxford English Dictionary:

> "exercise of authority or power in a burdensome, harsh, or wrongful manner; unjust or cruel treatment of subjects, inferiors, etc, or the imposition of unreasonable or unjust burdens."

However, the Court concluded that the appellant's confession had been admitted correctly in evidence by the trial judge who was satisfied that it was not obtained oppressively, despite the fact that the police had told lies in respect of her partner having an affair, who was also in custody. Conversely in *R. v Paris* [1993] 97 Cr.App.R. 99, the Court of Appeal accepted that the police do need to interrogate suspects with a view to establishing particular facts and are not precluded from doing so after the first, or several denials. However, it was oppressive conduct for the interviewing officers to continuously shout at, or bully a suspect and especially so as against a suspect who was mentally susceptible and who had denied any involvement in the brutal murder of a prostitute no fewer than 300 times.

The presumption of innocence, together with a qualified right to silence, safeguards the suspect from being forced or coerced into incriminating or implicating themselves. In *Saunders v UK* [1996] 23 E.H.R.R. 313, the ECHR recognised that these two rights and international standards are the bedrock of the notion of ensuring a fair trial. It is for the prosecution to prove its case and not to resort to tactics of extracting incriminating evidence from the accused, either by oppression or coercion. To do so would be in clear breach of art.6. It is the essential duty of the judge to protect the fairness of the proceedings and ensure that the defendant's safeguards have not been infringed. If a statement given by the defendant does not amount to a confession for the purposes of s.76, but was obtained by oppression, then in such circumstances, as stated in *R. v Z* [2005] 2 A.C. 467, recourse would lie with the, "unrestricted capability of s.78 to avoid any injustice".

Section 172 of the Road Traffic Act 1988 places an obligation on the owner of a motor vehicle to provide information to the police so as to indentify the driver of the vehicle at the time of a specified offence. If a motor vehicle is caught by a speed camera, then a notice of intended prosecution along with a s.172 notice is sent to the registered keeper. The standard statement as completed by the owner, identifying themselves as the driver amounts to a confession and if purported to be signed by them, is admissible evidence under s.12 of the Road Traffic Offenders Act 1988.

If the registered keeper fails to complete the form, then this amounts to an offence. If the registered keeper identifies another person as the driver, this does not offend the right against incrimination, either of oneself or of another (see *O'Halloran and Frances v UK* [2007] (App. 15809/02), discussed further in Chapter 8 at para.8.07). Further, in *Francis v DPP* [2004] EWHC 591 the High Court held that no caution is required for the s.172 notice, since Code 10.1 provides that a person need not be cautioned, if the questions are for "other necessary purposes", such as identification or ownership of any vehicle, or as in the case of s.172 to obtain information in accordance with a relevant statutory requirement.

4. Meaning of Unreliable

28.04 The more likely ground to be argued is that the confession was obtained in consequence of anything said or done, which in the circumstances, is likely to render it unreliable. This would also encapsulate any oppressive conduct by the interviewing officers. For the confession to be deemed unreliable, it must be as a consequence of anything said or done by the person in authority which may have prompted or caused an accused person to make a confession. Consequently, it is not what an accused person themselves may have said or done which is envisaged by the relevant statutory phrase. It is, as explained in *R. v Goldenburg* [1989] 88 Cr.App.R. 285, that the words establish a causal link between what was said or done and the subsequent confession.

The statutory words "anything said or done" must derive from something extraneous to the accused person. In dismissing the appeal the Court held on the facts that although the appellant was anxious to be granted bail or credit for assisting the police such requests were things done by him and neither offered or encouraged by the police extraneously to him? Moreover, in *R. v Crampton* [1991] 92 Cr.App.R. 369, the Court of Appeal held that the holding of an interview was not something done for the purpose of reliability and that whether a drug addict was fit to be interviewed, in the sense that his answers could in fact be realistically relied on, was a matter for those present at that time. The Court also took the view that unreliable means:

> "cannot be relied upon as being the truth, what the provision of subsection 2(b) is concerned with is the nature and quality of the words spoken or things done by the police which are likely to in the circumstances existing at the time, render the confession unreliable in the sense that it is not true."

In *R. v Barry* [1992] Cr.App.R. 384 the Court of Appeal allowed the appeal on the basis that it was impossible to be sure that the appellant, despite clear advice to the contrary, was not influenced by the promise of bail, if he made a full confession. Section 76(2) should be approached in a broad sense and not on the narrow issue of whether there had been an offer which was accepted unequivocally by the accused.

If the defendant raises an issue as to the reliability of their confession, then the court ought to adopt the following approach:

(i) Identify the alleged thing said or done. This will require the judge to take into account everything said and done by the police.

(ii) Consider objectively whether what was said and done was likely in the circumstances to render unreliable a confession made in consequence, taking into account all the circumstances.

(iii) Consider whether the prosecution has proved beyond reasonable doubt that the confession was not obtained in consequence of the thing said and done. This is clearly a question of fact to be approached in a common sense way.

28.05 In *Fulling* [1987] 85 Cr.App.R. 136 the Court of Appeal made it clear that there is no requirement to show that the confession was obtained in consequence of police impropriety. Section 76 can still invalidate a confession, even where there is no suspicion of police misconduct. If there is police misconduct, in the sense of breaches of the Codes of Practice, such as refusing or failing to advise a suspect of a right to seek free legal advice, this will make it all the more difficult for the prosecution to discharge its heavy burden (see *R. v Cheung* [1992] 92 Cr.App.R. 314).

Care must always be taken if (which is clearly safeguarded against in s.77) to recognise any mental or personality disorders pertaining to the suspect which may impact on the reliability of what they say to questions put to them. In all such cases, an appropriate adult must be present. In *R. v Ashley King* [2000] Crim. L.R. 835, on this very point, the Court of Appeal quashed the conviction of the appellant for murder in 1986, which rested entirely upon a signed written confession made by the appellant after a number of interviews. On receiving fresh psychiatric evidence that the appellant was significantly less intelligent and abnormally suggestible, which the Court found persuasive, Lord Bingham observed that the fairness or otherwise of police interviews should be considered both in the context of the procedures and the standards in force at the time of the trial, as against present day fairness and that had this new evidence been available at the time there would have been strong grounds for excluding the confession, thereby rendering the conviction unsafe (see also *R. v Foster* [2003] EWCA Crim 178).

In *R. v Cromer and Wahab* [2002] EWCA Crim 1570, the Court of Appeal took the view that a defendant having been given proper and realistic advice from a solicitor would not normally be a sufficient basis for excluding a confession now claimed to be unreliable by the defendant due to that advice. The Court, nevertheless, did not rule out the possibility of a confession from a vulnerable defendant, even after being advised as being unreliable.

5. Admitting a Confession Made by a Co-Accused and s.76A of PACE 1984

28.06 In *Myers* [1998] A.C. 124, the appellant had made admissions to the police that she had stabbed the victim. The prosecution did not intend to rely on the admissions as evidence due to breaches of the Codes of Practice. However, a co-accused, who contended that he had nothing to do with the killing, wished to adduce the admissions as evidence to support his defence. The judge refused to order separate trials and also allowed the co-accused to cross-examine the police officer to whom the admissions were made. The House of Lords, in dismissing the appeal, ruled that a defendant has an absolute right as, confirmed in *Lobban v The Queen* [1995] 1 W.L.R. 877, to lead all relevant evidence in support of their defence and that the trial judge cannot under any circumstances, including s.78, exclude such evidence.

A co-defendant is entitled to cross-examine any co-accused concerning a previous inconsistent confession they had made and if they deny it the co-defendant should be allowed to rebut that denial. Likewise, the House of Lords stated that a co-accused should be allowed to cross-examine a witness to whom the other co-accused had made a confession, provided that this is relevant to their defence and that the confession was not obtained in breach of s.76(2). To prevent such cross-examination could led to unfairness, since the other co-accused may decide not to give evidence in order to avoid the risk of being cross-examined themselves about the alleged confession.

To clarify and place this important rule of evidence on a statutory basis s.128 of the Criminal Justice Act 2003, which came into effect on January 29, 2004, inserts a new s.76A into PACE 1984, which states clearly that a confession made by an co-accused may be given in evidence against another jointly charged defendant in the same proceedings, provided it is relevant. Subsection (2) makes it clear that if such a confession was or may have been obtained either by oppression, or is unreliable in consequence of anything said or done, then the court must not allow the confession to be adduced, unless, the co-accused who wishes to rely on it can show on a balance of probabilities that the confession was not obtained illegally.

28.07 The court can of its own motion, even if there is no suggestion of illegality, require the co-accused to discharge this burden of proof. In *R. v Finch* [2007] 1 W.L.R. 1645, the Court of Appeal, when construing the expression "another person charged", held that it is a clear proposition of law that a person who pleads guilty and is therefore not facing a trial is not a person charged and therefore the intention of Parliament is clear. A defendant facing trial for an offence cannot under s.76A adduce as evidence a statement of exoneration of them in a confession by another, who has pleaded guilty. In this situation, the witness is compellable and therefore consideration will need to be given to a witness summons and hostility.

Of importance is subsection (4), which provides that if a confession is either wholly or party excluded, this does not impact on any facts that are discovered as a result of the confession. If the co-accused wishes to use that excluded confession to establish that the other accused speaks, writes or expresses themselves in a particular way they may only use as much of the confession as is necessary to do so. Section 128 does not affect the decision of the House of Lords in *R. v Blastland* [1986] A.C. 41 in which the defendant (having been charged with the murder of a boy with whom he admitted to having committed acts of indecency near to where his body was found, but denied being the murderer) wished to adduce the evidence of a witness who had heard a third person called Mark state that a boy had been murdered before any body was in fact found.

The purpose of this was to invite the jury to draw an inference from the knowledge of the unknown Mark, that he knew the boy was dead and must have been the offender, not the defendant. The House of Lords, in dismissing the appeal, confirmed that an accused person cannot adduce in evidence the confession made by another to the same crime. This clearly amounts to hearsay and is therefore inadmissible in the sense of being an implied admission of knowledge of the offence.

28.08 In *R. v Hayter* [2005] 1 W.L.R. 605, the House of Lords confirmed the existing principle of law that a voluntary out of court confession or admission is admissible as being an exception to the hearsay rule of inadmissibility. However, an admissible confession can only be used to implicate the person who made it and cannot be used to prove the case against another defendant, jointly charged. The judge must direct the jury to ignore the confession of an accused, when considering the case against another co-accused. The appellant *Hayter* was convicted of murder in a contract killing, he had acted as the middleman between a woman who wanted her husband dead and the actual murderer, who shot the deceased.

The principal offender had confessed the killing, to his girlfriend. By a majority of three to two, the House of Lords ruled that the judge was correct and had not infringed the rule above in directing the jury that only when they, on the evidence, found both the actual killer and the woman guilty of murder, would it then be open to them to consider, along with other evidence, the guilt of Hayter. The judge had correctly, in accordance with practice, told the jury to ignore the contents of the confession of the killer, when determining the case against Hayter. The position would be no different if the evidence was not a confession, but say a fingerprint or DNA sample. If needed, the majority were prepared to make a necessary and sensible adjustment or modification to the rule on out of court confessions. Their Lordships, in the majority, found further support in s.74, which would allow the conviction of the principal offender to be used in any subsequent trial of the others.

In a powerful dissent, both Lord Roger and Lord Carswell observed that the ruling of the majority would in effect turn what is inadmissible evidence into admissible evidence. It would require the jury to engage in mental gymnastics and to induce them into false sophistry. It would be impossible to envisage a jury first finding a defendant guilty based solely on their confession and then taking that finding of guilt into account in determining the case against another, but at the same time ignoring the confession that they have used to find the other accused guilty. In s.118(5) of the CJA 2003, Parliament had specifically preserved common law rules as to the admissibility of confessions or mixed statements. Accordingly, such a change as made by the majority was a matter, not for the House of Lords, but for Parliament. By making such changes this would lead to an increase in applications for separate trials, leading to uncertainty and confusing distinctions.

Another important statutory provision in relation to admission evidence is s.74 of PACE 1984, which was created to remove the exclusionary principle in *R. v Spinks* [1981] 74 Cr.App.R. 263. Section 74 allows the prosecution, if relevant, to admit the conviction of another as evidence to prove any issue against the defendant now being tried. For instance, if A and B are jointly alleged to have committed a street robbery. A pleads guilty, but B denies any involvement. To contradict this, the prosecution can seek to invite the judge to invoke s.74 and admit the conviction of A to prove B's involvement. Section 74 gives the judge a discretionary power which must be considered together with s.78, whether to allow such evidence and consider whether it would be highly prejudicial to the defendant. In *R. v Dixon* [2000] 164 J.P. 721, the Court of Appeal observed that s.74 should be used sparingly when admitting a confession in the evidence of a co-accused.

Section 74(3) allows a previous conviction of the accused themselves to be admitted, provided it goes to prove an issue in a subsequent trial and not a propensity to commit the kind of offence for which they are being tried. A vivid illustration of this provision is *R. v Shanks* [2003] EWCA Crim 680, in which the appellant had been convicted of the offence of possessing a firearm with intent to endanger life, although the jury could not agree on the charge of murder. He was subsequently re-tried and the prosecution sought to introduce the firearms conviction as evidence on the issue of whether or not he had the necessary intent to kill and was not suffering from diminished responsibility. The Court of Appeal ruled that the judge was correct to admit the firearms conviction.

6. Procedural Fairness and the Discretionary Exclusion of Evidence under s.78 of PACE 1984

28.09 The basic proposition in the law of criminal evidence is that if the evidence is relevant to the issue of establishing the ingredients of the offence, then it is prima facie admissible for that purpose, even if the evidence was obtained in a irregular manner. This point is clearly recognised in *Kuruma v The Queen* [1955] A.C. 197, when Lord Goddard, sitting in the Privy Council, emphasised that if the evidence is: "relevant to matters in issue", then it will be admissible and the court will not concern itself, "with how the evidence was obtained".

Notwithstanding this, Lord Goddard stated obiter that a judge did have a discretion in certain circumstances to exclude evidence: "if the strict rules of admissibility would operate unfairly against the defendant".

This may occur, for instance, where the evidence is obtained from the accused by deception or procured by a trick. In *R. v Mason* [1988] 1 W.L.R. 139, the Court of Appeal quashed the appellant's conviction for arson, when it was revealed that the police had, by a deliberate deceit, hoodwinked both the appellant and his solicitor into believing that they had found an incriminating fingerprint, which led to the appellant making an admission.

In *R. v Sang* [1980] A.C. 402, the House of Lords provided a useful review of the authorities on the approach to and the essential nature of the common law rule, by defining carefully the limits of the discretion. It was held unanimously that a discretion exists only where the evidence (admissible and relevant) sought to be adduced by the prosecution, has such a prejudicial effect that the prejudice it might create in the mind of the jury is out of all proportion to its evidential value. Their Lordships further concluded that except for confessions and evidence obtained from the defendant after the commission of the offence, there is no discretion vested in the judge to exclude non-confession evidence on the ground that it was obtained by improper or unfair means. Whilst s.82 of PACE 1984 preserves expressly the discretionary exclusion rule of the common law, s.78 is the principal provision on which the courts will rely, when exercising their discretionary power to exclude evidence, having regard to all the circumstances which would, if admitted, have an adverse effect on the fairness of the proceedings.

Section 78 is equally applicable to trials in the magistrates' court as well as the Crown Court. Guidance on how to approach an application to rule on the admissibility of evidence in the magistrates' court is given in *R. (DPP) v Acton Youth Court* [2001] 1 W.L.R. 1828. One of the problems with the magistrates' court is that the magistrates/District Judge are both judges of law and fact. Provided that the fairness of the proceedings is maintained, it is not necessary for a justice or judge to dismiss themselves once they have ruled evidence inadmissible, unless either actual or apparent bias is unavoidable. In *J v DPP* [2004] EWHC 1470 the High Court applied the decision in *Vel v Owen* [1987] Crim. L.R. 496 and ruled that the object is to ensure a fair trial and that the decision regarding an application under s.78 can at the court's discretion be taken as and when the application arises, or as in other cases, it may be more appropriate to delay the decision until the end of the hearing.

7. Police Breach of PACE 1984 and the Codes of Practice

28.10 The decision whether or not to exclude evidence under s.78 is a matter for the judge based on the individual facts of the case. The application of s.78 is wide in that proceedings, including all the preliminary steps up to and including trial and evidence, will include all information relevant to the case. If the police either breach a provision of PACE 1984, or alternatively, fail to follow the Codes of Practice (which are themselves admissible evidence at trial under s.67(11)) then the issue is whether any evidence obtained in consequence ought not to be excluded. Section 78 is not used by the court as a method of disciplining the police for what might be considered bad practice.

The essential issue is the fairness of the proceedings to a defendant and consequently there is a right to be protected by the court (see *R. v Quinn* [1990] Crim. L.R. 581 and *Chalkley* [1998] 3 W.L.R. 146–171). In *R. v Keenan* 90 Cr.App.R. 1, the Court of Appeal excluded the contents of an interview, on the grounds that the police had used the tactic of "verballing" (deliberate use of direct closed questions pressuring the suspect to provide an answer) on the appellant to such a degree as amounting to "significant and substantial" breaches of the Codes for which the judge should have excluded the confession. Likewise if the police and equally Customs Officers, such as in *Okafor* [1994] 99 Cr.App.R. 97, should demonstrate a lamentable and cynical disregard to the clear application of the Codes, then a confession or any other evidence should be excluded (see *R. v Canale* [1990] 2 All E.R. 187).

Similarly, in *R. v Walsh* [1990] 91 Cr.App.R. 161, the Court of Appeal observed that if there are significant and substantial breaches of either s.58, right to free legal advice, or the Codes generally then it would be unfair to admit any evidence obtained in consequence, (in contrast see *R. v Alladice* [1988] 87 Cr.App.R. 380). If the police fail to administer a caution properly, then this does not, as seen in *R. v Absolam* [1989] 88 Cr.App.R. 332 and *R. v Delaney* [1989] 88 Cr.App.R. 338, automatically render any evidence obtained subsequently inadmissible. However, in *R. v Kirk* [2000] 1 Cr.App.R. 400, the Court of Appeal, in allowing the appeal against conviction for offences of robbery and manslaughter, ruled that a suspect under both s.28 of PACE 1984 and Code C is entitled to know in general terms the seriousness of the alleged offence for which they have been arrested.

28.11 Where the police question, without cautioning, the suspect about a more serious offence of which they were not aware and therefore did not seek legal advice and the suspect gives critical answers in the interview that they might not have otherwise given, had they been aware of the offence to which the questions related, in such circumstances, that evidence ought to be excluded under s.78 as being unfair. Nevertheless, the training of police officers in terms of interview technique has improved significantly, in reducing the likelihood of a deliberate breach of PACE 1984.

In *Whitley v DPP* [2003] EWHC 2512, the High Court, having referred to the authority of *DPP v Kennedy* [2003] EWHC 2583, ruled that s.58 of PACE 1984 gives a clear and fundamental right of a suspect to seek free legal advice and under the Codes, a Custody Sergeant should act without delay and as soon as is reasonably practicable to obtain that advice. However, if having requested legal advice, the relevant officer informs the suspect that a breath test procedure will not be delayed in order to wait for the requested legal advisor, then, in such circumstances, the evidence from the breath test procedure is not automatically to be excluded under s.78. It is a question of fact and degree as to how the police responded to the request for legal advice.

The appellant must show that a court would conclude that the delay went beyond what was as soon as reasonably practicable. If this is demonstrated, then was the breach of s.58 and the Codes so significant and substantial as to justify exclusion? Again, this amounts to a question of fact and degree in all the circumstances of the case. In particular, the Court made it plain that whilst art.6 ensures a right to fair proceedings, it is a proportionate response for the police, in achieving the legitimate aim of suppressing drink driving in the public interest, to request that a suspect gives a specimen of breath while waiting for legal advice and will not amount to a reasonable excuse for refusing to comply (see also *R. v Forde v DPP* [2004] EWHC 1156 and *Myles v DPP* [2004] EWHC 594).

The difficulty sometimes faced by the courts when having to strike a fair balance between competing interests on the use of evidence, is illustrated vividly in *Attorney General's Reference (No.3) of 1999* [2001] A.C. 91, in which the police had obtained from an unlawfully retained sample (which should have been destroyed under statutory provisions) probative and cogent scientific evidence showing the defendant to be the offender in a violent and brutal rape. The trial judge excluded the evidence on the basis that s.64 of PACE 1984, at the time, forbade the use of a sample which should have been destroyed. However the House of Lords ruled that any evidence derived from an illegally retained sample was not to be treated as mandatorily inadmissible, but was instead to be considered at the discretion of the judge under s.78. Parliament has since amended s.64 by ss.9 and 10 of the CJA 2003, to allow the police to retain all samples taken regardless.

8. Section 78 and Entrapment/Agent Provocateur Evidence

28.12 It as been said on a number of occasions throughout this book that the court is always striving to strike a fair balance, between the three competing interests of the public, complainant and the defendant. The gathering of evidence and intelligence and the methods used in order to obtain such evidence are matters for the police as an agent of the State acting in the public interest. Certain serious criminal offences do not necessarily have a direct complainant who is able to provide crucial evidence. In other instances an increase in certain offences requires the police or other agencies (i.e. Customs and Excise) to instigate a planned operation with a given code name.

Such offences include street drug dealing, theft and or interference with motor vehicles, or shops selling alcohol to the under aged. In order to gather evidence sufficient to commence criminal proceedings this may require the use of undercover police officers. The public interest unquestionably demands such investigations to be carried out. The legal question is how far the police can operate in this manner without jeopardising the operation itself and falling foul of the rule of law. All law enforcement agencies must work within the legal framework and the important safeguards that form part of it. In what circumstances does a suspect commit a crime voluntarily or is otherwise enticed encouraged or even compelled by deception to commit a crime?

The leading authority on the legality of undercover police operations is *R. v Loosely* [2001] 1 W.L.R. 2060, in which the House of Lords first observed that there is no defence of entrapment for an alleged offence, as stated clearly in *Sang* [1980] A.C. 402 and *Smurthwaite and Gill* [1994] Cr.App.R. 437. However, if the defence claim that the evidence was obtained by way of entrapment, then the appropriate remedy is to make an application for the proceedings to be stayed as an abuse of process. Should this fail, an application ought then to be made for the judge to exclude the disputed evidence under s.78 as having, if admitted, an adverse effect of the fairness of the trial (see *R. v Shannon* [2001] 1 W.L.R. 51, where undercover journalist posed as a Arab Sheikh in order to uncover drug dealing). If this application is successful, then it will be a matter for the prosecution to decide whether there is other sufficient evidence to continue or appeal the decision under s.58 of the CJA 2003.

28.13 The House of Lords in *Loosely*, on a second point, made it clear that to allow the prosecution of "state-created crime" would amount to an affront to public conscience. It would be unfair and improper to do so in such circumstances. The test to be applied when determining whether the police have acted within the acceptable limits on the use of undercover investigations is that expressed by Lord Nicholls as needing:

> "to consider whether the police did not more than present the defendant with an unexceptional opportunity to commit a crime. I emphasise the unexceptional. The yardstick for that purpose of this test is, in general, whether the police conduct preceding the commission of the offence was not more than might have been expected from others in the circumstances."

It is clearly not unexceptional for the police by their direct involvement to incite, instigate, persuade or lure a person into committing a crime artificially and in an environment in which they would not have otherwise done so. Other important factors for the court are the assessment of whether the level or degree of intrusiveness deployed was proportionate to the legitimate aim to be achieved by the operation, i.e. the enforcement of regulatory offences, for instance, unlawfully selling alcohol, where test purchasing is legitimately deployed to aid investigation and detection, in which the child purchaser acts like any other customer is doing nothing unexpected. Another method is the use of pro-active techniques as opposed to passivity (see the decision in *Nottingham City Council v Amin* [2000] 1 Cr.App.R. 426, when two undercover police officers targeted unlicensed taxi drivers by using the service). Where the police acts are in good faith, what level of inducement is being used by them in order to gather the evidence against the target in question? The greater the intrusion, the more the court will scrutinise it, but what is unlikely to be relevant, unless linked to the reasonable suspicion of the alleged misconduct, is the defendant's criminal record. The overall consideration, according to Lord Nicholls:

> "is always whether the conduct of the police or other law enforcement agency was so seriously improper as to bring the administration of justice into disrepute."

Finally, their Lordships in *Loosely* made it clear that the principles of English law are entirely consistent on this issue with that of the European Court of Human Rights in *Teixeira de Castro v Portugal* [1999] 28 E.H.R.R. 101, and the right to a fair trial is maintained. In that case, the Court ruled that the defendant had not received a fair trial when, on the facts, the police officers had gone beyond the role of acting as undercover officers under supervision and acted improperly by instigating the alleged offence. The European Court emphasised that fairness and justice cannot give way to expedience and that the public interest can never be served, or justify the use of evidence obtained by police incitement. Any trial founded on such evidence would be tainted and deprive the defendant of a fair trial. To assist and ensure that any undercover operation is administered correctly, there is in place a manual entitled "Undercover Operations Code of Practice" issued by the Police and Customs and Excise.

28.14 Ultimately, each case must be dealt with in regard to its own particular facts. In *R. v Christou* [1992] 4 All E.R. 559, the Court of Appeal held that there had been no trickery or incitement to commit offences of handling stolen goods, when the police set up as a jewellers' shop, since the defendant freely entered it and offered the goods as being for sale. Similarly, in *Williams v DPP* [1993] 98 Cr.App.R. 209, the police had not acted improperly when they left a sting vehicle unattended, with empty boxes in the back of an unlocked van. Although no issue of entrapment was raised on the somewhat unusual facts in *R. v Elleray* [2003] EWCA Crim 553, the Court of Appeal stated that the judge had exercised his discretion correctly, by allowing in evidence the conversations that took place between the offender and his probation officer in a pre-sentence report for an indecent assault, in which the appellant admitted to raping the complainant.

In *R. v Stagg* [1994] (unreported), the trial judge excluded the evidence obtained by a undercover woman police officer who befriended the suspect in a deliberate attempt to get him to incriminate himself in the murder of Rachel Nickell. This amounted to a misleading, manipulative and unfair method of investigation. In respect of a psychological profile as possible supplementary evidence, the judge considered this to be, "redolent with considerable danger" and not to be encouraged as a form of expert evidence if indeed it could be so categorised.

In *R. v Jones* [2007] EWCA Crim 1118, the Court of Appeal, referring to the guidance in *Loosely*, dismissed the appeal against conviction for an offence under s.8 of the Sexual Offences Act 2003. The appellant had left graffiti messages in various locations inciting eight to 13-year-old girls to contact him for sexual activity. The appellant received a message from a girl he believed to be 12, but who was in fact an undercover police officer. The Court of Appeal concluded that the communications between the officer and the appellant, far from bringing the administration of justice into disrepute, were necessary to gather the evidence against the appellant before he committed the complete offence. The offence was instigated not by the police, but by the appellant's own actions. Accordingly, there was no abuse of power by the State so as to deny the appellant a fair trial.

9. Covert Surveillance and Interception of Communications

28.15 Similar, to the use of undercover police agents, so do the law enforcement agencies in certain situations resort to deploying covert surveillance techniques in order to gather compelling evidence, either by intercepting private communications, or by listening devices located covertly. The active use of such methods is highly intrusive into the private communications of others. By such conduct, there is a risk that the following rights of the suspect may have been breached: (i) art.8, a right to private and family life and (ii) art.6, a right to a fair trial, either by an abuse of process, or exclusion of the prejudicial evidence, including the right against self incrimination.

The statutory framework to authorise and control covert surveillance practices is found in Pt II of the Regulation of Investigatory Powers Act 2000 (RIPA 2000), which came into effect on September 25, 2000. The purpose of the Act was to consolidate and repeal the previous provisions found in the Interception of Communications Act 1985 and the Police Act 1997 and to ensure that a fair balance is stuck between protecting the rights of individual, whilst recognising the legitimate aim of the prevention and detection of serious crime as being necessary to the public interest. In *Attorney-General's Reference (No.5 of 2002)* [2004] [2005] 1 A.C. 167, the House of Lords found the provisions of the RIPA 2000 difficult to understand and apply, when having to determine the ambit of s.17, on the admissibility of evidence obtained through the interception of telephone conversations in a police station, involving the alleged corruption of certain police officers. The House of Lords held this to be lawful and a necessary and proportionate interference with art.8 and the right to privacy.

Section 26 allows for three different types of surveillance to be undertaken namely:

(i) directed but not intrusive;

(ii) intrusive concerning residential premises (this includes a hotel and a prison/police cell) and private vehicles, i.e. use of listening devices;

(iii) conduct and use of covert human intelligence sources, in which a person establishes and maintains a personal, or other relationship with another person, in order to obtain or gain access to information or the disclosure of such information by them.

For each method of surveillance the appropriate authorisation from a designated person (i.e. Secretary of State) must be obtained in order to make the activity lawful, otherwise it would be unlawful and may amount to an offence under s.1, if it involves the interception of communications by post or public telecommunications. Under s.17 such evidence obtained in consequence would be inadmissible. In *R. v E* [2004] 2 Cr.App.R. 29 the Court of Appeal gave a wide meaning to the expression "interception" which:

> "denotes some interference or abstraction of the signal, whether it is passing along wires or by wireless telegraphy, during the process of transmission. The recording of a person's voice independently of the fact that at the time he is using a telephone, does not become interception simply because what he say does not only go into the recorder, but, by a separate process, is transmitted by a telecommunication system."

28.16 Even if the evidence was obtained lawfully and not in breach of the RIPA 2000, the judge must always consider the discretionary power of exclusion under s.78 of PACE 1984 (see also *R. v Kennedy and Others* [2005] EWCA Crim 2859). In *R. v Allsopp* [2005] EWCA Crim 703, the Court of Appeal, having approved and followed the decision in *R. v E*, observed that it was not necessary for the defence to be given any significant detail upon which the prosecution relied in order to obtain the authorisation for the intrusion. The matters would be sufficiently be dealt with by the judge at the PII hearing, and that s.78 must always be considered. All these cases involved police investigations into conspiracy to supply a class A drug and the evidence obtained from a listening device in a vehicle or room which picked up conversations on a phone, and did not amount to an unlawful interception under s.1 of the RIPA 2000 (other authorities include *R. v Smart-Beard* [2002] EWCA Crim 217 and *R. v Hardy* [2002] EWCA Crim 3012).

The purpose of the authorisation and the regulatory provisions on covert surveillance is to ensure that those activities are necessary and proportionate and are undertaken in accordance with the law, so as to amount to a justifiable interference with a person's right to a private life contained in art.8, which is what occurred in *Khan v UK* [2001] 31 E.C.H.R. 45, *Taylor–Sabori v UK* [2003] E.C.H.R., *Hewitson v UK* [2003] E.C.H.R. and more recently *Elahi v UK* [2007] 44 E.H.R.R. 30. However, in *R. v Rosenberg* [2006] EWCA Crim 6, the Court of Appeal endorsed the refusal of the trial judge to exclude evidence of drug dealing obtained from a neighbour's CCTV on the grounds that it did not amount to police surveillance for the purposes of the RIPA 2000. The police had not actively encouraged, authorised, or instructed the filming. Further, the Court held that if the provisions of the Act applied, it did not breach s.26, since the surveillance was not covert, given that the appellant was aware of her neighbour's filming. Also, even if there was a breach of art.8, this does not render the evidence inadmissible; the issue being whether the appellant would receive a fair trial.

Further safeguards in the Act include the appointment under ss.57 to 64 of a Interceptions of Communications Commissioner, to keep under review the exercise of any of the powers under the Act and also under ss.65 to 70 the creation of a Tribunal to consider and determine a complaint from an aggrieved person, about the exercise of certain powers within the Act (Pt II is included in this). Likewise s.71 provides for the Secretary of State to issue a Code of Practice relating to the exercise and performance of the main powers under the Act, which includes Pt II.

Under the previous provisions in the Interception of Communications Act 1985, the House of Lords in *R. v Sargent* [2003] 1 A.C. 347, had found that the complainant as a telephone engineer had unlawfully intercepted a conversation that implicated his ex wife and new partner in an offence of arson on his property. Although compelling evidence this was admissible at trial under s.9. Nevertheless, it was further ruled that it is permissible for the police to use such evidence in interviewing when questioning the suspect and that any evidence gained in consequence would, subject to s.78, be admissible at trial (see also *Morgans v DPP* [2001] 1 A.C. 315).

10. Article 8 and Admissibility of Evidence

28.17 The leading authority, albeit now to be read in conjunction with the RIPA 2000, on whether any evidence obtained in breach of art.8 can still, nonetheless, be admissible at trial is *R. v Mason* [2002] EWCA Crim 385. The police launched Operation Brassica in order to investigate a series of burglaries and robberies in Coventry. Nine offenders were arrested. Covert audio equipment was installed in the custody suite, from which incriminating evidence was obtained. The Court of Appeal, whilst recognising that this occurred prior to the commencement of the RIPA 2000 which now provides the necessary legality for covert taping within the category of "intrusive surveillance" under s.26 held that it did infringe art.8(2), since it was conduct not in accordance with the law having no recognisable legal structure or authority in place.

However, whilst a breach of the right to privacy, the Court, in the judgment of Lord Woolf, held that this did not lead automatically to the exclusion of the relevant evidence at trial, since, following the decision of the European Court in *PG and JH v UK* [2001] E.C.H.R., the issue of admissibility of evidence was a matter for national law and the determination of the courts. Automatic exclusion would undoubtedly lead to a "greater injustice to the public than the infringement of art 8 creates for the appellants". However, the trial judge might take such an infringement into account when asked to exercise their discretionary power to ensure fairness under s.78 of PACE 1984.

11. Covert Surveillance and "Legal Professional Privilege"

28.18 Any communication between solicitor and client is protected by the doctrine of legal professional privilege in order to ensure the free and unhindered flow of information without fear or restriction. In *R. v Grant* [2005] EWCA Crim 1089, the Court of Appeal quashed the appellant's conviction for conspiracy to murder, as being obtained by an abuse of process, when information was obtained by the police through the use of covert listening devices with respect to legal professional privilege communications. On this point Laws L.J. made it plain that:

> "acts done by the police, in the course of an investigation which leads in due course to the institution of criminal proceedings, with a view to eavesdropping upon communications of suspected persons which are subject to legal professional privilege are categorically unlawful and at the very least capable of infecting the proceedings as abusive of the court's process."

In *R. v Derby Magistrates Court Ex p. B* [1996] A.C. 487, Lord Taylor, in considering legal professional privilege, stated that it is much more than a ordinary rule of evidence, "it is a fundamental condition on which the administration of justice as a whole rests".

12. Stay of Proceedings for an Abuse of Process

28.19 The court has a general common law power to protect the process of both law and justice and stay any prosecution if those who pursued it have acted outside and undermined the rule of law, in their endeavour to secure a conviction, by whatever means. In *Beckford* [1996] 1 Cr.App.R. 94 Neill L.J. stated that this amounts to a constitutional principle under which the courts have a duty to ensure that there is no unfair treatment of those who are brought before the courts.

In *R. v Horseferry Road Magistrates' Court Ex p. Bennett* [1994] 1 A.C. 42, as confirmed in *R. v Latif* [1996] 2 Cr.App.R. 101, the law relating to an abuse of process argument is well settled and is based on three components:

- (i) The court has a discretionary power to decide whether or not to stay proceedings as an abuse of process if this would amount to an affront to the public conscience, so that,
- (ii) a fair trial would be impossible, and
- (iii) it would be contrary to the public interest in the integrity of the criminal justice system.

In *R. v Beckford* [1996] 1 Cr.App.R. 94, in which the police had destroyed the car pre-trial, it was alleged that the defendant had caused the death of another by dangerous driving due to a collision, the cause of which was disputed by expert evidence. In dismissing the appeal, the Court of Appeal surmised that the court had a discretionary power to stay proceedings if it concluded that either the defendant; (i) could not receive a fair trial, or (ii) it would be unfair for the defendant to be tried.

In order to determine whether a fair trial is still possible, then the judge will need to strike a balance based on the triangulation of interests. On the one hand, the court needs to ensure that public confidence in the justice system is maintained at all times. Whilst it is not the function necessarily of the courts to discipline the police, any misconduct by them or the prosecution, strongly suggests the need to stay proceedings to prevent unfair treatment of the defendant, because of that misconduct. On the other hand, the court has a duty to protect the public from the commission of crimes, especially serious crimes, and if the circumstances allow, there may be refusal of a stay of proceedings on the premise that the inbuilt mechanisms of the trial process itself will ensure fair proceedings.

28.20 Each case is dependant on its facts and like s.78 the Appeal Court will only interfere with the exercise of the discretionary power if the judge has acted so unreasonably that no other court would on the facts, come to that decision. Arguments as to an abuse of process have been concerned predominantly with:

- (i) excessive delay in bring and concluding proceedings;

(ii) misconduct by either the police or the prosecution in their approach to the proceedings;

(iii) lost or non-disclosed evidence.

In *R. v Bloomfield* [1997] 1 Cr.App.R. 135, the Court of Appeal ruled that, in the particular facts, regardless of whether the defendant was prejudiced or not, it would amount to an abuse of process by bringing the administration of justice into disrepute to allow the prosecution to renege on its previous decision, of communicating to the defendant that they would be offering no evidence. In contrast, the Court of Appeal in *R. v Murphy* [2003] Crim. L.R. 471 dismissed the appeal against conviction for an indecent assault, an offence that had been added later in the Crown Court. The decision in *Bloomfield* does not create any general principle of law and certainly does not create a rule that the prosecution cannot later, having reviewed the evidence, add or amend an indictment. Likewise, as stated in *Ex p. Low* [1990] 1 Q.B. 54, the fact that either a summons or charge is withdrawn, does not prevent the subsequent issuing of a summons for the same offence (see also *R. v Ebrahim* [2003] EWCA Crim 1881).

Neither is it necessarily an abuse of process for the defendant to be tried for the same offence a third time. In *R. v Henworth* [2001] EWCA Crim 120, the appellant had originally been convicted of murder. This was set aside on appeal and after a re-trial, the jury could not reach a verdict, the jury having been discharged the prosecution sought a further re-trial. The Court of Appeal ruled that this, on the facts, did not amount to an abuse of process, since the pubic interest demands that those who are charged with serious offences, of which there is a case to answer, must be tried by a jury. The Court did nonetheless recognise that there may be situations where it would amount to an abuse of process, to allow the prosecution to try again. However, such cases will very much depend on there own particular facts, which will include factors such as:

(i) the overall period of delay and reasons for it;

(ii) the result of previous trials;

(iii) the seriousness of the offence; and

(iv) possibly any tactical advantage gained from the previous trial(s) that now allows the case to be presented differently.

13. Excessive Delay and Abuse of Process

28.21 If there is a substantial time lapse between the actual commission of the alleged offence and the subsequent commencement of proceedings, or proceedings having been commenced are then inexorably delayed, then in these situations, it may not now be possible for the defendant to have a fair trial within the reasonable time requirement contained in art.6.1. The leading authority is *Attorney-General's Reference (No.1 of 1990)* [1992] 95 Cr.App.R. 296, where Lord Lane stated on this particular issue that:

> "no stay should be imposed unless the defendant shows that on a balance of probabilities that owing to the delay he will suffer serious prejudice to the extent that no fair trial can be held: in other words, that the continuance of the prosecution amounts to a misuse of the process of the court."

His Lordship then went on that say that:

> "stays imposed on the grounds of delay or for any other reason should only be employed in *exceptional circumstances*. If they were to become a matter of routine it would be only a short time before the public, understandably, viewed the process with suspicion and mistrust."

Accordingly, the power of the court to stay or prevent a prosecution is one to be exercised sparingly and, according to Lord Lane, even if the delay is not justifiable, even more rarely should there be a stay, if the prosecution or complainant are faultless. If the delay is due to the fault of the defendant, then that should never be a foundation for a stay. One particular area of sensitivity is the long delay in a formal complaint of an alleged sex offence that occurred many years earlier. For the defence, the issue will usually be one of lies and that given the delay, they could not receive a fair trial, since not much more could be contended, other than the complainant is telling lies and cannot be believed. Given there may be no other supporting evidence, it would, according to the defence, be an abuse of process to allow such a prosecution, given the dangers involved.

In *R. v S* [2006] 2 Cr.App.R. 23, a case involving offences of rape and indecent assault of a brother against his two sisters that had occurred some 25 years earlier, the formal complaints were made when it came to light that the appellant had sexually assaulted the daughter of his partner. In dismissing the appellant's appeal, Rose L.J., who gave the leading judgment, considered the previous authorities on the issue of delay and stated that the discretionary power as to staying proceedings is one to be determined not by burden and standard of proof, but by:

> "judicial assessment dependant on judgment rather than on any conclusion as to faced based on evidence."

Applying the decision of Clarke L.J. in *R. v EW* [2004] EWCA Crim 2901, the essential question to be asked by the judge is whether in all the circumstances and despite the delay, it is still possible for the defendant to receive a fair trial. His Lordship then provided the following guidance as to the correct approach based on the previous authorities of *R. v Smolinski* [2004] EWCA Crim 127, *R. v Hooper* [2003] EWCA Crim 1270 and *R. v B* [2003] 2 Cr.App.R. 13. A judge ought to bear in mind when determining an application to stay proceedings due to delay:

(i) even where the delay is unjustifiable, a permanent stay should be the exception rather than the rule;

(ii) where there is no fault on the part of the complainant or the prosecution, it will be very rare for a stay to be granted;

(iii) no stay should be granted in the absence of serious prejudice to the defence so that no fair trial can be held;

(iv) when assessing possible serious prejudice, the judge should bear in mind his or her power to regulate the admissibility of evidence and that the trial process itself should ensure that all the relevant factual issues arsing from the delay will be placed before the jury for their consideration in accordance with appropriate direction from the judge;

(v) if, having considered all these factors, a judge's assessment is that a fair trial will be possible, a stay should not be granted."

28.22 On whether and in what terms a judge should give an appropriate direction to the jury, the Court of Appeal in *R. v M* [2000] 1 Cr.App.R. 49 ruled that the decision in *Percival* [1998] *The Times*, July 20, 1998, did not lay down any prescribed formula as to summing up cases involving delay. This is a matter for the judge based on the particular facts of the case. If there is a substantial delay between the date of the alleged offence and that when it was formally reported, then it will usually be desirable to give a clear warning on any impact upon the memories of witness and the potential difficulties placed upon the defendant in challenging the allegations. A useful starting point is the Judicial Studies specimen direction. Not every case will require a warning, especially where there is cogent evidence and any failure to give a warning will not necessarily render any conviction as unsafe (see also *R. v Brizzalari* [2004] EWCA Crim 310).

In *Attorney–General's Reference (No.2 of 2001)* [2004] 2 W.L.R. 1, the House of Lords considered the issue of a delay caused by the prosecution in either instigating proceedings, or once commenced in pursuing the matter to a timely conclusion. Such delay may infringe a defendant's right to a fair trial being determined within a reasonable time frame. By a majority, Lord Bingham, giving the leading speech, ruled that if there is a recognisable breach of the reasonable time requirement, then dependant on the nature of the breach, when it arose and all the circumstances of the case, an appropriate remedy would, under s.8 of the HRA 1998, be a public acknowledgement and grant of bail, action to expedite the proceedings, a reduction in sentence or payment of compensation to an acquitted defendant. But a stay of proceedings will not be in the public interest as amounting to an appropriate remedy and it is not incompatible with art.6, even if there is a breach of the reasonable time requirement for the prosecution to continue, or indeed entertain a prosecution subject to that breach, unless a fair hearing is no longer possible, or it would be unfair to actually try the defendant. Such cases would, according to his Lordship, be:

"very exceptional, and a stay will never be the appropriate remedy if any lesser remedy would adequately vindicate the defendant's convention right."

For Lord Bingham, any breach relates not to the actual hearing itself, but to the accrued delay encountered. In a powerful dissenting judgment, Lord Hope disagreed with this assessment in that the reasonable time requirement cannot be detached in that way from the clear right to a hearing being fair. The reasonable time requirement is a free standing right and does not require the defendant to show that as a result of its breach, it would no longer be possible to have a fair hearing. On a second point on which all their Lordships were agreed, it was observed that that the relevant time starts from the point when the defendant is officially alerted to the likelihood of criminal proceedings being commenced. Ordinarily this would be either when charged or on summons.

In *Miller v DPP* [2004] EWHC 595, the High Court ruled that a delay of some two years from the appellant pleading guilty by post for three offences of speeding, to the actual execution of a warrant backed for bail to secure his attendance for the purposes of possible disqualification, was disproportionate, given the nature of the case and clearly in breach of art.6.1. In this instance, the appropriate remedy for the breach was a reduction in the disqualification period.

14. Malpractice and Abuse of Process

28.23 The court must protect the criminal process from any malpractice or manipulation of it by the prosecution and must not be seen to condone such conduct. If the misconduct of the prosecution is such so as to deprive the defendant of any protection under the law and therefore suffer unfairness, then the proceedings ought to be stayed as an abuse of process. This clear principle of law is summarised in *R. v Latif* [1996] 2 Cr.App.R. 92 and *Derby Crown Court Ex p. Brooks* [1985] 80 Cr.App.R. 169.

On the point of whether a defendant would suffer unfairness or prejudice as a result of either the loss or destruction of evidence that may have had relevance to assisting the defence, the High Court, having reviewed the previous authorities in *R. (Ebrahim v Feltham Magistrates' Court* [2001] 1 W.L.R. 1293, gave the following general guidance. If the defence allege that a failure of the prosecution to retain video recordings or forensic evidence amounts to an abuse of process, making it impossible for the defendant to have a fair trial, then in such circumstances, the court will need to consider the code of practice issued under the CPIA 1996 and the obligation of the police/prosecution to obtain and retain the evidence in question. If there is no obligation, then no unfairness arises.

If however, there is a duty to obtain and retain the evidence, then in deciding whether or not to exercise the discretionary power to stay the proceedings the court will need to strike a fair balance between the competing triangulation of interests. This will require the court to consider the need to safeguard the defendant from any prejudice arising from the failure or breach, whilst at the same time ensuring that the interest of the public is maintained in the prosecution of a criminal offence and also consider any impact upon the victim, should the proceedings be stayed. Ultimately, each case will depend on its own particular facts.

28.24 In *R. v Sadler* [2002] 166 J.P. 481, the police, in breach of their obligations, had delayed in obtaining video evidence from a nightclub in which the defendant had allegedly committed a serious assault. Likewise, there was a failure on behalf of the prosecution to provide the details of witnesses who had not provided statements and also with regard to the destruction of a broken bottle, being the possible weapon, together with the shoes and socks of the defendant. Despite these breaches, which the court stated amounted to negligent failings and thoroughly reprehensible, it was not so serious as to deprive the defendant of a fair trial. The Court observed that whilst there is authority for a stay of proceedings being possible in the absence of bad faith, such cases would be rare and only where the misbehaviour of the prosecution was so serious that it would be wrong to allow the prosecution to still benefit from this, to the detriment of the defendant. An application to stay proceedings on the failure to obtain and retain evidence, contrary to the Code of Practice, requires there to be:

> "conduct involving some degree of deliberate manipulation of the pretrial process by the police or prosecution *and* that the question is whether what happened prejudiced the defendant in such a way that he could not receive a fair trial."

The discretionary power to stay is a power to be used sparingly and only where it is compelling that the defendant would not receive a fair trial, or that it would because of the conduct of the prosecution, not be fair to try the defendant. This is seen clearly in *R. v Latif and Shahzad* [1996] 2 Cr.App.R. 92, where the House of Lords refused to interfere with the decision of the trial judge to refuse to stay the proceedings, despite the fact that Shahzad had been lured to the UK through an agreement by a paid informer to import drugs. The Lordships concluded that the judge had balanced the competing elements of justice and policy properly.

Although concerning a claim for compensation for a miscarriage of justice, the Court of Appeal in *R. (Raissi) v Secretary of State for the Home Department* [2008] EWCA Civ 72 highlighted serious default by both the police and CPS in the conduct of extradition proceedings, which according to the Court, were brought for an ulterior motive against the claimant, and for which there was no evidence or prospect of bringing serious charges. This amounted to an abuse. The Court noted that there was false evidence in respect of a flight log book given by the Metropolitan Police, that contributed to the decision to refuse bail. Neither could the CPS, in the view of the Court, be absolved of any responsibility. The CPS had simply relied and acted upon the unsubstantiated assertions of the US Government. It was the duty of CPS to disclose evidence that they knew of and which destroyed, or seriously undermined the evidence which the US Government relied upon. If the CPS knew or ought to have known of this serious default, then that would constitute an abuse of process.

15. Submission of No Case to Answer

28.25 Usually, at the conclusion of the prosecution case, the defence may feel it appropriate to make a submission of no case to answer, in that the prosecution have failed to prove the elements of the offence. This may be because the witnesses called by the prosecution have failed to come up to proof, due either to lack of consistency or credibility. The leading authority on the principles for making such an submission is *R. v Galbraith* [1981] 2 All E.R. 1060, in which Lord Lane set out the principles of law in the following terms:

> "How then should a judge approach a submission of no case to answer?
>
> (1) If there is no evidence that the crime alleged has been committed by the defendant, there is no difficulty. The judge will of cause stop the case.
> (2) The difficulty arises where there is some evidence but it is of a tenuous character, for example because of inherent weakness or vagueness or because it is inconsistent with other evidence.
>
> (a) Where the judge comes to the conclusion that the crown's evidence, taken at its highest, is such that a jury properly directed could not properly convict on it, it is his duty, on a submission being made to stop the case.
> (b) Where however the crown's evidence is such that its strength or weakness depends on the view to be taken of a witness's reliability, or other matters which are generally speaking within the province of the jury and where on one possible view of the facts there is evidence on which a jury could properly come to the conclusion that the defendant is guilty, then the judge should allow the matter to be tried by the jury.
>
> There will of cause as always in the branch of law, be borderline cases. They can safely be left to the discretion of the judge."

In applying the test above, the court must ask itself whether there was evidence of the offence and if there was, whether taken at its highest, a jury properly directed, could properly convict upon it. Ultimately, a case ought to be left with the jury, if the strength or weakness of the evidence depends on the view the jury takes of a witnesses' reliability or other matters.

In *Galbraith* Lord Lane made it clear that:

> "Where on one possible view of the facts there is evidence on which a jury could properly come to the conclusion that the defendant is guilty, then the judge should allow the matter to be tried by the jury."

Nevertheless, *R. v Shipley* [1988] Crim. L.R. 767, a ruling of a High Court. Therefore does not necessarily have great value as precedent, where it was said that the requirement of taking the prosecution's case (evidence) at its highest did not mean, "picking all the plums and leaving the duff behind".

In other words, a judge should not ignore the weaknesses in the case for the prosecution. The instant case involved a serious rape; an allegation which was based virtually on the uncorroborated evidence of the complainant. At the close of the prosecution's case, this was shown to be significantly at variance with other supportive evidence and therefore incredible to such a degree of inconsistency as being unable to establish an allegation of rape.

As with an application contending an abuse of process, the assessment of whether there is a case to answer will be at the discretion of the judge applying the broad principles in *Galbraith*. Only if that decision is unreasonable, would a appeal court interfere with it. In *Moran v DPP* [2002] 166 J.P. 467, the High Court ruled, on a case stated appeal, that the magistrates had not acted unlawfully by failing to give reasons as to why they refused to allow a submission of no case to answer. The Court ruled that there was no legal obligation on the magistrates to give any reasons, since the summary trial procedure is highly specific and given that the justices are both the tribunal of law and fact, it would in those circumstances be undesirable for them to give detailed reasons in their assessment of the evidence and the witnesses at the end of the prosecution case, on a submission of no case to answer. For this reason there is no breach of art.6. The defendant had still received a fair trial. If convicted, the justices would then be legally required to give reasons for their decision as to a finding of guilt.

INDEX